ADVERTISING THE AMERICAN DREAM

ADVERTISING THE AMERICAN DREAM

MAKING WAY FOR MODERNITY, 1920–1940

ROLAND MARCHAND

University of California Press

Berkeley   Los Angeles   London

University of California Press
Berkeley and Los Angeles, California
University of California Press, Ltd.
London, England
© 1985 by
The Regents of the University of
California
Printed in the United States of America

1 2 3 4 5 6 7 8 9

Library of Congress Cataloging in Publication Data

Marchand, Roland.
    Advertising the American dream.

    Bibliography: p.
    Includes index.
    1. Advertising—United States—
    History. I. Title.
HF5813.U6M26 1985   659.1'0973
84-28082   ISBN 0-520-05253-6

To Sue and Jeannie

CONTENTS

ACKNOWLEDGMENTS

After enjoying the assistance of many individuals and institutions during nearly a decade of research on the history of American advertising, it is gratifying to have the opportunity to acknowledge formally their indispensable support, cooperation, and advice.

A Humanities Fellowship from the Rockefeller Foundation brought this project to fruition by providing me with an uninterrupted year in which to complete my research and write a first draft of the book. Patient support from the Academic Senate Committee on Research of the University of California, Davis, enabled me to visit the various corporate and agency archives and maintain my momentum over an extended period of research.

I greatly appreciate the privileges and courtesies extended to me by several advertising agencies. The J. Walter Thompson Company, by establishing a professionally supervised archive, has recently taken a major step to remedy the neglect of the historical record common to most agencies. I am particularly gratified by the precedent which J. Walter Thompson has set by extending me the privilege of consulting and quoting from the confidential verbatim minutes of the meetings of its creative staff and its account representatives during the 1920s and 1930s. The J. Walter Thompson archivist, Cynthia G. Swank, and her assistant, Annemarie Sandecki, provided expert help in identifying the relevant materials and verifying the accuracy of references. During a research trip before the formal establishment of the JWT archive, N. Terry Munger and Mary Gegleys of J. Walter Thompson kindly provided me with convenient access to historical materials in the JWT library.

I was generously given access to historical agency materials by N. W. Ayer and Son, by Batten, Barton, Durstine and Osborn, by Foote, Cone and Belding, and by Young and Rubicam. I am indebted to Mr. Brad Lynch and Mr. John Kaufman of N. W. Ayer and Son for taking an interest in my project and providing me access to materials still retained by the agency; and to Ms. Tony Falcone, Ms.

Terry Glenzole, and Ms. Lindsey Cohen for helping me identify specific files and boxes of Ayer correspondence and publications. At BBDO, Mr. Ray Maloney, Ms. Ann Heitner, and Ms. Paula Brown furnished me with working space and access to historical materials in the BBDO information center during two research trips. Robert J. Koretz of Foote, Cone and Belding Communications informed me of the existence of a comprehensive collection of scrapbooks of the ads of Lord and Thomas, the agency which subsequently became Foote, Cone and Belding. He also kindly shared with me his recollections of the Lord and Thomas years and his manuscript recounting the agency's history. John Kok of Foote, Cone and Belding assisted me in using materials in the agency library, and Joe Lentino initiated me into the mysteries of the cellar crypt where the Lord and Thomas scrapbooks are entombed. At Young and Rubicam, Ms. Celestine Frankenberg graciously found working space for me in the agency's tiny archive and made special provisions to enable me to make efficient use of the archives in the time I had available. Ms. Ina Geske of Kenyon and Eckhardt took the time to copy and pass on to me the meager historical data retained by that agency.

Several major corporate advertisers have also been generous in their cooperation and interest in my project. Since I have simultaneously been conducting specialized research on institutional advertising, the extent of my indebtedness to many of these companies will become apparent only upon the completion of a subsequent book. Mr. Hubert M. (Bart) Snider provided me access to the General Electric Company library and archives on institutional advertising, and also shared with me his own research into the company's history. Mr. Julian E. Aurelius of E. R. Squibb and Sons, Inc., took the time to familarize me with the scope and organization of that company's extensive archive. At the Hoover Worldwide Corporation, Mr. R. W. Gillman and Mrs. Helen Magaw were particularly accommodating in helping me use Hoover house organs and other historical materials. Mrs. Claudia Penna at the American Telephone and Telegraph Company archives and Ms. Margaret Hall and Ms. Gerry Flanzraich at the Metropolitan Life Insurance Company library gave me valuable assistance in locating correspondence files and house organs in those companies' substantial collections. Mr. Ed Rider provided me with useful materials from the Procter and Gamble Company files, and Ms. Helen Vincent, editor of *True Story Magazine,* gave me access to the backfile of *True Story Magazine* at the Macfadden publishing offices and permission to reproduce a 1929 magazine cover. Many of these businesses are not organized to accommodate academic scholars. I greatly appreciate the special efforts they made to provide me with working space and access to little-used files and collections.

Many scholars and friends have made the most indispensable of intellectual contributions to this study—a willingness to listen sympathetically yet critically to my ideas. David Brody, Daniel Brower, Daniel Calhoun, T. J. Jackson Lears, and Michael Schudson read major portions of the manuscript at various stages in its development. Each alerted me to further interpretive opportunities or stimulated me to search for a more cohesive integration of my materials. Michael Schudson and Richard W. Pollay generously shared their unpublished work-in-progress with me. Many friends and colleagues, including William Bowsky, Paul Goodman, Norma Landau, Eugene Lunn, Ruth Rosen, Lorenz Schultz, Lenora

Timm, and Merline Williams, read segments of the manuscript or listened to my dilemmas and offered astute advice. Richard Schwab and K. C. Liu took a special interest in my project and provided vital assistance in bringing my work to fruition.

Stanley Burnshaw and John Caples took the time to answer my questions and share some of their recollections of agency work in the late 1920s and early 1930s. Robert J. Koretz not only shared his recollection of Lord and Thomas with me, but later assisted me in ensuring the accuracy of detail in my accounts of several incidents. Matthew Joseph shared with me both his warm hospitality and his intimate knowledge of the Bruce Barton Papers. Professor Richard Tedlow helped me arrange a most profitable exploration of the various sources of the Harvard School of Business Administration, and Ms. Jen E. Sullivan helpfully guided me in the use of the school's unpublished Case Study files. The librarians and archivists of the State Historical Society of Wisconsin, the Baker Library of the Harvard School of Business Administration, the New York Public Library, the Arthur and Elizabeth Schlesinger Library, and the California State Library have all given me indispensable assistance. I am indebted to Donald J. Kunitz of the Special Collections Department of the Shields Library of the University of California, Davis, and to Ms. Sabra Basler, Ms. Marcia McCune-Feldman, and Mr. Levi Phillips of his staff, for accommodation and assistance during the time I was writing the book. Ms. Faye Vierra and Ms. Gladys Taylor of the interlibrary loan department at the University of California, Davis, patiently responded to my heavy demands on their services.

I have frequently benefited from the support of individuals who have loaned or given me useful materials. Mrs. Enola Hicks, Mr. Robert Powell, Mrs. Terry Richard, Mr. Max Rothe, Mr. Michael Woodard, and Mrs. Freida Young have all sustained me with their contributions and their interest. Several research assistants, including Carolyn Brown, Wendy Gamber, Jim Lapsley, Sue Lehmer, Frank Lortie, and Karen March have aided me in various aspects of my research. I am also indebted to Bill Antaramian, Karen Hairfield, Carole Hinkle, Phyllis Graham, Katherine Hill, Diane Dean, and Evelyn Echevarria for their patient work in converting the scrambled segments and insertions of various drafts into a readable manuscript.

Working with the University of California Press has been a pleasure. Mr. James Clark, the Director of the U.C. Press, has particularly sustained me through the last stages of my work with his enthusiasm for the project and his specific suggestions. I have benefited from the opportunity to work with editor Marilyn Schwartz and production manager Chet Grycz. As copy editor, Gene Tanke astutely and persistently guided me toward greater clarity in style. It has been a pleasure to work with someone so sensitive to nuance and so adept at straightforward expression. In preparing the illustrations, I have been fortunate in being able to draw upon the expertise and patience of Richard Kulmann and the staff of Illustration Services, University of California, Davis. The enthusiasm of Steve Renick, Art Director of the University of California Press, and his sensitivity to the unique pictorial qualities of the ads of the 1920s and 1930s have made the task of designing and coordinating the illustrations a stimulating experience.

I owe my deepest gratitude to my family for sustaining me through the long period of research and writing. My mother, Mildred Marchand Watson, and my stepfather, John L. Watson, have supported me with their unflagging interest and confidence. My daughters, Sue Marchand and Jeannie Marchand, have not only stimulated me with their critical eye for contemporary advertising, but have willingly submitted themselves to my requests that they serve as sounding boards for my ideas and as critics of my esthetic and literary judgments. My wife, Betsy Marchand, has sustained me with the love and confidence that she has brought to all of our truly mutual endeavors. In addition, by sharing with me the full texture of her experience in elected political office, she has constantly reminded me of some of the realities of American life against which I might appraise the semblances and fantasies of that life that have constituted modern advertising.

INTRODUCTION

In 1926 the venerable Philadelphia advertising agency of N. W. Ayer and Son made the following bold prophecy: "Historians of the future will not have to rely on the meagre collections of museums, will not have to pore over obscure documents and ancient prints, to reconstruct a faithful picture of 1926. Day by day a picture of our time is recorded completely and vividly in the advertising in American newspapers and magazines. Were all other sources of information on the life of today to fail, the advertising would reproduce for future times, as it does for our own, the action, color, variety, dignity, and aspirations of the American Scene."[1]

I began to study the social content of American advertising in the 1920s and 1930s in much the same spirit of naive optimism exhibited in this self-congratulatory agency pamphlet. I marveled that historians could have written so much about social values and popular attitudes without examining the ads—a profusion of documents aimed precisely at reflecting those values and shaping those ideas! In my more romantic moods, I saw myself as a crusader charging off to rescue all those neglected damsels, the advertisements, from the dungeons and dustbins of history.

My quest for the lost historical treasures of advertising led me first to an intensive survey of the ads of the Great Depression. By the early 1930s advertising had progressed far beyond the age of the poster and the slogan. For more than two decades, artists and copywriters had been perfecting techniques of suggesting consumer benefits. Ads now regularly portrayed the lives of "typical" consumers as enhanced by the use of the product. Surely, I thought, the advertising tableaux of these years, as mirrors of society, would reflect the momentous changes of circumstance and attitude wrought by the depression.

But any naive assumptions I harbored about the character of advertising as an authentic and uncomplicated social mirror were quickly dashed as I immersed myself in the ads. Year by year, from the stock market crash of 1929 through the mid-1930s, advertising themes and motifs remained remarkably consistent. The social content of the ads changed far less than did the styles of layout and illustration; in fact, the attitudes and values conveyed by the ads proved exceptionally persistent. Certainly the ideas and images in the ads changed much more slowly than the attitudes of most Americans are generally thought to have changed. In some cases, the advertisements of the early 1930s even reiterated, with increased intensity, certain attitudes and values associated with the pre-depression era. From this discovery, one might conclude that the early years of the depression had no more than a slight effect on American ideas and social values. This hypothesis was not entirely implausible—Robert Lynd arrived at much the same conclusion when his research team revisited "Middletown" (Muncie, Indiana) in the mid-1930s to analyze changes since the 1920s.[2] But another, more disconcerting, hypothesis could not be ignored: perhaps the ads did not provide an accurate reflection of social reality after all.

I broadened the chronological boundaries of my intensive survey to include the 1920s as well as the 1930s. My sample expanded to include substantial selections from *Good Housekeeping*, *Ladies' Home Journal*, *Better Homes and Gardens*, *Fortune*, *True Story Magazine*, *Redbook*, *Literary Digest*, *Photoplay Magazine*, *McCall's*, *Delineator*, the *American Weekly*, the *Chicago Tribune*, and the *Los Angeles Times*, as well as comprehensive coverage of every issue of the *Saturday Evening Post* and the *American Magazine* from 1923 through 1937—in all, an approximate total of 180,000 ads of a quarter-page or larger. The addition of a large segment of advertising from the 1920s not only provided a basis for judging the modification or persistence of themes and attitudes during the depression; it also extended my survey to include the crucial period during which advertisers brought to maturity their techniques for depicting the product or its benefits "situationally"—that is, in the life of the consumer.

Still, I only encountered new perplexities in my quest for the social mirror that would "completely and vividly" reflect the times. No wonder so few had taken up the challenge of reconstructing the attitudes and values of an era from its ads! Quandaries and imponderables loomed on every side. Did the content of advertisements mirror the consumers' actual conditions and behavior—or their fantasies and aspirations? Or did the ads reflect, even more faithfully, the particular values and preoccupations of advertisers, advertising agents, and copywriters? Of what value was a systematic analysis of the overt elements of the content of advertisements when subtle nuances often lay at the heart of their appeals? Almost by definition, nuances defy quantification and categorization. Moreover, even a plausible explanation of the content of a group of advertisements, as intended by their creators, would prove nothing about the impact of the messages in those ads on consumers. If sales increased during a particular advertising campaign, other factors in merchandising, distribution, economic conditions, or social fads might have triggered this response. Even if advertising could be isolated as the crucial factor in the "merchandising mix," the placement, frequency, special offer, or eye appeal of a given ad might have influenced consumers far more than any aspect of its implicit or explicit social content.

I regret to say that I have not resolved these dilemmas. I cannot prove conclusively that the American people absorbed the values and ideas of the ads, nor that consumers wielded the power to ensure that the ads would mirror their lives. In fact, as advertisers quickly perceived, people did not usually want ads to reflect themselves, their immediate social relationships, or their broader society exactly.* They wanted not a true mirror but a Zerrspiegel, a distorting mirror that would enhance certain images. Even the term Zerrspiegel, denoting a fun-house mirror, fails to suggest fully the scope of advertising distortions of reality. Such a mirror distorts the shapes of the objects it reflects, but it nevertheless provides some image of everything within its field of vision. Advertising's mirror not only distorted, it also selected. Some social realities hardly appeared at all. One has to search diligently in the ads of the 1920s and 1930s to find even fleeting glimpses of such common scenes as religious services, factory workers on the job, sports fans enjoying a boxing match or baseball game, or working-class families at home.

The angle of refraction, and hence the degree of distortion of these advertising images, was determined not only by the efforts of advertisers to respond to consumers' desires for fantasy and wish-fulfillment but also by a variety of other factors. The most obvious source of distortion in advertising's mirror was the presumption by advertisers that the public preferred an image of "life as it ought to be, life in the millennium" to an image of literal reality. "The people are seeking to escape from themselves," concluded a writer in *Advertising and Selling* in 1926. "They want to live in a more exciting world." Working under this assumption, ad creators tried to reflect public aspirations rather than contemporary circumstances, to mirror popular fantasies rather than social realities.[3] Advertisers recognized that consumers would rather identify with scenes of higher status than ponder reflections of their actual lives. In response, they often sought to give products a "class image" by placing them in what recent advertising jargon would call "upscale" settings.

Even apart from such upscale strategies, advertisements of the 1920s and 1930s were likely to convey unrepresentative class images. Most advertisers defined the market for their products as a relatively select audience of upper-class and upper-middle-class Americans. Even had they sought to depict the lives of these consumers with absolute fidelity, their ads would have mirrored only this select audience rather than society as a whole. Moreover, most ad creators occupied a class position and displayed cultural tastes that distanced them from popular conditions and values. Not only were they likely to portray the world they knew, rather than the world experienced by typical citizens, but also they sometimes allowed their cultural preferences to influence their depiction of society. Their "elite provincialism" and their tendency to create ads that satisfied their own tastes further distorted social reality.

Most powerful of all in distorting advertising's social mirror were specific merchandising strategies. The central purpose of an ad was not to reflect reality but to "move merchandise." Often the strategy of an advertiser would dictate a deliberate distortion of reality—for example, the repeated depiction of women

*Although the term "advertisers" is often understood to apply specifically to companies that offer their own goods and services for sale, I have used it somewhat more broadly, to include all those people who conceived, executed, and approved advertising content, whether they worked in corporate advertising departments, in advertising agencies, or on contract.

gazing spellbound into their open refrigerators, or lovers rejecting potential mates solely because of bad breath. Background elements of the ad that were not critical to the selling message were often determined by pictorial convention or artistic convenience rather than by close observation of contemporary life. The required background of "a family" or "a city" often assumed a conventionalized form. Attempts by historians to find in the ads of any era certain truths about family size or the spacing of children, for example, would be quickly thwarted by requirements of specific merchandising strategies (show children of different ages to demonstrate the broad age appeal of the product) and of artistic economy (include only enough figures to convey the idea of children).

In the process of selling specific products, advertisers also communicated broader assumptions about social values. Implicit value statements, passed along unconsciously as givens, usually carried an ideological bias toward "system reinforcement." Manufacturers and ad agency leaders recognized their stake in the contemporary configuration of economic and social institutions, and thus found little reason to portray realities that might bring the system into question. Advertisements therefore promulgated what Jacques Ellul has characterized as "integration propaganda"—that is, ideas and images that reinforce and intensify existing patterns and conceptions.[4] To the extent that contemporary business ideology led advertisers to exclude aspects of a broader, more diverse social reality, the ads failed to hold up a true mirror to society. In this sense, the relation of advertising images to contemporary social realities is best suggested by the phrase Michael Schudson has coined to describe American advertising art: Capitalist Realism.[5] Like the paintings and murals of Socialist Realism, the illustrations in American advertising portrayed the ideals and aspirations of the system more accurately than its reality. They dramatized the American dream.

Despite these serious distortions in advertising's mirror, some of them virtually inherent in the nature of advertising, the case for advertisements as useful historical documents may not be entirely without merit. Advertisements present problems that differ more in degree than in kind from those involved in interpreting social reality from more conventional historical sources. We may not be able to prove the specific effect of an advertisement on its readers, but neither can we prove the effects of religious tracts, social manifestos, commemorative addresses, and political campaign speeches on their audiences. We like to believe that the content of movies, popular literature, and well-attended amusements reveals something about the attitudes and values of audiences during a given era, but we cannot prove this from their content. Bruce Kuklick and Jay Mechling have judiciously warned us that even such apparently revealing documents as jingoistic campaign speeches or advice books for mothers, whatever their measurable popularity, cannot be taken as authoritative evidence of the ideas of those who heard or read them. As Herbert Gans succinctly warns: "The critics' practice of inferring effects from content is not valid."[6] Advertisements merely share the characteristics of many other suspect forms of evidence about popular attitudes: we do not know exactly why they were popular or successful; we do not know if audiences shared or adopted the ideas presented; and we have reasons to suspect that the authors had motives and biases that did not completely coincide with those of the audience.

making the case for studying Ads!

Once we have placed advertisements in the same category as many traditional historical documents, it may be possible to argue that ads actually surpass most other recorded communications as a basis for *plausible inference* about popular attitudes and values. Among elite communicators, advertisers have been motivated by a particularly direct and intense need to understand and communicate effectively with their audiences. Certainly they have had few rivals in the expenditure of money and effort in assessing audience response. Deficient as their early methods were, advertisers still tested the effects of their communications more often and more rigorously than novelists, writers of magazine fiction, newspaper editors, movie directors, cartoonists, or even politicians. And they had reasons for taking these "reality checks" seriously.[7]

Advertising leaders recognized the necessity of associating their selling messages with the values and attitudes already held by their audience. They sought to strike only those notes that would evoke a positive resonance. As one agency ad reminded advertisers: "You must not implant the smallest grain of disagreement in a reader's mind. . . . There are certain things that most people believe. . . . The moment your copy is linked to one of those beliefs, more than half your battle is won."[8] Whatever the results in ad content and audience reaction, advertising people clearly invested more time, energy, and money than any other mass communicators in the effort to discover such fundamental beliefs.

Sometimes advertising content directly reflected the consumer attitudes reported in surveys and questionnaires. For its 1926 Pyrex campaign, the Corning Glass Ware Company sought to place the product in the context of the housewife's immediate reality. After determining which dishes housewives prepared most often, the company used the five most common ones as illustrations in all Pyrex ads.[9] Advertising artists carefully reproduced the exact details of current fashions in dress, furniture, and home decoration, although comparisons with home inventories would reveal that such illustrations more accurately reflected the living conditions of the wealthy and avant-garde than the tastes of typical Americans. The 1929 Harvard Awards Committee for advertising suggested the probable degree of refraction in the mirroring of living conditions in ads. It noted approvingly that a series of Armstrong Linoleum ads had depicted "rooms not sufficiently out of the ordinary to be regarded by the representative reader as unobtainable."[10]

In a variety of ways, advertisements provide glimpses of past social realities. Illustrations of eager delivery boys with baskets of groceries, or formally attired department store clerks with a deferential hunch to their shoulders, remind us of economic services and social relationships that once existed for certain segments of society.[11] Such illustrations would not have appeared without some basis in actuality. Advertisements quickly reveal that bridge and golf were current fads. Yet such ads fail to provide a mirror, because they offer no accurate measure of how many people played golf or bridge, or how often they did so. At the minimum, however, ads do reveal what products and services were sold during a given era, when new products first attained mass distribution, and what explanations and suggestions were offered for their use. Testimonial ads tell us which public figures a well-informed and highly motivated advertising elite believed the consumers would identify with and accept as adequate authorities.

Another argument for the contribution of advertisements to an understanding of social realities rests on certain unprovable but commonsense assumptions about the broad impact of advertising. Few students of mass communication now accept the "hypodermic-needle" theory, which emphasizes the power of media images to inject certain attitudes and ideas into the minds of audience members. But scholars do acknowledge the power of frequently repeated media images and ideas to establish broad frames of reference, define the boundaries of public discussion, and determine relevant factors in a situation. (Advertising research has repeatedly confirmed that ads emphasizing the aroma, taste, or texture of a food product, though not necessarily effective in shifting brand preferences, do successfully establish the criterion they emphasize as the relevant one for the consumer making a choice.)

Certainly few images have buffeted the consciousness of twentieth-century Americans as repetitively as advertisements. As Walter Benjamin observed of architecture and film decades ago, they have been largely perceived by the audience in an inattentive "state of distraction."[12] Still, they may have shaped the audience's frame of reference all the more effectively for being passively absorbed rather than actively contemplated. As I shall argue later, by disseminating certain incessantly repeated and largely uncontradicted visual clichés and moral parables, the ads were likely to shape or reinforce the same popular attitudes they sought to reflect.

Advertisements also contributed to the shaping of a "community of discourse," an integrative common language shared by an otherwise diverse audience. Except in movie theaters, advertising maintained a highly visible and nearly ubiquitous presence in all the popular media of the 1920s and 1930s. Through repetition, bold display, and ingenuity, advertisements infused their images and slogans into America's common discourse. If the metaphors, syntactical patterns, and verbal and visual "vocabularies" of our common language establish our parameters of thought and cut the furrows along which our ideas tend to flow, then advertising has played a significant role in establishing our frames of reference and perception.[13]

In my survey of advertising content in the 1920s and 1930s, I have sought to interpret some of the major contributions advertising has made to the vocabulary and syntax of American common discourse, and thus to the framing of basic societal assumptions. I have not tried to make a case for the probable impact of specific ads, or even of single campaigns. Rather, through a process of total immersion, I have sought to recognize and analyze certain persistent patterns of verbal and visual expression. Although I became more conscious of the distortions in advertising's social mirror as my study progressed, I have sought to determine what can be salvaged from advertising "reflections" by plotting the probable angle of refraction or direction of distortion in the Zerrspiegel of advertising. By examining the social backgrounds of those who shaped the advertisements and by listening to their shoptalk about themselves, their audiences, and their working conditions, I have tried to assess their biases and the accuracy of their perception of social realities. In interpreting advertising content, I have tried to work backward to the underlying social realities by correcting advertising's depiction of American society for the refractions introduced by such biases, motives, and assumptions.[14]

One significant bias of advertisers deserves particular attention; and it is a bias that, paradoxically, offers us the prospect of using the advertisements of the 1920s and 1930s more confidently as a key to understanding certain realities of American culture. The ad creators of that era proudly proclaimed themselves missionaries of modernity. Constantly and unabashedly, they championed the new against the old, the modern against the old-fashioned. This bias, inherent in their economic function, ensured that advertisements would emphasize disproportionately those styles, classes, behaviors, and social circumstances that were new and changing.

This bias toward modernity, although it further amplified advertising's distortions of typical social circumstances, ironically served to enhance the fidelity of ads as mirrors of a wider cultural ethos. As apostles of modernity, advertisers paid close attention to signs of consumer resistance to their messages and thus acquired a particular sensitivity to certain consumer discontents with modernity. Although consumers responded positively to the claims of modernity in technology, in style, and in ways of doing things, and although they appreciated the benefits that economies of scale brought to their standard of living, still they resented certain "indignities of scale" that accompanied modernization. Through consumer response, through trial and error, and through close observation of the other media of popular culture, advertisers gradually observed and responded to a popular demand that modern products be introduced to them in ways that gave the appearance and feel of a personal relationship. People craved opportunities, through vicarious experience, to bring products within the compass of their own human scale.

At the same time, advertisers came to recognize certain vacuums of advice in modern society. They had always offered advice in a narrow, prescriptive sense: use our product. Now they discovered a market for broader counsel and reassurance. In response, they gave advice that promoted the product while offering expertise and solace in the face of those modern complexities and impersonal judgments that made the individual feel incompetent and insecure. Advertisers, then as now, recognized a much larger stake in reflecting people's needs and anxieties than in depicting their actual circumstances and behavior. It was in their efforts to promote the mystique of modernity in styles and technology, while simultaneously assuaging the anxieties of consumers about losses of community and individual control, that they most closely mirrored historical reality—the reality of a cultural dilemma. Yet even here, we must still reckon with some refraction in the advertising images. Although the ad creators sought, above all, to discover and empathize with public needs and anxieties, they most convincingly portrayed those anxieties that closely approximated their own.

In view of both the opportunities and the obstacles presented by advertisements as reflections of American culture, I have concluded that the 1920s and 1930s provide the optimum era for exploring this approach to historical interpretation. American advertising took on a new scope and maturity during these years. Not only did the number of advertisements, the variety of products advertised, and the media available to advertising expand dramatically; in addition, advertisements increasingly gave predominant attention to the consumer rather than the product. In their efforts to win over consumers by inducing them to live through experiences in which the product (or its absence) played a part, advertisers offered detailed vignettes of social life. This evolution toward an emphasis on consumer anxieties and satisfactions, which culminated by the 1930s, was what made American advertising "modern." It also made advertising more useful than ever before to the cultural historian.

Of particular assistance to the historian is the sense of innocent self-assurance about their cultural mission that many advertising people retained during this period. Despite a rapidly growing sophistication within advertising agencies, many ads still conveyed their messages far more ingenuously and explicitly than would be the case several years later. Advertising leaders took delight in the new maturity and power of their profession. They anxiously explored the possibilities and perils of acting as intimate advisors to the fickle, suggestible, and inexperienced new masses of economically enfranchised consumers. Their excitement led them impulsively to fill the pages of the trade press with revealing gossip about their techniques, their perceptions of the audience, and their own motives.

The advertising of the 1920s was the response of advertising agents, representing the economic and cultural elite, to their perception of a new consumer constituency in much the same way that Jacksonian politics and the Whig "Log Cabin" campaign of 1840 represented the response of a political establishment to perceptions of a new political constituency. In both instances, the established elites felt some sense of distaste for the ignorance and vulgarity of their new constituents. The advertisers, however, made greater efforts to examine the full dimensions of the needs and desires of their new constituency, and then not only to "pander" to it but also to counsel and uplift. Their motivation was no less self-interested than that of the early Democrats and Whigs, but the frequency and variety of their campaigns led them to search diligently for unfulfilled needs that they might promise to satisfy. Discovering vacuums of advice and psychological deprivations in modern society, they accepted a therapeutic role in helping Americans adapt to new social and technological complexities. The American dream, they promised, was a thoroughly modern dream, adaptable to a modern scale. It offered new and satisfying forms of individualism, equality, personal interaction, and cost-free progress within the emerging mass society. We may discount the solutions they offered to modern problems. But we would be unwise to neglect their diagnosis of the needs and desires of the expanding consumer society, or to ignore the refracted images of it that they projected in their advertising tableaux.

APOSTLES OF MODERNITY

The American advertising man of the 1920s was the most modern of men.* He claimed that distinction for himself with much bluster and self-confidence—but also with considerable justification. Not only did he flourish in the fast-paced, modern urban milieu of skyscrapers, taxicabs, and pleasure-seeking crowds, but he proclaimed himself an expert on the latest crazes in fashion, contemporary lingo, and popular pastimes. As an exuberant apostle of modernity, he excitedly introduced consumers to the newest in products and confided to manufacturers the newest in popular whims. In fact, he based much of his claim to professional expertise on his particular sensitivity to changes in public tastes.

Other professional elites—scientists, engineers, and industrial designers—also claimed to epitomize the dynamic forces of modernization, but advertising agents insisted that they played a crucial role. Scientific inventions and technological advances fostered the expectation of change and the organization for continuous innovation that characterized modern society. But inventions and their technological applications made a dynamic impact only when the great mass of people learned of their benefits, integrated them into their lives, and came to lust for more new products. Modern technologies needed their heralds, advertising men contended. Modern styles and ways of life needed their missionaries. Advertising men were modernity's "town criers." They brought good news about progress.

In a structural sense, the advertisers' claim to modernity rested on their role in pushing economic modernization further along its logical course of develop-

*Although a small minority of women played a role in shaping the content of national advertising, as described in Chapter 2, I have occasionally resorted to the phrase *advertising man* to epitomize the profession. Despite its generic inaccuracy, this gender-specific phrase does provide an occasional reminder of the overwhelmingly male dominance of the process of creating and approving advertisements. It also dramatizes an important aspect of the social context in which the ads of the 1920s and 1930s must be understood. As I explain in detail in Chapter 3, the advertisements of this era were generally perceived by their creators as communications from a rational and therefore putatively masculine elite to the emotional, "feminine" masses.

ment.[1] An economy organized for efficient production through economies of scale, rationalization of the working place, functional specialization, and a rapid and integrated flow of materials and communications also needed a high "velocity of flow" in the purchase of goods by consumers.[2] Ad creators were becoming the highly specialized facilitators of that process. As some business leaders in the 1920s began to worry about the dangers of over-production, advertising agents gained increased respect for their role as guardians of uninterrupted progress.

New industries were surging to the forefront in the 1920s. Nearly all of the glamor industries of the era—automobiles, radio, chemicals, movies, drugs, and electrical refrigeration—had established what George Mowry calls a "face-to-face relationship" with the consuming public.[3] Industrial giants like General Electric and Westinghouse, once primarily suppliers of equipment to other industries, increasingly sold products directly to individual consumers. The special modernity of advertising agents seemed exemplified by their strategic position on the interface of this dynamic new relationship between big business and its public.

In their efforts to speed the flow of goods through the national marketplace by eliminating any friction from consumer resistance, advertisers sought the ultimate realization of those qualities that had characterized the whole process of modernization. Presiding over the immense, impersonal marketplace that marked America's emergence as the world's most modern society, advertisers worked to further the processes of efficiency, specialization, and rationalization. More information about more products, they argued, would further rationalize the market. It would remove "the waste and lost motion in the channels of trade."[4] As more brands achieved national recognition, customers would enjoy a further expansion of choice. Consumer choices, in turn, would reward the best and most efficient producers, increasing their sales and enabling them to achieve new economies of scale in production. These producers would then lower prices, giving everyone the opportunity for a higher standard of living.

Advertisers thus celebrated the complexities and interdependencies of modern society, seeking to further rationalize the operations of the marketplace, to lubricate its mechanisms, and to achieve greater control over its functioning. With the maturing of industrialization, the consumer remained the most unpredictable and thus the most disruptive element in the economic system. If advertising agents could induce consumers to answer their needs by depending on more products offered them impersonally through the marketplace and could educate them to a predictable and enthusiastic demand for new products, then they would enhance the rationality and dynamism of the modern business system.

Picking Up the Tempo

For most advertising leaders of the 1920s and 1930s, it was hardly necessary to step out of character to preach a gospel of modernity. If modern society was distinctively urban, the people in advertising were quintessential city people. If modernity implied youthfulness, mobility, optimism, and a tolerance for diversity and speed of change, most advertising leaders immediately recognized such qualities in their self-portraits. When the copywriter A. B. Carson sketched for his colleagues a day in the life of John Smith, "typical citizen of this restless republic," he instinctively took the ad man as his model of an American attuned to the modern tempo:

> Whang! Bang! Clangety-clang! Talk about the tempo of today—John Smith knows it well. Day after day it whirs continuously in his brain, his blood, his very soul.
>
> Yanked out of bed by an alarm clock, John speeds through his shave, bolts his breakfast in eight minutes, and scurries for a train or the street car. On the way to work his roving eye scans, one after the other, the sport page, the comic strips, several columns of political hokum, and the delectable details of the latest moonshine murder.
>
> From eight to twelve, humped over a desk in a skyscraper, he wrestles with his job to the accompaniment of thumping typewriters, jingling telephones, and all the incessant tattoo of twentieth century commerce. One hour off for a quick lunch, a couple of cigarettes, and a glamorous glance at the cuties mincing down the boulevard. Jangling drudgery again from one until five. Then out on the surging streets once more.
>
> Clash, clatter, rattle and roar! Honk! Honk! Honk! Every crossing jammed with traffic! Pavements fairly humming with the jostling crowds! A tingling sense of adventure and romance in the very air! Speed-desire-excitement—the illusion of freedom at the end of the day! The flashing of lights of early evening—Clara Bow in Hearts Aflame! Wuxtry! Wuxtry!—Bootlegger Kills Flapper Sweetheart! Clickety-click, clickety-click—John Smith homeward-bound, clinging to a strap and swiftly skimming through the last edition.[5]

Carson's cameo strikingly captures the mood of dozens of self-portraits drawn by other advertising writers of the era. All recounted the hectic pace of their lives, the tense competition. But despite their allusions to "jangling drudgery" and "jostling crowds," they responded enthusiastically to the modern tempo. The rapid pace of urban life matched the tempo of their jobs. The complexity and diversity of the city provided the stimulus for new "angles" and ideas. They prided themselves on their cosmopolitanism, their independence from traditional mores and maxims, their tolerant acceptance of whatever motif of "smartness" was borne aloft by the latest wave of fashion.

In their anxiety to stay alert for any signs of change and in their urgency to impress prospective business clients with the indispensability of their expertise in interpreting current tastes, advertising leaders in the 1920s heralded a new society transforming itself at breathless speed. "What an age," gasped a columnist for *Advertising and Selling*. "Photographs by radio. Machines that think. Lights that pierce fog. . . . Vending machines to replace salesmen. . . . The list of modern marvels is practically endless." Everything now had to be "quick," observed another advertising writer: "quick lunches at soda fountains . . . quick cooking recipes . . . quick tabloid newspapers . . . quick news summaries . . . quicker novels . . . quick-drying furniture paint . . . quick-smoking cigarettes . . . quick-service filling stations."[6] Robert Updegraff, author of the most quoted article of the 1920s in *Advertising and Selling*, warned of a "new American tempo" that had given American life "the turbulence of shallow water." No one could predict what might next evoke the public's enthusiasm or sudden indifference, he observed. People were worried that the "stream of life" would surge past them, that their neighbors would leave them behind. This made them "quicker to take up new ideas, to sample new products, to test new services, but quicker, also, to toss them aside." Advertising, warned the agency president Earnest Elmo Calkins, was "the only means by which a manufacturer can quickly refocus his attack."[7]

[margin note: people worried life would leave them behind]

While advertising agencies and the media undoubtedly hyped "the new tempo" in an attempt to stampede businessmen toward their services, the perception of a new pace of life was not mere advertising puffery. For more than a century Americans had been chronically self-conscious of the speed of change in their society, but the 1920s brought a new onslaught of that obsession. Everywhere they looked, Americans saw striking technological advances. In their everyday lives, they experienced the impact of disruptive social changes. A national network of new highways visibly symbolized a world now moving at a pace set by the automobile. Cities everywhere had suddenly acquired skyscraper skylines and rings of suburbs. As industrial production doubled during the 1920s, electrification and the assembly line proceeded apace. Everything seemed to operate on a new scale. In "Middletown" (Muncie, Indiana)—a city selected by the sociologists Robert and Helen Lynd in the mid-1920s as "having many features common to a wide group of communities"—the largest factories now employed between one and two thousand workers compared to approximately two hundred a generation before. Industrial hierarchies of technically trained managers were multiplying; employers no longer knew their workers. Larger, less "personal" chain stores steadily supplanted independent retailers: during a ten-month period in 1924–25, four new chain stores entered the small city of Muncie. New forms of consumer credit accelerated economic activity. By the end of the 1920s, Americans were buying over 60 percent of their cars, radios, and furniture on the installment plan.[8]

The exhilaration created by the new pace of technological change and economic activity coexisted with deep anxieties about social disorder—anxieties symbolized by prohibition, immigration restrictions, and warnings of the dangers posed by the "new woman" and "flaming youth." Jazz, bobbed hair, cosmetics, the hip flask, and sexual frankness all flouted traditional moral standards and seemed to threaten family stability and paternal authority. The new media of movies and radio were nationalizing American culture, creating the specter of a country whose masses could be easily swayed by the latest fad.

[margin note: social panic]

Ad creators seized on the public's sense of an exciting yet disconcerting new tempo, reinforcing and amplifying this perception for their own purposes. They welcomed the economic forces that were propelling advertising toward an enhanced position of power and status in the society, and they explored strategies for transforming their clients' products into plausible solutions to the anxieties and dilemmas that arose from the pace of life and the scale of institutions in the new era. In the process, American advertising matured in style and content, gradually assuming what we now recognize as distinctly modern forms.

Practical Heroics and Versatility

To gain full stature as the vanguard of American business in the 1920s, advertising first had to prove its worth on pragmatic economic grounds. It had long since accomplished this in product areas ranging from railroad lines to breakfast foods. But the second decade of the twentieth century witnessed an impressive expansion of the successful application of national advertising to the promotion of a much wider range of products and causes.[9]

Even before World War I, several large companies had begun to use advertising to do more than simply sell a product. In 1908, for example, American Telephone and Telegraph launched a continuing campaign of institutional advertisements to persuade the public of the virtues of a regulated private monopoly. The campaign also instructed the public in proper telephone etiquette and reminded AT&T operators of their responsibilities to the public. Several public utilities and railroads launched similar institutional campaigns with more limited political objectives. The meatpackers turned to advertising to defend themselves against government investigations and threats of antitrust prosecution. The notion gained credence that advertising could influence public attitudes as well as sell products.[10]

But the merchandising of products remained advertising's central function. Here advertising began to demonstrate its amazing flexibility in the years just before World War I. Burgeoning sales of an array of new electrical appliances seemed to prove the efficacy of the large advertising campaigns that had launched them. Procter and Gamble tutored the business community in the power of planned promotion for a new product when it spent $3 million in a step-by-step campaign to launch Crisco. Advertising also found ways to show its muscle in the promotion of old products. Textile mills began to trademark and label their products and to seek brand loyalty through national advertising. The California Fruit Growers Exchange (Sunkist) demonstrated that even fresh produce could successfully be branded and advertised. By the early 1920s, products ranging from walnuts to household coal were ingeniously being individually branded and nationally advertised. Few products seemed beyond the pale of advertising after 1909, when the National Casket Company embarked on a national magazine campaign.[11]

Even products rarely purchased as separate units began to seek a place in consumer consciousness. The Timken Roller Bearing Company and the Timken-Detroit Axle Company pioneered the way, beginning in 1912. Consumers were likely to purchase axles and ball bearings only as component parts of automobiles or other pieces of machinery. But Timken hoped, by creating a national reputation, to cement the loyalty of auto manufacturers to well-known components. By the early 1920s, a half-dozen manufacturers of component auto parts, from upholstery to door handles, were expressing their faith in advertising by purchasing expensive full-page ads in the *Saturday Evening Post*.[12]

World War I provided American advertising with new opportunities to exhibit its power and flexibility. Organizing themselves into a National War Advisory Board, advertising leaders offered to help the government raise funds and recruit military personnel. Eventually incorporated into the government's public relations program (as the Division of Advertising of George Creel's Committee on Public Information), agency leaders mounted impressive campaigns to sell war bonds, enlist army and navy recruits, enhance worker morale, and promote conservation of food and resources. Their propaganda packed evident emotional power; the war bond campaigns were a conspicuous success. As the J. Walter Thompson agency observed, the war gave advertising men "an opportunity not only to render a valuable patriotic service . . . but also to reveal to a wide circle of influential men . . . the real character of advertising and the important function which it performs." *Printers' Ink* later concluded that advertising had fully capitalized on its opportunity. Wartime advertising had shown that "it is possible to sway the minds of whole populations, change their habits of life, create belief, practically universal, in any policy or idea." Moreover, reflected Theodore Mac-Manus, the genius of Cadillac advertising, the patriotic propaganda campaigns had accustomed people to the notion that "any surface and every surface, and all approaches through the senses" were appropriate for advertising.[13]

A wartime excess profits tax, which defined advertising expenditures as exempt business costs, encouraged experimentation with new or enlarged advertising budgets. As the agency president and advertising historian Frank Presbrey observed, this tax policy, which continued through 1921, "set new standards in the use of space." Timid advertisers now burst forth with full-page displays. They liked the ego-satisfaction of such "dominance" as well as the resulting sales returns. In 1919 and 1920, advertising volume broke all previous records. After a brief downturn in 1921, the economy boomed, the real income of most Americans expanded, and installment-plan selling gained momentum. In an essay subtitle, *Printers' Ink* dubbed 1922 "The Dawn of the Distribution Age," an age in which advertising would play a central role.[14]

Mounting statistics revealed how successful advertising had been in proving its practical power. Daniel Pope, in a recent attempt to correct incomplete and suspect statistics, estimates total advertising volume in the United States to have increased from $682 million in 1914 to $1,409 million in 1919 and to $2,987 million in 1929. The ratio of advertising costs to total distribution costs, according to Pope, rose from 8 percent in 1919 to 14 percent in 1929. Newly emerging national advertisers increased their advertising appropriations by geometric proportions. Maxwell House Coffee, for example, expanded its magazine budget from $19,955 to $509,000 during the years from 1921 to 1927 alone. The Crane Company (plumbing fixtures) appropriated $436,000 for advertising in 1925 compared to only $79,000 in 1921. Mushrooming activity brought unprecedented boosts in agency salaries and fees for artists and photographers. Agency costs in producing advertisements, as one critic put it, "hit the ceiling, broke through, and sailed off into the empyrean."[15]

Meanwhile, the advertising trade was gradually becoming more consolidated and complex. During the first year after the war, two dynamic new agencies, Barton, Durstine and Osborn and Newell-Emmett, appeared in New York City. Within two years, J. Walter Thompson, the largest New York agency, increased its staff from 177 to 283. During the previous decade, Philadelphia, and especially Chicago, had challenged New York in claims to leadership in national advertising. As late as 1926, two of the nation's three largest advertising agencies were still headquartered outside New York City: the venerable N. W. Ayer and Son maintained its main offices in Philadelphia, and Lord and Thomas had its head-quarters in Chicago. But both now expanded their branch offices in New York City. The term "Madison Avenue," which first came into passing use in 1923 as shorthand for advertising agencies, steadily came to reflect accurately the concen-tration of advertising expertise in uptown Manhattan.[16]

As the 1920s progressed, the rise of radio advertising and the corporate mergers that brought more companies under Wall Street influence tended to centralize national advertising in New York City. By the late 1920s, 247 Park Avenue, 285 Madison Avenue, and the Graybar Building on Lexington Avenue near 42nd Street had become the three points of a triangle of bustling advertising activity. The number of agencies and accounts mounted; the migration of accounts and personnel between the agencies intensified. In June of 1926 *Advertising and Selling* announced a new service to readers—a News Digest section that would catalogue for quick reference the proliferating agency and personnel changes.[17]

It was also in 1926 that another significant sign of advertising influence and maturity appeared. In that year the *Saturday Evening Post*, the nation's advertising showcase and the largest weekly in circulation, began to carry a regular Index of Advertisers as well as an index to its editorial content. In the same year the *Post* first offered four-color pages to advertisers at a rate of $11,000 per page.[18] Already magazines and newspapers had become bloated with advertisements. In 1926 a single issue of the *Saturday Evening Post* often exceeded 200 pages. In the April 1926 *Ladies' Home Journal*, the largest issue yet published, advertisements com-manded 162 of its 270 pages. National magazine advertising had increased 600 percent in the decade since 1916, and newspaper advertising had doubled. Amer-icans could hardly fail to notice this testimony to business confidence in the power of advertising. Trade leaders, and even the Secretary of Labor, proclaimed the end of business cycles. The bold application of advertising, they claimed, would counteract business downturns and prevent future depressions.[19]

The climactic event in the demonstration of advertising's economic power came early in 1927, with the capitulation of Henry Ford, advertising's most prominent hold-out. Except for a large but temporary campaign in 1924–25, Ford had largely shunned national advertising. Advocates of advertising as the ultimate economic force found Ford's success a thorn in their side. In mid-1926 he had impetuously eliminated nearly all of his advertising budget, exclaiming, "Cut it all out; it's an economic waste and I never did believe in it." The advertising trade press, stung by Ford's actions and remarks, exploded in jubilation the next year when Ford announced a massive advertising campaign in support of his new Model A. The last great unbeliever had been converted.[20]

Erasing the Barnum Image

Many advertising leaders in the 1920s did not remain content with the wide-spread recognition of advertising's economic power. If advertising had proved itself economically as "the Archimedean lever that is moving the world," then

perhaps such leverage could also be employed to elevate its status as an occupation.[21] Patent medicines had loomed large in nineteenth-century American
advertising. The lingering effects of that association continued to fuse images of
the modern advertising man with recollections of carnival barkers, snake-oil
salesmen, and such celebrated promoters of ballyhoo and humbug as P. T.
Barnum. Advertising leaders chafed under public suspicion of their craft. Move-
ments for professionalization and respectability, such as the pre–World War I
quest for professional standing as a "science" and the "truth in advertising"
movement of 1912, had testified to the depth of their concern about this image
problem.[22]

Service with the Committee on Public Information during World War I helped
bring advertising men new stature. George Creel, chairman of the CPI, concluded
that their war service had won advertising men new prestige as professionals. In
their successful promotion of Liberty bonds, military enlistments, and civilian
morale, they had convinced the nation that advertising could instill new ideas and
inspire people to patriotic action. Comparable war work also significantly elevated the status of advertising men in Britain. The wartime crusades proved that
advertising was no mere commercial tool, but a great moral and educative force,
capable of serving "unselfish social purposes."[23]

Capitalizing on their wartime elevation in status, advertising leaders in the early
1920s began to seize every opportunity to associate themselves with high culture
and "business statesmanship." In 1921 the Art Directors Club of New York
initiated exhibitions to demonstrate advertising's contributions to artistic excellence. In 1924 the trade established a "Harvard connection" with the announcement by the Harvard Business School of awards for various phases of advertising
excellence. By the mid-1920s, agencies had been able to lure such prestigious
illustrators and photographers as Maxfield Parrish, Norman Rockwell, Walter
Briggs, Edward Steichen, Anton Bruehl, Bernice Abbott, and Frank Lyendecker
from their magazine-cover and studio work to contribute to the prestige and
allure of the advertising pages. No less an institution than the Metropolitan
Museum of Art appointed a liaison officer to help advertisers use its resources.[24]
Agencies boasted of their dignified and high-minded new institutional campaigns
on behalf of E. R. Squibb and Sons, General Motors, General Electric, and the
Metropolitan Life Insurance Company. Advertising's rising star was hardly
dimmed when Bruce Barton, a partner in the flashy young agency handling the
General Electric and General Motors institutional accounts, hit the top of the
nation's nonfiction bestseller list in 1926 with *The Man Nobody Knows,* in which
he portrayed Jesus as the archetypal, advertising-minded businessman.[25]

The climax of advertising's rise to new heights of influence and stature came
with President Calvin Coolidge's address to the convention of the American
Association of Advertising Agencies in the fall of 1926. For more than a decade,
advertising leaders had been claiming recognition as a preeminent civilizing and
modernizing force. By educating consumers in everything from the use of toothpaste and higher standards of dress to a love of beauty and a "cultivation of the
mind and the social graces," they were harnessing America's modern industrial
system to the uplift of its citizenry.[26] President Coolidge defined their con-

tribution to modern society even more impressively. If the "life of trade" had once been competition, the President observed, it was now advertising. Advertising men were "molding the human mind." Upon the advertising profession had been thrust "the high responsibility of inspiring and ennobling the commercial world." In a sanctification of their occupation that even advertising writers would find hard to surpass, the President concluded by defining their work as "part of the great work of the regeneration and redemption of mankind."[27]

The Advertisement Becomes "Modern"

What made American advertising "modern" as an economic force and "modern" as a promoter of new urban habits of hygiene, dress, and style consciousness was not what made it "modern" in content and technique. As an economic force, advertisements functioned as efficient mass communications that rationalized and lubricated an impersonal marketplace of vast scale. They facilitated the exchange of goods and services between multitudes of strangers on a national (and even international) level. The resulting economies of scale and efficiencies of specialization generated those increases in the American standard of living that President Coolidge undoubtedly had in mind when he spoke of "regeneration and redemption." Advertising also stimulated the popular conviction "that what was new was desirable," the attitude that J. H. Plumb describes as crucial to an acceptance of modernity and that twentieth-century advertising leaders saw as indispensable to mass production and economic growth. Thus advertising fits comfortably into the concept of "the modern" as expressed in the term *modernization*.[28]

But "modern" also means "characteristic of the present time, or time not long past."[29] In the 1920s and 1930s, as in several previous eras, the attitudes, fashions, modes of artistic expression, and fads in popular psychology that were "characteristic of the present" were as likely to contradict the process of economic and industrial modernization as to reinforce it. The "modernity" of advertisements that were "characteristic of the present" often found expression in styles and appeals that catered to yearnings unfulfilled by efficient, rationalized mass production and distribution. Thus in content and technique, American advertisements can be said to have become "modern" precisely to the extent to which they transcended or denied their essential economic nature as mass communications and achieved subjective qualities and a "personal" tone. As it came to accept the paradox of its role as both apostle of modernity and buffer against the effects of modern impersonalities of scale, and as it developed strategies for accommodating the public to modern complexities, American advertising in the 1920s and 1930s took on what we now recognize as a distinctly modern cast.

Advertising content and style had changed gradually but decisively during the first two decades of the twentieth century. Older styles and techniques were seldom discarded entirely and sometimes experienced revivals, but the main

1.1, 1.2. *Between 1916 and 1926, Procter and Gamble abandoned its detached, "reason-why" tone of voice (Fig. 1.1) for less product-oriented ads, with person-to-person illustrations and copy (Fig. 1.2).*

thrust of change was unmistakable. At the beginning of the century advertisers had sought simple brand-name publicity through advertising jingles and poster-style displays. Then advertising copywriters had turned to "salesmanship in print" with hard-selling copy full of reasons and arguments in place of rhymes and slogans. These arguments and reasons, as Daniel Pope and Jackson Lears have observed, were not necessarily "rational"; influential copywriters and advertising psychologists had already concluded that consumers acted less from logic than from "nonrational yearnings." The new "reason-why" approach took as its model the salesman, foot in the door, overcoming buying resistance with an arsenal of factual and emotional arguments. Already, copy experts were admonishing each other not to think of their audience as an anonymous crowd, but rather to imagine themselves selling the product to an individual customer. To induce consumers to read advertising copy that was often long and argumentative, the advertiser-as-salesman was encouraged to use imagination and a "human-interest" approach to appeal to their emotions.[30]

By about 1914, a few advertisers had begun to appreciate the advantages of selling the benefit instead of the product—illumination instead of lighting fixtures, prestige instead of automobiles, sex appeal instead of mere soap. (Woodbury's pathbreaking slogan, "The Skin You Love to Touch," first appeared in 1911.) Still, the great majority of advertisements remained product-centered. Only occasionally did human-interest advertising move beyond appealing illustrations of children, animals, and trade characters.[31] A comparison of advertisements of 1915–16 with those of a decade later presents striking contrasts (Figs. 1.1, 1.2). For all of the new emphasis on advertising psychology in the years just prior to World War I, the ads of that period largely featured the product itself; most gave little attention to the psychic byproducts of owning it.

Product

Personal Benefit

The freshest and cleanest writing paper

WHEREVER you find Highland Linen Writing Paper—and you find it nearly everywhere—you always find it fresh and crisp and clean. Monthly shipments constantly replenish every dealer's stock. Dainty attractiveness is the chief charm of Highland Linen. We cannot let that daintiness be marred by shop-worn goods. Highland Linen is always fresh. You can send out your letters on it with the calm assurance that it will reflect credit upon you and convey a compliment to your friend.

EATON'S
HIGHLAND ✦ LINEN
The writing paper for particular people

1919

Would you criticize a Friend behind her back?

OF COURSE, you wouldn't! You may not be a stickler for propriety, you may do many things that are modern, things that violate some people's ideas of the conventions, but disloyalty to a friend—never!

But how about disloyalty to yourself? Are you always sure that you are not thoughtlessly laying yourself open to criticism? Are you not often guilty of reflecting on your own good taste and good sense?

Does your writing paper talk about you behind your back? Does it say to your friends what they are too loyal to you to say—that you lack taste or that you are indifferent to the good taste of others?

Every letter on cheap, gaudy paper, every note hurriedly scrawled on a pad or whatever is handy and mailed in a misfit envelope carries with it a reflection on the taste of the sender and implies an utter disregard for the taste of the one to whom it is sent.

No girl can afford to misrepresent herself in this way. And it's so easy to have the right paper at hand—it costs so little and saves so much trouble and so many embarrassing situations. Just ask for Eaton's Highland Linen at any store where good stationery is sold. You will be shown a number of pretty, correct shades in a variety of correct shapes and sizes.

And—if you're in the least doubt about social usage in letter-writing, I have a little book called "Correct Social Correspondence" that I'll be glad to send you on receipt of 50c. It tells most everything you might want to know about all those so-small but so-important niceties of correspondence. Or if you wish, I will personally answer any question about letter writing.

Caroline de Laney

Address me in care of
EATON, CRANE & PIKE COMPANY
225 Fifth Avenue, New York City

Eaton's Highland Linen in five smart envelope styles and all the fashionable shades may be bought wherever stationery is sold.

Style is a greater Social Asset than Beauty

1923

1.3, 1.4. Compare Eaton's genteel 1919 ad (Fig. 1.3) with its invitation to consumer participation in 1923 (Fig. 1.4). The advertiser-as-adviser now asked solicitously, "Does your writing paper talk about you behind your back?"

Most advertisements, even into the first years of the 1920s, still retained the quality of announcements. While they did occasionally show people enjoying the product—dancing to the phonograph or riding in the car—they rarely invited the reader's engagement and empathy with detailed vignettes of group conversations, family activities, or moments of social triumph or humiliation. In contrast to the dominant mode of ads after the mid-1920s, they provided more objective information about the product than subjective information about the hopes and anxieties of the consumer (Figs. 1.3, 1.4).

In an attempt to define what was new about advertising content and technique in the 1920s, *Printers' Ink* retrospectively pointed to such criteria as the shift from the "factory viewpoint" to concern with "the mental processes of the consumer," from "the objective to the subjective," from "descriptive product data" to "talk in terms of ultimate buying motives." Recently, Richard Pollay has characterized these changes toward an emphasis on the benefits of consumption, portrayals of consumers using the product, and "emotive" copy styles as a transition from "a production or selling orientation" to a "marketing orientation."[32] Ads increasingly included what might be called "participatory" anecdotes and illustrations. These changes manifested themselves by the mid-1920s in ads with such headlines as "Are You Sure You Know Your Type?" "Little Dry Sobs Through The Bedroom Door," "And he wondered why she said No!" and "Sh-h-h, he's coming." People rather than products dominated illustrations as advertisers sought to induce the potential customer to play a vicarious, scripted role as protagonist in the ad. A 1928 headline, "Be the Leading Lady in this Little Modern Drama," only made explicit the invitation to consumer participation that many advertisers now sought to imbed in their illustrations and copy.[33]

Advertisers had come to appreciate the advantage of inducing the reader empathetically "to have *lived through an experience*—an experience planned by the advertiser to prove a sales point."[34] Reciprocally, consumers, through responses measured in sales results, personal letters, and coupon returns, were persuading advertisers that they wanted to comprehend the product on a "human scale" and thus, perhaps, gain confidence in their capacities as individuals to retain a sense of control in an expanding mass society.

Americans had traditionally welcomed modernization. They had celebrated the contributions of new technologies to prosperity, convenience, comfort, and a faster pace of life. But many had accommodated uneasily to the new scale of social and economic life occasioned by technological advances. People had responded with both excitement and suspicion as new forms of transportation and communication invaded local communities. As powerful external forces seemed to gain increasing power over their lives, Robert Wiebe observes, people "groped for some personal connection with that broader environment, some way of mediating between their everyday life and its impersonal setting." The giant industrial organizations that emerged with technological advance could easily diminish the individual's sense of autonomy and control. As Daniel Bell has pointed out, the new world of large-scale organizations—the world of coordination and bureaucracy—was one in which men were often "treated as things because one can more easily coordinate things than men." And the rationalization and depersonalization of increasing portions of people's lives made it more difficult to find emotional satisfactions. During the late nineteenth century and the early years of the Progressive Era, many Americans had vented their anxieties about the increasing complexity and scale of their society by protesting against the engulfing tides of unrestricted immigration, by launching anti-monopoly attacks against the great corporations, and by seeking, in quests extending from political reform to mind cure, some reassurance that opportunities still existed to achieve autonomy and to gain recognition for qualities of individual character.[35]

World War I brought an end to widespread distrust of big business, and postwar legislation curtailed the influx of immigrants. But perceptions of a quickened tempo of change in the 1920s intensified people's fears of failing to keep pace with new complexities and of becoming "lost in the crowd." Societal trends toward

large bureaucratic organizations, high mobility, and more anonymous and seg-
mental relationships persisted, even accelerated. Even in the late nineteenth century, a "tangled and distended" network of economic and social relationships and
a crumbling faith in "communal, ethical, or religious frameworks of meaning"
had cut many Americans adrift from a secure "sense of selfhood." Now, increasingly, many Americans pursued their search for a secure identity, for
"self-realization," by seeking clues and advice in those sources most conveniently
and ubiquitously available—the mass media.[36] Advertisers gradually recognized,
consciously or subconsciously, that the complexities of an increasingly urbanized,
specialized, interdependent mode of life were creating a residue of unmet needs.
Perceiving new vacuums of guidance and personal relationships, they stepped
forward to offer their products as answers to modern discontents. Thus what
made advertising "modern" was, ironically, the discovery by these "apostles of
modernity" of techniques for empathizing with the public's imperfect acceptance
of modernity, with its resistance to the perfect rationalization and bureaucratization of life.

Some ad creators, undoubtedly, simply assumed that their new strategies
reflected a gradual awakening of copywriters to psychological truths about human
nature. But others recognized that the success of the new subjective, personalized,
and "participatory" techniques stemmed from ambiguous popular reactions to the
modern scale of things and the modern tempo. The inferiority complex had come
to be "a valuable thing in advertising" noted William Esty, a J. Walter Thompson
account representative, in an agency meeting in 1930. Was that not due, he asked,
to "the fact that this standardized age has made people feel inferior?"[37]

Advertisements in the new copy styles set forward a model of life's struggles
that was well-tailored to strike a responsive chord among people conscious of the
increasing dependence of their life ambitions on large organizations and impersonal judgments. This model portrayed the typical life-situation as that of an
individual facing an external task or goal. An objective test or impersonal decision
determined whether the protagonist of the story—the consumer's stand-in—
successfully met the challenge. Disinterested, judgmental people would determine whether one succeeded in contests for business success, popularity, social
standing, beauty, even love. "They" would determine by rigid standards—
without the possibility of personal favoritism or the sympathetic excusing of
faults—whether one's teeth, breath, "intestinal vigor," bathroom fixtures, silverware, or automobile polish "met the test." Having scripted a confrontation between the consumer and an impersonal test, the advertiser quickly befriended the
consumer. Assuming the role of coach and confidante, he offered the consumer
advice and encouragement as together they faced the external challenge.

Side by Side with the Consumer

As copywriters evolved from salesmen to confidantes, they began to perceive
other advantages in this new "side-by-side" approach. Argument, no matter how
amiable and persuasive, had a polarizing tendency that pitted advertising persua-

siveness against buyer resistance. Too much argumentative reliance on reasons induced the reader to generate counter-reasons. Advice or "coaching," on the other hand, aligned advertiser and potential consumer on the *same side* in opposition to a task or problem confronting the consumer. As society's increasing pressures and complexities made the consumer uneasy, the advertiser intervened with sympathetic advice on how to triumph over the impersonal judgments of the modern world.

"Scare copy," which became increasingly prominent as the 1920s progressed, was simply one variant of this side-by-side positioning. Known in trade jargon as the "negative appeal," scare copy sought to jolt the potential consumer into a new consciousness by enacting dramatic episodes of social failures and accusing judgments. Jobs were lost, romances cut short, and marriages threatened. Germs attacked, cars skidded out of control, and neighbors cast disapproving glances.[38] In each instance, the product stepped forward—not to argue with the reader, but to offer friendly help. Scare copy posited a universe in which the fate of each consumer lay in the hands of external disinterested forces and unsympathetic, judgmental observers, a world of normative expectations applied with unmerciful severity. By contrast, the advertiser was solicitous and caring, a friend in need (Fig. 1.5).

Increasingly during the 1920s, this friend was recognizable by name. It might be Betty Crocker or Mary Hale Martin or Nurse Ellen Buckland or any of a score of (usually fictitious) advisers and confidantes who "personally signed" their company's ads. Or it might be someone you "knew well"—a prominent society figure or movie star whose familiar presence could give you a sense of receiving advice from a real person.[39]

Personal endorsers in the advertisements acquired a new sort of realism. The conventionalized character types of only a few years before—the stencilled and standardized doctor, businessman, druggist, and housewife—were vanishing from the ads, the *Printers' Ink* art reporter noted in 1926. As photographers turned away from professional models and as artists perfected refinements in expression, he claimed, people in advertisements seemed less commercial. Now, "familiar faces smile out at you; old friends bow recognition. . . . The little lady in the shoe advertisement is almost a likeness of a friend's daughter who lives down the suburban street." Not only were the faces of people in the ads coming to look friendly and familiar. They were also acquiring the power to induce readers to "smile with them, frown with them, suffer with them." By the beginning of the 1930s, one critic was praising Unguentine ads for "studies in expression . . . so catching' . . . that the reader is swept along by them despite himself."[40]

Advertising copy could also *create* ordinary folks as "real people" to personalize the helpful advice. Procter and Gamble advertisements for laundry soap reported in chatty informality on a series of "Actual Visits to P & G Homes." "Mrs. Lewis" in P & G home no. 3 recalled her experiences with "little Dorothy's" rompers, and "Mrs. Moore," encountered in home no. 5, offered friends an ironing hint (See Fig. 1.2). Names were crucial, concluded William Esty several years later. In comparative tests with copy returns, an ad with a person's name always outpulled an ad without one, regardless of the selling message.[41] Readers hungered for a personal touch. Mobility, greater generational separation, and modern complex-

"She looks old enough to be his mother"

A CATTY REMARK—but this time it's true. And actually she is five years younger than her husband!

And the pity of it is that, in this enlightened age, so often a woman has only herself to blame if she fails to stay young with her husband—and with her women friends.

Today science has applied itself to those delicate problems of feminine hygiene upon which so much of a woman's good health and youthfulness and charm depend.

Today there need be no misconception of the true facts. The makers of "Lysol" Disinfectant offer you a booklet called "The Scientific Side of Health and Youth" which gives the correct information and simple rules which every woman should have for constant reference. It is sound professional advice, written for women by a woman physician. It is free. Simply send the coupon below. The booklet will reach you in a plain envelope.

In the meantime, don't take needless chances. Buy a bottle of "Lysol" Disinfectant today at your drugstore. Complete directions come with every bottle.

"Lysol" Disinfectant is sold at retail *only* in the *brown* bottle packed in the *yellow* carton.

Made by Lysol, Incorporated, a division of Lehn & Fink Products Company. Sole distributors: Lehn & Fink, Inc., Bloomfield, N. J. In Canada, Lysol (Canada) Limited. Distributed by Lehn & Fink (Canada) Limited.

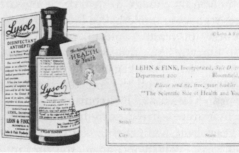

Lysol Disinfectant

LEHN & FINK, Incorporated, Sole Distributors
Department 200   Bloomfield, N. J.
Please send me, free, your booklet
"The Scientific Side of Health and Youth"

Name

Street

City   State

1.5. *Dramatizing a world of harsh but valid external judgments, advertisers stepped forward as advisers and confidantes. If she ignored them, the consumer had "only herself to blame."*

ities of living had created a vacuum of personal advice. In responding to that need, advertisers explored new ways to personalize their relationship with the consumer.

How did the ad creators *know* that consumers thirsted for the subjective, personalized, "realistic" vignettes of the emerging modern style of advertising? Certainly they paid close attention to the returns from coupon offers of booklets and samples. And they noted the apparent reflection of popular tastes in the movies, tabloid newspapers, and other burgeoning forms of popular culture. But above all, they paid attention to the most dramatic successes among other advertising campaigns. Advertising leaders had experimented with the human-interest approach in the decade before 1920, but it was the spectacular sales success of several specific campaigns in the early 1920s that now spurred a host of advertisers to adopt the modern mode in advertising.

Three Legends in the Making

Within a single year in the early 1920s, major advertising campaigns emerged for three products that were unknown, obscure, or facing declining sales. In each case, the product achieved spectacular sales increases by the middle of the decade. Since advertising seemed primarily responsible for each of these success stories, other advertisers pondered the lessons they offered in modern advertising content and technique.

Fleischmann's Yeast, the first of these emerging advertising legends of the 1920s, had been "something merely to bake bread with—until Fleischmann advertisements said otherwise." In the face of a steady decline in home baking, even Fleischmann's lofty characterization of its product as the "Soul of Bread" had not proved inspiring enough to stem declining sales. Social trends offered little hope for a resurgence in home-baked bread. Prohibition had largely destroyed another sales outlet for yeast. Could the sales of a product so tied by tradition to very specific functions be salvaged by its promotion for some new use? In 1919 the Fleischmann Company began to explore that possibility with a medicinal appeal.[42]

Within a year, with the impetus supplied by its new agency, the J. Walter Thompson Company, Fleischmann's advertising had transformed its product into a food to be eaten directly from the package as a potent source of vitamins. Two years later, with the market saturated by new vitamin products, Fleischmann's Yeast evolved once again, this time into a natural laxative. A prize contest brought in hundreds of usable testimonials for the product's newly advertised propensities. From 153 of the winners, the agency gained permission to use their letters and "illustrate them in any way we saw fit."[43]

Fleischmann advertising moved into the costly but highly visible rotogravure sections. Photographs replaced drawings to give the ads a greater aura of realism. Soon photographers' models gave way to "candid" photographs of the actual endorsers. Capturing the tempo of popular journalism, the J. Walter Thompson copywriters established a tabloid format for the Fleischmann campaign. They

1.6. In a format easily mistaken for a feature story, Fleischmann's encouraged readers to share the experiences of a hunter, a mother of four, and other familiar folk who had "corrected clogged intestines."

1.7. Despite cries of "tastelessness" and AMA criticism of medical testimonials, Fleischmann's pursued sales by combining the aura of European medical authority with attention-grabbing, "scientific" diagrams.

injected as much human interest and eye appeal as possible by using multiple photographs and succinct, first-person testimony (Fig. 1.6). Sometimes the ads recapitulated the layout of the magazine or newspaper so perfectly that the reader might become thoroughly immersed in the ad before discovering that it was not an editorial feature.[44]

By 1926 the Fleischmann Company had become one of the nation's ten largest magazine advertisers and a major purchaser of newspaper space. With no other new factor in its merchandising effort, sales turned upward. By the spring of 1926 sales had increased 130 percent over 1923, when the candid, man-in-the-street testimonials had begun.[45]

When sales threatened to recede, the Thompson agency called doctors to the rescue. Authoritative physicians in white coats explained how the pressures and complexities of modern civilization had led to constipation and advised readers to eat half a cake of yeast three times a day to counteract "intestinal fatigue." One agency executive affirmed the effects of the modern tempo in tracing the logic of the newly labeled disease. "Fatigue is universal; we simply have to credit it to the intestines, that's all."[46] Ignoring complaints about a violation of Victorian delicacy, the agency dramatized the role of the intestines by superimposing bold diagrams of "where the trouble starts" over photographs of lovely young women (Fig. 1.7). Such diagrams might help readers picture more clearly the source of their own modern troubles. Undaunted by the American Medical Association's outrage and its prohibition of testimony by its members, the agency turned for paid testimonials to European doctors. Their impressively unpronounceable names, prestigious hospital affiliations, and stern visages reinforced their authoritative presence.[47]

The success of Fleischmann's Yeast in the 1920s seemed to confirm the power of advertising. It had become a popular remedy despite formidable obstacles. Its price was high and its taste so repulsive that backsliders had to be reconverted to its medicinal benefits again and again. Other challenges, a copywriter reflected, were the "necessity for frequent purchase and the almost complete absence of *quickly apparent* results."[48] Advertising alone had enabled the company to increase sales in spite of these difficulties and the decline of its prime home-baking market.

The success of the Fleischmann campaign was overshadowed, however, by the even more spectacular story of Listerine. The profits of the Lambert Pharmaceutical Company, manufacturers of Listerine antiseptic, mushroomed from approximately $100,000 per year in 1920 and 1921 to over $4 million in 1927.[49] Not surprisingly, the company's style and strategy gave rise to a whole school of advertising practice.

Listerine was not a new product in 1920. For years it had been merchandised perfunctorily as a general antiseptic. Initially, the three men who transformed Listerine into the marvel of the advertising world—the copywriters Milton Feasley and Gordon Seagrove and the company president Gerard B. Lambert—did not so much convert the product to a new use as induce the public to discover a new need. After a year of comparatively awkward and old-fashioned human-interest ads for Listerine as a mouthwash, the copywriters hit upon a winning formula. The picture of a lovely girl introduced a story cryptically entitled "He Never Knew Why." The hero of the story, a rising young businessman, was spurned by the "luminous" but "charmingly demure" girl of his dreams after a single romantic encounter. He seemed to have every advantage in life, but he labored under one insurmountable handicap. He had "halitosis."[50]

The term "halitosis" (exhumed from an old medical dictionary) had a scientific sound, and thus took some of the coarseness out of a discussion of bad breath. Mimicking the tabloids' personal-interest stories and advice to the lovelorn columns, the ads took the form of quick-tempo sociodramas in which readers were invited to identify with temporary victims in tragedies of social shame. Now the protagonist was not the product but the potential consumer, suffering vicariously a loss of love, happiness, and success (Fig. 1.8). As *Printers' Ink* reflected in a tribute to the copywriter Milton Feasley: "He dealt more with humanity than with merchandise. He wrote advertising dramas rather than business announcements—dramas so common to everyday experience that every reader could easily fit himself into the plot as the hero or culprit of its action."[51]

Feasley and Seagrove constructed the Listerine ads in a way that resembled scientific efforts to control for independent variables. The heroine or hero of the story invariably possessed all the qualities needed for success—wealth, good looks, attractive personality, high social standing. Thus the only possible cause for a personal failure had to be the inexcusable fault of halitosis.

By 1926 *Printers' Ink* was eulogizing Feasley for having transformed people's behavior. He had "amplified the morning habits of our nicer citizenry—by making the morning mouthwash as important as the morning shower or the morning

What secret is your mirror holding back?

NIGHT after night she would peer questioningly into her mirror, vainly seeking the reason.

She *was* a beautiful girl and talented, too. She had the advantages of education and better clothes than most girls in her set. She possessed that culture and poise that travel brings.

Yet in the one pursuit that stands foremost in the mind of every girl and woman—marriage—she was a failure.

Many men came and went in her life. She was often a bridesmaid but never a bride. And the secret her mirror held back concerned a thing she least suspected—a thing people simply will not tell you to your face.

* * * * *

That's the insidious thing about halitosis (unpleasant breath). You, yourself, rarely know when you have it. And even your closest friends won't tell you.

Sometimes, of course, halitosis comes from some deep-seated organic disorder that requires professional advice. But usually—and fortunately—halitosis is only a local condition that yields to the regular use of Listerine as a mouth wash and gargle.

It is an interesting thing that this well-known antiseptic that has been in use for years for surgical dressings, possesses these peculiar properties as a breath deodorant. It halts food fermentation in the mouth and leaves the breath sweet, fresh and clean. So the systematic use of Listerine puts you on the safe and polite side. You know your breath is right. Fastidious people everywhere are making it a regular part of their daily routine.

Your druggist will supply you with Listerine. He sells lots of it. It has dozens of different uses as a safe antiseptic and has been trusted as such for half a century. Read the interesting little booklet that comes with every bottle.—*Lambert Pharmacal Company, Saint Louis, U.S.A.*

★ **For HALITOSIS use LISTERINE**

1.8. By emphasizing "your mirror," an early (1923) Listerine ad involved each reader vicariously in the tragedy of a girl with every advantage who failed to marry because of one unsuspected fault.

shave."[52] But Gerard Lambert had not been content to wed the fortunes of his product to *one* new habit. To maintain momentum, he had quickly introduced new uses for Listerine. Halitosis had hardly become an advertising byword before Lambert began to proclaim Listerine's virtues as a cure for dandruff. Between 1921 and 1929 the American public also learned the virtues of Listerine as an after-shave tonic, a cure for colds and sore throats, an astringent, and a deodorant (Figs. 1.9, 1.10). (If Listerine's claims to versatility seemed audacious, they paled in comparison to those of Linit, long advertised as a starch, which courted "Fastidious Women" in the mid-1920s with pretensions to newly discovered qualities as a beauty bath.) Lambert capitalized on the new fame of his product to market a Listerine toothpaste, which brought even greater financial returns. The Listerine advertising budget mounted from $100,000 in 1922 to $5 million in 1928.[53]

The financial feats of the Listerine campaign held the advertising trade enthralled. Although Lambert claimed to have contributed to company profits through innovations in cost accounting and production efficiency, observers justifiably attributed his success to the power of advertising. Phrases like "the halitosis style," "the halitosis appeal," and "the halitosis influence" became standard advertising jargon. In unmistakable tribute, copywriters soon discovered and labeled over a hundred new diseases, including such transparent imitations as "bromodosis" (sweaty foot odors), "homotosis" (lack of attractive home furnishings), and "acidosis" (sour stomach) and such inventive afflictions as "office hips," "ashtray breath," and "accelerator toe."[54] Needless to say, most of these new diseases had escaped the notice of the medical profession. Even more influential than the halitosis ploy was Listerine's effective use of copy that presented the consumer-surrogate as protagonist. Scores of converts to "Listerine copy" offered their sympathy and advice to readers who faced those intrusive, impersonal judgments of their skin, teeth, figure, clothes, furniture—even their choice of car polish and house paint—that modern life occasioned.

The promoters of Listerine were not the first to discover the sociodrama as an advertising technique—just as they had not pioneered the appeal to social shame or personal fear. In advertisements headlined "Within the Curve of a Woman's Arm," the deodorant Odo-ro-no had earlier confronted the threats to romance posed by underarm perspiration.[55] But Listerine purchased larger space in a wider variety of publications. Its expanding appropriations and spectacular profits impressed the business community. The J. Walter Thompson Company summarized the new perception of proper advertising techniques in 1926: "To sell *goods* we must also sell *words*. In fact we have to go further: we must sell *life*." Listerine had vividly demonstrated how to "befriend" consumers by inducing them to experience vicariously the barriers and the avenues to "a romantic way of living" through the ads.[56]

A third widely heralded triumph of advertising in the early 1920s was the almost instant success of a new product of the Cellucotton Company: Kotex. Advertising had long proclaimed its role in ensuring rapid, deserved success for superior new products as one of its major social contributions. The inventor Elias Howe had died a pauper, advertising writers reminded the public, because the

*1.9, 1.10. As Listerine claimed new qualities as a dandruff cure (Fig. 1.9)
and deodorant (Fig. 1.10), it explored new visual techniques: accusing
fingers to dramatize external judgments and close-up photographs to promote reader involvement.*

virtues of his unadvertised sewing machine had too long remained unknown to
the nineteenth-century public.[57] Not so the disposable sanitary napkin in the
1920s. Even though the delicacy of the subject of menstruation placed formidable
barriers in the way of an advertising campaign, the Lord and Thomas agency
accepted the challenge.

The first Kotex ads, which appeared in 1921, cautiously employed a string of
circumlocutions. The first ad in *Good Housekeeping,* under the headline "Meets the
Most Exacting Needs," pictured young women skating. It said only that Kotex
"completes toilet essentials" for active schoolgirls, "guards against emergencies,"
and "has been accepted as the most satisfactory article of its kind."[58] As a publicity
article sent to the dealers explained, the ads simply set forward the general value
and convenience of the product in an inoffensive, scientific way. Facts were
presented "thoroughly yet without unnecessary detail. If possible the reader is left
to draw her own conclusions from her intimate understanding of the subject."
Some letters of protest did greet the appearance of advertising for so intimate a
product, but the negative reaction was far milder than either the manufacturer or
the advertising agency had expected.[59]

Encouraged by this response, the Cellucotton Company pushed ahead. It enlisted the hand of "Ellen J. Buckland, Registered Nurse" to sign the advertising

copy and give readers a personalized yet professional and scientific figure to whom they could write for booklets on such an intimate subject (Fig. 1.11). Appropriating the theme of the modern tempo, the Lord and Thomas agency began to tie Kotex to the image of the modern woman who "lives *every day* of her life" and "fills every day with activity." "Today, with Kotex," Nurse Buckland promised in 1923, "you need never lose a single precious *hour*." By 1925 she was able to keep pace with changing times by assuring, "You never lose a single *moment's* precious charm." Several years later, Kotex further incorporated modern advertising techniques by replacing Nurse Buckland with "Mary Pauline Callender," who adopted the chattier, more intimate style of the advice columns.[60]

By 1927 Lord and Thomas claimed that "over 80 percent of the better class of women in America today employ Kotex." Even discounting the expected agency puffery, the sales results were impressive. Cellucotton changed its name to the Kotex Company. Albert Lasker, the president of Lord and Thomas, took tremendous pride in the Kotex campaign. It was a "simon-pure" advertising triumph, achieved in the face of a tabooed topic that "admitted no definite descriptive words in the headlines."[61] Advertising had not only publicized and gained widespread use for a practical new product; it had also stepped forward to fill one of the many vacuums of adequate communication and advice. It had assured women, through the intimacy of friendly chatter, that the correct product would enable them to keep pace with their changing society.

Selling Satisfactions

The spectacular sales results of the Fleischmann, Listerine, and Kotex campaigns had won the practical flattery of a host of imitators by the late 1920s. Personal confidantes and advisers proliferated, warnings of probing scrutiny by others mounted, and the personal testimonial enjoyed a dramatic revival. *Printers' Ink* noted that the Fleischmann "news-picture" style had attained "high favor" by 1928.[62] Inspired by these campaigns, advertisers of a wide variety of goods found ways to empathize with the anxieties of consumers who sought to keep pace with the tempo of modern life and to overcome its impersonal judgments.

Still, these three campaigns were hardly typical of the advertising of the era. Product-oriented "announcement" copy still appeared regularly. Although the Jordan Motor Car Company had been titillating the trade for several years with copy emphasizing "the enjoyment of something besides mere transportation" and the feel of a "personal, individual intimate car," Buick, Chrysler, and Chevrolet still greeted 1926 readers with pictures of their factories.[63] In the mid-1920s the more subjective, intimate style of the Fleischmann, Listerine, and Kotex campaigns still represented only the leading edge of change in a diverse body of advertising. Some advertisers, concerned about the prestige of their products and the status of their profession, found such copy too reminiscent of the patent medicine era. The sales figures were impressive, but could "participatory" copy work for most products?

1.11. *Kotex ads stressed the product's "modernity" through associations with busy urban scenes, high fashion, and "Better-Class Women." "Nurse Ellen Buckland" provided an aura of professional yet personal advice.*

By the end of the 1920s, the answer to that question by the advertising business was unquestionably Yes. Negative or scare appeals might often be inappropriate, but empathetic depiction of consumer experiences, instead of the product itself, gained steadily in favor. "Show consumer satisfactions" increasingly became the rallying cry for advertisers. The organizer of a J. Walter Thompson door-to-door survey returned early in the decade from the land "behind the doorbell" to report breathlessly that "members of the Consumer Family do not want for its own sake the product which they buy."[64] Soap ads should sell "afternoons of leisure," advised one copywriter. Copy should wrap the product "in the tissue of a dream." The *Chicago Tribune* provided a lesson in the new orthodoxy for anyone who had missed the message. It demonstrated the potential of its rotogravure section for radio advertising with a sample illustration captioned, "Here is a picture, not of a radio, but of keen enjoyment."[65]

consumers point of view over the producer

Obviously the illustrations for such ads should emphasize people more than products. They should picture situations of fulfillment or cautionary scenes of humiliations easily avoided by use of the product. Advertising agencies prided themselves on having begun to modernize industry by introducing the consumer's point of view to correct the producer's self-centered myopia. "The happiness of the reader should be the real topic of every advertisement," concluded Earnest Calkins in 1926. "The happiness of the advertiser should be carefully camouflaged." Writers in the advertising journals recounted a standard scenario of modernization in advertising: it began with ads depicting the bewhiskered founder and his factory, then moved to illustrations of the housewife pushing a vacuum cleaner or otherwise using the product, and finally arrived at scenes of fulfillment—the housewife's friends blinded by her gleaming floor or her children enjoying her company on an outing to pick wildflowers.[66]

The result of this trend toward emphasis on consumer satisfactions was called "dramatic realism"—a style derived from the romantic novel and soon institutionalized in the radio soap opera. It intensified everyday problems and triumphs by tearing them out of humdrum routine, spotlighting them as crucial to immediate life decisions, or fantasizing them within enhanced, luxurious social settings. In selling leisure, enjoyment, beauty, good taste, prestige, and popularity along with the mundane product, advertisers assumed that the customer was "pre-sold" on these "satisfactions" as proper rewards for the successful pursuit of the American dream. But in dramatizing the American dream and giving it pictorial form, advertisers also further defined the specific meanings of such qualities as good taste and enjoyment. By attempting to "fit the product into the life of the consumer," advertising, in Otis Pease's phrase, had come "to traffic in beliefs concerning the Good Life."[67]

But *whose* beliefs about the good life were these? Did copywriters and advertising artists, as apostles of modernity, measure the good life by its conformance with rational efficiency, technological sophistication, and the tempo of urban life? If so, was that good life really "pre-sold" to consumers whose emotional, irrational, and even archaic yearnings were seen by advertisers as shaping the appeal of the modern advertisement? Were images of the good life *imposed* on an unsuspecting public, or were they *drawn from* the lives of the people themselves by experts in the synthesis and articulation of inchoate popular lore? What relationship did these images bear to actual social conditions or cultural dilemmas? We can begin to suggest answers to these questions only when we know more about the creators of advertising—who they were and how they defined their relationship to their audience. That will be our task in the next two chapters.

MEN OF THE PEOPLE:
THE NEW PROFESSIONALS

Nothing irked advertising leaders of the 1920s more than the public's habit of referring to advertising as "a game." They found it particularly galling that even bright young aspirants to agency jobs spoke of "breaking into the advertising game." This popular expression, they felt, denied the occupation its true seriousness, its progress in craftsmanship, and its economic impact, and it encouraged young people to approach advertising careers nonchalantly, ignorant of the hard work and intensive preparation that were now required. It falsely suggested "a kind of gay adventure, an outlet for the spirit of ballyhoo and medicine man," and it invited the public to retain suspicions of advertising as "a racket."[1]

Most advertising leaders spoke confidently in the late 1920s of the increased prestige their occupation had gained as it had enhanced its economic role. But they remained sensitive to those slights and taunts they continued to face. *Who's Who* continued to ignore the advertising profession. A "mere advertising man," no matter how prominent, could not gain admission, complained *Advertising Age,* "but if he becomes president of the horseshoe pitchers' association or otherwise distinguishes himself, the magic portals promptly swing open." Even Bruce Barton had gained admission to the select circle as an "author" rather than as the leading figure in a major advertising agency. Novelists and playwrights portrayed the advertising man with "little of the solid sterling worth of the banker, the lawyer, or the engineer," thus denying him a proper dignity. In response, advertising leaders denounced all references to the "advertising game," shunned the popular term "ad" in favor of the more dignified "advertisement," and, in a few instances, even sought to rechristen "ad men" as "consumption engineers."[2]

Two Routes to Professionalism

While they agreed on the seriousness and stature of their occupation, however, advertising leaders held two distinct and conflicting interpretations of "professionalism." One viewpoint emphasized educational standards, public service, and cultural uplift. The other stressed the narrower professionalism of the "real pro" who loyally supplied his client with practical expertise. These conflicting ways of seeing themselves as modern professionals led advertising agents into arguments over the content and style of advertisements as well as over professional behavior and concepts of service.

According to the first model, advertising agents should claim status as professionals by acquiring a learned expertise through advanced education.[3] Advertising writer Albert E. Hasse reported favorably in *Printers' Ink* on a plan proposed in Britain to give examinations and set standards that would attract "men of education and ability" to the profession and set them "apart from the sloganeer, the adsmith, and the amateur."[4] Earnest Elmo Calkins of Calkins and Holden proposed that the Association of American Advertising Agencies define and classify the kinds of knowledge necessary to enter the profession and pass on the qualifications of prospective advertising agents. Another agency president called for a professional education for advertisers that would "compare favorably with that of the so-called learned professions—Medicine, Law, and the Pulpit."[5]

As early as the mid-1920s, Stanley Resor, president of the J. Walter Thompson agency, pointed proudly to a staff that included 105 college graduates, including five Ph.D.s. Others, associating higher education with the realm of high culture, reinforced the claim to professional status by cultivating higher standards in advertising art and prose. The Harvard Awards, established in 1924 to reward advertising excellence, epitomized this claim. Professor Neil Borden, who administered the awards on behalf of the Harvard Business School, urged advertising agents to believe what they said when they spoke of copywriting as an art. The preparation of an advertising booklet, he insisted, required an ability equal to that of writing a book. *Advertising and Selling* ranked the Harvard Awards with the Nobel and Pulitzer Prizes, saying that they encouraged advertising to rise "to a higher level of intelligence, decency, and appreciation."[6]

Some copywriters proudly compared the purposes and challenges of their craft to the labors of Shakespeare, Stevenson, and Dickens. They fondly quoted Aldous Huxley's statement that "the advertisement is one of the most difficult of modern literary forms. . . . The problem presented by the sonnet is child's play compared with the problem of the advertisement."[7] Earnest Calkins noted in 1930 that such experts as Rudyard Kipling, Brander Matthews, and H. L. Mencken had "expressed admiration for the literary quality" of much recent advertising. Such men had applauded the virtuosity of the copywriter, his ability to produce any desired effect in a few paragraphs. Moreover, the "stigma once attached to advertising art" had vanished, Calkins argued. Commercial artists were no longer failures in "real art," but artists who would have been famous as sculptors, portraitists, or muralists in an earlier age. The N. W. Ayer and Son agency sought to confirm the new status of the advertising illustrator, and enhance its own prestige in the process, by creating its own gallery. Here, in high-ceiling rooms suggestive of museums of high art, it staged regular exhibitions of advertising artists. (Fig. 2.1).[8]

2.1. The art gallery of the N. W. Ayer and Son agency suggested a link between "professionalism" in advertising and the standards of high culture.

   This model of professionalism, which stressed advanced education and high culture, found ultimate expression in assertions of advertising's status as a public service. If doctors, lawyers, and the clergy gained status from the association of their work with a higher calling, then advertisers could make similar claims. Bruce Barton proclaimed advertising to be "the voice of business' better self." Advertising agents were the idealists of business, he argued. By encouraging businesses to promise high standards and high business ideals in their ads, advertising agents pressured manufacturers to live up to these promises, thus constantly "urging them to be something more and finer." By bringing businessmen in contact with the best artists, Earnest Calkins contended, advertising had brought beauty into the machine age. It had engendered new styles in hundreds of products and raised the level of public taste.[9]

   In sharp contrast to the proponents of professionalism through education and uplift, the "real pros" denied that the status of advertising could be divorced from its paramount commercial function. In their view, professionalism meant sticking faithfully to the business at hand—providing expertise to the business client. An advertising agent under contract to a business firm was professional in the same

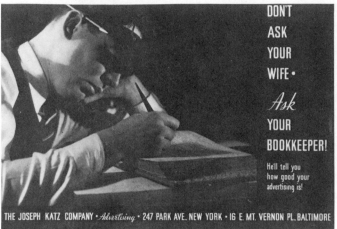

DON'T
ASK
YOUR
WIFE •
Ask
YOUR
BOOKKEEPER!

He'll tell you
how good your
advertising is!

THE JOSEPH KATZ COMPANY • *Advertising* • 247 PARK AVE. NEW YORK • 16 E. MT. VERNON PL. BALTIMORE

2.2. In contrast to Fig. 2.1, this agency ad insisted that professionalism in advertising found its test in client sales, not in the esthetic judgments of wives or other cultured critics.

sense as a law firm under contract. Both applied their specialized knowledge and technical skills solely on behalf of the client's best interests. "After all," wrote one advertising man to *Advertising and Selling Fortnightly,* "advertising is advertising," and attempts to "dignify it" only "lead away from profits" (Fig. 2.2).[10]

Proponents of this narrow, or commercial, conception of advertising professionalism constantly warned against viewing advertising as an end rather than a means. Too many people, they argued, still thought of advertising as an "economic waste." Advertising agents could justify their claim to recognition as professionals only by demonstrating their power to increase sales. Pretensions to art or public service too often diverted agencies from techniques that would maximize sales for their clients. The desire for public recognition and admiration, the effort to appear more creative than competitors, the "mad rush for fame and glory" threatened to turn the attention of advertising writers away from the sales chart.[11]

Nothing so infuriated the advocates of a narrow professionalism as the various awards for advertising excellence that first appeared in the 1920s. The Harvard Awards, the annual awards of the Art Directors' Club, and the exhibitions of fine art, writing, and typography in the the Ayer gallery epitomized the high-culture claim to professional stature, the effort to make advertising an art rather than a trade. John R. Caples, a recognized genius in mail-order advertisements, called upon the devotees of such awards to examine their professional responsibilities. Answer this question, he challenged them: "Shall I spend my client's money to raise the tone of the advertising business? Or shall I spend the money to increase his sales?"[12] Kenneth Groesbeck, vice-president of the McCann-Erickson agency, summarized the attack on the mystique of advertising awards: "Prizes are awarded for originality, for beauty of layout and illustration, for typographic charm, for striking headline, for everything under the sun except the only thing that matters a whoop; the sale of the product. . . . This emphasis on the *manner* of our work and this ostrich-like sticking of our heads into the sand as to its *result,* is holding us back from professional standing."[13]

Ambassadors of the Consumer

The debate over whether advertisers should base their claims to a new status on their expertise as "real pros" or upon their increased ability to measure up to certain standards of art or public service permeated every level of internal controversy within the trade. Arguments over copy styles, media choices, and agency selection echoed the same themes. Individuals sometimes wavered between the two viewpoints. But in their struggle to define their claims to enhanced status and social recognition, advertisers did discover one unifying conception with which both viewpoints were compatible.

The burden of this unifying idea was that a new mode of social communication had now come to maturity, and that the creators of advertisements played a pivotal role in it. Through the services of the advertising agent, manufacturers and retailers now talked directly with an expanded and economically potent buying public. Advertising had been chosen to preside over a communication process that was essential to national prosperity and business modernization and was also ripe with potential for social betterment.

From the standpoint of one party to this communication system, the manufacturer, the function of the advertising agent was increasingly indispensable. Mass production required mass demand. Since 1921, at the least, the American economy had been a buyer's market. Production had soared, and only advertising could bring about a balancing level of consumption. So important was this function that advertising leaders predicted they would inevitably gain positions at the center of corporate leadership. By 1926 some thirty advertising men were already serving on corporate boards of directors. A knowledge of consumer desires was becoming increasingly crucial to decisions not only about *how much* to produce but also about the details of *what* to produce. As "an ambassador of the final consumer" the advertising agent could tell the manufacturer how and when to change his production machinery.[14]

In 1928 Kenneth Goode, a prolific writer on advertising topics, predicted that by 1950 the advertising expert, acting as a "psychological engineer," would have the power to see that "popularity and publicity and proper prices" were "manufactured into" the product. Five years later he was even more confident. Within the next decade, he wrote, "advertising-minded" men would become the top executives in every business. With more than a hint of contempt for the geniuses behind the great corporate mergers, *Printers' Ink* suggested in 1927 that someday these "great financiers" might "learn almost as much about what the people of the United States really know about and are interested in as does the junior copy writer of a fourth-rate advertising agency."[15]

Such expectations of predominance within the business community rested on assumptions about the special qualities of the relationship between the advertising agent and the American public. Trade journals and advertising leaders sought to describe the role of advertising agents with a variety of terms. They were advance agents for the public, solicitors before the court of public opinion, liaison officers, interpreters of the consumer viewpoint, experts in consumer reaction, ambassadors of the final consumer, consumption engineers.[16] Such self-conferred titles carried many different implications. Did advertising writers exercise power *over*

Beg,
Budget or Steal
an Advertising Test Fund!

2.3. This trade journal illustration epitomized one popular self-image among advertising agents: the all-powerful manipulator. See also Fig. 6.8. For contrasting images see Figs. 2.4 and 2.5

consumers or did they derive their power *from* them? In their quest for a new professional stature, advertising leaders brashly tended to answer, "Both" (Figs. 2.3, 2.4, 2.5).

Certainly the advertising agent's power was, in its origins, a delegated power. Agency leaders were particularly fond of explaining the role of advertising through analogies to political democracy. Advertising, Bruce Barton wrote, had been "voted for, and elected" as the method by which people wished to learn of new things to buy.[17] Advertising agents constantly spoke of the consuming public as a constituency. They shouldered a dual responsibility: to determine the wants of their constituents, and then to propose new or improved products to the manufacturer who could satisfy those wants. The agent's chief asset and major source of influence in working with the manufacturer was a sensitivity to consumer attitudes, an ability to provide an outside view. Recognizing the nature of this delegated power, advertising agents should "interpret, and cater to, the consumer viewpoint."[18] Just as citizens had a representative in Congress looking out for their needs and interests, so consumers had a representative in the highest councils of business, demanding that their desires be satisfied.

Much as they sought to impress corporate executives with their credentials as knowledgeable representatives of the consumer viewpoint, most advertising agency leaders did not allow the notion of delegated power to restrict their claims to stature as the new movers and shakers of American society. Advertising writers not only reflected consumer demand, they claimed, they also helped make it more intelligent, more modern. By selling ideas and stimulating the demand for goods, they revealed themselves as the geniuses behind a newly discovered economic

2.4, 2.5. Those who advertised services or products to other businesses,
such as the DuPont Cellophane Company and the N. W. Ayer agency,
often portrayed the consumer as an exacting, imperious judge, thus relegat-
ing the advertising agent to solicitor.

perpetual-motion machine. By stimulating desires for a higher standard of living,
they inspired people to work harder. Hard work then contributed to new levels
of production, for which advertising agents would find buyers by stimulating a
new pitch of consumer desire. Manufacturers merely made products, Kenneth
Goode observed, but advertising writers operated on a higher level of production:
they manufactured customers.[19]

Obvious ambiguities, perhaps deliberately courted, characterized the advertising leaders' most widely shared claim to new stature. Positioned at the crucial
juncture in the network of economic communications, they claimed preeminent
status both as faithful representatives of a sovereign public and as elite benefactors
who promoted prosperity and civilization by "molding the human mind."[20] Both
the ambiguities and the hubris of such a position were epitomized in a pro-
nouncement by the Barton, Durstine and Osborn agency early in the 1920s:

> The product of advertising is something . . . powerful and commanding—it
> is *public opinion;* and in a democracy public opinion is the uncrowned king.
>
> It is the advertising agency's business to write the speeches from the throne
> of that king; to help his subjects decide what they should eat and wear; how
> they should invest their savings; by what courses they can improve their
> minds; and even—for so far has advertising advanced—what laws they should
> make, and by what faith they may be saved.
>
> Archimedes asked for a lever long enough and strong enough to move the
> world. We have a suspicion that if he lived today he would apply for work in
> an agency.[21]

Such a declaration only began to reveal the perplexities arising from the role claimed by the advertising agent. For example, although it was democracy that had made public opinion a "king," members of that public were actually "subjects" who looked for guidance to a king who had been "produced" by advertising and armed with speeches prepared by ad agencies! Unquestionably advertising agents had found a strategic niche for themselves as crucial mediators in the vast national marketplace. Their role was, indeed, ambiguous. They served their clients as intelligence agents, yet the test of their intelligence-gathering lay in their success in presenting products in the words and images that consumers most cherished. What particular attributes of background, personality, or training had fitted advertising agents for this sensitive function? Did they share certain cultural and demographic characteristics with the mass of American consumers, so that their particular fluency made them accurate articulators of a "public" opinion? How did the structure and internal pressures of the emerging advertising profession affect their relationships with the consumer masses that they intended not only to represent but also to modernize and uplift?

Atypical Men—and Women

In sketching a composite portrait of the advertising profession of the late 1920s, I have focused primarily on one select group—those responsible for the content of national advertising. In this group we find the agency heads, account representatives, and creative staffs of the larger agencies and the advertising managers of individual corporations. I have largely ignored vast segments of the trade: the staffs of retail and other local advertisers, the space buyers and media representatives, and all agency personnel not engaged in creating or gaining approval for advertising content. I have also excluded those who worked exclusively in mail-order advertising or in the "industrial" advertising directed at business rather than at the public at large.

I wish primarily to describe the backgrounds, occupational attitudes, and social and institutional ties of persons in the twenty largest advertising agencies. These were the advertisers who acted as the "advance agents of the public" for the bulk of the new advertising that sought to depict the product within the life of the consumer. A list of these agencies, roughly in the order of their size in 1927, might look like this:[22]

1. J. Walter Thompson Company
2. Lord and Thomas and Logan
3. N. W. Ayer and Son
4. George Batten Company
5. The H. K. McCann Company
6. Barton, Durstine and Osborn
7. The Blackman Company

8.   Campbell-Ewald Co.

9.   Theodore F. MacManus Co.

10. F. Wallis Armstrong

11. The Erickson Company

12. Erwin, Wasey and Company

13. Young and Rubicam

14. Calkins and Holden

15. Gardner Advertising Co.

16. Henri, Hurst and McDonald

17. Williams and Cunnyngham

18. Newell-Emmett Company

19. Pedlar and Ryan

20. Ruthrauff and Ryan

Even the most cursory survey would show that the people in these agencies were hardly representative of the American public in any demographic sense. For one thing, the creators of advertising were overwhelmingly male. In the context of a society in which every aspect of business was predominantly carried on by men, this was hardly surprising. In fact, by the late 1920s women probably played a more influential role in advertising than they did in any other major industry— with the possible exceptions of publishing, movies, and department store retailing. Several fragmentary sources provide a rough sense of the numerical representation of women in the profession. Although *Who's Who in Advertising, 1931,* noted almost apologetically that it had included sketches of 126 women in a volume that gave profiles of 5,000 advertising men, a more accurate estimate of their participation above the secretarial level can be gained from records of two of the largest agencies.[23]

At the time of its 1928 merger with the George Batten Company, the Barton, Durstine and Osborn agency listed twenty "executives," all men, and forty-five assistants, of which seven were women. All twenty-six members of its art department were men. Subsequent BBDO ads often pictured from eight to ten members of the company staff; typically, one of these was a woman. The ads appear to have reflected accurately a staff ratio of about ten to one.[24] At J. Walter Thompson, minutes of the meetings of leading staff members in the late 1920s normally listed approximately twenty persons in attendance. Of these, three were women—two heads of copy groups and the president's personal secretary. The list did not reflect, however, the powerful role within the agency of Mrs. Helen Resor, the president's wife. A survey of the advertising profession in Detroit in 1928 found 18 women among the 200 persons surveyed, reinforcing the impression of a ten-to-one ratio of men to women.[25]

Numerical ratios, however, tell us little about status and influence within the profession. Here, the evidence is ambiguous. Unquestionably advertising provided some women with career opportunities that they could not easily attain elsewhere. In a survey of fifteen agencies in 1926, Aminta Casseres of J. Walter

Thompson found women soliciting new business, heading research departments, and acting as space buyers. She counted "four full-fledged and highly successful women account executives."[26] Dorothy Dignam, a leading copywriter for N. W. Ayer and Son, drew a salary of $7,800 in 1930, which placed her solidly among the top 5 percent of all families and individuals in annual income.[27] But the attainment of such authority and compensation still did not establish even the most successful women in a central position within the profession or place them on a status of equality with their male colleagues.

Segregation in local advertising clubs clearly signaled a status differential. In some of the less prominent cities, such as Hartford, Kansas City, Portland, and Fort Worth, women were included within a single club structure. But in the major centers of national advertising, the gender line was firmly drawn. The founder of the New York League of Advertising Women recalled the necessity of launching a women's organization because all the men's organizations barred women from membership and refused to "countenance women" at their meetings. When Jane Martin launched the New York League, members of the men's club dubbed it "Jane Martin's Sewing Circle."[28]

Although a few advertising women drew large salaries by the standards of business pay for women of that era, even the best-paid women copywriters lagged far behind their male counterparts. Comparisons from agency to agency and position to position are difficult to make, especially in a business where it is impossible to disentangle individual creative contributions from the group effort. But William Benton, as a young man with the George Batten agency, increased his salary to $5,000 in less than three years in the early 1920s, whereas Dorothy Dignam, widely recognized as one of the leading copywriters by the end of the 1920s, worked for long hours and under intense pressure for nearly a decade at the McJunkin and Ayer agencies before passing the $5,000 mark. During the same period Jim Ellis at the Wm. H. Rankin agency boosted his salary from $3,120 to $11,000 in less than six years. Dignam noted in 1931, while making no complaint herself, that women were irked by salary discrimination. The 1928 Detroit survey revealed that although 50 percent of the men were then receiving salaries of over $5,000 a year, no woman was being paid more than $3,500. "Groucho," a regular columnist for *Printers' Ink,* readily confessed that the "girl with all-around talents . . . gets about a third of what she's worth."[29]

Rare was the advertising woman who escaped being typecast as an expert on the "woman's viewpoint." In fact, the very presence of women in other than secretarial positions stemmed largely from the recognition that women were the primary purchasers of most consumer products. Agency and company leaders feared that without expert feminine guidance, they might strike the wrong fashion note or make "social errors" in illustrations of table settings. The "main reason" that women were employed in advertising, Ruth Waldo of J. Walter Thompson acknowledged, was because they had "intimate knowledge of women's habits and desires."[30] The George Batten Company, in a 1927 agency ad, noted that women talked only among themselves about such things as garter runs, the color of a chair that got on one's nerves, the way straps of underthings fell off one's shoulders, and the problems of a kitchen sink placed too low. "Here is where the woman in advertising offers you her experience," the agency concluded. "She takes part in just such conversations. . . . A thousand and one intimacies she gives to you and your advertising."[31]

If such expertise provided the entering wedge for women in the advertising profession, it also defined their proper sphere. Copywriting, which usually involved no executive responsibility, was "woman's happy hunting ground" as Aminta Casseres put it. A woman's other major role was in "research," because she could more easily gain entree to homes to "chat with women on domestic problems and get them to open up."[32] Assigned largely to "women's product" accounts, women seldom became generalists and rarely became account executives. And the more a woman seemed intuitively to reflect the "feminine point of view," the more likely she was to confirm expectations of a lack of general business judgment. Thus most advertising women occupied what Ruth Waldo characterized as "the lesser and run of the mill" positions under male department chiefs.[33]

Despite their resentment of personal slights and institutional patterns of discrimination, advertising women advised a pragmatic acceptance of things as they were. "If the advertising agency merely wanted a *copywriter,*" Dorothy Dignam pointed out bluntly, "they'd hire a man!" She urged her female colleagues to dress well and "keep a stiff upper lip, with some lipstick on it."[34] Bernice Bowser counseled advertising women to remember: "We work on the premise that the masculine is the superior sex. We never make the silly mistake of competing with men. We stick to our knitting and work only on those things [on] which we, as women, must be able to do a better job than men because of the thousands of years of conditioned thinking which lies behind us. . . . Listening is the way most wives, and all mistresses, hold their jobs."[35] Advertising men accepted their small contingent of "experts on the feminine viewpoint" largely on those terms. Only rarely did the profession bestow its ultimate accolade on one of the "girls"—as it did upon Aminta Casseres in 1930 when a writer in the J. Walter Thompson *News Bulletin* proclaimed: "She is a swell advertising man!"[36]

If women gained only limited representation and influence in advertising, most ethnic and racial groups gained even less of a foothold. In the 1920s and 1930s, for example, Jews played only a minimal and peripheral role in the field of national advertising, in which they were later to excel. Daniel Pope and William Toll found only 92 out of 5,000 men in *Who's Who in Advertising,* 1931, who were identifiably Jewish. Less than 10 percent of these 92 worked for large agencies, despite the increasing concentration of the large agencies in New York City.[37] The remarkable success of Albert Lasker as head of Lord and Thomas did not pave the way for any immediate surge of Jews into the major agencies.

Nor were other ethnic groups visibly represented. A survey of the names mentioned in the trade journals and those included in the 1931 *Who's Who in Advertising* yields virtually no names of agency personnel that are manifestly Italian or Polish, or of other Eastern or Southern European origin. The editors of the 1931 *Who's Who* described the profession as dominated by a blue-eyed, Nordic strain. There is no evidence that blacks did anything other than janitorial work for agencies during the 1920s and 1930s.[38]

The large advertising agencies were probably little more exclusive ethnically than most other large businesses of the era. Pope and Toll suggest that the personalized hiring practices of ad agencies and their lack of explicit educational or bureaucratic requirements reinforced this ethnic exclusiveness. An old-boy network operated with little challenge from objective measures of qualifications.[39] In fact, in a line of work where personal contacts with clients were crucial, any ethnic characteristics that might discomfort the client were positive disqualifications.

Much of the exclusiveness was undoubtedly unconscious, but some of it was quite deliberate. Trade journal ads occasionally stipulated that a position was open to a "Christian man." In 1939 the head of N.W. Ayer hotly denied that his agency still investigated church and YMCA affiliations in its hiring, as it had in the past. But historian Ralph Hower, who had intensively investigated the agency's operations, discounted the denial as inaccurate for the early 1930s. The Ayer president confessed that some people still carried the impression that Ayer was "unfavorable to Catholics and Jews." The most suggestive evidence of widespread prejudice appears, interestingly enough, in an advertisement that deliberately sought "Jewish brains" for an agency partnership. Jewish merchandising experience was "inborn" and ran "in the blood," the unnamed agency declared. "Therefore, whereas the usual advertisement calls for Christians, this one calls for Jewish talent."[40]

Although the large advertising agencies of the 1920s and 1930s did not draw personnel from the burgeoning ethnic populations of the urban centers in which they were located, they were nevertheless fated by the nature of the national communications industries to assume an unrepresentative position of metropolitan "provinciality" with respect to the country at large. By the census definition of "urban" (places of over 2,500 population), an increasing majority of Americans were urban residents after the beginning of the 1920s. But this was a far cry from making New York City or Chicago a typical living environment, or from making the daily lives of the agency copywriters similar to those of their national audience.

The large agencies realized that their centralized locations, especially in New York City, left them vulnerable to the charge that they were isolated from their clients' markets. Occasionally a businessman would touch a raw nerve by commenting that "the worst thing that could happen to a business" would be for its leaders to make judgments based on New York experience, or by suggesting that agency copywriters, having been "soaked in big-city consciousness," had become addicted to sophisticated "city-minded copy."[41]

Some agencies sought to blunt such criticisms, or to turn them against competing agencies, by stressing the representative backgrounds of the people on their staff. President Batten of N. W. Ayer argued in the late 1930s that while many agencies had acquired staffs of "local people who have a big-city tenement point of view," Ayer had long made a deliberate effort to hire people "from every state in the union." William Benton recalled that while he was a partner in Benton and Bowles, the men of the Frigidaire company in Dayton had accused him of heading a contingent of "city slickers"; he met the challenge by replying that "the biggest town any one of them comes from is Cloquet, Minnesota." Batten, Barton, Durstine and Osborn claimed in 1931 that its agency staff included someone who had been born, raised, or educated in every state of the union. The implied contention in each of these "defenses" was that the big-city environment had no power to cloud the broad understanding of the country and its people among agents "spawned on the frontier, on the farms, and in the small towns."[42]

The apparent complacency of these claims to geographic representativeness was belied by the fears of urban provinciality that advertising professionals expressed to each other. A woman in the George Batten Company returned from a trip to warn that even in the large cities of the Midwest, women's thoughts and behavior were so different from what they were in New York that the agency would have to learn to talk their language in order to reach them.[43] The idea of the rest of the United States as "another country" was set forth even more dramatically in a 1927 article in the J. Walter Thompson Company *News Letter* entitled "Have You Been in the States Recently?" New Yorkers, the author noted, were deeply impressed by the "modern tempo." They responded to "certain jokes, allusions, ways of thinking and feeling." But the American people at large lived "uncomprehendingly in their own highly satisfactory world. And it is in that world that we must meet them." It was just possible, he concluded, that everyone was in step but New York.[44]

The sense of distance from the American people created by the geographic concentration of advertising's creative elite actually bred less anxiety within the profession than the distance created by their class standing. This was a sensitive matter, because the conventional portrait of the advertising man emphasized a mystique of social representativeness. He was the man who knew what the public wanted because he talked with "bank presidents and elevator boys, debutantes and stenographers, magazine representatives and taxi drivers." Of all businessmen, he was "the greatest democrat and best 'mixer.'" Among businessmen, it was he who purported to know intimately "the great mass of common everyday folks."[45]

But if such intimacy required sharing the cultural tastes and economic circumstances of the common people, most of the creators of national advertising scarcely qualified. In the late 1920s, when the median family income in the nation was below $1,600 a year, Detroit advertising men earned a median annual salary of $5,167. Although copywriters often complained that they were badly paid in comparison with account executives, still the salaries of experienced copywriters and art directors easily placed them in the nation's upper 10 percent in personal income.[46] When advertising agents illustrated their arguments with anecdotes from their personal lives, the frequent mention of household servants revealed a style of life appreciably above a "representative" mode. At the depth of the depression, one agency man noted that the wives of twelve men in his office employed chauffeurs.[47]

Nor were the educational backgrounds and cultural tastes of advertising copywriters and executives representative of national patterns. Advertisers often came into the trade from newspaper writing or sales work. But after 1920 an increasing

As ad men became more renowned, they were less in touch w/ the general public

number of them also entered with a college education. In fact, despite the stigma of a tainted past, advertising began to draw heavily upon Ivy League graduates. James Webb Young of J. Walter Thompson reminisced later about his "bull pen" of young copywriters "not too long out of Harvard, Yale, and Princeton." Alex Osborn of Barton, Durstine and Osborn remarked on the apparent inability of the many Harvard and Princeton men in the office to outgrow the collegiate mentality.[48] The new Benton and Bowles agency of 1929 rested on a Yale connection. And the cultural tastes of men and women in the large agencies tended toward modern art and the opera. Their listening tastes ran to symphonies, their reading tastes to the *New York Times*.[49]

Another indication of the class position of advertising men was their obsession with golf. In the weekly section of "Advertising Club News" in *Printers' Ink,* only notices of the elections of new officers in local clubs outnumbered the news items on the clubs' golf tournaments. When a *Printers' Ink* editorial proposed that advertising men pre-test their copy on the public for credibility, the writer could think of no more appropriate audience than "fellow golfers" in the locker room. Even the joke columns in trade journals were occasionally dominated by golf.[50] Advertising men, it seemed, didn't notice (or didn't care) that their mania for playing golf, talking about it, and picturing it in their ads was not shared by the majority of Americans at the time.

A speaker at the private J. Walter Thompson "forum" summarized the problem of remoteness from the masses. Were New York copywriters representative or typical? Some 66 percent of New York copywriters had domestic servants, he claimed, compared with 5 percent of all homes. Far more than half had *never* lived within the confines of the average national income, "and half can't even remember any *relatives* or *friends* who live on that figure!" Some 40 percent of the New York writers had not visited any of the "remoter sections" of the United States more than once in the previous ten years. Some never had. And the evidence of unrepresentative behavior continued to mount: "None of our New York writers belongs to a lodge or a civic club; only one in twenty-five attends a political meeting; not one ever goes to a public picnic. Only one out of five goes to church except on rare occasions. Half never go to Coney Island or to a similar resort; the other half go once in one or two years. This—in a nation that can almost be described by such experiences."[51]

In communicating with a broad national audience, those who created and approved national advertising campaigns thus appeared to face a formidable barrier. The new advertising called for intimacy with consumers—seeing the product from their viewpoint and imaginatively portraying its result in their lives. If it was to succeed, the distinctive and unrepresentative demographic characteristics of advertising men (and sometimes women) had to be surmounted. Advertising leaders might introduce themselves to the public as "jes folks," but among themselves they were likely to panic at the suggestion that they had lost their touch by failing to mingle. When the Ruthrauff and Ryan agency opened a trade journal ad with the questions "Ever stand around a factory at noon?" and "Ever chat with the men at the noon hour?" it must have prodded many a guilty conscience.[52]

The Agency Subculture:
Courtiers and Creators

If distinctive characteristics of class, culture, education, gender, ethnicity, and urban provinciality separated members of the creative advertising elite from major segments of their audience, how did the ambiance of the advertising agency affect their capacity to bridge this gap? Copywriters, art directors, and agency officials not only worked amid the influences of a metropolitan environment; they also worked within the structural constraints of a client-agency system, with its particular pattern of personal relationships. Some of the rewards and pressures of this system helped insure that agency writers and artists would use their utmost resourcefulness to overcome the demographic distance between themselves and the average consumer. Other pressures and rewards, however, encouraged the qualities of detachment and cynicism that some observers described as characteristic of the "provinciality" of the metropolitan advertising agent.[53]

Since early in the twentieth century, the staff of a company's advertising agency had come to perform the bulk of the creative work on national advertising campaigns, but this had not always been the case. The pioneer advertising agencies of the nineteenth century had been primarily brokers of space. They had bought newspaper columns and magazine pages in wholesale quantities at a discount, and then resold portions of that space to individual advertisers at whatever profit margin they could negotiate. The individual advertiser had written the ad. However, as competition for consumer favor intensified and more sophisticated forms of copy appeal emerged, agencies had begun to compete with one another by offering their clients expert advice in the preparation of advertisements. And as agencies expanded their art and copy departments to provide this specialized service, their client companies began to avoid expensive duplication by keeping their own internal advertising departments small.[54]

The exact apportioning of responsibility for creative work between agency and client was a matter for informal negotiation, and it varied greatly from company to company. Trade journals described the ideal relationship as a creative partnership: the corporation advertising department supplied expert knowledge of product characteristics and cumulative merchandising experience, whereas the agency contributed a sophisticated knowledge of media and the crucial understanding of the consumer viewpoint—the so-called "outside view." In the late 1920s most major advertisers relied on their advertising agency both for overall strategy and for the detailed content of each ad.

One crucial function that the client retained in every case, whatever the distribution of creative effort, was final approval of the advertising campaign, which often included approval of every detail in each individual advertisement. Thus any longings for creative expression among agency copywriters and artists were constrained by the task of meeting a series of challenges to final approval. These challenges might come from the agency copy chief, the agency art director, the agency account executive or contact man for that client, the other agency executives who would have to present the ads to the client for approval, the client's advertising manager, its sales manager, and often other executives of the client company, up to the president. "Trying to please them all," wrote John Caples, an admired and experienced copywriter, "is like trying to drive a croquet ball through a dozen arches at one shot."[55]

The personal relationships involved might range from harmonious to exceedingly prickly. But the very necessity of running such a gauntlet of approval often bred a sense of frustration among copywriters, and it could utterly humiliate an unfortunate contact man. BBDO actually seemed to breathe a sigh of relief when one of its long-standing clients, Atwater Kent, went out of business in 1936: an agency partner praised the long-suffering contact man for eleven years of "continual punishment," for taking it on the chin "week in and week out, in all seasons."[56]

Of course an agency could refuse to accept a submissive role. Some agencies did break their ties with the more demanding or ungrateful of their smaller, less remunerative clients. But the large national advertisers possessed an intimidating financial leverage. They could always make an abrupt change of agencies, and they exercised this power with unsettling frequency. Ralph Hower estimates that N. W. Ayer clients between 1921 and 1931 stayed with the agency an average of less than four years. A trade journal survey placed the typical client-agency connection, even in the palmy 1920s, at only forty-two months.[57]

Many agencies derived most of their revenues from a handful of their largest clients. The loss of a single large account could decimate an agency. The announcement of an agency-client divorce—or even the rumor of one—sent tremors of insecurity through the agencies. The very structure of agency-client relationships was calculated to produce what the *Printers' Ink* columnist "Groucho" characterized as the two abiding realities of agency life: the fear of losing accounts and the resulting "client prostitution"—the ingrained habit of paying constant deference to corporate advertising managers.[58]

The tensions and indignities of these relationships were often heightened, in the view of advertising agents, by the arbitrariness, egotism, narrow vision, or judgmental incompetence of the advertising managers and other executives of their corporate clients. These people rejected inventive ideas and made detailed changes in copy out of personal taste, or on the basis of what their wives thought. "It would be interesting to watch some of these morons edit Shakespeare's copy," fumed one copywriter in *Printers' Ink Monthly*. Arbitrary and irrational advertisers provoked copywriters to private explosions of exasperation. Clients often changed their minds overnight, and refused all constructive recommendations. They were apt to propose a fear campaign for mustard simply on the ground that one had worked for birdseed.[59]

The implications of the structure of agency-client relationships, especially for the doubly or triply subordinated copywriter, have been suggestively outlined by the sociologist Joseph Bensman in his reflections on the advertising profession of the post-World War II era. Bensman, who worked as an ad agency executive, explores the client-agency relationship through a king-and-courtier analogy. The advertising man, he suggests, is a "marginal man," because his "very existence depends on the 'favors' bestowed." In a business situation characterized by irrationality and personal caprice, where there are "great opportunities for total defeat and loss," the pressures for deference are intense. The main outlet for a sense of pride and accomplishment lies in in-group displays of virtuosity.[60]

Using a more modern political metaphor, Giancarlo Buzzi reminds us that the power of the advertising agent is a "delegated power," granted not by consumers but by the industrial elite. Advertising agents act within a limited tactical sphere. They may occasionally flatter themselves with the claim that they are shapers of public opinion, but in fact their "sphere of discretion" is small.[61] Their boastings and preenings, to return to the earlier analogy, are like those of courtiers outside the hearing of the king. In the everyday world of the 1920s advertising agency, the rejection or disfigurement of copy and the circulation of intimidating rumors of account losses constantly reminded agency personnel of the delegated nature of their power.

The resulting agency sensitivity and resentment was occasionally expressed when copywriters and agency leaders could speak in private or from the safety of historical distance. One particularly revealing example is the confidential "account status" summary prepared by the Batten Company in 1928, when it merged with Barton, Durstine and Osborn. Prepared as background information for their new BDO colleagues, the long account summaries often devoted more attention to personality profiles of client executives than to the details of advertising strategy. In the summaries of many accounts, the message was clear: successful agency service depended primarily on knowing the personal idiosyncrasies of client executives who had to be stroked or circumvented. The acerbity with which several of the client personality portraits were sketched suggests deep reservoirs of frustration within the agency.[62] Similar exasperation with the indignities of courtier-like subordination emerged in an outburst entitled "My Boy a Copy Writer? Never!" by an anonymous "veteran copy writer" in *Printers' Ink Monthly*. "I have tiptoed to clients and been browbeaten by account executives like every good copy writer should," he confessed.[63]

The personal indignities of subordination, however, were not always foremost among the dissatisfactions of agency copywriters and artists. Just as frequently, copywriters bemoaned the stifling of their creative impulses. Their creations were not merely criticized; they were judged by improper standards, emasculated by revisions, and given no credit. Bernice Fitzgibbon reiterated the copywriters' credo when she commented, "They say that the best stuff written in advertising agencies never gets into metal type."[64] The trade journal *Tide* speculated in 1930 that if copywriters should ever form a union, their first demand would not be for shorter hours or higher pay "but for more freedom in writing copy." Some months later, an art director made a comparable plea for greater creative autonomy in an attack on "art butchering" by manufacturers and their advertising managers. All advertising men, one agent wrote, "hanker for a little unbiased approval of our work to offset the caustic criticism of the client and his minions." One agency writer was even so brash as to suggest that copywriters ought to be allowed to sign their copy.[65]

Such a proposal threatened deeply ingrained conventions. Custom and practicality imposed a lid of repression on the desires of copywriters to escape the oblivion of anonymity. A powerful faction within the trade, including many copywriters, regularly arose to defend its own idea of professional craftsmanship

2.6. Agencies and their clients worried
that their biases and instincts for self-
expression might distort the appeal to the
consumer. Visually, this three-page ad
(pp. 42–43) dramatized the dangers of
shedding a "cloak of anonymity."

**Does Your Customer See Himself
in Your Advertising?**

by denouncing the literary pretensions of those who sought individual pride of
authorship and public recognition. Expanding upon the arguments for a narrower
professionalism, they deplored the tendency to confuse copywriting with self-
expression and advertising with high art. Advertising agencies, one writer of this
persuasion complained, had unfortunately been infiltrated by "unappreciated po-
ets and unstaged dramatists." They were "full of copy men who fully expect—
some day when they are no longer beggars on horseback—to write The Great
American Novel." Such copywriters, he and others warned, set false and inappropriate standards that diverted attention from the true source of pride for the
professional craftsman. They were "slightly ashamed" of the advertising business.
Some even considered copywriting "prostitution" and denigrated their temporary
positions as those of "literary courtesans."[66]

Critics of the passion for self-expression reminded their restive colleagues that
an advertisement was "not a personal thing" but was best produced by group
effort. Its purpose was not self-expression, but the sale of goods and services.
Readers should not say "What a fine ad," but "What a fine thing to buy!" (Fig.
2.6).[67] If a copywriter cast aside his "cloak of anonymity" and placed his signature
on the ad, it "would look as though a sort of literary gunman had been hired to
do the job," warned one writer: "Imagine five or six advertisements of different
products in one magazine all signed by the same copywriter." Even without such

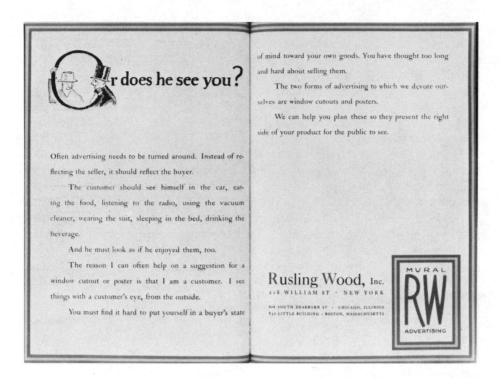

comparisons, another advertising man pointed out, a signature would introduce an obvious middleman between manufacturer and consumer and thus destroy the desired intimacy of a "direct-to-reader tone."[68]

Those who deplored literary pretensions proposed a more circumscribed conception of the copywriter's task and challenge. It was satisfying and character-building, they argued, to try to excel in the creation of effective copy within the confines set by practical constraints. Frank Fletcher, who made a fortune as a freelance copywriter, gloried in the creative training imposed by his first advertising assignment. It consisted of saying "the same thing differently three times a week for twenty years" in three-inch, single-column newspaper spaces.[69] Good copywriters, asserted an advertising man in *Printers' Ink,* were not made out of men who sought "to imitate Turgenev or Shakespeare or even Stevenson." They arose, another writer added, from the ranks of those who realized that a copy-writer was not primarily a writer but a salesman. This did not diminish the creative challenge; it magnified it.[70]

These appeals to pride in a narrowly defined professional craftsmanship usually carried implications of dedication to a career of sacrifice. The copywriter must accept anonymity and repress the desire for self-expression; loyalty to the team and its sales task should outweigh any desire for individual credit. "Ours is essentially a workshop, not a scenic background for a Personality," proclaimed a

BBDO publication. Individual credit, it added, was "no longer one of the rewards of agency work." Although criticism was never pleasant, the member of a creative team should welcome it. "Ours is no place for a sensitive soul who craves appreciation," BBDO assured its clients.[71]

But even the most persuasive appeals to copywriters to repudiate the sirens of self-expression, and to take pride in the challenges of a narrow craftsmanship, failed to satisfy their hunger for creative fulfillment. The very frequency and fervor of the attacks on self-expression and literary aspirations in the trade journals and house organs suggest the persistent strength of sinful hankerings to escape the "hard knocks" of the profession. One ad man publicly warned his son, "The necessity for subordinating one's ideas to those of others which you cannot accept, your own work garbled and mangled, those inevitable failures to satisfy a client or hold an account—all are the lot of the advertising man."[72] But advertising men would continue to try to escape the frustrations of this lot through various forms of self-expression. And given the many ways in which their backgrounds, tastes, and social circumstances differed from those of the public at large, each successful dash of self-expression would again pose the question of their capacity to serve as "men of the people."

Competition, Craftsmanship, and Cynicism

The particular incentives and demands arising from the character of agency work may have induced some self-selection among those who entered the field. But it is clear, despite the stereotypes of a dozen plays and novels, that no single personality-type dominated the profession. Fast-livers, puritans, and recluses were all represented among the profession's elite. Conventional wisdom associated different agency functions with distinct personality types. The account executive or contact man should be a good mixer, a bustling optimist; the copywriter might either be slightly withdrawn and studious or a wisecracking, idea-a-minute cynic; the advertising artist might be something of a bohemian. In reality, of course, even these more specialized stereotypes failed to reflect the diversity of personalities. Of all advertising men and women, fewer than 25 percent had planned on an advertising career; most had gravitated into advertising through chance opportunities from disparate fields. If anything united them, beyond the general demographic convergences of class, gender, and metropolitan environment, it was the impact on their diverse personalities of some common pressures of their working situation.[73]

Advertising men and women pursued their careers in an atmosphere of high tension and insecurity. No advertising leader has characterized the competition within the profession as anything but intense. "Fierce and unrelenting," Fairfax Cone described it in a memoir celebrating the profession. Rosser Reeves, another enthusiast, remembered his learning process as "a hard school" in which "Darwin's law of survival of the fittest is at work every minute of the day." So intense had been the devotion demanded by his agency chief, an agency radio expert explained in 1932, that staff members were obliged to put their work before home, wife, or children. "A Young and Rubicam widow was a much more poignant spectacle than any golf widow," he recalled.[74]

Old pros regularly warned young aspirants of the "terrific pace" at which they must expect to live. Like war stories, accounts of the terrifying pressures of speed and competition were often recounted with a survivor's pride. "If you have never wrapped a cold towel around your head at three o'clock in the morning in an effort to get a piece of copy ready for delivery before nine," Jim Adams wrote, "you have never given it your all."[75]

In an atmosphere of deadlines and competition, the loss of a major account—or even the fear of it—could intensify the pressure. Nothing, said Fairfax Cone, could compensate for "the awful feeling that comes to every advertising agency person when the announcement is made that an account is leaving. It comes like a hard blow in the pit of the stomach." And well it might, particularly to the less-entrenched agency personnel. Layoffs were likely to follow any major client defection, the only consolation being the prospect that the client's new agency would simultaneously be beefing up its staff to handle the account. This was one source of an inherent instability which saw 37 percent of the profession change jobs every year.[76]

Another cause for the large floating population in the profession was the steep salary gradient within the agencies. Young copywriters and researchers often began at very low salaries. Those with obvious talent and capacities for self-promotion could advance rapidly, but often only by moving to other agencies or advertising departments. One of the most celebrated creative men of the late 1920s and early 1930s was reputed to have held thirteen different jobs in fifteen years.[77] Among higher agency executives, some would split off to form their own agencies. Account executives with a particular account "in their hip pocket" made deals to shift both themselves and their client to a new agency. The constant flux of people and accounts evoked a sense of personal precariousness. One newspaper writer who had spent a year working consecutively for two advertising agencies in search of bigger money returned to his editorial desk with a sigh of relief. "It was like riding a merry-go-round in an insane asylum," he gasped. "Most agencies thrive on two or three fat bread-and-butter accounts and they're neurotic with fear of those clients. Consequently, advertising men eat too fast, smoke and drink too much, suffer from telephone madness, and Bermuda is their sanitarium."[78]

Given such pressures and insecurities (undoubtedly enhanced in the telling by the qualities of dramatic exaggeration that served so well in advertising copy), it is hardly surprising that advertising gained a reputation as a "young man's profession." Some described this phenomenon in positive terms: advertising agents reached their prime at an early age. Others looked at the flip side of the coin: advertising agents were washed up at forty. In 1931 *Printers' Ink* quoted the comment of a prominent New York agency man that an ad agency was no place for anyone over thirty-five. That was the same age at which the hero in *The Hucksters,* the controversial 1946 novel of the advertising scene, declared himself to be "old" as an advertising man.[79] A survey of the BBDO staff reported that 54 percent of the agency members fell between the ages of twenty and twenty-nine; only 12 percent were forty or older. Statistics on Detroit revealed an average age for advertising men of thirty-three, with 80 percent falling under the age of forty. When the George Batten Company used a youth theme in its 1928 advertising, it reported complaints from within the profession. One of them read: "The man of forty-five has a hard enough time as it is now. Stop telling the world that as a copywriter he lacks potency. What is to become of the upper-middle-aged if this stuff is kept up?"[80]

But the emphasis on youth did not subside. Agencies often insisted on a "young man" in their employment ads. As a BBDO executive remarked, agencies were wise to seek young people with "a physique and temperament that can stand long strains without cracking." When they succeeded in hiring such youths, they boasted about it to prospective clients. Not only did youth signify energy and enthusiasm, it also suggested adaptability, freshness, and an awareness of the newest in lifestyles and conversational patter. Several sage elders might be useful for balance in an agency, but few were likely to survive the pace beyond middle age. Stanley Burnshaw, a copywriter for the Biow Agency in the late 1920s before embarking on his career as a poet and the editor of Dryden Press, recalls the "common belief" that a copywriter or layout man could expect little more than a ten-year career before being "thrown on the ashheap."[81]

Indeed, agency life, as portrayed in many first-hand accounts, was so demanding, nerve-wracking, and insecure that a reader finds it hard to understand why anyone would want to pursue it for long. In fact, many did flee the pressure, and others led careers interspersed with nervous breakdowns. Such advertising luminaries as Claude Hopkins, Albert Lasker, Fairfax Cone, and Bruce Barton suffered major mental crises or persistent bouts with neurosis. Cone attributed the prevalence of breakdowns among agency men to the fact that they were "continuously perched on the edge of anxiety," their lives subject to decisions rarely made in their presence.[82]

Others found ways to escape from the strain and tension, but left the trade anyway out of a sense of futility or disenchantment. William Benton, a spectacular success as a young advertising man, began to complain early of the "ephemeral, unsubstantial" character of his work. Soon after founding a thriving new agency, he abruptly sold out his partnership. Benton's partner, Chester Bowles, also disliked the profession, and found it necessary to escape it entirely for several months every year; he left it permanently several years after Benton. (Benton subsequently served as vice-president of the University of Chicago, chairman of Encyclopaedia Britannica, and U.S. Senator; Bowles went on to become the wartime head of O.P.A., Ambassador to India, and Under Secretary of State.) The celebrated copywriter Theodore MacManus found advertising—and business generally—dreary and cheapening. He trudged on, he confessed, only because he could not escape "the iron clutch of circumstances."[83]

Few artists and copywriters, especially as they approached middle age, could avoid wondering whether they might have built themselves a more satisfying reputation in "serious" art or literature. Even Claude Hopkins could not decide

Comment on society
↳ social history

whether the copywriting career that had made him a millionaire and a legend in the profession had brought him solid satisfaction. In his autobiography he boasted of his many advertising triumphs and told how his lonely pursuit of ambition had led to "happiness in abundance and absolute content," but he also confessed that he envied his old friends who had found equal joys without the wracking illnesses and distractions of a "turbulent life."[84]

But like Hopkins, whom Albert Lasker lured back into the "serfdom" of advertising after one of his breakdowns, many advertising agents persisted in the trade despite its psychic toll. Besides the possibility of great financial rewards, the —the mush!! profession offered a variety of other satisfactions. Particularly in the 1920s, when business basked in the radiance of widespread public approval, advertisers could sit near the thrones of power and share in their luster. They consulted with business moguls at the scene of action in the society, and they were central participants in the process of social interpretation, a function that subsequent studies have suggested is an important key to a sense of high status. "Advertising is the epitome of all that is brave, adventurous, and interesting in business," exulted the BBDO house publication; "it affords the fun of running the loco-motive." William Esty, the vibrant copy chief at J. Walter Thompson, described his work as "the supreme thrill."[85] "Groucho," the *Printers' Ink* columnist, ex-plained what made it all worthwhile. "We shy away from the idea of leaving this kind of business cuz we're playing every day with the hopes of rich manu-facturers, pepping up dealers, lecturing to consumers, working up schemes to make people happy with all kinds of toys from nail files to airships. We are in the thick of where things are going on."[86] — hmm

While "Groucho's" tone of voice carried a hint of self-parody, an attitude of cynicism was far from essential to the careerist in advertising. Like the public relations men described by Richard Tedlow, many advertising agents found themselves capable of "psyching themselves up," throwing themselves into their work with unapologetic zeal, and convincing themselves that their client, their client's product, and the broad social functions of advertising were all syn-onymous with the public interest. "By a process of self-hypnosis they became deliriously enthusiastic about whatever they were obliged to sell at the moment," former ad man James Rorty commented sourly.[87] In fact, it was their conviction about the ultimate righteousness and social contributions of advertising that en-abled advertisers to build justifications for the devious tactical moves they occa-sionally needed to make. Like lawyers pursuing every trick of the trade in defense of their clients, advertising agents could seek justification in the ultimate beneficence—or necessity, at least—of the larger system.

But what many advertising agents seem to have found most attractive in their work was the element of risk and adventure. Although they deplored as degrading and trivializing any portrayal of advertising as a "game," they seem themselves to have found its game-like aspects most compelling. Life in an advertising agency accentuated, more than most occupations, the elements of chance, risk, high stakes, great rewards, and challenging limits. And the absence of objective stan-dards (who could say, especially before publication, which was the "perfect" ad?) cast a game-like aura of unreality over the whole creative process. The acceptance of a kind of existential absurdity—created by the arbitrariness of clients, the seeming fickleness of the public, and the lack of verifiable measures of what would "work" in advertisements—encouraged creative people to develop a private ethic of amoral craftsmanship.[88]

Benign Deceptions

Once one came to believe in the larger functional necessity or social beneficence of advertising—or simply stopped considering such wider implications—the actual creation of campaigns and individual advertisements could be played like a game, with the same exhilarating sense of freedom from ethical consequences. Although they craved social approval as public benefactors, advertising agents also took particular delight in seeing themselves as "players," in showing off their virtuosity by devising the best strategies for hands dealt to them by particular clients, their products, and the nature of the public.

Kenneth Boulding has astutely observed that every trade and profession is inherently inclined to organize itself into some kind of "a conspiracy against the public." In the very process of developing a self-consciousness, a profession begins to exclude nonmembers from knowledge of its particular skills, its tricks of the trade.[89] Thus advertising was hardly unique among professions in developing a private ethic that could justify a detached or manipulative stance toward outsiders. Like the theater troupes of sociologist Erving Goffman's examples in *Frame Analysis,* or like professionals in law, academia, and medicine, the creators of advertisements assumed that their tricks were, in Goffman's phrase, "benign deceptions." Such tricks were required by their specialized functional role and were conducive to the public's welfare.[90] Just as actors had to create illusions and employ deceptions in order to give the audience the enjoyment it expected, so advertising agents had to excel in strategies of manipulation in order to carry out their social function.

But actors primarily play to *one* "outside audience." Advertising, as the experienced agency man James Webb Young observed, involves two "arts" and two audiences: the "art of advertising" involves selling goods to the public, while the "art of the advertising business" aims at selling the advertising agency to its business clients. Both arts are essential to agency success. In explaining the high reputation of the radio department of the rival BBDO agency, a J. Walter Thompson staff member noted caustically that although there was "not much showmanship in the creation of the program . . . there [was] a good deal of showmanship for the benefit of the client." While admitting that JWT radio men also did a lot of "galloping around" and mysterious whispering, he claimed that at least "our young men *know* that these extraordinary manifestations of speed and energy don't mean anything." It all went to show, he said, that both the wider radio audience *and* the client audience had to be humored with "a certain amount of bunk."[91]

In *The Presentation of the Self in Everyday Life,* Erving Goffman employs the theatrical metaphor of a "performance" to describe how people constantly cast themselves in various public roles and then seek opportunities to retire to some backstage area "where the impression fostered by the performance is knowingly contradicted as a matter of course."[92] If the acting profession provides the most concrete illustration of the function of the "backstage," the advertising agency affords one of the most striking examples of the need to draw psychic sustenance from backstage camaraderie. Creative workers in advertising were engaged in two arts, two performances. They found it expedient, though not always possible, to shield each audience from a view of the performance intended for the other.

Thus, agents writing in the narrowly circulated trade journals were apt to boast to advertisers of their power to mold behavior and create new desires—their power to make an impact. But to wider audiences, and occasionally among themselves, they confessed impotence before the will of the masses and described themselves as mere representatives or "ambassadors" of the consumer viewpoint. This dual performance intensified the importance of the agency "backstage," an arena in which to relax from posing and find compensation for the indignities suffered in playing the role of pleader, courtier, or clown.[93]

Two of the many stories once told backstage at the agencies suggest the satisfactions to be found in displays of survival techniques and professional virtuosity. The first of these commented ironically on a performance for consumers. The J. Walter Thompson radio director came to a staff creative meeting one day to report smugly on the successful creation of a new format and a new public image for the Rudy Vallee show. He said that the public, which adored Vallee, liked the new format because Vallee was presented as having chosen all the acts and stars personally. Vallee now introduced his guests informally to the audience through conversational repartee that revealed how he had met them and recognized their talent. It had been essential, the radio director argued, that all credit for the ideas, the script, and the selection of the stars and acts go to Vallee. So successfully had this been done "that all the theatrical publications are now hailing Vallee as the greatest showman in radio." It was all "quite a compliment" to the agency, he concluded: "The facts are that Vallee doesn't know now what is going to be rehearsed this afternoon. He doesn't write one word of the script. All of the things about how he first met these people, etc., we make up for him."[94] Thus the client was served and the audience more fully entertained. Backstage, in public anonymity, the agency man took pleasure in the craftsmanship of manipulation.

The second story concerns a performance for a client; it has been recalled by Robert Koretz, noted for his work on the Kotex account, who began work as a copywriter for Lord and Thomas in the early 1930s. He recalls the talents that agency president Albert Lasker employed to gain approval from an arbitrary client who lacked good judgment on copy but enjoyed the exercise of authority. In one instance, Lasker was presenting a series of ads to this client. Lasker had not had time to review the ads beforehand, nor did he know that the copy for all the ads in the series was identical, except for illustrations, headlines, and subheads. As he reached the midpoint of the first ad, the client reacted with almost violent rejection. Calmly and confidently, Lasker remarked: "I just read you that for contrast so you could appreciate the really fine copy in these other ads which I will read to you." Then he read a second ad, identical except for illustrations and headlines, and won the client's enthusiastic assent for the entire series. While the client had gained a satisfying sense of making a crucial decision, agency workers backstage could enjoy a sigh of relief and join in admiring their leader's skill in handling a client who held power over them but who lacked the sophistication to criticize agency craftsmanship. Lasker's tactics were another "benign deception"; the client was well served because the agency knew best how consumers would respond to this particular copy, which had proved its "coupon-pulling power" in controlled tests.[95]

The folklore of backstage tales is endless. Milton Feasley entertained guests at parties by reading aloud his halitosis copy for Listerine. Advertisers seem to have far surpassed other professions in the frequency of their self-parodies. Jokes in the trade journals lampooned copywriters and account executives as well as clients and consumers. An ad man might even invite a snicker at the entire industry's claims to professional respectability by remarking that advertising might be "the youngest profession," but it had "a lot in common with the oldest."[96] Humor, self-directed, could also accentuate the challenges of professional craftsmanship, as in an anonymous poem entitled "The Advertising Man" in *Printers' Ink:*

> Glorifying pink chemises, eulogizing smelly cheeses,
> Deifying rubber tires, sanctifying plumbers' pliers,
> Accolading rubber panties, serenading flappers' scanties,
> Rhapsodizing hotel fixtures, sermonizing on throat mixtures;
> Some call us the new town criers,
> Others call us cock-eyed liars![97]

Given such challenging products, and the accompanying client pressures, some ad writers cultivated a backstage view of themselves as neither criers nor liars, but as agile survivors and virtuoso players.

Sometimes a survival ethic dominated the backstage conversation of advertisers. Cynical comments abounded, expressing admiration for such triumphant survivors as the bald copywriter who had tried all the hair restorers without success yet still wrote powerful and convincing hair-tonic copy. Even the *Printers' Ink* columnist "Groucho" admitted that in a "driving, feverish business" the advertising man could not be fair-minded, and thus might need to fall back on an expedient cynicism. "He is compelled," Groucho explained to agency clients, "to see the consumer as one who has to be brought into your camp by hook or crook." Still, heavy reliance on the satisfactions of backstage confessions, a tendency implicit in the very structure of agency operations, did not necessarily connote a pervasive cynicism. Most of the advertising elite saw themselves engaged in creating benign deceptions. "Hook or crook" tactics served a larger, positive purpose.[98]

The larger purpose, stated in its exemplary form, was to sell a product that would improve the buyer's standard of living. As apostles of modernity, advertisers would persuade consumers to avail themselves of each modern advance. Could dedication to that purpose surmount the barriers between the advertising elite and its "constituency" of consumers—barriers erected by differences in class, gender, geographic location, and cultural tastes? Certainly the advertisers were eager enough to understand the public and to present readers with slice-of-life images they would immediately recognize as relevant to their own lives. But how successfully could they capture the realities of consumers' lives amid work pressures that encouraged them to withdraw into a narrow circle of fellow-conspirators for enhancement of their self-esteem and recognition of their craftsmanship?

Certainly agency pressures and the demographic characteristics of advertising agents should alert us to the likelihood of distortion in the "mirror" images of society in the ads. Yet, in one particular sense, advertisers were favorably situated to provide an accurate revelation of underlying cultural realities. As the "most modern of men," they experienced with particular intensity many of those qualities of modern life that had gradually been coming to unsettle the wider society. They worked under severe pressures of time, competition, and unsympathetic external judgment. They were forced to acknowledge limits on their own creativity and personal control. When Fairfax Cone spoke of the anxiety created by a sense of impotence in the face of distant, impersonal decisions, he described an experience that advertisers shared with other Americans who were steadily being initiated into more complex and impersonal modes of modern life.

As veterans in assimilation to modernity, advertisers could offer knowing advice on how to adjust the pace and the scale of modern life. Their responsibility to pay attention to consumers' reactions also reminded them of the psychological costs of such adjustments. As mediators of modernity as well as its apostles, they adopted modes of appeal that never could have been predicted through logical extrapolation of theories of modernization. The actual content and style of "modern" advertising, and its capacity to reflect accurately the lives and aspirations of Americans in the 1920s and 1930s, would depend heavily on the way advertisers understood their relationship to the consumer audience and how sharply they kept that audience in focus.

KEEPING THE AUDIENCE IN FOCUS

In January 1928, a young woman in the J. Walter Thompson advertising agency, who described herself as "an inexperienced but struggling enthusiast," challenged the recent trend of her own agency's advertising style. The agency was already facing increasing criticism in the trade for its heavy reliance on paid testimonials. In such a setting an attack from within, even one printed anonymously in the agency's confidential newsletter, represented a bold reproach. Why, she wanted to know, had the recent layout and copy of the campaign for Fleischmann's Yeast "deteriorated . . . to such an extent that they have assumed the appearance of a *True Story Magazine* insertion"? Was it to appeal to "the minds of those morons . . . who daily dole out their 2 cents to secure the latest news not only unadulterated but graphically portrayed"? Had the agency lowered itself to producing "tabloid copy for tabloid readers"?[1]

The agency's response, written by the experienced copywriter Gerald Carson, was immediate and devastating. In so skeptical an age, said Carson, people should welcome "any manifestation of idealism as precious, there is so little of it." Nevertheless, the stern demands of duty required the agency not to indulge its preferences, but to advance the sale of Fleischmann's Yeast. This duty could be performed only with copy "comprehensible to the plain people." It might be more pleasant to "advertise exclusively to 'nice' people," such as the girls at Sweetbriar or Vassar (a direct hit, perhaps, at "struggling enthusiast's" alma mater). But advertising success was "too dependent upon the franchise of the common people for us to cherish a purpose so aristocratic." Carson eagerly accepted the challenge for the agency. Yes, by all means, "tabloid copy for tabloid minds."[2]

Much the same debate over the characteristics and tastes of the audience for advertising regularly stirred the trade press. As the 1920s progressed, each of the various advertising media sought to capture its own definition of the audience in a pithy slogan. "Tell It to Sweeney," urged the king of the American tabloid newspapers, the New York *Daily News.* "Sweeney," who might live in Brooklyn, Staten Island, the Bronx, or Upper Manhattan, and whose real name might be Muller, Cohen, Nelson, or Smith, symbolized the common man, now economically enfranchised, who read the *Daily News.* Wise advertisers would seek to tell their sales stories to "Sweeney" in his own language and in his favorite media.[3] On the contrary, *Harper's Bazaar* urged advertisers to cultivate the "inner circle," the class with "the *most influential* purchasing power," which set the example for the rest of society. By making no "editorial concessions to the masses" *Harper's Bazaar* achieved the tone necessary for an effective appeal to this discriminating class.[4] By the late 1920s scores of magazines and newspapers steadily harangued advertising agents with similar slogans and arguments. Each claimed to have discovered and captured just the audience to which they should appeal.

The private dialogue over style within the J. Walter Thompson agency and the clamorous competition of the media to define the optimum audience posed questions that never ceased to trouble the creative elite of advertising. What was the class structure of the buying public? What were its tastes and desires? How did you go about discovering them? Might your own situation and your range of personal contacts distort your vision of that audience? Working in the rarefied atmosphere of an advertising agency, how could you be sure that you were keeping your picture of that audience and its tastes properly in focus?

Even these questions did not measure the extent of the dilemma. Once the advertising copywriter had defined and analyzed the audience, how should he proceed if its tastes, motivations, and capacities differed from his own? How could he speak as a "man of the people" once he recognized a gap to be bridged—a gap that seemed to widen into a chasm as he moved from the "inner circle" toward Sweeney and the "tabloid mind"? To understand how the creative elite of advertising dealt with these problems of measuring, evaluating, and responding to an inscrutable consumer audience, we can best begin by looking at two phenomena of popular culture in the 1920s that fascinated the advertising elite and intensified its problem of defining and identifying with the consumer audience: the tabloid newspaper and the confession magazine.

Keys to the Consumer Mind: Confessions and Tabloids

True Story Magazine and the *Daily News* first appeared within weeks of each other in May and June of 1919. Together, they would profoundly influence the notions of the leading agencies about advertiser-audience relationships. *True Story* was the offspring of the magazine *Physical Culture,* published by the flamboyant strongman and health enthusiast Bernarr Macfadden. For several years Bernarr's wife Mary had been reading the letters and manuscripts that poured into the *Physical Culture* offices. In many of these, women brokenheartedly confessed their true experiences. Mary Macfadden's own instincts, and the responses of other young women working in the *Physical Culture* offices, convinced her that this was saleable material. As one staff member remarked: "Everybody will want to read *that* one. All the working girls go through the same love troubles. This one will be about themselves and *written* by themselves."[5] Bernarr Macfadden adopted the first-person, confessional formula for the new publication. *True Story* later touted its contents as "the first folk-literature since the days of the Bible—a literature written *by* the people themselves and responded to by the people." The stories of girls gone astray, of jealous husbands intent on revenge, and of sublime love transformed to hatred gained emotional force from illustrations that broke away from the idealized art style of most magazine fiction and used dramatic photographs of models in menacing poses or love clinches.[6]

Bernarr Macfadden unflinchingly aimed *True Story* at an audience of young, working-class women. Insisting that the stories came from "common people," Macfadden tested any copy that sounded too high-brow on the office elevator operator. Anything that puzzled him was rejected—a practice that provoked one irreverent staff member to compose his own underground confession story: "How I was Demoted to Editor of *True Story* and Worked My Way Up to Elevator Man Again."[7] Although it was not sold by subscription and carried a high newsstand price (20 cents at first, compared with 15 cents for the dominant *Ladies' Home Journal*), *True Story* soon revealed an impressive market. By 1924 it had pulled even with the reputable *Good Housekeeping* at a circulation of about 850,000. By 1927 it was boldly challenging *Ladies' Home Journal* and *McCall's* for first place in national circulation among women's magazines, with newsstand sales of over two million per issue (Fig. 3.1).[8]

True Story held fast to its astoundingly successful formula—women's personal, confessional accounts of temptations, love triangles, and tragic adventures. Again and again, the "simple, trustful humans" who were *True Story*'s heroines fell victim to the perils of a bewildering and complex modern world.[9] In George Gerbner's epitome of the genre, the heroine of the confession, "buffeted by events she cannot understand," began a "headlong flight down the line of least resistance," which ended in "her inevitable sin." Punishment, physical or moral, was immediate and severe. Although *True Story* disavowed any intention to preach, every story turned out to be "a powerful sermon."[10]

Might the success of such a formula carry important lessons for advertising? A sophisticated young lady like J. Walter Thompson's "struggling enthusiast" might recoil from the literal-mindedness and sensationalism of *True Story*'s lurid style. But millions of people did not. In a series of sociological sermons to the trade, *True Story* ads proclaimed the magazine's discovery of the once-downtrodden. *True Story* readers constituted a whole new market: the wives of skilled workmen, women who "can't comprehend the more sophisticated 'silk worm' magazines written for white collars." These women were not yet deafened by the "billion dollar din of repeated advertising." They were more likely to live in a modest frame house on Main Street than in "a palace on Lake Shore Drive" but they had plenty of money to spend on cars, radios, and appliances, as well as on soup, soap, and breakfast food.[11]

3.1. *A 1929 cover suggests the newsstand appeal of* True Story, *now boldly priced at 25 cents. Its first-person, confessional stories attracted an immense audience, one that advertisers could not ignore despite their disdain for its low tastes.*

At first, advertising agencies hesitated to buy space in *True Story* despite its mounting circulation figures. Its style and tenor seemed incongruent with the copy they were producing for most of their clients. Self-consciously guarding their new respectability, advertising agents were reluctant to use a medium so redolent of a shady past; both they and the products they advertised might lose caste through such an association. Could you do a serious, businesslike job of selling in such a lurid atmosphere? Besides, who could demonstrate that *True Story* readers were a distinct market with adequate buying power? As late as 1926, with a circulation approaching two million, an issue of *True Story* often carried less than a dozen full-page or half-page ads for national advertisers. It still drew the bulk of its considerable advertising revenue from smaller ads for bust developers, weight-reducers, cures for bunions or baldness, and money-making schemes.[12]

By the beginning of 1928, however, when "struggling enthusiast" was bemoaning J. Walter Thompson's new "tabloid" style, *True Story* had clearly won many converts within the agencies. After a period of cultural lag, during which advertising agencies, somewhat aloof and aghast, had curiously eyed *True Story*'s rising circulation, they began to grasp the implications of the magazine's appeal. Here was one successful form of the more personal, intimate approach they had been seeking. Here was a new *reading* public. Never mind how meager its vocabulary or narrow its interests; it could actually *read* advertisements, if properly written in the *True Story* style of "short words and shorter sentences." If the steady stream of statistics on rising wages did not lie, this audience could afford to buy the brands it chose. Coupon returns from advertisements demonstrated the power of *True Story* to elicit reader inquiries. By 1928, Fleischmann, Kotex, Lux, Pond's, Jell-O, Pepsodent, Cutex, Squibb, Lysol, Forhan's, Bayer, Wrigley, Camels, Old Golds, and the Cleanliness Institute, as well as more than a dozen others, had joined *True Story*'s roster of national advertisers.[13]

The idea of not only reaching the huge *True Story* audience, but reaching it with advertisements in the *True Story* formula, now began to take hold. The J. Walter Thompson agency, which was already placing ads for several clients in *True Story*, initiated seminars for its copywriters on the *True Story* approach. Copywriter Gerald Carson, a recent acquisition from Calkins and Holden, opened up "whole new vistas" with a talk on "The Mental and Emotional Life of a Tabloid Reader." Other agencies, too, excitedly discovered this new audience, which obviously craved the "dramatic realism" and personalized approach that recent theory had certified as the optimum advertising strategy.[14]

The headlines of advertisements in *True Story* now began to echo the titles of its confessional stories: "Could she be the Helen Brown I used to Know?" (Golden Glint Shampoo). "Because I confessed . . . I found the Way to Happiness" (The Borden Company). "I Deceived My Husband and I'm Proud of it!" (The Postum Company). "Some Wives Do it, but I wouldn't dare" (Wheatena Corporation). (See Figs. 3.2, 3.3.) The same or similar confessional ads soon appeared in newspapers and in such staid women's magazines as *Good Housekeeping, Delineator* and *Ladies' Home Journal*. Perhaps, advertisers began to surmise, the "tabloid mind" defined a much wider segment of the consumer audience than even the circulations of *True Story* and the tabloid newspapers revealed.[15]

95

Because I confessed

...I *found the* WAY *to* HAPPINESS

Modern to her fingertips, Julie fell in love with a man who demanded the old-fashioned virtues in a wife. What was she to do?

"MADGE, I'm going to tell you something I wouldn't tell another soul," I said. "I'm in love with Paul Blake—and if I weren't quite so frivolous, I think he'd admit he loves me. . . . You see, he believes in old-fashioned girls—girls who are good cooks, for one thing. He told me he just wouldn't *marry* anyone who couldn't cook."

"Shucks," said Madge. "I couldn't boil water when I was married, and look at my well-fed husband now. I'll admit I use my head, and every new short-cut I hear about. . . . Julie, that gives me an idea! You're both going to the dance with us to-morrow night, aren't you? Well, afterward—the plot begins!"

She talked on and on. Her last words were, "I'll send the book over right away, with the pages marked; and don't be afraid—you *can't fail!*"

⸎　⸎　⸎

The dance was over. By the time we had reached my house we were all half frozen, and my suggestion that the crowd come in for a hot drink was met with enthusiasm.

I disappeared into the kitchen, and there, with Madge's precious book before me, my fingers flew. In just nineteen minutes I wheeled in a tea wagon that was hailed with shouts of delight.

"Julie, this is the most de-*licious* hot chocolate I ever tasted!" "Julie, these luscious coconut macaroons are *warm!* You've a chef concealed in that kitchen!"

"Those things! Oh, I just tossed them together myself," I said carelessly.

"Impossible!" exclaimed the crowd's best cook. "You were gone less than twenty minutes."

Paul took my arm. "I appoint myself a committee of one," he said, "to search Julie's kitchen, chaperoned by Julie herself. Then I'll report the number of chefs concealed about the premises. . . . I've an idea she's some little chef herself!"

A call from Madge woke me the next morning. "What I want to know is," she demanded, "*were* you proposed to in that kitchen—or weren't you?"

"Well—not exactly. But he's coming over tonight, and—"

"Enough," said Madge. "My engagement present to you, my child, is the condensed milk cookbook I intended simply lending you. John will die till I get another, but never mind."

"It's the only book I ever saw that simply *makes* you turn out good things in no time," I said. Suddenly I blushed furiously. "—And Madge—did you ever hear such an appropriate name—'New Magic in the Kitchen'?"

⸎　⸎　⸎

You can have magic at your own fingertips, simply by using the cookbook Julie used—and Eagle Brand Sweetened Condensed Milk.

Eagle Brand is not plain canned milk. It is fresh, full-cream country milk *ready-blended with fine sugar*—two ingredients in one. This smooth, rich, creamy mixture is highly nourishing, remarkably easy to digest. And it makes possible a wonderful new way of cooking!

"New Magic in the Kitchen", with its 175 economical, quick, simple new recipes, is yours for the asking—absolutely free. Just fill in the coupon, and mail it today!

Here's one recipe!

COCONUT MACAROONS

¼ *cup Borden's Sweetened Condensed Milk*
1 cup shredded coconut
¼ teaspoon vanilla
1 egg white, stiffly beaten

Mix condensed milk and coconut. Add vanilla. Fold in egg white. Drop by tea-spoonful on a well-buttered pan. Bake until lightly browned in a moderate oven (about 10 minutes.)

To serve eight people, Julie doubled this recipe.

You can get 174 others, just as good, by mailing the coupon!

C.-T.S.-2-29

THE BORDEN COMPANY,
Borden Bldg., 350 Madison Ave.,
New York, N. Y.

Please send me FREE your new recipe booklet, "New Magic in the Kitchen".

Name

Address

City and State

3.2. As advertisers discovered the vast True Story audience, they also experimented with its personalized, confessional copy style.

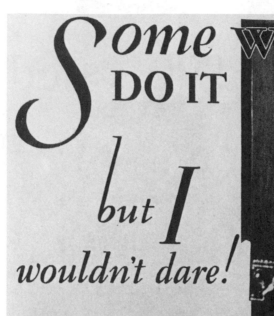

Some WIVES DO IT but I wouldn't dare!

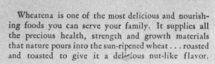

SOME wives I know treat their husbands shamefully. Off they're sent—every morning—with little more than a cup of coffee, a few bites of toast and a kiss. They show it, too! They have that lean and hungry look.

Not so with *my* husband. I wouldn't dare serve him such a flimsy breakfast. His health—and our happiness—are too precious for me to gamble with.

Early morning appetites *simply have to be pampered*—so I try to select breakfast dishes that are not only nourishing but also enticing. And that's why I serve Wheatena *regularly*. It's the only cereal my husband really enjoys—and the children just love it, too.

My discovery of Wheatena is due entirely to our doctor. He recommended Wheatena when my first baby reached the cereal age. He said Wheatena was not robbed—like so many cereals—of the minerals, vitamins, and other valuable food elements of the whole wheat.

For variety sake—I prepare Wheatena in a number of delicious ways. Sometimes I cook it with just water—other times with half milk and half water—and in summer I often serve it chilled with fruit.

And one of the nicest things about Wheatena is that it is so *quick cooking*. In just 2 minutes of boiling and bubbling, it's ready for the table.

Perhaps you, too, have this problem of selecting breakfast dishes that are not only nourishing but also enticing.

Wheatena is one of the most delicious and nourishing foods you can serve your family. It supplies all the precious health, strength and growth materials that nature pours into the sun-ripened wheat . . . roasted and toasted to give it a delicious nut-like flavor.

And no matter how you serve Wheatena — steaming hot or chilled, with fruit — it's equally delicious, equally nourishing, equally easy to digest and assimilate.

Wouldn't YOU like to try this wonderful cereal? Just mail the coupon below and we'll send you 3 generous servings. Or, better still, get a full-size package from your grocer today so you'll have it for breakfast tomorrow.

3 Delicious Servings

FREE

THE WHEATENA CORPORATION
Wheatenaville, Rahway, N. J.

Gentlemen: Please send me, by return mail, one of your friendly little packages of Wheatena . . . the sun-browned wheat cereal . . . sufficient to make three generous servings.

Name ....

Address ....TS 5-30

3.3 Even wholesome Wheatena turned to a hint-of-scandal confession to appeal to the "tabloid minds" of True Story readers.

3.4. *This 1920 issue of the* News *adopted a typical, four-photograph, tabloid format. In later years, a single photograph and a bold headline often constituted the tabloid's entire first page.*

Meantime, the conception of a "tabloid audience" had gained even greater credibility from the prosperity of the tabloid newspapers themselves. *True Story* was a national magazine. The *Daily News* gained its sensational success right in New York City, where no New York advertising agent could ignore its flamboyant presence, or that of its blatant imitators. First introduced in 1919 as the *Illustrated Daily News,* the *Daily News* surged to prominence on a wave of popularity even more impressive than that enjoyed by *True Story.* In two years it was selling more copies than any other New York newspaper. By 1925 it approached a million in daily circulation, far surpassing any other daily paper in the United States. Tabloids had now appeared in eleven other American cities. In June 1924, William Randolph Hearst launched his own New York tabloid, the *Daily Mirror,* and Bernarr Macfadden, the publisher of *True Story,* joined the New York tabloid competition with the *Daily Graphic.* By 1926 the *Daily News* and the *Daily Mirror* were New York City's two largest papers.[16]

The term "tabloid" had originally denoted the smaller-than-normal page size of the new papers. But the popular impact of these papers quickly transformed the word into an adjective suggesting their particular style and sensational mode of appeal. As the phrase "tabloid minds" suggests, the term also came to characterize the audience that responded to this appeal. Photographs dominated the news presentation and layout of the tabloid (Fig. 3.4). So thoroughly did the *Illustrated Daily News* devote itself to pictures that the word "illustrated" was soon dropped from the masthead as superfluous. Its front page consisted entirely of pictures and a single headline to rivet attention. The "extravagant emphasis" of each issue of the *Daily News* on a single major story derived from "the reasonable assumption that the average mind is incapable of becoming deeply interested in more than one thing at a time."[17]

Tabloid news stories were extremely brief. The discovery of techniques for introducing a "news" aspect into any account of sex or violence soon made the standard news story almost obsolete. Regular tabloid features included "Heart to Heart Talks," an advice column for young women, and "Real Love Stories," to which readers were encouraged by $5 prizes to contribute personal stories.[18] The *Daily Graphic,* drawing on the *True Story* experience, "adapted the confession-story technique to the news," recounting the day's sensational stories in first-person accounts ghosted by the newspaper's reporters but by-lined by the participants. The *Graphic* also introduced the "composograph," a photograph of models posed in a dramatic reenactment of "what was believed to have taken place." In picture and prose, the tabloid spoke in the language of the man on the street.[19]

The tabloids of the early 1920s, with their circulation triumphs in New York City, surpassed even *True Story* in their impact. The advertising agencies reacted at first with shock and skepticism. Like most of the respectable elite, advertising leaders disdained the tabloid as vulgar and depraved.[20] The *Daily News* gained major advertisers very slowly at first. Space buyers, one observer comments, apparently assumed at first "that the paper, plumbing the lower depths, had discovered a subhuman race which was of no account to anybody who wanted to sell something."[21] But advertising agents had an obligation that others of their education, tastes, and class position did not: they had touted themselves as experts on the consumer mind. As the circulation of the tabloid newspapers mounted, they dared not ignore the fact that more than three times as many New Yorkers read the tabloids as read the *New York Times,* the tastes of advertising agents notwithstanding.

By the mid-1920s advertising leaders were watching the tabloids with rapt attention as well as lingering distaste. *Advertising and Selling Fortnightly* noted early in 1926 that the tabloids were now "overriding the delicate sensibilities of advertisers and agents," convincing them no longer to "disdain to practice their art in terms of the lowest common denominator." In the same year, *Advertising and Selling Digest* predicted that the *Daily Graphic,* the lowest-pitched and most sensational of all the tabloids, would be copied with success in all the nation's major cities. The *Digest* based its prophecy on the fact that the *Graphic*'s publisher, Bernarr Macfadden of *True Story,* "knows what the public wants—and gives it to them."[22]

In its continuing "Tell It to Sweeney" campaign, the *Daily News* boasted that the tabloid had uncovered not merely new dimensions of audience tastes, but a whole new consumer audience. Like *True Story,* the *Daily News* emphasized the free-spending qualities of the newly prosperous common man, the "plutocrat in overalls." But the *Daily News* also offered advertisers assurances that its audience did not exclude the affluent. Its readership, it claimed, included "the milkman and the magnate, the shopgirl and her most extravagant customer," and it even enjoyed wide circulation among the city's business elite. (These gentlemen presumably kept it discreetly folded inside the *New York Times* or pretended to have picked it up only because the maid or the wife had left it around.) The implication for ad writers, if they accepted this claim, was that a tabloid style might well have universal appeal. As the *News* succinctly put it: "Tell It to Sweeney; The Stuyvesants Will Understand."[23]

The campaign by the tabloids and *True Story* to induce the advertising trade to accept their image of the consumer audience was reinforced by the efforts of such publications as the *American Weekly*. Commanding an immense audience through its inclusion in the Sunday editions of all newspapers in the Hearst chain, the *American Weekly* provided a weekly reading and pictorial diet best characterized by a list of the headlines for the articles of a sample issue. The issue for March 28, 1926, included:

> "Killed Herself to Spite the Man Who Spurned Her Love"
>
> "Marjorie Rambeau's Bad Luck. Accused in Court of Being a Love Pirate; Loses Her Fiance and Her Broadway Play Flops"
>
> "Unexpected Surprise That Betrayed the Grave Robber"
>
> "Why the Whipping Post is More Dreaded Than a Prison Cell"
>
> "His Revenge—In the Play—In Real Life: Story of the Lover Who Burned Out the Eyes of the Sweetheart Who Had Blinded Him"
>
> "Why Dancing the 'Charleston' is Sometimes Fatal"
>
> "Newest Earrings to Match Your Gown"
>
> "To Show Us How the Savior Really Looked"
>
> "Married the Chimney-Sweep's Daughter"
>
> "Lady Cathcart's Own Story"[24]

Such content, the *American Weekly* reminded advertisers, reflected the "reading taste of average men and women." Like *True Story* and the *Daily News,* the *American Weekly* warned advertisers to focus their sights on the rising economic power of ordinary folks. After all, it catechized the advertising trade several years later, "How Many Cigarettes Can a Dowager Smoke?" Like the *Daily News,* the *American Weekly* also claimed its share of devoted readers among the "quality" families of the "high-brow clubs and blue stocking societies," who shared the common taste for seeking life "Just the Way You See It In the Movies."[25]

The Matinee Crowd

By evoking the image of the movies, the *American Weekly* associated itself with the most influential popular medium of the age. Even before the 1920s, elites had cast a disdainful eye on the cultural tastes of the moviegoer; now the tabloids and confession magazines reinforced their negative impressions of the matinee crowd. The people in Hollywood knew how to find "the least common denominator" in an audience of billions, one agency man pointed out. That denominator was crassly emotional. To capture the movies' appeal, advertisers might well seek to stimulate "an occasional heart-throb." Like the tabloids, the movies provided a stern lesson in audience mentality, the Ruthrauff and Ryan agency noted. Once a copywriter recognized that the subtitles stayed on three times as long as it took him to read them, he would realize "how slowly most minds work."[26]

Probably the most striking lesson to be learned from the movies, advertisers somewhat reluctantly concluded, was that the audience valued opportunities for illusion and escape above all else. A speaker at a meeting of the creative staff of the J. Walter Thompson agency urged his colleagues to imagine "Main Street at night in a little town in Kansas or Nebraska or New Mexico." The scene's only suggestion of glamor was the blazing facade of the "Palace Theater." Inside, the screen conveyed romance, beauty, and adventure—"everything that is missing from the lives of the people out in front, who are escaping from grocery bills and the daily grind." Advertising agents might wish to take themselves and their business more seriously, but the people, as represented by movie audiences, wanted "more romance and less reality." From the movies, more than from any other source, magazine editors and advertising writers drew their image of the consumer audience as trapped in plain, even "drab" environments, bored and depressed by the "humdrum of existence" and filled with secret desires for illusions and romance.[27]

Nor could advertisers overlook the possibility that the vulgar emotionality or escapist illusions of the films might both stimulate and provide clues to the buying impulse. As a newspaper film critic pointed out in a *Printers' Ink* ad, the movies usually showed life at its best. People wore the latest, most tasteful styles against backdrops of exquisite furnishings and the most modern home accessories. And the movie "palaces" seemed to reveal the hunger of the audience for luxurious surroundings and the attentions of a servile class in the form of bowing ushers (see Fig. 7.7). Here was a promise of opportunity for the advertising agent: he might draw attention to his client's products by similar "entertainment" appeals based on the movie formula of "Luxury, Lackeys, and Love."[28]

Other movie "formulas" reinforced the ideas for advertising formats that copywriters had drawn from the tabloids. Even more than the tabloid, the movie screen revealed the power of dominating pictures. Advertisers quickly recognized audience fascination with the "close-up." As an advertising technique, the close-up not only attracted attention, it also fostered the habit of intense self-scrutiny. Advertising artists and photographers also sought to emulate the movies in what Neil Harris describes as their capacity to emphasize the "sensuous properties" of seemingly mundane articles. The movie-star phenomenon reminded advertisers of the popular hunger for personalities. And the power of quick-pacing and captions that drew the spectator along predetermined lines of thought and associations inspired advertising writers to ingenious efforts at capturing the essence of the movie in print (see Fig. 9.7).[29]

Film critics later recognized the impulse to audience involvement created by the fact that the moving picture, unlike the painting, had no fixed frame: the edges of the screen functioned like "a piece of masking" that prevented the viewer from seeing the wider, extended reality of which the screen image seemed only a portion.[30] In seeking to capture the "realism" of the movies, advertising artists in the 1920s increasingly shunned borders in their ads and used more photographs and striking visual juxtapositions. Above all, they sought to create "dramatic scenes" to tell emotion-laden stories. And they increasingly did so with the movie-matinee audience in mind.

If advertisers had considered only the lessons of the new popular media, they would have faced problems enough in keeping their audience in focus. But advertisers were also assailed by the insistent voices of hundreds of newspapers and magazines, many of them with claims to the patronage of a "quality" audience. These publications argued that sophisticated luxury-buyers were growing in numbers. "The Man with the Hoe dons a Dinner Jacket," proclaimed a *Better Homes and Gardens* ad in 1917, "and there are a million like him." "What's Become of the Four Hundred?" asked *Cosmopolitan* magazine rhetorically. The nation's once-tiny social elite, it quickly replied, had now grown to one million—all readers of *Cosmopolitan,* of course. *Vogue* coined the phrase "the art of gracious living" to suggest a social atmosphere of luxury and leisure desired by highly cultivated men and women who commanded concentrated buying power.[31]

The argument for emphasis on a "class" audience did not rest solely on the purchasing power of the carriage trade itself. This class, the quality publications insisted, also exercised *influence.* These were "the key-people of the country." A wealthy social class of about 500,000 people, N. W. Ayer and Son pointed out, sponsored fashions for the nation, popularized new forms and places of amusement, and pioneered new styles of living. The rest of the country soon followed. Where salesmen failed, Ayer argued, advertising could slip past the protective butlers of this influential class. No one could deny the popularity of the movies, admitted an ad for the "quality group"—*The Atlantic Monthly, Harper's Magazine, Review of Reviews, The Golden Book Magazine, Scribner's Magazine,* and *The World's Work.* But those who attended museums, "while far fewer in numbers, are vastly more effective in thinking power, in purchasing power, and in the power of leadership."[32]

The Limits of Consumer Citizenship

Besieged by the various media with these conflicting sociology lessons on social structure and the flow of cultural influence, advertisers gradually formed their own tentative consensus about the consumer audience. Of course, that audience differed for each product. No one was more aware of the multitude of overlapping audiences for different goods and services than the advertising agent. But copywriters and artists also formed images of general audiences for a large variety of products. These revolved around the conception of two broad categories: class and mass.

Before advertising's creative elite had arrived at this bifurcation of the nation's consumers, however, they had subscribed to an even more fundamental assump-

tion. Drawing by analogy upon the political concept of citizenship, they constructed an image of a market democracy, in which advertisers appealed to constituen-
cies of consumer citizens and won election of their brands as popular products.
Representation in this theoretical consumer republic rested on the "one dollar, one
vote" principle. Some people could cast far more votes than others. As *The
Literary Digest* noted, one man's patronage was not just as valuable as another's.
"Democracy will not stretch so far as that. It admits equality in the inalienable
rights to Life and Liberty, but not in the Pursuit of Merchandise."[33] Those whose
income fell below the effective equivalent of "one dollar" in the marketplace were
disenfranchised. Thus the first basic distinction lay not between class and mass
buyers, who at least were buyers at the minimum one-dollar level, but between
buyers and those who economically did not qualify as "citizens" at all.

Controversy occasionally flared over the minimum qualifications for consumer
citizenship. The high courts of national advertising were known to send down
split decisions. In American metropolitan centers, insisted the Portland *Oregonian,*
"only half of the population falls in the Able-to-Buy class." In the low-rent
sections of the city, families were not markets (consumer citizens) "in the ordinarily accepted sense of the word." Their incomes were too low. Another periodical excluded only 37 percent from the ranks of "worthwhile" consumers. But a
writer in *Advertising and Selling* granted consumer citizenship to less than one-
third of the nation's families in 1934 when she brusquely informed her "Prep
School for Copy Cubs" that families with incomes below $1,000 a year were
"omitted from this lesson." Consumer citizenship, by many of these definitions,
was a minority privilege.[34] Other writers in the trade journals specified particular
disenfranchised groups—tenant farmers, Negroes, and those without an easy
command of English. The exclusion of blacks is confirmed by the meager national
advertising in black newspapers such as the *Chicago Defender* and the *Pittsburgh
Courier.*[35] Generally, the criteria for disenfranchisement encompassed a far wider
population than these seemingly obvious ineligibles. Although the estimates of
the extent of consumer disenfranchisement ranged widely—from a low of 30
percent up to a high of nearly two-thirds of the population—the general notion
of a "citizen-noncitizen" distinction gained nearly universal assent. It is therefore
essential, as we examine advertisers' images of the class and mass audiences, to
remember that between 30 and 65 percent of the people had already been excluded
from consideration. The term "mass audience" thus referred primarily to those
Americans with higher-than-average incomes. When the trade journal *Tide* noted
that the Erwin, Wasey agency had "talked class to the masses," it defined the
"masses" as the readers of the *Saturday Evening Post.*[36] "Mass" was defined not in
terms of the population as a whole but in relation to the narrow elite that had
preoccupied the attention of many advertisers before the economic changes of the
1920s.

When it came to distinguishing between a class audience and a mass audience,
two practical considerations influenced the advertising trade. Each of these led to
somewhat different conceptions. The first consideration was the choice of media
for advertising a given product. Some luxury products did not justify advertising
beyond the circle of the wealthy few; other products could survive only with the
widest distribution. In the choice of media, agencies and manufacturers paid close

attention to the newspapers' and magazines' various claims for the class standing of their readers.

Publications aspiring to a class image constantly sought new ways to dramatize their superior selectivity. Some personalized their image by portraying their typical reader as sophisticated, affluent, and compulsively intent on possessing whatever was modern. Others portrayed their publication as a giant magnet pulling only the best out of the city's population, or claimed that they obtained their subscribers by getting debutantes to enroll their friends.[37]

Although *Cosmopolitan* and *Literary Digest* insisted that their readers were selected on the basis of "sophistication" or "alertness" rather than mere wealth, the bottom line in calculating which media provided a class audience was family income or wealth. Agencies usually segregated survey questionnaires into three or four categories on the basis of family income. The J. Walter Thompson agency based its distinctions on the rental value of the home, classifying homes in categories from A to D. Its A category, characterized as "homes of cultured people with large incomes" and at least one servant, corresponded roughly to the trade's conception of the class audience.[38]

An influential survey of consumption patterns by Pittsburgh families in 1931, utilizing three categories of social class, concluded that 5.2 percent of the city's families qualified as "Class A families" of higher business and professional positions. Of these families, 83.2 percent owned cars and 57.2 percent owned electric refrigerators, compared with only 47.6 percent and 18.9 percent respectively for families in the next-lower B category.[39] Such a 5 or 6 percent elite among an urban population represented the broadest possible definition of the class audience to gain credence within the advertising agencies. This left the term "mass" to represent all those families that fell between the top 5 or 6 percent and some equally arbitrary definition of a minimum level of income for consumer citizenship.

The advertising elite also considered distinctions between class and mass audiences when choosing what type of advertisement to use. Would a class audience respond to a different style than a mass audience? Here, the tendency to differentiate clearly between class and mass was less common than in the choice of media. Advertisers talked about the presumably singular qualities of the masses—particularly their susceptibility to emotional appeals—but then proved increasingly unwilling to delineate a class audience that would not respond to the same approach. Copy styles with a tabloid flavor gradually made their way into general magazines and occasionally into class publications. In some product categories, class-mass distinctions were preserved. A silverplate manufacturer explained his choices: modernistic illustrations and male servants to appeal to the most exclusive sophisticates; maids and more conservative art for "quietly prosperous" Mary Smith; suburban chintz curtains, bright peasant ware, and no maid for Mary Jones with her nice little house and garden; and movie-star testimonials for Mary White. But many campaigns used the same copy for all publications. Procter and Gamble, for instance, employed identical copy in 1930 for Camay ads in *Cosmopolitan*, the *Saturday Evening Post,* and *Photoplay.*[40]

The justification for this frequent refusal to differentiate mass and class appeals was often compressed into one of the advertising profession's most common figures of speech: "the Colonel's Lady and Judy O'Grady" (characters from Kipling) were "sisters under the skin."[41] This saying neatly encompassed both the notion of a distinct social hierarchy and the insight that, on some level of consciousness, such distinctions disappeared. For advertisers, "under the skin" clearly referred to the level of basic emotions. Since the classes and the masses (individualized as the Colonel's Lady and Judy O'Grady) shared the same basic instincts and emotions, and since an appeal to the emotions was the most effective way to stimulate action, advertisers often saw little need to differentiate copy appeals.

Sizing Up the Constituency: The Feminine Masses

How, then, did the creative elite of American advertising in the 1920s and 1930s characterize its audience? After the economically unqualified had been put out of mind and the class audience partly fused into the mass, on what salient traits did ad writers base their generalizations?

The pairing of the Colonel's Lady with Judy O'Grady pointed to the most striking single quality of the consumer audience. The choice of this particular figure of speech may have been fortuitous, but its imagery was significant: the word picture that served to collapse the class audience into the mass audience was female in gender. The consumer, whether class or mass (but intrinsically mass), was a "she." As one ad in *Printers' Ink* succinctly put it, "The proper study of mankind is *man* . . . but the proper study of markets is *woman*."[42] No facet of the advertiser-audience relationship held such consequence for advertising content as the perception by the overwhelmingly male advertising elite that it was engaged primarily in talking to masses of women.

Demographically, of course, women comprised no more than a razor-thin majority of the nation's population—or of any of its mass or class segments. But statistics indicated that women did the bulk of the nation's retail buying. A constant agency cliché referred to women as the "purchasing agents" of their families, an analogy that suggested near-total responsibility for expenditures. The advertising trade journals commonly attributed 85 percent of all consumer spending to women. Scarcely anyone estimated women as comprising less than 80 percent of the consumer audience.[43]

Once the audience was understood to be overwhelmingly female, certain implications for copy content and selling appeal seemed evident. Advertisers could draw upon a long tradition, British and French as well as American, for viewing women as fickle and debased consumers. In a tone of scientific assurance, advertising leaders of the 1920s and 1930s added that women possessed a "well-authenticated greater emotionality" and a "natural inferiority complex." Since women were "certainly emotional," advertisements must be emotional. Since women were characterized by "inarticulate longings," advertisements should portray idealized visions rather than prosaic realities. Copy should be intimate and succinct, since "women will read anything which is broken into short paragraphs and personalized."[44]

Although the women's magazines regularly pictured their sophisticated readers as leading busy, diversified, action-packed lives, advertising agencies generally adopted a very different model of the typical woman consumer. This model owed more to the contemporary stereotypes of the movie-matinee fan and *True Story* reader than to the bustling, self-confident women shown in ads by *McCall's* and *Ladies' Home Journal.* "We must remember," wrote a *Printers' Ink* contributor, "that most American women lead rather monotonous and humdrum lives. . . . Such women need romance. They crave glamour and color." The advertising pages, he argued, should become "the magical carpets on which they may ride out to love." They should cast such magical spells that housewives and women workers could "daily see themselves as *femme fatales,* as Cleopatra or Helen of Troy."[45]

Advertisers derived another appraisal of the consumer audience from various estimates of its level of intelligence. Army tests during World War I had recently startled Americans. A shocking percentage of prospective inductees had not possessed the minimal level of intelligence to qualify for military service. The burgeoning science of psychology was perfecting its measurements of I.Q. or mental age. Advertising writers followed these revelations and discoveries with curiosity, if not always with discerning attention. Repeatedly they reminded their colleagues of the latest figure which had lodged in their memory: "Most of us have the mind of a child of ten"; "Remember, the average citizen has the mentality of a child of twelve"; "It has been established that the average intelligence of the American people is that of a thirteen-year-old child."[46] Estimates of average mental age ranged from nine to sixteen. Occasionally trade journals protested that these figures distorted advertising by setting the level too low. But the constant citing of such figures had a cumulative effect upon the consciousness of advertising writers.

The content of the popular press reinforced this image of an unintelligent public. Several advertising writers recalled that Arthur Brisbane, the editorial genius of the Hearst papers and the guiding spirit of the tabloid *Daily Mirror,* had shown his insight when he had posted a sign in the Hearst city room that read "You *cannot* underestimate the intelligence of the American public." *Time* magazine, which shared the tabloids' dedication to an image of speed and brevity, concluded that the most striking way to describe its distinctive "class" audience to the trade was to proclaim its contempt for tabloid "heart-advice departments" and to refuse to dilute its news content with "a multitude of features dedicated to Mr. and Mrs. Moron and the Little Morons."[47]

Movie content, also, provided a measure of public intelligence. "We say Hollywood people are stupid, the pictures are stupid," reflected one agency representative. "What we are really saying is the great bulk of people are stupid."[48] The Ruthrauff and Ryan advertising agency, flaunting its own success in following the example of "editors, movie directors, and popular novelists," instructed the trade in the deplorable but inescapable facts of life: "After all, men and women in the mass are apt to have incredibly shallow brain-pans. In infancy they are attracted by bright colors, glitter, and noise. And in adulthood they retain a surprisingly similar set of basic reactions."[49]

Closely related to the theory of the limited mental capacity of advertising's audience was the assumption of public lethargy. "The mass mind is averse to effort," an experienced woman copywriter warned agency novices. "Women don't like to think too much when buying," added a contributor to *Advertising Age*. Popular culture and preferences for routine work revealed the public's resistance to originality or mental effort, its reluctance to "try to take in anything new." George Gallup, reporting on his polling information for the Young and Rubicam advertising agency, suggested that the success of the New York *Daily News* was related to the tendency of "whole legions of women to read only the headlines except in the case of a juicy crime story where their interest overcomes their mental inertia." Gallup concluded that "nothing short of a terrific blast attracts their attention or seems to register on them." The prolific advertising writer Kenneth Goode reminded the trade in *How to Turn People into Gold* that "man in the mass," except when caught up in emotion, "won't exert himself beyond the line of least resistance."[50]

In envisioning one particular segment of the mass audience, advertisers were inclined to associate the characteristic lethargy of the consumer with exclusion from the cosmopolitan life. Advertising writers occasionally reminded each other that they must not allow their own metropolitan world—the culture that shaped so many of their conclusions about the mass mind—to blind them to the fact that much of their audience was composed of "the folks back home" who lived in smaller towns and cities or on farms. If urban masses displayed the lethargy of conformity and mental torpor, rural folk exhibited the phlegmatic qualities of a slower pace of life and an even greater resistance to modern change. Of course, the creative advertising elite did not always depict country life and country folk in a negative light; some advertising writers sentimentalized rural and small-town life. But images of rural consumers usually reminded the advertising agents of their mission on behalf of modernity. The farmer and the small-town resident gained their most unqualified tributes in the advertising journals when they displayed just as much interest in modern goods and styles as did city folk.[51]

In viewing the urban masses, advertisers associated consumer lethargy as much with weak-kneed conformity as with cultural backwardness. The masses never looked beyond the need for immediate gratification. They would greet with suspicion any invitation to differ from the crowd. Often they were irritatingly slow to accept modern ideas. Subtleties entirely escaped their "careless, uncomprehending mentality." They refused to respond to anything but the most sensational stimuli.[52] In trying to capture a sense of the culture of the "people," a Ruthrauff and Ryan ad verbally panned across the advertising audience for a quick, movie-like impression:

> Perspiring thousands at Coney Island. . . . Gaudy pennants. The crunch of peanut shells underfoot. Chewing gum. Mustard dripping from hot dogs. People struggling for a view of some queer freak in a side show. Red-faced men elbowing and crowding for the vicarious thrill of a cooch dancer. . . . Stopping for the shudder of gaping at a gory accident. . . . Women tearing other women's clothing in the scramble at a bargain counter . . . huddling at

a radio to hear a crooner drone Tin Pan Alley's latest potion of vapid sentimentality. . . . Waiting in line for hours to view the saccharine emotional displays
of a movie idol. Taking a daily dose of culture from the comic strips.[53]

Although such vulgarities were partly counterbalanced by popular qualities of
"heroism, self-sacrifice, generosity, and tenderness," one general conclusion
seemed inescapable: advertising writers were addressing an audience that lived not
by logic and reason but by "its rather raw and crude emotions."[54]

Academic psychologists had been stressing the efficacy of the emotional appeal
in advertising ever since Walter Dill Scott's *The Theory of Advertising* in 1903.
Throughout the 1920s advertising agencies intensified their rival claims to superiority in creating emotional copy. One agency claimed that it based its effort to
dramatize each advertising story on the scientific fact that "for every act based
upon *reasoning* we perform *twenty* acts as a result of our *emotions.*" William Esty
of J. Walter Thompson reminded his colleagues that the unanimous conclusion
of all the experts they had recently consulted on public opinion was "that it is futile
to try to appeal to masses of people on an intellectual or logical basis." Emotion,
or what one of those experts had referred to as the public's "childish love of . . .
raw sensation," was the only sure avenue of influence.[55]

This growing consensus about audience emotionality helped fuse the other
observed audience traits into a composite conception. Popular convention defined
emotion as a particular characteristic of women—and the advertising audience
was overwhelmingly female. In fact, nearly every characteristic commonly attributed to the masses was also conventionally a "feminine" trait—capriciousness,
irrationality, passivity, and conformism. A blatant appeal to the emotions, moreover, epitomized the vulgarity in taste that was common to the masses. Emotional
appeals succeeded because only by seeking this lowest common human denominator could the advertiser shake the masses from their lethargy without taxing
their limited intelligence. Despite occasional protests against this audience image,
advertisers of the 1920s became increasingly committed to a view of "consumer
citizens" as an emotional, feminized mass, characterized by mental lethargy, bad
taste, and ignorance.

"Oh, What Do the Simple Folk Like?"

How did the creative elite of American advertising, confronted with the task of
preparing messages for this audience, understand its own relationship to the
consumer masses? A few advertisers used the collective pronoun "we" in dis-
cussing consumer traits, on the democratic assumption that if the masses were
emotional and lethargic, it was because those qualities were common to all
people—even advertising writers. But in the overwhelming majority of their
descriptions of the consumer masses, advertising leaders used the pronoun "they"
and drew clear distinctions between the capabilities, tastes, and mental processes
of the creators of advertisements and those of consumers.

In describing the consumer audience, advertising leaders almost invariably assumed it to be socially inferior. "Who are those people who crowd Market Street," asked the N. W. Ayer and Son agency, with the clear implication that advertisers would be quite unfamiliar with people who were carpenters, mail carriers, machinists, and clerks. *Tide* characterized tabloid readers as reaching "with their grimy hands into their patched pockets." Other trade journals frequently reminded advertising men that only about 1 percent of the population were college graduates, that more people still took a bath only on Saturday night than bathed daily, and that the worker, although now a "marketing factor," was "socially and intellectually . . . still a Wage Earner, in every sense of the phrase." *Advertising and Selling Digest* suggested obliquely that "Few people live in the skyscrapers of New York. Most of them live on the street level."[56]

But the class distinctions that advertising writers drew between themselves and their broad audience were not nearly as sharp as the disparities they perceived in intelligence and in cultural tastes. In describing the types of copy appropriate for the unlettered, emotional masses, advertising men emphasized the wide cultural gulf separating them from those to whom they must appeal. In *Psyching the Ads,* Carroll Rheinstrom spoke matter-of-factly about "women of the financially modest—and, correlatively, mentally modest—groups." George Gallup, employed by the Young and Rubicam agency, confessed himself unable to account for the amazingly low level of taste of the typical woman newspaper reader. But he noted that his interviews found "stupid women" in city after city who consistently preferred vulgar, sensational stories of baby-killers to momentous items of world news. Even Claude Hopkins, himself the creator of many simplistic copy slogans, confessed that he personally disliked "these tales of broken homes, wrecked romances, ruined lives" in human-interest advertising. But, he argued, advertising men should suppress their own values and "give them what they want." Afterward, he continued, "we can retire to our libraries and read philosophy."[57]

Scores of others among advertising's creative elite echoed Hopkins's suggestion. Advertisers must suppress their own revulsion against the vulgarity and emotionalism of the masses and talk in the language of the audience, even though such advertising was "crude" and "low-brow." As one writer put it, "it isn't the taste of the angler that determines the kind of bait to be used, but the taste of the fish."[58] Ruthrauff and Ryan, which scored one advertising triumph after another by aiming lower in style and appeal than other agencies, constantly stressed the we-them disparities. "We must not forget that many things which are well-known to us are beyond the horizons of the multitude," it cautioned. "In addressing the large audience, we cannot ignore . . . the mental and emotional limitations of the great mass. . . . Our choice of appeals, copy ideas, headlines, and illustrations must embody concessions to popular taste—whether we, as individuals, endorse that taste or not."[59]

"Concessions" was the key word. Advertising leaders, in fact, were far better educated than the average member of the consumer constituency. A writer in *Printers' Ink* may have exaggerated the comparison with the average consumer when he wrote, "While he is intellectually twelve, you are intellectually thirty."

But he unerringly reflected the creative advertising man's perception of cultural distinctions when he continued, "We come from another world, all right."[60] Advertising agents readily confessed that the styles and appeals they found themselves impelled to adapt from *True Story,* the movies, and the tabloids were "in very rotten taste," "lacking in beauty," full of "obvious banalities," and "sloppily emotional." "Aesthetes may weep," *True Story* magazine taunted them, "*But business men will stop and think!*"[61]

Advertising men sometimes wished they could direct all their campaigns to such "thinking" businessmen who made decisions on the basis of logic rather than unreasoning emotion. The Henri, Hurst and McDonald agency explained that its January 1927 ad in *Printers' Ink* was a rare exception to proper reliance on the emotional appeal because it addressed a "limited group of men," the controllers of advertising budgets, who "deal in cold facts and logical conclusions, else they would not be at the top." The agency obviously relished this opportunity to speak man-to-man to the rational elite. But such rarefied advertising could never meet the needs of the emotional masses. Reason, explained the executive of another leading agency, was a "faculty . . . reserved only for a few, the advance guard who suffer for their ideals."[62] It was again *True Story* that recalled the advertising men to their role as mediators between the business elite and the unsophisticated, emotional masses. "Socially these people are strangers to you," *True Story* pointed out. "Culturally, their tastes are quite different from your own. But economically they are your bread and butter."[63]

Such economic dependence on the consumer audience, coupled with social distance, inclined advertising men to contemplate the power and vulgarity of this new economic "citizenry" in the 1920s with a mixture of fascination and disgust. Their attitudes bore a resemblance to the demagoguery to which the Whig Party had turned in the 1840 "Log Cabin" campaign as it acknowledged a new political constituency. In a vaguely parallel sense, a "newly enfranchised" consumer constituency had mushroomed in the two decades preceding 1930, just as the enfranchised political constituency had expanded between 1815 and 1840. Much as the bumptious vulgarity of the new Jacksonians had alarmed fastidious gentlemen in the 1820s and 1830s, so the emotional and tasteless new consumers of the 1920s offended the sensibilities of a more sophisticated, and better-educated, advertising elite. A new democracy with "a deafening clatter and a disregard of the sanctities" now confronted the business world, a national advertising leader noted with mixed feelings in 1927. "Deplore and deprecate them as we might, we had opened the doors to the hobnail and the hoi-polloi and they came crowding toward the peak." Little wonder that Jose Ortega y Gasset's *The Revolt of the Masses,* which warned of democracy's contribution to the influence of the culturally barbarous masses, gained attention among a few of the more philosophically inclined advertising leaders.[64] As we shall see, however, many advertising men staved off fears of a debasing cultural engulfment by clinging to a more congenial vision: they might close the cultural gap by using advertising to uplift the tastes of the masses.

As a last resort, in the protection of their self-esteem and as a psychological weapon against cultural engulfment by the tastes of the consumer masses, advertisers could always emphasize the stereotyped gender distinction between advertisers as men and consumers as women. This distinction shielded the advertising elite not only from being debased by the vulgarity and backwardness of the consumer masses but also from being debauched by the lesser frailties of the "class" audience. Although the "class" audience shared with the advertising elite such qualities as cosmopolitanism, high social status, tastefulness, and sophistication, still it was primarily female. Thus it exhibited a degree of frivolity, emotionality, and mental inertia from which most advertising leaders, as men, considered themselves immune. It was both a comfort and a challenge to conclude that even "the Colonel's Lady" must be addressed in a language different from that normally spoken among advertising men.

"Getting to Know Them"

Advertising leaders were intensely aware of the problems presented by their social, cultural, and intellectual distance from the mass of consumers. Trade journals abounded with sermons on the text "Know thy audience." These arose from the shared conviction that myopia was the profession's besetting sin (Fig. 3.5). Ruthrauff and Ryan, a small but aggressive agency that prided itself on the common touch, seemed to taunt the other agencies by probing their perpetual vulnerability to fears of a loss of audience contact. "Ever shake hands with your customers?" the agency inquired, with a meaningful side-glance at its sophisticated, cultured, stuffed-shirt competitors.[65] The Lillibridge agency dramatized the issue by creating a new ailment—"desk disease." The failure to get out and circulate among the people, it warned, often created mental paralysis in advertising agencies.[66]

The critics of advertising's ingrown perspective agreed on one thing: copywriters were the worst judges of the merits of their own work. Since merit in an advertisement was determined by sales, it was the unsophisticated consumer whose judgment was crucial. The critics of too "artistic" an advertising craftsmanship gleefully reported instances in which judgments by professionals and consumers differed. In an exhibition of advertising art, Kenneth Goode revealed, ad managers and visiting artists had given almost unanimous first-place votes to one illustration in an ad directed toward women. Meanwhile, he continued, "women visitors—the people to whom that picture was designed to appeal— placed it ninth on their list!" Eastman Kodak reported that a jury of consumers had scored 69 in accurately predicting sales results from a group of ads while ad men had scored only 26.[67] In 1935 the Lydia Pinkham Company, after years of relying on its executives to choose "suitable" ads, agreed with its new advertising agency to "disregard all personal likes and dislikes" as unscientific and to rely instead on measurements of consumer inquiries. As the Ruthrauff and Ryan agency suggested, the proper prescription for avoiding the afflictions of ingrown thinking and "desk disease" was "Don't take your *own* pulse—take the consumer's."[68]

But the prescription was easier to write than to administer. Just *how* did an agency take the consumer's pulse? One common agency answer was to propose

From these shelters
Beauty comes forth to buy

Every year American womanhood spends 4½ billion dollars strictly on American womanhood. Cosmetics and clothes. Most of this money does not come from the men signs on the hill. It comes from the grey herds of houses in the valley. Beauty lives down by the railroad tracks.

This is not something that Newell-Emmett thinks. It is something that Newell-Emmett knows. We have recently gathered a third of a million coupons on a "loveliness appeal." A man was sent out to photograph a few hundred of the addresses on the coupons. Above are some of his pictures.

To reach this market is more than a job of selecting the right magazines and newspapers. It is a matter of developing the right appeal. Putting the right pictures and the right words together to interest these women and girls.

Any thinking on this subject is valueless unless it is based on a sure knowledge of what *they* think and *how they* think. These are known factors at Newell-Emmett.

NEWELL-EMMETT COMPANY
ADVERTISING   NEW YORK

· 111 ·

3.5. Agency ads frequently appealed to clients' fears of elite myopia. Unlike other agencies, Newell-Emmett implied, it recognized that consumers lived in "grey herds of houses . . . down by the railroad tracks."

experience in ringing doorbells and face-to-face selling as an optimum seasoning process for the prospective copywriter. *Printers' Ink* recorded the career of "John S. Advertissimo," a mythical "advertising superman," as having begun with stints as a reporter and advertising solicitor on a suburban newspaper, as a retail clerk in a large store, and as a salesman "on the road."[69] Such seasoning behind the counter, on the road, and in the hinterlands was primarily prescribed for youthful beginners. But the J. Walter Thompson agency took special pride in reprogramming Dr. John B. Watson, the famous behavioral psychologist and chairman of the Johns Hopkins Psychology Department, when he joined the ad agency. Watson served first behind the retail counter at Macy's and then on the road selling coffee to retail dealers and conducting a survey on drugs. Although agencies rarely required such a seasoning, many talked about its desirability and seem to have assumed that a knowledge of the public thus acquired would last a copywriter's lifetime.[70]

One common prescription for agency "staleness" was a smaller dose of the same across-the-counter, door-to-door medicine. Even experienced copywriters could regain their touch and discover new copy appeals by getting out of the office temporarily and selling the product or observing it in use. Dorothy Dignam of N. W. Ayer and Son described how she regularly worked in a department store or dimestore to maintain a feel for the "customer's viewpoint." Ads for the George Batten Company (later BBDO) described how copywriters got up at six in the morning and donned uniforms to work with a biscuit company salesman, or worked underground in a coal mine for two weeks to learn to write copy for Exide batteries in the language of miners.[71]

Undoubtedly agency copywriters did occasionally undertake such forays, but scattered evidence suggests that "across-the-counter" experiences played a larger role in advertising talk than they did in agency practice. A *Printers' Ink* columnist recalled for agency executives their standard advice to young men and women to "go out and get some first-hand selling experience" and then concluded: "I won't be so cruel as to ask whether you have done the same." A copy chief at J. Walter Thompson confessed that the burden of closing dates and office work had made any plan to release copywriters for selling experience impractical. Moreover, he allowed, in many cases they would find such consumer research "distasteful."[72]

BBDO was still bragging in a 1933 promotional presentation about the copywriter who "recently covered up his typewriter, went to Pennsylvania, got into miner's clothes," and carried out an underground investigation for Exide battery copy. The story was strikingly similar in every detail to one that the pre-merger George Batten Company had first recounted in an ad in 1928. Likewise, the legend of the early-rising copywriters who joined the National Biscuit Company salesman on his rounds, first reported in a George Batten Company ad in early 1928, still gained billing as recent news in a BBDO ad in mid-1932.[73] Such agency human-interest stories of face-to-face encounters with the masses apparently gained a timeless, mythic quality in the retelling.

Another commonly prescribed cure for the out-of-touch copywriter can best be classified as "mingling." Copywriters or agency executives might not "live with the mass" but they should "mingle with it, listen to it, observe it, talk to it." Contributors to the trade journals constantly scolded copywriters for living "too narrow and restricted a life." They should be present where the crowds of common people congregated. The copywriters' school should be the railway station, wrote one commentator; they should "go sit in the waiting rooms for an hour a day." Others suggested a department store, a subway, or the lobby of a movie theater. To gain the common touch, such advice continued, copywriters should deliberately go slumming a bit to ensure that they were among the masses. They should sit in the bleachers rather than the grandstand; they should choose a second balcony seat over one in the grand tier. If they watched the crowds and mingled with the throngs, then in their copy they would speak to the mass audience not as intruders but as intimates.[74]

Such rebukes for aloofness and admonitions to "live close to the people" probably tell us more about agency anxieties than they do about copywriters' normal practice. Of course, we have no reliable data on the frequency with which advertising agents attended dance halls and amusement parks. We do not know how many left their desks to watch the crowds in railroad stations and movie lobbies. The few diaries and autobiographies that exist do not mention such behavior, although they do afford glimpses of advertising men and women at art exhibitions, at the opera, and on European tours. As one agency man commented, the tendency, as in every business, was for advertising leaders to grow more remote from the masses as they advanced in position. By and large, he noted, "we try to avoid being where the mass is."[75]

Probably advertising agents were no more inclined than others to initiate unconventional social contacts or attend entertainments they did not enjoy. Their acclaim for mingling served to impress prospective clients and to remind themselves of their functional duty to present the "outside view." The effect, if any, of such "hands-on" experience on advertising content and style is impossible to estimate, since tributes to the value of "mingling" never described the specific observations drawn from such reacquaintance with the consumer public.

Detached observations of the mass public offered advertising agents a less provocative image of their own social role, and a less dramatic story to relate to clients, than adventure stories of forays into the haunts of the masses. But various forms of remote observation proved more convenient than "rubbing up against life" in dance halls or bleachers. The copywriter could find out "what people are like" by investigating what books they read, what movies and magazines they preferred.[76] In the late 1920s the J. Walter Thompson agency began inviting figures from the world of popular culture—editors from the tabloids, movie distributors, comic section editors—to speak to the agency staff. At one point, one of its copy groups made an intensive study of the *True Story* editorial techniques. In 1929 the trade gave a warm reception to Robert and Helen Lynd's sociological study *Middletown*. Here, the reviewers suggested, was a good tool for correcting illusions about the nature of the broad consumer audience.[77]

The research study, of course, was a vehicle that the advertising agency itself could, and did, employ. But the bulk of what passed for advertising research throughout the 1920s did not explore the subjective qualities of the masses. Most agency research was market research. It compiled indexes of buying power in various areas, cataloged media coverage, and tabulated brand preferences at representative retail stores. Researchers categorized selected audiences by occupation and class but did little else that would give copywriters a feeling for the "mass mind."[78]

The predominant form of copy testing was the "keyed" advertisement with a coupon that could be cut out and returned for a product sample, information booklet, or special premium. Agency researchers tabulated the returned coupons, each keyed by means of a special post-office box number or similar device, to evaluate the relative "pulling power" of various media and appeals. Identical ads were inserted in different magazines; ads with different copy and art work were tested against each other in the same media. Such tests provided a rough notion of audience preferences, although advertising writers argued vehemently over whether those who returned coupons were in fact representative of the whole readership of the publication and whether coupon returns bore any conclusive relationship to eventual sales.[79]

Several agencies boasted of other forms of research into consumer attitudes in the late 1920s, but their crude, slapdash methods made these "surveys" of questionable value in providing accurate feedback. One agency reported that it could obtain quick, inexpensive results in investigations involving only a few questions by having all members of the staff send questionnaires to their friends. A silver manufacturer first submitted a variety of possible copy illustrations to ten young women in its own offices and then "cross-checked" the results by testing the same illustrations on a larger sample of young women in the office of its advertising agency.[80] *Printers' Ink Monthly* recounted in doggerel verse the role of "representative consumer" often played by "the ad man's wife":

> This is the tale of an Ad man's wife
> A tragic glimpse into her life
> A jibe at the Fates that Cruelly doom her
> To play the role of the "Great Consumer"
> Of how her advertising spouse
> Goes snooping for copy around the house
> While he drives her near the brink of distraction
> With his "Dear, I'd like to get your reaction!"[81]

When agency men searched further afield for reactions of "typical" consumers, their research methods still invited criticism. One agency set up an outside "consumer jury," but it selected that jury from the names of those who had written in response to advertising by one of the agency's clients. General Electric pre-tested one batch of copy on advertising classes at Columbia University and a New York City night school, hardly a national cross-section of consumers.[82] None of these methods afforded a glimpse of a wider consumer audience. In fact, they encouraged the very myopia that agencies were presumably trying to avoid. Concern for gaining an accurate image of the audience was not lacking; but few agencies had the capacity to bring research to bear on that elusive task.

We should be cautious, however, about assuming that we can measure accurately the degree to which the creative advertising elite of the 1920s and 1930s succeeded, as it often claimed it did, in gaining an intimate knowledge of its audience. Our own knowledge of the "reality" of that audience springs largely from sources used by the advertisers themselves: popular media of the era, sociological surveys such as *Middletown,* the content of the era's popular culture, and various measures of buying habits, attendance patterns, and social participation. Historical distance colors our own impressions and precludes the immediacy of direct perception. Nevertheless, recalling the fact that some advertisers recognized their demographic, educational, cultural, and geographical distance from the bulk of their audience, we can ask whether the various contemporary techniques of audience contact—seasoning, mingling, observation, and research—promised to succeed in overcoming that distance. By present-day standards, certainly, the research efforts of agencies were infrequent and often crude, and "mingling" appears to have been honored more in promotional efforts than in practice. Were the advertisers' other resources—observation and intuition—sufficient to bridge the social and cultural gulf between these creators of a modern "folklore" and the "folk" whose values and desires their advertisements sought to reflect?

In Search of the Typical Consumer

One possible test of the success of copywriters in accurately gauging their audience would be to compare their portraits of the typical consumer with estimates drawn from other sources. Such a comparison is useful but presents serious difficulties in interpretation. Depictions of the typical consumer, both verbal and pictorial, abounded in the advertising press. But many of these were created by individual newspapers and magazines bent on convincing manufacturers and agencies that their readers were ideal consumers, with modern ideas and plenty of purchasing power. In conformity to the logic of the new advertising, they drew portraits of the typical consumer with which *their* potential customers, the agency leaders and advertising managers, could readily identify.

Thus the media offered the copywriter a picture that recapitulated his own fondest images of the consumer. *True Story, American Weekly,* and the tabloids, of course, seemed eager to shock advertisers with the reality of a working-class consumer audience. But even they often spruced up their Mr. and Mrs. Sweeneys with refinements in lifestyle that would satisfy the expectations of an advertising agent. Thus media portraits of the typical consumer were often skewed by the desire to entice the advertiser. Their usefulness in appraising the accuracy of the profession's audience image stems only from the tendency of the ad creators to absorb such images and echo them in their own consumer stereotypes.

Deliberate efforts by the media to depict their readers as a "class" audience were predictable. Far more intriguing were their portraits of the "modest" or "typical" consumer citizen. In 1926 the Cincinnati *Enquirer* ran a series of ads in the trade journals in which it personalized each Cincinnati suburb from which its readers were drawn. Most of the depictions, such as those of Mrs. Hyde Park, Mrs. Mt. Auburn, and Mrs. Wyoming, were rarefied "class" portraits. Mrs. Oakley, on the other hand, was introduced as a "salt of the earth" type, yet the *Enquirer's* description of her could be considered modest only by contrast with its image of the aristocratic Mrs. Wyoming. Mrs. Oakley, the most humbly situated of all of the *Enquirer's* typical readers, owned her own "homey white cottage" with a "velvety lawn," was a leader in civic activities, and kept her living room, dining room, and kitchen each looking "like a picture from *House and Garden.*"[83]

The *American Weekly,* claiming to represent the mass tastes of "5,000,000 typical American homes," nevertheless described its readership as far more educated and prosperous than any census statistics could have predicted. Ads in 1926 and 1927 depicted the *American Weekly's* common man in a business suit, returning home on a front path that appeared to wind about one hundred feet from porch to street.

3.6. Advertisers had trouble
keeping their audience in focus
when mass publications like
Hearst's Sunday supplement,
American Weekly, bom-
barded them with upscale portraits of typical consumers.
(Compare Fig. 3.5.)

His wife, well-dressed and coiffed, stood on the commodious front porch of a
house that one imagines to be comparable to the large residence across the street
(Fig. 3.6).[84] The Chicago American's "typical" Morton family displayed standards
of dress and patterns of family democracy likely to be found only at the upper-
most reaches of the middle class.[85]

The Merrill J. Browns of Indianapolis, whom the American Magazine nomi-
nated for typical American family in its ads, lived in "an eight-room frame house,
with bath, steamheat, electric-sweeper, washer and ironer, automatic refrigerator, telephone, and radio." Mr. Brown, a sales manager, golfer, and tennis
player, had a "moderate income" of about $5,000 a year in 1931. Census statistics,
by contrast, would have placed this "typical" American family within the top 12
percent in income even in the more prosperous year of 1929. As for Mr. Brown's
recreational activities, they appear far more typical of the interests of advertising
men than of the habits of the consumer audience as a whole. A 1930s survey
numbered golfers at less than 2 percent of the population. As late as 1950, when
the golfing population had expanded considerably, Gallup pollsters found that 93
percent of their respondents never played either tennis or golf.[86]

Certainly any sophisticated advertiser should have discounted these portraits of
the typical family as distorted, self-serving fabrications by the media. But other

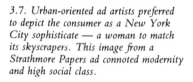

3.7. *Urban-oriented ad artists preferred to depict the consumer as a New York City sophisticate — a woman to match its skyscrapers. This image from a Strathmore Papers ad connoted modernity and high social class.*

3.8. *Even outside unmistakable New York settings, the typical consumer remained urban — and female. The consumer is also defined as female in Figs. 2.3, 2.4, 2.5, and 3.5.*

images of the typical consumer that circulated within the trade did not differ appreciably from these models. Perhaps the constant barrage of media-contrived stereotypes had a hypnotic effect on copywriters. More likely, in their eagerness to personalize a typical consumer so that their communications would be intimate and sympathetic, copywriters and agency art directors found it congenial— perhaps inescapable—to picture someone with a living style and tastes similar to their own. In describing a "typical father" one contributor to *Advertising and Selling* described the coming of a baby in his home as inspiring the hiring of a nursemaid at $60 a month and another servant at $40 a month. An ad by the Lennen and Mitchell agency associated the increasing "average income" with the need for a second car, "so that Mother and Daughter may motor out to the Country Club."[87]

Advertising agencies almost invariably depicted typical consumers as urbanites. Mr. McGroucher, Pillsbury's "likeable representative" of typical "me-and-you folks," was a white-collar commuter who had to hurry in order to catch the 7:43. The agency for Strathmore Papers stereotyped "your customer" as a stylish woman shopping in skyscrapered streets that could only represent New York City (Figs. 3.7, 3.8).[88] Other generalized images of the consumer provided more detailed impressions of what was typical. The Batten, Barton, Durstine and

Osborn agency seemed incapable of presenting the typical consumer as anything but a golfer. It spoke of "one hundred and thirty million people, all living about the same kind of lives" and noted that they all yearned for "comfort, pleasure, travel . . . and more distance off the tee."[89] A significant graphic image of typicality appeared in a Campbell's Pork and Beans ad. The illustration depicted a national sample of American consumers who "overwhelmingly" preferred the product. Of the thirty-two consumers, two were children and twenty were women, all dressed to suggest a status of upper-middle class or above. Of the ten men, all were attired in topcoats or business suits and ties except for the four in leisure dress, three of whom were engaged in such genteel forms of recreation as hiking, tennis, and golf (Fig. 3.9).[90]

Even those who attacked their colleagues for nurturing too lofty a view of the typical consumer often failed to surmount their own restricted vision. One writer in *Printers' Ink* vehemently protested against all the illustrations of servants and evening clothes in advertisements, only to proclaim that art directors should depict "the rank and file of our Americans . . . playing bridge as they do with their most intimate friends."[91] In *Selling Mrs. Consumer,* Christine Frederick excoriated advertising men "who carry in their minds completely erroneous pictures of Mrs. Consumer in the mass." In preferring to think of her "as a woman of their own class or nearly so" they were ignoring statistics that revealed her fourteen-year-old mentality, and her failure, on the average, to adopt even such minimally civilized habits as brushing her teeth. Some 200 pages later, however, Mrs. Frederick had gravitated back to describing this same archetypal "Mrs. Consumer" as centering her social life around the country club, and as perhaps having bought "*several* pianos of different shapes and woods in recent years." "Mrs. Consumer" might be mentally deficient, but she seemed easier to call to mind when she possessed upper-class status and modern tastes.[92]

One explanation for such inconsistencies and distortions of vision may be that advertising artists and writers were frequently unable to maintain distinct, separate images of a class audience and a mass audience. Perhaps as they shifted their gaze from one to the other, their vision blurred and the two unfocused images tended to fuse. But to explain their dilemmas on the simple basis of these two conspicuous audiences is to stop short of comprehending the complex, conflicting pressures they faced. If advertising men had difficulty keeping the consumer audience in focus, it was partly because they were anxious to please and identify with other, less evident, audiences: their clients, their high-culture critics, and not least of all, their colleagues and themselves.

Feedback from Secondary Audiences

Raymond Bauer has argued persuasively that the style and content of a mass communication message is rarely conceived with only a "single manifest audience" in mind. Secondary audiences, consciously or subconsciously imagined, may determine the communicator's approach. Ithiel de Sola Pool and Irwin

America OVERWHELMINGLY PREFERS THESE PORK-AND-BEANS

they're slow-cooked ·· *they're* golden brown ·· *they're* steeped in tomato sauce

LOOK FOR THE
RED-AND-WHITE
LABEL

Years ago tastes for beans varied in different parts of the country. Certain sections were justly proud of the way they cooked and served them. But today there's no doubt whatever about the pork-and-beans the whole country prefers. There's a national taste in beans extending from the Atlantic to the Pacific, from the north to the Gulf of Mexico. The overwhelming majority eats Campbell's — slow-cooked and with sparkling, taste-tempting tomato sauce. We point with pardonable pride to the record—for they are by far the best-liked and largest-selling beans the nation over.

Slow-cooking makes every bean mellow, golden-brown, nut-like in its richness — tender, yet whole —

firm, yet delightfully smooth to the tongue. The famous tomato sauce, made from Campbell's exclusive recipe, flavors each bean through and through. There's the savor of the pork — and a seasoning as mild as it is delightful.

The way America likes beans is the way *you* like beans. Taste Campbell's—and see!

Campbell's Pork-and-Beans
··· *the way America likes beans*

3.9. Campbell's "America" reflected the advertisers' favored image of the consumer constituency: predominantly female and clearly upper middle class in dress.

Shulman examined this hypothesis in their study of "newsmen's fantasies." They concluded that news reporting was heavily influenced by reporters' mental images of the anticipated audience. That audience, as Bauer noted, was rarely the "average middle-class man who buys this newspaper." Images of secondary audiences determined what the communicators remembered as well as how they organized and phrased information for presentation. The influence of such secondary audiences or reference groups lies in their power to offer rewards to communicators or deflate their self-esteem through disapproval.[93] Like news reporters and other mass communicators, the women and men in advertising faced secondary audiences whose explicit or imagined approval was crucial to their careers and to their self-esteem.

Advertising agencies had to produce advertisements that pleased the client or lose the account. And clients, in the view of many advertising agents, were notorious for accepting distorted views of the audience and indulging in self-satisfying rather than sales-producing advertising. *Printers' Ink* recounted with satisfaction W. K. Kellogg's confession that dramatic sales results finally persuaded him to abandon an earlier style of advertising, based on a false audience-image, that had won him many ego-inflating words of praise from his fellow businessmen. The not-uncommon client who continued to listen to the advice of his wife and the flattering comments of his friends could exert the influence of a very powerful "secondary audience" on the creative advertising elite.[94]

Even more influential than clients were colleagues. Because of the multiplicity of factors affecting sales, estimates of the success of an advertising campaign were bound to be highly subjective. Attempts to evaluate the impact of a single ad, or a single aspect of an ad, were even more problematic.[95] A noticeable sales increase might reflect only the magnitude of an advertising effort rather than any particular aspect of the illustration or copy. Members of the creative staff of an agency could rarely count on sales results to stimulate appreciation for their specific contributions. In most cases only another professional could recognize them as the writer or artist of a particular ad and judge their inventiveness or skill of execution. And the only words of praise or disdain that were likely to reach their ears came from their professional colleagues.

The audience of colleagues embraced not only the staff of a copywriter's or art director's own agency, but those of other agencies and companies as well. They were professionals whose acclaim was highly valued and whose recognition might shape one's career. The primary audience of consumers was so distant, and evidences of its approval so impersonal and uncertain, that the creative elite became heavily dependent on this secondary audience of colleagues. Sales results might challenge or verify the accuracy of copywriters' images of their public audience in the very broadest terms; but for all the creative nuances involved in the style and detailed content of an illustration and the phrasing of copy, the most powerful audience was other advertising professionals.[96]

Many of the standards of this audience of colleagues were, in turn, set by another secondary audience—that of the nation's educated elite, including the high-culture critics of advertising. Again and again, advertisers displayed an extreme sensitivity to criticism, a sensitivity all out of proportion to the capacity of critics to interfere with advertising practice. Writers in the trade journals counterattacked with vehemence when critics questioned the economic role of advertising. But when critics ridiculed or rebuked advertising for being tasteless, idiotic, silly, or deceptive, agency leaders more typically replied with *mea culpas* and calls for higher standards.

This response is not surprising if we recall that the creative elite in advertising shared the tastes of the high-culture critics to a far greater extent than they shared those they perceived in the consumer audience. Copywriters and artists tended to be well-educated. They shared the educated elite's disdain for vulgarities of taste, excessive emotionalism, and mindless banality. Most were embarrassed to be chided by their colleagues for having produced what was known in the trade as "buckeye," or corny, advertising.[97]

Yet buckeye advertising seemed to be just what the "tabloid mind" demanded. Thus copywriters and artists often found themselves engaged in what the high-culture elite could only characterize as pandering to the mob. The very word *pander,* with its connotation of playing the pimp and catering to low tastes and vile passions, dramatized the advertisers' dilemma in keeping their consumer audience in focus. If they accepted at face value the image of the audience gained from popular culture and from "scientific" assessments of public intelligence, they faced the prospect of being charged with pandering to the vulgar tastes and ignorant irrationalities of the crowd; they invited the contempt of their educated peers and the pangs of their own consciences. But if they rejected that audience image, they faced the hazardous prospect of retreating into insularity. Then they might defeat the whole effort to communicate by constricting their view of the audience to a mere projection of their own cultured, educated, cosmopolitan self-image.

Folk Wisdom, Uplift, and the Irresponsible Public

Both the presence of diverse audiences and the recognition of a significant cultural gap between the creative advertising elite and its primary audience of consumers pose problems for present historians, just as they did for advertising writers and artists of the 1920s and 1930s. For historians, the problems are simple to state but difficult to solve. Since we know that creative advertising people avidly sought audience feedback in order to mirror popular attitudes, we may assume that we can learn something about social realities from the content of advertising. That assumption is tenuous enough, given the deficiencies of the feedback process in the twenties and thirties and the likelihood that advertisers sought to "mirror" aspirations more often than realities.[98] But even if we accept it, we must then face the more complex question of determining *which* audiences were supplying the most influential feedback in any given instance.

The sociologist Hugh Duncan has noted that it is hard to communicate frankly and unequivocally to one audience when other audiences are listening in.[99] Advertising writers and artists, speaking to several audiences at once, created advertisements that depicted as "reality" a set of social relationships and values that was partly reflective of their own narrow circle, partly reflective of their conception of the desires of an ideal audience, and partly reflective of the characteristics they disdainfully attributed to the mass audience. None of the resulting "images of society" were undistorted mirror images. All were refracted to some degree by the biases and preoccupations of the advertising elite. Probably the most accurate reflections occurred when the concerns and attitudes of the various audiences coincided. This conjunction, I believe, was most likely to take place in the area of basic cultural anxieties and dilemmas. Such considerations will guide my consideration of advertising as a historical "mirror" in subsequent chapters.

The problems that diverse audiences and a "cultural gap" created for contemporary advertisers were both more complex and more immediately pressing. They demanded a practical response. "If we believe that the voice of the people is the voice of God," writes Duncan, "we address them very differently than if we believe them to be fools, children, or beasts."[100] But copywriters of the 1920s and 1930s could not select their content and choose their tone of voice according to such an exact distinction. The consumer audience seemed to be at once a foolish beast and the voice of God.

From one standpoint, much of the advertising elite looked down upon the throng of consumers with bemused contempt: these masses were ignorant, tasteless, emotionally foolish, and essentially "feminine." Drawing pay and professional prestige from their association with the (presumably) rational elite, they could hardly escape sharing some of their clients' scorn, as producers, for the less rational, more self-indulgent, and seemingly dependent role of consumer. Yet from another vantage point, still envisioned as located symbolically "above" the consumer masses, they assessed with awe the economic power of these millions. Just like a mob, Christine Frederick warned, "Mrs. Consumer in the mass has an ominous, ruthless power."[101] From this perspective, advertising agents might well wish to view themselves as ambassadors from these consumer citizens. In such a role, the advertising agent would translate the welling voices of the crowd for business clients and the educated elite, bringing them the voice of God, whose commandments had to be followed if the economic system were to prosper.

In one sense, the emerging image of an audience of "tabloid minds" reinforced the importance of the ad agents' mediating role. They might have preferred to communicate with audiences composed exclusively of rational, sophisticated, modern business leaders like themselves. But such a task would not have demanded special skills that the manufacturer could not have provided himself; simple announcements would have sufficed. However, reaching an emotional, sensation-seeking, uncomprehending audience that seemed to prefer its economic information wrapped in dramatic, personalized packages required special expertise. The more "debased" the audience, the greater the challenge to those playing the crucial role of economic mediators and missionaries of modernity.

Still, the image of a tabloid audience did confront advertising agents with a dilemma of means-ends relationships. If advertising writers produced "buckeye" copy on the "moron level," could they retain their self-respect and continue to pride themselves on "educating the masses"? If they resorted to sob-sister copy and the pseudo-gemeinschaft of intimate personal talks, were they really serving as apostles of modernity?

One response to these questions, though certainly not the most common one, might be characterized as the "salt of the earth" or "folk wisdom" theory. By celebrating the virtues and instinctive good sense of the common people, the advertiser could argue that it was no disgrace, but rather an honor, to talk to the mass audience in its "own language." If the readers of tabloids were, as the *Daily Mirror* described them, "intensely human," then any stigma should rightly fall on the snobs who "high-hatted" them and pretended to be more than human. Typical members of the consumer audience might not be "refined," but they were "plain folk" with common sense. "Regardless of outward noisy indications to the contrary," avowed one agency president in the mid-1920s, most people were "decent, courteous, kind, well-mannered, and considerate." Paraphrasing Kipling, another agency confidently assured advertisers that they could "walk with crowds and keep the kingly touch."[102]

A much larger segment of advertising's creative elite gave occasional lip service to the "folk-wisdom" pieties but found it impossible to identify sympathetically with the "tabloid mind." With a mixture of disappointment and cynicism, they accepted an "irresponsible public" as an inescapable reality. Consumers simply were not serious or rational. They preferred silly things and fell for ridiculous appeals. The radio programs they liked best, such as "Thirty Minutes of Sunshine," were "just terrible, awful." By the standards of advertising agents, such entertainment was "unspeakable stuff." People refused to buy products on their merits, choosing them instead for frivolous, emotional reasons and shifting their allegiances on the slightest whim.[103] John Benson, the president of the American Association of Advertising Agencies, confessed in 1927: "To tell the naked truth might make no appeal. It may be necessary to fool people for their own good. Doctors and even preachers know that and practice it. Average intelligence is surprisingly low. It is so much more effectively guided by its subconscious impulses and instincts than by its reason."[104] Most of the ad agents who accepted the "irresponsible public" viewpoint were inclined to interpret Benson's phrase "for their own good" not as suggesting a hope for intellectual or cultural uplift of the mass audience but rather as recognizing the need to stimulate consumption in order to maintain prosperity.

To their secondary audience of the educated elite, these advertising writers seemed to say, "I hate tabloid copy as much as you do, but people are like that and progress must be served, so what else can I do?" The successful freelance copywriter Frank Fletcher expressed this viewpoint with biting acerbity in an imaginary dialogue:

Myself: Truth in Advertising is the heraldic device of a forgotten family connection.

Felicia: But don't you believe in it yourself?

Myself: From a moral point of view, implicitly; from a practical point of view its merit is still unproved. Advertising is still largely a lever of lies resting on a fulcrum of falsehood.

Felicia: That is a serious charge to bring against your own profession.

Myself: The charge is not against the advertising profession but against the public it must appeal to. Most advertisers want to tell the truth, but there is no market for it. A rising sales curve derives its impulse from the false, not the true. Nowhere is the will-to-illusion more manifest than in the wide public acceptance of what isn't so.

Felicia: But is not such a state of affairs deplorable?

Myself: On the contrary, if exaggeration will induce a million people to brush their teeth every morning, [people] who would otherwise neglect that office, then the end justifies the means.[105]

Some adherents to the "irresponsible public" point of view simply accepted this consumer image with a shrug of acquiescence. They retained a rather contemptuous view of the consumer, produced what the consumer seemed to want, and employed their skill to keep their attitude from becoming too apparent in their copy. By concentrating on a craftsmanship that would win backstage approval from their colleagues, they modulated their cynicism and achieved a certain narrow sincerity of purpose.

For others, however, disappointment in the audience engendered a deeper cynicism and anger. A *Printers' Ink* columnist may have revealed an underlying psychological truth when he offhandedly linked the words "audience" and "enemy." The consumer, even if ignorant and vulgar, was nevertheless powerful. It was degrading to live at the whim of mass consumers and to have to "transgress the laws of good taste" in order to pander to their fickle passions. "What a way to sell goods!" lamented one writer repeatedly. "What a way to sell goods!"[106]

Could logically minded, educated, adult men spend most of their time talking down to an audience of fickle, irrational, child-like women without losing their self-respect? Many adherents of the "irresponsible public" school feared they could not. The most effective ideas in reaching that audience, Frank Fletcher confessed, "are those that fill an intelligent man with secret embarrassment and shame."[107] The sociologist Erving Goffman notes that if a loss of self-respect results "when the audience must be accorded accommodative face-to-face treatment," the team members who must engage in such communication may often ridicule, caricature, or curse the audience, as a form of compensation, when they are "backstage where the audience cannot see or hear them."[108] This hypothesis not only describes the nature of backstage gossip about the consumer audience within the advertising trade, but goes on to predict the maxims about the audience that many advertisers found incisive and captivating.

One defense against the deflation of one's self-image through pandering, Goffman suggests, is to create "a backstage image of the audience which makes the audience sufficiently inhuman to allow the performers to cozen them with emotional and moral immunity."[109] Such audience "dehumanizations" are used by many "performers," from movie directors to news reporters, from college professors to politicians. But advertisers did it with a flair. For the edification of colleagues searching for advertising appeals, one writer in *Printers' Ink Monthly* revealed the secret of the world's champion hog caller: "You've got to convince the hogs you have something for them."[110] The Young and Rubicam agency made a similar point with a change of imagery. "Make a noise like a Moose," advised an agency ad. "There are sounds more pleasing to the human ear than a moose call. The clear, true tone of a French horn, for instance. To get results, however, the guide uses the call that will make the strongest appeal to the moose."[111]

Such passages may reinforce stereotypes about the eternally manipulative advertising agent. But we must remember that such expedient "dehumanizations" of the consumer audience were the copywriters' defense against their own dehumanization. The advertising elite may have interpreted its audience unfairly, by condemning consumers as lethargic, stupid, and fickle when they were merely inattentive, refusing to treat brand choice as seriously as the advertiser expected. But copywriters were not mistaken in seeing a threat to their self-respect in the necessity of communicating with a mass audience whose tastes might be as different from their own as a moose call from a French horn cadence.

Many advertising leaders refused to accept either of the two extreme responses to the image of the consumer audience revealed by the tabloids, movies, and confession magazines. They could not comfortably identify with the "humanity" of this tasteless, emotional mob; but neither did they wish, by yielding to a cynical view of an irredeemably irresponsible public, to abandon their sense of a higher calling as apostles of modernity. A popular compromise position was the "uplift" approach.

This view accepted the evidence of the new popular media. Unquestionably the audience was intellectually inferior, culturally backward, emotional and tasteless. But could not this mass audience be seen as the latest and largest of a series of nouveau riche classes? The nouveau riche had traditionally been vulgar and inferior, but it yearned to display modern tastes and possessed a powerful instinct for improvement. Already, asserted a *Printers' Ink* editor, national advertising had improved the popular taste for quality, smartness, and beauty "by leaps and bounds." Advertising, by linking itself with civilizing influences, could thus serve a redemptive function. It would not only improve the economic well-being of the consumer masses; it was destined to raise their cultural and intellectual standards as well.[112]

It might seem that all the evidence from the popular culture of the early 1920s militated against such a view. How could advertising leaders sustain faith in the capacity of consumers for cultural improvement when the success of *True Story* and the tabloids revealed an opposite trend—toward cultural debasement. Could they ignore the lessons conveyed by the success of those colleagues and competing agencies whose ads "aimed lower" in taste and intelligence?

Even the most genteel of advertising leaders could not, and did not, ignore such lessons. Exaggerated claims and blatantly emotional appeals steadily became more common. Yet in their desperate search for some image of an audience that they could address without losing dignity—an audience with sufficient reason and self-control to be susceptible to uplift and modernization—the "uplift" faction among advertisers found one ray of hope. Tabloids and confession magazines were not the only new media of the early 1920s. An even more exciting new medium loomed on the horizon, and it seemed to provide evidence of a mass audience of very different qualities. That medium—their "great genteel hope" —was radio.

ABANDONING THE GREAT GENTEEL HOPE: FROM SPONSORED RADIO TO THE FUNNY PAPERS

Radio was the most tantalizing, yet most perplexing, new medium ever to confront advertisers. No other media had offered such potential for intimacy with the audience. Radio surpassed all others in its capacity to deny its own status as a *mass* medium. Moviegoers congregated in public crowds, and newspaper and magazine readers were affected by the "distancing" qualities of print. But radio carried the human voice directly into the privacy of the home, to the center of the revered family circle. In that setting, listeners might readily imagine that the speaker was talking personally to them. Moreover, the level of concentration required by early radio ensured the listener's undivided attention. But radio's tempting strategic position within the family circle also created dangers for the advertiser. Any false note on such an inherently "intrusive" medium might bring a very negative reaction.[1]

To add to this perplexity, radio posed the issue of the relation of advertising to entertainment in the bluntest possible way. After the first few tentative years, during which radio manufacturers found it expedient to produce radio programs in order to stimulate the sale of receivers, no one stepped forward to provide the entertainment to gather an audience for the advertiser. If radio was going to serve as an advertising vehicle, the advertiser would have to attract his own audience, playing the role of entertainer as well as that of serious salesman.

As close observers of popular culture, advertising leaders at first took a strikingly different attitude toward radio than they had taken toward other new media. Whereas they had often viewed the movies with disdain, they approached radio with reverence. The tabloids and confession magazines, they concluded, revealed the ignorance and tastelessness of the people; radio, however, promised their cultural redemption. There were several reasons behind these emphatic distinctions among the media. One was the diversity of their social origins. The background of the movies was plebeian: they had emerged from the nickelodeons patronized by the urban masses. *True Story* and the tabloids had aimed at working-class audiences. The ownership of radio sets, by contrast, gradually spread from the wealthier classes to the less affluent, thus suggesting an initial elite audience. Such distinct class origins fit nicely with implications that arose from the apparent nature of the various media themselves. Movies played to a crowd in a garish public setting; they seemed to reflect the indiscriminate tastelessness and sensuality of people in the mass. Tabloids and confession magazines conveyed the aura of subways, screaming newsboys, and crowded newsstands. Radio, by contrast, reached its audience as individuals, or in small family groups, insulated by the home setting from any of the base passions of the mob.[2]

Sponsorship Only:
Radio as Cultural Uplift

Historians of broadcasting have sometimes dramatized the contrast between the early dreams for radio and its ultimate commercial reality by describing radio mogul David Sarnoff's vision of radio as a philanthropically supported public service, or by quoting Herbert Hoover's comment that it would be "inconceivable that we should allow so great a possibility for service to be drowned in advertiser chatter."[3] Such pious declarations might lead us to suspect that these "good intentions" for the future of radio must have been undermined by a conspiracy among advertising agents.

But the advertising industry did not set out in the early 1920s to capture this new medium. Quite the contrary. The overwhelming majority of advertising leaders held just as lofty a view of radio as anyone else. Eventually most agencies had to be ardently wooed before they took up with the new medium. In 1922 and 1923 *Printers' Ink* editorialized against radio as an "objectionable advertising medium." Twice in 1925 it rejected broadcasting as a "legitimate advertising medium" and insisted that it did not belong in advertising accounts. While admitting the "alluring" attractions of radio, the journal emphasized the dangers of creating public ill-will and reminded the profession that "the family circle is not a public place, and advertising has no business intruding there unless it is invited." A contributor to *Advertising and Selling* in 1922 issued a similar warning against any commercial "intruder" into the sanctity of the home. Advertising should refrain from any association with radio unless it could discover a way to do so without the slightest debasement of radio's "refinement and general satisfaction."[4]

Meanwhile, however, tentative experiments with advertising on the air had begun, in spite of the "almost universal" opposition expressed at the first Radio Conference in Washington, D.C. Station WEAF in New York City, the experimental station of the American Telephone and Telegraph Company, invited all comers to pay to enter WEAF's radio "phone booth" in order to deliver a message. Takers soon appeared. Within a year or so, several advertisers, including the National Carbon Company (Eveready batteries), Ipana Toothpaste, and Cliquot Club Ginger Ale had begun to sponsor programs of musical entertainment.[5]

Still, opposition to radio as an advertising vehicle remained strong in most advertising circles. To sponsor a program as a public service was commendable, but a direct pitch for a product would debase the medium. As late as 1926, a writer in *Printers' Ink* wrote that while he was intrigued as an advertising man by the "immediate possibilities of radio advertising," he still concluded "as a family man and radio enthusiast" that the medium would be imperiled "if advertising were ever permitted to touch radio even remotely." *Printers' Ink,* reviewing the dangers of "an invasion of the home," warned that the injection of advertisements into every communications medium would "breed public resentment" against all advertising.[6] By the mid-1920s a consensus had emerged; it disapproved of any "direct advertising" of products on the air but acknowledged the merits of commercial sponsorship. Radio's sole value to the sponsor, which might be destroyed by any direct advertising, was the creation of public goodwill.[7]

The "sponsorship only" theory of radio advertising, which predominated in the advertising press from 1923 until 1927, reflected several propensities of big business and advertising in the mid-1920s. One of these was the ideal of business paternalism. Invigorated by the challenges of World War I and schooled by an era of muckraking and antitrust agitation, many corporate leaders had entered the 1920s with a sense of their responsibility to conduct business as a public service. Having experimented with such welfare capitalism programs as profit-sharing, pension plans, and immigrant "Americanization," many of these leaders prided themselves on a capacity to uplift the masses. Prominent among the spokesmen for a public-service vision of business were the leaders of General Electric and AT & T—both of which played a major role in the development of radio. Owen D. Young, the chairman of General Electric and the chairman, in 1926, of Radio Corporation of America, regarded RCA's new subsidiary, the National Broadcasting Company, as a "semi-philanthropic" activity.[8]

Few new media have enjoyed an aura of cultural uplift comparable to that of radio in the mid-1920s. Technology seemed to be fulfilling its destiny as a civilizing force. A National Carbon Company ad, after alluding to famous orchestras and classical arias, concluded: "The air is your theater, your college, your newspaper, your library."[9] In part, the vision of radio as uplift may have arisen from a moral resolve to see that this technological miracle was used only for the loftiest purposes. To an equal degree, I suspect, the image of radio as a civilizing force derived from its early broadcasts of classical music. Radio would provide the widening audience an opportunity—perhaps its first—to listen to "good" (classical) music, with all its calming, enlightening, and culturally uplifting qualities.

On the flimsiest of evidence, advertising journals claimed radio's success in the elevation of popular taste. *Advertising and Selling* boasted in 1926 that "radio has transformed numberless homes from deadly monotony into enjoyment of the finest things in life" through such experiences as listening every Sunday night to "the world's greatest musicians."[10] *Judicious Advertising* presented the optimistic assessment of David Sarnoff, the general manager of RCA: "Countless thousands whose musical experience had never transcended the phonograph and the local town band have learned to enjoy the music of a symphonic orchestra; vast numbers whose tastes had been limited to popular music have been initiated into

4.1, 4.2. Who could doubt the uplifting potential of radio when they regularly saw ads which associated it with awe-inspiring "music rooms" and refined postures and expressions?

opera."[11] The George Batten agency claimed that surveys corroborated this elevation of taste. Whereas 75 percent of those surveyed in 1923 had indicated a preference for jazz music and only 20 percent for symphonic music, radio had so enhanced public discrimination that by 1925 the preference for symphonic music surpassed jazz by 50 percent to 10 percent.[12]

Nowhere was the vision of radio uplift so vividly conveyed as in advertisements for radio receivers. The stately home interiors in these ads often assumed mansion-like proportions; their walls, sumptuously yet tastefully decorated with oil paintings or tapestries, often rose out of the viewer's sight to heights of at least fourteen feet. The radio audience usually consisted of two couples or a man and several women. If early radio announcers dressed in tuxedos to perform at the microphone, this imagined listening audience dressed in formal elegance as well, so the ads implied. The men stood stiffly, in deference to the solemnity of the occasion; the ladies, more emotional but nevertheless refined and decorous, draped themselves gracefully over the huge chairs and divans, staring pensively into space. Such illustrations conveyed a sedate and ethereal mood (Figs. 4.1, 4.2).[13]

If one accepted this image of a radio audience immersed in an atmosphere of spirituality, dignity, and stately luxury, there could be no question of the incongruity of direct advertising. A company might legitimately wish to sponsor radio broadcasts, especially programs of elevating music, in order to publicize the corporate name and earn the gratitude of the public. But this creation of good will, the Crosley Radio Corporation warned the trade, "must not bear the stigma of direct advertising. It must be done in a manner so subtle as not to be objectionable." As the president of NBC put it, "The finest results have been with the most delicate announcement in putting over the name."[14] Advertising agencies listened nervously as the excessive advertising of a few radio sponsors began to inspire audience complaints in the mid-1920s. Such protests reflected their own "class image" of the medium.[15]

The extreme sensitivity of advertising leaders to complaints about radio advertising again reflected the influence of "secondary audiences" on their image of the consumer public.[16] By 1926 radio reached about 20 percent of all American families, and by 1928 it would reach over 30 percent. Yet in judging audience preferences and resentments, advertising men consulted the reactions of their friends and the friends of their clients. Having defined radio as an agency of uplift, they remained, at least briefly, captives of their own image-making. They accepted too uncritically a survey by Daniel Starch, which concluded that metropolitan radio listeners preferred semiclassical and classical music and grand opera. As other polls and the trends in radio programming soon revealed, Starch's interviewers were probably learning not what people really preferred, but what they *thought* they should prefer or what would fulfill the interviewers' expectations.[17] In any event, the advertising profession tiptoed into direct advertising on the radio with a trepidation unjustified by any subsequent negative effects on sales.

Very practical considerations soon reinforced the advertising agencies' early bias against direct radio advertising. One was the opposition of newspapers to radio as a competitive medium. Publishers feared the loss of advertising revenues. They often refused to print radio schedules and sought to discredit commercially sponsored shows. Some encouraged listeners not to be "imposed upon" by radio advertising. Advertising agencies hastened to assure the press that radio could never become anything but a goodwill supplement to print advertising.[18]

Most agencies, moreover, were not prepared to handle large-scale work in the new medium. Agency radio departments were scarce in the mid-1920s, and some of them were one-man departments. As one agency man later recalled, early radio departments often served as "pigeon holes for relatives" or "broken-down actors" or old and ineffective staffers.[19] NBC, according to its chief promoter, had to plead to arouse advertisers' interest. Agencies were suspicious of radio and rarely welcomed a radio solicitor. They complained of clients with "acute inflammatory radioitis." Radio disrupted old agency routines, required "very adroit" new copy techniques, and gradually brought new types of employees to the agency. Moreover, agencies lacked expertise in production and in judging the value of the listening audience they were buying. Only in late 1928 did a national network of stations become available to advertisers. Even then it was difficult to know how much to discount the overblown, unverifiable estimates of audience size.[20]

Despite these objections and inhibitions, however, experiments with program sponsorship had led advertising to the threshold of new discoveries about the profitable fusion of advertising and entertainment. Very cautiously, advertisers tested the limits of mere sponsorship. When those limits were reached, they began exploring unobtrusive methods of integrating advertising and entertainment.

Always, agencies worried about the overly commercial "false step" that would trigger audience resentment.

It was radio's special promise of intimacy that ultimately lured advertisers toward a mutual seduction. Even the staunchest critics of direct advertising noted that radio programs had made "thousands of people feel free to sit down and write a friendly and personal letter to a large corporation." Howard Dickinson, an agency man and contributor to *Printers' Ink,* marveled at the "intimate disclosure of personal wishes" conveyed in the floods of "chatty, friendly" letters. Thousands of such "personal, intimate, and cordial" letters might arrive in response to a single program. Radio was "humanizing" the image of business. It was restoring the "personal touch" of earlier days.[21] Virtually every ad for a radio receiver conveyed the image of listeners giving rapt attention to every word and sound from the radio. It was difficult not to lust after such an audience. If some advertising leaders concluded that radio's very intimacy precluded any direct sales pitch, others were tempted to invade a "psychic space previously unreachable."[22] Wasn't that what an empathetic, "side-by-side" advertising strategy was all about?

From the beginning, advertisers drew a distinction between daytime and evening radio. In the evening, the aura of the family circle must remain inviolate. But during the daytime, when women were busy with housework, a self-interested but tactful informational talk by an advertiser might prove a real service.[23] Obviously, a "bold and pointed selling talk" would not be acceptable, but a low-key approach held promise. The J. Walter Thompson agency explained that in presenting early talks for women by Swift and Company, the introduction of the talk by a station announcer saved the speaker "from appearing in the role of an aggressive salesman." The entire introductory "advertisement" on a Swift show in the fall of 1923 read as follows:

Announcer: Perhaps the biggest problem of the housewife who is trying to keep down food bills and still to serve three delicious meals daily is the problem of meat. It's an absolutely necessary part of her menu and often an expensive part. This morning Mr. William Johns of Swift and Company has some *Practical Suggestions for Reducing Your Meat Bill.*—Mr. Johns.

The program concluded with a statement by the station announcer that "Mr. Johns of Swift and Company has told me that I may offer a pamphlet of recipes. . . ."[24]

Such advertising restraint was understandable when the entire substance of a radio "talk" on cooking or nutrition essentially constituted an advertisement. But what of the evening entertainment shows? Station WEAF, the nation's leader in sponsored programs, prohibited sponsors from offering samples, quoting prices, or describing their products. Only identification for goodwill purposes was allowed. Here, and on other stations, advertisers found they could best gain brand recognition by naming the show after their product. This at least provided numerous opportunities during the show to mention the brand name. Thus, early sponsored shows featured such musical groups as the Ipana Troubadours, the A & P Gypsies, and the Cliquot Club Eskimos. Palmolive Soap pushed the brand-name repetition technique to the limit by giving its soloists Frank Munn and Virginia Rea the new names of Paul Oliver and Olive Palmer.[25]

A few advertisers, impatient with such contrivances, began in about 1926 to experiment with "direct advertising." But they were cautious about violating radio's mystique of gentility. As late as April 1928 the producers of Listerine, already a trade legend for dramatic, hard-selling, and highly personal print advertising, broadcast their shaving cream commercials in a high-culture atmosphere and with a sedate style:

Closing Announcement: With the playing of selections from Rubinstein's Ballet, the curtain is drawn on the Carnival of Music. In presenting the Carnival the Lambert Pharmacal Company of St. Louis, Missouri, acquaint you with their Listerine Shaving Cream. The Shaving Cream that has much to bring you of smoothness and coolness and speed in your daily shaving. New as it is, your druggist has it.

The Lambert Pharmacal Company welcome [sic] comments on the program. Address your letters or cards: Listerine, L-I-S-T-E-R-I-N-E, Listerine, St. Louis, Missouri, or to the station to which you are listening.[26]

Similarly, James Gray describes the first radio singing commercial, broadcast late in 1926 by General Mills for Wheaties, as "a model of decorum, courtesy, and effectiveness."[27]

Even so, most critics in the trade journals in 1925 and 1926 continued to worry about audience resentment. Entranced by the aura of radio, they warned that increasing flirtation with direct advertising would provoke a "strong and general prejudice against all forms of advertising on the radio." Such resentments, others feared, would carry over into a reaction against all advertising. Besides, advertisers who engaged in such dalliance might stray from rational, business-minded practicality. Was even brand-name publicity worth enough, asked one skeptic, for advertisers "to go into the theatrical business?"[28]

Super-Advertising and the Specter of Saturation

At the height of the prosperity of the 1920s, a foreboding seized advertising leaders that overcame many of their inhibitions about an aggressive exploitation of radio. This anxiety also led them to experiment ever more boldly in print media with a variety of increasingly dramatic and emotional appeals. The name most frequently given to the source of this apprehension was "saturation."

Ironically, the very success of advertising as a whole now loomed as a threat to the effectiveness of any given campaign. The public was becoming so saturated with advertisements that each advertiser had to overcome formidable competition just to gain a moment of the consumer's attention. Magazines had become so overweight with ads that the president of the Association of National Advertisers wondered out loud "just how many people see our individual advertisement and how much of an impression it can possibly make." In newspapers as well, on page after page, ads crowded each other for attention. A 1927 cartoon in the *Saturday Evening Post* shows a man standing in his living room in newspapers up to his shoulders; to his astonished wife, he explains, "I Lost Control of the Sunday Paper." The cost of advertising space escalated, the "visibility" of each ad declined, and the trade journals fretted about "diminished returns." "We have to step on the gas in our advertising," warned one advertising leader, "if we are going to get people to stop, look, and listen."[29]

Other fears reinforced anxieties about the surfeit of advertising. In 1927 the economy suffered a downturn; concerns about overproduction intensified. Manufacturers looked to bold initiatives in packaging, industrial design, and advertising to prevent slippage in demand. The automobile industry, the nation's economic bellwether, feared the approach of a saturation point at which all families with adequate buying power would already possess a car. The annual rate of increase in car registrations declined from 24 percent in 1923 to 5 percent in 1927.[30] The obsession of advertising journals in 1926 and 1927 with issues of saturation also provoked a heightened consciousness of the comprehensive scope of product competition. A piano manufacturer did not contend for sales merely with other piano manufacturers. He also competed with producers of radios, automobiles, movies, and bridge tables. As the Batten, Barton, Durstine and Osborn agency warned in its house organ, "the paint dollar . . . must fight the car dollar, the radio dollar . . . and the savings bank dollar."[31]

Not only did advertisers face competition from *all other products,* but their ads had to contend with *all other diversions* for the reader's time and attention. Given the tempo of the age, this was a formidable challenge. "Advertising in this jazz age must hit us as we run," one writer warned. People had less time for reading. Tabloids and news digests had made them impatient with anything that could not be grasped at a glance. Distractions crowded people's lives. Dancing, movies, the radio, outdoor sports, automobile riding, and card playing consumed ever larger portions of time. Some movie palaces now opened at nine in the morning, a copywriter grumbled in 1928. Others had added special midnight performances.[32] Another copywriter exclaimed with mingled awe and exuberance: "These are times when the earth revolves twice as fast upon its axis. The three o'clock brunette is the four o'clock blonde. The spirit of the hour is, 'Cut it short or cut it out.' The Babbitry and Boobery, no less than the *Hoi Aristoi,* demand to be moved, or piqued, or stirred, or even jarred or thrilled by advertising—or they won't read the stuff."[33]

By 1929 anxieties over saturation and the resulting "mad scramble" to gain the modern reader's attention had stimulated a variety of bold advertising forays.[34] These were most conspicuous in the print media, but they were also influential in the evolution of radio advertising. Undoubtedly the most garish and controversial of these initiatives were those launched by George Washington Hill, who had taken over the presidency of the American Tobacco Company from his father in

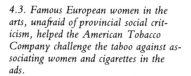

4.3. Famous European women in the arts, unafraid of provincial social criticism, helped the American Tobacco Company challenge the taboo against associating women and cigarettes in the ads.

1925. Shortly before, Albert Lasker, head of the Lord and Thomas agency, had convinced Hill and his father to concentrate their advertising appropriation on a single product—Lucky Strike cigarettes. The rise of the American Tobacco Company to advertising notoriety began modestly enough in 1926 with a flood of testimonial ads and a musical variety program on radio (which was described as including not a single "commercial note" beyond repetition of the words "Lucky Strike").[35]

A venerable advertising technique, the testimonial or endorsement had gained new popularity during the 1920s as advertisers searched for a personal approach. As Stanley Resor, the president of J. Walter Thompson, later argued, people had demonstrated again and again that they wanted their "news, education, and entertainment conveyed . . . through the medium of personalities." Throughout history, from ancient legends to current movies and tabloids, Resor noted, people had always been most eager to hear about other people and to see "virtues and vices . . . *personified.*" Moreover, the eternal "search for authority" led people to revere whomever in a democracy could best fill the traditional role of aristocracy.[36] In the late 1920s, Lucky Strike followed this prescription. It extracted endorsements from an amazing assortment of public figures, from business tycoons and society women to athletes and movie stars. A roster of prominent Americans who did *not* appear in Lucky Strike testimonial ads would be a select list indeed.

4.4. In this famous 1926 poster, Chesterfield had already found an indirect but sensuous way to advertise cigarettes to women.

But Lucky Strike had thrown its energies into a technique that was already controversial in 1927 and soon became the source of bitter wrangling. Luckies began with the "precious voice" campaign, in which actors, broadcasters, popular singers, and opera stars testified to the value of Luckies in protecting their throats (Fig. 4.3). Coaches and athletes recommended Luckies for throat protection. The enlistment of singers suggested another endorsement angle—the exploitation of the growing market for cigarettes among women. Other cigarette manufacturers had approached this subject with great caution—as witnessed by Chesterfield's "daring" 1926 poster (Fig. 4.4). Albert Lasker and George Washington Hill now perceived an opportunity to evade the taboo against associating women and cigarettes in ads: they could use testimonials by women who did not fear social censure—that is, European women of artistic fame and high society.[37] However, one of the first of these forays, a testimonial by the European opera singer Madame Schumann-Heink, complete with her photograph and signature, confirmed the fears of many advertising leaders that testimonials posed a threat to the credibility of all advertising. Madame Schumann-Heink repudiated her endorsement as having been obtained through a hoax.[38]

Meanwhile, other campaigns were blackening the reputation of the advertising testimonial. Queen Marie of Romania had given her blessing (at a price) to so many products that she became a joke in the advertising trade. Gossip about professional solicitors of endorsements, the high prices paid for testimonials, and endorsements by non-users of the products had become widespread. As early as 1926, *Printers' Ink* reported on a football player who had received $4,000 for a cigarette testimonial (presumably Lucky Strike) "notwithstanding the fact that he has never smoked and admitted that he couldn't discriminate between the aroma of a burning mattress and that of a dollar perfecto." At this rate, the public would soon conclude that "all testimonial copy is faked," warned *Printers' Ink*. Some

4.5. Lucky Strike's diet suggestion — "Reach for a
Lucky instead of a Sweet" —
provoked the confectioners to
this spirited defense of candy
as the "mainstay" of a scientific "reducing regime."

observers predicted that the testimonial vogue would sink beneath a tide of public
ridicule after the October 29, 1927, issue of *Liberty* magazine displayed movie star
Constance Talmadge's photograph and endorsement in *"eleven different advertisements of eleven different products!"*[39]

Embarrassment over this exercise in overkill slightly dampened the testimonial
craze of the late 1920s. But not for George Washington Hill. He not only sustained
his testimonial barrage; he turned to "competitive copy"—one of the trade's most
entrenched taboos. "Competitive copy" is advertising that attacks or makes comparisons with another brand or product. Such a tactic, critics warned, invited
counterattacks and slurs that would eventually destroy all public trust. But Hill,
exhibiting a promotional flair worthy of P.T. Barnum, recognized the potential
of controversy as an attention-getting device. "A good advertising fight helps
both sides," Hill replied to his critics.[40] In 1928, in pursuit of the women's market,
Hill declared war on the candy industry with the slogan "Reach for a *Lucky*

4.6. When American Tobacco exploited front-page news to identify Lucky Strikes with rescue-at-sea heroism, many advertising leaders warned that dubious paid testimonials would undermine the credibility of all advertising.

Instead of a Sweet." Recognizing the increasing appeal to women of an image of slenderness, Hill solicited the testimonials of society women, actresses, and athletes on the dieting effect of substituting cigarettes for candy.[41]

Genteel advertising leaders frowned on such tactics. The candy industry exploded in a frenzy of protest and attempted retaliation. Hill remained unruffled. When the National Confectioners Association augmented its protests with ads that defended candy as a diet food and told consumers, "You can get thin comfortably 'on candy'" (Fig. 4.5), Hill declared ingenuously that he had never intended to attack nonfattening products, and would be happy to change his slogan to read "Reach for a *Lucky* Instead of a Fattening Sweet." The added adjective only reminded consumers of their long-standing assumptions about the fattening effects of candy and further infuriated the confectioners.[42]

Then, in February 1929, while this controversy still seethed and Luckies raked in huge profits from increased public attention, Hill opportunistically revitalized the testimonial campaign by gaining endorsements of Luckies from the captain, first officer, and boatswain's mate of a ship that had just returned from a well-publicized rescue-at-sea mission. Captain George Fried of the U.S.S. *America* reported that Lucky Strikes had enabled him to maintain "nerve control" during the crisis (Fig. 4.6). (According to one report, Fried later regretted signing the

Lucky endorsement for $1,000; he actually smoked Old Golds, which had offered him $2,000, but too late.)[43] First Officer Harry Manning confessed:

> When I climbed aboard the *America* after those cold, strenuous hours getting the men off the freighter *Florida,* there was nothing I wanted so much as a *Lucky.* . . . As an actual fact in returning to the *America* I noticed one of our men rowing with one hand and lighting a *Lucky* with the other.[44]

The one-handed rower, Boatswain's Mate Aloys A. Wilson, added his (richly rewarded) thoughts to another ad:

> So many people have made a fuss over me because in rowing back to the *America* after we had picked up the *Florida* survivors, I was smoking a *Lucky Strike.* I can't see why there should be any excitement about this—it was the natural thing for me to do. Before we started out from the *America* I made sure that my pack of *Luckies* was with me—I wanted the comfort and pleasure of *Luckies* no matter what happened. . . . As long as I live, I'll never get another kick as I did from the sweet old toasted flavor of the *Lucky* as we were tossing about on the old Atlantic. I'm a hundred percenter when it comes to "reach for a *Lucky* instead of a sweet." I lay off the things that would make me flabby and light up a *Lucky* instead.[45]

Defenders of the good name of advertising bemoaned this cavalier assault on public credulity. The next month editor Frederick Kendall of *Advertising and Selling,* with the support of several leading agencies, launched an all-out campaign against paid testimonials.[46] But Hill remained undaunted. He now assaulted the refined sensibilities of genteel advertising leaders on other fronts. First, on behalf of Cremo cigars, he self-righteously undertook a graphic crusade against spitting in public places. With the slogan, "Spit is a horrid word, but it is worse on the end of your cigar," he denounced this vile and disease-spreading habit while implying that all cigars except Cremo were manufactured in filthy shops by disgusting men who spit on the ends to seal them.[47] Then, while critics contemplated this new abyss of advertising vulgarity, Hill recharged Lucky Strike's anti-sweets campaign with a series of visual blockbusters. Under such headlines as "Foiled by Moderation," "Pretty Curves Win," and "Coming Events cast their shadows before," startling black silhouettes of impending triple chins, bloated paunches, and "fat, clumsy ankles" reminded readers to "avoid that Future Shadow" (Fig. 4.7).[48]

By this time the trade press was fuming over the abuses of "super-advertising"—a term that encompassed bad taste, exaggerated claims, the escalation of superlatives, and the paid testimonial. Worried critics concluded that the "quickened tempo" of life had led to an "over-anxiousness to sell" and "circus advertising."[49] But criticism of Hill and the aggressive new tactics was far from unanimous. Once the tidal wave of denunciation had subsided, advertisers began to give attention to the financial reports of the American Tobacco Company. On the strength of Hill's aggressive advertising, the company had built up a sales

4.7. With the theme "Avoid that Future Shadow," Luckies broadened its attack from sweets to overindulgence. It preached moderation while shocking readers with silhouettes of the triple chins and bloated paunches of their future selves.

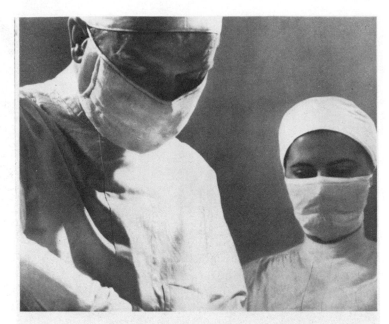

... and the trouble began
with harsh toilet tissue

SURGICAL treatment for rectal trouble is an everyday occurrence in hundreds of hospitals. Specialists who perform these delicate operations estimate that 65 per cent of all men and women over 40 years of age suffer from some form of rectal affliction.

In many of these cases inferior toilet tissue is directly blamed. In every case inferior toilet tissue seriously aggravates the trouble.

Unaware of these facts, millions of women continue to buy toilet tissue which they believe to be safe . . . but which is actually unfit for use—harsh, non-absorbent, full of impurities.

As a safety precaution, millions of other women

SCOTTISSUE, an extremely soft, pure, white, absorbent roll containing 1000 sheets
2 for 25¢

WALDORF, soft and absorbent, yet inexpensive. Any family can afford this fine tissue
3 for 20¢

use ScotTissue and Waldorf—specially processed bathroom tissues that meet every medical requirement of purity, softness and absorbency.

These two health-protecting tissues are made from fresh new materials fabricated on special machinery that makes them softer and twice as absorbent as ordinary toilet tissues.

To have either of these two famous health products in the bathroom brings a comfortable sense of security—an appreciation of their better quality.

Don't take chances. Scott Tissues cost no more than inferior tissues. Always ask for ScotTissue or Waldorf when ordering. Scott Paper Co., Chester, Pa. In Canada, Scott Paper Co. Ltd., Toronto, Ont.

Doctors. Hospitals. Health Authorities approve **Scott Tissues** for Safety

4.8. Few ads gave readers a more intimate sense of "participation" than the sociodramas of the "scare campaigns." Who would have expected brand choice to be fraught with such consequences?

momentum that defied the onset of the depression. For the first six months of 1930, as the campaigns against spit and overweight gained momentum, American Tobacco Company profits rose 100 percent over the same months of 1929.[50]

Most advertising leaders deplored George Washington Hill's "vulgarity," and many continued to disdain the paid testimonial. But none could ignore the pressures for more powerful copy created by fears of saturation. As the competition for attention had intensified, scare campaigns for a variety of products had tested the limits of public credulity. A toilet soap warned "every woman" to take to heart the lesson provided by a dancer who had collapsed and died onstage from "clogged pores." Listerine sought to shock *Colliers'* and *True Story* readers by recounting an equally awe-inspiring tale. In "Her Last Party," the heroine neglected to gargle after she caught a chill waiting for a taxi ride home from the party. Ten days later, ignorant or neglectful of the virtues of Listerine, she lay

4.9. *Which is the feature story? Which is the ad? By mimicking familiar magazine layouts and typography, the Pond's ad (right) attracted readers with its "editorial" style.*

dead. The Scott Paper Company abandoned its genteel copy on softness and purity in 1928 in favor of a scare campaign on rectal trouble. "Now doctors ask you: 'Is your bathroom paper safe?'" warned Scott ads. Masked doctors and nurses looked down grimly at patients on the operating table, mercifully obscured from the ad reader's view (Fig. 4.8). "A single contact with inferior toilet tissue may start the way for serious infection—and a long, painful illness," warned one ad. The advertising agency would have preferred more pleasant copy, one of its leaders noted, but scare campaigns proved more effective in commanding attention and increasing sales.[51]

More significant than the scare campaigns was a gravitation toward increased and innovative use of what the trade called "editorial copy." In pictures and layout, such copy attempted to compete for attention with the popular features of magazines and newspapers through "camouflage" or editorial imitation. As one advertising writer put it, "if the editorial 'dyes its whiskers green,'" then advertisers should do the same. Palmolive Soap adopted a format for newspaper ads that was almost indistinguishable from an advice column. Packer's Tar Soap did the same in *Ladies' Home Journal.* Pond's Cold Cream ads in the *American Weekly* and women's magazines mirrored the editorial features; they carried no large logotype and mentioned the product name only in the text of interviews with countesses or "talks" by society matrons on skin care (Fig. 4.9). Illustrations in ads

4.10. McClelland Barclay's "Fisher Body Girl" was one of the most prominent advertising characters of the late 1920s.

sometimes deliberately mimicked the illustrations for short stories. McClelland Barclay's Fisher Body girl beguiled her way onto the *Saturday Evening Post* cover as an anonymous beauty and then resumed her well-known advertising persona (Figs. 4.10, 4.11).[52] The J. Walter Thompson *News Letter* noted that since the reader of the rotogravure section was "in the mood for pictures," the advertiser should adopt the same mood. A Fleischmann's Yeast ad in the New York *World*, the agency boasted, had so perfectly captured the rotogravure style that the *World* had felt compelled to insert the word "advertisement" above the Fleischmann headline. "Sometimes you have been lured halfway into the text," one advertising writer exclaimed in mock protest, "before you realize that you are reading a vulgar advertisement which is trying to sell you some merchandise." Here was an attractive alternative to the garishness of George Washington Hill. By blending ads with editorial features and styles, advertisers might compete for attention while avoiding the "advertising tone of voice."[53]

THE SATURDAY EVENING POST

JULY 27, 1929

4.11. Occasionally the "Fisher Body Girl" helped blur distinctions between advertising and other magazine content by appearing as an anonymous cover girl.

UP TO NOW—By Former Governor Alfred E. Smith

Interweaving the Commercial

The idea of blending the ad into the other content of the media quickly found its most promising application in radio. Among the print media, even the tabloids and confession magazines had not introduced product messages into the texts of their news stories, confessional memoirs, or frothy fiction. But no inviolate line between "editorial content" and advertising characterized radio in the years following 1928. Advertisers, as Raymond Bauer and Stephen Greyser have pointed out, found the very "intrusiveness" of radio, which had inhibited direct advertising, a source of fascination.[54] If only advertising could be done in such a way as to preserve radio's aura of refinement and its mood of relaxed entertainment, then it could reach the listener in an intimate, attention-absorbing way. If people liked a program, perhaps they would not resent advertising that preserved its continuity of setting, character, and mood. In radio, advertising men applied the lessons of "editorial copy" by experimenting with techniques of "interweaving" entertainment and advertising.[55]

Radio commercials increasingly sought to capture the mood, setting, and momentum of non-commercial scenes. On the Chesebrough "Real Folks" show, one character in the plot, a local barber, would suggest in passing how Vaseline could be spread on the face to facilitate shaving. Another character would cut his finger and need Vaseline applied. Entertainers on the Blackstone show dropped Blackstone cigars on the ground and even walked on them, at moments "spontaneously" occurring during the plot. This gave the characters an occasion to mention the cigar's "Cellophane coat of armor" during the flow of the entertainment.[56] The Maxwell House program, a pioneer in the interwoven commercial, scrupulously maintained the continuity of mood. Program characters delivered the commercials as they gathered around the table with the program host, the Old Colonel, to share coffee and reminisce about olden days at the Maxwell House Hotel (the program's setting), when Teddy Roosevelt had characterized the coffee as "Good to the last drop."[57]

Soon the interwoven radio commercial became a standard formula. An agency man, reflecting on the frequent discussion of "nice and white" shirts on one program, christened it the "Rinso school of the theater," which he defined as "a radio play in which the product itself is tossed into the story regardless." Another copywriter expanded the concept of interpenetration between entertainment and advertising by proposing an hour-long "family life" drama show in which the products of *six* different companies, each incapable of supporting its own radio campaign, would all be interwoven into the plot. The agency for Simmons Mattresses toyed with the idea of a program with the single theme of fatigue; the central character would be a kindly old doctor who was concerned with "people's souls and their psychology." Every week a story, such as that of a woman losing her husband's affection because of fatigue, would proceed inexorably "down the copy slant to a commercial which does not seem like an intrusion."[58]

The J. Walter Thompson agency, a deft experimenter in the techniques of interweaving, discovered a technique in 1929 for involving listeners and creating a kind of "plot," even in a musical variety show. The show was set in a club. During a simulated intermission the host, crooner Rudy Vallee, sauntered among the tables introducing his guest to fans until they happened to overhear a conversation at one table. Vallee said, "Let's listen," to his friend (and to the radio audience). A change in tone quality signaled a change in microphone; then the radio listener found himself joining Vallee in eavesdropping on a young couple who were marveling at the man's great success in business since he had been taking Fleischmann's Yeast.[59] Advertisers had already recognized the power of the "overheard conversation" to induce reader involvement (Fig. 4.12). Here was a demonstration that radio was a more natural medium than print for luring the consumer into a conspiracy to eavesdrop. The listener became the host's unwitting accomplice in a trick that subtly shifted the scene from entertainment to a commercial vignette. Having assented to the initial titillation of eavesdropping, the consumer could not even plead entrapment.

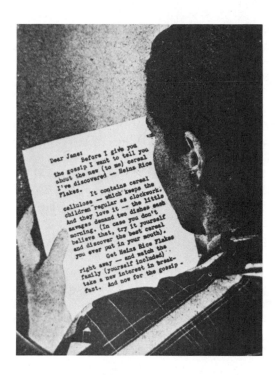

Dear Jane:
    Before I give you
the gossip I want to tell you
about the new (to me) cereal
I've discovered — Heinz Rice
Flakes.   It contains cereal
cellulose — which keeps the
children regular as clockwork.
And they love it — the little
savages demand two dishes each
morning. (In case you don't
believe that, try it yourself
and discover the best cereal
you ever put in your mouth).
    Get Heinz Rice Flakes
right away — and watch the
family (yourself included)
take a new interest in breakfast. And now for the gossip -

4.12. This print advertisement resorted to a "typewriter of . . . Gargantuan proportions" to involve readers in an over-the-shoulder glimpse of personal mail. Radio more easily lured listeners into a conspiracy to eavesdrop.

Demands for such delicate dovetailing of entertainment with advertisement stimulated agencies to expand their radio departments and assume broader control over program production. Agencies should master broadcasting technique, argued Roy Durstine of BBDO, in order to produce a program with the right emphases and omissions to fit the client. During 1927 and 1928 a number of agencies created new radio departments and others rapidly expanded their skeleton staffs. Agencies whose clients had previously been content to sponsor "studio programs" produced by the networks now assumed more control over program content.[60]

The mushrooming of agency radio departments coincided with the final steps in linking together networks that could provide nationwide coverage. It reflected a growing recognition that, contrary to genteel assumptions about radio, "direct advertising" over the air could produce sales. In fact, ads might not even *have* to be subtly interwoven. In the fall of 1928, the American Tobacco Company temporarily suspended nearly all other advertising for Lucky Strike cigarettes in order to test the power of radio. Using testimonials taken from its aggressive print campaign, Lucky Strike increased its sales by 47 percent within two months. Lord and Thomas, the Lucky Strike advertising agency, now proclaimed: "broadcasting is a profitable advertising medium when used frankly and fearlessly as such."[61]

Most other advertisers feared to invade radio with such boldness. But clearly, by 1929, insistence on "sponsorship only" had faded. The guardians of radio's sanctity now asked only for moderation. Roy Durstine, a leader in BBDO radio programming and advertising, quickly revised his judgment of only a year before. In May 1928 he had warned that frequent references to a sponsor or "direct forms of advertising on the air" were inadvisable and self-defeating. By June 1929 he concluded that consumers had "come to expect and accept infinitely more advertising in a program than would have been considered tolerable even a year or so ago."[62] Radio, so recently the " great genteel hope" of cultural redemption for the millions, now seemed to many, as one columnist noted, simply a billboard in the living room. Even so, its evolution had only begun. From the perspective of 1932, *Fortune* would look back on radio in 1930 as having still been polite and genteel, "a guest in the home, not the salesman on the doorstep."[63]

Many of the advertising practices that further undermined the gentility of radio by 1931 and 1932 were direct effects of the intensified competition generated by the depression. NBC, partly in reaction to competition from the fast-rising CBS network, and partly in response to pressures from hard-pressed advertisers and agencies, relaxed many of its restrictions on advertising. Selling talk became longer and more intense. National polls of program popularity, beginning with the Crossley telephone interviews in 1930 and supplemented in the mid-1930s with surveys by Daniel Starch, Clark Hooper, and *Variety,* sensitized advertisers to the less elevated tastes of the expanding radio audience. Program content itself shifted rapidly toward comedy, light drama, and variety shows. Popular music gained an edge over symphonies. "Amos 'n' Andy," a broadcast amalgam of blackface minstrelsy and family comedy, won unprecedented popularity through raucous humor. Other situation comedies of less quality followed.[64]

Agency leaders often blanched at the low taste exhibited by some of the new programs, but they adjusted the tone and extent of the selling message to match the less cultured atmosphere. Expenditures on radio advertising continued to grow through 1931 and the first half of 1932 while other advertising expenditures decreased sharply.[65] A contributor to *Printers' Ink* noted that radio ads were not merely growing longer but that "selling sense" was "permeating program after program." The radio columnist for *Advertising and Selling* groused about the "bogus entertainment which turns out to be direct advertising."[66]

Crooners and Commercials: From Intrusion to Intimacy

A major trend in radio advertising by 1932, which some saw as a lowering in tone, stemmed from further explorations into the special affinity of radio for the personalized approach. A successful radio performer sounded as if he or she spoke to each individual on a one-to-one basis. Millions came to feel that they knew such radio "personalities" intimately. The providential ambiguity of the second-person pronoun in English—the "you" that embodied both the intimate, singular *tu* and the impersonal, plural *vous*—allowed the advertiser's spokesman to use a form of address that was both mass delivered and highly personal. As Leo Lowenthal was later to complain, "especially for you" meant "all of you."[67]

Radio thus approximated the one-to-one relationship between salesman and prospect; a lofty, remote, or preaching tone of voice was even more inappropriate here than on the printed page. Agencies first began to request the same station announcer for every one of a client's programs; next they replaced station announcers with special artists who could create a "voice personality" for the sponsor.[68] Then they sought greater intimacy through the folksy, conversational approach epitomized by the opening lines of this script for Tony Wons, the special announcer on the "Camel Quartet Hour" in December 1931: "Are you listenin'? That's Morton Downey, the silver-singing Camel Minstrel. This is Tony Wons speaking. And say—I'll bet you hear a lot and read a lot these days about what it takes to make a cigarette good, and I'll bet a lot of you folks are wondering what it's all about, hummm?"[69]

In his discussion of the voice personalities created through such conversational copy, Herman Hettinger, an early historian of radio advertising, provocatively discusses "crooning" by radio singers in conjunction with broadcast advertising.[70] If, as subsequent critics have suggested, the key to the success of the crooning style, from Rudy Vallee and Morton Downey to Bing Crosby and Frank Sinatra, was not merely the relaxed mellowness achieved by sliding into notes but also the performer's capacity to make each member of the audience perceive the song as an intimate, individual communication, then singers and advertising agencies seem to have perceived the special qualities of radio at about the same time. It was no coincidence that the Rudy Vallee show became one of the biggest radio and advertising successses and that the J. Walter Thompson agency quickly arranged for Vallee, rather than an impersonal announcer, to introduce the advertising. Certainly Tony Wons' announcement, in the excerpt above, represented an effort to introduce the qualities of crooning into the commercial.

Through a variety of techniques, radio advertisers in 1931 and 1932 expanded upon the experiments in interweaving and crooning to personalize the commercial and blend it with entertainment. Program stars such as Ed Wynn, Heywood Broun, and Jack Benny were induced to "kid" the sponsor's product during their comedy skits and routines, thus associating the product with their own personalities.[71] The "dramatized commercial" also made its debut. Here, in a pattern now traditional on television, a short mini-drama, distinct from the program content, provided the sales message in the guise of entertainment. Sometimes the program characters continued their roles into the commercial mini-drama, as when Sherlock Holmes and Dr. Watson discussed the virtues of George Washington brand coffee as Holmes answered Watson's puzzled queries about details of the preceding mystery story. The sponsor, according to *Tide*, had embarked on this experiment very cautiously, "wondering if listeners would resent talent forsaking art for a two-minute sales talk." But the result was a "signal success."[72]

By the mid-1930s advertising leaders were generally agreed that since the public obviously preferred entertainment to edification, agencies should not hesitate to carry out their economic function by means of showmanship.[73] Beyond this, some disagreement persisted. Those with lingering notions of the dignity of radio still feared that too obvious a commercialization of the medium might make it a nuisance within the home. They preferred to camouflage or "sugarcoat" the sales message through interweaving.[74] Others, concluding that the public did not resent commercials, discounted the cultural pretensions of radio sufficiently to equate it with the door-to-door salesman. "You must go right to bat and sell your goods," advised one agency man, "after you get in the house by way of the radio." Agency men should stop listening to the criticism of their friends, one radio chief insisted. In fact, the commercials that advertising men found most offensive were the ones that worked best. Talks carried "to the point where it is nauseating" brought the most replies.[75] Deliberately intrusive commercials, such as the "Call-l-l . . . for-r-r Philip Mah-ra-hiss!" cry of Johnnie the bellboy, made a positive and telling impression on listeners. *Fortune* magazine confirmed the re-assessment of radio as a direct advertising medium when it commented in 1932 that since most listeners seemed "actually to like" advertising, the sponsor was "likely to lose more listeners by adding a symphony than adding a sales talk."[76]

Entertainment Triumphs:
The Descent into the Funny Papers

As radio, in the eyes of the more genteel advertising leaders, descended from the sublime to the ridiculous, the concept of a redeemable audience, susceptible to cultural and intellectual uplift, suffered an even more grievous blow from another quarter. Early in 1931 George Gallup made public the findings of his first research study—an analysis of newspaper readership in Des Moines, Iowa. No statistics from the survey so startled advertisers as those on readership of the Sunday comic section. People had known that the comics were popular, but they had carelessly assumed that the funnies served primarily to make the newspaper a "family paper" by broadening it to include the interests of children. Now Gallup's study indicated that adults liked the comics too—in fact, they preferred them to the leading news stories by an overwhelming margin. Even the least popular comic strip surpassed the main news story in popularity among readers of Sunday editions in Des Moines.[77]

Gallup's findings and his further studies, many conducted for the Young and Rubicam agency, confirmed the image of a "tabloid" audience. Lofty misconceptions about radio had simply postponed the acceptance by some advertising leaders of the audience image that their colleagues had earlier drawn from an assessment of the movies, tabloids, and confession magazines. Given their recent disillusionment with the tastes of the radio audience, they should have expected Gallup's findings that the comic and rotogravure sections had virtually universal appeal and that the "advice to the lovelorn" column was preferred two to one over any item of foreign news. But Gallup's findings did more than provide "scientific proof" of a low level of public taste; they also seemed to demonstrate that the "tabloid mind" was neither a class phenomenon nor confined to the urban masses. Bankers and professors read the comics as eagerly as waiters and truck drivers. Midwestern Iowans had tastes similar to those of the tabloid readers of polyglot New York City.

In response to Gallup's findings, alert agencies immediately launched an invasion of the funny papers. Until 1931, advertising had rarely appeared in the Sunday comic sections. Only a handful of products had experimented with cartoons as ads. Old Gold Cigarettes employed cartoon-strip ads in the magazines in the late 1920s, and Ted Geisel (Dr. Seuss) had begun his career by drawing advertising cartoons for Flit insecticide. At the outset of the 1930s, the down-to-earth, tabloid-minded Ruthrauff and Ryan agency had begun telling (for Lever Brothers) the story of how Rinso banished washday blues through cartoon strips in which ordinary women exchanged complaints and advice in speech balloons. Encouraged by favorable sales results, Lever Brothers had soon set the agency to work preparing comic-strip mini-dramas of love-lost-and-regained through the conquest of B.O. (Body Odor) by Lifebuoy Soap. Still, as late as 1930, the comic-strip ad remained something of a curiosity in the trade. Advertising aspired to be serious; comic strips suggested frivolity and childish escape. Generally the two maintained their distance.[78]

In 1931, however, as Gallup's survey gained attention in the trade press, the intense competition of the deepening depression dissolved the scruples of advertisers and agency men about debasing their brand names and their own reputations by peddling products in the funny papers. On May 17, 1931, an unassuming General Foods comic-strip ad for Grape Nuts, entitled "Suburban Joe," made its debut. Hearst's Sunday *Comic Weekly* promptly opened one page and then two pages to advertising. Furthermore, it reinforced Gallup's conclusions by reporting a survey of its own. One of its papers had experimented on 1,000 subscribers by omitting the main news section on one Sunday, the magazine section on another Sunday, and the Sunday comic-strip supplement on a third occasion. Only 45 readers contacted the paper to complain when the news section was omitted, and only 240 complained about the absence of the magazine section; but an impressive 880 out of 1,000 subscribers protested the omission of their comic section. The *Comic Weekly* proclaimed itself the new "greatest common denominator" for advertising. People wanted entertainment above all else, it argued. Advertisers should take off their top hats, associate themselves with such popular entertainers as Tillie the Toiler and Felix the Cat, and join in providing entertainment themselves.[79]

It is hard to say whether, in more prosperous times, the advertising agencies would have listened to such impertinent but tantalizing affronts to their business dignity. But in 1931, with commissions declining and clients nervously shifting agencies in search of quicker sales results, few agencies proved too dignified to accept the challenge. By the end of 1931 Hearst's *Comic Weekly* had sold 111 pages of advertising, and other Sunday papers had opened their comic supplements to advertisers. General Foods reported early in 1932 that in six months after entering the comic pages it had transformed a steady 13 percent decline in Grape Nuts sales to a handsome increase.[80] It quickly added Postum, Jell-O, Minute Tapioca, and Post Toasties to its roster of comic-section advertisers. Lever Brothers bought a full page in September 1931 for two comic strips featuring Lifebuoy and Rinso, and it steadily increased its number of pages over the next year. By September

1932 the expanded *Comic Weekly* counted 27 advertisers who had taken full pages. Soap, food, and drug products led the way, but fountain pens, razors, and typewriters joined in.[81]

Enthusiasts for the comic section as an advertising medium quickly discovered that in the comic-strip format, the best techniques learned from other sources could be combined. From the movies came the ideas of continuity of action, quick-cutting from scene to scene, and focusing attention through the occasional close-up. From the confession magazines came the power of personal testimony and the intimate drama. From the tabloids came an emphasis on brevity and pictorial imagery. And from radio came the persuasiveness of a conversational style and the seductiveness of eavesdropping.

Testimonials for a product carried the least credibility when delivered by the producer or his sales representative. They were more effective when delivered by an apparently disinterested party, particularly a celebrity. But the most powerful testimonial of all was the one embedded in an ostensibly private conversation that the advertiser arranged for the consumer to overhear. "Most people find it hard to resist" reading a speech balloon, noted a *Comic Weekly* editor. "It seems to promise a glimpse into what people really are thinking, a peep into the other fellow's private view of the universe."[82] An agency copywriter marveled at the "almost hypnotic factor in the ease with which one of these squares leads to the next." Print advertising now seemed to have found a way to capture the qualities of movement and dramatic action so apparent in the movies and radio. "You can see the possibility of leading the reader through a series of steps right up to the point of sale," mused the copywriter, and "then having him go out to do the same thing in a sort of hypnotic trance." But, he added ruefully, no concrete evidence yet existed that such a process was producing sales.[83]

Most advertising agency leaders did not stop to worry about the exact method by which the comics "worked." Spurred by the deepening depression, they rushed to join the funny-paper bandwagon at the first news of sales success from pioneers like Grape Nuts and Rinso. *Advertising and Selling* passed along the word from one disgusted agency man that comics had been considered for every account at the agency. Some people at J. Walter Thompson were "debating whether all of our money should go into comics." By early 1933 advertising space in the *Comic Weekly* and other nationally syndicated Sunday comic supplements was selling for $16,000 to $17,500 a page, compared to page rates of $11,500 and $12,500 for national circulation in old standbys like the *Saturday Evening Post* and the *Ladies' Home Journal*.[84]

Even if the comic-strip craze had been confined to the funny papers, it would have been a milestone in advertising. But the new style quickly spilled over into other print media (Figs. 4.13, 4.14). Comic-strip ads soon appeared in mass circulation magazines and even in the business press. Artists superimposed speech balloons over a series of small photographs to create mini-dramas with an aura of realism. *Advertising and Selling* charted an abrupt rise between January and May of 1932 in the number of speech balloons in advertisements in the *Ladies' Home Journal* and *Woman's Home Companion*.[85] By 1935 the staid *Saturday Evening Post*—

4.13. Comic-strip formats (like radio commercials) afforded ads a time dimension. Even a staid baking company might lure newspaper readers into the "almost hypnotic" sequence of squares that told of a marriage imperiled by "bargain bread."

4.14. *There was nothing genteel or uplifting about comic-strip copy, but surveys showed that readers loved those "speech balloons." Confessions added a* True Story *appeal and photographs introduced "realism."*

the criterion, in the words of the editor of *Comic Weekly*, "by which all advertising is measured"—was carrying as many as three full-page comic-strip ads per issue and at least a half-dozen other ads with balloons, sequence pictures, or other derivatives of comic-strip technique.[86]

Now that radio had descended to the popular level, the comic-strip technique provided an effective means for creating advertising "tie-ins" among the media. Several advertisers translated their radio-program characters into the protagonists of their comic-strip copy in magazines and newspapers and on product packages.[87] In this way, readers of their print advertising could be converted into part of the audience for their radio shows and vice versa. The "voice personality" of many radio characters was now linked to an engaging cartoon caricature.[88] If advertising had "gone entertainment," as some critics of the trends in radio and comic sections lamented, then entertainment figures, from comic-strip heroes to radio crooners and comedians, had reciprocated the gesture: they now animated products by infusing them with their own personalities.

For some advertising leaders, the comic-strip craze perfectly symbolized the deterioration of standards in a profession brought low by the depression. They had long worried that the trade could be debased by its association with frivolous entertainment, and now the worst had happened. Advertising had reached its nadir. It was completely fused with entertainment of utter mindlessness and the lowest taste. But others listened sympathetically to arguments that the comic-strip had coaxed copywriters and advertising artists toward a new realism. It had forced them to present their messages in an "orderly, direct, one-two-three-four arrangement" without strained visual analogies, longwinded introductory paragraphs, or purple prose. It had given them a sobering glimpse of an audience that was "far more simple in thought and emotion than most of us realize." Finally, it had driven home the same maxim that the evolution of radio had put forward: "The appetite of the public for entertainment is insatiable."[89]

The new media of the 1920s and early 1930s taught a harsh lesson to advertising leaders who prided themselves on their rationality and seriousness of purpose. Nothing in the logic of modernization had suggested that big business should engage in "show business." But the popularity of the new media demonstrated again and again, in the words of Leo Rosten, that the public preferred "the frivolous against the serious, 'escape' as against reality . . . the diverting as against the significant."[90] Just as the newspaper reader chose the tabloid picture over the serious story and the comic page over the foreign news, and just as the radio audience turned its dial to tasteless comedy rather than classical music, so the consumer would not accept serious advice about products *in any medium* without a dream world of frivolity and fantasy to go with it. People seemed to want escapist fantasy, a feeling of personal identification with fictitious characters and celebrities, even more than they wanted products. Such irrationality was unfortunate, perhaps, and advertising agents liked to think they did not share it. But it was an irrationality they could not afford to ignore.

The cumulative experiences of a decade in radio had crushed the vision of advertising as a broad educative force that would lift consumers to higher esthetic tastes and intellectual pursuits. First the tabloids and confession magazines, and then radio itself, had exposed an audience with such persistently low taste in all media as to appear impervious to such education. Who could sustain hopes of cultural uplift in the face of radio-station ads that urged advertisers, "Ditch Dvorak. They want Turkey in the Straw"?[91] And after the success of the comic-strip techniques, even the emergence of the radio soap opera in 1933 would come as no surprise. What advertisers had learned from radio's collapse as a "great genteel hope" was that any reputation advertising might acquire as a "serious" and respectable endeavor would have to come from an appreciation of its basic economic function, not from its public image.

Any hope for uplift, for the missionary effect of the adverising writer, would have to come, if at all, not from the impact of the advertisements on the consumer's mind but from the new behavior and tastes that the ownership of products would induce. Since the products themselves would be the agents of uplift, advertisers could best carry out their mission as modernizers and civilizers by employing the most effective means—including frivolous entertainment and the "inferred intimacy" of crooning—to put the products in the consumer's hands.[92] In serving the cause of modernity, American advertising modernized its techniques. Ironically, it did so by responding to some of the most archaic qualities of a seemingly unsophisticated, emotional, intimacy-hungry public.

THE CONSUMPTION ETHIC:
STRATEGIES OF ART AND STYLE

In 1928 a vice-president of the American Telephone and Telegraph Company boldly proposed that the giant corporation overturn tradition and adopt "a changed psychology toward the telephone." The public, unfortunately, had come to look upon the telephone as a necessity. Although this "psychology" was exactly the state of mind that AT & T had sought to inculcate over several decades, it had now, in the late 1920s, ironically become a barrier to progress. The power of advertising to change public habits and ideas, argued Arthur W. Page, Vice-President for Publicity, should now be employed to transform the consumer image of the telephone from that of a necessity to that of a convenience, even a luxury. A "changed psychology" would lead "normal" families to seek "all the telephone facilities that they can conveniently use, rather than the smallest amount they can get along with." Nor did Page's challenge to hallowed utilitarian tradition stop here. AT & T, he suggested, might even wish to entice the public to buy colored hand sets as "outward and visible signs of an inward and spiritual grace."[1]

Prior to this time AT & T advertising had been primarily institutional, supplemented by promotion of its long-distance lines. Its institutional campaigns made no direct pitch for increased usage or sales; they focused on creating a personable corporate image and on protecting the company from political attack by justifying its status as a private monopoly. Now, at the 1928 AT & T General Commercial Conference, Page sought to justify a new "comfort and convenience" advertising campaign that would persuade the public to adopt higher standards of "adequate service."

Page made his case on firm merchandising principles. The company needed increased sales for growth and stabilization. A major potential market lay untapped among the affluent who could well afford additional telephones, extensions, and intercom systems. But, as Page elaborated at a subsequent conference, additional telephone extensions competed for consumer dollars "with everything from cigarettes to a trip abroad." Until they shed the image of dull necessity, telephones were unlikely to win the competition with more glamorous conveniences and luxuries. What was more, Page added, the modern consumer was critical of the price and quality of things purchased as necessities, but liberally purchased whatever contributed to comfort and convenience. AT & T, he implied, might even enhance its corporate image and strengthen its political armor by transforming its image from that of a monopoly controller of a necessity to that of a provider of attractive accessories for gracious living.[2]

Page alluded to the 142 different kinds of switchboard cables that AT & T made available to associate companies. "That was quite a degree of personalization," he observed. Yet to the public AT & T offered merely "one black desk set, a hand set, a wall set, and one of those black buttoned inter-communication systems." That hardly represented the personalization the public sought or the image of luxury for which it was increasingly willing to pay.[3] Anticipating some skepticism, Page pointed to the most celebrated merchandising lesson of the era, the contrast between General Motors and Henry Ford. With the consumer inducements of multiple colors, new styles, accessories, and a variety of technical improvements, General Motors had first forced the once-dominant Ford to adopt colors and then to shut down entirely in 1927 to produce a Model A that would more nearly meet the public demand for style and convenience. Page clinched his case by conjuring up the parable of Henry Ford and the new consumer of the 1920s: "He made one little black instrument, too, and it did just what ours did: when it got started, it went fine, and so did ours. But, you know, Henry has recently come to the point where he realized he had to make a change and I think now that he has made a lady out of Lizzie, we might dress up these children of the Bell System."[4]

Symbolically what Page proposed, and what the entire advertising and merchandising world of the late 1920s appeared to affirm, was that business should cast off its sober, utilitarian outlook in favor of a new, more pleasure-minded, consumption ethic. The idea had too long persisted that the telephone should not be used for "frivolous conversation." Page snorted: "That is about as commercial as if the automobile people should advertise, 'Please do not take this car out unless you are going on a serious errand.'"[5] In order to break down the older attitude "that the telephone is a necessity not to be trifled with," Page explained, AT & T would experiment in 1929 with a "comfort and convenience" advertising campaign that might eventually make it "the style" for an average home to have two or three telephone extensions and an affluent home to have as many as fifteen. At least the company would have responded to the public's new taste for style and luxury by attempting to "give the public what they *desire*."[6]

A brief flurry of enthusiasm greeted Page's proposals. The comfort and convenience campaign went forward in a number of women's and "class" magazines. In 1929 another leading AT & T officer spoke enthusiastically of a further "personalization" of service through styling. Color choices could be supplemented by alterations in shape and size, so that the same type of telephone no longer need appear in both the fish market and the bank president's office.[7] Even so, AT & T stopped short of exploring the full implications of Page's proposals. Another company official noted that if the Bell system had a competitor who

5.1. In the late 1920s, AT&T promoted the consumption ethic in a genteel way by associating multiple telephones with maids, "smartness," and houses where a single phone would have required "long trips . . . to distant parts."

marketed "beautifully decorated hand sets," AT & T would undoubtedly join in the competition. But he admitted that colored phones sounded "a little silly." In fact, AT & T did not advertise colored phones until the late 1950s. Even then, some company traditionalists distrusted color as a sign of "depravity."[8]

Arthur Page himself was an intellectual, a Virginia gentleman of the old school, and the son of an ambassador to the Court of St. James. Until he joined AT & T in 1927 he had been the publisher of *The World's Work*. When he said "give the public what they *desire*," he envisioned providing suitable accessories for gracious living to the affluent, but not sensual frivolities for the masses. The "radically different" AT & T comfort and convenience ads embraced the consumption ethic only to the extent of catering to a refined taste for luxury and convenience among the thoroughly respectable. Extension phones would facilitate conversations with the maid, cook, or butler "while you are dressing for dinner." A separate telephone could insure that servants' calls would not intrude on the peace of the family. Telephone extensions would characterize homes that were models of "subtle management" in which there was "no bustling confusion, no shouting from room to room, no scurrying to and fro." "Enough telephones are an essential of the well-ordered home," AT & T ads counseled readers. "They prevent the little annoyances that destroy pleasant moods."[9] (See Fig. 5.1.)

Despite its muted, genteel response to the issues raised by Arthur Page, AT & T's awakening interest in a comfort-and-convenience approach is significant. Largely insulated from the pressures of competitive merchandising, AT & T was hardly typical of manufacturers of consumer goods in the 1920s. Yet, so powerful was the tide of enthusiasm for style, color, and beauty in the advertising and merchandising of the era, that it touched even this conservative monopoly. And so pervasive was the notion that the public must be reeducated to imagine how much it might pleasurably consume, rather than how little it might get by on, that even AT & T glimpsed the possibilities of expanding its sales and further personalizing its service by advertising images of style and luxury.[10]

Advertising and the Color Explosion

The notion that the introduction of certain qualities of style or "fashion" into a product could enhance its value to the consumer is a very old one. Anne Hollander, in *Seeing Through Clothes*, attributes the historical intensification of the "visual need" for new style in clothing both to increases in social mobility and to "the lust of the eye for change." Whether or not such a "lust" is, as Hollander implies, an innate instinct, it is clear that it can easily become a self-fulfilling expectation in the marketplace. Once the expectation of a "new look" takes hold in a society, Hollander observes, it seems as though "artists build into their compelling interpretation of the look of the moment the necessity for a different look in the next moment."[11] By the beginning of the twentieth century, both the relative social fluidity of the upper ranges of American society and the pace of technological change had conditioned Americans to expect and relish each "new look" created by mechanical improvements in goods and by changes in style in such accepted fashion goods as clothing, furniture, and home decorations. What the 1920s contributed to the triumph of style was to expand enormously the range of goods merchandised on this basis.

Advertising had an important stake in promoting elements of style in all categories of products. As an editorial in *Advertising and Selling* put it, the enemy of style was price. The advertising press steadily proposed strategies for lifting business out of the "price rut."[12] As long as competition between producers remained on the level of comparative prices, the role of advertising was limited. It could play a critical role in achieving nationwide distribution and public awareness of a brand, and it could publicize favorable price differentials for its client. Beyond this, however, clients might well reject increases in the advertising budget in favor of cost-cutting measures that could give them price advantages against their competitors.

An advantage in the imponderable realm of style, on the other hand, might lift a manufacturer out of the welter of price competition. It would attract consumers to buy his product at a price somewhat above that of less fashionable versions of the "same" product. Exactly how much higher he could price his product depended in part upon the degree to which advertising could convince consumers

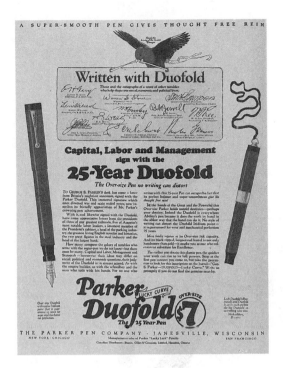

5.2. The attention-grabbing power of color in the predominantly greyish magazines of the early 1920s helped stimulate Parker to put color in both product and advertising.

that elements of style and beauty had transformed his product from merely an expensive version of the "same thing" as a competitor's product to an essentially "different" product with added qualities. Through the merchandising of style, advertising might virtually create business for itself.

One obvious method of creating a sense of style, as Arthur Page had recognized in reappraising the utilitarian telephone, was to introduce a choice of colors. But even this degree of style variation required manufacturers to make a mental leap. They had to persuade themselves that their products belonged to the realm of "fashion" goods. In this process, the advertising agent played an important role. This was not because advertising agents knew that consumers *wanted* their fountain pens, roofing shingles, underwear, and ovens to come in a variety of colors. No advertising research of the era explored this issue. Rather, agencies were always looking for "news" about the product, which they could then publicize. They also recognized the value of color in attracting attention to the advertising page. As magazine advertising had mushroomed in the early 1920s, the percentage of ads in color had advanced hesitantly to levels between 12 and 38 percent. As late as 1924, however, an issue of the *Saturday Evening Post* might include color in less than one-fourth of all full-page ads. Only 20 pages in a 160-page magazine would contain any color but white, grey, or black. Against the greyish blandness of such a background, a colored product could immediately and ingeniously provide an eye-catching advertising advantage (Fig. 5.2).[13]

5.3. The Fisher Body Corporation rejected pictures of the product in favor of elegant images that said "style." Its logo connoted craftsmanship by evading the imagery of mass production.

Still, in order to persuade many manufacturers to invest in the new technologies for introducing color and to hire style experts, it was necessary to show them how color could convert utilitarian products into fashion goods. The major breakthroughs in both color and design occurred at an accelerated tempo between 1924 and 1928. After Willys-Overland pioneered with the colored Red Bird car in 1923, General Motors, with the new Duco synthetic lacquers, introduced multiple colors in its 1924 models with gratifying results. Meanwhile Fisher Body ads accentuated the association between automobiles and high fashion (Fig. 5.3). The Parker Pen Company had recently demonstrated that consumers would respond to the attractions of a bright terra-cotta red barrel on so mundane and utilitarian an instrument as a fountain pen. The Crane Company began offering booklets on color in the bathroom in 1925, and Hoosier Kitchen Cabinets tested the market

5.4. Cannon towels instructed women in such consumption-expanding modern styles as that of having the bathroom "appear in towels bordered with blue and orange one week, lavender and green the next."

5.5. As staples were transformed into style products with harmonized images, advertisers stressed the individualizing potential of style motifs. "There is one for every style of bathroom," promised Martex towels.

for color ever so cautiously in late 1924 by coming out with units in "French Gray."[14] Meanwhile, academic psychologists such as Albert Poffenberger encouraged the interest in color by analyzing color preferences by sex and class, the attention-getting power of various colors, and the "feeling-tone" of various color combinations. By 1927 a writer in *Printers' Ink* had enthroned color as "the sex appeal of business."[15]

The evolution of Cannon and Martex towels in the 1920s illustrated the speed with which tentative ventures into color and style could kindle the flame of esthetic sensibility into the raging fire of a full-blown consumption ethic. In the early 1920s a bath towel was still a utilitarian staple and was available only in plain white. Even those who wished to be "high hat" could obtain nothing more stylistically distinct than Turkish towels with a plain red or blue border. Typically, the makers of such "staples" did not advertise.[16]

But in 1924 the Cannon Manufacturing Company cautiously initiated consumer advertising, and by 1926 it was trading heavily on style. Cannon produced a "class" towel at four times the average retail price and introduced not only color but decorative designs. It employed a professional designer from Macy's to plan decorative motifs of whales, flamingos, dolphins, ships, and lighthouses (Fig. 5.4). Meanwhile, Martex towels had already engaged René Clark, a prominent artist and designer with the Calkins and Holden advertising agency, to convert its "staples" into images of exotic sensuality. Martex advertisements displayed towels with feathery fronds and band of clear blue water in a bathroom with "a sea-blue wall covering and green fish at the water spouts." The whole scene, commented a *Printers' Ink* columnist, "suggests the luxury of semi-tropic bathing" (Fig. 5.5).[17]

5.6, 5.7, 5.8. Models of bathroom luxury ranged from the coup d'oeil in
colored fixtures (Fig. 5.6) to the evocation of classical grandeur and sensuality (Fig. 5.7) and the modernistic tribute to thematic harmony
(Fig. 5.8).

Cannon now escalated its merchandizing drive. By 1928 it was subtly promoting increased bathing through advertisements that praised readers for their
"wisdom" in adopting the habit of a bath a day. Since more baths would mean
both more comfort and more towel usage, Cannon even suggested more than one
bath a day. It explained the consumer benefits from such indulgence through a
series of "bathing recipes" with cautionary advice: "Because the first towel ab-
sorbs impurities from the skin it must never (under any circumstances) be used
again before washing."[18] Such an appeal to abundant use of the product revealed
a transparent merchandising strategy; it also symbolized the tendency of the style
appeal to lead to the embrace of a wider consumption ethic. A plain white Turkish
towel might be "good enough for drying anybody's back," a successful copywriter later observed, "but what does it do for your soul?"[19] A willingness by the
consumer to pay for the added values that came with "smart," soul-satisfying,
stylish goods presumably indicated an openness toward personal indulgence.
Such susceptibility could be cultivated on behalf of the additional luxury and
convenience of multiple purchases.

The textile manufacturers were not alone in the color crusade to emancipate the
bathroom from prim utilitarianism. By the late 1920s the Crane Company, the
Kohler company, and the American Sanitary Manufacturing Company were
advertising color options in plumbing fixtures and tantalizing the public with

5.9. So absorbed did advertisers become
in the consumption-promoting rage for
color harmonies that they sometimes induced the lady of the house to dress to
match her bathroom's color scheme.

luxurious full-color illustrations of model bathrooms (Figs. 5.6, 5.7, 5.8). These
prototypes of "good taste" in home decoration banished all connotations of shame
and reticence. The lowly bathroom rose to the status of a showplace of style and
opulence. The American Radiator and Standard Sanitary Corporation dazzled
readers with ornate depictions of its Roman Style with Pompeian motif and its
neoclassic Pembroke Model in a Directoire setting. Kohler celebrated its Impera-
tor Bath with fixtures in lavender.[20] As early as 1927 a Cannon ad proclaimed that
the "pistachio and orange" bathroom had supplanted older "plain vanilla affairs"
in the public imagination. By 1929 Standard Sanitary had moved on to Vincennes
Orchid and Clair de Lune Blue. These model bathrooms, while largely dependent
on striking colors for their impact, also emphasized the importance of style
elements in line, pattern, and decoration. So zealously did such models emphasize
the stylistic principles of thematic unity and color coordination that some illustrations even used the lady of the house as a prop to contribute to the bathroom's
larger harmony of color and pattern (Fig. 5.9).[21]

By the end of the 1920s, the presumption of color had triumphed in the
advertising of all bathroom accessories. Kohler offered fixtures in green, brown,
gray, ivory, lavender, and blue. The C. F. Church Manufacturing Company
advertised colored toilet seats in "nine pastel shades and nine sea-pearl tints." The
rise of the bathroom as a setting in which consumers were encouraged to indulge

5.10. According to this 1928 ad
in House Beautiful, *even the
cellar boiler could not escape the
modern mandate for color and design harmonies "decreed by
leading architects."*

in modest visions of luxury and sensuality undoubtedly owed part of its stimulus
to the movies, in which bathing scenes suggested opulence and sexuality. The
model bathroom extravaganzas also represented efforts, like the avowed strategy
of the Cannon Manufacturing Company, to create a prestige image for the entire
product line.[22]

The triumph of color in the bathroom encouraged advertisers and designers to
explore other mundane areas of life in which the element of style might successfully elevate consumption levels above those of mere utilitarian serviceability. At
a certain stage in distribution, the potential profits in expanding the total market
for a product seemed less than those to be gained from reselling current users on
the desirability of replacing present fixtures, towels, and so on with those that had
soul-satisfying colors or newer styles. A booklet by the Henri, Hurst and Mc-
Donald agency soon announced, "There is *Style* in most everything." Certainly
imagination need suffer few constraints now that tinted toilet seats, in Arthur
Page's borrowed phrasing, had successfully achieved the status of "outward and
visible signs of an inward and spiritual grace."[23]

The triumphal march of color soon invaded the kitchen, the bedroom, and even
the cellar (Fig. 5.10). Christine Frederick, a home economist and advertising
counselor, later recalled that manufacturers had responded with icy indifference
in the early 1920s when she proposed that they copy recent European ventures

into colored enamelware in pots, pans, and utensils. But by the mid-1920s color in low-cost kitchen items had been widely introduced. In 1926 the J. Walter Thompson advertising agency, after experimenting with copy themes of sanitation and efficiency for Hoosier kitchen cabinets, convinced its client that appeals based on beauty and color brought a larger response. By 1928 the company was advertising the "new Hoosier Beauty" in such exotic colors as "Venetian green with Oriental red interior."[24] Early in that same year *Printers' Ink* informed readers that "the humble gas range" was about "to blossom riotously in rainbow hues." Several electric refrigerators appeared in 1928 in "four intriguing colors." G. I. Sellers and Sons promoted its colored kitchen cabinets by promising, "The colorful kitchen is more than *stylish* . . . it is *inspiring*." Commentators began to worry about how the bedazzled housewife would ever harmonize the diverse hues of her cupboards, appliances, and utensils; some manufacturers began offering matching color schemes in ranges and cookware.[25]

In the bedroom, advertisers found that the introduction of color and style could lift even items not visible to public display out of price competition and enhance consumption levels. Sheets and pillowcases had previously been "bulk" goods, unbranded and undecorated. But grasping its inspiration from the towel manufacturers, the Pepperell Manufacturing Company brought out the Lady Pepperell line of colored sheets and pillowcases in 1928. Within three months, competitors had announced their own colored lines. Pepperell promoted a booklet entitled "Personality Bedrooms" that described the superior value of colored sheets. They would harmonize with the complexions of individual women and carry a personalized decorative scheme throughout the room. "Every woman's sleeping-room should express her personality," the Pepperell booklet insisted. Charts in the booklet keyed color choices to complexions and personalities. The "daintiness of orchid," for instance, made it "particularly suitable for the 'feminine' type of woman, the woman with delicate, fair skin, small features, and a figure of slight proportions." It was suitable for "blue eyes, black eyes, and gray eyes—if the lashes are dark." The added value of such personalization of the product through color seemed apparent.[26]

Uplifted Tastes and Borrowed Atmospheres

Color was often the easiest and most advertisable way of converting staple products into fashion goods. But the quest for a style appeal advanced beyond mere color in search of lines and shapes that would bring added value to the product through the resonance of its form with the vivifying images of the age. Two stylistic motifs contended for supremacy in the late 1920s: the classical, embodying the notion of timeless beauty; and the modernistic, employing sharp angles, geometric forms, and streamlined silhouettes suggestive of the dynamic movement of the new society.

Classical imagery and allusions offered the nouveau-riche "masses" the assurance that they had purchased products that exemplified their mature taste and their recognition of the eternal qualities of high art. Modernistic shapes and patterns catered to the "lust of the eye" to carry the visual excitement of the hard-edged, motion-filled lines of speeding airplanes and soaring skyscrapers into other accoutrements of a modern life. Occasionally overshadowing both of these motifs loomed the American fixation on Paris as the symbol of fashion in the two most prominent categories of "style goods"—women's clothes and furniture. Whatever a product's shape or color, advertisers would concoct a credible reference to Parisian styling authorities to convince consumers of enhanced value. By the early 1930s Dupont was even tracing its new "opale" colors for automobile finishes back to Parisian dressmakers and salons.[27]

Throughout the late 1920s, manufacturer after manufacturer experimented with variations on these motifs to lift products into the style goods category. Sometimes the search for a style image led to new product design; in other instances it focused on package design or on advertising imagery. Advertising agencies often inspired the search for style. A number of artists gravitated into the new field of industrial design in the late 1920s after working in ad agencies. Walter Dorwin Teague spent a long apprenticeship in the art department of Calkins and Holden. Raymond Loewy worked for both Lord and Thomas and Lennen and Mitchell during his evolution from a department store advertising director to an industrial designer.[28] By 1931 Young and Rubicam had reclassified its art director as a Vice-President in Charge of Design. The heir to the new title, Vaughn Flannery, predicted that art directors throughout the agencies would soon follow his own course, evolving from buyers of illustrations to product stylists and designers.[29]

Even before the introduction of the colored chassis, the automobile had been advertised on the basis of style. But after the mid-1920s, partly as a result of the way in which color called attention to style, this emphasis accelerated. Willys-Overland advertisements in 1926 introduced the "premier interior decorator," Miss Elsie de Wolfe "of Paris, London and New York," to testify to the "fitness of things" in the new Willys-Knight Six. The Franklin Automobile Company sought to establish a style image with ads that showed its cars against cubistic backgrounds.[30]

But it was Chrysler Motors that made the most significant bid for stylistic distinction. Proclaiming that "Chrysler beauty is no chance creation," the company's advertisements offered readers a lesson in the motifs of classical art. A 1929 ad displayed the Chrysler against the backdrop of the Parthenon. Diagrams illustrated how the principle of repeated motifs in the Parthenon's frieze had been replicated in Chrysler's matching of the "slender-profile radiator with the cowl bar moulding." Other ads, also with classical backgrounds, described how the Egyptian lotus-leaf motif had influenced the front elevation of the new Chrysler and how the "dynamic symmetry" of its fenders and wheels recapitulated the success of classic masterpieces in using the "wave border" to capture "the very essence of life and motion" (Fig. 5.11). By 1930 Chrysler was proclaiming "a new style as distinctive and charming as the newest creations of Paquin and Worth are among Paris gowns."[31]

While some manufacturers experimented with extremes in industrial design to give their products a classic, streamlined, or "skyscraper" look, others searched

CHRYSLER
BEAUTY *is no chance creation*

For the first time *in the history of motor car design an authentic system has been devised based upon the canons of ancient classic art*

The most modern thing in motor car design —Chrysler's matching of slender-profile radiator with cowl bar moulding—has its artistic origin in the repetition of motif in the historic frieze of the ancient Parthenon.

Note the dynamic symmetry of Chrysler fender contours and wheels, counterparts of the "wave border" of the classic masterpieces of architecture and design.

The Chrysler front elevation indicates the influence of the Egyptian lotus leaf pattern. Applied with consummate artistry in blending beauty and utility.

Artists know this as a "rising, diminishing series." The level road, the bumper, the tie-rod above, and radiator form a series in perfect harmony.

CHRYSLER designers realize fully that beauty is an elusive thing and that the pursuit of it in motor car design must not be hampered by too rigid adherence to laws and conventions ... But Chrysler also has found that there are so many glorious precedents and inspirations in art, architecture and design, that the search for authentic and harmonious symmetry can actually be reduced to something like a scientific system in which results are certain ... Chrysler has left nothing to chance ... Chrysler has not relied alone upon the inspiration of individual designers ... Chrysler has sought instead to do something never done before in motor car design — to search out authentic forms of beauty which have come down the centuries unsurpassed and unchallenged and *translate* them in terms of motor car beauty and motor car utility ... The lengths to which Chrysler designers have gone in this patient pursuit of beauty will doubtless prove a revelation to those who have probably accepted Chrysler symmetry and charm as fortunate but more or less accidental conceptions ... The Chrysler process goes far deeper than any charming but accidental conception.

New Chrysler "75" Coupe (with rumble seat) $1535. Wire wheels extra

All Chrysler models will be exhibited at the National Automobile Shows; and at special displays in the Commodore Hotel during the New York Show, January 5th to 12th and in the Balloon Room and entire lobby space of the Congress Hotel during the Chicago Show, January 26th to February 2nd.

5.11. *In 1929 Chrysler crowned the car's transformation to "style goods" by proudly tracing its style elements to the classical authority of the Parthenon frieze and the Egyptian lotus leaf.*

for a shortcut to style status through various forms of association. The Colonial Manufacturing Company claimed to have introduced the "swirl of style" in its new clocks by picturing them against a stylized "modernistic" backdrop of sky-scrapers, airplanes, and criss-crossing beams of light. The Elgin Watch Company, in 1928, promoted its Parisienne watches as much by emphasizing the names of such designers as Agnes, Lanvin, and Molyneux as by illustrating the lines of the watches themselves.[32]

One agency described the importance of association in a 1927 crash campaign to create a fashion image for a client. Realsilk Hosiery had been "caught by surprise" in the shift to shorter skirts. Sheerness and fashion in hosiery now counted more than durability and price. Since the product contained no style superiority, the agency had been forced to "borrow an atmosphere" that would conjure up "an impression of style, quality, sheerness, etc., that we could not create by direct claims." The agency hired five people to form a Realsilk Fashion Committee—two to forecast styles and three to approve.[33] The resulting adver-tisements depicted the Realsilk company at the hub of a web of communications from the "playgrounds of the world." Alluding pretentiously to "the centers of the truly smart," such as Venice, the Lido, Cannes, and Newport, the ads as-serted: "In these centers, the Realsilk Fashion Committee, members themselves of this exclusive world, now forecasts the hosiery mode—for you. . . . An artist of international renown, a debutante, a brilliant actress, contribute individual ver-sions of the mode—each from her own *chic* circle."[34] In this instance, as in several others, the style advisors—who had been created solely for advertising purposes—actually came to play a role in product styling. Advertising agencies took pride in pointing to instances in which they or their hired committees of advisors, as "ambassadors" representing the consumers' desire for color and style, had gained a voice in their clients' actual product design.[35]

While advertising agents sometimes claimed to be speaking on behalf of the consumer and her thirst for stylish fashion and harmonious decoration, they opted just as often for the self-image of cultivated imposers of good taste from above. Just as they had nurtured a vision of cultural uplift through classical music on radio, so one faction of advertising leaders contemplated an uplift of popular tastes through product design and advertising art. The infusion of beauty into the product and its advertisements would educate the tastes of the newly "enfran-chised" consumer masses. Earnest Elmo Calkins, the profession's foremost spokesman for beauty in advertising, hailed the advertising agency as the potential savior of beauty in the age of mass production. In a machine age, he pointed out, the workman had become a machine-tender who could no longer create beauty in the product through his craftsmanship. "If we are to have beauty in the machine age," Calkins concluded, "it must be imposed at the top by the fiat of a man who owns the machines." For manufacturers to impose beauty, they would have to be convinced of its economic value. That was the role of the advertising agent, who often forced the manufacturing company "to live up to its advertising" by sug-gesting nuances of style or color in the advertisement that were later adopted at the factory.[36]

Others joined Calkins in entrusting their hopes for uplift of the tasteless masses to advertising artists and industrial designers. Julius Klein of the Department of Commerce assured readers of *Advertising and Selling* that art in industry was demonstrating that a mechanized society could still be "luminous-majestic-vivid-satisfying." Another contributor to the trade press affirmed, "Those in control *can* improve the taste of the mob." He pointed to the lampshades, dress goods, neckties, and kitchen furniture of 1929 as evidence that an ordinary person without any taste could hardly find tasteless versions of such items available in any store. Art directors, he added, should insist on artistic illustrations and layouts, impose a new standard of how things should look, and "make 'em like it."[37] As early as 1926, a woman writing in *Printers' Ink* confirmed with some chagrin, advertisers had intensified their efforts to impose good taste by instilling narrow standards of stylistic "smartness" in both retailers and consumers. If the ads were to be believed, she concluded, the consumer could purchase only smart things, since the shops offered nothing else. She proposed a revised maxim for the style-conscious new age: "Some people are born smart, some attain smartness, and others have smartness thrust upon them."[38]

If some advertisers saw the introduction of greater style and beauty into products and advertisements as a deliberate campaign of esthetic uplift, others were content to endorse the new trend simply as pragmatic merchandising strategy. Beauty paid; it brought increased coupon returns. Style induced increased consumption. Neither was justified except on these grounds.[39] Some even worried that a good thing might be carried too far. The proliferation of colors and styles taxed the production capacities of the manufacturer. Whimsical shifts in taste and fashion might bring disaster to businesses unable to adapt themselves almost overnight. If fashion could serve as the instrument of the producer to expand consumption, it might also become the weapon by which a frivolous public eradicated reputable businesses in favor of newer fads. Style might become a "fickle dictator" that would serve the unpredictable masses rather than a conservative business elite.[40]

Imbedded in assumptions about the role of style, either as an agent of cultural uplift or as the plaything of the changeable masses, lay ambiguous conceptions about that perplexing creature, the female consumer. Women were viewed as virtually the sole buyers of "style goods." To incorporate style into a product was to give it a "feminine appeal." According to the observer's degree of sympathy, women were seen either as possessing "a sixth sense for what is stylish, for what is good, for what is beautiful" or as displaying a particular weakness for the whims of fashion.[41] The first of these judgments reaffirmed the stereotyped conception of women as the preservers of beauty and culture in an industrial society. The second judgment simply elaborated the advertisers' conception of women as emotional, irrational, and lacking in self-control.

Sometimes these two judgments were so subtly merged as to defy distinction. Was the advertising analyst Carroll Rheinstrom speaking in a tone of admiration or contempt when he observed that the housewife had "proved herself susceptible to peach-toned saucepans, old-rose refrigerators, and baby-blue bathtubs"?[42] The kitchen and bathroom had become more attractive, yet the phrasing carried a suggestion of condescension. All that could be said for sure was that no man would have taken such a statement as a compliment. The competing conceptions of the relation of women to style were resolved, if at all, through an appeal to class distinctions. Women of the upper classes brought gracious living to the society through the exercise of their refined sense of taste; other women thoughtlessly followed the latest fad. Yet advertising men labored under a powerful impulse to see Judy O'Grady and the Colonel's Lady as "sisters under the skin." This insured that only a fine, indistinct line would separate style and color appeals that could be confidently construed as contributions to good taste from those that pandered in a manipulative way to frivolous self-indulgence.[43]

The Mystique of the Ensemble

The crowning achievement of advertising's emphasis on color, beauty, and style in the 1920s was its popularization of the idea of the ensemble. A passion for harmonies of color and style among a variety of accessories swept through one product area after another, resulting by 1929 in a number of major merchandising successes. Before 1920 the idea of stylistic coordination had only affected the buying of such traditional style goods as women's clothes and furniture. Now it governed the advertising and merchandising of such diverse products as galoshes, clocks, bedsprings, and automotive accessories. More than any other phenomenon of the era, the success of advertisers in selling the esthetic of the ensemble to consumers epitomized the contributions of color and style advertising to the ascendance of a mature consumption ethic. The popularization of the idea of the ensemble not only expanded the definition of consumer "necessities" and schooled the eye in the recognition of obsolescence; it also represented a notable success in the transfer of elite tastes and ideas to the consumer masses and provided a new vehicle for the "personalization" of mass-produced goods.

Women's apparel led the way in the ensemble parade. One expert observer of fashion pinpointed the 1926-1927 season as the year of take-off in ensemble selling of women's wear. But Robert Lynd, selecting statistics on the output of purses as a likely indicator of consumer response to the idea of matching ensembles, suggested a broader, more sustained trend. Based on a normative index of 100 for the year 1925, the production of women's purses increased from an index of 28.1 in 1921 to 146.9 in 1929. Only the production of radios and electric refrigerators increased at a faster rate. By 1930 the *Buyer's Manual* of the National Retail Dry Goods Association reflected nostalgically on those days not too far removed "when a hat was a hat, and a bag was a bag" rather than each serving as "only one link in an ensemble."[44]

In women's hosiery, so rapidly did shades and textures expand to meet the needs for precise matching with other elements of the clothing ensemble that the number of separate items produced by the Holeproof Hosiery Company mushroomed from 480 in 1920 to 6,006 in 1927. A *Printers' Ink* writer noted in 1928 that expensive jewelry had largely given way to the preference of women for a large variety of rings, bracelets, and necklaces to harmonize with each of their various ensembles.[45] The Calkins and Holden advertising agency established a Fashion Coordination Bureau that supplied 1,200 department stores with fashion charts explaining "how every unit in the fashion ensemble from the draping of an evening gown to the buckle of a shoe should be coordinated into a correct and harmonious whole." By 1930 advertisements for lipsticks, compacts, watches, and even cameras were promising color and style choices that would contribute to the harmonious unity of the consumer's ensemble. Elgin advertised women's watches in several "Parisienne" styles. Each was designed by one of the "great couturiers of the Rue de la Paix to join your hat and your handbag, frock and flower, shoes and shingle, in composing the perfect *ensemble*." Although the watch still had a vestigial functional value, its preeminent role was to provide the "fashionable touch that emphasizes your entire smartness as an exclamation point accents a sentence." A Parisienne watch, Elgin advised, would serve "to point the time to you and your timeliness to everyone."[46]

Meanwhile, the idea of the ensemble marched on the heels of color into the automobile, the kitchen, the bedroom, and the bathroom. With Corona's offer of a choice of six typewriter colors for "perfect harmony" with the user's environment, it even invaded "that little nook of a study where you write." The Ternstedt Company introduced the ensemble into automotive fashion with built-in "ensemble sets" of vanity and smoking cases. It urged consumers to notice how perfectly the paneling and the "theme design wrought into the metal" of the cases harmonized with each automobile's "interior color scheme and appointments."[47] Dupont, the manufacturer of Duco refinishing paint, beckoned the "gypsy-hearted motorist" to reflect on the changing natural hues of Indian summer. "Your car—it too can change its garment"; it could have one of the modern, harmonious color schemes suggested by "the golden orange of the hills or the soft gray of the fields."[48] The Hupp Motor Car Company went further. With a flourish of high fashion, one Hupmobile ad introduced the perfect union: "Evening Ensemble by Jenny; Car . . . by Hupmobile." (For a similar ad, see Fig. 6.18.) In the same key, another Hupmobile advertisement proposed that consumers judge an automobile by the same standards as they would a Paris frock: "Does the contour reflect the modern mode for restrained and governed grace? . . . Are the accessories placed where they accent the design as tellingly as the correct shoes, hat, and handbag point a costume? . . . Are the metal trimmings chosen to touch the ensemble with brilliance as skillfully as you choose your jewels?"[49]

In the bathroom, now heralded as the showplace of the home by towel and fittings manufacturers, the campaign for color quickly engendered ensemble appeals. By the beginning of the 1930s, Kohler was promising fittings with "an advanced color harmony, blending the softer, clearer tones of Kohler enamel and vitreous china into a background of harmoniously tinted tile." At the same time, Carter Brothers was advertising ensemble sets of bathmats, rugs, lid covers, and stool covers. Cannon Mills developed a seven-piece Tritone bath set, packaged in cellophane, to sell as an ensemble purchase. Even the venerable cleanser, Bon Ami, donned a new "rich black and lustrous gold" container in order to harmonize with all the fashionable color ensembles in modern bathrooms and to "take its place in the fashionable society of gay bottles" on the bathroom shelf.[50]

5.12. A woman need hardly be interested in photography, Kodak implied, to crave such a chic "addition to one's ensemble" as the Vanity Kodak — in five colors.

Perhaps the most inventive manufacturers to catch hold of the color-ensemble bandwagon were the Eastman Kodak Company and Oneida Ltd., the makers of silverware. Since women sometimes carried cameras as well as handbags, Kodak reasoned, why should this additional accessory be allowed to disrupt the unity of the ensemble? In 1928 the company brought out the Vanity Kodak, a "highly ornamental and intensely personal" camera "designed to echo the color scheme of the particular costume." These "smartest manifestations of the mode" came in five colored leathers—"Sea Gull (gray), Cockatoo (green), Redbreast (red), Blue-bird (blue), and Jenny Wren (brown)" (Fig. 5.12). Men seeking to purchase gifts, Kodak pointed out, would readily see that such harmonious accessories would be "welcomed by any woman not blind to the dictates of Dame Fashion."[51] Apparently pleased with the results of ensemble merchandising, Kodak returned the next year with a new "Paris-inspired" contribution to the smart woman's ensemble, the Kodak Petite, which came "in five alluring colors." Women would treasure them, Kodak promised, "not only for what they do but for what they are

5.13. By adding color to design, even silverware could provide "the delicate last touch of modernity to a modern woman's table," proclaimed Oneida Ltd.

. . . exquisite little costume accessories."[52] These ads seemed calculated to convince even women who were disinclined to photography to purchase several Kodak Petite cameras purely for use as ensemble accessories.

Silverware might appear even less amenable than cameras to the new strategy of merchandising on the basis of color harmonies, but Oneida Ltd. remained undaunted. Since the mid-1920s Oneida had subscribed to a theory of advertising based on the use of harmonic "overtones" of style and theme to intensify the "subconscious emotional appeal." By 1928 its search for an advertising atmosphere that would authenticate a new fashion of color ensembles in silverware led to the depiction of two women of towering, aristocratic stature and exquisite dress. These women, said Oneida, were "the Fashionables returning from Paris." The advice they brought from the center of world fashion was to use silverware with colored handles to form a tasteful ensemble with other table accessories. Handles with the "translucent rose-red of rubies, the clear blue of sapphires, or the scintillant green of emeralds" would blend with the silverware "in chords of color" (Fig. 5.13).[53]

5.14. Since a woman should envision the total ensemble when choosing linoleum as well as clothes, a perfect blend of floor and mistress helped this advertiser evoke the aura of the harmonized ensemble.

Perhaps the Oneida company's officers had read the ads of Chicago department stores that encouraged Chicago hostesses who cared about "harmony in appointments" to extend the unified ensemble effect even to their maids' uniforms by purchasing "maidservant's attire in delicate tints to match the color schemes of both drawing and retiring rooms." In any event, hardly one reader in a million was likely to reflect on the striking contrast between the stark simplicity of the nineteenth-century utopian community in New York from which Oneida Ltd. had emerged and the Oneida advertising of the late 1920s. Now, through the "harmonics" of the ensemble and the "overtones" of the consumption ethic, the commercial descendants of those austere and egalitarian utopians sought "by implication" to lift all users "to the Landed Gentry Class."[54]

Reason might suggest that the rage for color ensembles could go no further. But by the beginning of the 1930s this advertising theme had also come to embrace women's galoshes, men's suspenders (in a comeback campaign against the belt), automobiles, clocks, women's make-up, men's and women's underwear, and linoleum floors (Fig. 5.14). Despite its disclaimer in small print that "of course, no woman would buy a car merely to create a color ensemble," the Reo Motor Car Company bragged that its car finishes had subtly recaptured the season's new fall tones from Paris designers. Reo proclaimed: "A woman's car today should be her most charming background." The B.V.D. Company even suggested that a wife should exercise her esthetic sense by making her husband part of the bedroom ensemble. "Keep him decorative even in his underwear," urged B.V.D.; "Make him a better boudoir decoration." Carters Ink Company discovered a ready market when it brought out a "Jewel Case Assortment" of colored inks to create an ensemble effect with "different writing papers, moods, or whatsoever." Advertisers who had exhausted the possibilities of color ensembles turned to ensembles of matched scents or paired colors and scents. Cannon Mills paired lavender towels with lavender-scented cachets. Hosiery manufacturers experimented with scented hose. Matching scents in powder and perfume were "the latest thing in *chic*," observed Coty knowingly: "Every lady knows clashing scents are taboo."[55]

The idea of the ensemble also gave rise to the merchandising of the prepackaged gift ensemble, advertised at the point of sales as "Sets for Her" and "Sets for Him." While the idea of the ensemble unquestionably appealed to advertising leaders on esthetic grounds and as a contribution to the education of consumers in good taste, its virtues as a merchandising strategy were at least equally attractive. In some industries, the ensemble provided a welcome solution to the problem of inducing people "to use more and more, in order to escape the bugaboo of market saturation."[56] For the woman who aspired to a stylish image, the purchase of a new dress now involved the additional purchase of matching shoes, hat, handbag, and color-coordinated hosiery and jewelry. She might even realize a need for new shades of underwear, make-up, lipstick, and fingernail polish as well. A stained or worn-out bathroom rug or towel now required the replacement of an entire seven-piece bathroom ensemble. Observers noted how a new appliance or a new piece of furniture made everything else in a room seem obsolete and out of harmony with the new style or color. Once accepted, the ensemble idea profitably increased the average size of each consumer's purchase. The woman whose fleeting mood or tinted writing paper required ink of "Chinese Jade" would have to buy Carters' whole "Jewel Case" of four fashion colors to satisfy her need. The prepackaged ensemble was perfect, noted a writer in *Printers' Ink Monthly*, for the retailer "who wants to sell a customer as much as he can in the shortest time with a minimum of floor and counter space."[57]

Department stores, which had pioneered in rudimentary forms of ensemble advice to customers, now capitalized on advertising's massive promotion of the ensemble idea.[58] They supplemented their buyers with "stylists" who bore the responsibility for coordinating merchandise stylistically. These stylists applied good taste to the display and the advertising of prestige goods, and kept a finger on the "style pulse of the public." Manufacturers began to hire style experts and industrial designers. Then they added style forecasters. Manufacturers' representatives and department-store stylists gave seminars to retail clerks so that they could parrot advertising copy about the current mode in Paris and Deauville when explaining the units of an ensemble to a customer. Some enterprising manufacturers, who despaired of so monumental an educational program, provided retail clerks with elaborate color-coordination charts so that they could authoritatively demonstrate to customers the absolute need for harmonious hosiery or a coordinated necktie.[59]

One contributor to *Printers' Ink Monthly* even carried the logic of style and ensemble selling to the point of questioning the traditional attire and social status imposed upon the retail clerk. She complained that the clerk, even in women's wear departments, "still reflects only too well the shadow of her past." Traditionally viewed as a servant of both the proprietor and the "class" customer, she still wore the dreary black dress or uniform of the servant (see Fig. 6.29). But the theory of the ensemble asserted that the product was known by its associations; therefore it should be surrounded with an appropriate "atmosphere." Retailers should supplant the clerk-as-servant with the clerk-as-model. Replicating the atmosphere created by advertisements and window displays, she should project an image of "color, personality, harmony in attire."[60]

The notion of "uplift" infused the entire ensemble movement. The argument that ensemble merchandising, carried to its logical conclusion, required a new, elevated status for the salesperson exemplified this propensity. Ideas of the unified and harmonious image, and the presentation of oneself as an esthetic masterpiece, had their sources in elite sensibilities. They connoted the bringing of order out of chaos, the molding of an image of "fittingness" and harmony—traditional concerns of social elites. The consumer's rampant accumulation of things, otherwise apt to offend refined sensibilities as vulgar and grossly materialistic, need not disturb the most esthetically inclined advertising writer or artist when such things harmonized to create a unified, artistic whole. Creative advertising men and women, as representatives of a cultural elite, had hoped to impose their esthetic vision on the rising consumer masses. Few of their efforts proved so successful as the campaigns for ensembles and color coordination.

The ensemble, properly authenticated by an authoritative source, offered the consumer "an education in good taste" and a defense against social disapproval.[61] It defined the rooms of the house as tests of the housewife's capacity to appreciate the qualities of harmony. And it interpreted the human body itself as analogous to a lump of clay to be self-sculpted into a work of art. Little hope for such a result could be placed on the tastes of a buying public confronted by a proliferating welter of choices. Authority must come from above, imposing itself through the initial selection and coordination of new styles and colors by manufacturers and their stylists and through the authenticating imagery of the advertising pages. Even the lowly retail clerk, now envisioned as a model and an authority on style, ought logically to be elevated in status above the consumer whose role became that of confused seeker of esthetic uplift.

If the ensemble idea reeked of cultural uplift and even of the imposition of conformist standards, advertising writers soon discovered that it could also be presented as a new contribution to the consumer's quest for the personalization of modern life. Soon after the triumph of color, advertising writers discovered that the new tints could be further vivified and personalized by giving them "nicknames." Such evocative nicknames as "robin's egg blue" and "sea foam green" served less to distinguish shades of color than to "bring them alive" or "give them personalities" endearing to the reader.[62]

More directly, as in the promotion of Lady Pepperell orchid sheets as particularly flattering to women with a certain stature, coloring, and personality, advertisements offered ensembles as extensions of the consumer's personal attributes.

5.15. *Should Milady buy a different car for each mood? Paige-Jewett judiciously declined to elaborate on its claim to individualization. But other advertisers pursued the idea of the "mood ensemble."*

In 1928 Jantzen Knitting Mills adopted the slogan, "Your type determines the color of your Jantzen." Its swimsuits provided different "color harmony sets" for blondes, brunettes, and redheads. Some cosmetic companies were content simply to promote different shades of make-up to coordinate with dress ensembles or with complexion tones inspired by the suntan fad.[63] But Hudnut discovered that each woman had "a definite personality color" that required a personalized ensemble of cosmetics, and Paige-Jewett, advertising automobiles in fourteen body types, promised a car that would "match milady's mode" (Fig. 5.15). Pepperell promised that its colored sheets would "make your bedroom express your personality," and the Arden Lipstick Ensemble claimed the power "to change your personality to suit your mood—or your gown."[64] With a deft advertising touch, the mystique of the ensemble thus promised to enhance individuality. Paradoxically, mass production would rescue consumers from drowning in mass society's sea of conformity. The ensemble promised to confer the authority of correct taste, yet magnify and vivify the individual personality of the consumer.

Modern Art and Advertising Dynamics

In few spheres of the creative "high arts" did upper-middle class Americans of the late 1920s gain so constant a familiarity with the styles of the avant-garde as in the realms of photography and modern art. Almost weekly, they came into at least fleeting visual contact with examples of cubism, futurism, vorticism, impressionism, Art Deco, and expressionism (Figs. 5.16, 5.17). Regularly they viewed the newest work of such photographers as Edward Steichen, Charles Sheeler, Margaret Bourke-White, and Anton Bruehl, and occasionally they spied copies of the styles of Picasso, Charles Sheeler, or Charles Demuth (Figs. 5.18, 5.19, 5.20). They gained this familiarity not through visits to galleries or even through art magazines. Instead, consumers engaged in these visual adventures as they thumbed through the advertising pages of such magazines as *Ladies' Home Journal* and the *Saturday Evening Post*.[65]

The flirtation of advertising with modern art reflected the same passion for alluring atmosphere and class association that characterized ensemble selling. The principle of the ensemble had suggested that a product drew its style image from association with its surroundings. When an advertising art director sought to create an aura of style around a product that did not itself convey an adequate prestige image, he was likely to turn to high art for the desired association. Modern art, in particular, offered the aura of both rarefied esthetic quality and an up-to-date tempo.

We have observed advertising's surge of enthusiasm for color and style in the mid-1920s. Even earlier, the competition of advertisers for attention in the expanding magazines, and the development of an adequate process for reproducing color on the magazine page, had inspired what *Tide* later dubbed "a frenzy for Art." Oil paintings attained early popularity as advertising illustrations because of their vivid hues and prestigious, "high-art" connotations.[66] What the product acquired from such illustrations was not so much a particular style image as an imputed prestige from its proximity to a work of fine art. It might also gain an aura of romance, or warmth, or exquisite brightness from the "feeling-tone" of the painting. The sophisticated legacy of the painting in oils persisted through the 1920s in Maxwell House Coffee scenes of Old South hotels and hospitality; in interpretive depictions of musical themes, such as Rockwell Kent's interpretation of Stravinsky's "Fire Bird Suite" for Steinway pianos; and in the costume studies of the old guild masters employed by Gruen Watches. As *Tide* later observed, the oil painting served best in campaigns with "literary and sentimental overtones."[67]

5.16, 5.17. Chrysler's futurism and Johnson's Baby Powder's impressionism were among the many modern art styles conveyed frequently to readers through the advertising pages. See also Figs. 5.18, 5.19, 5.22, and 5.27.

5.18, 5.19, 5.20. Advertising illustrations familiarized Americans who
never attended modern art galleries with styles ranging from those of
Picasso (Fig. 5.18) to those of Charles Sheeler (Fig. 5.19) or Charles
Demuth (Fig., 5.20).

As the 1920s progressed, the oil painting steadily gave way to simpler, less
formal modes of illustration such as the wash drawing. An economy of line and
detail allowed the artist to direct the reader's eye more effectively. And the
pragmatic introduction of arrows, "danger lines," and daydreamed words or
images seemed less a violation of the sacred integrity of a work of art when printed
over a wash drawing. As the prestige-oriented oil painting declined, a new mode
of creating a more specific style atmosphere emerged to take its place. This was
the striking use of the formulas and motifs of modern art. Ads adopted abstract
cubistic forms, zig-zagging lines, asymmetrical layouts, futuristic borders, surrealistic juxtapositions, and montages of centrifugal images. The modernistic
illustration insinuated style and emotion into the product, thrusting it into association with the "smartness" of novelty, fashion, and the latest mode. It infused it
with the excitement of movement and tempo.

By the middle of the 1920s modernistic styles had already sufficiently infiltrated
advertising art to raise a clamor of excited comment and dismayed alarm. Reviewers for the trade press noted that the Art Directors' Annual Exhibition of
Advertising Art in the spring of 1926 had revealed "more or less conclusively"
that modern art forms were the predominant trend. Later that year, a writer for

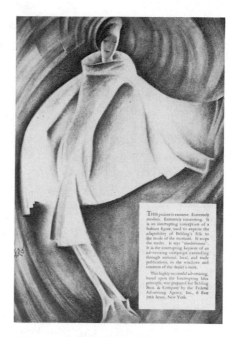

5.21. As early as 1926, the Federal Advertising Agency prided itself on an ad that sold a client's "modernness" through the unbalanced, distorted, kinetic imagery of modern art.

Printers' Ink breathlessly reported the appearance of "dream stuff . . . nightmare art . . . purposely exaggerated and distorted" in newspaper advertising. The public seemed to want "atmosphere," particularly in fantastic and eccentric forms. Futurism met the demand. Two weeks later a contributor to *Advertising and Selling* recounted his discovery of modern art in one advertising illustration after another in the current women's magazines.[68] Already, the Federal Advertising Agency had employed the motion lines of the new style to catch the attention of prospective clients and to assert its own modern consciousness (Fig. 5.21).[69]

The elements of an advertising illustration that artists employed to "say modernness" comprised an eclectic assortment of spatial configurations and motifs drawn primarily from the phase of Art Deco style that David Gebhard has labeled Zig Zag Moderne. Entranced by images of the skyscraper, the airplane propeller, and—in Jeffrey Meikle's phrase—"the staccato rhythm of the mass production assembly line," artists of the Art Deco school had sought to recapture the vibrating rhythms of the machine in a style that combined simplicity and dynamism.[70] Commercial artists freely imitated them in the use of triangular shapes, hard edges, high-polished surfaces, and striking contrasts of light and shadow. The artist and industrial designer Walter Dorwin Teague characterized the new style as "a maze of intersecting planes and solids" that conveyed an image of movement and speed.[71] An editorial in *Printers' Ink* described the disconcerting dynamism of modernistic layout: "Pictures run in one direction; actions in another; headlines dash off pell mell in another direction, while type blocks, sublimely aloof from any responsibility to any of these factors, tilt and stagger across the page."[72]

The adaptability of modern styles to advertising illustration lay primarily in five salient characteristics. One was the dominance of the diagonal line. Previous advertising art had favored squared-off pictures conservatively anchored by rectangular layouts and borders. Now, artists striving to command the attention of distracted readers and to suggest the tempo of changing fashions rejected such pictures and layouts as static and unexciting. They might suggest prestige, but they did not project vitality.[73] By contrast, the diagonal line created a sensation of motion. It captured the eye—a crucial prerequisite in a period of intensified competition for consumer attention in the bulky magazines and newspapers. Carefully executed, it might take "command of the eye" and lead it directly to the central sales message. Commercial artists had regularly employed straight lines as subtle "arrows." These pointers insured, as the *Printers' Ink* art critic put it, that "with target-like certainty, you look where the artist has willed that you should look." The diagonal line added a more dynamic sense of movement to such "visual path-blazing." In addition to its workmanlike proficiency in arresting attention, the diagonal line contributed to the atmosphere of the modern. For that reason, diagonals and the "bias cut" also characterized the latest styles in dressmaking and furniture.[74]

The off-center layout, a second prime characteristic of the modern style, paralleled the diagonal line in aura and psychological effect. The unbalancing of picture, text, and even letters in the typeface introduced a dynamic quality of unresolved tension. As the reader's eye struggled to restore balance to the layout, the ad captured his attention long enough to impel him toward the selling message. The combination of asymmetry and diagonal lines created an illusion of movement, even when the object or person stood motionless. Ads with modernistic illustrations often also used the simplified, dynamic new typefaces from Germany. Balanced composition might have been suitable for "the leisurely contemplation of an earlier generation," commented one authority on typography, but the new age called for deliberately setting type out of balance, on an "off-center . . . asymmetric axis" to create a "factor of tension, or suspense, like the strained pose of the runner awaiting the starting signal."[75]

Advertising illustrators sought to capture the essence of what designer Lucien LeLong called the "kinetic silhouette"—a pleasurable, though disquieting, image of forms in motion. Anne Hollander has detected this kinetic silhouette in the new forms of women's dress from this period and Elizabeth Kendall has discovered it in modern dance. Kendall describes how Martha Graham trained the members of her dance troupe at the end of the 1920s to develop the strength "to hold themselves off balance" so that they could express the dynamic, attention-compelling, modern qualities of "suppressed actions with stopped resolutions, or actions reiterated with fanatical insistence." Advertising art directors sought to create a similarly evocative and compelling imagery through the asymmetrical layout.

SNOWDRIFT

for making cake, biscuit,
pie crust and for whole-
some frying. Snowdrift is
so dainty and fresh and
good-to-eat that it makes
fried food a real delicacy.

*5.22. Snowdrift sought to put some
"soul" into a mundane product with
modernistic renditions that first shocked
and then impressed many art directors.*

The unresolved tension inherent in the disequilibrium of the ad, they hoped, would suggest modernity and induce audience involvement.[76]

Unresolved tension was also the seeming intent of the deliberate discontinuities of modern art, a third quality often appropriated by advertising artists. Such discontinuities emerged in the dissonant juxtapositions of the montage, in the simultaneity and rejection of sequential logic in surrealism, in futurism's immediacy and lust for impact. Modernists, in Eugene Lunn's analysis, sought to reshape perceptions through "defamiliarization"—the shocking disruption of "the expected and ordinary connections between things in favor of new, and deeper, ones." In its impulse to "break up ordered space," according to Daniel Bell, modernism found a new esthetic in fragmentation— "in the broken torso, the isolated hand, the primitive grimace, the figure cut by the frame." In the service of high art, modern artists employed such discontinuities to make the work of art "difficult"—to shock the audience into fresh perceptions, and to insist, through a refusal to resolve tensions and ambiguities or provide catharsis, that the work of art be "completed by the audience." But the same techniques, advertising artists discovered, could also serve commerce without calling the audience to so arduous a task or so profound a goal. Advertisers, too, often wished to lift a mundane product out of the familiar, to reshape perceptions of it, to "put some soul into the commodity" (Fig. 5.22). They also found discontinuities useful in seizing the attention of the audience, in associating a product with the excitement of modern, urban diversities and tempos, and in inducing new perceptions, particularly those of self-scrutiny. They did not, however, refuse to provide catharsis. After discontinuities and unresolved tensions had captured attention or created the right atmosphere, they were eager to promise consumers easy consolation. Consumers could easily and quickly "complete" these commercial works of art by purchasing the products.[77]

A fourth appealing characteristic of modern art, from the standpoint of the advertising illustrator, was the license it gave to "expressive distortion," to exaggeration even to the point of caricature. Rejecting the standard of mimetic fidelity to nature, modern art sought to capture the essence of form, of color, and of spatial and psychic relationships through abstracted or symbolic representations. While devotees of modernism in the fine arts often employed distortion and abstraction as an expression of a subjective esthetic experience, commercial artists found that such techniques also gave an emotional dimension to commodities. Distortions, like discontinuities, could put "soul" into products.[78]

Reason could not impel people to buy fashion and style goods. But emotion and imagery could. The zig-zag art styles, a writer in *Advertising and Selling* observed, merely offered "caricatures or hasty character-sketches of the products." Drawing on what Meyer Shapiro has called "the emotional suggestiveness of forms," these abstracted and expressively distorted shapes evoked a feeling of speed, of height, of vibrant energy. Modernism, as Jackson Lears concludes, offered "not information but feeling." Modern art, Earnest Calkins noted, "offered the opportunity of expressing the inexpressible, of suggesting not so much a motor car as speed, not so much a gown as style.[79] Modern art encouraged distortions of the human form that allowed a smart, up-to-date woman to rise to heights of eight feet or more (Fig. 5.23). One agency art director described the women sitting down to tea in a typical advertising scene as "a head taller than Nature really made them." Cars assumed an elongated elegance that no measure of actual wheelbases could corroborate. Montages of abstract shapes or of machines, skyscrapers, and airplanes could suggest an association with the dynamic forces of the society. Modern art, concluded one agency art director, afforded a way to "suggest novelty without the use of words."[80]

The final quality that advertising artists claimed to have derived with profit from modern art was simplicity. The older illustration, in its aspirations toward realism, had included too much distracting detail. Everything in the picture seemed to have an equal value. Conversely, the style of modern art enabled the illustrator to exalt the "most important selling quality" of the product by cutting out all unnecessary details. Likewise, the "absolute simplicity" of the new sans-serif typefaces sought to respond to the demands of the age for a fast tempo of reading based on "effortless simplicity" in the type.[81]

The advertising world's enthusiasm for a new simplicity in illustrative style, however, concealed some confusion and disagreement over the nature of the appeal of modern art. Some praised the new style as a means of simplifying the message to the consumer. As a letter to *Advertising and Selling* argued: "Modern art makes things easy for the reader; it tells him at first glance just what the picture is trying to express." But others praised the new simplicity primarily for its esthetic purity: "In the absolute elimination of all unessentials," wrote one art director, "modern art . . . has acquired the aristocratic mien."[82]

To some advertising theorists, successful evocations of the aristocratic air—of the "atmosphere of delicacy, smartness, luxury"—represented the epitome of the

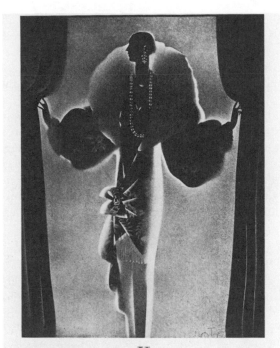

HERE is art, but not for Art's sake. You saw this picture, you stopped, and now you read . . . Such illustrations, new, smart, and exactly expressive of "La Loie Silvel" durable Transparent Velvet, are among the *interrupting* features of the advertising prepared for The Shelton Looms by the Federal Advertising Agency, Inc., at 6 East 39th Street, New York.

5.23. Even a modest infusion of modern art could transform a woman into a design element. The demands of style rather than realism determined her height and proportions.

"style appeal." Simplicity was the result when everything was eliminated but the exaggerated lines, shapes, and angles that contributed to the "larger sphere of emotion." The added value of style in a product could not be conveyed by presenting a written argument or a literal picture of the product, but only by associating the product with suggestive forms and kinetic silhouettes that were recognizably modern.[83]

But critics of modern art as an advertising tool worried that the achievement of an "aristocratic mien" revealed more about the esthetic pretensions of the artist than the tastes and buying impulses of the public. Kenneth Goode, a prolific writer on advertising, warned that the modern artist's absorption in self-expression, and scant concern for communicating his ideas to others, might infect the modernistic advertising illustrator.[84] Agency president Lynn Sumner questioned whether people were "imaginative enough to fill in the gaps" and concluded that the only manufacturers who successfully advertised with smart, modish pictures also sold "very smart, modish, modern merchandise." Writing in 1928, Sumner puzzled over such recent advertising images as: "advertisements of luggage where the modest overnight bag was lost in a maze of what seemed to an untutored mind to be skyscrapers; advertisements of toilet preparations in which a deftly placed container of the precious scent was multiplied a millionfold by trick mirrors and then played hide and seek with its own repeated shadows."[85] If this was "simplicity" and good sales technique, he implied, why did not such illustrations appear in the catalogs and ads of the mail-order houses, businesses that really measured direct returns? Could it be, he asked, that the "territory for modern art selling" actually ended "west of the Hudson and north of the Bronx"?[86]

Criticisms of modernism in advertising art persisted, even as the rage swept through agency after agency. Art directors, the indictment charged, had given too much allegiance to art with a capital A—at the expense of loyalty to advertising. The trend toward modernism had encouraged the art director to fill the magazines with pictures and layouts that were "planned to be good-looking to himself and to persons of equal intelligence and taste in design and pictures." The consumer audience, however, had been nourished culturally on the art of magazine covers and sentimental favorites; the pictures it prized were "naturalistic and pretty, or else broadly comic." *Printers' Ink,* after reviewing Daniel Starch's compilation of *300 Effective Advertisements,* concluded that the public liked the "homely humanness" of illustrations that were "Norman Rockwellish rather than Rockwell Kentish." Several years later, in an article entitled "They still like Grandma," a *Printer's Ink Monthly* editor sympathetically agreed with the Art Directors' Club that the public was undoubtedly "wrong," artistically, in preferring Norman Rockwell tableaux to striking modern illustrations. But, he warned advertising artists, "unfortunately in this age of crass commercialism, it is the public that buys the merchandise." The public preferred sentimental realism to cubism or impressionism. To the chagrin of advertising artists, the Victor Company's dog in "His Master's Voice" was "advertising's great art" for the masses.[87]

The critics of modernistic styles in advertising art alertly perceived that the creative leaders of advertising, in their cultural insularity, were once again self-indulgently pursuing their own unrepresentative tastes. But those who carried their criticism to the point of urging a return to pictorial literalism, a fidelity to "the correctness of things," failed to appreciate the important shift in advertising strategy that the turn toward modern art had reinforced.[88] Many products, when measured solely by their utilitarian value, were nearing a stage of consumer saturation. Only a successful "style appeal" could induce a woman to buy four or five purses, or several bottles of nail polish in a variety of colors. Some products could increase their value and escape the effects of severe price competition only by offering the consumer the additional satisfactions of esthetic pleasure and enhanced social prestige. Only the operation of a mature consumption ethic that placed a constant premium on the new and the stylish seemed capable of absorbing the nation's output of goods and ensuring dynamic growth. As missionaries of modernity, advertising men bore the major responsibility for nurturing the consumption ethic to maturity by educating the audience in the satisfactions to be derived from style and beauty. Creative advertising men and women often erred when they attempted to say "style" in an artistic language that was too rarefied and abstract for much of their potential audience. But they did sense the readiness of the public to respond to messages that said, in effect, "Woman does not live by bread—or even plain black galoshes—alone."

Photography as Sincerity

Zig-zag art was one way of saying "modern" or "stylish." Another way, though seemingly opposite, was to use photographs. In the early 1920s the photograph was still the exception in advertising art. This was particularly true in newspaper advertising. As late as 1925 only 6 percent of national ads in newspapers used photographs. In magazines, which faced fewer technical problems in reproduction, the use of photos still advanced haltingly.[89] In the mid-1920s most advertisers ranked color and modern art above photography as means of arresting attention. But toward the end of the decade photography began a distinct rise in popularity. *Advertising and Selling* reflected the changing sensibilities. Photographs appeared on fewer than 20 percent of the journal's covers in 1926, but on over 80 percent in 1928. During the depression, photographs won increasing favor, partly because they were cheaper than drawings or paintings. By early 1932 over 50 percent of the advertising illustrations in a typical issue of the *Ladies' Home Journal* were photographs. Whereas the first Art Directors' Exhibition of Advertising Art in the early 1920s had included only four photographic entries, the tenth annual exhibition in 1932 boasted an entire photography section. George Gallup confirmed the merchandising prudence of the trend toward photography; his 1932 survey of 4,000 reader reactions ranked photographs as more effective than other illustrations.[90]

Common sense attributed to photography a literal, matter-of-fact realism that contrasted starkly with the exaggerated and emotion-laden abstractions of modern art. But photography had developed its own artistic self-consciousness by the 1920s. None of the canons of this new art defined the photographer as merely a passive recorder of literal fact. Romanticized as artists, photographers assumed the role of active manipulators of their subjects. They accepted as few "givens" as possible and employed extreme strategies of camera perspective, variant focus, light and shadow, and compositional juxtapositons to startle the eye or evoke a mood. Far from simply registering an image of the literal "face" of things, photographers now used the camera to reveal people's feelings and character (Fig. 5.24). By examining configurations and textures, they probed the inner essence of things. In the hands of an artistic professional, the camera could rival a modern painter in its capacity to "emotionalize" subjects or create a sense of style through abstraction.

Like modern artists, photographers sought to see things in a fresh way— whether by distortion, abstraction, attention to microscopic detail, or unexpected angles of vision. But, in contrast to modern artists, photographers commonly declined to draw any distinction between their medium as a fine art and as a commercial tool. Like their contemporaries—the artists, typographers, and photographers of the Bauhaus and Russian constructivism—many American photographers found advertising art thoroughly compatible with the modernist urge "to teach men to gaze unconventionally." But most American "art photographers" did not conceive of their search for new visual experiences as part of any larger program of social reconstruction. As they employed their cameras to explore the qualities and textures of materials and the depths of human personality, they attracted the patronage of advertising agencies. Advertisers, too, were eager to persuade people to see things (their products or surrogate consumers expressing their ecstasy) in exciting new ways. The photographers Edward Steichen, Anton Bruehl, and Margaret Bourke-White contributed directly to new trends in advertising illustration.[91]

One obvious contribution of the photograph to the selling argument was its connotation of authentic "news." The tabloids and rotogravure sections had educated the public to expect the latest news in photographic form. So conventional was the association of the photograph with a sense of the "new" in this era, that "before and after" parables of historical progress—in product improvement or in ways of doing things—typically contrasted a pen drawing of the "old" with a photograph of the "new." An even more striking attribute of the photograph as a selling tool, art directors never tired of repeating, was its "sincerity." For understandable reasons, they used the word "sincerity" to denote effect rather than intention: the photograph was "sincere" because people accepted it as showing the literal truth. "Buyers do not question *photographic* evidence of merit," the Photographers' Association of America reminded advertisers. "They *believe* what the camera tells them because they know that nothing tells the truth so well." As Susan Sontag has observed, the photograph has seemed to capture real experience so ingenuously that often "it is the reality which is scrutinized, and evaluated, for its fidelity to photographs."[92]

If the power of the advertising photograph lay in the viewer's conviction that it did not lie, its effectiveness in conveying a sense of style or in inspiring emotion lay in its capacity to tell any one of a thousand truths. Modern art could capture attention and suggest an atmosphere by eliminating details, juxtaposing images, and exaggerating shapes and sizes. So could a clever photographer. "Even the most prosaic of products acquires an added appeal when deftly photographed," advised the Photographers' Association. Descriptions of such deftness were widely publicized in the advertising trade journals. Extreme camera angles could dramatically foreshorten or elongate photographic subjects. Photographers painstakingly constructed miniature scenes and then injected the look of reality with lighting techniques. By effectively using light and shadow, the photographer could capture the simplicity and sense of dynamic movement of modern art. As early as 1927 the art critic for *Printers' Ink* was already describing the special techniques of "futuristic" advertising photography. Distorting lenses, artificial sets, and cubistic backdrops could create distinctive images. "The camera can be made to do almost anything," he concluded.[93]

Experiments testing the creative possibilities of photographic "sincerity" inevitably ensued. A contributor to *Printers' Ink* described how "mosaic photography" could be used to obtain a satisfactory advertising photograph. For instance, a skilled developer could patch together several photos of a factory to eliminate "disturbing elements" in its surroundings. Several testimonial advertisers found that many of their users who gave testimonials were "too old, too young, too fat, too hopelessly ugly," so they employed "situational" photographs—photos of more attractive surrogates whose images would "carry home the copy idea in pictorial form."[94] The Hoover Company pulled off a "brilliant stroke of adver-

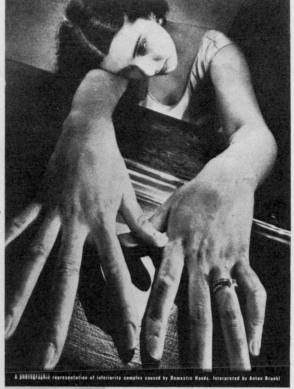

5.24. The popularization of Freudian ideas and the romanticization of the photographer as creative artist justified Anton Bruehl's photographic distortions to illustrate a larger psychological reality: the inferiority complex.

5.25. If a central quality of
the photograph was its presumed sincerity, then
photographic comparisons of
"embedded dirt" surely did
not lie.

tising genius" by varying the light in developing the photographic plate. A
photographer took a "human-interest" shot of a child playing on a rug and
developed it in three different shades ranging from very dark to clear. The clarity
of the third photograph symbolized—and might be misunderstood to scientifically depict—the amount of dirt and dust removal achieved by the Hoover in
comparison with other cleaners (Fig. 5.25). Art directors took delight in recounting how they had created "impossible" advertising photographs by superimposing one photograph on another, and they praised retouchers for "putting
inspirational touches to the frankly prosaic subject." The Monroe Calculating
Company described its composite effects as "dramatized" photographs. Another
advertiser spoke of "strengthening the realism of a particular [photographic]
scene" by the deft addition of additional artifacts with pen, brush, or superimposed photo.[95] So obscure became the distinction between realism and artifice
in advertising photography that a columnist for *Printer's Ink* could blandly advise:
"Moods . . . [are] not easily manufactured. If they are to appeal to the reader as
genuine and unposed, they should be based on absolute sincerity. Thus the special
staging."[96]

The very ambiguity of the relationship between things-as-they-are and things-
as-we-like-to-fantasize-them was the quality that came increasingly to endear the
photograph to advertising. The advertiser could use the photograph to select a
particular visual "truth" about the product, or to place the product within a staged

but "truthfully recorded" social or natural scene of optimum appeal. The photograph, with its aura of literal and objective reproduction, then shouldered the burden of conveying this selective, idealized image to the consumer as a representative, unexceptional, and therefore realizable "truth." The viewer of a pen or brush illustration was unlikely to forget the deliberate artifice employed by the creator of the illustration. But the photograph, except for extreme experiments in futuristic and "artsy" effects, did not provoke the viewer to conjure up an image of the photographer who devised it. Rather, it encouraged the viewer to remain unconscious of any intervening, manipulative creator and to experience the voyeur's sense of directly glimpsing the world's reality.

The result, if well executed, was an illustration that merged two disparate forms of appeal into a mode of "dramatic" or hyped-up realism. The advertising photograph idealized the product by choosing just the right lighting and angle of vision or dramatized its effect by selecting the most charming expression of satisfaction. The photographic image itself became a "consumer product." By association, it lent an added value to the product in the form of a pleasing fantasy. Yet, as an "actual photograph," it ingenuously denied the image's inaccessibility as fantasy (as might be the case in a painting) and insisted that this vision faithfully represented a reality purchasable at the local store.[97] In embracing photography, advertisers did not repudiate the idea of using modern art to stimulate a demand for style and beauty in products. Rather, they discovered a more subtle and durable mode of pursuing the same end.

Art and the Consumption Ethic

Advertisements of the early 1930s signaled the decisive triumph of art over copy. Enthusiasm for modern art had advanced this trend in the 1920s; the continuing surge toward photography after 1930 confirmed it. The success of the tabloids, the movies, and the rotogravure sections pointed to the public's desire to absorb new ideas and information in visual form. If nothing else, the intensified competition for a few seconds of the consumer's attention gave primacy to the illustration. It was the picture that had to capture the reader's fleeting glance and lead her toward the sales argument in the text. Only an eye-stopping illustration could place an advertisement in tempo with the age. As one advertising manager observed, "Advertising isn't read much any more. . . . It is seen."[98]

Steadily the size and number of advertising illustrations increased at the expense of copy. Reports on coupon returns almost invariably favored those ads with prominent illustrations. By 1926 a contributor to *Advertising and Selling* was arguing that consumers made purchases on emotional impulse and then justified them with "reason-why" rationalizations. Convincing copy was needed, but mainly as a follow-up to confirm the consumer's choice after the emotional appeal of the illustration had made the sale. Epitaphs for the copywriter appeared regularly in the early 1930s. One *Printers' Ink* contributor described the vestigial responsibilities of the copywriter under the sardonic heading "A Suitable Caption Goes Here." Copy, he complained, had been "stepped down" in size to allow more room for illustration. It had been compressed into grotesque shapes "to gratify the errant whim of a visualizer straining to be different." Another critic moaned, "Millions for Artwork—But Not One Cent for Copy." *Tide* reminisced about the halcyon days before the copywriter had become merely "an adjunct to a $1,500 illustration and a million-dollar idea."[99]

But nostalgia for a golden age of copywriting hardly slowed the march of advertising from text to picture. Advertisers had come to recognize the need to add value to certain products by "fortifying" them with images, much as breakfast cereals were now fortified with vitamins. Word images simply could not give the same fillip to the consumption ethic as illustrations could. Prose was more adapted to logic; pictures spoke the language of emotion. As they appraised the capacities and desires of the growing mass audience, few advertising leaders could doubt the permanence of art's supremacy over copy.

Proponents of the visual image as advertising's main vehicle of communication advanced a number of explanations for their bias. One advertising executive defended an early experiment with a textless cartoon ad on the simple grounds that "the eye gets the facts quicker and more graphically than the mind." Charles Kettering of General Motors noted that "people positively do not speak the same language." Words invited argument and diverse interpretation. Therefore, Kettering concluded, "the fewer words an advertisement contains, the better it will be." Many advertising experts agreed. Words divided people; pictures united them. *Advertising and Selling* praised the psychology of a 1934 campaign for Spud menthol cigarettes that dispensed with all but a few words of copy; the Spud ads sought to convey an idea of "coolness" with full-page photographs of water lilies and snow-covered roofs. "It is easier to transfer an eye impression to the palate direct, without going into the ratiocination department," it observed.[100]

Pictures were easier to understand than copy, many observers noted. They inspired belief ("people believe what they *see*") and aroused less psychological resistance. As Stephen Baker later pointed out, "No schoolmarm or any other superior person has ever embarrassed us for 'misusing' the picture, let alone mispronouncing it or misspelling it." Not only did people lack the ability to argue with pictures, as Marshall McLuhan later observed, they did not approach them, as they did words, with feelings of insecurity and distrust. Slowly, advertising artists perceived another positive dimension to the illustration as a stimulus to more bountiful conceptions of consumption. Pictures surpassed copy not only in their ability to intensify emotion but also in their capacity to say several things at the same time.[101] Visual imagery effectively reached the less literate portions of the population. It also conveyed dense messages. By setting up harmonics of atmosphere and imagery that resonated at a variety of levels, visual images also obscured problems of internal contradiction or irrational association.[102] Such harmonics were exactly what gave style products their added value beyond pragmatic utility. Evocative pictures upped the consumption ante by inducing the customer to obtain the fullest satisfaction by "buying the ad" along with the product.

Finally, pictures easily demonstrated their superiority to copy by cultivating a consciousness of obsolescence. Advertisers had long realized that no text could

5.26, 5.27. *These ads exemplify the use of backdrops to convey an aura of modernity—through skyscrapers and airplanes or dynamic geometric shapes.*

compare with pictures in dramatizing the time-honored "before and after" story. By the late 1920s, the before-and-after story had transcended its weight-reducer, hair-restorer origins to become part of the implicit argument in most advertisements that suggested product style. Occasionally, advertisements depicted both the old and the new in technology, ways of life, or product design in order to associate the company with progress. This was particularly true in the "institutional" or corporate-image ad. More often, ads simply associated the product pictorially with such symbols of modernity as the skyscraper, the airplane, the dirigible, or the angular, elongated "modern woman." Or they defined the product as modern by placing it in a visual field, sometimes photographic, which was characterized by diagonal or zig-zag lines and geometric or streamlined shapes (Figs. 5.26, 5.27). The vivid "look" established by the product's own lines and its association with other objects of "modern" style, through constant repetition, educated the viewer's eye to recognize products with slightly differing lines as obsolescent. Just as a piece of furniture of a distinctively new style will make all the familiar furnishings of a room appear dowdy and old-fashioned, so the advertising illustration contained a power, unrivaled by prose, to engender an immediate recognition of stylistic obsolescence—and perhaps an emotional revulsion against it. The more that visualizations of the ensemble educated the consumer's eye, the more readily any new product, even if purchased for its technological superiority over an older model, made its surroundings look unacceptably inharmonious and out of style.

Progressive Obsolescence

Americans had long revered the notion of technological obsolescence. By the end of the nineteenth century the equally venerable upper-class tradition of creating clothing obsolescence through fashion had attained sufficient prominence to provoke Thorstein Veblen's withering attack in *The Theory of the Leisure Class*. But it was during the 1920s, in company with the accelerated merchandising of style, that advertisers undertook to promote modernity by educating the new consumer masses in a broad ideology of stylistic obsolescence. Reassuringly, they explained its economic necessity to those business leaders who still harbored doubts about an idea so dangerously suggestive of wastefulness and improvidence. The word "obsolescence" still carried a sufficiently pejorative air that evangelists of the new ideology such as J. George Frederick, President of the Business Bourse publishing house, and his wife Christine Frederick, a prominent home economist and advertising counselor, coined the phrases "progressive obsolescence" and "creative waste" to inspire a reappraisal of persisting negative connotations.[103]

Style obsolescence promised to solve the problem of overproduction. Thus it was hardly surprising that the automobile industry pioneered its advance from clothing to a wide range of other goods. By about 1926 automakers had begun to worry about "saturation" of the middle-class market for cars—the market that had spurred the dynamic growth of the previous decade. What would happen when everyone who could afford one of the cheapest models already owned a car? The replacement market for cars worn out from long use could hardly sustain current rates of growth. In 1927 auto production fell for the first time. Car registrations in that year surpassed those of 1926 by only 5 percent.

General Motors led the drive to introduce preplanned obsolescence to the industry. It adopted regular changes in both technology and style. Charles Kettering, who defined the mission of his General Motors Research Division as the organized creation of dissatisfaction, had long campaigned for the annual model, and by 1927 GM president Alfred Sloan had unreservedly adopted the principle of the yearly style change, which Jeffrey Meikle has called "artificial obsolescence." Already General Motors' model changes were bringing gratifying results. At the beginning of the 1920s, the Model T Ford had outsold all General Motors' models combined; but by the spring of 1927, Chevrolet had overtaken the Model T in one of the most startling reversals of brand preference in merchandising annals.[104]

In practice, Henry Ford grudgingly gave way to the demands of style obsolescence. In principle, he continued to despise it. Although Ford has sometimes been characterized as the very epitome of the shift from the self-absorbed, production-minded entrepreneur to the consumer-oriented, distribution-minded businessman, he also personified the resistance of many businessmen to the luxury-minded softness of the consumption ethic. Ford was alternately the despair and the delight of the advertising press. For a decade preceding 1924, he had disdained general advertising. When he launched a million-dollar advertising campaign in 1924, advertising men rejoiced. But their joy turned to aggrieved

Greater Even Than Its Beauty is the Reliability of the New Ford

THE NEW FORD SPORT COUPE IN THE POPULAR ARABIAN SAND COLOR

WOMEN'S eyes are quick to note and appreciate the trim, graceful lines of the new Ford, its exquisite two-tone color harmonies, the rich simplicity and quiet good taste reflected in every least little detail of finish and appointment. ... than this be... the me-

know that your Ford will take you safely, comfortably and speedily to the journey's end.

For the new Ford has been built to endure. Its beauty is not confined to... ... only, but go...

Ford

FORD MOTOR COMPANY
Detroit, Michigan

hydraulic shock absorbers; the Triplex shatter-proof glass windshield; the standard selective sliding gear shift; the ¼ irreversible steering gear; th... horse-power engine; the ...le bro...

5.28. With the Model A, Henry Ford seemed to capitulate to style-consciousness and the consumption ethic. This agency artist enlisted a maid, a chauffeur, and an antique urn to create a "class image."

resentment once again in 1926 when Ford reversed himself and eliminated most of his advertising budget.[105] Then, in a tone of defiance toward the advertising press, his infuriatingly successful competitors at General Motors, and the segment of the public seemingly seduced by the new consumption ethic, Ford threw down the gauntlet in an all-print, no-frills advertisement. It read in part: "The stability of the substantial bulk of the American people is most definitely evidenced by the continued leadership of Ford. Despite confusion, in the minds of many, of extravagance with progress, a vast majority cling to the old-fashioned idea of living within their incomes. From these came and are coming the millions of Ford owners. . . . They possess or are buying efficient, satisfactory transportation."[106]

But consumers were voting in the marketplace every day for style, beauty, "extravagance," and the installment plan. They were voting against automobiles defined simply as "satisfactory transportation." Despite the bravado of his manifesto, Ford had already recognized the impending eclipse of his leadership. When he accommodated himself to the "confusion" of the public with a new, up-to-date Model A in late 1927, Ford's new advertising agency, N. W. Ayer and Son, worked to transform the Ford image into that of a "smart and stylish car." Significantly, it was the illustrations of these ads, with their depictions of elegant social settings, that carried the main burden of creating a new class image for the Ford (Fig. 5.28). One Ayer copywriter even developed a variety of proposals to link the Ford car with fashion shows.[107]

Outward signs to the contrary, however, Henry Ford had not taken to heart the new fashion of style obsolescence fueled by advertising. Far from accepting the annual model idea, he immediately froze the design of the new Model A. On the eve of its unveiling, he contradicted the implications of his style advertising by proclaiming his intention to make the new car "so strong and so well-made that no one ought ever to have to buy a second one."[108] A more explicit repudiation of the ideology of obsolescence can hardly be imagined. Of his concessions to the rage for stylistic fashion he grumbled, "we are no longer in the automobile but in the millinery business." Christine Frederick paraded forth Ford's statement as evidence of "Mrs. Consumer's" power to bring the "mighty Ford . . . to his knees," but Ford continued to disdain artificial obsolescence, to distrust advertising, and to wage a public, rear-guard battle against the forces of frivolity and extravagance.[109]

Henry Ford was unique in the public vehemence of his condemnations of the extravagance of the consumption ethic. But his views were not necessarily antithetical to those of other businessmen, or even to those of many advertising agents. It is true that most business leaders adapted their own firms to the style emphasis and selling appeals of the consumption ethic more readily than Ford, and even the bankers eventually accommodated themselves to the moral degeneracy of installment buying by christening it the "new thrift."[110] Still, many harbored deep reservations. The term "businessman" connoted efficiency, self-control, rationality, practical common sense, and a hatred of waste. Most businessmen treasured this self-image. Less ostentatiously than Ford, they clung to a "producer ethic." Whatever compromises with the consumption ethic they forged out of opportunism, they wished to hold themselves aloof from its complicity in catering to the weak-willed self-indulgence of the consumer masses.

For advertising agents of that era, the apparent popular enthusiasm for the consumption ethic created a potentially agonizing dilemma. They bore the responsibility for devising appeals that would whet the public's appetite for extravagance and engender a contempt for yesterday's styles. Yet few advertising leaders had adopted the bohemian philosophy of hedonism. They shared with other businessmen a deep suspicion of the impulses toward what could be considered self-indulgence, frivolous wastefulness, and decadent extravagance, and all of these seemed to lurk within the consumption ethic. Inescapably, they seemed confronted by the paradox of modernization: the forging of the final link in an efficient, rationalized system of mass production—its stabilization through the creation of predictable, expanding consumer demand—now required the nurture of qualities like wastefulness, self-indulgence, and artificial obsolescence, which directly negated or undermined the values of efficiency and the work ethic on which the system was based. And advertising agents of the 1920s were certainly unwilling to abandon allegiance to the work ethic. Like their business clients, they saw themselves as producers, not consumers. They sought self-fulfillment in hard work, in carrying out what they instinctively defined as serious, purposeful tasks. They shared the producer's almost ascetic contempt for the weak-willed, dependent consumer.[111]

Some agency leaders distinctly disapproved of some of the very actions their ads sought to induce. President William Johns of the George Batten agency regularly preached sermons on the tenets of thrift to his employees in the agency newsletter. He warned them to "learn to distinguish between luxuries and necessities" and not to abandon their judgment to "the seeming pleasures of the moment." Bernice Fitzgibbon, the creator of hundreds of retail ads intended to stimulate a lust for consumption, confided that her personal advice was "learn early that it's smart to defer gratification." Indeed, she continued, "deferring gratification is a good definition of being civilized."[112] Although their ads roundly condemned "drudgery," few advertising leaders spoke an ill word against "work." Bruce Barton proclaimed that "all work is worship," but nowhere did he confer such a distinction on consumption. In fact, once while watching a crowd of Easter shoppers, perhaps buying merchandise advertised by his own agency, Barton remarked disgustedly to a friend how "dreadful" it was to see these women wasting their husbands' earnings. In *Advertising and Selling*, Floyd Parsons lamented the passing of the self-containment of a previous age that had not felt the "need for constant thrills." He deplored the "present terrific urge to meet rising standards of life" and the "high-powered salesmanship" that induced the masses "to buy silly things and imperfect products."[113]

Even Christine Frederick recoiled against an overemphasis on color and style. She could fondly describe the "creative waste" of a woman who rejected her stylistically obsolete piano "of excellent tone" and had "perhaps bought *several* pianos of different shapes and woods in recent years." Yet she winced at ads that featured only stylistic externals, denouncing ads for washing machines in "Karnak Green" and "Galahad Grey" and ads for gas ranges that stressed "the delicate tracery of the design on the splasher back." Women whom home economists had educated to be "trained buyers" were being asked "to fall for 'color' with as little intelligence as a child puts out its hand for a bright toy." "Does the range roast?" she inquired. "Is it economical of fuel? Is it well insulated? Alas, we shall never know. But of its 'delicate tracery' of design the advertisement glowingly informs us."[114]

Did advertising leaders, despite these personal reservations, still conspire to seduce the public into accepting a self-indulgent consumption ethic—on the theory, incisively phrased by Rosalind Williams, that economic stability required that "the relative asceticism of the producers has to be balanced by the hedonism of the consuming masses"?[115] Certainly some theorists in the trade press clamored for a frontal attack on the old values and argued that advertisers needed to teach Americans to play "cheerfully-comfortably-confidently" and to "spend with faith."[116] But most individual advertisers recognized only a minor stake, if any, in the promotion of a broad consumption ethic. They were anxious to persuade consumers to loosen their purse string—or even to buy on credit—in order to obtain their own product. If desire for this product required a new sensitivity to the pleasures of style and luxury, they were eager to promote that consciousness as well—but usually with the cultivation of a taste for their specific product narrowly in mind. A deliberate intention to instill a consumption ethic should logically have prompted advertisers of labor-saving devices to depict housewives using their new leisure for exciting shopping forays. But this did not happen. Instead, such ads favored non-consumption-oriented activities like picking wildflowers or reading to children. Propaganda for a comprehensive attitude favoring extravagance and self-indulgence arose more from the cumulative effects of thousands of individual appeals than from any concerted effort to promote consumerism.

In effect, then, advertising's contribution to the advance of a consumption ethic stemmed less from any conspiracy than from the inevitable consequences of scale. As a mass communication, each ad that responded to the active desires of *some* consumers to be titillated by images of new choices and indulgences also exercised its seductive powers on thousands of *others* who had not yet experienced such desires. A kind of Epicurus's Law insured that each response to the whispered desires of a few would take the amplified form of a siren call to the millions. Thus each consumer would find in the advertising pages not only the enticing images of his or her own active consumption fantasies but entrancing images of the fantasies of all other consumer–citizens as well. A beckoning glance from a single window, so to speak, prompted a seductive song from the troubadours of advertising to the entire dormitory. And advertisers gallantly defended such "freedom of speech" against those puritanical consumer advocates who sought to impose utilitarian rationality on the masses by requiring that such songs be translated into a dull drone of specifications.

Although many advertising leaders personally deplored the self-indulgence of the masses and feminine appetites for frivolous goods, still they prided themselves on their tolerance in accepting human foibles. Moreover, they reasoned, it was absurd in a prosperous society to attempt "to draw a line between essential and non-essential things—between material wants and luxuries." As the advertising writer Kenneth Goode succinctly put it, "every free-born American has a right to name his own necessities."[117] Or, to phrase it another way, every consumer had the right to decide when to cooperate in the pleasure of his own seduction. But the image of the (welcomed) seducer, though popular in cynical backstage chatter, was not one that most advertising agents found permanently satisfying nor one that would be reassuring to the public. The trade searched for a more wholesome image that would free advertisers from any association with the degenerate aspects of consumption. In the process they discovered a variety of ways to get around the "inherent contradiction" of modernization.[118] In a series of evasions, advertising leaders of the 1920s and 1930s found that they could temporarily avoid confronting the challenge that the consumption ethic posed to the work ethic and to the vision of a rational, uplifting modernity.

The Gospel of the Full Cereal Bowl

Some advertisers needed to inspire a consciousness of style obsolescence to enlarge their market. They found they could evade any direct moral responsibility for promoting wastefulness by treating artificial obsolescence as inevitable. Society demanded it, they asserted. In 1927 the Elgin Watch Company waged a campaign that copywriters privately nicknamed "the clodhopper series." "Was your present watch in style when *Uncle Tom's Cabin* came to town?" asked one of the ads. "Did your watch ride with you . . . on a bicycle built for two?"

5.29. Here a stylish modern woman demonstrated how increased consumption could be placed in the service of democratic family values. The trek to the country for wildflowers beguiled the era's advertising artists.

inquired another. Elgin reminded the reader that others regarded his watch—like his car, house, and clothing—as an "index to your business and social standing." His watch might be a "splendid timekeeper . . . an old and faithful servitor," yet be so anachronistically out of style as to create an unfavorable impression.[119] In 1929 Standard Plumbing Fixtures set forth as fact, rather than as stylistic judgment, the observation that "bathrooms have aged more in the past year than in all the twenty before." Atwater Kent merely suggested that an older model radio "would look funny now." That legendary, normative, and perpetually mobile American family, the "Joneses," had built three new homes but had moved out of two of them in the last twelve years, Christine Frederick noted, simply "because they seemed obsolescent to this family so rapidly moving up on the social scale."[120] By attributing this judgment of obsolescence to vaguely defined public impressions, advertisers might argue that they were only bending to the will of consumers who valued luxuries over necessities.

Another way to promote the consumption ethic, yet not castigate still functional products as obsolete, was to argue that an adequate standard of living now required the purchase of a second model of the product. Beginning in 1927, first Marmon, then Jordan and Hudson, and finally General Motors began to stress the theme of the two-car family (see Fig. 5.29). General Motors empathized with the "marooned" wife who was denied her own personal car. "A car for her, too" was "becoming a necessity," insisted Chevrolet in 1928. Soon AT&T discovered the need for several telephones in a home.[121] Atwater Kent proposed an additional upstairs radio set or two for putting children to sleep with soothing music. With another set, parents could avoid the downstairs jazz program and ease family competition for control of the single dial. Gruen explained "why every man needs two good watches," and Jantzen announced, "Beach uniforms are out! Beach styles are in!" to encourage consumers to buy several different swimsuits for each "place and occasion." The Cleanliness Institute of the Soap and Glycerine Producers even applied the several sets idea to bathing—a prime consumer of soap. Since there were many kinds of baths—cold, cool, tepid, warm, and hot—for many purposes, consumers had good reasons to indulge in more than one bath a day.[122]

Advertising men found considerable solace in the belief that families who bought second models of the product, or responded to the pressure to avoid style obsolescence, worked harder than ever to afford their new styles and (necessary) luxuries. "Advertising has stimulated more work," rejoiced the Ayer agency. Americans so valued labor-saving devices that they were "willing to work harder for them."[123] Howard Dickinson, of the George Batten agency, happily pictured Americans on a progressive treadmill in which desires for style inspired more work so that "even our extravagances turn more wheels" and "we lift ourselves by our boot straps."[124] Thus appeals to style and "progressive obsolescence" actually promoted the work ethic. Even an ad like "Some Day your Boy will own a Buick," which seemed to epitomize the shift of goals away from those of a producer (to become head of the company) to those of a consumer (to possess the right product), did not preclude the possibility that much hard work would be required by the boy before he enjoyed the promise of the consumption ethic.[125]

Advertising leaders also fell back on their occupational assumptions to evade the challenge of the consumption ethic to the work ethic and a modernity of rationality and self-control. One of these was the faith that even the hedonism of the masses would not prevent a rational elite from guiding the society to progress. Uplift might fail, but paternalism would save consumers from the potential consequences of their self-indulgence and weakening of character. Another compatible assumption rested on observations about the susceptibility of women to advertising and the consumption ethic. As a 1937 *McCall's* ad put it, "categorically . . . man is always the producer . . . woman, the consumer."[126] The world of manliness might thus stand aloof from the threats posed by the new ethic's feminine tendencies toward frivolousness, emotionality, and effusive adornment. The notion that extravagances in consumption were the particular vice of women served opportunely to spare advertising men from concerns that the new ethic might plunge the entire society into an abyss of hedonism. Men might safely overindulge women if they walled off the sphere of consumption from their own sphere of work and rational control.[127]

Many of these evasions of the challenge to refined modernity posed by the consumption ethic were flawed by their failure to completely free advertising men from the taint of association with fickle tastes, stylistic superfluities, and artificial obsolescence. But in 1932 the editor of *Printers' Ink* discovered a morally irreproachable image that freed the consumption ethic from such disconcerting connotations. In place of the old symbol of the "full dinner pail"—an image evocative of the production-oriented worker, satisfied with mere subsistence—the editor proposed a new, consumption-oriented symbol: the "full cereal bowl." It was the full cereal bowl, not the dinner pail, he argued, that now dramatized "the future of America, the dream of the pioneers for a better and richer life." The hope of the future lay in a new generation of children, raised on the heavily advertised cereals. Nurtured on advertising, they would march forward "with fearless eyes" from the wondrous moment at "the point in life where they can read for the first time about the product some manufacturer has made for their comfort and pleasure" to their final, triumphant entrance "into the class of full-fledged consumers."[128] The image of the cereal bowl conveniently evaded the issues of extravagance, obsolescence, emotionality, and feminine frivolity. Cereal represented no threat to the work ethic; most ads for breakfast cereals in the 1920s and early 1930s stressed their crucial contribution to the energy needed for a day of work or study. In an age still innocent of Cocoa Puffs and Captain Crunch, who could remain squeamish about promoting the march toward consumption when its robust, young participants drew their nurturing inspiration from so wholesome a source as the full cereal bowl?

ADVERTISEMENTS AS SOCIAL TABLEAUX

The scene opens upon the covered veranda of a spacious country club. In the foreground, two women and a man are seated in large, smartly designed wicker chairs around a low table. They are carrying on a casual but obviously engaging conversation. A waiter in a white coat, black bow tie, and slicked-down hair stands near the table, opening a bottle. A golf bag rests beside one chair. The two women are seated with their backs to us, but their stylish cloche hats, their trim figures, and the slightly angular but nevertheless graceful way in which one leans forward toward the gentleman who is speaking unmistakably suggest fastidious demeanor and social confidence. The man faces us. He is impeccably dressed in a summer suit with his handkerchief precisely squared in his coat pocket. He has a tiny, trimmed mustache. As he speaks, he projects an image neither aggressive nor retiring, but simply confident and relaxed. His hands rest comfortably on his crossed knees.

The larger setting is opulent and refined. In the foreground and to the extreme right, a distinguished-looking man in knickers, seated in a wicker chair, serenely puffs a pipe and rests his book in his lap. He gazes out through the veranda's pillars toward the lawn, the boxed and sculpted trees by a low wall, and the golf course beyond. In the far background more waiters hover about several tables of genteel club members, as yet another couple emerges onto the veranda from the club-house doors. Everything suggests spaciousness as well as leisure. The central figures are well separated from each other with ample "talking room" and sufficient privacy from other tables. They are small, yet not dwarfed by the clubhouse. The pillars at the right, with several Italian cypress trees interspersed, open out for the entire length of the veranda, as far back as we can see, on the expansive open areas of the golf course. Several indistinct figures of golfers can be vaguely glimpsed. Although no color is apparent, the tiled floor of the veranda, the vines covering its roof and the grassy expanses convey a sense of vivid opulence. Tiny goblets on the table of the three characters in the foreground complete the image of fastidious restraint.

Having taken in the scene, we then learn something about the sprightly conversation that is unfolding at the table in the foreground and about some other characters soon to make an appearance: "A woman's laugh falls gaily upon their ears, and the company learns of a well-played match. The talk turns to yachting and a youth tells of winning the King of Spain's cup. Fleet horses engage their interest and a Master of Hounds recounts a thrilling hunt in Maryland."[1]

The scene just described might have served as the opening tableau for a play, reproduced in precise detail from the instructions of a playwright who wished to convey an immediate impression of the characters and their society at the raising of the curtain. In fact, it appeared in a 1929 Canada Dry Ginger Ale ad from the *Chicago Tribune.* Advertising tableaux such as this confront us directly with the dilemma posed by the rather offhand but frequently repeated truism that "advertising reflects society."

We should recognize, first, that advertisements may be said to reflect society in several ways that have little relevance to the problems raised by the Canada Dry tableau. Advertisements depict and describe the material artifacts available for purchase at a given time. They reveal the state of technology, the current styles in clothing, furniture, and other products, and sometimes the relative prices commanded by various goods. Whereas archaeologists must deduce the probable social uses of the artifacts they unearth, and then interpret from them the economic and social structures of the society, advertisements provide us with ample guidelines to the social functions (or at least the suggested uses) of various products. They can supply this information about a society without depicting either a person or a social setting, merely by displaying and describing the products themselves.

Another way that advertisements can "reflect society" without actually depicting any social setting is through the testimonial ad. The endorser may be quoted without illustration; or he or she may be shown in close-up, with no suggestion of social context. But the choice of endorser will tell us what sort of person the advertising professionals, from their highly motivated study of popular attitudes and perhaps through sales or coupon tests, have determined that the public will best accept as an "authority." If the trend in testimonials moves away from business figures toward movie celebrities, we have glimpsed one reflection of attitudinal changes in the society.[2]

The Concept of a Social Tableau

But the advertisements we are most likely to think of when we speak of ads as "reflections of society" are those, like the Canada Dry ad, that may be defined as "social tableaux." Within this category fall all advertisements in which persons are depicted in such a way as to suggest their relationships to each other or to a larger social structure. The depiction of a single person may qualify if that person is placed in a setting suggestive of social relationships with others.

I have adapted the phrase "social tableau" from the term "tableaux vivants" or "living pictures," a genre of theater entertainment that enjoyed a moment of popularity toward the end of the nineteenth century. The tableaux vivants were elaborately costumed and staged representations of familiar scenes, accomplished through the grouping of models who held sustained, motionless poses while the curtain remained open on the scene. Their entertainment value stemmed from the shock of recognition of a familiar scene suddenly "brought to life" in three dimensions with real persons. The scenes, therefore, had to be familiar to the audience. They usually consisted of famous paintings, historical or biblical scenes, or esthetically pleasing fantasies of "moonlight" or "springtime."[3]

Playwrights still occasionally employ the tableau technique to etch a scene vividly in the audience's memory. The actors are frozen in place as the curtain opens or the stage lights come on. They hold their poses for several seconds before the action and dialogue begin, so that the audience may take in the atmosphere of the stage set and the implications of the depicted social situation. These theater tableaux seem to me the genre most nearly analogous to printed advertisements that depict social scenes. Though both are static, both are as suggestive as possible of impending or arrested action.

The social tableau advertisement usually depicts a contemporary "slice-of-life" setting rather than a work of art or a legendary scene. But it still relies on scenes sufficiently stereotypical to bring immediate audience recognition. Just as the tableaux vivants were defined as "vivid" representations, so the advertising tableaux often enhance social scenes through their brilliance of imagery and intensity of focus. With a little imagination, we might even interpret the texts of those ads as analogous to the program notes or spoken narratives that sometimes accompanied the nineteenth-century tableaux vivants.

But did the social tableau advertisements of the 1920s and 1930s serve, as they might seem to promise, as "mirrors" of American society in those decades? They usually purported to depict real, contemporary social scenes. But the Canada Dry tableau, which was not entirely unrepresentative of most advertisements, seemed to "reflect" only one very narrow stratum of American society. Other social strata, as manifested in urban slums, or working class households, or even apartment-house dwellers and families with boarders, found no reflection in advertising's "mirror." So prevalent was a "class atmosphere" in these social tableaux that a historian relying exclusively on their manifest evidence could only conclude that most Americans of that era enjoyed an exceedingly affluent and leisured mode of life.

Thus, before we attempt to evaluate the "evidence" of these social tableaux, we must recall that "reflecting society" was not the purpose of these ads. The content of a social tableau advertisement was determined primarily by merchandising strategy. Its purpose was to sell a product. Within the boundaries set by that strategy, its content was further shaped by pictorial conventions and by the desire to provide consumers with a scene into which they could comfortably and pleasurably place themselves. Given the assumption of advertisers, constantly reinforced by their observations of popular culture, that people preferred to identify with portrayals of themselves as they aspired to be, rather than as they "really were," we must assume that most social tableaux aimed at depicting settings at least "a step up" from the social circumstances of the readers.

If social tableau advertisements are too unrepresentative of social reality to provide us a "slice-of-life" semblance of America, perhaps they can be salvaged as evidence by interpreting them as reflective of the "reality" of the social aspirations of American consumers. After all, the tableaux were reflections of *something*, even though that something is more accurately described as "social fantasy" than "social reality." Fantasy images of "a step up" may also conceivably be employed to estimate the reality of the step below. Even highly selective and idealized images of one elevated rung of the social ladder may provide information on assumptions about class relationships and social structure that ad writers believed their audiences would accept without dissent.

But these "reflections" in the ads must still be evaluated in the light of another possible source of distortion—the impact of the advertisers' mission as apostles of modernity. The social tableaux depicted an ideal modern life—one to which consumers presumably aspired, but also one specifically discerned by the eyes of ad creators. As we explore the social roles portrayed by the players in these tableaux, we will find instances in which the distortions created by merchandising strategies and by the occupational biases of advertising agents resulted in images that accurately reflect neither the actual lives nor the authentic aspirations of consumers. But we may also discover situations in which the tableaux, because they sought to relate products to social needs, did graphically reflect central social and cultural dilemmas of the age.

Modern Woman as Businesswoman: "The Little Woman, G.P.A."

The leading lady claimed the largest role in the advertising tableaux. Her qualifications for stardom were scarcely debatable; everyone acknowledged that she made at least 80 percent of all consumer purchases. To foster identification and illustrate consumer satisfactions, advertisers kept her in the limelight. Although stereotyped characters abounded in the tableaux, the portrait of the American woman that emerged from the ads of the 1920s and 1930s is striking in its complexity. No other figure in the tableaux shifted roles and appearances so frequently. Yet the ultimate boundaries on the leading lady's scope of action were so clearly drawn that this apparent diversity of roles eventually came to seem less impressive.

The decisive separation of workplace and home during the previous century had inspired extremely polarized conceptions of the proclivities and capacities of men and women. Man's proper sphere had been increasingly defined by a life away from home in a world of ambition, severe competition, and the efficient, unsentimental manipulation of people and objects. In compensation, the home, now defined as the woman's sphere, had assumed the character of a sanctuary. Here the woman preserved the "softer" and more "cultured" qualities of sentiment, beauty, and repose, while progress proceeded apace in the "real world" outside.[4]

The home and its perpetual occupant, the wife, had thus acquired an archaic aura. According to this convention the home was not an agency of modernization, but rather a buffer against the harsher thrusts and shocks of progress. The women who guarded these havens did not contribute to the progress of the modern world. Rather, they preserved those qualities that helped to soften the necessary dislocations caused by progress and to salve the psychological wounds they inflicted.

Most social tableau advertisements of the 1920s and 1930s perpetuated the notion of polarized sexual spheres. But advertisers strenuously resisted the implication that women represented archaic qualities. Jealous as they were of their self-proclaimed status as the most modern of men, advertising men still labeled women as the more modern of the sexes. Advertisers not only complimented women on their superior responsiveness to new ideas, they also made them *look* modern. Although Santa Claus retained his traditional girth and white hair in advertising tableaux and usually displayed an archaic, puckish charm, advertisers who employed "Mrs. Santa Claus" as a merchandising assistant insisted that she be a slim, chic, "modern little lady . . . who is up-to-the-minute on all present day matters."[5]

Once again, however, the ambiguities of the concept of modernity intervened to prevent women from gaining complete respect for their apparent superiority. Ideas of modernity carried connotations drawn both from the realm of modern business progress (efficiency, control, rationality, technological sophistication) and from the realm of fashion (expressiveness, changeability, extravagance). Advertising tableaux cast women in "modern" roles in both of these senses of the word. But women's modest attainments in the higher, business sense of the term "modern" never achieved sufficient scope or stature to compensate for the unserious implications of their modernity in fashion. In fact, the more that women achieved recognition for their modernity in consumption, the less they qualified for any true equality in the broader quest for modern progress.

This is not to say that women gained no recognition from advertisers for their progress in business skills in the 1920s. Quite the contrary, copywriters constantly congratulated women for their presumed new capacities for management. But the proper field for these managerial talents remained the home. Nowhere did advertising men display so sincere a desire to flatter women for having achieved modernity than in the frequency with which they recast the old role of housewife as "family G.P.A." or general purchasing agent.[6] To view the home, by analogy, as a business concern and the housewife as a business executive seemed, in a business-minded age, to banish the archaic aura of the home. As purchasing agents, women could command respect for exhibiting qualities previously honored primarily in men—capacities for planning, efficiency, and expert decision-making. In its ad "The Little Woman, G.P.A.," N. W. Ayer and Son stationed the housewife at the controls of a domestic communications center, and appended prestigious initials after her name in the same way that a professional man might add LL.D. or M.D. (Fig. 6.1). "Businesses may have their treasurers, their controllers," noted Ayer. "But homes have their wives who do the same work in 25 million independent businesses, the households of America."[7] An appliance company congratulated "the modern homemaker" for running her home "quite as

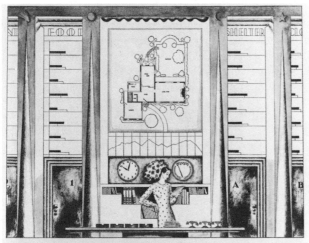

The Little Woman, G · P · A ·

Businesses may have their treasurers, their comptrollers, even their boards of directors who watch expenditures. By careful perusal of charts and graphs, by weighty conferences, they determine how annual income is to be spent.

But homes have their wives who do the same work in 25 million independent businesses, the households of America. Without elaborate research, without the counsel and the conferences of big business, these executives spend annually 40 billion dollars. They spend it amazingly well, too, though they are not specialized purchasing agents any more than they are specialized cooks, or interior decorators or educators or furnace tenders.

Their decisions are governed by the welfare of their families. "Is this breakfast food better for my children to eat?" . . . "Will this davenport and these curtains, this lamp and this piano, make my home a pleasanter place to be?" . . . "Will this school give my daughter what I know she needs?" . . . "Would another kind of heating equipment make our home more comfortable, more healthful next winter?" These are samples of the questions they ask.

Always they visualize the ideal, these wives and mothers, before they consider economies. But they watch for economies as few business men do. By aptitude and training they are excellent shoppers. The

competition for their attention, the courting of their favor, is tremendous. The way to their hearts and their purses is not easy, but it is clear. These general purchasing agents are readers of advertising, consistent, critical readers of advertising. It has been estimated that they buy more than eighty per cent of all advertised merchandise.

Addressing the women of America on the printed page is an art, but an art that can be applied with almost the exactitude of a science. Already it has meant the growth and continued success of many concerns who manufacture products useful in the business of making a home and rearing a family.

N. W. AYER & SON   ADVERTISING HEADQUARTERS PHILADELPHIA
NEW YORK   BOSTON   CHICAGO   SAN FRANCISCO

6.1. When advertisers sought to dignify housework, they resorted to business analogies. Against a backdrop of graphs, charts, and telephones, the home's "General Purchasing Agent" acquired new prestige.

efficiently as her husband does his business—perhaps more so." Scores of tableaux disclosed the housewife planning expenditures or paying bills at her home desk and labeled her role "manager" or "executive."[8]

Social tableaux also frequently portrayed women demonstrating their new competence as purchasing agents in forays outside the home. In an ad headlined "Women know these things now," Veedol Motor Oils complimented women on their refusal to "rely on the men folk for every little thing as women did a generation ago."[9] Similarly, Piggly Wiggly stores, the pioneers in self-service food markets, congratulated women for their "self-reliant" new skill in shopping. "The women of yesterday probably could not have done it at all," Piggly Wiggly began patronizingly. "For the woman of today it is both easy and pleasant. Her new, wide knowledge of values, her new ability to decide for herself, is one of the wonders of the world we live in." By selecting products off the shelf with "no clerk to persuade her," proclaimed Piggly Wiggly, "she has astonished her husband . . . and the world."[10]

If her husband was astonished, still he suffered no loss of traditional dominance. If his wife was the home's purchasing agent—and thus analogous to a business

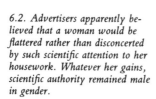

6.2. Advertisers apparently believed that a woman would be
flattered rather than disconcerted
by such scientific attention to her
housework. Whatever her gains,
scientific authority remained male
in gender.

executive of modest power—the husband was more elegantly defined, either
implicitly or explicitly, as the home's "treasurer" or its "president."[11] The wife's
expertise and efficiency within the realm of day-to-day consumer decision-
making warranted praise, but her ultimate subordination to a higher executive
remained unchallenged. As for her heralded new competence in decision-making,
Piggly Wiggly characterized it as fully expressed in her "endorsement" of the
Piggly Wiggly plan, and Veedol suggested that she exercise her new independence
by relying on Veedol ads rather than on the advice of "men folk." For the
upper-middle-class housewife, the new ascribed status of "purchasing agent" was
particularly ironic. Just as she was receiving recognition with a managerial-
sounding title, as Ruth Schwartz Cowan points out, she was often losing help
from servants, relatives, and commercial service agencies and was slipping into a
less managerial role as an unspecialized, "proletarianized" household worker.[12]

Even though the "President of Home, Inc." occasionally called her to account
on expenses, the efficient home manager's goal was as much to save time as to
save money. A "clever manager" not only claimed respect for her businesslike
modernity, she also emancipated herself from withering isolation and cultural
deprivation by creating time for outside activities. This she accomplished by
giving housework even more attention but turning it into a science. So systematic
was one home manager, in the fond vision of an advertising agent for a washing
machine, that "when she shopped, she bought in twos. Two shirts exactly alike.
Two sheets exactly alike. Two towels, two pairs of pajamas, two pairs of hose."
She saw that each article had similar wear. "But one she sent out by the pound and

the other she had washed at home with her electric washer. . . . Then she balanced her cost—operating cost of machine, maid's time at 50 cents an hour, . . . machinery depreciation."[13] For a somewhat less self-reliant but still eagerly scientific young housewife, Old Dutch Cleanser provided a white-coated scientist with a stop watch to measure her cleaning speed (Fig. 6.2).[14]

Leisure—For What?

The merchandising strategies of manufacturers of foods, soaps, waxes, disinfectants, and similar products usually dictated tableaux that elevated the standards for respectable housekeeping. Like the home economists, whom they often employed, these advertisers exalted "homemaking" as a career. As Ruth Cowan remarks, the image of housework changed: "it was no longer a trial and a chore, but something quite different—an emotional 'trip.'"[15] And if the positive rewards of scientific perfection were not sufficient, there was always the goad of possible failure. "By Their Floors Ye Shall Judge Them," admonished one floor polisher ad. "It is written that floors are like unto a mirror, reflecting the character of the housewife."[16] But emphasis on higher standards of housework was not the main thrust of ads to women in the 1920s and 1930s. Scores of advertisers, including the producers of new home appliances, promised that their labor-saving products and services would bring women the most fulfilling reward—leisure time.

It is in the delineation by social tableau advertisements of these new self-fulfilling activities for women that we discover one of the purest instances of advertising as a social mirror. The particular merchandising bias of the advertisement for a time-saving home service or a drudgery-removing appliance was largely exhausted in the argument that it could, in fact, produce the desired increase in a woman's "free" time. How the leading ladies in these tableaux *used* the new discretionary time represented the best estimate by advertising copywriters and artists of the uses of discretionary time that women would find most attractive.

Many of these ads now *showed* the housewife enjoying her leisure—with the picture of the product absent or subordinated. The desirability of the depicted substitute activity was the very essence of the ad's appeal: to show women using their free time for gardening when most actually longed to go shopping for clothes would be an advertising blunder. If advertising men ever faced a situation in which their overriding task was to depict exactly what the audience wanted, uncontaminated by their own or the manufacturer's ulterior motives, these portrayals of the uses of leisure would seem to have offered that occasion.

Using these assumptions, we can attempt to reconstruct the aspirations of women readers of mass-circulation magazines in the 1920s from the advertising campaign of the American Laundry Machinery Company. This campaign stressed the time saved by sending family washing to a commercial laundry and described the activities women might choose in their free time. Each ad usually included three or more illustrated testimonials in which women described the particular joys of their expanded leisure. Since the ads included a large number of examples, we may be able to infer from them not only which activities women most desired, but also the boundaries of such desires. What these ads did *not* include may be as significant as what they specifically portrayed.

What uses of leisure time did the women in these ads find most appealing? A compilation of all activities described or depicted in eight of these ads in 1926 reveals that leisure for reading and for spending more time with their children far outranked all other choices, with twelve mentions each. Participation in club activities gained six mentions; golf, sewing, and part-time work outside the home numbered five each. Visits with friends, concerts and plays, home decoration, music, motoring, and sports other than golf all appeared in at least three testimonials or lists of possible leisure activities. No testimonial mentioned a career. Civic affairs gained only a single reference, and shopping and charity work each appeared only twice (Fig. 6.3).[17]

A survey of ads for other labor-saving devices and services between 1926 and 1928 reveals an even heavier emphasis on "more time to devote to your children" or "companionship with your children" as the most desired benefit. Visits with friends, clubs, reading, golf, the theater, and bridge received lesser attention; part-time work, shopping, and civic affairs received none. Several years later, a *Woman's Home Companion* study of women's use of free time resulted in "a list so long and a range so wide that even we staunch believers in feminine progress were surprised." But the magazine still implicitly preserved certain outer boundaries of women's proper sphere by noting that the gamut of leisure activities extended from "kitchen to golf course—nursery to club room."[18]

This evidence could support the argument of Ruth Schwartz Cowan and others that new theories of child care—which called for expanded, expert attention to the child and the cultivation of a feeling of companionship between child and mother—had persuaded many women simply to shift their time from house maintenance to child nurture. Certainly advertisements seemed calculated to encourage that process. Social tableaux regularly offered warm scenes of mothers sharing their children's enjoyment of a book, a picnic, or a romp through a field of wildflowers (see Figs. 5.29, 8.18). Ads warned that during children's early "plastic years . . . when they need 'mothering' most," a woman had precious little time to exert that crucial influence that would guide her children "safely through the shoals and narrows of childhood" and fortify them against the multitude of competing influences and attractions that might later induce them to "drift away."[19]

The social tableaux will not tell us, however, whether these visions of a new companionship with children actually came to pass. Nor will they reveal whether these choices for leisure time were authentic reflections of women's real attitudes. We must still take into account possible refractions in advertising's "mirror image." The testimonials may have revealed women's notions about praiseworthy uses of leisure time more clearly than it showed their real preferences. Certainly it is striking, despite mounting box-office figures and frequent comments in the trade press about the movie-madness of the age, that no women in these tableaux confessed to using their new leisure time to go to the matinee.

The American Laundry Machinery testimonials were undoubtedly edited by copywriters to avoid undue repetition and to establish the range of alternatives they wished. The resulting priorities may well have represented a judgment by

"Might-have-been hours"…*how many of them are* YOURS ?

"I MIGHT have done that"—"I might have gone there"—there are so many "might-have-been hours" in every woman's life! All because some household task—washing, ironing, cooking, cleaning—demands attention.

But how to take care of these duties, and still have time for the "might-have-been" pleasures? Electricity and all the servants it puts at your command will shorten much of your daily work. And the modern laundry, greatest time-saver of all, will actually give you a whole day of leisure every week.

Think of the many things you can do with this new time. Perhaps, like Mrs. Schwinn of New York City, you will use the time for music; or, like Mrs. Jones of Covington, Ky., you may devote the time to school and civic activities; or maybe, like Mrs. Looker of Hollywood, Calif.,

"Send it to the Laundry"

the time can be used to improve your health and your finances.

Home, husband, children, books, the theater—myriad happy duties and pleasures await you.

Today, just phone a modern laundry in your city—they will tell you about a washday service exactly suited to your needs, at a price within your reach. Then try this service—at least for one day every week, the laundry will take the 'might' from your "might-have-been hours."

How three women took the 'MIGHT' from their "might-have-been hours"

"My husband is a teacher in the high school and naturally I am supposed to attend the receptions and parties at the school, and to take part in civic activities. Yet for years I couldn't seem to find time for such things. Then I sent my washing to the laundry, rearranged my weekly schedule and discovered that I had plenty of time for all my social and civic obligations."

Mrs. Wm. M. Jones,
Covington, Ky.

"From girlhood I have been fond of music; I even used to dream of a 'career.' Then I married and said goodbye to my music; I had no time for it. But I couldn't forget it. Finally, I turned my washday tasks over to the laundry and gave the time thus saved to music. With my new leisure, I have been able to practice regularly, join music clubs, and even sing in concerts, and at church."

Mrs. D. L. Schwinn,
New York City

"I can't begin to tell you what a wonderful help the laundry has been to me, both from a health and from a financial standpoint. The time the laundry gives me I have used in cultivating a vegetable garden. The open air exercise has been decidedly beneficial to me—doctor bills are a thing of the past—while the vegetables I have grown have more than cut our grocery bill in half."

Mrs. N. Looker,
Hollywood, Calif.

Published in the interest of the public and on behalf of the Laundry Industry by The American Laundry Machinery Company, Executive Offices, Cincinnati, Ohio

6.3. The vignettes of golf, the theater, and reading to children in this prototype American Laundry Machinery Company ad reflected advertisers' assumptions about women's preferred and proper uses of leisure.

Just what is it to be
A Good Wife *in this*
MODERN AGE?

*D*EEP down in your heart—in the heart of every woman—is that eager, wistful wish to be *a good wife*—a partner in your husband's plans; his cheery companion in leisure hours.

You realize that in this advanced age your husband needs a mate as modern-minded as himself; a wife whose tastes and temperament are attuned to the present-day pace. He is moving ever forward. *You* can not afford to lag behind.

In the world of Business, men have banished the dragon of Drudgery. But what of *your* world? Are you still hampered by heavy household tasks that take your time and sap your strength?

Does the weekly washday take its heavy toll of hours that you could spend so joyously, so profitably in other ways?

>>>>><<<<<

TUNE IN ON LAUNDERLAND

Hear the lads and lassies of Launderland broadcast for all the family every Saturday evening at 8:30 o'clock, Eastern Time and at 9:00 o'clock Pacific Time. Tune in on your favorite station of the National Broadcasting System for a real musical treat.

>>>>><<<<<

Are you passing up enjoyable, stimulating, youth-bringing pleasures and pastimes because of this heavy burden? It is no wonder then that washday steals more of Youth and Beauty than the other six days can restore!

Washday in your home is doomed—a day of rest and recreation is assured—if you will decide now to *get the facts;* to see for yourself just what the modern laundry has to offer. In place of drudgery you are given a full day of freedom; happy hours for those pleasant pursuits —those gracious arts—that make one a truly good wife—a worthy companion of the twentieth century husband.

You will find there is a laundry service that *exactly* meets your needs; one that fits snugly into your Family Budget. Moreover, in this progressive day, the laundry can be relied upon to wash clothes clean and make them last long. The health of your family is safe-guarded with every scientific aid. Modern laundry service really *costs less* in the long run.

At the other end of your telephone there is a laundryowner who will gladly continue this story. Talk with him— this morning. Let him send you the delightful journey booklet of "Alice in Launderland." It's the next thing to visiting the laundry yourself.

LET THE Laundry DO IT

SPONSORED BY THE ASSOCIATION OF THE
LAUNDRY OWNERS NATIONAL UNITED STATES AND CANADA

6.4. *A woman needed leisure simply to fulfill her obligation to remain a stimulating evening companion with modern tastes. Her husband was "moving ever forward." She must not "lag behind."*

male copywriters about what women *ought* to want. Finally, although these ads addressed women of middle-class status and above, the class and educational biases of advertising men still had a distorting effect. Whether golf really played so substantial a role, even in these women's *fantasies* of leisure, is certainly open to question. The extraordinary emphasis on reading may have been influenced by copywriters' own association of reading with enjoyable leisure, and by the frequency with which their trade journals bombarded them with clichéd pictures of the faithful woman subscriber to the advertised publication intently reading in her chair.[20] This emphasis may also have arisen from the traditional convention of depicting the stereotyped woman-at-leisure as reposing in a chair or reclining in a chaise lounge, with one hand holding a book or magazine and the other poised over a box of chocolates nearby.[21] In short, I suspect that female readers of these advertisements harbored real desires that were less refined, less intellectual, less golf-oriented, and perhaps even more consumption-minded than the ads suggested.

Many of the advertising tableaux presented women's new leisure pursuits as acts of individual self-expression. One American Laundry Machinery Company ad, having contrasted "Mrs. Weary Wife at Home" and "Mrs. Wise Wife at Liberty," suggested an open-ended, self-justifying notion of "female freedom" in a world of recreation and amusement where "there is so much to learn, so much to do, so much to see and hear."[22] But more common were the tableaux that brought women back full-circle to their traditional roles: the new range of activities made them "better wives and mothers."

In the modern, bureaucratized, less provincial business world, the ads warned women, their husbands might quickly outgrow them in sophistication, class standing, and breadth of tastes and experiences. To retain their husbands' affection, modern wives had to find time to educate themselves to be stimulating social and intellectual companions. They needed to preserve their youth so that they could beautify their husbands' lives and keep pace with them during evenings of dancing and theater (Fig. 6.4). The Laundry Owners Association promised "the woman who could never think of reading *like this* on washday" that with her wash at the laundry, her new leisure would keep her "young-minded, fresh, and radiant." You will be, they told her, "a real partner in your husband's interests; a true companion to your children; an even better homemaker than you have ever been."[23]

In the crucial endeavor of becoming good companions and partners to their modern husbands, the tableaux further suggested, women's business efficiency in the home held value only as a necessary means. The new woman must apply the time saved through modern management to the cultivation of broader interests and a youthful, modern look. Diversification of her activities and her mastery of business methods did not alter the reality of a woman's "world." It was a world, in Roland Barthes' phrase, "entirely constituted by the gaze of man," one in which "man is everywhere around, he presses on all sides, he makes everything exist." Lady Esther Face Cream expressed the idea more hauntingly: "Men's eyes are magnifying mirrors."[24] Borrowing from a tradition well established in art, advertising illustrators generously supplied their female subjects with mirrors as surrogates and symbols of those judgmental gazes of the world outside the boudoir

6.5. The omnipresent mirror reminded each woman of her central "duty"—to be beautiful. See also Fig. 6.9.

(Figs. 6.5, 6.6). Some advertisements clearly conveyed the idea that in presenting the formulaic scene of the woman seated before her dressing-table mirror they had captured the essence of "Woman" (Figs. 6.7, 6.8). For the male copywriter or illustrator, the mirror served to epitomize women's supposedly unrivaled addiction to vanity; for a woman, it served as a reminder of an inescapable "duty" beyond that of efficient homemaking—the duty "to catch and hold the springtime of her beauty."[25]

Advertisers insistently reminded women that they might lose the very opportunity to embark on their "great adventure" of homemaking or fail to hold their treasured positions as companions unless they repeatedly won these privileges in the ongoing "beauty contest of life." The warnings could be positively intimidating. "What Do Men Think When They Look at You?" asked one Camay soap ad. "You against the Rest of Womankind; your Beauty . . . your Charm . . . your Skin," warned another. "Someone's eyes are forever searching your face,

6.6. *By surrounding women with mirrors, advertisements reinforced each reader's sense of living constantly under the world's judgmental gaze.*

6.7. *The Sun bluntly equated multiple mirrors with the very essence of "Woman."*

6.8. *Radio Sales, Inc., suggestively associated a woman's narcissism with the ease with which others could "make up her mind."*

The Eyes of Men ··· the Eyes of Women
Judge your Loveliness every day

You can hardly glance out of the window, much less walk in town but that some inquiring eye searches you and your skin. This is the Beauty Contest of life. Not even a queen escapes it. And a modest country girl can win it ··· if her skin is lovely and deserving.

★ *Make a rich lather with Camay, a soft cloth and warm water, gently massaging it into your skin. Rinse well with cold water. Then note how soft and fresh your skin feels.*

★ *This is creamy-white Camay, the famous beauty soap that thousands of lovely women use for their complexions, for their hands and in their bath. A finer, gentler soap was never made!*

Copr. 1931, Procter & Gamble Co.

You may be sprightly and sixteen; fair and forty; or serious and sixty, yet you cannot deny that every pair of eyes that looks at you commends your beauty or regrets its lack. For life is a Beauty Contest for every woman. And she whose skin is soft and fresh has a wonderful advantage.

THE SOAP OF BEAUTIFUL WOMEN

To possess a lovely, clear complexion take infinite care in choosing your beauty soap! Use gentle,

creamy-white Camay, the Soap of Beautiful Women! Its lather is rich as cream ··· luxuriant in any kind of water. Camay is made of pure, delicate oils, safe for the most delicate feminine skin.

NEW LOW PRICES

Never in all your lifetime have you known a soap of such exquisite quality to cost so little! The price of Camay is now so low you will want to buy a dozen cakes today!

CAMAY
THE SOAP OF BEAUTIFUL WOMEN

6.9. Life was a "Beauty Contest," the advertisers frequently reminded women. "Not even a queen escapes it," but with the product's help, "a modest country girl can win."

"I'M STARTING YOUR BEAUTY PLANS NOW"

SIXTEEN years from now, Mary Ann, you'll be powdering your nose for your first real party! Now cuddle up and listen to your mother— I'll tell you why Ivory Soap will help you keep your lovely complexion! You'd be the silliest baby alive if you didn't stay true to Ivory Soap. Why, doctor prescribed Ivory for you

when you were 48 hours old. He knew that a sensitive skin needs a pure soap! Don't let your mother find you experimenting with colored or perfumed soaps. For it's priceless to your complexion to remember that Ivory is pure. Besides, mother's own, I have proof for you that Ivory is the real beauty soap. Smooth your cheek against mine.

Why, Ivory is a beauty secret that runs in our family! It has been taking care of my complexion since I was a baby! You're too small a chick now to realize what a clear sparkling complexion will mean to you some day. But I promise you that a lovely skin starts heart trouble with men. And if you don't believe me, ask your father!

Keep a baby-clear complexion with the baby's beauty treatment · Ivory Soap · 99 44/100 % pure   IVORY SOAP

6.10. If a woman's life was to be simply a never-ending "Beauty Contest," it only made sense to train for the competition early.

comparing you with other women."[26] (See Fig. 6.9.) A corset manufacturer added that the "beauty contest of life" was an equal-opportunity competition, in which women must acquire beauty "as a personal achievement . . . not a birthright." Ivory soap rushed to the aid of mothers seeking to protect their daughters from failure in the most important "battle" of their lives. To gain a headstart on the competition, the mother in an Ivory tableau told her infant daughter, "I'm Starting Your Beauty Plans Now" (Fig. 6.10).[27]

Grotesque Moderne

Exactly what "look" women should adopt to play their modern roles was defined less by the close-ups of soap and cosmetic ads than by the stances, silhouettes, and accessories of women in the whole range of social tableau advertisements. The "Fisher Body girl" established the normative image for women in the late 1920s and early 1930s. The creation of illustrator McClelland Barclay, this

*O*f all those
who express motor car body
preference . . 95% Prefer "Body by Fisher"

An investigation made by a disinterested agency and reaching into every county of every state in America, has revealed that the vast majority of motor car prospects select a car with its body attributes foremost in mind. It also established that 95 per cent of all motor car buyers who are influenced by the body in purchasing a motor car, prefer Body by Fisher.

When the American people—who *know* motor cars—exhibit

CADILLAC · LA SALLE

such solid and pronounced preference for any automotive product, there is only one answer: *That product must be unmistakably superior.*

As a matter of fact, the super-quality and super-value of Body by Fisher have been evident from the first. So evident, that Bodies by Fisher were early demanded by the manufacturers of the finest motor car chassis. Inevitably, Fisher thus became associated years ago in the public mind not only with better

bodies—*but with better motor cars* as well.

Note the result: When General Motors gathered the finest motor car in each price class into one great organization, these better cars were already equipped—had long been equipped—with Body by Fisher. That is one reason why today the emblem "Body by Fisher" is the unfailing guide to the better motor car in every price field—a fact which is very plainly apparent when you glance at the list printed below—of cars equipped with Body by Fisher.

BUICK · OAKLAND · OLDSMOBILE · PONTIAC · CHEVROLET

BODY by FISHER

GENERAL MOTORS

6.11. *Whether attended by maid or male escort, the Fisher Body girl accentuated her angular lines by indulging in self-dramatizing stances and gestures. See also Figures 4.10, 4.11, and 5.3.*

His first love

Mother—radiant and youthful, with the charm of that schoolgirl complexion. This simple daily rule is known to thousands:

KEEP THAT SCHOOLGIRL COMPLEXION

*6.12. Mothers looked "softer"
than the norm for modern women
and rarely indulged in dramatic
poses or gestures. They were
shorter, rounder, more likely to
appear in soft focus. Compare
Figs. 6.10, and 6.12 with Figs.
5.4, 5.14, 6.13, and 6.14.*

heroine of the Fisher Body ads was slender, youthful, and sophisticated. Her finely etched facial features formed a slightly aloof smile, suggesting demure self-confidence in her obvious social prestige and her understated sexual allure. Attired elegantly, but not exotically, she stood tall and angular, her fingers and toes tapering to sharp points. In her role as a model of the proper feminine look, she gained credit for attracting the attention of women as much as men (Fig. 6.11).[28]

In one direction, this modal image of modern woman shaded off into that of the housewife and mother. Her outlines were usually softer and slightly more rounded than the Fisher Body girl. Her posture was less self-consciously canted or accentuated, her neck and limbs slightly shorter (Fig. 6.12).[29] In the other direction, the divergence from the Fisher Body model moved more abruptly toward striking "high-fashion" extremes, until the "modern woman" approached the status of a geometric abstraction.

It was in the increasingly abstract portrayals of this "high-fashion" version of the American woman that advertising men effectively propagated their contention that the "beloved buying sex" must also be the most modern.[30] Men were sometimes depicted in modernistic illustrations. But never did advertising artists distort and reshape men's bodies as they did when they transformed women into Art Deco figurines. Women in the tableaux, as symbols of modernity, sometimes added more than a foot to their everyday heights and stretched their elongated

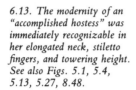

6.13. The modernity of an
"accomplished hostess" was
immediately recognizable in
her elongated neck, stiletto
fingers, and towering height.
See also Figs. 5.1, 5.4,
5.13, 5.27, 8.48.

eyes, fingers, legs, arms, and necks to grotesque proportions (Figs. 6.13, 6.14).
The proportions of some women in the tableaux suggested a height of over nine
feet. In deference to the geometric motifs of popularized modern art in the 1920s,
women's legs sometimes extended in cantilevers or absolutely straight lines from
thigh to toe. Their pointed feet and toes appeared to have emerged fresh from a
pencil sharpener. Foot-long fingers similarly tapered into icy stilettos. As for their
legs, one advertising writer observed that they were "just as long as the artist cares
to make them, and evidently he is paid by the running foot."[31]

Thus the woman of high fashion—and, by implication, all women of high
social status—appeared in advertising tableaux as physically distinct from the
woman of lower social position. By a Lamarckian process of natural selection, the
lady of high class had acquired an elongated neck to accentuate her pearl necklace
and her hat, and a body tall enough for the artistic drape of an evening dress. Her
sculpted head evoked images of Grecian culture and aristocratic poise; her brittle,
tapered appendages conformed to Thorstein Veblen's specifications for the look
of conspicuous leisure. So extreme were some of these distortions that a comparison of advertising drawings with contemporary advertising photographs is
often startling, even though the photographs themselves were often taken at

Maybe white is her lucky color. For here she is again in a white dress by Lucien Lelong. Again is precisely the word, since the first time this country saw her she wore a white dress by Lelong while singing her famous song "I Don't Know." And the dress too was named "I Don't Know," after the song she sang. She has played in "Candlelight," "The Battle of Paris," a talking picture, "Charlot's Revue," "The Treasure Girl" and "Oh, Kay!" This portrait especially painted by M. Reynaldo Luza, celebrated Parisian artist. Observe the Parisienne watch, vivid against the whiteness of the glove.

6.14. The "smartness" of actress Gertrude Lawrence, like that of the Oneida hostess (Fig. 6.13), was revealed in bodily proportions that suggested a height of at least eight feet.

6.15, 6.16. Despite the photographers' use of flattering angles, women in full-length photos utterly failed to live up to the ad artists' models of the modern woman. Compare Figs. 5.4, 6.13, 6.14, and 8.48.

extreme angles, in an effort to approximate the fashionable ideal. Even next to the moderately high-fashion drawings of the retail advertisements, women in the advertising photographs look squat, neckless, and beefy (Figs. 6.15, 6.16).[32]

What relationship did the modern woman of these illustrations bear to social realities? Certainly the physical resemblance was meager. Fashion economist Paul Nystrom estimated in 1928 that only 17 percent of all American women were both "slender" and over 5 feet 3 inches in height.[33] The emphasis on youth and slimness, however, did reinforce the notion of women's new freedom of physical activity; and like the cut of women's clothes, the stance of fashion models, and the postures of modern dance, it fostered the image of the woman in actual or impending motion—the woman on the move.[34] The tubular shapes and angular lines also suggested a rejection of the traditional motherly image. In fact, advertising tableaux that cast women in maternal roles with children usually modified the modern image appreciably, rounding out the figure, bringing the proportions back toward normal, and softening the lines (see Fig. 6.12). Perhaps significantly, mothers looked like women of more modest social status.

If extreme height and exaggerated "artistic" postures gave the modern woman of the ads a certain claim to elegance and prestige, still she gained stature mainly in comparison to other, non-fashionable women. In relation to men, as Erving Goffman has intriguingly suggested in *Gender Advertisements*, distortions of women's shapes and gestures often convey messages about social subordination. Women, Goffman argues, appear in poses that are more "canted," more exaggerated and grotesque, more off-balance and tentative than those assumed by men. These stances and gestures imply a sense of dependence on the man for stability

6.17, 6.18. No men appeared in advertising art in postures so grotesque or canted as did women. Only women could appear so unserious and purely decorative. See also Figs. 5.21, 6.6, and 6.33

and balance, a willingness to make oneself into an interesting "object," and a greater vulnerability to the caprices of a dominating emotionality (Figs. 6.17, 6.18).[35]

Particularly common in the illustrations of the 1920s and 1930s is the contrast, which Goffman noted in the 1960s, between the predominance of a solid, firmly planted stance for men and an unbalanced stance for women. Men in the tableaux usually balanced their weight on both feet. Women placed their weight on one foot while the other leg indulged in a "bashful knee bend" or complimented the supporting leg and foot by posing at an artistic angle (see Figs. 9.10, 10.3). If such off-balance and tentative stances implied, as Goffman argues, a status of dependence and a "foregoing of full effort" to prepare for assertive, self-reliant action, then illustrators of the 1920s and 1930s certainly exaggerated these qualities in depicting the modern woman.[36]

Advertising illustrations thus reinforced the tendency to interpret woman's modernity in a "fashion" sense and to define the status of "decorative object" as one of her natural and appropriate roles. Women took on the contours and angles of their modern art backdrops more decisively than men, suggesting their pliability in the service of art. In some tableaux, women with less distorted shapes and postures still functioned as decorations for the depicted room, as much as did the sculptured art objects or the curtains (see Fig. 5.23).[37] Even the distortions of body proportions, which elevated women of fashion and status to awesome heights of eight or nine feet, served more to accentuate their decorative potential than to suggest their commanding presence as new women of broader capacities and responsibilities.

Anticipations of Superwoman:
Finessing the Contradictions
of Modernity

The compulsion of advertising men to relegate women's modernity to the realm of consumption and dependence found expression not only in pictorial styles but also in tableaux that sought to link products with the social and political freedoms of the new woman. Expansive rhetoric that heralded women's march toward freedom and equality often concluded by proclaiming their victory only in the narrower realm of consumer freedoms. In "When Lovely Women Vote," an immaculately groomed modern woman, well-educated and active in civic affairs, gazed idealistically outward and upward in the pose more recently adopted for political candidates with "vision." However, the question on which she was asked to vote was "What toothpaste do you use?" (Fig. 6.19).[38] Cannon Mills recalled that since women had first exercised the vote for political candidates in 1920, "that year we decided to let them vote on towels too."[39] The frequent conflation of consumer and sociopolitical freedoms found provocative expression in a 1930 *Chicago Tribune* ad entitled "Feminine Values": "Today's woman gets what she wants. The vote. Slim sheaths of silk to replace voluminous petticoats. Glassware in sapphire blue or glowing amber. The right to a career. Soap to match her bathroom's color scheme."[40]

Although a devotion to matching soaps might seem trivial to some, women's responsibility for home decoration was linked with a much more significant issue. Whatever range of outside activities they might enjoy, women still bore full responsibility for maintaining the "saving atmosphere" of the home. In an age of rapid tempo and distracting amusements, women needed to respond to such centrifugal forces by making their homes adequate counter-attractions. Only by making her home a haven of beauty and cleanliness, and herself an energetic and alluring companion, could a wife shoulder that "burden of making a marriage successful [which] must always be chiefly on the woman."[41] Ads for products ranging from laxatives to varnishes agreed that "one person" alone was responsible for the family's happiness. No tableau ever portrayed a housewife enjoying golf, a club meeting, or even a frolic with the children at the *expense* of her homemaking responsibilities. Nor did any tableau exempt her from the responsibility of beautifying herself and her surroundings. Men, the tableaux reiterated, fell in love, and stayed in love, with the beauty-minded, and ultimately home-oriented, "womanly woman." "Watch that you don't disappoint him," they warned.[42]

Thus the chain of women's roles in the tableaux came full circle: from the "business modernism" of the efficient home manager to the personal modernity afforded by leisure time and outside activities, then to the fashion modernism of the decorative object, and finally back to the hearth as home-beautifier and anchor against the winds of modern distractions. A woman's enthusiasm for stylistic modernity revealed a proper instinct for beautification, but it also inspired suspicions about her helpless susceptibility to the whims of change. It was not a modernity that contributed to significant social and economic progress.

When lovely women vote

To thousands of women of this type—charming, educated, well-to-do, prominent in the social and civic life of her city, we put this question: What tooth paste do you use?

To our delight, the majority answered Listerine Tooth Paste. Certainly to women of means, the price of 25¢ could not possibly have been a factor in deciding upon a tooth paste. Obviously, the quality of the dentifrice itself and the brilliant results it accomplished were responsible for their choice.

Won't you try Listerine Tooth Paste? See how thoroughly it cleans. How swiftly it erases blemishes and discolorations. How gleaming white it leaves the teeth. How it refreshes the mouth and sweetens the breath. Bear in mind, incidentally, that it costs you but half of what you would ordinarily pay for tooth paste of equal quality. Lambert Pharmacal Co., St. Louis, Mo.

LISTERINE TOOTH PASTE the quality dentifrice at 25¢

6.19 Listerine blithely introduced the theme of woman suffrage only to flatter the majority of women on their choice of toothpastes. Consumption was the true realm for a modern woman's decision-making.

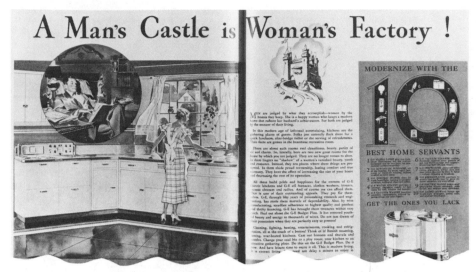

6.20 *An efficient housewife might create more leisure, but she could entertain wider aspirations only in defiance of authoritative warnings: "Men are judged by what they accomplish—women by the homes they keep."*

In tableaux with titles such as "Her home is still her castle . . . but it has a drawbridge now," advertisers celebrated a woman's new freedom of activities.[43] But the drawbridge also led back into a castle (sometimes called a woman's "factory" in other tableaux) in which she was to continue to play the roles of queen and castellan (Fig. 6.20). A truly modern woman would be so efficient as a "home manager and hostess" that she could blithely tee off at the fourteenth hole at four o'clock and still arrange a "dinner at seven for eight."[44] Sacrificing none of her former responsibilities as housewife, doting mother, and vision of loveliness, this modern superwoman would simultaneously display her talents as sportswoman, clubwoman, hostess, sophisticate, and home decorator. In advertising's fond reflection of "progressive" American ideology, she could attain every promise of the new while sacrificing nothing worthwhile of the old. Advertising men, it appeared, were not only apostles of modernity; more significantly, they were mediators who counseled women on how to adapt without cost to a consumption-oriented modernity that was appropriate for feminine instincts and capabilities.

The Businessman as Generic Man

In contrast to the women of the advertising tableaux, most of the other characters played less striking and less ambiguous roles. Men appeared almost as frequently as women, but often in nondescript, standardized parts as husbands or as businessmen at work. When the advertising message called for it, men appeared in a much larger variety of occupational roles than women—an accurate reflection of social realities. As doctors, dentists, or business executives, they might endorse

This worker scorned Safety Goggles—

"SAFETY Goggles, huh? Don't need 'em, Boss. Been working with bare eyes for ten years, and I blind yet!"

During 1924, in the State of Pennsylvania alone, 658 eyes were lost by factory workers. Under the Workmen's Compensation, eyes cost over $1,000,000.

6.21. Dave, the protagonist in this American Optical Company ad, was not even a foreman. But on his return home he became a consumer and, thus, presumptively middle class. No man in overalls and cap could be a consumer surrogate.

the product; as truckers, delivery men, house painters, or mechanics they joined the tableaux to demonstrate the product's manufacture or use. But working-class men never appeared as consumers; an unspoken law decreed that the protagonist (and consumer surrogate) in every ad must be depicted as middle class (Fig. 6.21). Not one motorist in a thousand, for instance, ever appeared in anything but a suit, tie, and hat or elite sporting togs.

When merchandising strategy did not call for a particular occupational function, the leading man, as Everyman, tended to conform to a single stereotype. Whenever his occupation was revealed, the man who played the role of husband was almost invariably identified as a businessman. Advertisers sought to flatter their male readers by opening the sales argument with "You are a business man." Remedies for nerves, fatigue, and constipation regularly attributed such ills to the "stress of business."[45] Among hundreds of thousands of advertisements in the 1920s and 1930s, I have yet to discover a single one in which the husband or the ambitious young man is defined as a factory worker, policeman, engineer, professor, architect, or government official, and I found only one in which he is a lawyer. Even doctors and dentists appeared only in their functional roles—not as typical husbands. As a *McCall's* advertisement put it, in an offhand manner that reflected the conventionality of this advertising stereotype: "The average man is just a business man."[46]

Within the role of businessman, some slight differentiations emerged. Older men were likely to be cast as business executives. Young men were often salesmen, aspiring to the popular intermediate step of sales manager on a stereotyped business ladder. When husbands telephoned their wives to expect a dinner guest, they always brought home either a "sales manager" or a "client." Whatever his level of achievement in business, advertising's Mr. Everyman always left home bound for "the office," never for the shop, the factory, the garage, the courthouse,

6.22. Telephones, ticker-tape, and leisured luncheons defined the quintessential man as urban business executive. Was that his wife in different outfits, or had she failed to keep pace as an evening companion? See Fig. 6.4.

or the store. Copywriter A. B. Carson's "John Smith—typical citizen" worked "humped over a desk in a skyscraper." Coming home or leaving, he invariably wore a business suit. In the evening, at dinner parties, bridge games, or in restaurants and nightclubs, he usually adopted formal attire. One tableau defined the class position of typical men by describing the spectrum of their possible activities in the phrase "wherever they may be, at their desks or on the golf course." Advertisements that chronicled "a day in the life of a businessman" typically portrayed him at his desk, taking a customer out to dine, perhaps reading the ticker tape, and escorting a woman out for the evening (Fig. 6.22). His office window, with its view of the tops of nearby skyscrapers, defined his employment as urban and his business affiliation as more likely a large corporation than a small retail concern. (See Figs. 8.6, 8.22.)[47]

In contrast to many women of the advertising tableaux, men rarely assumed decorative poses or exaggerated bodily proportions. Their hands exemplified the contrast between the functional grasp of the male and the ethereal gesture of the female. In the struggle of business, suggested by harsh, competitive grasps, the man had often lost "a bit of the sentiment that used to abide in his heart," several ads noted. He had been "shackled to his desk" and might even need to slacken his pace, get to know his wife and children again, and experience those softer sentiments preserved within the shelter of the home.[48] But only for a brief respite. The competitive world of business helped make him a true man, and advertisers occasionally worried that the attempt to pretty him up for the collar ads and the nightclub scenes would sissify and weaken man's image, tailoring it too much to feminine tastes.[49]

One collar manufacturer, seeking "to avoid the obvious danger of effeminacy" when women were introduced into collar ads, found a way to emphasize sexual differentiation by displaying the girl in color with many decorative accessories. She was looking at a man in a black-and-white photograph whose portrait, with its severe lines and matter-of-fact atmosphere, stood out in "virile contrast to the feminine charm of the girl and her colorful surroundings."[50] Edgeworth Smoking Tobacco even suggested that the growing number of women smokers had effeminized cigarettes; men should respond by turning to pipes. In a rare but strategically understandable display of pique at the recent advances of women, Edgeworth proclaimed: "A man looks like a man when he smokes a pipe."[51]

Men could dress conservatively, avoid distorted, modernistic poses, and return to traditional habits like pipe smoking because they did not have to *prove* themselves modern. All middle-class and upper-class men were businessmen, the tableaux implied. A businessman exemplified efficiency and control. If a woman's modernity was primarily decorative, a man's was primarily functional. In modeling the typical man on themselves, advertising men distorted the realities of occupational and class structures. By refusing to give men a distinct "look" as consumers, they preserved the assumption that dominant male instincts for production and functional modernity would counter any decadent tendencies of the consumption ethic.

Supporting Players

Of the supporting actors and actresses in the social tableaux, few were more stereotyped than the children. Two children invariably meant a boy and a girl, never two girls or two boys. Virtually never were children described or depicted in such a way as to suggest distinctly individual personalities. Except when the selling message specifically dictated otherwise, children were healthy, fastidiously groomed and attired, and impeccable in behavior. Magazines of the 1920s often conveyed "an image of youth out of control."[52] Not so the advertising tableaux. Except on the few occasions when children or young people were called upon to influence the family's buying decisions through pleading or protest, they happily deferred to parental authority.

The elderly found their leading roles largely limited to ads for life insurance and grave-vaults; occasionally they gained "sit-in" parts as grandparents. Older men enjoyed a little greater latitude, since a silver-haired man could still find occasional work as a business executive, doctor, or experienced craftsman. Women whose hair had whitened found parts only as widows or grannies. Nothing so uniformly characterized the tableau roles of the elderly as a seemingly compulsory seated position. An observer from another century might well conclude, from studying advertisements alone, that men and women of the 1920s and 1930s lost the power of locomotion and upright stance after the age of fifty-five. Grandmothers sometimes still did handwork and both grandmothers and grandfathers held young children or read to them. Grandmothers bestirred themselves once or twice a year to put holiday turkey in the oven, but aside from that, most of them apparently did little more than daydream about the past (Fig. 6.23). As if to confirm their distance from modernity, the elderly never appeared in explicitly urban settings.[53]

If American films of the era, as Martha Wolfenstein has argued, placed their spotlight entirely on the younger generation and emphasized the discontinuity between present and past, advertising did so even more emphatically.[54] The elderly were not model consumers. Their needs and desires were less pressing than those of the younger generation and their ideas and habits were out-of-date. Usually, and perhaps mercifully, advertisers either removed them from sight or allowed them to sit quietly by the fire, rather than parading them on center stage as horrible examples. It would be easy to interpret a neglect of the older generation, and the prevalence of families with only one or two children, as an accurate reflection of certain social realities of the age: certainly nuclear families increasingly lived apart from grandparents, and the middle and upper classes adopted the ideal of the small family and practiced contraception.[55] But we must remember that the tactical considerations of advertising played as large a role as social realities in shaping such illustrations.

Children or the elderly usually gained parts in the tableaux for the limited purpose of conveying a single visual message—such as "family" or "child" or "extended family." Children appeared frequently, but in numbers no greater than needed to convey the required message. Only rarely did a family with more than two children appear, even in ads by newspapers and magazines that stressed the buying power of their subscriber families. Nor was the three-generation family called upon to convey an image of family buying power. Part of the reason stemmed from a law of artistic economy: don't clutter the picture with several figures when one child will adequately say "family" to the audience, and when a boy and a girl with parents will symbolize the whole universe of possible nuclear-family roles. A desire to focus the viewer's attention could lead to the decision to employ only a single child. Then, with the eyes of both mother and father turned solicitously toward the child, readers would be induced to look where the parents looked. (See Figs. 7.11, 8.15.) Such a focus of attention also carried the side effect of emphasizing the child's right to the parents' attentive concern.[56]

The other reason for limiting the number of children and the appearances of grandparents was more attuned to social realities—or at least to the real attitudes of advertisers. To the upper-middle class, with its ideal of the smaller and more "democratic" family, a picture of a family with three or more children might suggest an absence of middle-class status. And the presence of three generations—except in the formulaic holiday dinner scene—might indicate an overcrowded and less affluent household. Social tableau families were the idealized families of artistic economy and social aspiration. Grandparents were removed from sight and mind and a favored child or two might receive doting attention.

Ethnic and racial minorities found virtually no employment in the advertisements of the 1920s and 1930s. The names and facial features of the central and supporting figures in the tableaux never suggested Southern or Eastern European origins. The names given to "typical" families or other leading figures tended heavily toward such standards as Brown, Anderson, Smith, Morton, and Jones. (Among these fictional names, the most suggestive of ethnic diversity I have encountered were Dougherty and Joyner.) Two rare tableaux allowed Italian men

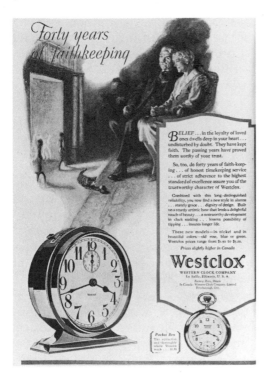

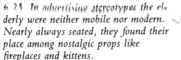

6.23. In advertising stereotypes the elderly were neither mobile nor modern. Nearly always seated, they found their place among nostalgic props like fireplaces and kittens.

6.24. Blacks and other racial minorities occasionally gained servile supporting roles, but they never appeared as consumers.

to speak broken English.[57] Asians found no role whatsoever in the ads; one "Mexican" washerwoman and an Eskimo washlady made single appearances as archaic foils for modern washing methods in a Procter and Gamble series. American Indians played their stereotyped roles in historical scenes, but they never appeared as contemporary figures. Categorically, ethnic and racial minorities failed to qualify as modern. Nor did crowd scenes depict racial and ethnic diversity, as they frequently do today. To immigrants, the message of advertising was implicit: only by complete fusion into the melting pot did one gain a place in the idealized American society of the advertising pages.[58]

For blacks, the available roles in advertising, outside of those in the black press itself, were severely limited in scope as well as number. Finding little reason to use caricatures of blacks for humor, as other forms of popular culture did, advertisements largely confined them to roles as contented porters, janitors, washwomen, and houseboys (Fig. 6.24). A few black trademark figures, such as Aunt Jemima and Rastus, the Cream of Wheat cook, at least managed to preserve a measure of humble dignity. Blacks never appeared as consumers, or as fellow workers with whites, or as skilled workers.[59] Primarily, they functioned as symbols of the capacity of the leading lady and leading man to command a variety of personal services. Certainly the tableaux distorted the diversity of functional roles that blacks played in the society and the extent of their satisfaction in servile positions, but the occasional presence of blacks did offer one perspective on the spectrum of social classes in that era. Perhaps if we turn from the predominantly stereotyped individual roles of the advertising tableaux to their broader delineations of classes and class relationships, we will find images more reflective of reality in advertising's "mirror."

Social Class in Advertising Tableaux

In *People of Plenty,* when David Potter defined advertising as the characteristic institution of an affluent society, he also suggested indirectly the affinities between advertising and a society of high social mobility and insecure social status.[60] Expectations of mobility create the necessary openness to change; insecurities suggest an avenue of advertising appeal. It was particularly in a society of shifting relationships, without a fixed social hierarchy or authoritative standards, that products most readily served as an index of status.

Judging by the social tableaux of the 1920s and 1930s, advertisers had evidently concluded that American consumers hungered for an authentic, certified social aristocracy against which they might measure their own gains in status. For women, who constituted the huge bulk of consumers, the pursuit of modernity offered fulfillment only if it brought secure social status in reasonable proximity to an authentic social aristocracy. The tableaux steadily promised such fulfillment in scenes of ornate hotel ballrooms, exclusive restaurants and cabarets, and country club verandas like the one presented in the Canada Dry Ginger Ale tableau described at the beginning of this chapter.

These tableaux, and many others of less pretentious social scenes, disclose a society that saw differences of social class more distinctly than we do now—and a society that often spoke frankly about them. Frankness, of course, is not a salient quality of advertisements in situations where the advertising writer or art director has any reason to suspect that it will provoke even the slightest negative reaction. But advertisers in the 1920s and 1930s apparently had no qualms about flaunting the image of an opulent, exclusive, and clearly defined elite class before their audience. According to the tableaux, "society", in the narrow, elitist sense of the word, deserved popular veneration. Illustrations pictured an American social aristocracy; advertising texts unflinchingly labeled it as "high society." Although illustrations of mansions, liveried chauffeurs, and polo matches would seem to have been sufficient to create the desired impression, copywriters sometimes bluntly underlined the point by referring explicitly to "the rich" and "the wealthy." In the depths of the depression, staff members of one advertising agency voted a preference for advertising copy for a baking powder that claimed the patronage of 36 out of 39 "millionaires in one square mile" over copy that simply implied the same thing by referring to homes in "the finest residential section of Brookline."[61]

The "society" of the wealthy, moreover, was an organized society. As revealed in advertisements, it had distinct boundaries and standards of admission. People who were "in society" could be confidently labeled as such; others could be

6.25. When the wealthy exhibited such grandeur in living and such exquisite taste in modern products, Freed-Eisemann concluded, they should be
proudly acknowledged as an "aristocracy." See also Fig. 9.3.

described as seeking to "break in." For their own tactical purposes, advertisers
simultaneously stressed both the clarity of such boundaries and the ease of crossing them—the first to enhance the exclusiveness and desirability of the life of the
rich, and the second to suggest how easily the advertised product would eliminate
barriers to upward mobility.

The ads that depicted America's wealthy elite never carried the least implication
of satire. Nor did they suggest that the rich held any power—except, of course,
the power to shape the esthetics of the society. "The rich" and "the fashionable,"
explicitly so labeled, strutted through the advertising tableaux as though ex-
pecting bedazzled deference from the audience.[62] Since no formal aristocracy
existed in America, advertisers felt impelled to certify the rich as having gained
that status. The Packard Motor Company and Freed-Eisemann Radio specifically
designated their patrons as "America's Aristocracy" (Fig. 6.25). The Willys-
Knight Motor Car Company counted among the admirers of its new "Great Six"
the "world's elect," which included "those who by birthright move in America's
most select social orbits."[63]

In their campaigns to establish a socially authoritative American aristocracy,
advertising men freely drew upon the aid of European kings, queens, dukes, and
duchesses. If traditional American patriotism had prescribed a self-respecting,
republican contempt for decadent European aristocrats, advertisers nevertheless
sensed a powerful and insufficiently repressed American undercurrent of veneration for a titled nobility. Oneida silverware claimed a baronness, a princess, and
a duchess as patrons. Pond's Cold Cream combed Europe for testimonials from
titled ladies. Queen Marie of Romania replenished the royal coffers from her
many appearances on American advertising pages. When Fleischmann's Yeast and

Palmolive Soap sought expert testimony in Europe they chose an ample number of doctors and beauty advisors who were "graced by royal patronage."[64]

Although endorsements by prominent American socialites drew gratifying responses in advertising coupon tests, the public seemed to prefer authenticated nobility. A study of the "pulling power" exerted by the various endorsers in Pond's Cold Cream ads in 1925 showed that European royalty and nobility held three of the top four positions, with Princess Marie de Bourbon well on top. Another study four years later revealed a commanding lead for the Duchesse de Richelieu, with Mrs. Reginald Vanderbilt narrowly edging out the overworked Marie, Queen of Romania, for second place. Given this bias for titled Europeans, advertisements regularly cast the mantle of aristocracy over rich American social-ites by gossiping about their social intimacy with European nobility.[65]

Yet few European duchesses or aristocratic American socialites dared appear before the consumer audience merely as grande dames in static, courtly tableaux. Despite their fastidious demeanor, they were also horsewomen, golfers, and tireless travelers, living activity-filled lives, fully in pace with the tempo of the age. The "gay round" of one "charming cosmopolitan," the audience learned, included "Newport for the brilliant summer season . . . a whirl of early autumn festivities in New York, then on to Melton Mowbray, England, for the fox hunting, winter in Italy or Egypt . . . spring in Paris."[66] Thus the dignity of inherited social eminence was fused with expertise on the up-to-date and fash-ionable. Moreover, any taint of decadence that might have been attached to unproductive, pleasure-seeking women of wealth and title was deflected by the strenuous activity they undertook. In seeming anticipation of the "fun morality" that Martha Wolfenstein discerned in American popular culture in the late 1940s, copywriters made their duchesses and debutantes work extremely hard at keeping up with the hectic pace of high society. Perhaps advertisers felt more comfortable glorifying these prototypes of a triumphant consumption ethic when so much "hard work" was involved.[67]

Having conferred upon America's wealthy the qualities of aristocratic stature and a sensitivity to the pace of modern life, advertisers then added a few finishing touches before setting them before the public as models and advisers. The wealth these people enjoyed, the advertisements pointed out, enabled them to choose products without regard to price; their social lineage gave them an "instinctive" sense of taste. Their fastidiousness and discrimination made them the "best people" in every conceivable sense. Thus the aristocratic rich were always the first to recognize products of quality; news of their choices gradually trickled down to influence the consumer masses. Advertisers found no reason to imagine that this picture of a superior social elite as supremely "in the know" might provoke skepticism or resentment in the broad consumer audience.

The word "fastidious" in an advertisement was always the highest compliment; it never suggested an irreverent snicker, as it might today. The fastidious ones were "people who know their way about in the world," people "with whom excellence in all their material possessions is a fetish." Canada Dry never doubted that "our best people" had the discrimination to select the best ginger ale. Camel cigarettes assured readers that "those who live well" easily recognized those "subtle differences in flavor . . . lost on some people." Kotex bluntly and repeti-

6.26, 6.27. These ads appeared not in Vogue *but in* True Story, *where working-class readers, these advertisers concluded, preferred glimpses of the rich to reflections of their own lives.*

tinusly told readers both in upper-class women's magazines and in *True Story* that "women in the better walks of life" or "better class women" had overwhelmingly adopted Kotex. (See Fig. 1.11.) So blithely did they assume that all new products of any quality must gain acceptance by the general public through the example of their social betters, that advertising writers greeted the success of vivid colors in Cutex nail polish as a surprising new phenomenon—a product that had actually moved up in social acceptance from below.[68]

The use of high-class social tableaux and high-society social models did not always follow the pattern of indulging the prospective consumer in a fantasy of merely moving "one step up" through acquisition of the advertised product. Sometimes the social fantasy assumed Cinderella proportions. Tableaux of rarefied high society and European aristocracy appeared almost as frequently in *True Story* or *Photoplay* as they did in *Ladies' Home Journal* or *McCall's*. Through *True Story* advertisements, young, working-class "Judy O'Gradys," as *True Story* often described its readers, learned how Lady Buchanan Jardine led "the gay whirl of smart young English society at balls and dances, famous race meetings, hunting and house parties" and how Mrs. Cornelius Vanderbilt, Jr., "modern to her finger tips" and "ever on the wing," remained "entrancingly beautiful as this romantic world would wish her to be." Listerine Tooth Paste spoke frankly to *True Story* readers of "the dentifrice of the rich," and Camels depicted those discerning Camel smokers who were "to the manner born" (Figs. 6.26, 6.27).[69]

Young working girls, advertisers calculated, savored social tableaux of high society just as much as those in the upper-middle class who might more realistically aspire to live the aristocratic life. "The average life is drab," observed a president of the American Association of Advertising Agencies. The average family needed alluring dreams to compensate for its low income. Cecil B. De-Mille had already demonstrated the popularity of opulent movie scenes that provided modest housewives and working-class girls a glimpse of the life of the rich. Although agency people were indifferent to many such movies, an art director argued, they should take a lesson from Hollywood and give this matinee audience the same opportunity to participate vicariously in a life of fashionable luxury through advertisements.[70]

Were these social tableaux, though unrepresentative of American society as a whole, at least accurate depictions of the nation's wealthiest families or faithful mirrors of the social fantasies of the public? Idealized though these scenes were, they did reflect a wider tendency of the media of the age to portray the wealthy, in Frank Fox's phrase, "as a separate genus of man."[71] The "smart set" was still a highly visible and relatively cohesive group. Whether or not the pre-1929 rich truly "glittered as they walked," as Caroline Bird later recalled, advertising writers and artists strongly encouraged American consumers to think of them that way. Advertising not only reflected but exaggerated and embellished the steeper social pyramid of the late 1920s.[72]

Still, while the social tableaux of the aristocratic rich undoubtedly provided satisfying social fantasies for the wider consumer audience, the particular needs and biases of the ad creators shaped that fantasy in ways that may not have reflected accurately even the "realities" of the public's fantasy life. Distinctly absent from these tableaux were displays of the more vulgar tastes of some of the nouveau riche or any suggestion of those naughty escapades of the rich that so attracted tabloid readers. The need to protect the reputation of the product and confirm the reasonableness of its price ensured that advertisers would place it in the company of only the most discriminating among the rich. One suspects that this made the aristocrats of the advertisements more fastidious than their "real life" counterparts. It also may have made them less extravagant and sensual in their tastes than they would have appeared in social fantasies of the public's own making.

Social tableau advertisements thus emphasized the importance of class distinctions and provided a flattering and conservative portrait of the lives of a "natural aristocracy" composed of the very rich. But what did they reveal of the larger class structure? Some tableaux suggested the extent of the class spectrum, although from a rather foreshortened viewpoint. Advertisers tended to make only gross distinctions below a level roughly constituting the upper-middle class.[73] One scheme of stratification identified the aristocratic rich with butlers and man-servants, the affluent or upper-middle class with maids, dinner parties, and tuxedos and evening dresses; the middle class with a white collar, home-loving existence—with, perhaps, a single maid—and the remainder of society as working class. Only those of the middle class and above ever appeared in the tableaux as consumers. Illustrators and copywriters frequently defined this spectrum of significant social classes through a mansion-bungalow comparison. The initial term of this comparison—the mansion—suggested that the contrast would span the universe of possible social stations. By implication, then, the cozy bungalow or "cottage" constituted the society's opposite pole of possible living standards.

From hundreds of coffees, a few were chosen and mingled

6.28, 6.29. Ad artists found frequent use for scenes of eager service to the wealthy. The chauffeur in a Maxwell House Coffee tableau doubled as a butler to make a proper picnic possible while a clerk in the illustration for a store equipment ad assumed a deferential posture.

The inhabitants of these far-from-tiny bungalows were inevitably a young middle-class couple. The husband, like all tableau figures with ambitions of mobility, was invariably depicted as *already* middle class in clothing, occupation, and social setting.[74]

The working class appeared in advertising tableaux only in supporting, functional roles such as garage mechanic, house painter, truck driver, store clerk, or household servant. Some of these supporting players—delivery boys, tailors, maids, and scrupulously attentive sales clerks—remind us of the reality of the far greater amenities of deferential personal service that were then available to those of the middle class and above.[75] Working-class people, including the emerging white-collar class of clerks and office employees, were never shown off the job in home situations or enjoying recreational pleasures. The task of depicting a home scene of a working-class family would have severely challenged the illustrators' capacities for social imagination. There is no evidence that they found occasion to attempt it.

Although the advertising tableaux of the 1920s and 1930s spoke far more explicitly than their present-day counterparts about class position and frequently depicted characters who wore unmistakable badges of their exact class status, they never suggested that wide discrepancies in position should breed class resentment. On the contrary, the very tableaux that most vividly depicted the extent of the class spectrum often used the contrasts not to separate but to unite. Chauffeurs, maids, grocers, and department store clerks happily and deferentially served their exquisitely dressed patrons (Figs. 6.28, 6.29). The ad creators sufficiently shared the class prerogatives of the upper and upper-middle classes to wish to believe that those who provided menial services to their betters did so fondly and thankfully.

If advertisements, as Jib Fowles argues, serve as the clearest indicators of a society's unfulfilled needs, then prominent among those needs in the 1920s and 1930s was the need for a sense of confidence in having secured a hold on a clearly demarcated place in the social hierarchy.[76] Ads did not necessarily promise consumers a position in the highest echelons. The tableaux often assumed that members of the consumer audience would continue to admire the upper crust of high society from afar. But advertisers offered viewers who used the product the prospect of a secure foothold on *some* elevated rung of the social ladder.

The attainment of such a status, moreover, was clearly a palpable pleasure. Recent advertisements often celebrate pleasures of comradeship, sexuality, or gastronomy by showing people enjoying them either entirely independent of any particular class setting or in a variety of class settings. In contrast, the tableaux of the 1920s and early 1930s associated all other pleasures with an explicit "class" setting. Although ads portrayed people having fun at restaurants, ballrooms, nightclubs, and dinner parties, the major satisfaction they conveyed was that of *simply being there,* securely installed in the proper class setting, among the proper people, and appropriately defined as "belonging" by their attire. Advertisers assumed that their audience craved vicarious participation in displays of class standing and that it gladly imbibed the frank portrayals and discussions of the class hierarchy that were necessary to define the setting of the tableaux. Modernity in the realm of consumption, the wanton pursuit of style, did not afford complete gratification; some ultimate reward was required. The ads confidently addressed an audience willing to believe that class position itself constituted the supreme pleasure. All other pleasures contributed to it or flowed from it. The "good life" in these tableaux was a life lived in evening clothes (Fig. 6.30).

Modern Maids and
Atavistic Ambitions

Visual confirmation of a secure, elevated social status often called for the inclusion of a final supporting player in the social tableau—the modern maid. Ballrooms and polo fields provided a setting and required an attire that immediately conveyed the class atmosphere of a tableau. A maid provided the same visual index of class in a domestic scene. Although they served mainly as props and rarely gained speaking parts, these maids deserve our attention. Their prevalence in the advertising tableaux of the 1920s and early 1930s, and their particular physical characteristics, dramatically illustrate both the extreme distortions of reality sometimes reflected by advertising's "mirror" and certain larger truths about the society's cultural dilemmas.

If advertisers, as apostles of modernity, wanted to acquaint American society with the logical outcome of the process of industrial modernization, they should have emphasized the leveling of the hierarchy of classes and the fading of visible class distinctions. They should have reflected the tendency for people to find their identity more in occupational groups than in explicit distinctions of social class.

The
HAWK — the newest after-dark
ARROW—and the first dress shirt ever
Arrow-Sanforized-Shrunk - guaranteed
for permanent fit. The bosom is smartly
tapered for wear with the fashionable
high-rise trousers. The fabric is a beautiful French pique. *The* HAWK—with its
new bosom-shape and its opening-at-
the-back—is easily the smartest and most
comfortable dress shirt ARROW ever
made. Three dollars and fifty cents. (The
correct new Arrow Wing Collar is HAIG.)

CLUETT, PEABODY & CO., INC., TROY, N. Y.

ARROW SHIRTS

6.30. *The American dream meant belonging to the right class. To live the
dream was to spend one's life in evening clothes. See also Figs. 4.10,
10.3.*

They should have explained that "exclusiveness" through external display was necessarily declining with the advance of mass production and mass consumption. And they should have accurately recorded a decline in personal servants.[77] But they sensed that their audience was not eager to listen to such blunt messages. If Americans were not yet prepared to relinquish the vision of a highly visible and elegantly enthroned social aristocracy, even as the price for a presumed democratization of society, advertising men were willing to indulge them in nostalgic social fantasies. Again, advertising leaders acted more as mediators than as apostles of modernity, providing the audience with fantasies that would buffer their adaptation to modern realities.

The "modern maid" of the advertising tableaux epitomized the adaptive social fantasy in its nostalgic or atavistic form. One might have expected that the high demand for maids as a means of establishing a "class" atmosphere would have provided employment in the tableaux for many black and immigrant women. But such was not the case. In defiance of the realities of the American domestic working force, advertisers insisted upon the image of the "French maid" as the standard for social respectability. In *Selling Mrs. Consumer*, Christine Frederick conjured up images of domestic maids with such names as "Bridget, Maggie, Hulda, or Annushka," but the poise, demeanor, and facial characteristics of most advertising maids hardly suggested recent immigrant stock.[78] A few black women did make an appearance as maids or cleaning ladies, but they were outnumbered more than ten to one by young white women in immaculate caps and aprons. White maids older than thirty-five or with physiognomies distinctly different from that of the lady of the house were even scarcer than blacks.

Again and again, in advertisement after advertisement, the maid was young, poised, and slender. She possessed finely chiseled facial features and a smartly modern hairdo. Except for her dress, she was indistinguishable from the leading lady. Even in photographed tableaux, the models who posed as lady of the house and as the personal maid could have been interchanged (Figs. 6.31, 6.32). Of 186 advertising illustrations of maids I have recorded, 158 show maids who are young, white, slender, and have facial features very similar to those of the leading ladies, occasionally differing from them only in looking slightly younger or having a different hair color. In 13 instances the maids are somewhat dissimilar to the smart young leading lady, but are still young, white, and slender. In only 15 cases is the maid black, plump, or noticeably older than the mistress.[79]

Such a phenomenon cannot be explained by any theory of advertisements as direct reflections of social realities. Most female domestic workers in the United States in the 1920s and 1930s were not young "French maids." In fact, most were blacks or recent immigrants. According to the 1930 census, 18 percent of the women listed under "other domestic and personal service" were foreign-born and 39 percent were black. By 1940 the percentage of blacks among female domestic servants would surpass 46 percent. Nor were the majority of actual maids young women in their early twenties, as the ads seemed to suggest. In 1930, 39 percent of female domestic servants were over thirty-five years of age. By 1940, those over thirty-five had increased to 47.8 percent.[80] The likelihood of an urban upper-

6.31, 6.32. Advertising's maids lost some of their youth and poise in photographs (compare Figs. 5.1, 6.11, and 6.33), but they still looked like their mistresses, not like real maids of the era—who were usually immigrant, black, or older.

middle-class family securing a maid who met all of the typical tableau specifications—slim, white, between twenty and thirty years old, and possessed of finely etched facial features—was slender indeed.

The persistent presence of maids in the advertising tableaux, moreover, contradicted broad social trends. The ratio of domestic servants to households had fallen sharply in the United States in the decade before 1920. In that year, according to figures cited by David Katzman for five Northern cities, female servants ranged from 35 to 79 per 1,000 families. Markedly lower ratios characterized rural areas. Although the number of female servants took an upturn in the 1920s, it had slumped again by 1940. Never after 1920 did female domestic servants exceed a national ratio of 67 per 1,000 households. Meanwhile, wages for domestic help increased in the 1920s. As a writer summarized the "servant problem" for the *Saturday Evening Post* in 1926, "only the very wealthy can afford the luxury of being insulted by high-priced domestics."[81]

Advertisers perceived that the public found fantasy fulfillment in visions of stylish maids, especially when they connoted both modernity and willing subordination. Upper-middle-class families were facing a complex "servant problem" to which the producers of household appliances were offering only a partial solution. Some of these families now did without full-time, live-in servants because of the shortage of cheap household labor and the acquisition of labor-saving products. They sought to get by with the once- or twice-a-week black washerwoman or immigrant cleaning lady.[82] But the absence of a maid provoked

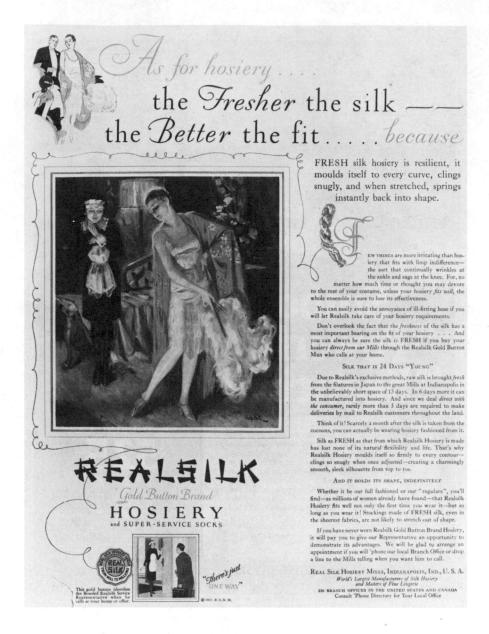

6.33. *What could feed fantasies of class harmony and personal status more powerfully than an attentive, worshipful maid whose "at-your-service" stance complemented her mistress's dramatic pose? See also Figs. 5.1. and 6.11.*

fears of social inferiority. Through coupon tests, the J. Walter Thompson agency discovered that the most effective headlines for Lux dishwashing soap were "Do Women with Maids Have Lovelier Hands?" and "Need Your Hands Say 'I Have No Maid'?"[83] Consumers liked to think of themselves as entering that social class whose status was still symbolized, as a result of a kind of cultural-pictorial lag, by the visible presence of idealized, prestige-enhancing maids.

Even those who still retained domestic servants did not appreciate being reminded by the advertising pages of their problems with uncongenial, hard-to-manage, and less-than-exquisitely presentable household help. The tension-filled relationship of mistress and maid continued to be, in David Katzman's phrase, "an arena of intense cultural, racial, religious, and class conflict."[84] In short, this was an era in which the satisfactions of being attended by a maid were likely to be far greater in vicarious experience than in the reality. If the advertising tableau was going to depict a maid, there was ample reason not to stir the ill-humor of the reader by reminding her of such unpleasant realities as her dependence on ethnic minorities and blacks or on unstylish and hard-to-manage older women for domestic help. Instead, a parade of smart, efficient, and subservient young French maids might provide welcome psychological relief from the irritations and indignities of the "servant problem."

But the smart young maid, despite her passive role as a dehumanized stage prop, did more. Her modern, often glamorous, beauty added a Veblenesque increment to the image of conspicuous leisure in "class" advertisements. Her streamlined figure complemented the modern artifacts surrounding the leading lady of the tableau in an ensemble effect that would have been disrupted by the authentic depiction of a typical real maid of the era. The French maid's usual roles as dutiful, conscientious servant and ego-enhancing personal attendant offered readers a chance to retain in fantasy something that appliances-as-servants could not provide—the psychological pleasures of solicitous personal attention from an obvious subordinate (Fig. 6.33).[85]

Thus the advertising tableaux, despite their distortions of reality, did sometimes explore basic social dilemmas of the era. Modernization, in the form of mass production, improved standards of living; new leisure-creating technologies seemed to promise an opportunity to rise in society. But middle-class and upper-middle-class families were likely to find those promises a bit hollow unless that rise could be certified by visible signs of social arrival (such as a French maid). The ultimate reward they sought for modernity in style was ascension into a secure, exclusive level of society, enriched and made visible by dominion over attractive and attentive personal servants. Then they would be presumed tasteful and modern by instinct and birthright.

Logically, apostles of modernity should have characterized maids and other visible signs of aristocratic exclusivity as passé. Nothing in the theory of modernization suggested that women should look to Princess Marie de Bourbon, or even Mrs. Reginald Vanderbilt, for authoritative guidance. But if consumers wanted to believe that exclusiveness was still fully compatible with an age of mass-produced goods, advertising leaders were not prepared to undermine such expectations. On the contrary, they began to find a larger social function in accommodating their advertising strategies to any wistful fantasies and illogical faiths that would ease the continuing transition to modern society.

THE GREAT PARABLES

There were two mothers, and each had a sickly young son. The first mother summoned her son and said: "Thou art spindly and underweight. Verily, I fear for thy health. Here, take and eat these nutritious vegetables." But the boy sulked and put them aside with harsh words. And his mother said: "Trouble me not. Except as ye eat these bitter viands, which I have prepared for thine own good, ye shalt have no desserts nor any other good thing." The mother continued to coax and threaten, but the boy ate not the vegetables and he waxed exceedingly cranky. But the mother relented not, for she feared for his character.

The second mother observed this and she said to herself, "Verily, I will seek a better way." And she arose and went to the wise elders. As she drew near, the elders cried, "Behold, take and try this new substance which is named 'soup.' Receive it with gladness, for in it are nutritious vegetables, disguised and hidden among mystic letters and other curious things." And she said to her son, "Do not fret, for the eating of this soup shall be fun, and for each bowl thereof thou shalt receive a gold star. And when thy chart overfloweth with stars, thou shalt arise and enter the great club and the elders will reveal unto you the secret handshake." And it came to pass that the boy waxed exceedingly robust and strong.

The first mother thought to condemn her child, for he was puny beside the other, he brought home ill news from school, and he desecrated the dinner hour with loud complaining. But the second mother chastised her, saying, "Blame not the child. Thou hast led him in the harsh olden ways, but at a cost that is not meet. Behold the new way which I have shown thee. My child partakes of what is best for the sake of fun, and there is no bitter cost. Fail no more. Go and do likewise."

Thus, had it been translated into biblical prose, might have read one of the great parables of American advertising in the late 1920s—the parable of the Captivated Child. Didactic advertising tableaux may be called "parables" not because they conform to prevailing definitions of Jewish, New Testament, or secular parables in every respect, but because they attempt to draw practical moral lessons from the incidents of everyday life. Like the parables of Jesus, these advertising stories employed stark contrasts and exaggeration to dramatize a central message. And, like the parables of Jesus, they sought to provoke an immediate decision for action.[1]

Of course, we must not ignore the important respects in which advertising tableaux like that of the Captivated Child did not conform to the model of the biblical parables. The advertising parables offered comfortable rather than distasteful truths. They usually sought to persuade more through insinuation than confrontation, and they sought unthinking assent rather than active thought or new insight. They encouraged readers to assimilate the product into their present lives, not, as Sallie TeSelle writes of the biblical parables, to tear apart the "secure, familiar everydayness of their lives" in order to force them to a decision to live "by a different logic."[2] The individual advertiser sought no such reorientation to a new "moral logic." The usual extent of his message was "same logic, plus new product." Whereas the biblical parables have aptly been characterized as encounters with our sense of the limitations of reality, the parables of advertising promised readers no insurmountable limitations and offered a reality easily within the reach of their hearts' desires. In short, advertising parables bore much the same relationship to biblical parables as melodrama has traditionally been understood to bear to high art or tragedy.[3]

Advertisers found themselves attracted to this form, which we might now characterize more strictly as the "melodramatic parable," for practical reasons. As a story without an identifiable author, often presented in such a manner as to suggest either distilled folk wisdom or suprahuman insight, the parable served to divert attention away from the advertiser as interested "seller" and toward the ad's message. Moreover, it was well adapted to the task of luring readers into active involvement.[4] The parable, as one theologian notes, was "ordered in such a way as to get in gear with the hearer, engage him in the movement of the story, and release him at the end back into his own situation in such a way that the parable happens to the situation."[5]

That was just the kind of inducement to action that advertisers wanted. The parable invited the use of vivid, radical comparisons that would arrest attention. And the exaggerations and hyperbole of the biblical parables, which induced hearers to momentarily suspend disbelief for the sake of a dramatic presentation of the central moral point of the story, found a resonance in the melodramatic parables of advertising. Advertisers, too, wished to employ poetic license in conveying a lesson about the perfection or indispensability of the product. In adopting a form like that of the biblical parables, they often asked their audience to suspend incredulity as part of the "rules of the game" of parable-telling. Joseph McFadyen portrays Jesus as implicitly asking his listeners to discount the dramatically useful exaggerations and dislocations of his parables by understanding each parable as though it began "It is as if." Advertisers found the parable form convenient in seeking the same "as if" suspension of skepticism from the audience.[6]

The parable flourished in American advertising in the late 1920s and early 1930s. Several advertising parables were so frequently repeated and so effectively reduced to formulas that their entire story could eventually be suggested by a phrase or two. These I have designated the "great parables" of the age. They did not directly invite interpretation on more than one level or challenge the audience to accept a new moral logic. Yet they did, in spite of their narrow, practical intent, incorporate some wider dimension of meaning. They reinforced (and even encouraged conversions to) a modern, secular "logic of living," as we shall see once we have examined them one by one.

The Parable of the First Impression

A flush of anticipation colored the cheeks of the beautiful young lady as her escort seated her at the elegant table. It was her first important dinner among the fashionables of the city's smart set. But as the butler served the first course, her thrilled excitement turned to terror. "From that row of gleaming silver on either side of her plate, which piece shall she pick up?" Suddenly she sensed, as a knowledgeable mother would have been able to advise, that her chance of being invited to such an affair again—in fact, her whole future popularity—would be determined by this crucial first impression of her "presence." As her social destiny hung in the balance, "She could feel every eye on her hesitating Hand."[7]

Even if she passed the test of "the Hesitating Hand," a young lady was certain to encounter many other fateful first-impression judgments. In "the Open Door" she and her husband faced the greatest social crisis of their five-year marriage: they had taken the bold step of inviting the vice-president in charge of sales and his wife to dinner. For days, the eager young wife planned the dinner menu. Her husband researched and rehearsed several topics for appropriate conversation. But both completely forgot about their tasteless front doorway, with its lack of beautifully designed woodwork. And neither realized how dreary and out-of-date was the furniture they had purchased soon after their marriage. Thus, all of their efforts at preparation came to naught, for their guests formed an indelible impression during "those few seconds" from "the touch of the bell" to their entrance into the living room. No feats of cooking or conversation could counteract that first impression of dowdy tastelessness and lack of modernity. It fatefully bespoke a deficiency in character and ambition. Twenty years later, with the husband still third-assistant for sales at the small branch office, they anxiously passed on to their children a hard-won bit of wisdom: "Your Future may rest on what the Open Door reveals."[8]

These re-enacted conflations of late 1920s "tragedy of manners" advertisements suggest the drama and pathos with which copywriters could recount the popular parable of the First Impression. According to such tableaux, first impressions brought immediate success or failure. Clearly, the scenarios were fantastical. Yet the parable of the First Impression, for all its exaggerated dramatics, drew much of its persuasive power from its grounding in readers' perceptions of contemporary realities. In a relatively mobile society, where business organizations loomed ever larger and people dealt far more often with strangers, many personal interactions were fleeting and unlikely to be repeated. In large organizations, hiring and promotion decisions now often seemed arbitrary and impersonal. No

Ever tried selling *yourself* to *YOU*?

Is yours a smile that would help . . . or hinder?

Favorable first impression is the greatest single factor in business or social success

For WHITER TEETH there's a way all men should know

RULES we apply, judging others, are nearly always applied by others, judging us.

's why it pays a man to check 'lt. freo' ana.

be. Correct daily brushing, *with the proper brush*, will polish teeth to amazing new whiteness.

For these reasons, millions use the mo² ¹r. West's to¹

You can see, in the small diagram near by, how these advantages give you whiter teeth, quickly.

All druggist² Toothbrus¹

Dr. West's ¹ ¹ ¹

7.1. *In the parables of the First Impression, such as this ad for Dr. West's toothbrushes, a smile or a smooth shave replaced old-fashioned character as the key to success. See also Figs. 7.3. and 8.22. For this parable with a woman as protagonist see Fig. 9.10.*

longer were they generally predictable on the basis of accumulated personal connections and past interactions. The reasons why one man gained a promotion or one woman suffered a social snub had become less explicable on grounds of long-standing favoritism or old family feuds. In the increasingly anonymous business and social relationships of the age, one might suspect that anything—including a first impression—had made the crucial difference.

Warren Susman and Daniel Rodgers suggest the context of popular ideas within which the parable of the First Impression found ample sustenance when they describe the new advice manuals of the early twentieth century. These manuals revealed a fundamental shift: from a nineteenth-century "culture of character," which stressed morality and work discipline as prerequisites for success, to a new "culture of personality," which emphasized the cultivation of one's ability to please others.[9] Paula Fass's study of the peer society of college students in the 1920s indicates a high potential susceptibility to the parable of the First Impression among these business-oriented youths. She notes their emphasis on "externals of appearance and the accessories of sociability," their "scrupulous attention to grooming," and their heavy reliance on instantly recognizable displays of status calculated to create a desired impression.[10] Like many others, they perceived that the rapid tempo of the age, and the larger scale and relative impersonality of business and social life, invited decisions based on anonymous judgments and quick impressions. One was never sure what minor and superficial considerations one's casual acquaintances might take into account.

Sensing its power in these circumstances, a variety of advertisers made use of the parable of the First Impression. Often they modified the basic formula of the tableau slightly to fit their particular product. Clothing manufacturers stressed overall appearance; gum, toothpaste, and toothbrush makers promised a "magic road to popularity in that first winning smile" (Fig. 7.1). Williams Shaving Cream recommended that powerful initial impact of "the face that's fit" for the "double-quick march of business." All agreed that "it's the 'look' of you by which you are judged most often."[11] One of the most important effects of preparing carefully for that crucial first impression, many of the ads suggested, was the sense of self-confidence it created. "The man who looks like business, meets *better* business more than half-way," assured Williams Shaving Cream. A lovely frock, washed in Lux, would enable any woman to overcome an inferiority complex and feel a "deep, sure, inner conviction of being charming," Dorothy Dix counseled readers of the *Ladies' Home Journal*. The House of Kuppenheimer confided to the up-and-coming young man that "someday your father may tell you how a certain famous letter 'k' in his inner coat pocket . . . put confidence in his heart . . . the confidence born of good appearance. And so helped him land his first job."[12]

The disastrous results of a similar case, in which the leading man had failed to prepare himself for a positive first impression, were graphically displayed by the Cleanliness Institute of the Association of American Soap and Glycerine Producers. In the tableau, a salesman sitting in front of the desk of a business executive glanced back nervously over his shoulder at a huge specter of himself posed with one hand to his face in an embarrassed, self-conscious gesture. As the executive's impression formed, the salesman realized why he was failing to "put it over" (Fig. 7.2).[13]

Capitalizing on an increasing public uncertainty that true ability and character would always win out in the scramble for success, advertising parables of the First Impression stressed the narrowness of the line that separated those who succeeded from those who failed. Many men possessed relatively equal abilities. The intensity and evenness of the competition gave great import to every detail of one's appearance. Far from deploring the apparent trend toward judging people on superficial externals, advertising tableaux often suggested that external appearance was the best index of underlying character. People were always—necessarily and appropriately—looking for quick clues to your taste and character. If they found these in the cut of your clothes, the brightness of your teeth, the age and taste of your furniture, your inept choice of silverware, or the closeness of your shave, they judged appropriately in a world of quick decisions. If your outer appearance, and that of your home, failed to reflect your true qualities of taste and character, you had no one to blame but yourself.

The power of the parable of the First Impression stemmed from the presumption that these impressions, any one of which might constitute a crucial victory or defeat, occurred constantly and almost instantaneously. Only because she was constantly prepared could the heroine of a Dr. West's toothbrush tableau pass "The Smile Test" during that moment when a handsome man picked her up from a fall off a speeding toboggan. "How often trivial incidents change the whole course of our existence," philosophized Dr. West. Such "great moments" allowed no opportunity for last-second preparations and no second chances. Like death or the "Second Coming," the impression that might determine one's opportunity for social acceptance, marriage, or a promotion might come at any time, in its terrible swiftness and finality, catching one unprepared for social salvation. "In the flicker of an eyelid," warned Camay soap, "a man—another woman—will appraise your looks." A "charming hostess" who failed to obtain stylish new furnishings would

He had to fight himself so hard...
he didn't put it over

YES, he was his own worst enemy. His appearance was against him and he knew it. Oh why had he neglected the bath that morning, the shave, the change of linen? Under the other fellow's gaze it was hard to forget that cheap feeling.

There's self-respect in soap and water. The clean-cut chap can look any man in the face and tell him the facts—for when you're clean, your appearance fights *for* you.

There's self-respect in SOAP & WATER

PUBLISHED BY THE ASSOCIATION OF AMERICAN SOAP AND GLYCERINE PRODUCERS, INC., TO AID THE WORK OF *CLEANLINESS INSTITUTE*

7.2. Advertising's parables often invited the negative or "scare" approach. Even in the age of Eugene O'Neill, advertising managed to surpass the theater in graphic materializations of the subconscious.

henceforth be condemned to "lonely afternoons, dreary evenings" for being un-prepared for acquaintances who "called once out of courtesy" but never came again.[14] One ardent suitor completely destroyed the good impression he had built up over months "when she noticed a hint of B.O." as he knelt to pop the question. There was no appeal from such judgments, no way to escape the constant surveil-lance. Throughout life, the Cleanliness Institute counseled, "Everywhere we go the people we meet are sizing us up. Very quickly they decide whether we are, or are not, from nice homes."[15]

As advertisers of home furnishings came to recognize the persuasive power of the parable of the First Impression, judgments about "niceness" pushed beyond the test of personal appearance, even beyond first impressions of entranceways and parlors, to include the entire home. Its external appearance and internal furnishings revealed the taste and character of the family within. Johns-Manville argued that roofing shingles bespoke "the taste and standing of the family," and Sherwin-Williams cautioned that "many a man has been rated as lacking in com-munity spirit . . . even as a business failure—merely because of a paint-starved house."[16] One cement manufacturer even challenged readers: "Would you will-ingly be judged by the looks of *your basement walls*?" Furniture manufacturers warned that since people used their homes "for social and business advancement . . . interesting, worthwhile people judge *you* by what your rooms reveal." Since the whole atmosphere of the home was "so clearly linked with the personality of its occupants," each room might well "betray owners laggard in ambition and insensitive to beauty, charm, and uplifting influence."[17]

Advertisers of bathroom furnishings and fixtures boldly applied the parable of the First Impression to the innermost recesses of the home. If every room told a story, then this most hidden and intimate of rooms would most clearly reveal family character. In "The Room You Do Not Show," discerning visitors would find a quick, authentic index to your standards and "your beliefs on how a civilized person should live." "Would you like to have visitors go into your bathroom and see the towels that are there all the time?" inquired Cannon Towels challengingly.[18] The Kohler company, manufacturer of bathroom fixtures, noted: "Quality tells—quality shown not so much by the coat you wear and the car you drive, the things the grocer's boy can see, but in the more intimate evidences of training and insight, in the vital corners of the home that give away your true philosophy of life. No room in the house is more expressive than the bath-room."[19] The C. F. Church Manufacturing Company narrowed the focus even further: "The bathroom, most of all, is a clue to the standards of the household and the most conspicuous thing in the bathroom is the toilet seat." Little wonder that the man in the Brunswick-Balke-Collender Company tableau, who had just learned of the impending visit of an influential business associate, thought first of the "old-fashioned wood toilet seat" as his mind's eye quickly scanned his house for social flaws.[20]

Such social tableau advertisements convinced economist Paul Nystrom that advertising was "necessarily the enemy of privacy."[21] "Critical eyes are sizing you up right now" was an integral element in the parable of the First Impression (Fig. 7.3). In advertising tableaux, friends, casual acquaintances, and strangers peered under people's rugs or inspected their handwriting for such signs of deficient

7.3. "Let your face reflect confidence—not worry! It's the 'look' of you by which you are judged most often," warned the text. Such judgments—by impersonal others—were always probing, critical.

character as might be revealed by a leaky pen. They retreated with disgust from bathrooms in which the "otherwise perfect appearance" had been spoiled by a "mussed towel" or a "slow-draining, gurgling lavatory."[22] Kohler headlined one advertisement with the inviting phrase "our neighbors are the nicest people." But a wary reader, well-schooled in the parable of the First Impression, might have quickly turned the page, not wishing to be reminded that the nicest people were also those most likely to invade the "vital corners" of one's home to judge one's character and standards.[23]

No other medium of popular culture preached the parable of the First Impression with the insistence of advertising. From no other source did people receive such frequent reminders that other people were constantly sizing them up and whispering about them behind their backs, or that they had so many possible reasons to feel a sense of social shame. Movies and comic strips sometimes depicted "love at first sight" or invited their audiences to join protagonists in making snap judgments. But these media usually subsequently revealed that initial impressions and assumptions had been inaccurate, thus conveying—often through humor—a moral lesson against the hasty judgment. Romantic magazine fiction, and later the radio soap operas, often emphasized the cutting social judgments of whispering gossips. But the gossips in these genres were nearly always cast in stereotyped negative roles.

The advertisements, by contrast, rarely questioned the truth of the parable of the First Impression. By clear implication, they accepted the efficacy and validity of the gossips' judgments (see Figs. 1.4, 1.5). Most ads equated other people's judgments with correct standards of appearance, cleanliness, taste, and modernity. Occasionally, superficial judgments might be characterized as unjust, but they were nevertheless presented as inevitable. One paint industry advertisement conceded that two gossips might be "unfair" in concluding that another family "must be hard up" because their house needed a new coat of paint. "But unfair or not," the ad gravely admonished readers, "we cannot escape the opinion of other people."[24]

The merchandising strategy underlying the parable of the First Impression was obvious. People would certainly display more concern for the details of their personal appearance and that of their home if they could be induced to scrutinize themselves through the eyes of other people and to conceive of every aspect of external appearance as an index to their true character. But such an appeal could only succeed in a society which had come to doubt that a person's true character and worth were adequately revealed and judged in other, less superficial, ways.

Advertising men knew from their personal experience in the business world that first impressions *did* make a difference. The shifting, uncertain relationships in the field of advertising, the processes by which advertisements gained approval from clients, and the apparently fickle tastes of consumers in response to various advertising appeals, all encouraged them to conclude that, in many aspects of life, externals counted for more than intrinsic qualities. Working in an urban, sophisticated milieu, and impressed by the increasing complexity and ambiguity of business and social relationships, advertising men sensed that the parable of the First Impression had become a plausible explanation for how things worked in this "new world" that they knew and that others were increasingly coming to encounter.

Externals *were* more significant in a mobile, urban, impersonal society. As a leading citizen of "Middletown" commented to a member of Robert and Helen Lynd's research staff in the mid-1920s, "You see, they [people] know money; they don't know you."[25] By applying that money, through products, to your wardrobe, your face, your automobile, or your bathroom, you might manipulate their judgments in your favor. It might have been pure fantasy to suggest, as Tumbler Car Polish did, that a woman would break a social appointment because her husband had bought the wrong car polish and thus invited a bad first impression through "motor car dullness," or to imply, as Paris garters did, that a woman would reject the marriage proposal of an otherwise desirable mate simply because his socks sagged (Fig. 7.4).[26] But the parable of the First Impression would never have appeared in such extreme variations if advertisers had not sensed that it reflected a common public perception of how society really worked in an age of shifting relationships.

In their own pragmatic search for merchandising triumphs, advertisers were exploring the implications of changing conceptions of the relation of the individual to society that later writers were to characterize as a shift from a "character ethic" to a "personality ethic." Already in the late nineteenth century, T. J. Jackson Lears notes, the interdependence fostered by urban, market relationships had

—and he wonders why
she said "NO!"

Could he have read her thoughts he would not have lost her. A picture of neatness herself, she detested slovenliness. And not once, but many times, she had noticed his ungartered socks crumpling down around his shoe tops. To have to apologize to her friends for a husband's careless habits was too much to ask. So she had to say "NO" and in spite of his pleading couldn't tell him WHY.

No SOX Appeal Without

PARIS
GARTERS
NO METAL CAN TOUCH YOU
25c to 82
Dress Well and Succeed

SINGLE GRIP   DOUBLE GRIP

© 1928—A. STEIN & COMPANY·MAKERS·CHICAGO, NEW YORK, LOS ANGELES, TORONTO

7.4. *Even if she could have learned to tolerate his "slovenliness," a woman had to consider how her life might be blighted by her husband's bad first impression on others.*

undermined individual autonomy and engendered the idea of a fragmented "discontinuous self," comprised only of "a series of manipulatable social masks." Modern identity, in Peter Berger's phrase, had become "peculiarly open." In an interdependent world of fragile institutions and shifting opportunities, individuals had to be prepared to transform themselves for new roles and new opportunities, thus making themselves "peculiarly vulnerable to shifting definitions" of themselves by others. Moreover, modern life induced a perception of living "constantly in a crowd," Warren Susman argues. This inspired individuals to play roles or create traits that would distinguish them from the mass and make others think of them as "somebodies."[27]

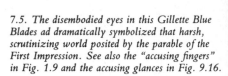

7.5. *The disembodied eyes in this Gillette Blue Blades ad dramatically symbolized that harsh, scrutinizing world posited by the parable of the First Impression. See also the "accusing fingers" in Fig. 1.9 and the accusing glances in Fig. 9.16.*

When Dale Carnegie's bestseller, *How to Win Friends and Influence People,* appeared in 1936 it seemed to epitomize the new "personality ethic." Carnegie emphasized the responses of other people as the main obstacle to success. But advertisers, in parables of the First Impression, had already thoroughly explored the merchandising possibilities inherent in a modern fragmentation of selfhood. Ads with such leading questions as "Do you know how to be yourself?" and "Can a woman change a man's idea of her personality?" had explained how a perfume or nail polish might resolve a woman's identity crisis.[28] Like other versions of the parable of the First Impression, such ads reinforced Americans' growing perception that they must create their own identities in the face of superficial and unsympathetic judgments by impersonal others. Advertisers did not create the modern "identity crisis," but they welcomed the opportunity to dramatize it. They then stepped forward as personal counselors on how to meet the scrutiny of judgmental others and how to succeed by "looking the part."

Thus the parable of the First Impression dramatized popular apprehensions about a society moving toward depersonalization. Frequently reiterated, in ever-expanding conceptions of possible sins against good taste and social presentability, these "tragedy of manners" tableaux increased public awareness of the ways one could offend others or fail to live up to their expectations. To some, the parable of the First Impression may have stimulated the hope that they could win out over the potentially unfair judgments of an anonymous society. Through a self-conscious attention to putting on the right face, they might turn the tables and manipulate the attitudes of those who scrutinized them so constantly but so superficially. To others, the cumulative effect of sundry advertising versions of the parable of the First Impression must certainly have been to intensify their sense of social insecurity. Martha Wolfenstein and Nathan Leites have noted a frequent pattern in American movies of the 1920s through the 1940s in which the audience was invited to identify with innocent characters who "are accused by a leering or ostracizing or punishing world with which they struggle to clear themselves." They attribute these "nightmarish" but eventually triumphant encounters of the innocent with unfair judgments of guilt to "intense self-accusations" by Americans.[29]

At most, advertising could only have acted as one of a number of forces in American society contributing to a tendency toward self-accusation. But it had obviously discovered a sensitive social nerve to stimulate and exploit. Whereas movies and soap operas often provided vicarious experiences of triumphs over society's false accusations, advertisements emphasized the power, validity, and pervasiveness of the world's judgmental scrutiny. With headlines such as "When they look at your feet on the beach," "Suppose you could follow yourself up the street. . . . What would you see?" and "more searching than your mirror . . . your husband's eyes," they encouraged the transformation of this scrutiny into self-accusation.[30] Their cumulative effect was more likely to reinforce the readers' impression of being surrounded by a host of accusing eyes than to reassure them that new furniture, familiarity with good silverware, or "a face that's fit" would testify to their "innocence" and spare them social shame (Fig. 7.5).

The Parable of the Democracy of Goods

As they opened their September 1929 issue, readers of the *Ladies' Home Journal* were treated to an account of the care and feeding of young Livingston Ludlow Biddle III, scion of the wealthy Biddles of Philadelphia, whose family coat-of-arms graced the upper right-hand corner of the page. Young Master Biddle, mounted on his tricycle, fixed a serious, slightly pouting gaze upon the reader, while the Cream of Wheat Corporation rapturously explained his constant care, his carefully regulated play and exercise, and the diet prescribed for him by "famous specialists." As master of Sunny Ridge Farm, the Biddles' winter estate in North Carolina, young Livingston III had "enjoyed every luxury of social position and wealth, since the day he was born." Yet, by the grace of a modern providence, it happened that Livingston's health was protected by a "simple plan every mother can use." Mrs. Biddle gave Cream of Wheat to the young heir for both breakfast and supper. The world's foremost child experts knew of no better diet; great wealth could procure no finer nourishment. As Cream of Wheat's advertising agency summarized the central point of the campaign that young Master Biddle initiated, "every mother can give her youngsters the fun and benefits of a Cream of Wheat breakfast just as do the parents of these boys and girls who have the best that wealth can command."[31]

While enjoying this glimpse of childrearing among the socially distinguished, *Ladies' Home Journal* readers found themselves schooled in one of the most pervasive of all advertising tableaux of the 1920s—the parable of the Democracy of Goods. According to this parable, the wonders of modern mass production and distribution enabled every person to enjoy the society's most significant pleasure, convenience, or benefit. The definition of the particular benefit fluctuated, of course, with each client who employed the parable. But the cumulative effect of the constant reminders that "any woman can" and "every home can afford" was to publicize an image of American society in which concentrated wealth at the top of a hierarchy of social classes restricted no family's opportunity to acquire the most significant products.[32] By implicitly defining "democracy" in terms of equal access to consumer products, and then by depicting the everyday functioning of that "democracy" with regard to one product at a time, these tableaux offered Americans an inviting vision of their society as one of incontestable equality.

In its most common advertising formula, the concept of the Democracy of Goods asserted that although the rich enjoyed a great variety of luxuries, the acquisition of their *one* most significant luxury would provide anyone with the ultimate in satisfaction. For instance, a Chase and Sanborn's Coffee tableau, with an elegant butler serving a family in a dining room with a sixteen-foot ceiling, reminded Chicago families that although "compared with the riches of the more fortunate, your way of life may seem modest indeed," yet no one—"king, prince, statesman, or capitalist"—could enjoy better coffee.[33] The Association of Soap and Glycerine Producers proclaimed that the charm of cleanliness was as readily available to the poor as to the rich, and Ivory Soap reassuringly related how one young housewife, who couldn't afford a $780-a-year maid like her neighbor, still maintained a significant equality in "nice hands" by using Ivory.[34] The C. F. Church Manufacturing Company epitomized this version of the parable of the Democracy of Goods in an ad entitled "a bathroom luxury everyone can afford": "If you lived in one of those palatial apartments on Park Avenue, in New York City, where you have to pay $2,000.00 to $7,500.00 a year rent, you still couldn't have a better toilet seat in your bathroom than they have—the Church Sani-white Toilet Seat which you can afford to have right now."[35]

Thus, according to the parable, no discrepancies in wealth could prevent the humblest citizens, provided they chose their purchases wisely, from retiring to a setting in which they could contemplate their essential equality, through possession of an identical product, with the nation's millionaires. In 1929, Howard Dickinson, a contributor to *Printers' Ink,* concisely expressed the social psychology behind Democracy of Goods advertisements: "'With whom do the mass of people think they want to foregather?' asks the psychologist in advertising. 'Why, with the wealthy and socially distinguished, of course!' If we can't get an invitation to tea for our millions of customers, we can at least present the fellowship of using the same brand of merchandise. And it works."[36]

Some advertisers found it more efficacious to employ the parable's negative counterpart—the Democracy of Afflictions. Listerine contributed significantly to this approach. Most of the unsuspecting victims of halitosis in the mid-1920s possessed wealth and high social position. Other discoverers of new social afflictions soon took up the battle cry of "nobody's immune." "Body Odor plays no favorites," warned Lifebuoy Soap. No one, "banker, baker, or society woman," could count himself safe from B.O.[37] The boss, as well as the employees, might find himself "caught off guard" with dirty hands or cuffs, the Soap and Glycerine Producers assured readers of *True Story.* By 1930, Absorbine Jr. was

You'd like to be
in this man's shoes
. . . yet he has
"ATHLETE'S
FOOT"

7.6. *A negative appeal transformed the Democracy of Goods into the Democracy of Afflictions. Common folk learned from this parable that they could inexpensively avoid afflictions that beset even the yachting set.*

beginning to document the democratic advance of "athlete's foot" into those rarefied social circles occupied by the "daintiest member of the junior set" and the noted yachtsman who owned "a railroad or two" (Fig. 7.6).[38]

The central purpose of the Democracy of Afflictions tableaux was to remind careless or unsuspecting readers of the universality of the threat from which the product offered protection or relief. Only occasionally did such ads address those of the upper classes who might think that their status and "fastidious" attention to personal care made them immune from common social offenses. In 1929 Listerine provided newspaper readers an opportunity to listen while a doctor, whose clientele included those of "the better class," confided "what I know about *nice* women."[39] One might have thought that Listerine was warning complacent, upper-class women that they were not immune from halitosis—except that the ad appeared in the *Los Angeles Times,* not *Harper's Bazaar.* Similarly, Forhan's toothpaste and the Soap Producers did not place their Democracy of Afflictions ads in *True Story* in order to reach the social elite. Rather, these tableaux provided enticing glimpses into the lives of the wealthy while suggesting an equalizing "fellowship" in shared susceptibilities to debilitating ailments. The parable of the Democracy of Goods always remained implicit in its negative counterpart. It assured readers that they could be as healthy, as charming, as free from social offense as the very "nicest" (richest) people, simply by using a product that anyone could afford.

Another variation of the parable of the Democracy of Goods employed historical comparisons to celebrate even the humblest of contemporary Americans as "kings in cottages." "No monarch in all history ever saw the day he could have half as much as you," proclaimed Paramount Pictures. Even reigning sovereigns of the present, Paramount continued, would envy readers for their "luxurious freedom and opportunity" to enter a magnificent, bedazzling "palace for a night," be greeted with fawning bows by liveried attendants, and enjoy modern entertainment for a modest price (Fig. 7.7). The Fisher Body Corporation coined the phrase "For Kings in Cottages" to compliment ordinary Americans on their freedom from "hardships" that even kings had been forced to endure in the past. Because of a lack of technology, monarchs who traveled in the past had "never enjoyed luxury which even approached that of the present-day automobile." The "American idea," epitomized by the Fisher Body Corporation, was destined to carry the comforts and luxuries conducive to human happiness into "the life of even the humblest cottager."[40]

Even so, many copywriters perceived that equality with past monarchs might not rival the vision of joining the fabled "Four Hundred" that Ward McAllister had marked as America's social elite at the end of the nineteenth century. Americans, in an ostensibly conformist age, hungered for exclusivity. So advertising tableaux celebrated their ascension into this fabled and exclusive American elite. Through mass production and the resulting lower prices, the tableaux explained, the readers could purchase goods formerly available only to the rich—and thus gain admission to a "400" that now numbered millions.

The Simmons Company confessed that inner-coil mattresses had once been a luxury possessed only by the very wealthy. But now (in 1930) they were "priced so everybody in the United States can have one at $19.95." Woodbury's Soap advised the "working girl" readers of *True Story* of their arrival within a select circle. "Yesterday," it recalled, "the skin you love to touch" had been "the privilege of one woman in 65," but today it had become "the beauty right of every woman."[41] If the Democracy of Goods could establish an equal consumer right to beauty, then perhaps even the ancient religious promise of equality in death might be realized, at least to the extent that material provisions sufficed. In 1927 the Clark Grave Vault Company defined this unique promise: "Not so many years ago the use of a burial vault was confined largely to the rich. . . . Now every family, regardless of its means, may provide absolute protection against the elements in the ground."[42] If it seemed that the residents of Clark vaults had gained equality with the "400" too belatedly for maximum satisfaction, still their loving survivors could now share the same sense of comfort in the "absolute protection" of former loved ones as did the most privileged elites.

The social message of the parable of the Democracy of Goods was clear. Antagonistic envy of the rich was unseemly; programs to redistribute wealth were unnecessary. The best things in life were already available to all at reasonable prices. But the prevalence of the parable of the Democracy of Goods in advertising tableaux did not necessarily betray a concerted conspiracy on the part of advertisers and their agencies to impose a social ideology on the American people. Most advertisers employed the parable of the Democracy of Goods primarily as a narrow, non-ideological merchandising tactic. Listerine and Lifebuoy found the parable an obvious, attention-getting strategy for persuading readers that if even society women and bankers were unconsciously guilty of social offenses, the readers themselves were not immune. Simmons Mattresses, Chevrolet, and Clark Grave Vaults chose the parable in an attempt to broaden their market to include lower-income groups. The parable emphasized the affordability of the product to

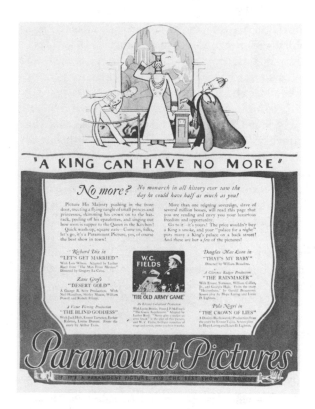

7.7. Of course, real kings
had never shared their status with crowds of other
"kings." But the parable
of the Democracy of
Goods offered a brief,
"packaged experience" of
luxury and preference.
See also Figs. 9.2 and
9.3.

families of modest income while attempting to maintain a "class" image of the product as the preferred choice of their social betters.

Most advertisers found the social message of the parable of the Democracy of Goods a congenial and unexceptionable truism. They also saw it, like the other parables prevalent in advertising tableaux, as an epigrammatic statement of a conventional popular belief. Real income was rising for nearly all Americans during the 1920s, except for some farmers and farm workers and those in a few depressed industries. Citizens seemed eager for confirmation that they were now driving the same make of car as the wealthy elites and serving their children the same cereal enjoyed by Livingston Ludlow Biddle III. Advertisers did not have to impose the parable of the Democracy of Goods on a contrary-minded public. Theirs was the easier task of subtly substituting this vision of equality, which was certainly satisfying *as a vision,* for broader and more traditional hopes and expectations of an equality of self-sufficiency, personal independence, and social interaction.

Perhaps the most attractive aspect of this parable to advertisers was that it preached the coming of an equalizing democracy without sacrificing those fascinating contrasts of social condition that had long been the touchstone of high drama. Henry James, writing of Hawthorne, had once lamented the obstacles facing the novelist who wrote of an America that lacked such tradition-laden

as a sovereign, a court, an aristocracy, or even a class of country
Without castles, manors, and thatched cottages, America lacked those
positions of pomp and squalor, nobility and peasantry, wealth and
at made Europe so rich a source of social drama.[43] But many versions
ible of the Democracy of Goods sought to offset that disadvantage
aining James's desired "complexity of manners." They dressed up
America's wealthy as dazzling aristocrats, and then reassured readers that they
could easily enjoy an essential equality with such elites in the things that really
mattered. The rich were decorative and fun to look at, but in their access to those
products most important to comfort and satisfaction, as the magazine *Delineator*
put it, "The Four Hundred" had become "the four million."[44] Advertisers left
readers to assume that they could gain the same satisfactions of exclusiveness from
belonging to the four million as had once been savored by the four hundred.

While parables of consumer democracy frequently used terms like "everyone,"
"anyone," "any home," or "every woman," these categories were mainly intended to comprise the audience of "consumer-citizens" envisioned by the advertising trade, or families economically among the nation's top 50 percent.[45] Thus
the *Delineator* had more in mind than mere alliteration when it chose to contrast
the old "400" with the new "four million" rather than a new "one hundred and
twenty million." The standard antitheses of the Democracy of Goods parables
were "mansion" and "bungalow." Advertising writers rarely took notice of the
many millions of Americans whose standard of living fell below that of the cozy
bungalow of the advertising tableaux. These millions might overhear the promises of consumer democracy in the newspapers or magazines, but advertising
leaders felt no obligation to show how their promises to "everyone" would bring
equality to those who lived in the nation's apartment houses and farmhouses
without plumbing, let alone those who lived in rural shacks and urban tenements.

In the broadest sense, the parable of the Democracy of Goods may be interpreted as a secularized version of the traditional Christian assurances of ultimate
human equality. "Body Odor plays no favorites" might be considered a secular
translation of the idea that God "sends rain on the just and on the unjust" (Matt.
5:45). Promises of the essential equality of those possessing the advertised brand
recalled the promise of equality of access to God's mercy. Thus the parable
recapitulated a familiar, cherished expectation. Far more significant, however,
was the parable's insinuation of the capacity of a Democracy of Goods to redeem
the already secularized American promise of political equality.

Incessantly and enticingly repeated, advertising visions of fellowship in a Democracy of Goods encouraged Americans to look to similarities in consumption
styles rather than to political power or control of wealth for evidence of significant
equality. Francesco Nicosia and Robert Mayer describe the result as a "deflection
of the success ethic from the sphere of production to that of consumption."
Freedom of choice came to be perceived as a freedom more significantly exercised
in the marketplace than in the political arena. This process gained momentum in
the 1920s; it gained maturity during the 1950s as a sense of class differences was
nearly eclipsed by a fascination with the equalities suggested by shared consumption patterns and "freely chosen" consumer "lifestyles."[46]

The Parable of Civilization Redeemed

In 1930 the pharmaceutical firm of E. R. Squibb and Sons sought to capture the attention of readers for a dramatized version of a now-familiar fable. Employing a touch of the popular "believe-it-or-not" mystique, it introduced a note of mystery and irony into its advertising headline: "The interesting story of how man outwitted nature—and *lost!*"[47] The revelation it had to offer, Squibb boasted, would be "another of those thrilling stories from the annals of modern science," a story of "how man, in his struggle to be civilized, became his own arch-enemy." In the beginning, Nature had prudently placed essential vitamins in the "coarse, plain foods she intended us to eat." But man, captivated by new and tempting tastes, had sought to make such foods more appetizing. In the process, he had "cooked and refined out of them" the very vitamins that Nature had foreseen would be necessary for good health. "Today," Squibb sermonized, "we are paying the penalty for this mistake. 'Civilized ills' plague us—ills caused by an incomplete diet of highly refined foods."[48]

Had the story ended there, the parable would have remained a simple jeremiad. It might even have suggested a return to the purer, less decadent practices of yore. But the fable contained a second irony. If Nature, in its instinctive wisdom, now sought to punish civilized mankind for its waywardness, then Civilization, in its own sophisticated wisdom, had found a way to regain Nature's intended gifts without sacrificing the fruits of progress. Squibb's Vitamin Products would lift the curse that Nature had unthinkingly sought to inflict on Civilization.[49]

Such was the parable of Civilization Redeemed. A familiar theme in the advertising tableaux, it usually varied from version to version only in the extent of its elaboration and in the particular form taken by Nature's curse. In proclaiming the victories over threats to health and beauty that the products of civilization now made possible, these parables of Civilization Redeemed never sought to denigrate Nature. In an era when the suntan first became fashionable and the ultraviolet ray an object of veneration, the virtues of Nature were not lightly dismissed. The point of the parable was that Civilization, which had brought down the curse of Nature upon itself, had still proved capable of discovering products that would enable Nature's original and beneficent intentions to triumph. Since it was inconceivable that civilized traits or habits, once attained, would ever lapse or be renounced, it was necessary for progress that they not come accompanied by the unacceptable penalties that an uncomprehending Nature sought to impose. The parable of Civilization Redeemed taught that the advance of civilization, temporary afflictions notwithstanding, need never exact any real losses. Civilization had become its own redeemer.

One of the deleterious by-products of civilization most often lamented in the advertising parables was the physical "softness" that came with refined, over-cooked foods and a decline in physical exercise. Pebeco toothpaste deplored the lack of exercise for mouth glands that had come with the "soft foods" of the modern diet. Without exercise to keep these glands "young" and active, tooth decay quickly ensued. Wrigley's Gum agreed that civilization had created grave threats to the health and beauty of mankind because of "the lack of chewing required by our modern, soft foods." Since "charming lips" constituted the main factor in a woman's beauty, her charm was likely to fade rapidly under modern, civilized conditions that cheated facial muscles of the exercise needed to keep them supple. Wrigley urged readers to follow the example of the girls of the high-kicking chorus line, who recognized the necessity to "take every precaution to look and keep fit" in all respects, and therefore avoided "flabby face lines" by chewing Wrigley's Spearmint Gum for exercise.[50]

In their anxiety to dramatize the potential dangers of modern habits and conditions, advertisers occasionally identified civilization with images of sloth or decadence. In an attack on the "soft fare of civilization," Ipana toothpaste introduced a hint of degenerate luxury by populating a restaurant scene with a heavy-set waiter, several languid ladies lounging about the central table, and a corpulent couple in the background. In another restaurant tableau, Ipana warned, "Eating today is a lazy pleasure."[51] Other advertisers contrasted the physical "laziness" of modern civilization with the hard work that Nature had originally intended for such parts of the body as the teeth, the gums, the eyes, and the intestines. Grape-Nuts reminded readers that "Nature's plan" intended teeth for "hard work—and plenty of it." A Squibb Liquid Petroleum ad warned: "Civilization has *cheated* you. . . . Your intestines have gone lazy." Summing up the effects of overeating, insufficient sleep, and lack of exercise, Postum concluded: "Health is natural. Sickness is man-made."[52]

The parable of Civilization Redeemed not only contrasted a healthful, hard-working past with an indolent, potentially degenerate present; it also seemed, on occasion, to elevate ancient or "natural" men over civilized moderns. One Dentyne Gum advertisement contrasted scenes of a contemporary girl lying listlessly in a sickbed and cavemen vigorously consuming their "tough wild meat" (Fig. 7.8). Another Dentyne ad contrasted "Mrs. B," who has "spent hundreds on her teeth and has six fillings and a bridge," with an Eskimo girl, "untouched by civilization," whose teeth remained perfect without dental work.[53] A General Electric ad idealized the Indian's power of distant vision before man moved into the dim light of an artificial, indoor world. And General Foods created a new, youthful, slender, and feminine image of the advertisers' favorite representative of natural vigor, the caveman (Fig. 7.9).[54]

Few advertisements compare the past favorably with the present, but the parable of Civilization Redeemed diverged from this pattern. Many advertisements in the 1920s had betrayed an ambiguous attitude toward the traditional American virtue of hard work; several bluntly condemned hard work after expediently renaming it "drudgery." But when the parable of Civilization Redeemed associated the ancient past with the vigorous hard work of physical exercise, it clearly implied the moral superiority of the "natural" past over certain soft and lazy qualities of the present. Even so, the parable contemplated no turning back. "We could hardly revert to a diet of raw roots and unpeeled fruits," exclaimed Ipana.[55] The "superiority" of the past was a narrow, particular one; it did not have to be sacrificed on the altar of progress. Civilized man could enjoy both soft foods and tough gums, both "refined dishes" and healthy elimination. The advertised product offered the solution.

7.8, 7.9. *The parable of Civilization Redeemed deplored the apparent
depredations of modern progress only to conclude, triumphantly, that civilization entailed no necessary losses. The product would restore primitive
virtues. See also Fig. 1.7.*

Physical softness, however, was not civilization's only affliction; the hurried,
nervous pace of modern society also threatened people's health. Advertisers had
frequently expounded on the nervous tempo of modern society and on the intense
pressures of speed and competition in their own profession. They found it easy
to evoke images of a frantic, nerve-shattering modern pace of life, especially when
the product could be interpreted as an antidote. Ads for laxatives and vitamins
conjured up vivid images of "hurried nervous lives" and "quick-step times," of
people who "drive themselves until they drop."[56] Squibb's Vitamin Products
depicted a "perilous" modern living regime: "Twenty-four hours of . . . noisy,
crowded streets. Of dust and gas-ridden air. Of machine-made speed. Of strain.
Of nervous tension." In prose that similarly matched the tempo of modern
civilization, Post's Bran Flakes added its warning: "So the pace is fast; everything
is abbreviated. The very food you eat is concentrated."[57]

Advertisers of laxatives and "natural bulk" foods united in laying the blame for
constipation directly at the doorstep of modern civilization. Fleischmann's Yeast
eagerly quoted a British doctor's charge that constipation was "civilization's
greatest curse" (see Fig. 1.7). Plugged intestines seemed both a literal and a
symbolic manifestation of "the poisons of waste which too civilized people accu-
mulate within themselves." Moreover, it proved easy to draw causal relationships

between the modern tempo and constipation. Men and women who were constantly "on the go from morning until night" became irregular in their habits. Because of "the strain and complexity of modern living," people were "daily driven to neglect." "Life is too crowded, too hurried, too soft," moaned E. R. Squibb and Sons, manufacturers of Petrolatum. Such a life condemned men and women to "constipating, concentrating foods" with the result that "you suffer from sluggish intestines . . . you pay that price to civilization."[58]

Other advertisers discovered the effects of a hurried pace and nervous tension in other symptoms. Hurry and strain slowed up the action of mouth glands, causing tooth decay. Fatigue, overwork, and "rush eating" precipitated cases of "American Stomach," requiring Ovaltine as an antidote. The "nerve-wracking" speed of modern life dictated that the best workers would be the "high-strung" and the "sensitive-nerved," reported Herbert Tareyton cigarettes. Tareytons promised to soothe and steady the nerves of nurses, pilots, radio operators, stockbrokers, and those in hundreds of other tension-filled modern occupations.[59] Even the pavements of modern civilization brought a "jumpiness" and "irritability" not known to native African bearers who made their long safari treks, as nature intended, "on springy turf." As the United States Rubber Company, the maker of Spring-Step Rubber Heels, concluded: "Nerve exhaustion is the price we pay when we depart from nature's plan."[60]

Still, advertisers did not seek to slacken civilization's hurried pace of life. In fact, the very ads that blamed civilization for the ills of constipation and nervous fatigue often took delight in the pace of modern American life. Post's Bran Flakes glorified its protagonist, "Thompson," who was "head of a world-business, director in a dozen corporations, capable of long hours at fever pitch." Sal Hepatica encouraged women to keep "on the go," rushing "from one activity to another." Squibb declared, "Every hour of the twenty-four is precious!" and suggested that a woman who did not keep pace would miss "countless moments of gaiety and joy."[61] Nujol, a laxative, greeted the new tempo with something approaching ecstasy: "Three times the amount of living crammed into every twenty-four hours; the pace of ten years ago is tripled. Between business and evening affairs is merely time for changing clothes. Thus, night after night. Morning finds men and women rushing joyously through daily tasks. And they thrive on the pace that dizzies bystanders."[62]

Far from questioning the course of civilization, then, advertisers encouraged readers to indulge even more fully in those modern habits that invited Nature's curse. Rather than avoid soft foods or slacken their pace, men and women could pursue their civilized habits and tastes with abandon, confident in the capacity of the advertised product to save them from any ill consequences. Since advertising men worked amid the atmosphere of deadlines and conflicting pressures, they could vividly convey the deleterious qualities of a fast-paced, "overcivilized" social and business life. By raising the specter of civilization destroying the balance of nature, they gave dramatic and sometimes exaggerated expression to the uncertainties of a wider public. After this cathartic airing of anxieties, they offered assurances, through the parable of Civilization Redeemed, that the apparent costs of progress could be avoided. Civilization and Nature were not antithetic. No brakes need be applied to the wheels of progress.

7.10. In the mental climate of the 1920s and 1930s, reinforced by the parable of Civilization Redeemed, an outlying park seemed entirely adequate to solve the problem of "air" created by modern civilization.

Advertising stories do not have unhappy endings; nor do advertising parables preach hard lessons. The parable of Civilization Redeemed was no exception. It confirmed Americans in one of their treasured common beliefs—the belief in unequivocal progress, in the compatibility of technology with the most desirable qualities of Nature. Squibb's headline—"The interesting story of how man outwitted nature—and *lost!*"—was a striking attention-grabber precisely because of its preposterous, believe-it-or-not quality. The content of every medium of American popular culture of the era affirmed that man was constantly outwitting nature through technological advances and never "losing" as a consequence. By exploring *apparent* and incongruous exceptions to the principle of progress without cost, and by demonstrating man's capacity to prevent these unnecessary discontents of civilization, the parable of Civilization Redeemed buttressed a central tenet of American folk wisdom.[63]

The ideology of advertising is an ideology of efficacious answers. No problem lacks an adequate solution. Unsolvable problems may exist in the society, but they are nonexistent in the world glimpsed through advertisements. Thus the parable of Civilization Redeemed simply stated explicitly the implicit message of all advertising. Many advertisements of the late 1920s that did not state the parable directly nevertheless reinforced its reassurances. The Scripps-Howard newspaper chain, for instance, advertised its civic-minded editorial policies by depicting a girl running through a park glen in healthy delight, while her family picnicked nearby. The city in the distance lay under the heavy smoke of urban pollution. Yet a park on the periphery of such a city, the ad implicitly concluded, provided a complete solution for city workers and their families (Fig. 7.10). Meanwhile products ranging from yeast to Radiant Fire gas heaters promised to fully restore the sun's "vital rays" and "mysterious power" to a "sun-starved" modern race living indoors in schools, factories, homes, and offices.[64]

Sometimes, "solutions" to the apparent ills of civilization failed to bring the promised relief; yet even here, a *new* solution always appeared to resolve the apparent problem. During the early 1920s, motoring had been promoted for its health value. People could refresh themselves and gain relief from nervous strain by motoring in the fresh air of the countryside. But such gains were often offset, warned Watson Stabilators (shock absorbers), because the need to constantly brace oneself "against a bad toss" had brought fatigue and "muscular tension." Yet motoring, as civilization's solution to the problem of tension-creating urban conditions, need not bring its own attendant ills. Watson Stabilators would cushion the ride and restore motoring to its promised role.[65]

Perhaps the consummate expression of the beliefs embodied in the parable of Civilization Redeemed appeared in advertisements in the early 1930s for Midol, a patent medicine for menstrual cramps. Warning that "Nature won't postpone her process to accommodate social engagements," Midol promised relief in seven minutes by working "directly on the organs themselves." In so doing, it proved the capacity of civilization's products to carry out the beneficent intentions of Nature. "The periodic process is natural," Midol explained, "but the painful part is not."[66] That pain in any form—physical, social, or psychological—was "not natural" was a proposition that Americans most devoutly wished to believe. Advertising, and particularly advertising tableaux of the parable of Civilization Redeemed, offered only encouragement to such wishful thinking.

The Parable of the Captivated Child

Mother was vexed, exhausted, almost driven to distraction. Bobby simply would not eat his carrots, even though mother had followed "all the suggestions laid down by authorities on child training." Her efforts to get him to eat the vegetables essential to his health had become a "pitched battle." This particularly disturbed mother since, as everyone now realized, forcing or strenuous coaxing would destroy her vital bond of companionship with her child. Equally upsetting was her realization that those "little outlaws," Bobby and his friends, were actively pursuing "their natural search for forbidden and untimely foods" away from home, outside of her control. Mother recognized her duty to shape Bobby's diet; yet angry confrontations and tearful refusals would prove her a failure as a mother. What to do![67]

Fortunately, just during Bobby's most difficult years—from 1929 through 1933—the Campbell Soup Company offered a strategy to solve mother's dilemma. Realizing the hopelessness of the "pitched battle," Campbell's Soup ads recommended enticement rather than confrontation to bring a prompt "surrender" by balky and roving outlaws. Attractive home meals of Campbell's Soups would captivate Bobby's appetite, restrain his search for forbidden foods, and eliminate the exhausting need for coaxing. "It's not 'vegetables' to them," promised Campbell's, "it's just good soup!" By following the simple strategy proposed by this parable of the Captivated Child, all mothers could mold their "little outlaws" into happy, healthy youngsters without the harsh discipline that might turn them into willful, "sulky foes." Mothers could avoid the negative effects of irritable coaxing and still bring "the end of the great rebellion!"[68]

In seizing upon the parable of the Captivated Child, Campbell's Soups and a score of other advertisers fashioned popular theories of child guidance into a cogent merchandising strategy. Child psychology was riding a wave of popularity as a behavioral science. As new appliances lessened the time required for other domestic tasks, doctors, dieticians, psychologists, and other "authorities" explained to women new standards of child nurture. Some of these involved painstaking expertise in establishing complex and rigid schedules; others required time-consuming devotion to the development of empathetic yet manipulative emotional relationships. All of the new responsibilities encouraged women to invest more emotional energy in their role as mothers and to recognize that they would be judged more heavily than ever by their successes or failures in this role.[69] As child guidance authorities discerned more and more difficult "problems" in attaining the proper diet for children and in properly molding their behavior without destructive discipline, advertisers eagerly publicized those problems and offered their products as solutions.

Among the ideas of child guidance most widely popularized by advertisements, four assumptions were particularly crucial to the parable of the Captivated Child. The first of these was the notion that parents should maximize the personal development of the child through increased attention and companionship. "She needs you so!"—the message of a 1927 Cream of Wheat ad—reiterated the constant refrain.[70] Children were malleable creatures; but their character was quickly set. "An hour of 'mothering' now is worth a year of advice later on," one advertiser warned. Unsupervised play was dangerous. "Far better when Mother is the companion. Far better when Mother guides the restless hands and moulds the plastic minds." General Electric warned that "the years of a mother's influence are only seven." In those first seven "fleeting years" a child's "dominant characteristics" were formed.[71]

Although the texts of such advertisements rarely explained the specific form that such parental influence should take, the illustrations suggested a kind of companionate guidance. Mothers, and occasionally fathers, were shown actively participating in play with the children—running with them through grassy fields, swinging them, gathering wildflowers with them, joining them in playing with a train. Other illustrations showed women reading to their children or simply watching them with full attention while they played. Some illustrations of mothers suggested a particularly solicitous attitude. They served or bent over children at the table with suppliant tenderness; they knelt almost reverently to adjust their clothes.[72] Occasionally, guidance experts in the ads besought fathers, too, to get down on the child's level and be good companions. In an ad entitled "Dear Fathers," Cream of Wheat quoted one educator: "This year, make friends with your son. Try to understand him and help him with his lessons, his conduct, his play. . . . Be a boy again."[73] The 1920s was an era of more democratic, child-centered family relations for middle-class families; the advertising tableaux reflected and endorsed that transformation.

According to a second assumption of the parable of the Captivated Child, children would inevitably choose the wrong diet or acquire undesirable habits if left to themselves. Children naturally rejected certain foods that were best for them and resisted certain good habits because they found them bothersome and restrictive.[74] Mothers bore a responsibility to protect each child's health and mold its character in defiance of the child's natural neglect or abhorrence of essential foods and habits.

A third critical assumption of the parable drew heavily on contemporary child-rearing literature. It barred parents from one method of acting in the child's own best interests by insisting that any attmept to "force" the proper diet and habits on the child would not only fail, but would undermine the empathetic approach to child nurture posited in assumption number one. "Don't make your children dislike you," warned Ex-Lax. Instead of forcing children to take "hateful doses and bitter cathartics that so often cause tears and tantrums," a wise mother should tempt them with a candy-like laxative. "They'll love it . . . and love you for giving it to them." Advertisement after advertisement condemned the "forcing" of the "old discipline." Don't force, don't coax, don't plead, don't scold, they repeated (Fig. 7.11).[75] Coaxing and forcing, argued General Mills (Wheaties), often did more harm than good. Such conflicts might unwisely turn "high spirited youngsters" into balky, tearful, even "perverse" children. Cream of Wheat fondly quoted the exclamations of the author of a child guidance book: "Bubbling over with mischief! How children chafe against restraint!" And rightly so. Restraint was unproductive and unnecessary. In many modern homes, according to another authority on child guidance, "sound habits are being learned—not through 'must' and 'must not' but by games."[76]

The woman, ignorant or neglectful of such advice, who scolded or coaxed her child was quickly relegated by advertising to the role of bad mother. Every tableau in which a mother punished, criticized, or showed bad temper toward her child characterized the mother as the guilty party (Fig. 7.12).[77] To scold one's child was to fail as a mother, to reveal one's incompetence in what should be a woman's most natural role. Often such behavior revealed a failure on the mother's part to inform herself about the "sane ways" of leading rather than forcing the child. Since children who developed the habit, through confrontations, of behaving badly at the table were "often hard to manage otherwise, too," good mothers never forced children to eat "a tasteless, unwanted cereal" for their own good.[78]

Given these three axioms—parents should be companions to their children; children do not choose what is best for them; and children should not be forced or coaxed—the final basic assumption of the parable of the Captivated Child emerged as the only apparent solution to the problem of child management. The mother must become a deft but loving manipulator. With the indispensable aid of enticing products, she should use her child's own tastes and interests to "guide

7.11. *Is father ignominiously reaching for a bribe when mother's coaxing provokes resistance? The parable of the Captivated Child offered a more pleasant and honorable mode of manipulation.*

7.12. *Mothers never won the approval of copywriters for scolding or punishing. Like Helen's mother, they eagerly confessed their guilt when they discovered how to captivate the child. See also Fig.9.7.*

him to the thing he should do." Such captivation was easy when mothers could count on a product like Wheaties, which was "as alluring and enticing to a child as a French Confection."[79]

Sometimes the mother's responsibility for solicitous manipulation required inventive approaches. Cream of Wheat suggested the use of games as the perfect way to maintain a sense of companionship while manipulating child behavior. Under the headline "Bubbling love of fun—how mothers harness it to guide their youngsters," one Cream of Wheat ad explained how to "make a game of important habits." Another tableau in the same series proclaimed triumphantly, "'Rules 'n' Regulations' now turned into play." Each month during the late 1920s Cream of Wheat introduced a new child expert to explain the ways in which parents were now "appealing to children's love of games and of achievement to *lead* them instead of *pushing* them in the old way." Cream of Wheat's Hot Cereal Breakfast Club offered mothers and children a "jolly plan," with gold stars, badges, and secrets, to make the hot cereal breakfast habit a "fascinating game." With such assistance women could remain good mothers, despite the new complexities and standards of proper child care. "Full of fun but scientific, too," promised Cream of Wheat.[80]

The parable of the Captivated Child, like the other parables, was not simply an invention of the advertising trade. It reflected the intensified "child-consciousness" of the decade which had gained popular expression in 1926 in the appearance of *Parents' Magazine* (initially entitled *Children; the parents' magazine*).[81] Before advertising elaborated the idea in its parables, leading psychologists had already prescribed the replacement of traditional discipline with psychological manipulation of the child's natural impulses for its own good. The same sensitivity to the increasing necessity, in a modern environment of complex, bureaucratic institutions, to mold people's behavior and facilitate their "adjustment" by psychological manipulation rather than authoritarian coercion was also finding expression in the 1920s and 1930s in the rising enthusiasm for professional "personnel management" in industry. The parable's emphasis on captivation rather than force coincided with the trend exhibited in the U.S. Children's Bureau bulletin, *Infant Care;* in the 1914–1921 period it had recommended that infants be forcibly restrained from thumbsucking and masturbation by pinning down or tying their arms, but by 1929 it advised mothers to divert children from such habits by keeping their hands occupied with toys. Martha Wolfenstein, who traced the development of a new American "fun morality" through changes in the successive editions of *Infant Care,* might have found even more telling evidence of the promulgation of this new ethic in the hundreds of advertising tableaux that reiterated the parable of the Captivated Child.[82]

Advertising parables of the Captivated Child did not simply mirror contemporary society. They promulgated a particularly indulgent version of current theories of child guidance and diffused it to a wide audience. And these tableaux provided the constant repetition that gave the new ideas the authority of omnipresence. Although women were probably most influenced by their own upbringing in their style of child care, still the advertisements enabled them to experience vicariously the failures and guilt feelings of mothers who ignored the new ways.

As an advertising tool, the parable of the Captivated Child gave special emphasis to certain aspects of the new child-guidance theories that the manuals and advice books had suggested with far less intensity. For obvious merchandising reasons, the ads advocated parental indulgence with far less qualification than the experts. Sensing that family democracy meant earlier and wider participation in the joys of consumerism, advertisers enthusiastically endorsed the idea of family conferences and shared decision-making. Advertising tableaux surpassed even the child-rearing manuals in placing total responsiblity on the parents for every detail of the child's development, thus magnifying the potential for guilt. And they exaggerated the ease with which children might be manipulated. Psychologists occasionally argued that the mother might need to assert her domination in a direct contest of wills with the child, but the advertising parable portrayed a parent-child relationship in which open conflict was always unnecessary. Above all, it encouraged mothers to define their role as that of guarantors of a conflict-free home through their mastery of the new methods and the available products for manipulation.

Guideposts to a Modern
"Logic of Living"

The parables of the First Impression, the Democracy of Goods, Civilization Redeemed, and the Captivated Child were only four of many parables in 1920s and 1930s advertising tableaux. Such variants as the parable of the Benighted Drudge and the parable of the Sagacious Child also gained familiarity through frequent retelling. In each case, the parable so succinctly and vividly encapsulated widely accepted ideas that it propelled them back into the society with a more compelling force and a more entrancing ambiance. Advertising parables did not challenge the society to overturn conventional ideas, but they did facilitate the spread of those subtle reformulations of old ideas and values endorsed by the most "modern" segment of the population. Frequent reiteration of each parable by a number of advertisers gave the pattern of thinking it embodied such an aura of inevitability that fundamentally different points of view became increasingly difficult to imagine. Popularized for a widening audience, the parables acquired the status of social clichés—notions with the quality of "givens" that established the ideological framework within which other ideas would be explored.

Why did advertisers return again and again to the same "great parables"? We know that their measures of feedback were too rudimentary and defective to demonstrate that the audience responded to these particular fables.[83] In the absence of such validation, copywriters fell back upon the expedient that had always served them in their creative decision-making—their own instinctive judgment, biased as it was by the conditions of their own lives. Advertising writers resorted again and again to the great parables and recited them with confidence because they found their lessons validated in their *own* lives. For instance, in their own careers—shifting and uncertain, constantly dependent upon the success of brief presentations to prospective clients—they had been forced to acknowledge the importance of appearances. What was more, the success of each of their creations, as the trade press constantly reminded them, was dependent on the first impression that it made upon a hurried, inattentive reader. The parable of the First Impression was preeminently a parable for the advertising trade itself.

So, too, in a metaphorical way, was the parable of the Captivated Child. Advertisers employed this parable to align themselves with the most up-to-date literature on child psychology and to pursue good merchandising strategy. But their enthusiasm for it may also have stemmed from the way in which its admonitions to parents resonated with the advice that advertisers regularly exchanged among themselves about how to approach the consumer audience. Readers, they reminded each other, could not be forced or bullied into buying. They had to be tempted, subtly manipulated, given an image of the pleasures and rewards they would gain—in short, captivated. A parable that pointed the way to human betterment and increased pleasure through manipulation was likely to seem axiomatic to a practicing advertising man.

The parables of the Democracy of Goods and Civilization Redeemed also gained authority in the minds of advertising leaders because they served as parables of the function of advertising itself. The Democracy of Goods sought to define social standing in terms of the consumption of specific products rather than by broader measures of wealth or occupational and civic stature. By transferring all significant competition and achievement out of the realm of production and into the realm of consumption, it exalted the process of advertising and distribution as the solution to all problems. The parable of Civilization Redeemed offered a similar therapeutic approach in a way that particularly touched the social experience of advertising agents. Its admonitions about the nervous tension of modern society and the dangers of degenerate softness seemed to diagnose the endemic ills of the advertising profession—insecurity, the pressure of deadlines, and the temptations of overindulgence in the pleasures of affluent and sophisticated urban living. Yet the parable offered catharsis by promising that these particular ills of civilization—and by implication, all perils arising from modernity—could be cured by advertised products.

Thus, although the great parables were employed on each occasion for a specific merchandising purpose, their cumulative effect was to educate consumers to the modernity epitomized by the advertising agent. In a manner far less radical than the biblical parables, they invited readers to a new "logic of living" in which the older values of discipline, character-building, self-restraint, and production-oriented achievement were subordinated to the newer values of pleasure, external appearance, and achievement through consumption. These were not the parables of a radical gospel, but of an optimistic and mildly therapeutic ministry.[84] Rather than challenging entrenched values and ideas, they brought a modern cast to the American dream by subtly redefining the terms of its fulfillment.

Eventually, the explicit great parables of advertising were to decline as more subtle techniques gained in popularity. Despite their generally uncontroversial messages, advertisers increasingly sought to insinuate their maxims through immediate impression, a style incompatible with argumentative copy. Moreover, the lengthy text common to most advertising parables lost favor as advertisers came to rely increasingly on the illustration to convey the message. The "visual cliché," the topic of the next chapter, steadily came to bear the burden of converting the verbal imagery of the explicit parable into less argumentative, more emotional, iconographic forms.

VISUAL CLICHÉS: FANTASIES AND ICONS

All of us have seen portrayals of certain scenes so many times that each new version evokes a flash of recognition. These visual clichés include such disparate images as the madonna and child, the dog tugging at the mailman's trousers, or the pop singer embracing a microphone. If the vast majority of traditional folk tales tend to fall into certain categories of "tale types," and if much of popular literature, as John Cawelti argues, follows certain basic formulas, then popular visual imagery may also be susceptible of analysis through identification and interpretation of its persistent patterns or clichés.[1]

The individual mind stores a variety of mental images as well as data in other forms. Exactly what role visual images play in conceptualization remains undetermined, but psychologists characterize visual imagery as "the predominant modality" for the kind of "thinking" involved in reverie and fantasy. Jerome Singer not only describes the creation of "pictures in the mind's eye" as integral to daydreaming but asserts that daydreaming and fantasizing represent part of the thinking upon which behavior is based. Daydreams, he argues, represent rehearsals and "trial actions" for practical future activity.[2] To the extent that individual daydreams are shaped by an available vocabulary of familiar images, the clichés of popular art of an era, particularly if they are dramatically and repeatedly paraded before the public eye, may induce individuals to recapitulate in their own fantasies some aspects of the shared daydreams of the society. By the 1920s in the United States, advertising had become a prolific producer of visual images with normative overtones, a contributor to the society's shared daydreams.

The "great parables" described in the previous chapter relied heavily on textual argument. Although occasionally enhanced by visual images, they rarely conveyed their moral lessons through illustrations alone. But as the technology for reproducing illustrations expanded, and as the use of color mounted, advertisers increasingly favored pictures over text. Psychologists had regularly advised that pictures could best stimulate the basic emotions. Alfred Poffenberger championed

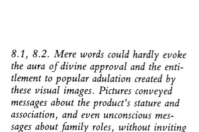

8.1, 8.2. Mere words could hardly evoke the aura of divine approval and the entitlement to popular adulation created by these visual images. Pictures conveyed messages about the product's stature and association, and even unconscious messages about family roles, without inviting debate.

the illustration in his 1925 edition of *Psychology in Advertising* and urged advertisers to "short circuit" the consumer's mind through vivid, pictorial appeals to fundamental emotions. "When the advertisement stimulates thought," he noted, "it stirs conflict and competition, instead of releasing a ready-made and predictable response."[3] Arguments invited counterarguments, and assertions might provoke skepticism. But pictures deflected criticism; they inspired belief. Moreover, they could convey several messages simultaneously. As Raymond Firth observes: "The symbol plucks all of the strings of the human heart at once; speech is compelled to take up a single thought at a time."[4]

The moral messages of the great parables were sufficiently conventional to be set forward frankly and literally in the text. The potential superiority of the "visual statement" became evident in cases where the advertiser's message would have sounded exaggerated or presumptuous if put into words, or where the advertiser sought to play upon such "inappropriate" emotions as religious awe or a thirst for power. For instance, a copywriter might well have hesitated to advertise a product as just the thing for the man who lusted after power over others. But an illustration with a man standing in a commanding position, perhaps overlooking an impressive urban vista, might convey the same message. Line after line of wordy sentimentality might never touch the reader's heartstrings with the impact of a single misty picture of the family at home. The agency president Earnest Calkins put it bluntly: "A picture . . . can say things that no advertiser could say in words and retain his self-respect."[5] Even at the height of the testi-

monial craze, no advertiser would have dared to present his product under the headline "God endorses." But a well-placed, radiant beam of light from a mysterious heavenly source might create a virtual halo around the advertised object without provoking the reader into outrage at the advertiser's presumption.

Thus, at a time when the advertising pages were heaping thousands of words of praise on automobiles, and when many agency leaders worried aloud about the undermining of public confidence by this flood of verbal superlatives, *Printers' Ink* noted that the Hupp Motor Car Company had transformed its car into a gleaming jewel simply by holding it aloft in an outstretched hand. Buick created a similar aura in a tableau in which an idealized worker-craftsman ascended over city and factory like a modern Apollo, upholding the luminous vehicle for popular worship while displaying a document that ambiguously suggested both manufacturing specifications and a poem of adulation (Fig. 8.1). The United States Rubber Company, without daring to argue that the automobile industry warranted a reverential patriotism, still managed to convey this message by depicting a family watching a parade of ever-improved automobiles go past in the sky against a resplendent background of clouds. The man in the scene gave a military salute while his son raised his arm in tribute (Fig. 8.2).[6]

These particular scenes were not repeated. But other scenes reappeared so often and in such predictable forms in the 1920s and 1930s that they came to qualify as clichés of advertising illustration. Some of these clichés were drawn from other popular media; several were the original contributions of advertising to the public's fund of familiar images. Whatever their previous dissemination, these clichéd images now occupied the advertising pages frequently enough to enter into the nation's visual vocabulary and assume a place within what Clifford Geertz calls "the social history of the imagination." Like materialized daydreams, they sometimes explored fantasies in time and space. Like religious icons, they often purported to symbolize some revealed truth or suggest the presence of a transcendent force. Almost always they conveyed the sense of some ineffable quality in the product or its users that lay beyond the power of mere words to explain.[7]

Fantasies of Domain: The Office Window and the Family Circle

I.   *Master of All He Surveys*

No advertising tableaux of the 1920s assumed so stereotyped a pattern as those of the typical man—Mr. Consumer—at work. In hundreds of scenes of manufacturing, delivery, and personal service, workers appeared in a variety of settings with many different props. But the man with whom the reader was expected to identify presented no such confusing diversity of semblances. Again and again, he reappeared in a setting so predictable that it became one of advertising's contributions to the nation's store of visual clichés. In his invariable role as a white-collar businessman, Mr. Consumer—the typical American husband, father, breadwinner, and man-on-the-make—did his work in an office. Almost as uniformly, his office contained a large window with a majestic view. His minimal but sufficient props included a telephone, the inevitable window, and a pristinely uncluttered desk.

Advertising strategies for particular products might suggest the presence of other men in the office to indicate an executive conference or a meeting with a salesman. Practical considerations might also require the addition of such props as a newspaper, an ashtray, or a photograph of the businessman's wife and child. But the window and the telephone were nearly always gratuitous embellishments. Rarely were they needed as props for the specific message. Rather, their presence stemmed almost entirely from the illustrator's sense of what was fitting to the image of the American man at work. Moreover, advertising strategy rarely determined the extent and content of the view through the office window. Yet, despite their freedom in choice of content, illustrators and agency art directors followed strikingly uniform patterns in depicting office-window vistas in their man-at-the-office tableaux. What assumptions underlay these visual clichés?

Both the telephone and the window-with-a-view symbolized prestige and power. Their combined presence adequately distinguished the executive, even the junior executive, from the mere salesman. The telephone placed the protagonist among those men in the firm whose rank entitled them to an individual extension. The telephone itself, as AT&T ads constantly emphasized, symbolized control, the ability to "multiply" one's personality and issue commands at a distance.[8] It

BROADER HORIZONS

MANY business men are discovering that their activities need no longer be limited to former boundaries. They are reaching out by telephone into new fields . . . developing new markets . . . finding new and unsuspected ways to make and save money.

Are you interested in increasing sales? By alternating telephone calls with personal visits, you can reach many more people, at lower cost. You can scout out new customers who formerly were beyond your reach. And you can give your old customers that prompt and satisfactory service which so often means repeat business.

Are you a merchant? The next time a customer asks for an article not in stock, telephone for it. This is direct evidence to him of your personal interest in his patronage.

Are you making purchases? By telephoning, you frequently can get better prices, or better delivery dates.

Wherever your own particular interest lies, the chances are you can extend your activities . . . broaden your horizon . . . with the help of Long Distance.

TYPICAL STATION-TO-STATION RATES

From	To	Day-time	7 P.M.	8:30 P.M.
New Haven	Boston	$ .70	$ .60	$ .40
Chicago	Grand Rapids	.75	.65	.45
St. Louis	Omaha	1.65	1.40	.95
Philadelphia	Jacksonville	3.00	2.45	1.65
San Francisco	Washington, D.C.	8.50	6.75	5.00

8.3. As "the master of all he surveys," that epitome of the American man, the business executive, commanded an unobstructed view.

also identified its user as "up-to-date," a participant in a network that transmitted the newest information. The window was even more symbolically significant. To command a view not only suggested high status within the firm (secretaries and mere salesmen almost never appeared next to large windows with views, except when they came into the boss's office); it also conjured up that ineffable sense of domain gained from looking out and down over broad expanses. Office-window illustrations inspired the welling up of a feeling best epitomized by the phrase, "master of all he surveys" (Fig. 8.3).

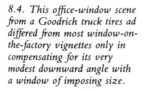

8.4. *This office-window scene from a Goodrich truck tires ad differed from most window-on-the-factory vignettes only in compensating for its very modest downward angle with a window of imposing size.*

In exploring the assumptions behind the illustrators' "free choice" of these props, I do not mean to imply that windows and telephones were imaginative embellishments of office scenes, unrelated to a contemporary reality. Undoubtedly, most business executives of the era enjoyed these prerogatives. But the persistence with which illustrators adopted an angle of vision which insured that these props would be prominently visible, the care they gave to putting the window exactly in the reader's line of vision, and the impressive scope and clarity of the view they provided through the window—all these suggest that their motive was not primarily fidelity to reality.

In these tableaux, the window shades were almost never drawn nor the blinds pulled shut. The window never appeared on the "wrong wall" of the office, where the reader could only glimpse its presence. The panorama view through the window was always expansive and usually from a considerable height. It was never obstructed by another skyscraper across the street or only a block away. Even the window panes regularly exceeded the size of those normally used in buildings of the era. This insured the business executive, and incidentally the ad reader, an unobstructed view. Occasionally the walls of the office would disappear altogether to provide the ultimate in expansive views for the businessman. The illustrator of ad executive Earnest Calkins' *Business the Civilizer* merely extended this imagery to its logical conclusion in 1928. Displaying an imagination as yet unmatched by architects of the era, he placed the advertising executive, as the archetypal modern businessman, in an office in which walls had given way entirely to a large-paned, ceiling-to-floor, wrap-around window.[9]

The content of the "view from the top" followed patterns almost as rigorously stereotyped as those of the office interior. Two basic motifs predominated. At first, in the early and mid-1920s, the most dominant was the view of the factory.

8.5. When corporation president joined research scientist, as in this illustration for a Celotex Company ad, beakers and microscopes temporarily supplanted the telephone. The agency lost no favor with its client by giving him so commanding a window on his domain.

The Power of *Practical* Imagination

TO ACCOMPLISH seemingly impossible things; to create, in a few short years, a huge industry of a known before; to satisfy certain *practical* quality of his imagination. These men have done many things that apparently "couldn't be done." They have squeezed of progress into m tus. At length the ideal material was found in bagasse, the shredded stalks of sugar cane remaining after the sugar h been ex d. These small f

By the beginning of the 1930s, this formula gave way to the other most common office-window motif—a view of the skyscrapered cityscape.[10] The decline of the first motif seemed to reflect, belatedly, a shift in business structure. The perception that real power resided in the central corporate offices located in metropolitan skyscrapers finally eclipsed the nostalgic image of the window-on-the-factory that was becoming anachronistic even during its period of greatest popularity.

The office window that looked out on the factory was identified explicitly or implicitly as the boss's office. As the visual representation of a lingering, slightly archaic, conception of business management, it implied a single factory with the business office located in an adjacent, somewhat taller building from which the boss could paternalistically oversee all the operations of his business. These tableaux, with the factory seen from a downward angle, suggested power over a very personal domain. They implied a direct, personal management in which the boss might still know by name the workers over whom he maintained his elevated surveillance. They also suggested an on-site managerial competence that could instantaneously judge production conditions by the smoke from any given factory chimney (Fig. 8.4).[11]

Although the text of the ad might deal with office supplies, advertising, or even personal goods or career advancement, the visual image clearly denoted the production-oriented businessman. In some cases, illustrators may have consciously or unconsciously intended to connote the majesty of the client himself. Certainly the immense window that an ad agency provided the president of the Dahlberg Corporation in a *Saturday Evening Post* ad seemed compatible with the agency's desire to flatter a client whom it viewed as seeking to compensate for his short physical stature with egomaniacal posturing (Fig. 8.5).[12] Other window-on-the-factory ads may have represented an agency's first step in luring the client away from old-fashioned scenes of "the founder" and "the factory." Above all, this visual cliché associated the businessman with control over an independent and autonomous domain. It established the standpoint from which the factory should be seen—the frame established by the window of the nearby, elevated executive office. No tableau that I have encountered in this era adopted an inverted point of view and showed the executive office window as seen from the factory grounds.

In reality, location of the main corporate offices at the factory site and personal supervision of production by the highest executives had already ceased to characterize most large corporations by the 1920s. Gradually, this clichéd scene of the window-on-the-factory must have come to seem archaic, even to artists who lacked the direct experience to make immediate corrections to traditional stereotypes of the business executive at work. By the mid-1920s, a picture of a skyscraper (along with an airplane and a dirigible) had become the artist's shorthand for the concept "modern." Since many corporate offices had moved to urban locations in recognition of the ascendant role of finance, advertising, legal expertise, and centralized communications in their operations, the steady drift toward the skyscraper as the locus of the typical office-with-window scene followed close upon trends in corporate structure.

Here, too, the ads gilded reality. Not all offices could occupy the topmost floors, but those in the advertising tableaux almost invariably gained this vantage. No rival skyscraper obstructed the view from these offices—although several such towers usually arose a dozen or more blocks away in order to provide an impressive cityscape.[13] The new businessman of the skyscraper office no longer looked out upon a scene of production under his control; neither did he look out upon scenes of consumption. It would have required an awkward angle of vision to encompass the streets below, and shoppers would have been too tiny to be distinct from such a distance. Instead, his window usually disclosed the tops of other skyscrapers and an occasional airplane. The view offered substitute satisfactions for a loss of individual autonomy in an age of business bureaucratization. The "company man," submerged in a large corporate hierarchy, could gaze out of his skyscraper window for compensatory visions of personal mastery. Once in a while, he might look past the fringes of the city to the landscape beyond. The horizon was broader than before; the domain more extensive but less under personal control. It suggested less a surveillance of present details than dreams of wider opportunities. In accordance with the enlarged role of planning and scientific research in business operations, the content and scope of the office view now suggested a window on the future (Fig. 8.6).[14]

Perhaps the infrequent exceptions to these two prominent office-window motifs best clarify the implications of these fantasies of domain. One exception was the business office with no view. Scenes of common office space—scenes of newspaper press rooms, typing and secretarial pools, or the desks of the sales force—do not really qualify here. But occasionally a tableau did appear of a single business office with no view. A few of these were photographs. Perhaps it was difficult to arrange the idealized, clichéd scene for the camera. Real office windows were not normally so large as illustrators liked to draw them; the vistas they afforded were unimpressive or hard to capture with clarity on film. Only with great ingenuity could a photographer capture executive, desk, window, and

Men who live for tomorrow

FOR certain scientists of the Gulf Refining Company, the present does not exist. Their eyes are on the future—for their duty is to forecast tomorrow's motoring needs.

These men must bring to their tasks a gift for scientific prophecy and a genius for perseverance. Theirs is a task in which science must live happily mated with imagination.

Will changing engine design call for a radically different motor fuel? These men must develop and perfect it. Will tomorrow's streamlined cars call for an oil able to resist airplane speeds? These men must make such oil a fact.

Already the results of their foresight have been notable. For out of the Gulf Research Laboratories came the Alchlor process of refining motor oil—probably the most significant single achievement in the history of lubrication.

From these laboratories came Gulf's process for retarding gasoline deterioration. From them, too, came a process which cut the cost ten times over of an essential industrial chemical.

Gulf products *could* be kept abreast of the times without the Gulf Research leadership, the laurels must go to the organization that walks with eyes fixed ahead.   ©1934, GULF REFINING CO., PITTSBURGH, PA.

GULF REFINING COMPANY

8.6. This "window-on-the-future" tableau fused business executive (with telephone at the ready) with company scientist. No window panes blurred his communion with the modernity of the airplane and the cubistic city.

8.7, 8.8. *Incompetents and failures had no right to windows on vast domains. They turned their backs on blocked views or gazed disconsolately at telephones they lacked the energy to use.*

external vista with proper lighting. More significantly, in the majority of non-photographic office scenes without views, the advertising text dealt with failure. In a Byers Pipe ad entitled "Couldn't the Engineer Foresee This," the executive confronted a man in overalls in an office with only a blank wall visible. In "Born Tired," Postum closed the curtains on a caffeine-drugged failure, and in "Wives must share this responsibility," Post's Bran Flakes washed out any window or view for the businessman who let down "on the very threshold of success," giving him no view of factory or city outside. The Monroe Calculating Company did provide its businessmen with a window in "A lot to pay for a needless mistake," but it denied them any vista by placing another building just beyond the window. The pattern seems clear. Failures did not look out over present or future domains (Figs. 8.7, 8.8).[15]

Another exception was the depiction of a woman working at a desk next to a window with a cityscape vista. I have discovered only two of these; secretaries normally gained such a view only when they were present in an executive's office taking dictation.[16] Of course, it is not surprising that women, who rarely occupied executive positions, did not enjoy such prerogatives. The secretary or file clerk did not need to exercise a magisterial surveillance over the factory. But the exclusion of women from the opportunity to stand or sit by office windows helped reinforce the notion of an exclusive male prerogative to view broad horizons, to experience a sense of control over large domains, to feel like masters of all they surveyed. (Figs. 8.9, 8.10).

Advertising tableaux rarely provided women with the opportunity to view *any* vista from on high, to gain a point of vantage from which to see into the future. When women did dream of the future, their vision normally appeared in a

8.9, 8.10. Even those rare ads that celebrated women in business did not
provide them with expansive and ego-enhancing office-window vistas.

thought–cloud above them. In movies, they occasionally looked out of second-story windows—usually only to spy their lover or husband with another woman in the garden below. In advertisements explicitly evoking a concern about the future, they gained the opportunity to stand hand-in-hand with their husbands, or under their sheltering arms, as the family stared out from a hill or uprising into the far distance. But in the advertising tableaux, women never gained the opportunity to look down with that magisterial sense of domain, control, and prospects for the future that the "typical" man obtained from his office window (Fig. 8.11). That difference reaffirmed which of the sexes was truly instrumental in making the world modern, whatever style choices women might make as consumers.

In one occasional variant of the "master of all he surveys" motif, advertising artists developed a visually provocative substitute for the office window. Once again, it excluded failures and women. In this visual cliché, a businessman, or more often several executives, loomed commandingly over a portion of the world miniaturized on a globe, map, or scale model. With giant hands and fingers they pointed to marketing targets, moved replicas of factories from place to place, or placed thumbtacks on cities or railroads. Sometimes they simply gazed intently at the various business options designated on a globe below them. At other times they reached out with huge hands over a scale model with a curvature at the top to indicate a broad segment of the world's surface.[17] Except for telephone operators, no women in the tableaux ever brought vast areas under similar symbolic control.

The telephone operator, of course, exercised such control only as the instrument of others. A 1929 AT & T advertisement spotlighted those whose power she represented. Six men, one with a telephone, surveyed a map on a conference table.

To all members of women's organizations in America:

THE advertisement below is one of a series now being widely published throughout the country. All thoughtful women realize that a cleaner world would be a better place in which to live; and to them such a campaign for cleanliness cannot fail to be of interest.

Furthermore these messages should prove a powerful reinforcement to the educational work being done by the Cleanliness Institute, in cooperation with social service organizations, departments of health, and schools, and through group leaders everywhere.

The Offices of Cleanliness Institute are located at 45 East 17th Street, New York City.

What do the neighbors think of *her* children?

To every mother her own are the ideal children. But what do the neighbors think? Do *they* smile at happy, grimy faces acquired in wholesome play? For people have a way of associating unclean clothes and faces with other questionable characteristics.

Fortunately, however, there's soap and water.

"Bright, shining faces" and freshly laundered clothes seem to make children welcome anywhere . . . and, in addition, to speak volumes concerning their *parents'* personal habits as well.

There's *CHARACTER* — in SOAP & WATER

PUBLISHED BY THE ASSOCIATION OF AMERICAN SOAP AND GLYCERINE PRODUCERS, INC., TO AID THE WORK OF *CLEANLINESS INSTITUTE*

8.11. *This housewife gained a window view only to recognize her guilt in the eyes of her neighbors (and her husband, judging by his glance) for her children's grimy faces.*

Planning high-speed business

An Advertisement of the
American Telephone and Telegraph Company

MORE than 95% of the telephone calls from one town to another in the Bell System are now on a high-speed basis. This holds whether the call is between neighboring cities or half way across the continent.

Even if it is a long call, the operator in many cases now asks you to hold the telephone while the call is put through.

Calls from one town to another used to be handled by one operator taking your order and giving it to another group of operators to put through. You now give your call direct to the operators who put it through—

and put it through fast while you are on the line. The average time for handling all toll and long distance calls in the Bell System was further materially reduced in 1928.

A high-speed service to all parts of the country—calls from one town to another as swift, clear and easy as local calls—that is the aim of the Bell System.

This is one of the many improvements in methods and appliances which are constantly being introduced to give high-speed telephone service. Better and better telephone service at the lowest cost is ever the goal of the Bell System.

"THE TELEPHONE BOOKS ARE THE DIRECTORY OF THE NATION"

8.12. Maps, graphs, globes, telephones, and office-window vistas of factories and skyscrapers all played a role in the imagery of a business command post. A woman's "command post" appears in Figs. 6.1 and 8.11.

Two pointed to specific objectives. A globe stood next to the table and maps and graphs covered the walls. Behind them, a window opened on a vista that included a factory chimney with smoke and a skyscraper (Fig. 8.12).[18] Such tableaux ranked with classic images of the enthronement of new elites. Anne Hollander has noted how artists employed the "immense expressive visual power" of draped cloth to convey the dignity and authority of rulers. And Herbert Collins has described how the new "sitting businessmen," the Dutch burghers of the paintings of Hans Holbein and others, were "enthroned" as a new social class through their portraits in impressive chairs, surrounded by the account books, coins, seals, and pens that suggested a world "susceptible to measurement and human manipulation."[19] In comparable fashion, advertising tableaux of the 1920s and 1930s offered powerful new visual images of man, as businessman, upraised to mastery. Telephones, huge fingers pointing to globes, maps, and scale models, and, above all, vistas through lofty office windows, provided the insignia that superseded the rich drapery and bulging ledgers of the past.

II. *Equality and Inequality in Soft Focus*

If the view from the office window defined the dominant fantasy of man's domain in the world of work, another visual cliché—the family circle—expressed the special qualities of the domain that he shared with his wife and children at home. During the nineteenth century, as a number of historians have pointed out, the notions of work and home had become dichotomized. The home came to represent a sheltered haven to which men escaped to find surcease from the harsh world of competition, ambition, and cold calculation. More than ever, the concept of the family circle, with its nuances of closure and intimate bonding, suggested a protective clustering—like the circling of the settlers' wagons—in defense of qualities utterly distinct from those that prevailed outside.[20]

This haven, in which men could experience sympathy and tenderness and refresh themselves to sally forth into the harsh "real" world outside, was understood to be another of man's domains in the sense of his ultimate authority. But the home had also come to be defined as woman's special domain. It was she who oversaw it throughout the day and imbued it with her singular qualities of softness, emotional warmth, and sacrificial love. She made the home an environment conducive to the molding of good character. Intellectual currents of the early twentieth century suggested that she and the children should exercise a larger degree of equality, at least within this domain and perhaps beyond.[21] In advertising tableaux of the family circle, these conflicting claims to governance, predominant influence, and democratic equality were subtly reconciled in visual images. The proposed reconciliations might have seemed far less congenial had they been reduced to explicit verbal formulations.

Like the fantasy of the office window, the fantasy of the family circle was conveyed almost entirely through visual imagery. Only rarely did the accompanying text attempt to further explain the meaning of the tableau. Nuances of medium, style, artistic technique, and composition often contributed as much to the meaning of a given image of the family circle as did explicit content. For instance, advertising illustrations emphasized the polarities between work and home as much through tonal qualities and atmospheric shading as they did through the depiction of the central figures.

The contrast in content was usually explicit enough. Instead of alertly surveying his domain or goading his ambition by gazing through the office window, the father, at home in the family circle, relaxed in a big chair with his wife perched beside him and his arm around his small son or daughter. But the contrast in atmosphere between home and work was even more dramatic. Instead of confronting the reader in the sharp-edged clarity of outline he had displayed in the austerity of his office, the father now appeared slightly blurred, surrounded by a sentimental haze similar in tonal quality to soft focus in a photograph.

Thus, "soft focus" defined the family circle tableau almost as readily as its specific content. Nostalgic in mood (by contrast, representations of the future in the 1920s and 1930s appeared in sparkling clarity with harsh lines and geometrical patterns), the soft-focus atmosphere suggested harmony and tenderness. It was as

8.13. A trade journal ad for Foldwell coated papers promised advertisers the emotional impact of soft-focus scenes like this.

though the artist, recognizing the moral ambience of the scene he was invading, deliberately averted the probing, judgmental gaze with which he viewed other vistas. Instead, he washed an affectionate, rosy mist over the scene. It was the family circle, rather than the home itself, that laid claim to the soft-focus treatment. Illustrations of the wife alone, or the wife and her friends in the home, rarely acquired the family-circle haze. They often depicted her efficiency as a consumer and home manager. Such tableaux, while often colorful, were more often glossy than misty. The addition of a child, connoting family, increased the likelihood of a soft-focus treatment. The addition of the father completed the circle, more or less assuring that the scene would fall into one of the sentimentalized categories of leave-taking, homecoming, the sharing of a meal, or evening leisure in the living room. On these occasions, and particularly in the evening scene, soft focus became common (Fig. 8.13).[22]

Of course advertisers did not limit the soft focus to family-circle tableaux. In other contexts it often represented an effort to imbue some other phenomenon with the emotional and moral qualities of the family circle. One series of tableaux employed the warm, misty atmosphere of the soft focus to contrast the personalized intimacy of the locally owned, independent grocery store with the cold impersonality of the externally controlled chain store.[23] Procter and Gamble introduced a blurry, soft-focus-with-highlights style for outdoor scenes of mothers, washerwomen, and children during happy washdays. When Arco-Petro Boilers demonstrated how to make the basement into a family "fun room," this formerly

8.14, 8.15, 8.16. *These three variations in the spatial organization of family-circle tableaux found a common unity in the warm, misty quality so typical of such scenes.*

cold and harsh setting suddenly acquired a soft, hazy, family-circle atmosphere.[24]

Although its atmosphere served other uses, the visual cliché of the family circle found its touchstone in the evening scene in the living room. All members of the family appeared in relatively close physical proximity. Father and mother were both present. And while it is difficult to explain exactly how this notion was conveyed, the reader felt assured that all their children were also present. So thoroughly were readers conditioned to accept such scenes as representing the completed family circle that no suspicion was likely to arise that another child might be upstairs or away from home. No toys rested on a section of the floor unoccupied by a child. No unfinished project or opened magazine lay on a table unattended by one of the visible family members. Never did picture or text suggest that other children had gone elsewhere in the house to amuse themselves or that mother and father might be worried about children who had not returned home on time. This was the family unified and intact.

Three variant groupings of family members dominated the family-circle tableaux: (1) father seated with mother and children clustered around him (Fig. 8.14); (2) both mother and father seated in oblique apposition to one another with the children completing a rough circle as they played on the floor (Fig. 8.15); (3) mother and father seated apart, each accompanied by a child (Fig. 8.16). In the latter case, the reader completed the "circle," which was often, more precisely, a kind of triangle. Merchandising strategy sometimes dictated a fourth formula in which the product—a radio, phonograph, room heater, or clock—joined the family circle as the focus of attention, the family forming a complementary semicircle with their backs partly toward the reader. Occasionally the artist made the imagery of the closed circle more explicit by superimposing swirling, concentric lines, a circular border, or an arc of light.[25]

Thus the visual clichés of the family circle stressed harmony, cohesion, and unity. This did not *necessarily* imply paternal domination. In fact, one variant of the family-circle tableau, the family conference, often advocated, by example, a policy of family democracy. Teenage and pre-teen children sometimes joined the conference, their inclusion depending on whether the advertiser, often a magazine publisher, wished to emphasize the influence of younger readers on family decisions. Sometimes these ads portrayed the politics of the family conference as consumer decisions by ballot, based on the presumption of one person, one vote. Father, apparently, had no alternative when outvoted but to submit to the majority decision.[26]

Although the father relinquished any clear claim to sovereignty in consumer decisions, he appeared to do so voluntarily—perhaps even with a bit of condescension. In the more common tableaux of the family circle during evening leisure, he usually retained his stature as the most important and *au courant* family member. Visual clichés of the family circle reconciled newer notions of family democracy with more traditional images of family governance. They placed the wife and children in less blatantly dependent and deferential postures than they occupied in mid-nineteenth century depictions of the family circle, yet they subtly reaffirmed the father's dominant role.

At least two visual indexes to dominance within the family can be detected in the family-circle tableaux. One of these is possession of the evening newspaper. The prerogative of first or major claim to the newspaper belonged to the family member most informed about important current matters, with whatever modicum of power such knowledge implied. The newspaper reader boasted the best preparation to act on behalf of the family on matters linking it to the outside world. Of the sixty-nine family-circle tableaux I have noted that depict newspaper

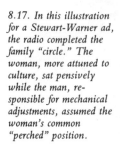

8.17. In this illustration
for a Stewart-Warner ad,
the radio completed the
family "circle." The
woman, more attuned to
culture, sat pensively
while the man, re-
sponsible for mechanical
adjustments, assumed the
woman's common
"perched" position.

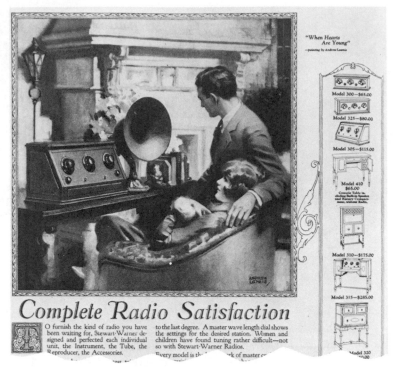

reading, thirty-three portray the husband holding exclusive possession of the
paper while the wife does handwork, reads a book, tells the children a story, or
otherwise busies herself with domestic tasks. Only twice does the wife have sole
possession. In twenty-six other instances, the husband sits in a chair with the
paper open and his wife looks on while sitting on the arm of the chair or standing
behind. Only three times does the wife sit reading the paper while her husband
looks on, and in only five cases do both possess separate sections of the paper
equally, despite the fact that several of these tableaux stress family readership of
a particular newspaper. Wives often read books—both in family-circle scenes and
in tableaux of women relieved from drudgery. But book reading suggested the
"escapism" of novels or the absorption in "culture" appropriate to the woman's
responsibility for refinement. Possession of the newspaper defined the member of
the family with priority to the right to know.[27]

The typical position of the wife in tableaux in which the newspaper is shared
suggests a second significant index to the subtle nuances of dominance and subordination that modified ostensible parity within the family circle. Two positions
within the living room scene carry clear implications of subordination because
they are frequently occupied by young children. These are the floor and the arm
of a chair or sofa. With rare exceptions, neither the wife nor the husband sits or
kneels on the floor. Such is not the case with the less humble, but nevertheless
subordinate, chair-arm perch so often occupied by children. Out of eighty-eight
family-circle tableaux in which only a single chair or sofa seat is occupied, the

Alone·· she faces this problem

And much depends on your wife's good judgment

8.18. Contrasts in tone, color, and focus distinguished father's cold, hard-edged domain of work from mother's circle of soft-focus warmth in this ad for A&P stores. Note how the window is treated in each vignette.

TO YOU, this morning was like a thousand other mornings. Up on time—breakfast in a hurry—off to business. Problems came your way. Some you handled alone. But o~

She must seek variety to tempt the appetites of the children, to keep them healthy and robust—to make your meals appetizing too. ʌ   ⁻ᵉ turns to ꓥ⸱⸱ᴰ for there she f

husband claims the right to the seat in sixty-five. In fifty-one of these instances, the wife perches accommodatingly on the arm of the chair or sofa, usually balancing herself by putting her arm lightly around her husband's shoulders. In fourteen instances, she stands behind him, diffidently bending or looking over his shoulder.[28] Interestingly, in nineteen of the twenty-eight contrary examples, in which the man balances on the arm of his wife's chair or stands nearby, the tableau advertised either a radio or a phonograph. Apparently, in the presence of culturally uplifting music, the woman more often gained the right of reposed concentration while the (more technologically inclined) man stood prepared to change the records or adjust the radio dials (Fig. 8.17).[29]

As in the case of the office window, the specific props and configurations of the visual cliché of the family circle derived primarily from the illustrator's free choice. Specific product strategies might require that a radio or a furnace be present, but these rarely determined the details of spatial arrangement or the nature of other props. In visually conveying the message "family circle," advertising artists drew upon a folk legacy of conventional images. Occasionally they modified these slightly to enhance the image of equality within the family and thus express the advertisers' partiality to a broader consumer democracy.

Despite the striking contrasts between the sharp, metallic tone of the office-window tableau and the soft-focus ambiance of the family circle, both constituted fantasies of domain (Fig. 8.18). The narrow domain of the family circle was almost invariably one of harmony. To the woman, the visual cliché of the family

For 1936 : a new outlook on life

THIS is a message to people who have been turning their backs on a very good friend the whole year long. ... a *symptom* ... me

resolutions for the future? Before the new year dawns, *do something about* that warning. Do the intelligent thing—*see your doctor.*

thus putting an unfair burden upon your heart. Or perhaps an examination will reveal some functional disorder which ... of reaching

tor's office, head high, unafraid, to face 1936 with the invigorating knowledge that you have the physical ... ment with ... ght for

8.19. In the visual language of advertising, the future was usually defined as a source of light, as in this illustration from an ad for the pharmaceutical firm of Parke, Davis and Company.

circle served as a reminder of her responsibility to ensure a setting of tranquil, tidy orderliness for the reunification of the family at day's end. To the man, it suggested that he should not survey this domain with the aggrandizing eye of ambition that he cast through the office window, but rather with a benevolent and forbearing regard, one that assumed but did not flaunt his authority.

The visual cliché of the family circle served to reconcile the past and the present, authority and democracy. It defined domain as security rather than as opportunity. Above all, it connoted stability. The products of modern technology, including radios and phonographs, were comfortably accommodated within the hallowed circle. Whatever pressures and complexities modernity might bring, these images implied, the family at home would preserve an undaunted harmony and security. In an age of anxieties about family relationships and centrifugal social forces, this visual cliché was no social mirror; rather, it was a reassuring pictorial convention.

The
new business
of retailing money

WITH THE RISE of the industrial age in the last half century has come a new need and a new business.

Into the lives of families that once produced their own food, built their own houses, wove their own cloth, has come a great change. Today, they work for wages, for money that in itself neither nourishes, clothes, nor shelters.

Frequently their pay envelopes and savings funds are not sufficient to pay for sickness, lay-offs, taxes, births, deaths. In such times of stress families must have extra funds to subsist.

No former plan of finance answered their necessity. Banks cannot afford to lend little sums at banking interest. Eighty-five per cent of ... ...lation have ... ...rity on which b... ...lend.

Pioneer and leader of this business is Household Finance Corporation. Twenty-seven states have now passed adequate small loan laws, and last year 148 Household offices in 90 principal cities of 13 states* served more than 400,000 families.

To them Household loaned approximately $80,000,000 in amounts up to $300, for provident purposes. Their required repayments over twenty months averaged under 6% of their incomes, enabling them to work their way out of debt aided by the Household budget plan.

No collateral was asked of them but the signatures of husband and wife, the security that is found in every home, and the ability to repay—the ... ...ndest basis there is for ... ... loan. More, the best ... ... back of the... ... ...

8.20. Frequently the source of light in images of the future was revealed as a gleaming city of skyscrapers.

Fantasies of Dimension:
The Future and the Eternal Village

I. *Toward the Heavenly City*

When father, mother, and child in an advertising tableau stood gazing off into the distance with their backs turned directly or obliquely toward the reader, it could mean only one thing. In the language of visual clichés, they were looking into the future. Perhaps deriving its inspiration from the hallowed image of the American frontiersman, first glimpsing the westward course of empire from the apex of a mountain pass, this visualization of the future objectified the linguistic bias that gave the future a spatial location. It was a place toward which one "faced" because it was "in front" of you.[30] Occasionally, advertising tableaux allowed the nature of the future to remain indistinct. The reader joined the protagonists in gazing toward a blurred line of horizon or a distant, mysterious light. More commonly, the future emerged as a towering and resplendent city (Figs. 8.19, 8.20). In both cases, when characters in the tableau stood facing the future, their faces were bathed in bright light.[31] To move toward the future was to move toward greater illumination.

In a few instances, the city in the distance took the shape of a fantasy city with an eclectic architecture composed of Byzantine, Egyptian, Gothic, and modern forms. But these images, as in the case of Postum Cereal's healthy city of Wellville, were usually allegories for specific fantasies rather than conceptions of the future.[32] By general consensus, the true image of the future was the skyscraper

SEVEN YEARS AGO, in these pages, we published an advertisement, headed "The Pioneer and the Vision,"* in which we paid tribute to those early pioneers who dared conceive of a mighty nation rising from tangled woods and fertile plains.

They were courageous, far-seeing men, but there was not one of them who possibly could have conceived the progress that has been made in the last one hundred years. Nor is there a man alive today who can draw an adequate picture of this country as it will be in 2026.

The dream of yesterday is a reality today—an accepted and almost commonplace achievement tomorrow. You need search no farther than the present-day development of radio to see how far the vision of the possibilities in just one field can widen in a few years. Yet there are those who catch the vision of a

THE WIDENED VISION

great success and those who pass it by.

It has been less than eighty-five years since bathtubs were taxed $30 a year as "a luxurious and undemocratic vanity," declared unlawful in at least one state, and banned by physicians as unhealthful.

It has been less than thirty years since the Captain of Park Guards in Fairmount Park, Philadelphia, wrote: "The automobile has not entered the park in sufficient numbers to warrant an expression as to

its safety to the public. . . . It seems to me a man versed in mechanics will have to be stationed in each district of the park to afford relief where the machine breaks down."

One of the most important functions of an advertising agency is to look ahead and anticipate the widened vision of each new decade or generation. To help the advertiser to keep his business so flexible and modern that he always will be a step ahead of changes in the public's opinions and needs. To be willing, yet not too eager, to discard old practices and adopt the new. To be able to distinguish between a mirage and a true picture of the coming years.

*In the issue of March 8, 1919, the first of this present series of N. W. Ayer & Son advertisements was published. For seven years our announcements have appeared each month without interruption. We speak from experience when we say "Keeping Everlastingly At It Brings Success."

N. W. AYER & SON
ADVERTISING HEADQUARTERS, PHILADELPHIA

NEW YORK   BOSTON   CHICAGO   SAN FRANCISCO

8.21. *The central vision and goal of America's celebrated frontier farmer, this N. W. Ayer and Son illustration implied, had been a future crowned with such towering cities as were to be expected at the end of rainbows.*

8.22, 8.23. Advertising leaders easily agreed: when Americans from pioneers to modern young businessmen looked toward the future for inspiration, they had inevitably glimpsed the skyscrapers of an alabaster city.

city (Fig. 8.21). With its gleaming white towers forming a single, symmetrical apex, this was the fabled "alabaster city" with machine-tooled edges and a burnished sheen (Figs. 8.22, 8.23). One popular convention, usually employed to visualize the future of an extant city, placed an idealized, skyscraper-dominated image of the present city in the middle distance with another taller, brighter, even more "inspirational" version of the same city rising up from this city into the clouds above. The future was not merely a skyscraper city; it was a super-city that thrust itself into the heavens by using the present city as a base.[33]

More detailed views of the interior of the future city presented an even more stereotyped vision of the cubistic urban future. Whereas the distant vision usually viewed the city from a low angle to emphasize its towering height, the internal vision looked sharply downward in order to include streets as well as towers. From this perspective, the visual impact of the freeways nearly equaled that of the skyscrapers. Criss-crossing at two or three levels, these broad, elevated highways often cut through the middle of the skyscrapers at heights ranging from the third to the thirtieth floor. The highways, crossing at exact right angles, contained no ramps or interchanges. The tableaux showed no device by which a car could change direction and move from one freeway level to another.[34] Cars and airplanes often appeared in such city interior scenes, but the viewer rarely caught a glimpse of human figures. When a person did become visible, as did a single master-controller of traffic in a Brunswick Radio ad, he acquired a futuristic

The Equitable looks back 75 years

... and 75 years ahead!

Not For a Day, But For All Time

visage that was vaguely "Martian."[35] Here was one way, at least, to translate the fantasy of domain from the present office window into a more centralized, mechanized future (Figs. 8.24, 8.25).

Much of the content of these visual clichés of the future seems quite unremarkable. It is hardly surprising that metropolitan advertising artists, in an age of advancing urbanization, should have depicted the future as a city. Such a vision has been popular even in some rural societies and in eras with very different conceptions of the city. Nor is it surprising that illustrators should have envisioned the city of the future by projecting the current wave of skyscraper construction on a bigger scale. As the famous architectural renderer Hugh Ferriss remarked in 1929, "the most popular image of the Future City . . . is composed of buildings which, without any modification of their existing nature, have simply grown higher and higher!"[36] That the future should appear as a source of light seems unexceptional in a society confident of progress. Seen either from an interior view or from afar, the city of the future connoted prosperity, cleanliness, order, efficiency, and inspiration—conventional values, all.

Equally conventional, but more instructive, was the manner in which such visual clichés of the future left a central problem unresolved. The geometric skyscraper city, seen from outside, presented an awesome spectacle. Its systematized interior conveyed a promise of efficient integration of mass activity. But, with the exception of the single, imperial figure of the traffic controller (an image

8.24, 8.25. Close-ups of the future city looked downward, associating the reader with those who would exercise control. Only separate nostalgic scenes provided the relief of a more "human" scale. Note the elevated highways that pierce the skyscrapers in both the segment of an Equitable ad and the Brunswick cityscape.

roughly analogous to that of the advertising man as manipulator and controller of "traffic" in goods and desires), no image appeared that revealed how this awesome, architectonic future city could be made compatible with life on a human scale. In his essay "Psyching out the City," William R. Taylor provocatively describes how American photographers struggled "to recover or re-create human scale" in the "disruptive visual setting" of the modern city.[37] It can hardly be said that the ad creators "struggled" with this problem. Rather, they evaded it. As expert manipulators they simply assumed that such problems could easily be finessed. Pictorially they distracted attention from the issue of human scale with resplendent visions of futuristic cities as symbols of progress. More significantly, they relied on separate, compensating images to retain the purity and simplicity of their vision. They relegated the responsibility for more consoling visual depictions of ongoing life on a coherent, neighborly scale to another visual cliché—that of the "eternal village."

II.   The World We Have Saved

Small towns in America did not remain static as the great cities expanded in the nineteenth and early twentieth centuries. New forms of transportation—canals, then railroads and highways—transformed their physical configurations and their economic roles. In grain-producing regions, the grain elevator became a common landmark in towns along the railroads. Tides of immigration often brought demographic changes to towns as well as to cities. Many small towns contained a cluster of families from at least one ethnic minority. As they grew modestly in size, some towns gained retail outlets by the 1920s for nationwide gasoline, dry goods, grocery, and drug chains. Many contained small factories, mills, or canneries. Other towns, their function undermined by changes in transportation, disappeared or slumped into a "spirit of decay." Many Americans concluded that small towns, as a reality, were "finished."[38]

But the economic transformation of "village America" hardly devitalized the American village as a visual cliché in advertising. Like a lingering ghost-image, the idealized American small town, with its connotations of unity, neighborliness, and comfortable human scale, became a sight more familiar to Americans through the advertising pages than through their direct experience. Few actual American villages of the 1920s and 1930s, with populations between 100 and 1,000 persons, could have seemed other than disjointed, slovenly, and discordant to those whose conception of the small town had been shaped by the advertising tableaux.

In most advertisements, the village appeared as part of the background rather than as the focus of attention. Often it was no more than a stylized miniature. Still, it helped evoke an atmosphere and contributed to a conventional perception of the American landscape. Certain stereotyped characteristics can be observed even in the most minute versions of this visual cliché. Almost invariably, the idealized village contained a single spire that towered above the other buildings. In most cases, this spire was identifiable as a church steeple. In other cases it was sufficiently indistinct to have been either a steeple or the spire of a town hall. In nearly every case, the houses of the town were grouped closely together, with the steeple or spire roughly in the center. Almost never did another prominent building appear—except in close-up illustrations of the main street with its bank, general store, and perhaps a gas station and movie theater. Grain elevators, mills, and other evidences of processing or production for export were virtually non-existent. If a highway entered the town, it usually followed a gently winding course (Figs. 8.26 through 8.29).[39]

These tableaux did not present idealized American villages as nostalgic images of the past. Although often stylized in appearance, these villages purported to represent part of the current landscape that consumers would experience while using the batteries, motor oils, tires, auto accessories, soaps, telephones, and other products featured in the ads. As they viewed repeated images of these pristine eternal villages, readers could find assurance that, despite the advance of awesome and impersonal skyscraper cities, their society still retained the qualities suggested by "village America."

The dominating steeple of the eternal village served both to symbolize a spiritual unity and to establish a comprehensible standard of physical scale. The single church (no village tableaux hinted at internal differences by depicting more than one church) suggested social harmony and the supremacy of higher, spiritual values. The clustering of houses around this focal point reinforced the image of unity and harmony. Huddled together, they implied neighborliness and demographic homogeneity. Although no inhabitant of the village could gain a sense

This man is in the business of making dreams come true

NO crystal gazer is this man —no prophet who can peer into the future. Yet to him falls the task of taking the uncertainty, out of tomorrow.

He deals with the plans and hopes about which lives are built in dreams of providing for the party to come. Of achieving security and peace of mind, of relieving a measure of life's comforts and anxieties. All these things can be realized with his help.

For this man is the instrument of a force which makes dreams come true—and that force is Insurance.

With insurance, and his knowledge of its application, he makes men sure of their goals years before they reach them.

Through life insurance he makes it possible for men to create estates, for their families without having misers to do it. Through retirement insurance he shows

those who dream of leisure in their sunset years the way to provide an income for those years—safely, scientifically.

Special income to send children to school and college, funds to meet unpaid portions of mortgages, life incomes for widows . . . all these he shapes insurance to cover.

Through other forms of insurance he frees people from the financial set-backs that emergencies so often impose. Automobile insur-

ance guards them while they drive. Fire insurance protects their homes. Accident insurance stands between them and hospital bills.

What your dreams for the future are, we do not know. But whatever they are, it's quite certain that this man—The Travelers representatives—can help you realize them.

The Travelers Insurance Company, The Travelers Indemnity Company, The Travelers Fire Insurance Company, Hartford, Conn.

MORAL: INSURE IN THE TRAVELERS

No Charge for Overtime

RIGHT among your friends and neighbors you will find plenty of car owners who have found that Exides outlast other batteries. Yet this overtime is not paid for by the Exide owner —it pays him.

The original price you pay for an Exide is extremely low,

and this rugged battery stays on the job so long that it proves most economical.

A nearby Exide Dealer has the economical battery for your car. You can also get a complete line of Exide Radio Batteries at Exide Dealers' as well as at radio dealers'.

THE ELECTRIC STORAGE BATTERY COMPANY, Philadelphia

THE LONG-LIFE BATTERY FOR YOUR CAR

Stranded in a Small town . . . He kept both Engagements by Telephone

A PLANT superintendent of a large tire company was on a business trip in Canada. He missed his connection and was stranded in a town with one train a day. Two important engagements loomed ahead—one in Toronto, the other in New York. He thought of the telephone. He called the two cities. He completed his business so satisfactorily in both places that neither of the trips was necessary.

The telephone is always ready to put important things through. A man in St. Louis was too busy to go to Memphis and back. He made the round trip by telephone. It resulted in $14,000 worth of business.

A Seattle lumber company received a carload order on condition that it could be shipped in five

days. Special items had to be cut. A telephone call to Portland, costing $1.15, found a mill that could do the work. The car was shipped in time. A Minnesota commission house invested $43.60 in nine telephone calls to five cities and sold 60 carloads—$14,640 worth—of potatoes.

What delay, worry or expense could you save today? Is there a misunderstanding to be adjusted, an important sale or purchase hanging fire? Calls are cheap. Typical station to station day rates: Chicago to South Bend, 60c. Peoria to St. Louis, 90c. Cleveland to Philadelphia, $1.60. Pittsburgh to St. Louis, $2.35. Boston to Chicago, $5.25.

Out of town calling is quick and calling by number takes even less time. Bell Telephone Service . . . Quick . . . Inexpensive . . . Universal

8.26, 8.27, 8.28, 8.29. Advertising's thousands of "eternal villages," almost invariably oriented around a single church steeple, suggested social harmony. For stylized background versions, see also Figs. 8.6 and 10.8.

When the sky signals, "It's going to rain," it also says, "Put on chains"

Wet Rubber Slips— WEED CHAINS Grip

The Correct Way to Put on Weed Chains

Drape chains over back tires with red connecting hook last resting on the road, toward the rear. Turk forward end of chains under tires.

Half car forward just enough to run over the slack ends so that the red connecting hooks are about a foot above the road

Connect the inside hook first, then the outside tight as possible by hand. When car runs the chains will have proper stretching action.

Made by the Makers of WEED Levelizers and WEED Bumpers

of hegemony by gazing down from some skyscraper window, still all residents, the tableaux implied, could shape their own destinies and enjoy congenial personal interaction with their neighbors on a warm, human scale. Advertising's eternal villages were invariably neat and trim, never decaying or funky. Nothing in the tableaux suggested that people were regularly leaving such towns for opportunities elsewhere, or that any reason existed why someone should wish to leave.

Whether advertising illustrators recognized that such eternal villages contained as much fantasy as their visions of futuristic cities is difficult to assess. Occasionally stylized images of the small town appeared in tableaux with equally stylized skyscraper cities, the contrasting visual clichés symbolizing the society's urban-rural spectrum (see Fig. 8.6).[40] E. R. Squibb and Sons employed these complementary images on an immense lighted sign that dominated the nation's most prominent advertising marquee—Times Square. A radiant sun, which was gradually transformed into the Squibb logo, arose from a body of blue water. Flanking the logo stood two glowing images, which together represented the entire nation—a "towering city" on one side and "a country village, with its cottages, trees, and a church steeple" on the other.[41] In such contrasts, village and city were equally idealized and stylized.

In other contexts, advertisers distinguished between the clichéd image of the eternal village and various actual small towns. In an Aluminum Company of America ad, which described how "smiling towns" could surpass their dingier neighbors through "the transforming power of aluminum paint," the idealized drawing of the archetypal "smiling town" at the top stood in pristine contrast to the less romanticized examples of the application of aluminum paint to lamp poles, water towers, and bridges in the pictures below.[42] More striking, in their divergence from the eternal-village image of the American small town, were the photographs of actual small towns in the advertisements by *Grit* magazine. Boasting of *Grit*'s coverage of such flourishing small towns as Bassett, Virginia, and Mount Jewett, Pennsylvania, these ads employed photographs that bore little resemblance to the conventional advertising image of the American village. The photographs showed bustling downtown shopping districts, parking lots, and factories. Not a single church steeple was to be seen (Fig. 8.30).[43]

But advertising illustrators ignored such glimpses of "real" small towns when called upon to depict rural landscapes. The villages in most advertising tableaux looked the way people wanted them to look—or at least the way advertisers assumed they should look. Such eternal villages assured readers that the qualities of life on a human scale were not lost in the midst of a "progress" symbolized by skyscrapers and elevated freeways. Could such assurances really make the depersonalized images of the city of the future more readily acceptable? All we can say for sure is that such visual clichés allowed readers to contemplate separately two idyllic settings that could not have been convincingly fused into a single image: the cold efficiency of the city of the future and the warm neighborliness of the eternal village.

Through compartmentalization, these visual clichés embraced and reinforced a popular ambition to gain the best of both worlds. One could more comfortably enjoy visions of a future amidst the thrilling towers and intricate networks of a

—typical of the 16,000 small towns where 500,000 families read GRIT every week

MAIN STREET BUSINESS SECTION

TANNERY EMPLOYS 185

GLASS WORKS EMPLOYS 125

TYPICAL HOMES

THE tannery is going full blast and so is the glass works. In a population of 1,379 there are only 290 families to provide workers for two large industries, so it is necessary to draw help from nearby towns.

Wages are good, living standards high. The local banker says business is better than it was in 1929.

Every week GRIT sells 155 copies in Mount Jewett — the broadest coverage in this town provided by any national publication.

Mount Jewett is just another of the 16,000 thriving, able-to-buy small towns where your business will be better when you put GRIT on your advertising schedules.

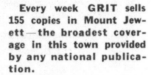

America's Greatest Weekly Newspaper!

8.30. GRIT, a national, small-town weekly newspaper, crowded its ads with photographs of factories and busy main streets. These demonstrations of buying power stood in stark contrast to the image of the eternal village.

dazzling but uncompassionate city if one could be sure that there were still neighborly villages to which one might occasionally retire, physically or psychologically, to regain contact with the sentimental side of life. Like the polarity of office and home, the implicitly complementary clichés of eternal village and skyscraper city encouraged a faith in the possibilities of progress without cost through broader, but highly segmented, lives. In subsequent decades, despite the growth of suburbia, Americans would not find it easy, or even entirely satisfying, to compartmentalize their lives in the quest for painless progress in the way that such scenarios seemed to envision.

Visual Clichés as Icons

At a certain point, almost impossible to define with precision, some of the visual clichés of the advertising pages acquired a liturgical dimension. Advertising, of course, did not deal with the conventional objects of religious worship. Advertisements were *secular* sermons, exhortations to seek fulfillment through the consumption of material goods and mundane services. Agency men warned their colleagues not to quote the Bible or otherwise invite religious controversy. Religious figures, including Jesus, Mary, the apostles, saints, and even contemporary ministers, almost never appeared in advertisements.[44] One might conclude that advertisers had accepted a doctrine of two distinct spheres—the material and the spiritual—and had resolved to confine themselves to "the things that are Caesar's."

But the silence of advertising on matters of religion did not entail so absolute a distinction between material and spiritual realms as might be imagined. By declining to compare the worth of their products with the worth of spiritual objectives, advertisers found themselves free to employ their fullest talents for glorification without incurring charges of idolatry. If an advertisement paid effusive homage to a door hinge or tube of toothpaste, it did not preclude the possibility, at least in theory, that an even higher pitch of adulation might be found for religious devotions. Leo Spitzer, the noted literary scholar, once suggested that popular convention permitted advertisers to exaggerate, as if all their statements were placed within qualifying "quotation marks." These invisible quotes—tacitly understood to exist by both advertiser and reader—said, in effect: We both know that the nature of advertising requires this statement to be exaggerated beyond all reasonable measure; therefore we both recognize that it must be discounted to some degree, and that the words and images glorifying the product are not to be taken quite at face value. With such quotation marks implicitly understood, products could virtually be deified in the "poetic" and "playful" language of advertisements without suggesting that they competed with religious figures as objects of devotion.[45]

Advertising leaders knew, however, that some Americans still worried that the goods exalted by advertising *did* compete against "higher goods" in seeking to tap a finite reservoir of public adulation. A few expressed fears that the booming voice of advertising would drown out spiritual appeals. Copywriters generally respected certain boundaries of the spiritual realm by declining to use words such as "worship," "pray," "bless," "revere," "bow down to," or even "adore" to describe the attitude the consumer should take toward the product. But illustrations did not observe such limits, and their subtlety in inducing a reverential attitude from the reader made it harder to discount their appeal to the proper degree. Such images as the family circle and the city of the future certainly invited attitudes of veneration or awe from the viewer. Several other visual clichés made products into virtual idols, creating a secular iconography for the age.

In her provocative essay "Advertising—Sacred and Profane," Marghanita Laski explains why it was virtually inevitable that advertisers would gravitate toward depictions of the product as idol. By asking in what context people typically find advertising offensive, she identifies a group of "numinous" situations and events that trigger "life-enhancing feelings" or "a passion of awe." (Rudolph Otto, in his study of the phenomenology of religion, first proposed the term "numinous" to characterize the nonrational elements of awe-inspiring "majesty," transporting "ravishment," and a sense of "absolute overpoweringness" in religious apprehension.) According to Laski, the realm of the "numinous" includes religion, royalty, art, education, national glory, natural beauty, love and marriage, childbirth, and childhood—all "sacred spheres" in which advertising is often seen as an incongruous and obnoxious intrusion.[46] Yet advertisers, she points out, although wary of the negative reactions they might provoke by invading such numinous realms, still recognize that people yearn to experience moments of enhancement, awe, and rapture. Given the power of such noncommercial aspirations, Laski notes, few advertisers will restrict themselves to appeals that belong only to the sphere of the marketplace. Not only do consumers want to believe that material goods will bring them transcendent, non-material satisfactions, but advertising men wish to see themselves as "creative men delivering not only the goods but the Goods."[47]

Advertisers, then, faced the strategic problem of identifying their product with life-enhancing moments without a blunt obtrusiveness that would destroy the quality of numinosity. To shout "Be patriotic; buy my product," or "Experience the sublime rapture of owning a product illuminated by God's holy light; send your money today," would embarrass any respectable advertiser. But visual clichés that employed vague forms of sacred symbolism rather than specific religious figures, icons, and relics might subtly infuse the product with numinosity. Such visual strategies sought to transform the product, in Laski's phrase, into a "surrogate trigger" for producing those life-enhancing feelings that consumers avidly pursued. As an ad in *Printers' Ink Monthly* offhandedly noted in 1926, advertisements were "beginning to occupy the place in inspiration that religion did several hundred years ago."[48]

I. *Heroic Proportions*

Some of the visual clichés that contributed to the numinosity of products were blatantly obvious. Many advertisers attempted to awe viewers with pure magnitude. Huge refrigerators towered above tiny towns of consumers; silhouetted against the starry sky, they stood guard over communities like giant sentinels. Immense cars straddled the rivers and towns of miniaturized countrysides below,

8.31, 8.32. One way to suggest the majesty and significance of the product or service was to enshrine it above a town or city in awesome size. Radiant beams from undisclosed sources further enhanced the effect.

symbolizing the command over the landscape obtainable through the automobile. Huge newspapers and magazines in the sky reflected illumination on cities and crowds below (Figs. 8.31, 8.32).[49] *Tide* described the fictitious salon that appeared frequently as the backdrop for automobile ads as dwarfing Madison Square Garden "to insignificance." Next to this "super showroom" of the tableaux, it observed, "many a stately cathedral would lose grandeur." (See Fig. 10.2.) In what one commentator described as a "burning in" campaign, the Goodyear Rubber Company erected its name in immense block letters on majestic mesas and mountains in the hope of imprinting this image indelibly on the reader's mind. In other ads, gigantic tires and batteries floated in the sky; colossal tubes of toothpaste and cans of car polish dwarfed their surroundings.[50]

No one expected consumers to be deceived by such images. The incongruous size of the product served to arrest the attention of the viewer who, knowing its real size, would make a substantial discount. But some advertising writers suggested that the "heroic-proportions" technique might earn the product an enhanced stature despite the viewer discount. To place a battery box in the sky above a busy metropolis and to surround it with miniature scenes, one commentator noted, "is to give great importance to a commonplace device."[51] Another critic of advertising art pointed out that the "kolossal" image was not only "almost overpowering in its demand upon reader attention" but also commanded "confidence and respect." Such an illustration, he continued, "figuratively batters down mental resistance by the sheer physical attributes of size, mass, bulk, and specific gravity." Rosalind Williams has recently characterized such tactics as an

8.33. It hardly seems surprising that a product of such heroic proportions and capable of emitting such lustrous beams should attract an adoring throng. Fortuitously, everyone so attracted looked prosperous enough to buy.

"esthetic of the primitive." Sympathizing with critics of ultramodern lighting displays in the auto salons of late nineteenth-century Paris, she observes that the "sheer disproportion of scale" in commercial displays served to display raw power and to "stun the spectator into a passive, confused stupor so that he is only able to look, look, look." Although "bigger-than-life" images in twentieth-century print advertisements lacked that degree of power and were undoubtedly discounted by readers as obvious visual puffery, they still conveyed impressions of the product as dominant or transcendent, if not awesome.[52]

II. *Adoring Throngs*

Advertising illustrators frequently introduced tiny human figures into the heroic-proportions displays in order to emphasize the awesome magnitude of the product. These dwarfed human figures served another purpose as well. They were the advertiser's shills, conveying by their demeanor a model for the appropriate attitude toward the product. A single individual would have been sufficient to establish the scale of proportion, but such illustrations often depicted large crowds swarming around the product or gazing up to it in a worshipful posture.[53] These "adoring throngs" manifested the manufacturer's fantasy of public response to his product and sought to sway consumers through a bandwagon appeal. Advertising agents must also have recognized the bewitching auxiliary effect of such illustrations on their clients' egos (Fig. 8.33).

You're NOT
just one of a crowd

When it comes to life insurance you need to be considered as an individual. You have ideas and ambitions of your own. Bend all your efforts to make them come true!

In order to be doubly certain, begin now by insuring these two desirable objectives:

(1) Financial Independence for yourself... and

(2) A program of protection for your family.

To help you achieve these objectives, The Equitable offers expert advice and guidance through its Case Method of life insurance planning—a method which gives you an individualized program at no extra cost. Equitable representatives are carefully trained to apply the Case Method to your life insurance needs.

You will be interested in reading how this Equitable service has benefited other men and women by providing them with solutions to their individual financial problems. Just fill in the coupon below and this valuable information will be mailed promptly. Send for it today.

THE EQUITABLE

FAIR – JUST

LIFE ASSURANCE

SECURITY – PEACE OF MIND

SOCIETY

MUTUAL – COOPERATIVE

OF THE U.S.

NATION-WIDE SERVICE

The EQUITABLE Life Assurance Society of the United States
Thomas I. Parkinson, *President.*   393 Seventh Avenue, New York, N. Y.

I am interested in your "Case Method" of adapting life insurance to specific needs. Kindly mail explanatory booklet.

NAME

ADDRESS   AGE

8.34. The power of this ad stemmed from its sensitivity to the rising fear among readers, dwarfed by the scale of modern mass society, of being submerged into "the crowd."

In their visual clichés of adoring throngs, advertisers expressed one facet of their understanding of the problem of man in the mass. Constrained by their economic function to move masses of people to action, and dependent on the theory of economic progress through mass consumption for self-justification, many advertising leaders nevertheless contemplated the rise of the modern mass man with fear and contempt. Bruce Barton prized José Ortega y Gasset's *The Revolt of the Masses* and recommended it to acquaintances; other advertising leaders reiterated Ortega y Gasset's warnings about the threat of the tasteless masses to the citadels of high culture. Like other elites, advertisers tended to identify crowds with unruly mobs and to preach the virtues of the man who pulled himself out of the masses through special effort. Recognizing, empathetically, a rising public fear of submergence in mass conformity (partly induced by their own successes in mass merchandising), advertisers frequently appealed to this concern by advertising products on the strength of their capacity to lift the individual out of the crowd (Fig. 8.34).[54] Significantly, visual depictions of the individual emerging out of the crowd never featured women.

There are no masses, Raymond Williams reminds us; "there are only ways of seeing people as masses."[55] Movie directors, beginning with D. W. Griffith, had given the public striking visions of the masses in motion—as festive celebrants in sacred and secular rituals, as dangerous agents of mass violence, as armies on the march, and as boisterous throngs in the marketplace. The poet Vachel Lindsay celebrated the "crowd splendor" of such whirling, handkerchief-waving, "sea of humanity" scenes as the major artistic and emotional triumph of early film-making.[56] But the "splendor" of crowds in advertisements was less turbulent and more statistical. Advertising crowds were passive and orderly. Often motionless, they occasionally moved in a trance toward the product-icon. These were well-dressed crowds—docile, respectful, even worshipful in demeanor. One senses their readiness to defer to leadership, to accept any proffered authority. The individual figures in these mobs were so tiny that readers were not invited to see themselves as members of the undifferentiated conforming throng. But they *were* expected to internalize the crowd's obvious sense of awe for the "bigger-than-life" product. In thus depicting the adoring throngs, advertisers expressed their fondest wishes for consumer pliability and sublimated their contempt for conformity and their fears of innundation by the mob.

Visual clichés of heroic proportions and adoring throngs represented elementary visual ways of conveying ideas that would have sounded ridiculous or authoritarian if stated verbally. Neither of these visual clichés has been entirely abandoned by advertisers, as evidenced by Jonathan Price's recent account of the troubles encountered in producing a television commercial based on "the idea of putting a five-story box of detergent out on an open plain, to be worshiped by hundreds of people."[57] But the massive crowds of tiny, undifferentiated figures paying homage to the heroically scaled product have appeared only infrequently since the early 1930s. This visual cliché may have faded as advertising leaders came to associate such images with totalitarian regimes or sensed that their audience was becoming increasingly fearful of the specter of conformity. Its decline may also have reflected the preference of advertisers for another visual cliché that offered a more individualized model for consumer behavior in the presence of the product.

III. *In Its Presence*

Within a single decade, beginning about 1920, one visual image became familiar to nearly all Americans through the efforts of advertising alone. This was the tableau of the small group clustered reverentially around the opened door of the new refrigerator. In their symbolic power and their zeal to inspire reverence in the viewer, the clichéd refrigerator tableaux generated a pattern of secular iconography.

All the mechanism is in here

It's all in a single hermetically sealed casing inside these coils . . . . there's no machinery underneath, none in the basement

YOU will notice that the unit of the new General Electric Refrigerator is on top of the cabinet. There are many important reasons why it should be there. General Electric engineers, in fifteen years of intensive research, found that the top-unit design was most efficient . . . and most economical.

With this arrangement, no heat is generated under the refrigerator. It all rises above. This cuts down current consumption. And the air-cooled coils also play an economical part in the running of the General Electric Refrigerator.

The top unit means no installation problem. All the mechanism—with a permanent supply of oil—is enclosed in one hermetically sealed casing. This is merely lowered into the top of the cabinet. There is no plumbing or assembling. There are no belts, pipes, drains or stuffing boxes. There is a constant circulation of air through the coils which actually prevents dust from settling.

This simplified refrigerator is unusually quiet. It is very economical. It is generously roomy because, with a given overall size, a minimum of space is occupied by the freezing chamber. Even the smallest model—the five-cubic-foot size—has a shelf area of nine square feet. Each

refrigerator is guaranteed by General Electric. There are many models. You will want to see them before you decide. Let us send you the address of the dealer who has them on display and booklet 9-S, which is interesting and descriptive.

Electric Refrigeration Department
of General Electric Company
Hanna Building   Cleveland, Ohio

G·E **Refrigerator**

GENERAL ELECTRIC

8.35. Even in the appliance store the electric refrigerator, as modern cornucopia, came amply supplied with food. Since the door did not hold food, it could be very narrow. Compare Fig. 8.37.

Several qualities of the electric refrigerator made it particularly eligible for the role of secular icon. As a protector of health through the prevention of spoilage, it served as the benevolent guardian of the family's safety. As the immediate source of a great variety of life-sustaining foods, it acquired the image of a modern cornucopia. No open refrigerator door in an advertising tableau ever disclosed a sparse supply of food. The gleaming white of the refrigerator's exterior suggested cleanliness and purity. And its size was sufficient to require a seated person (and the advertising illustrator) to view it at a slightly upward angle. Small wonder that the faces of the typical housewife and her friends in the advertising tableaux took on a rapturous glow when they beheld it, or that they chose to while away many an hour in the security of its presence.[58]

And this here
my good woman, is the Monitor Top

The what sir? The MONITOR TOP. *madam*
-the General Electric Monitor Top ......

THE language of this young gentleman may be a trifle inelegant—but his *facts* are right! That *is* the Monitor Top—hailed as the most outstanding combination of science to modern refrigeration.

It is the Monitor Top that is responsible for the General Electric Refrigerator's splendid record of service. In the Monitor Top, the General Electric Refrigerator's entire mechanism is *sealed in steel*—so that air, dirt and moisture are helpless to get inside. What comfort, what luxury, what true economy in owning such a refrigerator! The General Electric Refrigerator runs on a few pennies a day. How inexpensive it is to own! Prices now start as low as $205, at the factory—and most people buy on our easy time payment plan. How easy the General Electric Refrigerator is to buy!

Write us for the latest issue of our magazine, "The Silent Hostess." It will tell you a lot about the economy in modern, electric refrigeration. Address Section S-11A, Electric Refrigeration Department, General Electric Company, Hanna Building, 1400 Euclid Avenue, Cleveland, Ohio.

GENERAL ⒼⒺ ELECTRIC
ALL-STEEL REFRIGERATOR

Join us in the General Electric Program, broadcast every Saturday evening on a nation-wide N. B. C. network.

ELECTRIC WATER COOLERS   COMMERCIAL REFRIGERATORS   ELECTRIC MILK COOLERS

8.36. Did General Electric intend to mimic its earlier ads—or had the visual cliché simply frozen the artistic imagination? Note the high heels of the young initiates into the role of entranced consumer.

The visual cliché of the entrancing refrigerator appeared in several variations. Two of these predominated. In one, the salesman demonstrated the product while a young married couple or one or two women looked intently on. Often the women were seated like attentive students directly in front of the refrigerator. So clichéd did this scene become that the General Electric Company could effectively embellish it with a humanized touch (Figs. 8.35, 8.36).[59] In the other major variant, the wife or married couple brought guests to the kitchen to admire the new acquisition.[60] Convention dictated that in such tableaux no adult except the salesman could gaze in a direction other than at the icon itself. Convention also prohibited a husband from appearing in the company of a refrigerator without the presence of his wife. (An alien anthropologist might have identified this feature

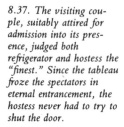

8.37. *The visiting couple, suitably attired for admission into its presence, judged both refrigerator and hostess the "finest." Since the tableau froze the spectators in eternal entrancement, the hostess never had to try to shut the door.*

as evidence of a cultural taboo.) Both men and women observed fastidious standards of dress in its presence (Fig. 8.37). Sometimes the expressions on the faces of the women suggested that they had glimpsed through the opened refrigerator door a secular revelation as spellbinding as any religious vision.

Such moments of secular epiphany were not confined to visions induced by refrigerator-icons. Other products could evoke similar reverence. The annunciation of the model 725 Hoover vacuum cleaner, for instance, disclosed the "finest portable electric cleaning machine ever made" on a small, raised platform around which four well-dressed women clustered in worshiping postures (Fig. 8.38). Few representations of the Christ child ever depicted a more rapt or focused attention by the assembled worshipers. The new Hoover lacked only a nimbus to complete the divine aura. Other Hoover ads revealed the same transfixed gazes on the part of husbands and wives who were prospective owners, the woman's expression being, as usual, the most suggestive of religious ecstasy.[61]

8.38. Advertising artists
would have been hard
pressed to discover more
worshipful expressions
and postures than those
with which they endowed
the figures in this ado-
ration scene.

It is unlikely that advertising illustrators, even when they created such tableaux as that of the communicants of the "new Hoover," saw themselves as appropriating religious imagery. Modern society saw little heresy in the most fervent adulation of the works of technological progress. Yet one doubts if copywriters could unabashedly have translated such scenes into comparable verbal expressions of awe and reverence. And one can imagine the quandary facing any artist required to search for postures and facial expressions that would convey a true religious ecstasy, something far surpassing the exaltation these consumers showed in the presence of a refrigerator or vacuum cleaner. Without directly competing with religion, advertising had appropriated the imagery of the sublime.

The detailed portrayal of exemplary facial expressions and body language in the product's presence, by figures who were simultaneously reader surrogates and advertisers' shills, clearly constituted an improvement over the "adoring throng" in effective advertising imagery. At its best, the adoring throng remained an abstraction. It was merely the visual equivalent of a numerical generalization about the millions who were devotedly choosing the product. The "in its presence" tableaux, however, personalized the proper attitude toward the product. By linking devotional imagery with the human-interest technique and the prescription to "show the results in the consumer's life," they encouraged viewers to identify with other "typical" men and women who were obviously entranced by the presence of the product. In these invitations to technological idolatry, no disturbing distinctions marked off the realm of the sacred from that of the profane.

IV. *Holy Days, Poignant Moments*

Readers of the July 1926 issue of the *American Magazine* encountered a unique illustration for a cigarette ad. The scene portrayed a colorful hometown holiday crowd of adults and children as they watched a fife and drum corps lead a Fourth of July parade. As the parade made its way down the tree-shaded streets of a small town or suburban neighborhood, the ad's headline encouraged readers to join in the spirit of the occasion: "When Fourth of July bands are playing—and the cannons are roaring out their celebration of another day of Independence and Freedom—have a Camel!" As the main text of the ad unfolded, Camel explained the less-than-self-evident connection. When readers thought about freedom, they should have a Camel. "For no other cigarette ever brought such liberation to so many millions of smokers. On the day of its birth, Camel decreed the end of tired taste, of cigaretty after-taste." Both the Fourth of July and Camel cigarettes symbolized freedom.[62]

Such were the tortuous associations often inspired by the advertisers' pursuit of the numinous. They neglected few chances to associate their products with the life-enhancing feelings already engendered in their audiences by holiday celebrations and historical symbols. Advertisers ran less risk of offense in appropriating political symbols than in employing explicitly religious imagery. But the lack of a visual cliché that effectively fused the product with the grandeur of the occasion could place an almost impossible burden on the text. Attempts to achieve numinous association through verbal explanations, as in the Camel ad, usually seemed awkward and forced. Still, the attraction of linking the product with "the finer feelings of the human heart" led the National Confectioners Association to proclaim October 8 as Sweetest Day—a day when each person could escape the rush and complexity of modern life and release the "little, lonely Cinderella lurking in the heart of every one of us who is gladdened by acts of kindness." A gift of candy, the Association noted in an apparent afterthought, was the epitome of such an act.[63]

In a number of instances, advertisers found it possible to appropriate an already secularized visual imagery that still evoked the numinous aura of communal celebrations. The religious numinosity of Christmas and Thanksgiving, in particular, might be tapped through symbols that could be employed commercially with little danger of offense. An ad in the 1931 Thanksgiving issue of *Saturday Evening Post,* for instance, offered readers a warm scene of a family Thanksgiving dinner with the pointed reminder that Camel cigarettes were "something to be

8.39. *Without any direct mention of religion, Listerine managed to inject its product into the most poignant of moments—mother and children warmly united at day's end in prayer.*

8.40. *A reader might doubt the text's assertion that candy bars could make "a cozy cottage seem the most desirable of fairy castles," but who could resist the illustration's enthralling ambience?*

thankful for." Sentimental scenes of family homecomings in the country, the family trimming the Christmas tree, or the extended family around the holiday feast had predated the new advertising; but advertisements were responsible for some touching twentieth-century renderings.[64] Santa Claus served so admirably as an advertising character that one trade-press critic expressed grave concern in the mid-1930s that he was being devalued by indiscriminate use. So common was the Santa Claus testimonial, in which Santa "endorsed" the product by using it in the advertising tableau, that the whole moral authority of Christmas might collapse as children caught glimpses of this "supreme arbiter of their rights and wrongs" racing his convertible at excessive speeds on behalf of high-octane gasoline, smoking a Lucky Strike, stealing a kiss "from a ravishing Old Gold Maiden," or gulping down "a straight slug of Old Drum blended Whiskey."[65]

Several advertisers recognized that in addition to times of traditional celebration, other poignant moments might provide effective visual clichés to convey numinous associations. A Listerine ad employed the powerful image of mother and children during bedtime prayers, with the small Listerine bottle inescapably visible in the medicine chest of the adjoining bathroom (Fig. 8.39).[66] Camel cigarettes insinuated themselves into those moments of communal bliss "when friends come in to share the warmth of your fire and your friendship," and the Curtiss Candy Company arranged the presence of Baby Ruth bars at a lover's tryst "on a winter's evening when lights are low" (Fig. 8.40). At such moments, the company explained to viewers who read beyond the romantic visual cliché, Baby Ruth inspired dreams that made "a cozy cottage seem the most desirable of fairy castles."[67] A *Printers' Ink* columnist described an ad for the "powdered brilliance" of new inside-frost electric lamps in which two lovers basked in the moonlight of an enchanted garden. The scene, he noted, had the effect of "surrounding . . . industrial subjects with a shimmering halo."[68]

In these sublime moments, as in the holiday scenes, advertising tableaux appropriated established visual clichés. Through advertising, such scenes became a more memorable part of the society's fund of visual images. In mellow four-colored reproductions, they often attained new evocative power. Products thus found their way into the secular iconography of communal celebration and romantic love.

V. Radiant Beams

The iconic visual clichés popularized by advertising illustrations were not all as obvious as the heroic-proportions tableaux or as derivative as the tableaux of sublime moments. Attempts to instill a "passion of awe" toward the product through numinous associations worked best when the imagery was abstract and when it was susceptible of both religious and secular interpretation. In such cases, the clichéd visual image could work its associative magic without the awkwardness of labored analogies or abrasive intrusions. A popular visual cliché of this type was the simple beam of light.

During the 1920s and 1930s, powerful beams of light steadily criss-crossed the advertising pages (Figs. 8.41 through 8.44). Often they streamed in from undisclosed sources, above and to either side, to spotlight the product. Some beams radiated outward from the product itself. A number of beams tapered to brilliant points; others broadened like searchlight rays. Several beams of light frequently intersected—often at the point where each illuminated the product, but sometimes randomly in mid-air. Beams of light entered rooms from directions in which no window was visible; powerful sunbeams simultaneously flooded buildings from opposite sides. Beams created sharply etched geometric patterns; they also diffused into misty aureoles of light around the product. Some took on that special radiance of a beam that has passed through a cathedral's stained-glass window (Fig. 8.45).[69]

Where did these beams come from? What did they signify? Since they often originated from sources beyond the border of the illustration, the viewer might unconsciously or inattentively assume various possibilities. One likely source was the sun. Another was some artificial source—a spotlight or searchlight. A purely figurative source was also possible, since the scenes themselves were sometimes more figurative than literal. For obvious reasons, this source was never portrayed visually or identified in the text. But sometimes the pervasiveness of the beams, their unnatural power, and their simultaneous points of origin in several undisclosed regions of the heavens clearly implied (but never argued) that they represented the holy light of God's favor.

Out of the Crowd — *the Man!*

WHAT A CAR
TO WIN SUCH PRAISE

OLDSMOBILE

TWO-DOOR
SEDAN
$925

WHAT ONE WOMAN RECOMMENDS TO ANOTHER

IMPROVED *Hand Dipped*
IN PURE MOLTEN ZINC

WHEELING CORRUGATING COMPANY, *Wheeling, West Virginia*

Kelvinator
The Oldest Domestic Electric Refrigeration

8.41, 8.42, 8.43, 8.44. *Radiant beams from undisclosed sources suggested the power of everything from individuals to garbage cans to command divine attention.*

*O*ver 6,000,000
motor cars enjoy
the enduring
beauty. . . the
protection of
DUCO

But that isnt
all! The benefits
of *DUCO* are
brought to you
on any number
of things that
come into your
home!

8.45. *Although some radiant beams gained the aura of having passed
through stained glass, the one in this illustration for a Duco ad proved, on
close inspection, to have entered the windows of an auto showroom, not a
cathedral.*

Were art directors conscious of employing religious symbolism in their use of radiant beams to evoke numinous feelings? Probably not. The subtly evocative power of the beam of light stemmed from the fact that it had become a secularized image without entirely losing its spiritual overtones. From one perspective, light beams in an advertising tableau might simply illustrate the sunbeam, a common natural phenomenon. Yet the way in which unnaturally distinct and powerful beams were drawn directly to the product, often illuminating a single car to the exclusion of the surrounding landscape or a single house in an otherwise overcast city, suggested a sun guided by moral considerations. Whatever the illustrator's conscious intentions, such distinctive beams seemed to signify celestial favor. Some light beams appeared to come from such melodramatic, yet unhallowed, sources as spotlights and searchlights. But these beams often fell upon objects that attracted other shafts of light from the heavens. Pictorial convention suggested that products capable of attracting the public favor symbolized by such secular beams must warrant attention from undisclosed heavenly sources as well.

Trade-journal discussions of these ubiquitous rays of light focused almost entirely on the issue of dramatic effect. Spotlighting the product through the "artifices of light and shadow" enhanced the importance of the product and focused the reader's attention. Small and commonplace products, such as the belt-buckle that barely peeked out from beneath a man's jacket, desperately needed dramatization. A beam of light could do this far more impressively yet unobtrusively than the old-fashioned, superimposed pointing finger.[70] Some advertisers used the beam of light simply as a visual substitute for the headline "Announcing." For others, it served as an element of design that conveyed an aura of modernity. One critic, exasperated with the imitativeness of modernistic advertising artists, reported that the only answer he received when he asked one artist "why he ran a handful of those radiant sun-explosive lines the way he did" was: "All right, then let's run them some other way." The radiant beam had become an unconscious, clichéd element in a variety of advertising tableaux. If asked to justify these conventional beams, advertising artists were most likely to cite their "vitalizing" effects.[71]

Thus advertising artists, if they gave any thought at all to this common visual cliché, considered it from a pragmatic standpoint. We should not read too much symbolic significance into a conventionalized image that had lost its original "meaning" and served merely to direct attention or elaborate a design. Still, the power of such beams to enhance products and provide drama stemmed in part from the more sublime harmonics with which they still resonated. Powerful beams of light had long represented divine force or influence; they had translated human "enlightenment" into pictorial form. Anne Hollander notes how seventeenth-century painters working in the style of Caravaggio employed beams of light instead of the traditional drapery to create awe-inspiring settings.[72] Elizabeth Kendall, in a description of an early twentieth-century Ted Shawn "sermon" in dance form, reveals how Shawn could employ a powerful beam of light from a hidden source off-stage in full confidence that the audience would immediately accept it as a symbol of the sublime. Shawn first interpreted a tortured soul. Then, "from the wings came a white light such as was used through the dramatization of Ben Hur; Shawn pulled himself to his feet, inflated his chest

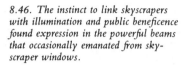

8.46. The instinct to link skyscrapers with illumination and public beneficence found expression in the powerful beams that occasionally emanated from sky-scraper windows.

and, set free from ignorance, walked off the stage into the heart of the hidden calcium [spotlight]."[73] The evocative, dramatic power of radiant beams did not arise merely from the physical impact of sharp contrasts of light and shadow on the viewer's cornea; it arose also from the suggestive, symbolic quality of the powerful beam of light, particularly when the source was hidden.

When they did not spotlight the product, radiant beams appeared most frequently in the company of one of the other secular icons of the age—the skyscraper. The vertical sweep and gleaming crowns of the new skyscrapers dominated the urban eye. Photographers in the 1920s paid them constant homage. Conveying a sense of both majesty and aspiration, the skyscraper seemed a vivid testimony to the power of man to manufacture the sublime. To characterize them as "cathedrals of commerce" was to express a perfectly proper reverence.[74] In the clichéd images of the city in the distance, these skyscrapers merged to form a crowning central apex. Their pinnacles often evoked a vision of the distant city as castle, a blending of modern aspirations with fairy-tale visions of the happy ending.[75]

The addition of radiant beams in crossing, angular lines dynamically complemented the skyscrapers' abrupt and static verticality. To the skyscraper's suggestion of man's domination, beams of light added the image of man's power to dispel darkness. And, while beams from within the city itself reflected man's power of illumination, rays of light from the heavens suggested that God and Nature approved the splendor of the scene below. In the visual clichés, this powerful conjunction of symbols found its crowning expression in radiant beams that traced their source to skyscraper windows. These beams equaled the power of those from the sky and those rising from ground level, presumably from

8.47, 8.48. *What copywriter could have conveyed so captivatingly those ineffable inner qualities of toothpaste tubes and sewing machines that these radiant beams revealed?*

searchlights. Only gigantic searchlights, mounted in the upper-story windows of these skyscrapers, could, in actuality, have produced beams of such intensity. Employed in this way, the beams gave testimony to the immense, benevolent power of the skyscraper and the business acumen and technological advances it represented. Skyscrapers possessed a celestial glow that radiated beams of great illuminating power (Fig. 8.46).[76]

Advertising leaders had an insatiable appetite for such images. Skyscrapers with radiant beams appeared even more frequently in trade-journal ads and illustrations than in the popular media. Denizens of skyscrapers themselves, advertising agents unsurprisingly found satisfaction in this sublime image of the business civilization they were helping to erect. They assumed that consumers would also find the skyscraper a compelling image of progress and modernity. On some occasions they even found it possible to combine the radiant beam or the skyscraper, or both, with the adoring throng.[77] Advertising men who had often worked late in these urban towers, or modest versions of them, may insensibly have enshrined themselves in such images. They, too, like the skyscrapers and the midnight beams, were firing the imagination of the American people.

If radiant beams carried a spiritual suggestiveness that consecrated skyscrapers, enthralled crowds, and transformed mundane products into secular idols, two variations of the radiant beam cliché carried even stronger religious overtones. In one of these, the beams radiated from the product itself. Such a phenomenon constituted a reasonable effort at literal rendition in the case of a light bulb. But it could only suggest some mysterious inner radiance in the case of automobiles, toothpaste tubes, sewing machines, or garbage cans (Figs. 8.47, 8.48).[78] In the other variation, beams from above or within the product created a hazy glow of

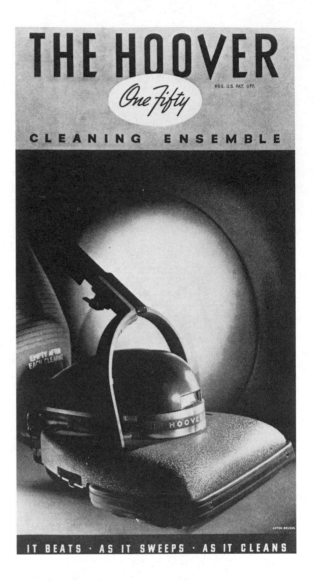

8.49, 8.50. Nimbus or aure-
ole effects (as in the Anton
Bruehl photograph for
Hoover) and radiant beams
from within the product suggested attributes that words
could hardly express. See also
Figs. 8.1 and 8.33.

light around the product that mimicked the traditional nimbus around the head
of Jesus, the Madonna, or the saints (Fig. 8.49).[79] So far as I know, no advertising
agency was ever accused of idolatry for putting the nimbus to profane purposes.
But the acquisition of such "outward and visible signs of an inward and spiritual
grace" represented a final step in the successful, though largely unconscious,
adaptation of religious imagery to the advertising tableaux, the modern icons of
a faith in mass consumption.

The relative power of such visual clichés to evoke numinous associations becomes apparent when we compare them with the awkward efforts of advertising
texts. When one toilet-seat manufacturer called his product "The Seat of Eternal

Whiteness," he was seeking to create the nimbus effect. But words invited the kind of snide reaction that a hazy halo of light did not. Similarly, words alone seemed inadequate to explain convincingly the contribution of Canada Dry Ginger Ale to "the soul and spirit of man."[80] Radiant beams probably enhanced the products of the McKinney Manufacturing Company with less likelihood of arousing skepticism than its advertising proclamation that "Hinges are no longer 'just hardware' . . . [but] the jewelry of the home" (Fig. 8.50).[81]

It was a testimony to the efficacy of the visual cliché that you simply could not put into words the same message, with all its nuances and associations, without sounding pompous, ridiculous, or just plain idolatrous. From 1926 to the middle of the next decade, writers in the advertising trade press regularly expressed alarm that advertising was courting public disbelief through exaggeration and "super-advertising." Incessantly, they warned against verbal superlatives and the attribution of vague, undemonstrable qualities to the product. But only three times in all those jeremiads have I discovered concerns about public responses to any of the iconic visual clichés: one critic worried about repetitious visual images, and two expressed concern about the overuse of the heroic-proportions cliché as a mental battering ram.[82]

Thus the visual clichés, through frequent repetition, became one of the most pervasive and least questioned contributions of advertising to the popular fund of images. That the family, the small town, or the future were understood to "look" a certain way did not insure that life would come to imitate popular art. On the contrary, the actual phenomena often changed while the picture remained the same. But the visual clichés helped establish the conceptual, and sometimes the moral, reference points in relation to which all changes brought about by the vicissitudes of modernity would be evaluated.

To the extent that they attained the numinosity of "sacred symbols," the visual clichés of advertising acquired what cultural anthropologist Clifford Geertz describes as the "peculiar power . . . to identify fact with value at the most fundamental level." In so doing, they pushed forward the process, described by Jackson Lears as already well advanced in the late nineteenth century, of appropriating traditional symbols for modern ends. The cultural impact was reciprocal. Products gained temporary enhancement, but traditional symbols were "trivialized."[83] And the process has continued, so that now, in our own time, it seems inconceivable that traditional and sacred symbols can be further impoverished. After the emergence of modern American advertising, as we now realize, there remained few ways of picturing religious inspiration that did not resemble some insurance tableau, nor could individuals easily daydream about poignant moments without recalling visual clichés from some coffee commercial or cigarette ad.

ADVERTISING IN OVERALLS:
PARABLES AND VISUAL CLICHÉS
OF THE DEPRESSION

"Every advertisement is an advertisement for success." Thus spake "Andy Consumer," typical American, created by the humor magazine *Life* in 1925 in an effort to win the goodwill of advertisers and their ad agencies. In his folksy way, Andy set forth a doctrine of the benefits of advertising to the common man. "Looking at the advertisements makes me think I've *got* to succeed," he confessed. "I guess one reason there is so much success in America is because there is so much advertising," he philosophized.[1]

Certainly advertising in the 1920s had incorporated Andy's creed in ways that went beyond his theory of ads as goads to success. Explicit formulas for success and the promise of progress without cost had permeated many of that decade's most persistent social parables and visual clichés. The Great Depression of the early 1930s, however, presented the American dream of individual success through equal access to ample opportunities with its most formidable challenge. Not only had advertising writers served as public spokesmen for a business system now brought under suspicion; they were now engaged, in their own agencies and corporate departments, in an increasingly desperate personal struggle for survival and success. It is therefore hardly surprising that they constantly reaffirmed and reinterpreted the success ethic in the dominant parables and iconographic expressions of advertising in the early 1930s.

Retrenchment and Morale Boosting

In the general prosperity of the late 1920s, American advertising had flourished as never before. Few agency executives or trade journal editors had been too modest to credit advertising with prime responsibility for the business boom.

Having freely predicted that advertising would prevent future depressions, some were even so bold as to welcome the 1929 stock market crash as "a magnificent opportunity for American advertising men."[2] Since the damage inflicted by the crash was primarily psychological, the president of the American Association of Advertising Agencies noted in mid-November, advertising, with its power to sway the public, was best prepared to deal with such a "mere state of mind." Never were advertising men more needed by the nation, one agency president wrote to the U.S. Chamber of Commerce, for never had there been "a slump so little related to business conditions." Since advertising writers specialized in deal-ing with states of mind, they could best reverse the depression mood by "hammering in certain points of view." Kenneth Goode called upon his fellow advertising men, as "the experts in this situation," to "volunteer to take charge of public sentiment" and thus demonstrate advertising's power. Advertising, Goode and several others implied, could handle the emergency almost singlehandedly.[3]

The Erwin, Wasey and Company advertising agency, seeking to turn the tide of public sentiment and earn the goodwill of business leaders, took the lead with a full-page ad in a number of newspapers in November 1929. "All right, Mister!" it challenged the reader, "Now that the headache's over, Let's Go To Work!" Denouncing the bull market as "the biggest crap game the world has ever seen," the agency called upon the reading public to get back to work to meet the continuing needs of the nation's "millions upon millions of regular folks." These inspirational ads, according to *Tide,* not only got the agency "talked about from coast to coast" but stimulated a host of other messages of reassurance: "Wall Street Bows to Main Street" ("things are as they should be west of Wall Street"); "Out From Under the Shadow of the Ticker"; "We Believe That Business Conditions Are Fundamentally Sound."[4] By early December, the Outdoor Advertising Asso-ciation of America had initiated a nationwide 50,000-billboard campaign in which a woman in flowing robes with a torch proclaimed "Forward America! Business is good—keep it good."[5] Despite their obvious failure to stem the onset of depres-sion, such inspirational ads never lost popularity with the advertising trade. Although they gradually took on a grim and beleaguered countenance, they reappeared frequently from 1931 through 1933.

As the depression deepened, advertising men found ample reason to favor inspirational messages. Most agencies had survived the 12–15 percent decreases in advertising lineage and revenue between 1929 and 1930 with little hardship. But the steeper declines of the next three years cut deeply into staffs, salaries, and self-confidence, creating an eager market for morale-boosting pronouncements. As early as April 1930, *Advertising and Selling* took notice of unemployment in advertising. Agency anterooms were crowded with applicants, it reported. The journal offered a free dinner to any ad man so unfortunate as to find himself in a breadline.[6] The journal's regular business columnist, Floyd W. Parsons, at-tempted to stimulate ingenuity and spread cheer by describing some of the new "Adventures in Earning a Living" to which recently unemployed individuals had successfully turned: running a snake farm in Texas, stunt-flying, working jungle cats in a circus, and buying walrus whiskers and selling them to Chinese restau-rants for toothpicks. With such opportunities for pursuing the American dream still open to the enterprising, Parsons implied, no one need despair.[7]

By 1932 nearly all the agencies were feeling the economic pinch. First they eliminated summer vacations. Then they cut salaries in an attempt to protect jobs. The huge N. W. Ayer agency spread the work by forcing staff members to take one day off each week without pay. In February 1932, Kenyon and Eckhardt, one of the twenty largest agencies, imposed a 10 percent levy on salaries for an agency reserve fund. In May, it boosted the "contribution" by another 10 percent. After making a "drastic cut in personnel," Erwin, Wasey slashed paychecks in half. A BBDO executive recalled that "people were disappearing from every aisle." Lord and Thomas employees suffered two salary cuts; then, on February 13, 1933, in the "St. Valentine's Eve Massacre," the agency summarily dismissed more than fifty employees, including executives with years of service.[8]

New tensions within the agencies surpassed even the salary cuts and dismissals as depressants on the morale of the surviving copywriters. Instability was rife. Into an already mercurial business, in which a high turnover of accounts stimulated frequent job shifts, the depression injected a new competitive intensity. Until the depression, most agencies had considered it vaguely unethical and dangerously wasteful of resources to attempt to lure an account away from another agency by presenting the prospective client with "speculative copy" —that is, specific examples of copy for an alternative advertising campaign. But now, as the *Printers' Ink* columnist "Groucho" warned in an article headed "Look Out! The Wolves Are Prowling About," manufacturers were regularly bombarded with speculative copy by "some of the biggest, best-known, and most gloriously ethical" agencies. "Rumor mongering is rife," complained the president of the American Association of Advertising Agencies early in 1932. The trade press frowned on the "orgy of solicitation" that was leading up to a "battle royal" for accounts.[9]

Every account was now "hot" all the time, a leading Lord and Thomas executive later noted. With its clients under steady solicitation by other agencies, each agency felt compelled to submit a steady stream of new plans, even when a good campaign was already in progress. Gone were the days when campaigns were approved and funded for an entire year. Now, clients demanded reviews of copy slants and appropriations on a monthly basis. Agencies no longer enjoyed slack seasons or the orderly process of general planning for a season. *Printers' Ink* lamented that the demand for more new ideas, more changes in plans, and more "sudden decisions" had intensified the "strain and worry."[10]

Nor could the agencies, faced with the steep decline in advertising appropriations and the competitive hunger of their fellow agencies, resist such pressures. In fact, they found themselves offering more and more free services to clients. Many manufacturers had responded to the depression by severely cutting back their own advertising departments, and then pushing a greater variety of merchandising tasks on their agency. Advertisers who had sharply cut appropriations, and thus their agency's percentage commission, still expected all the usual collateral services. Advertising, one unemployed ad man surmised, had become "a 'sweated' industry in which fewer and fewer people do more and more work." The new pressures and suspicions, warned *Printers' Ink,* destroyed harmonious working conditions and kept the agency's staff continually "on a dangerous edge."[11]

The Depression as Sales
Argument: Some
Parables Revisited

Eventually these economic and occupational pressures were bound to affect the style and content of advertising copy. Advertisers did not like to become the bearers of bad news; still, they needed to make the messages about their products "newsworthy." To do so often meant to show how the product—in price, function, or symbolic value—was particularly necessary or attractive "in these times." If readers were going to identify with their consumer-surrogates in the tableaux, copywriters would need to imbue these characters with some of the concerns and anxieties of a depression-shaken public.

No single trend in advertising content characterized even the gravest years of the early 1930s. Even in 1933, most national advertisements offered no direct reflection of the existence of the depression. But gradually, more and more advertisers sought to empathize with, and perhaps to reflect, public concerns about economizing and job insecurity and popular yearnings for compensatory satisfactions. In the process, they found two of the "great parables" of immense value.

The most obvious copy tactic was an appeal to economy. This took form most frequently in what conservative advertising men deplored as a shrill and blatant emphasis on price. In contrast to the 1920s, some automobile ads now began to feature a statement of price as the most prominent, attention-commanding element of the ad. Prominent dollar signs and even prices such as "67¢" now gave some national advertisements the look of retail ads. Crisco shortening made unabashed price appeals. "Take your pick of these three thrifty dishes," it suggested; boldly surprinted over the food dishes appeared the figures 49¢, 29¢, and 47¢. Some ads juxtaposed the new price with a crossed-out, previous price in the traditional format of the retail bargain offer.[12] The General Electric Company elevated thriftiness to a "thrill." Without quoting prices, A.1. Sauce consoled readers with the thought that "economy can taste good": housewives could defy the depression by seasoning hamburger to give "any porterhouse in the market a run for flavor."[13]

Meanwhile, the long-standing ban against any mention of price during radio commercials had begun to falter. Network executives had considered the quoting of prices incompatible with the elevated aura of radio and its status as "a guest in the home." More specifically, they had feared that allowing price appeals might invite advertisers to use radio only intermittently to announce special price reductions. Radio prospered in the early depression years while other media suffered, and for more than two years it maintained the ban. But in May 1932, for the first time in radio history, advertising revenues fell behind those of the year before. During the last half of 1932, billings averaged 10 percent lower than those of 1931. The response, as the *Advertising and Selling* radio columnist put it, was "immediate and emphatic." First came layoffs and salary cuts. Intense pressure from advertisers then induced the unnerved networks to lift their restrictions. In a time of fierce competition, the fading aura of radio gentility proved insufficient to deny advertisers an appeal to economy through sales pitches that quoted prices.[14]

9.1. *A depression consciousness appeared not only in father's expression but in the suggested uses for the $3 saved by buying Listerine. The utilitarian list included shoes, suspenders, underwear, and overalls.*

The appeal to economy was hardly *new* in the 1930s. Yet its intensification with the deepening of the depression was graphically demonstrated by the evolution of ads in the Listerine toothpaste series. As early as the fall of 1927, Listerine toothpaste had described examples of the additional products a consumer might buy with the $3 a year that could be saved by buying Listerine at 25 cents a tube rather than other brands at 50 cents. Yet, as hard times loomed, this explicit appeal to economy acquired a special depression consciousness. Whereas the pre-1931 ads had often mentioned only a few small extravagances that might be purchased with the $3 savings—a necktie, a scarf, or a pair of silk stockings—by 1932 some Listerine toothpaste ads were listing over forty different possible uses of the money, adding such mundane necessities as galoshes and underwear (Fig. 9.1). Some lists even included such subsistence purchases as milk, flour, lard, rice, and potatoes.[15]

In such ads as "Maybe I ought to thank the depression for a small, but worthwhile lesson in economy," Listerine tableaux invited readers to listen in on highly personal soliloquies or conversations about depression survival.[16] Far from ignoring or dismissing the depression, these ads brought it into center stage in an effort to communicate through empathy: "If there were only Mary and me, we wouldn't care if I got a couple *more* salary cuts. Didn't we get married during the 1921 slump—with me making only $35 a week? *We* didn't care. And we wouldn't care now—except for the children."[17] Scare campaigns aimed at job insecurity surpassed even economy appeals in the effort to empathize with, and capitalize on, depression fears. As early as the winter of 1930–1931 the Duofold Underwear Company shifted from a simple health protection theme to such scare headlines as "Look Out! Job in danger." The ads grimly reminded readers, "This is a year to *fight* for jobs! Don't take a chance on a single ordinary cold."[18] Other advertisers quickly concluded that if job insecurity could sell underwear, it might sell their merchandise too. Absorbine Jr. warned that people who allowed themselves to suffer from muscular pains often lost days of work. "Don't risk your job," the company cautioned. In "times like these" it was expensive and dangerous "to miss a single day."[19] Listerine tied mouthwash to depresson fears with a January 1931 ad entitled "Fired—and for a reason he never suspected," a theme that Lifebuoy Soap employed several months later in "Don't risk *your* job by offending with B.O." "Take no chances!" warned Lifebuoy. "When business is slack, employers become more critical. Sometimes very little may turn the scales against us."[20]

With the scales of success so easily tipped, the parable of the First Impression gained heightened significance. Since many men of equal qualifications in every other respect were now competing for the same jobs, the one quality affected by the advertised product loomed as more crucial than ever. Gem Clippers revealed how the careless neglect of fingernails had proved so devastating to the protagonist of one tableau as "to throw him out of several Good Jobs and the Social Register." Williams Shaving Cream adapted its "face-fitness" campaign of the late 1920s to the new age by stressing the importance of first impressions. "You can't afford to let down now," the company warned in 1932 with an eye to rising unemployment. Keeping "face-fit" was not vanity, cautioned another Williams ad. "It's good business—more so in these keenly competitive days than ever before."[21]

Hart, Schaffner and Marx, the men's clothiers, stressed the importance of a good first impression to the morale of men "battered" by the depression. In advertisements directed at women, the company stressed the responsibility of wives to "insist that their husbands maintain their morale in the face of the depression by looking prosperous." During times when the world seemed bent upon undermining everyone's self-confidence, a conscientious wife could at least make her husband "keep up his 'front' before the world by dressing like a successful man."[22]

If parables of the First Impression offered counsel in surviving the depression's threats to job security, the parable of the Democracy of Goods gained even greater use as consolation. Psychologically, the depression could be overcome through compensatory satisfactions. Certain products, affordable by all, could provide pleasures no millionaire could surpass. "One joy you can afford," insisted Vigoro

9.2. No housewife in a modest bungalow needed a lorgnette to feel equal to this wealthy dowager, the Hoover Company argued. Hoover cleaners united both in a Democracy of Goods.

fertilizer, "is a Beautiful Garden." "Here—write like a millionaire!" beckoned the American Pencil Company. "A millionaire may ride in a sportier car, live in a richer home, and work at a bigger desk . . . but he can't write with a better pencil than *you* can. . . . And the price is ten cents, to everyone."[23] Copywriters promoted easily affordable Edgeworth Pipe Tobacco not merely as a compensating pleasure but as a depression-inspired rediscovery of the truly satisfying. To the "thousands who had been swept away from the calmness and composure of pipe smoking by the speed of the Prosperity Era," Edgeworth offered an escape from "the tensions of work and business problems" and a return to "the solid things of life."[24]

Advertisements in the late 1920s had frequently described the luxuries of the wealthy in fond detail. But several Democracy of Goods campaigns of the early 1930s adorned the rich even more lavishly. In "Everything money can buy is hers," the Hoover Company endowed its wealthy dowager with an aristocratic lorgnette through which to peer haughtily out at the reader (Fig. 9.2). Ipana explicitly described the rich men who suffered the democratic affliction of "Pink Tooth Brush" as millionaires who owned yachts. With its typical egregiousness, Listerine toothpaste offered depression-stricken consumers a glittering portrait of their peers in the democratic fellowship of Listerine users: "Hundreds of the nation's tycoons last season took their ease at Palm Beach, Miami, Nassau, and other millionaires' playgrounds," it reported. "Their yachts, their horses, their cars, their planes were a brilliant part of the parade of wealth and society."[25] And to sharpen the contrasts between those wallowing in such riches and the common man or woman who might democratically share one of their possessions or

Vanderbilt..Morgan..Astor...

MRS. REGINALD VANDERBILT, née Gloria Morgan, was the wife of the third son of the late Cornelius Vanderbilt. Since her husband's death she has lived in Paris where she has captivated French society. She has wonderful dark eyes and a gardenia-petal skin.

MISS ANNE MORGAN, daughter of the famous financier, the late J. Pierpont Morgan, is widely known as the president of the American Woman's Association. Miss Morgan is an extremely distinguished figure, with her dark eyes, silvery hair and clear complexion.

LADY VIOLET ASTOR, daughter of an Earl, is one of the loveliest of England's noblewomen, charming, gracious, a brilliant hostess, active in good works, universally beloved. Hers is the classic English beauty; hair like spun gold, eyes violet-blue and exquisite rose-leaf skin.

afflictions, the depression parables also made the other end of the social spectrum more dramatically explicit. Advertising tableaux now contrasted the rich not merely with "women of modest means" but also with laborers, truck drivers, and even scrubwomen.[26]

One might question the advisability of associating one's product with such blatant economic distinctions during a time of depression. But two possible answers to that objection proved persuasive to many advertisers. First, as several observers argued, people had never been so eager to enjoy vicarious experiences of the life of the wealthy. The movies alone proved this conclusively. Moreover, women in particular had never surrendered their ambitions, despite hard times. "You see her wearing a plain little house dress," related the Hoover Company in explaining its new 1932 campaign to its salesmen, "but she sees herself someday in velvet and ermine."[27] Second, as the strategists behind the Democracy of Goods parables clearly perceived, the more dramatically the contrasts between millionaire and common man were portrayed, the more ultimately satisfying was that resolution of polarities in which consumers learned that they might share the same significant satisfactions or escape the same miseries that beset even a "wealthy dowager" or "a Big Shot in Steel."[28]

The Hoover vacuum cleaner campaign, which continued through March of 1933, demonstrated how the parable of the Democracy of Goods might reconcile middle-class consumers to an eclipse of economic mobility and still retain an upbeat flavor. Such tableaux as "Just starting out or 'arrived'" and "One thing she didn't have to wait to own" took the sting out of sharp class contrasts by making the wealthy woman much older than the young surrogate for the consumer. Thus, readers might cherish the expectation that the young housewife, in a "modest home" with "no corps of servants," would eventually realize her ambition "for the things riches can bring." One ad optimistically introduced the young

Belmont.. Drexel.. du Pont...

MRS. MORGAN BELMONT, wife of the son of the late August Belmont, is one of the most original and brilliant personalities in all New York society. Strikingly lovely, with intent green eyes, Titian hair and ivory skin, she is a keen sportswoman and a familiar figure at Belmont Park races.

MRS. ANTHONY J. DREXEL, JR., was Miss Marjorie Gould, daughter of the late Mr. and Mrs. George J. Gould. Her home is the Château Courbois, in France, but she spends much time cruising aboard her yacht. Her dark vivacious beauty is equally well-known in France, England and America.

MRS. ALFRED VICTOR DU PONT, of Philadelphia and Wilmington, is the former Miss Marcella Miller, of Denver, a recent graduate of Smith College. Widely traveled, a gifted hostess, she is also known for her charming poems. Mrs. du Pont is blonde with deep blue eyes and an exquisite fair skin.

9.3. Even during the depression, some advertisers did not hesitate to remind consumers of the yachts and jewels of the rich. Using Pond's would give readers much in common with those whom wealth had made "aristocratic."

housewife with the phrase, "No matter how wealthy she may be some day." In the meantime, Hoover promised its salesmen, its ads would "make her feel on a plane of equity with the wealthiest woman in the world, simply because she has a Hoover."[29]

This mansion-and-cottage campaign, the Hoover Company explained, would cover "the whole ground of feminine longing and feminine envy." Acknowledging that the average housewife pictured herself "surrounded with servants," it would tell her "in plain words—words that any feminine mind can grasp—that, while she may not have as fine a house or as fine furnishings as rich women have," she could take pride in owning that one possession "that the richest woman in the world can't outdo her in." In pandering to the "feminine mind," some advertising men concluded that they had found a way to keep alive the fires of ambition yet reconcile plain Americans to the full scope of current inequalities. *Advertising and Selling* pronounced Hoover's "Everything money can buy is hers" advertisement "a vivid and convincing page" (see Fig. 9.2). "Ordinary folks," it reflected, "are always pleased to know they can have the products good enough for Vanderbilts, Astors, Huttons, Mellons, and Fords."[30]

The notion that the deprivations and blocked mobility of the depression would only enhance the appeal of the parable of the Democracy of Goods led some agencies to create near-parodies on the theme of equal satisfactions. In "Rich Man—Poor Man," N. W. Ayer and Sons suggested that "whatever their fortunes," men who wore Hanes underwear would "*know* they are well off." Women could easily share the skin beauty of the aristocratic women of the Vanderbilt, Morgan, Astor, and DuPont families, with their "luxurious homes . . . private yachts, precious jewels," because those women also chose Pond's beauty preparations "despite their democratic simplicity and modest price" (Fig. 9.3). In a 1933 Goodyear ad, a young man in a working-class cap and sweater stopped to gape

9.4. *This young couple, defined as working-class by his cap, demonstrated how disappointed ambitions might be allayed by taking to heart the parable of the Democracy of Goods.*

at a luxurious new sedan with a uniformed chauffeur. "Anyhow," he boasted to his girl, "his Tires are just like mine!" (Fig. 9.4). Simmons Beautyrest Mattresses acknowledged that ordinary people and the very rich might be "far apart" during two-thirds of their lives, but anyone could enjoy "millionaire sleep" by buying a Simmons mattress. The company offered each consumer the chance to overcome class differences and depression frustrations with the slogan, "Live one-third of your life like a millionaire."[31]

Despite the dramatic contrasts of class position and the dubious promises of significant equality that characterized many depression versions of the parable of the Democracy of Goods, advertisers still universally accepted certain intriguing limits on the range of class contrasts. The tableaux continued to shy away from any mention of inferior housing conditions. Royal Baking Powder's contrasts between women of wealth and women of "modest circumstances" never ac-

knowledged a dwelling more lowly than a "modest three-room apartment." The Philadelphia *Evening Bulletin* somewhat archaically contrasted "the laborer in his cottage" with "the manufacturer on his estate."[32] In an age when writers and photo-journalists frequently confronted the public with views of urban tenements, Hooverville shanties, and sharecroppers' shacks, the Democracy of Goods ads continued to insist on the "bungalow" or "cottage" as the polar opposite of the mansion. The psychological strategy of the Democracy of Goods parable, as the Hoover Company explained it, was to "picture . . . the woman of wealth and the woman of little means . . . contrast their situation—show how great the gulf is between them—and then bridge that gulf" by showing that both owned a Hoover.[33] Any open acknowledgment of slums, shacks, and unemployment would suggest a "gulf" of conditions that even a vacuum cleaner, let alone a pencil or a pair of underwear, might not be sufficient to bridge.

Parables of the Depression:
Unraised Hands and Skinny Kids

The depresson not only inspired new elaborations and dramatizations of such parables as the Democracy of Goods; it also brought several new or little-used parables into prominence. One of these was the parable of the Unraised Hand. The school classroom, which had rarely served as a setting for advertising tableaux in the 1920s, now came into wider use. Poignant scenes of the student's arrival home with his report card, or humiliating comparisons of report cards, also became more common. The most striking of these tableaux began to appear in 1933 when Post's 40% Bran Flakes presented a "Real Life Movie" of "The Strange Case of Mary Dodd." In the most heart-rending scene of the "movie," little Mary sat listlessly while the other beaming children in the classroom eagerly raised their hands to answer the teacher's question (Fig. 9.5). Later that year, General Foods (Postum) confided sadly to the reader, "A Dunce they called him, . . . a sluggard," while depicting the poignant scene in which a teacher gazed judgmentally down at a discouraged boy kept after school to work alone at his desk amid the deepening shadows of a deserted classroom (Fig. 9.6).[34]

Each parable of the Unraised Hand delivered a predictable message: it scolded parents for neglect. Their child was failing through no fault of its own; its disadvantages could be easily removed by the proper parental purchases. In this respect, depression versions of the parable of the Unraised Hand departed not a whit from precursors of the 1920s. What did change was the new emphasis on academic failure. In 1929, only one advertiser, Compton's Pictured Encyclopedia, had centered a general magazine campaign on possible failures in school examinations. Two other advertisers, Corona Typewriters and Quaker Oats, had given momentary attention to "slow" children and "distressing" report cards. But by 1933 a wide range of advertisers, from breakfast cereals and vitamin supplements to pharmaceutical firms and toilet paper manufacturers, were preaching the parable of the Unraised Hand.[35]

Why this sudden emphasis on children's classroom performance? Advertising men during the depression were fascinated with the topic of competitive struggle. Moreover, they may have perceived that many parents, frustrated in their own ambitions, had now fixed their aspirations and competitive anxieties on their children. Since the next generation would now have to realize the parents' dreams, every aspect of the child's competitive progress came under intense scrutiny. In an increasingly complex society, with economic success more problematic, school marks gained added import as omens of the family's future. At the same time that parents were placing new competitive burdens on their children, advertisers deftly enhanced the parents' own anxieties by suggesting that it was the parents (who held the consumer purse-strings) who had heedlessly disadvantaged any failing student. That poor boy, struggling alone in the ignominy of after-school detention, was not a natural "Dunce"; only his parents' failure to substitute Postum for coffee had made him so.

Advertiser after advertiser, as the 1930s progressed, found a sales argument in the parable of the Unraised Hand. The Ralston Purina Company illustrated the potential effects of its wheat cereal by depicting two girls at their school desks, one

9.5, 9.6. The parable of the Unraised Hand, whether illustrated conventionally for Post's 40% Bran Flakes (Fig. 9.5) or through Postum's somber, dramatic epilogue (Fig. 9.6), targeted anxious depression parents who had increasingly displaced their aspirations onto their children.

alert with her hand raised and the other tired and dejected. "Parents!" the Royal Typewriter Company shouted, "Don't deny your students the advantages of this *vital* school need." A young student's mother in a Scott Paper Company ad confessed, "Mary was so fidgety she couldn't concentrate. . . . I was shocked to find that harsh toilet tissue was the cause."[36] The Eagle Pencil Company introduced parents vicariously to the terrible tensions of classroom competition: "Jim's in the 4th grade. . . . How he does bear down on that pencil! He must hang on hard, for pencils will slip through chubby, damp fingers! 15 examples in 15 minutes . . . will he make it? You can help him pass his test . . . make sure he has a smooth pencil, with a strong lead that won't snap in the middle of 4 × 4 and upset him."[37]

If the parents' guilt for their children's failures was not self-evident in such dramatic tableaux, other ads made it more explicit. "Many a bright child is unjustly blamed for dullness," the Metropolitan Life Insurance Company observed. General Foods headlined one tableau of a boy who had slumped in his school work, "scolded for mistakes that Father and Mother made." Here, the illustration intensified the parents' guilt by showing their harsh, unjust reaction when their son presented his report card.[38] In a Post's Bran Flakes version of the parable of the Unraised Hand, the guilty mother played a particularly villainous role. While several of little Sally's schoolmates laughed mockingly at her report card, Sally's mother shrieked: "Sally Lennox! I'm *ashamed* of this report card. What will your father say? I'm sure Barbara Weeks didn't bring home a report card like this. Why can't you do as well as she?"[39] Sally's mother *should* feel ashamed, the parable revealed, but for her *own* inattention in failing to recognize that Sally's real trouble was constipation. "Maybe you have a little girl like Sally," the company suggested, spreading the suspicion of guilt; "and perhaps like Sally's mother, you have been unjust to her" (Fig. 9.7).[40]

And so the message of the parable of the Unraised Hand continued to echo through the magazine pages with minor variations. In a tableau bluntly captioned, "Here are the report cards of Two Boys," General Electric contrasted the A's of the son of "thoughtful parents" with the C's and D's of the boy who studied in poor light. Remington Rand probed the pained conversation of two parents in "We tried to joke about it. . . . But *was* Joe really Dumb?"[41] Advertisers sensed that scenes of classrooms and report cards would evoke a sensitive response during this era. Many parents felt a need to make concrete contributions to their children's success, especially now that these children carried a larger responsibility for fulfilling their parents' aspirations. Advertisers threatened such parents with guilt. But they also offered them a means, by purchasing the right products, of making important contributions to their children's future.

Another closely related tableau, the parable of the Skinny Kid, gained remarkable momentum with the deepening of the depression. Advertisements had previously touted various food and vitamin products as correctives for underweight. But copywriters had never tortured mothers so frequently and unforgivingly for the sin of allowing their children to remain skinny as they did in the 1930s. Now a host of scrawny youngsters paraded before the consumer audience. Each spindly leg and gaunt chest testified to a mother's guilt.

A survey of the September through November issues of *McCall's* magazine discloses only two instances of the use of the parable of the Skinny Kid by a single advertiser during 1928 and only two instances by two advertisers during the same period of 1929. But by the fall of 1931, advertisers in *McCall's* were employing the parable of the Skinny Kid in six advertisements for four different products. And in the fall of 1932, five different advertisers presented the parable in eight individual ads.[42] Only a limited number of products could plausibly be touted as remedies for underweight. Nearly all the advertisers that could conceivably make use of the parable had joined the bandwagon by 1933. In "So Weak, So Wasted Away," the Ironized Yeast Company combined the Skinny Kid theme with the tragedy of dropping out of school. Like many of the other food supplements, Squibb's Vitavose neatly engrafted the newly popular parables of the Skinny Kid and the Unraised Hand onto the solid base of the familiar parable of the Captivated Child. Skinny, cranky, nervous children suffered from inadequate appetites. The resulting nutritional deficiencies would make a child frail, petulant, and a "laggard at school." "Is it fair to blame the child?" asked Vitavose.[43] The parable of the Captivated Child had prepared any experienced reader to answer, "No."

No copywriters imbued the parable of the Skinny Kid with more power as a weapon of reproach and persuasion than those of the Ruthrauff and Ryan agency in ads for the milk supplement Cocomalt. Utterly rejecting the warm, genteel tone of Cocomalt's previous sunlight-and-happy-healthy-children campaign, Ruthrauff and Ryan launched a continuing exposé of guilty mothers in the spring of 1931 with such headlines as "Whose fault when children are frail?" and "People

9.7. Unsurprisingly to those
familiar with advertising
parables involving children,
the "Truth about Sally" in
this Post's Bran Flakes
"movie" emerged as a truth
about her mother's guilt.

9.8. The depression brought increased concern about children's
weight and hardiness. Cocomalt's
tableau of parental guilt and redemption exemplified the "Parable of the
Skinny Kid." See also Fig. 9.16.

pitied my boy, he was so thin" (Fig. 9.8). Stark "slice-of-life" photographs and
vivid conversational frankness marked the new Cocomalt style. One mother,
stooping to pull up her boy's drooping sock, was "mortified" to hear one well-
dressed woman on a nearby park bench comment to another, "That child looks
half-starved." The mother of young "Dorothy" recalled how "I winced when
they called her 'skinny.'"[44]

The message of the parable of the Skinny Kid, as melodramatically epitomized
in the Cocomalt tableaux, was very similar to that of the parable of the Unraised
Hand. But the parable of the Skinny Kid explored new dimensions of social
shame. In a time of depression, thinness suggested impoverishment. Youthful
huskiness, by contrast, connoted not only a child's physical health but also the
family's financial well-being. The reason why it hurt "Dorothy's" mother "as
much as it did my little girl" to hear them call her "skinny" was that she feared,
perhaps irrationally, that others might take her child's frailty as an index to the
family's economic condition. Middle-class women have worried about their
children's lack of weight at many other times, but in the view of advertisers their
children's thinness had never made them so susceptible to fears of social
mortification as during the depression.[45]

Depression Advertising
as a Shift in Style

If we seek the most salient impact of the depression on the appearance of national advertising, we will find it expressed less in shifting parables or in appeals to economy and job insecurity than in advertising style. Depression advertising *looked* different. Of course, strategies for brand differentiation always insured that some advertisers would seek distinctive images by bucking style trends. But no one can glance through the advertisements of a 1932 issue of a popular magazine and mistake the prevalent style for that of a 1928 issue. Depression advertising was distinctively "loud," cluttered, undignified, and direct.

Like many Americans, advertising leaders found solace in interpreting the depression as a deserved chastisement for follies and excesses of the boom years. In the advertising trade, however, these blameworthy pre-depression practices were defined less as sins of speculation and high living than as ineffectual gentility in advertising technique. From 1930 through 1934, in a steady stream of articles and ads, advertising writers mercilessly lashed themselves—and, more often, their unnamed fellow "dilettantes" of the profession—for the "lazy, band-music advertising" of the late 1920s. Condemning the styles of the prosperity era as too abstract, too self-indulgently "beautiful," too "sleek and opulent," many advertising leaders now reacted to the depression by casting themselves in the role of "hardboiled" salesmen.[46] The time had come, a *Printers' Ink* editor proclaimed early in 1931, to buckle down to "shirt-sleeve advertising." The trade should forsake the "highly manicured appearance" and get some grease on its overalls.[47] Such images of working-class exertion and vitality seemed to provide catharsis for the hard-pressed, white-collar professionals of the advertising trade, struggling to regain a sense of potency. Advertising trade journals conjured up heroic images of ad men in dungarees, with sweat on their brows. In 1933, a journal contributor approvingly characterized the new hardboiled mystique as "Advertising in Overalls."[48]

One reason why copywriters had to figuratively adopt laborers' clothes and get down to "knuckle-bruising hard work," many advertising spokesmen assumed, was because strenuous efforts were needed to pry money out of the hands of a suddenly tight-fisted public (Fig. 9.9). Again and again, advertisers turned to the concept of a "buyers' strike" as the most plausible explanation for the circumstances they faced. Some complained about "hoarders," and one trade journal correspondent mused about the problem of "consumer constipation"; but the verbal imagery of the "buyers' strike" proved most persistent. The notion of a toe-to-toe confrontation between consumer and advertiser helped challenge the copywriter to marshal extra effort for a contest of wills. Some advertising writers did acknowledge that consumers might be out of work or have less spending money than before. But most focused their attention on those dangerous pessimists, the hoarders and the strikers, whose purses of ready money might still be pried open by copywriters worthy of their hire.[49]

Some gloomy prophets even goaded the trade to intensify its selling efforts lest a major degeneration of the consumption ethic ensue. Columbia professor Walter B. Pitkin warned in 1933 and 1934 of a potential "return to the primitive, a

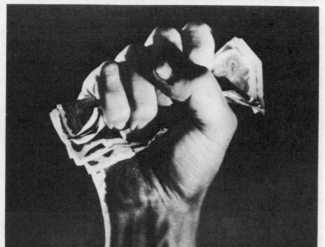

AMERICA HAS CLOSED ITS FIST

From a nation that spent money like a drunken sailor, we have become a people who think twice before we spend at all. • As a result, advertising to-day must not only move money in the direction of specific merchandise—it must first overcome the reluctance to part with that money. • This puts an added obligation on advertising. • It puts an added obligation on those who create advertising.

• It makes the choice of the right advertising agency more important than ever before.

YOUNG & RUBICAM, INCORPORATED · ADVERTISING
NEW YORK · PHILADELPHIA · CHICAGO

9.9. When speaking to potential clients—and when admonishing themselves—advertising agencies preferred to portray depression consumers not as impoverished or unemployed but as hoarders who resisted spending their money.

back-to-the-soil type of living" that would disdain progress and "the finer things." "Millions of rising consumers" might well relinquish "what we now consider the American standard of living," he declared.[50] A contributor to *Printers' Ink Monthly* challenged advertisers to overcome the "buyers' strike" by teaching consumers "to spend continuously." Hart, Schaffner and Marx tried to re-stimulate the buying instincts of men who were becoming accustomed to "skimping" on themselves, and American Telephone and Telegraph worried that people who gave up their phones during the depression years might lose the "telephone habit."[51] Not only had it become the fashion to be thrifty, complained advertising writer Robert Updegraff, but people were beginning to get "vain, virtuous, and vulgar about it in public." Advertising was going to have to work hard to combat this "degenerate type of social prestige," warned Professor Pitkin.[52]

Spurred to aggressive advertising tactics by account losses and specters of "buyers' strikes," advertising agents turned to more graphic, hardboiled advertising copy. The clean, esthetically pleasing layouts of the 1920s gave way to "busy," cluttered pages. White space dwindled as copywriters sought to make

9.10, 9.11. Depression
tactics included a shift
from clean, unified lay-
outs to busy, cluttered
pages of multiple photo-
graphs and "screaming,"
bold-face headlines.
Compare Dr. West's
ads of 1927 (Fig. 9.10)
and 1934 (Fig. 9.11).

every square inch of the ad do its share of sales work. Groups of small black-and-white pictures, often "news" photos or diagrams, usurped the place of single, large, eye-pleasing color illustrations (Figs. 9.10, 9.11). A statistical survey of one March and one September issue of the *Saturday Evening Post* for each year from 1925 through 1936 reveals that only 23 percent of all automobile ads during the 1925–1928 era contained more than one illustration. By contrast, car ads during the 1933–1936 period included two or more separate pictures over 48 percent of the time. In 1936, one-third contained *four* pictures or more. Such changes reflected the judgment that a multitude of pictures could best capture reader attention and illustrate more selling arguments. In other words, they were less pretty but could do more hard work.[53]

The use of "good art," traditionally viewed with disdain by one faction in the trade, now acquired the status of an unpatriotic act. Pre-depression advertising

had been too artistic, most critics agreed. It had contained "too many fancy pictures that no one could understand." No longer should artists be allowed to indulge themselves in creating "good-looking" ads and thus destroy advertising's reputation for hard selling.[54] By 1934, one art director was complaining that agencies and clients now "consciously strove for what was crude, ugly, and actually repellent." An agency consultant described her revulsion against "pages of action pictures and big black Gothic type—ugly pages that stare, that leap out at you."[55] But such "screaming, direct, ugly stuff" was often just the antidote for the pretty-pretty ads of the past that proponents of the hardboiled style were seeking. If an ad did "leap out" at the reader and command his attention, that was advertising's job. Tastefulness was for those who did not care about sales.

Thus, the new hardboiled advertising mystique brought a proliferation of "ugly," attention-grabbing, picture-dominated copy in the style of the tabloid newspaper. One study indicated that the average number of words in advertising texts declined from 290 to 212 between 1929 and 1933. Pictures so crowded the pages, one copywriter complained, that you couldn't find the text without a microscope.[56] Single illustrations fell under attack as less "hard-working" than multi-picture pages in the rotogravure style. So relentless was the trend toward the "busier" style of layout that by the end of the depression decade one agency president observed that the term "tabloid technique," which had once referred to sensational journalism, was now just a designation for a common display method.[57]

Depression conditions also stimulated a new surge of "competitive copy." This term referred to any advertisement that made explicit or implicit comparisons to the detriment of other brands or products. Traditional wisdom had counseled against the use of such copy as an invitation to mutual disparagement and thus to decreased public faith. But now competitive copy, when deftly applied, sometimes evoked praise and imitation. In the boldest "positioning" ploy until Avis plucked itself out of the pack of also-rans by "confessing" that it was only No. 2, the new Plymouth catapulted itself into the select circle of popular low-priced cars with a 1932 campaign that exhorted potential buyers to "Look at All Three." For a totally new automobile to "brazenly" demand equal attention with the two top-selling cars (Ford and Chevrolet) and implicitly invite comparison with them, the trade press agreed, was undoubtedly competitive copy. But it did not directly "knock" the other brands, and it worked. Few concealed their admiration.[58]

Depression advertisers were not only willing to become more competitive; they were also prepared to become more undignified. Having invaded the newspaper comic sections, as described in Chapter Four, they now flooded the sedate periodicals with ads in comic-strip or "continuity series" formats. One survey revealed that the cartoon style, virtually nonexistent in both 1924 and 1929, constituted 10 percent of ad formats in 1933. By 1935, an issue of that respectable showcase of advertising, the *Saturday Evening Post,* might contain as many as six continuity-style formats among forty full-page and half-page ads.[59] Such "strips" included from three to a dozen individual frames. Some replaced cartoon drawings with photographs on which speech balloons were superimposed. As copywriters became convinced that conversational selling was indispensable for a down-to-earth, personalized sales pitch, speech balloons began to appear everywhere. One writer observed that even Nipper, the famous RCA dog who had waited loyally and silently for so many years to hear "His Master's Voice," had suddenly burst into sales talk on radio and in magazine speech balloons.[60] Some advertising men, in dismay, christened the mid-1930s as the "balloon talk period" in advertising. Just as the comic-strip and news-photo styles constituted a "broken-copy" style, the balloons, superimposed captions, inserted boxes, and overlayed price-tags created a "broken-art" style. Rarely did any picture retain an isolated integrity. Nor did many advertisers genteelly refuse to engage in frivolous and "infantile" forms of address to the public.[61]

The mystique of hard work and the pressure to take advantage of any competitive margin encouraged agencies to exploit any new device that promised increased attention. Wrigley's Gum discovered the "unused" margins and gutters (inside margins by the fold) of newspapers and persuaded some newspapers to run

Wrigley ads sideways in color to fill these empty surfaces.[62] The *Saturday Evening Post,* in the effort to keep up revenues, invited advertisers to occupy more pages in front of the editorial material. It also, for the first time, violated the physical integrity of the editorial section by allowing ads to appear after the main section but before the commencement of several articles. *McCall's* responded to similar pressures by revamping its entire format. By segregating its articles into three separate sections, each related to one of women's three interests—romance, home, and self—*McCall's* promised advertisers the opportunity to "time" their ads in relation to the articles, so as "to strike home at the most favorable moment."[63]

The drive to utilize all possible space also led advertisers to take advantage of the new capacity of periodicals to print "bleed" pages in which the illustration extended past the traditional margin to the very edge of the paper. The *Saturday Evening Post* first offered bleed pages in 1933 for an extra charge of $2,000 a page. Several advertisers jumped at the opportunity to gain more display space and a margin of greater attention. Automakers, in particular, saw the technique as a means of showing their cars in larger size and greater "majesty." Some found bleed pages a striking way to amplify the effects of the tabloid style. Bleed photographs were particularly popular. Back in the mid-1920s, an agency artist had warned that any photograph that lacked a "holding border" would look incomplete. It would impress one as likely to fall to pieces. But most advertisers no longer sought completion or unity in layout. The dynamic, unsettling qualities of incompleteness would serve the purposes of advertising far better.[64]

Supplementing these aspects of depression style, and often superimposed on them, arose a "vogue of premiums" and a "contest rampage." Both the free premium and the promotional contest had been employed occasionally by advertisers throughout the 1920s. But in the early 1930s both techniques mushroomed in popularity. In theory, the depression had created a thirst for the premium as "something for nothing," and the monotony of enforced idleness had popularized the prize contest. By mid-1932, *Printers' Ink* was noting the unimaginative but regular increases in the "value and profusion of prizes." It feared that excessive use of the technique had led to "contest indigestion."[65] Premiums became so prevalent that in 1933 *Printers' Ink Monthly* began to devote regular sections of the journal to the topic. Cracker Jack began offering a *second* premium in each package, since its traditional technique had lost any distinctiveness. The immense popularity of both contests and premiums again revealed the readiness of advertisers to give any technique a try. One critic complained that prize contests destroyed all possibilities of "beauty and originality" in the ads: "You can't use a handsome layout. You can't use an original headline. You simply print the headline 'Win $$$' in big black type at the top of the page and write a set of rules."[66] But such an appeal to beauty, and to pride in advertising craftsmanship, was likely to fall on deaf ears in the mid-1930s. Ugly layouts and heavy black print held no terrors for the hardboiled advertising agent.

It was on radio that the rage for prize contests and premium offers first gained momentum in the early 1930s. And it was radio, as the agency president Raymond Rubicam observed, that had stimulated copywriters to inject more entertainment into advertising copy.[67] Before the depression, radio had already begun a rapid drift away from its elevated tone toward a more explicit commercialism. Even without the spur of the depression, the success of dramatized, conversational commercials on radio would have prompted advertisers to adapt this approach to print formats. The new comic-strip style of the early 1930s not only encouraged copywriters to carry the continuities of story-telling radio commercials over into print media; it also suggested a way to further publicize and personify fictional characters from popular radio programs. A number of radio characters had developed a close association with the sponsor's product. Advertisers often "concretized" such characters as cartoon figures in their magazine advertisements, thus reinforcing the impact of the radio show.

Broader in its impact on all advertising, but even more difficult to assess, was radio's reappraisal of audience tastes. Radio had nurtured fond hopes for audience uplift. Then came the 1929 success of "Amos 'n' Andy," followed by that of such "low taste" programs as "Clara, Lu, and Em," "The Eno Crime Club," and "Thirty Minutes of Sunshine."[68] Advertising men now revised downward their estimates of popular taste. Their hardboiled, depression-bred resolve not to be too proud to pander to the lowest common denominator of that taste shaped the tone and style of advertising in the 1930s. The competitive pressures of the depression accelerated these trends in print and radio alike. But new techniques in radio commercials and disillusionment with radio's potential for uplift made independent contributions to the new advertising styles that were almost as significant as the influence of the depression alone.

Many of the style changes of the early 1930s, advertisers regularly asserted, had stemmed from the resolve of shirt-sleeved copywriters to stop consulting their own tastes and to accept the public's preference for simple, comic-strip messages and sensational tabloid layouts. In style, they suggested, advertising had become more down-to-earth and democratic.[69] So, too, they argued, had the social content of advertisements. Certainly a few ads now revised their images of the "typical American" to a slightly lower social level. But there were telltale clues that imagery had changed much less than style. Until about 1937, maids and governesses continued to appear frequently, even in tabloid and comic-strip copy. Golf figured prominently in tableaux for such mass market products as Listerine, General Tires, and Dr. West's toothpaste. Dodge, for all its busy, tabloid pictures and heavy black headlines, still devoted the largest picture in an April 1935 ad to a scene of spectators at a polo match.[70] If its style bespoke the nervous tensions of depression-conscious copywriters, the social content of advertising still often reflected the self-images and social preoccupations of a hard-pressed but enduring advertising elite.

Upstart Agencies with That Depression Touch

Hard times and periods of upheaval often favor the rise of vigorous new firms in a field of business. Such was the case among advertising agencies during the early 1930s. Most of the large agencies, such as J. Walter Thompson, Lord and Thomas, and BBDO, continued to maintain their predominance in billings. In the

9.12. The J. Stirling Getchell style used bold photographs to tell a sequential story. It gave the "common man" a starring role.

long run these agencies may even have consolidated their position, as clients clung to the safety of a large, well-established agency while small agencies were weeded out. But the most sensational news stories in the trade press, both in trend-setting new campaigns and in dramatic victories in the battle for big-spending clients, revolved around a few new or dynamically expanding agencies.

One of these, widely heralded as the moving force in popularizing tabloid layouts, was the Sterling Getchell Agency, a 1932 product of depression upheavals. J. Sterling Getchell, its tactical genius, had embarked on a restless, transient apprenticeship during the 1920s, working successively at a number of major agencies, including Lord and Thomas, the George Batten Company, and J. Walter Thompson. Sidney Hyman describes him as the "ablest of the copywriters" at Batten in 1928.[71] But the depression years, and perhaps a mercurial temperament, brought adversity even to a brilliant copywriter like Getchell. According to William Benton, who had recently linked up with Chester Bowles to start a new agency, Getchell came to him in desperation in 1931 asking to be taken in. He had either quit or been fired from his last job, Benton recalled, and he confessed, "I've been everywhere twice. I can't go back to any of the big agencies. I've worked for all of them. They don't want me back." Benton declined to take Getchell in, but he did help him get a line of credit from the bankers to set up his own shoestring agency.[72]

Getchell launched the new venture rather inauspiciously with a contract to test and prepare copy for a famous but now fading nostrum, Lydia Pinkham's Vegetable Compound. (On the basis of copy tests, he recommended emphasis on such Pinkham headlines as "These Hysterical Women," "Quivering Nerves," "I Feel Full of Pep," and "Nearly Nervous Prostration.") Soon thereafter, however, he embarked on a remarkable rehabilitation from agency outcast to advertising prodigy. In the fall of 1932, on the basis of his imaginative work on his sole full-fledged account, the DeSoto division of Chrysler Motors, Getchell gained the account for Chrysler's new low-priced automobile, the Plymouth. His challenging slogan, "Look at All Three," promptly "created a sensation in both automotive and advertising circles" (Fig. 9.12). As advertising executive Fairfax Cone later described it, the "Look at All Three" campaign represented "the argument of a salesman in a showroom put into automobile advertising for the first time."[73]

Not only did Getchell employ hard-selling copy, he also personalized the company, transforming its president, Walter Chrysler, into an authoritative but affable head salesman. Featured in large, arrested-action photographs, Chrysler crowed about his company's engineering triumphs in defiance of the depression— "We Couldn't Have Done It In Any Other Year." He propped his foot, salesman-fashion, on the Plymouth's front bumper while he offered friendly, person-to-person invitations and advice to typical young American couples. Getchell had not quite put the president of Chrysler Motors in overalls; but he had, as *Printers' Ink* observed, figuratively put him out on the road as a salesman in a shirt-sleeved advertising campaign.[74]

By 1934, *Advertising and Selling* was crediting Getchell with having created a style vogue with his dynamic use of photographs as "bread and butter" illustrations. Whereas his bold, picture-laden copy had once "stood out like a mashed thumb in a manicure parlor," now scores of other advertisers were copying his style. The one agency that *Advertising and Selling* singled out as the major force in transforming Getchell's experiment into an advertising "bandwagon" was Ruthrauff and Ryan.[75] Others would have argued that this agency deserved recognition as more than a mere promoter and amplifier of Getchell's initiatives. In fact, Ruthrauff and Ryan's own advertising techniques had begun to inspire numerous imitations. So rapidly did this brazen, expanding agency add prestigious new clients in the early 1930s that an *Advertising and Selling* writer coined the term "Ruthrauff-and-Ryanism" to refer to the entire movement for "down to earth," shirt-sleeves and overalls advertising.[76]

Ruthrauff and Ryan was not a new agency. Throughout the 1920s, as a small and often disparaged agency, it had concentrated almost exclusively on mail-order advertising. Many leaders of American advertising looked rather disdainfully upon mail-order copy. It occupied small space, lacked any exciting display qualities, and often promoted products that were faintly disreputable. In short, it evoked unpleasant memories of the old patent-medicine era—and with good reason. Wilbur Ruthrauff had specialized in "symptom and cure copy" for patent medicines. Mail-order copy closely followed tested and proven formulas, allowing little scope for creativity. John Caples, who left Ruthrauff and Ryan in the mid-1920s to join Barton, Durstine and Osborn, has argued that the agency was unfairly and unwisely looked down upon. Ruthrauff and Ryan, he explains, was an excellent place to learn skills. But he recalls also that he was happy to move to BDO, where the products more often lived up to the ads.[77]

In the late 1920s, however, Ruthrauff and Ryan began to gain impressive sales results by applying its practical, hard-selling methods to several prominent, non-mail-order products. With the onset of the depression, it suddenly occupied the advertising spotlight. First gaining the Lever Brothers account for Rinso, a product with a lackluster sales record, Ruthrauff and Ryan proved successful enough by 1930 with cartoon ads and local newspaper testimonials to win another Lever Brothers account—Lifebuoy Soap. Here, a "buckeye" campaign against the threat of B.O. (Body Odor) in comic-strip formats, scare ads, and on radio brought sensational sales. The J. Walter Thompson agency nervously watched and crit-

9.13, 9.14. These 1931 and 1934 Dodge ads from Ladies' Home Journal *reveal the dramatic changes in style that made the Ruthrauff and Ryan agency a depression-era sensation.*

icized Ruthrauff and Ryan claims, technical expertise, and testing methods, out of fear of losing other Lever Brothers accounts to this upstart rival.[78] As if to prove that it could do just as "buckeye" and hardboiled a selling job as Ruthrauff and Ryan, JWT launched an "Undie Odor" campaign for its Lux Toilet Soap account. Other agencies and soap manufacturers complained about these offenses to good taste, but the depression encouraged attention to sales records rather than genteel standards of propriety. By 1933, *Advertising and Selling* was proposing a "21-gun salute" to Ruthrauff and Ryan and its cartoon-strip campaign for the "public service" of "scaring so many about B.O."[79]

Its record of effective sales in the face of an economic downturn brought Ruthrauff and Ryan a series of increasingly prestigious clients. Between 1930 and 1934, Dodge Brothers, the R. B. Davis Company (Cocomalt), the Goodrich Rubber Company, the Canadian Pacific Railway, Lehn and Fink (Hinds Honey and Almond Cream), the Gillette Safety Razor Company, and the Pennzoil Company all concluded that hard-selling copy in the spirit of the mail-order tradition was not too vulgar for their products. In a published interview with *Printers' Ink Monthly* entitled "Hard Times—Hard-Tack Copy," the agency's vice-president, W. F. Ruthrauff, welcomed the depression's "distinctly healthful influence on advertising." It had brought the triumph of a practical, unidealistic style over the old pattern of "easy but lovely copy."[80]

Two campaigns epitomize the tactical and stylistic transformations that made Ruthrauff and Ryan a major force behind depression copy trends. One of these was the copy for Dodge. Ruthrauff and Ryan abandoned large, exquisite illustrations in favor of a black-and-white, tabloid format with numerous action photographs and thick, black headlines. Never before had automobile copy in magazines adopted a "news" appeal with so bold and brassy a look (Figs. 9.13, 9.14). Between 1932 and 1933, Dodge dramatically boosted its relative sales position from ninth to fourth. *Advertising and Selling* lauded the agency's tabloid technique as "a genuine contribution to automobile advertising."[81] Meanwhile, Ruthrauff and Ryan had transformed the advertising style of Cocomalt (a vitamin additive to be mixed into milk). In 1929 Cocomalt had courted readers with warm, refined portrayals of children spotlighted by rays of sunshine (Fig. 9.15). In 1930, under the guidance of Ruthrauff and Ryan, it began to shock them with photographic melodramas in which mothers suffered public shame or lost their tempers because of fussy, undernourished children who refused to drink their milk (Fig. 9.16).[82] Cocomalt sales defied the depression, rising to a new peak in 1933. A Gallup survey of *Liberty* magazine reported that Cocomalt ads captured "nearly 150 per cent more reader interest than the average." Ruthrauff and Ryan proclaimed its "real understanding of people" and boasted about "countless imitations" of its campaigns. Few contested such assertions.[83]

No pairing of agency and client in the early 1930s quite attained the made-for-each-other quality of the business "marriage" revealed in April 1933 when the Gillette Safety Razor Company announced the appointment of Ruthrauff and Ryan as its advertising agent. Gillette was struggling and in disarray. It had barely survived a recent mismanagement scandal and a near takeover by the Autostrop Company. In desperation, the company brought in as president a flamboyant outsider who dramatically insisted on receiving no salary until the company's yearly profits rose above five dollars a share. At that time, he would receive 20,000 shares of company stock as his reward.[84] Gillette's new president was none other than Gerard B. Lambert, the erstwhile head of the Lambert Pharmaceutical Company and the celebrated merchandiser of Listerine.

Lambert was intent upon writing his own advertising. Initially he hired a small workmanlike agency to handle the routine details. Almost immediately, Gillette advertising took on an unmistakable "Listerine flair." A campaign with the theme "If Men Only Knew" employed poignant photographs of excruciating moments to warn that "It Wasn't the Depression" that cost young men their jobs. (It was their bristly jowls.) A woman's agonized face revealed her fear that her husband's careless, stubble-chinned appearance proved that he no longer cared.[85] Such copy suggested that Gillette hardly needed help in achieving the Ruthrauff and Ryan touch. Nevertheless, the seemingly inevitable perfect marriage soon followed. Lambert and Ruthrauff and Ryan launched a new series of buckeye melodramas in 1934. In "realistic," slice-of-life photographs, husbands turned away from be-stubbled business associates to whisper to their wives, "Don't worry . . . I won't bring *him* again." Men revealed that their bosses or prospective employees had told them to "spruce up *or get out.*"[86] Just as Ruthrauff and Ryan had successfully united the comic strip and the social melodrama in Lifebuoy's "B.O." advertising, so it joined with Lambert to perfect that fusion of social melodrama with action photography that it had used with telling effect for Cocomalt.

Other agencies that flourished during the depression often did so less by creating sensational and distinctive copy styles than by promptly developing new skills. Many advertisers in the 1930s sought specialized expertise in research and in radio. Benton and Bowles, a new agency, won a series of accounts on the basis of a flair for comic-strip "situation copy" and for soap opera development for radio. It also attracted clients with its special claim to expertise in the new fields of product research and consumer studies.[87]

9.15, 9.16. *This transformation of Cocomalt's style between 1929 and
1931 foreshadowed the shift in style from "pretty art" to photographic
melodrama and comic-strip balloons that would characterize much depression advertising.*

Young and Rubicam, already one of the dynamic, rising agencies in the late
1920s, hired George Gallup to supervise its Copy Research department in 1932.
On the basis of Gallup's work, Young and Rubicam touted itself as a leader in
"scientifically" measuring radio audiences and "reading and noting" newspaper
and periodical ads. George Gallup's early survey forms and summary sheets are
still proudly preserved in Young and Rubicam archives.[88] Batten, Barton, Durstine and Osborn, threatened with decline because of its disdain for some of the
more sensational new stylistic modes, still retained an image of modernity by
building on its early reputation for expertise in radio.[89]

Meanwhile, radio was providing the avenue by which the previously unheralded agency of Blackett-Sample-Hummert suddenly attained depression-era
prosperity. An agency with only eleven unimpressive accounts in 1927, Blackett
and Sample gained immediate stature by adding Frank Hummert as a full partner.
Hummert was the genius behind the early Kotex and Kleenex advertising for
Lord and Thomas and reputedly the "most highly paid advertising writer in the
world."[90] In the early 1930s, Hummert began to adapt his copywriting skills to
radio scripts and to the development of a new genre in radio programming. Soon
Hummert and his wife, Anne, ranked among the most prolific writers of radio
soap operas. In 1930 Blackett-Sample-Hummert had produced only one radio
program with 22 broadcasts; in 1933, it produced 55 different programs with
3,594 individual broadcasts. Advertising placed through the agency increased a
spectacular 167 percent in value during the desperate years of 1930–1934.[91]

If there were spectacular agency success stories during the depression, there were an even greater number of casualties. The depression accelerated a merger movement under the shadow of the "economic shotgun." Many small agencies simply collapsed. Even the giants often made drastic cutbacks in personnel and salaries. Erwin, Wasey and Company endured the most dramatic setback among the major agencies, barely surviving a series of disasters. As *Tide* later observed, "1932 was a pretty awful year for almost everybody. But it was a holy terror of a year for Erwin, Wasey and Company." Having already lost the Philco account late in 1931, the agency then reeled in mid-1932 with the news that General Foods had withdrawn all six of its accounts, a loss of millions in billings. Then, in the fall, it suffered another blow. William Esty, the inventive and tabloid-minded account representative at J. Walter Thompson, suddenly quit the agency to set up his own business. By submitting speculative copy plans for Camel cigarettes, Esty stole this huge account from Erwin, Wasey. Despite what copy chief Jim Ellis described as "probably the greatest exodus of accounts in history," Erwin, Wasey staggered through, only to suffer decimation again in 1935 when both Arthur Kudner and Leo Burnett left to set up their own agencies, each taking several accounts and skilled people with him.[92]

Such startling dramas of feverish success and headlong descent gave those in an already nervous, superheated occupation the sensation of having embarked on an endless roller-coaster ride. It was hardly surprising that many responded with shouts of bravado and an anything-goes, survive-at-any-cost attitude. Figuratively donning overalls and rolling up one's shirt sleeves represented, in part, an effort to retain an image of professional commitment, personal control, and serious social production while gripping the roller-coaster security-bar for dear life. The outpouring of sensational, "screaming" copy was hardly a surprising consequence. Some ad writers came to cherish the roller-coaster ride, to thrive on the opportunities for exciting new tests of public response to the blatant, the simplistic, and the spectacular. But others, particulary within the trade press and among the larger, somewhat more staid, agencies, began to voice hopes of regaining a little stability and calm judiciousness in the profession. They warned against advertising abuses that might sacrifice long-range credibility for immediate sales, citing visible evidence that the public would not forever tolerate the rising challenges to its intelligence, good taste, and credulity.

Ballyhoo, Organized
Consumers, and the New Deal

During the summer of 1931, an irreverent new magazine entitled *Ballyhoo* exploded like a bombshell in the advertising scene. An overnight financial success, this unlikely depression phenomenon offered vivid evidence of a latent public skepticism of all advertising. Launched as a humor magazine, *Ballyhoo* relied for laughs entirely on lampoons of notorious advertisements. Its parody of Listerine toothpaste's what-you-can-buy-with-the-money-you-save campaign proclaimed the wonders of "Blisterine": "Buy yourself some false teeth with the money you

Buy yourself some false teeth
with the money you save on tooth paste!

Why Buy
Tooth Paste?

Don't buy any!

Feel your mouth grow healthier!

TAKE that money you save by not buying our tooth paste, and buy yourself a nice set of store teeth. There! Is that big hearted, or isn't it!

No more tooth-aches, no more gas from dentists, no more pyro—you know what we mean.

Blisterine Tooth Paste saves you $3 a year, but if you don't buy any, you save $6!

However, spend it as you please. This is merely a suggestion.

You can get a good bottle of Scotch for what you save!

9.17. Ballyhoo *managed to parody both Listerine's sales pitch and the disembodied teeth and mouths of other toothpaste ads. See Fig. 9.1. for an example of the Listerine series.*

save on toothpaste" (Fig. 9.17). In "How Georgie Cursed when Milktime Came," *Ballyhoo* lampooned the new Cocomalt style with a worried-mother ad for Creme de Cocoa: "Georgie's weight has gone up a pound a week . . . since I began giving him milk this easy way. . . . You'll be surprised what Creme-de-Cocoa will do for your baby. It will darn near knock him outen his little bassinet!" Movie star "La Belle Zilch" kept her girlish figure by bathing "every fortnight" with "Lox Toilet Soap." Nine out of ten stars, *Ballyhoo* announced, really "clean up" with paid "Lox Toilet Soap" testimonials.[93]

With copy of this character, the initial edition of *Ballyhoo* (August 1931) sold out the entire run of 150,000 copies in a few days. It simply burst into existence, an agency executive complained, "like some rank tropical flower." The September issue sold 275,000 copies. October brought another sellout, this time of all 650,000 copies. Within five months, *Ballyhoo* magazine, with a circulation of a million and a half, had become one of the most sensational new business enterprises to defy the depression. The publisher began accepting paid ads at $3,750 a page. He required that all ads adopt an appropriate satirical approach.[94]

Ballyhoo also gained overnight success within the advertising trade. Everyone talked about it, joked about it, and shuddered a bit at its ultimate implications. Some advertising men enjoyed *Ballyhoo's* farcical renderings of their competitors' copy and found catharsis in devising their own take-offs. But others anxiously viewed *Ballyhoo* as the emerging tip of an iceberg of public cynicism. "Anyone with two eyes in his head can see that the public is getting restive," warned H. A. Batten of N. W. Ayer and Son. *Advertising and Selling* sensed a growing public skepticism that regarded advertising as "a great joke." It was all right for advertising agents to enjoy private lampoons at their own expense, but quite a different story when millions paid to read advertising's "high-priced pages" turned into "a coarse and disrespectful horse-laugh."[95]

An even more disturbing symptom of rising public distrust of advertising emerged in the form of a fledgling consumer movement. In 1927, the flustered advertising trade had reacted with a flurry of censure, ridicule, and counterattack to Stuart Chase and F. J. Schlink's muckraking book, *Your Money's Worth.*[96] Chase and Schlink had suggested that consumers create a test service to provide an objective source of information about products. Public response to the book encouraged them to expand their initial "Consumers Club" in White Plains, New York into a national organization known as Consumers Research. The new organization employed technical experts, set up a laboratory, and published a newsletter. Its membership reached 12,000 by 1930. With the impetus of the depression, Consumers Research doubled its membership in 1931.[97]

Meanwhile, other organizations with similar goals of consumer education had also emerged. A Consumers Cooperative movement was expanding. In 1933, F. J. Schlink and Arthur Kallet published *1,000,000 Guinea Pigs,* a sensational account of the misleading advertising of drugs and cosmetics. The trade press erupted with "wrathful denials." But some advertising leaders interpreted the incipient consumers movement as a symptom of a public skepticism induced by the heavy-handed advertising of the early 1930s. Devoting its first page of copy to an unprecedented lead editorial, *Advertising and Selling* alerted readers that its October 1931 article on the work of Consumers Research had evoked more concerned responses than any article since the paid testimonials controversy of the late 1920s. Psychologist Henry Link reported survey results which indicated that only 4 to 5 percent of the public believed certain current advertising assertions. Even the most credible assertions convinced only 37 percent of those surveyed. *Printers' Ink Monthly* noted the growth of Consumers Councils and warned the smug creators of "misleading, vulgar advertising" that "a movement of this kind grows with the geometrical rapidity of a snowball."[98]

The tiny new consumer organizations came to inspire fear in the advertising trade by the mid-1930s because they threatened to pursue their objectives through the new regulatory powers of the federal government. The Roosevelt administration proposed to extend the powers of the Food and Drug Administration to cover cosmetics and to regulate advertising as well as labeling. It also called for government-enforced grade-labeling of food. What would happen to brand-name advertising, many advertisers wondered, if people were induced to base their buying decisions on a grading system defined by the government? Would it destroy all advertising that celebrated, by implication, the superiority of Jones's grade-A canned peaches over the grade-A peaches by Brown? And once the regulation of drug and cosmetic advertising began, would not other inhibiting forms of regulation follow? Moreover, organizations such as the Parent-Teachers Association and the Home Economics Association were gaining a sympathetic hearing from Senate committees for their denunciations of distasteful and mis-leading advertising. And the federal government itself was now contributing bulletins to the flood of informational materials that "cast doubt on advertising and advertisers."[99]

As early as the fall of 1932, *Advertising and Selling* had begun to warn that such "pseudo-scientific" scare campaigns as the Scott Tissue ads, which dramatically warned of the dire results of using the allegedly arsenic-laden brands of toilet paper sold by competitors, represented "a direct invitation to government regu-lation." The New Deal proposals for the expansion of FDA regulation inspired calls for preventive self-regulation within the industry. A contributor to *Adver-tising and Selling* warned that the 1934 elections would bring a new Congress and "a flood of social legislation which will place advertising on a hotter seat than it has ever been on before."[100] In an editorial entitled "Let's Face the Music," *Printers' Ink* noted the growing number of dignified organizations now testifying to their skepticism of advertising before the Senate Commerce Committee. The specter of advancing government regulation provoked the editor to call upon "honest, intelligent, and high-minded advertisers" to silence "the fakers, charlatans, and crooks" of the trade.[101]

Medicine-Man Tactics and Self-Esteem

By 1933 there had emerged among advertising leaders a powerful wave of sentiment that conflicted with the hardboiled, advertising-in-overalls posture. This was their mounting concern about advertising abuses. Many agency execu-tives and copywriters resented the pressures and "competitive fright" that had pushed "nervous manufacturers" to insist on vulgar and ludicrous copy. The more conservative agencies, in particular, denounced the unscrupulous tactics used by their dynamic competitors to stimulate immediate sales for their clients. Such techniques and appeals might win more sales in the short run, they argued, but they would also breed public skepticism. They would soon bring all adver-tising into further disrepute and under government regulation. Some critics even glimpsed, in the exaggerated claims and "bombastic ballyhoo" of depression styles, a threat to the whole effort of the previous two decades to cast off the lingering aura of "patent medicine days."[102]

Theodore MacManus, long esteemed as a copywriting genius, attacked the merchandising tactics behind an antiseptic "originally introduced as a mouth wash and now sneakingly promulgated as a preventive of conception." Much recent

9.18. The depression so degraded taste and ethics in advertising that many leaders feared a "national nausea." They pointed to such outrages as the use of sexy models to sell caskets.

advertising, he complained, assumed that people were "lapsing rather rapidly into a state of grinning imbecility." Others denounced the "advent of Casket Cuties" (bathing beauties used to gain attention for coffins) as evidence of misplaced faith in the "erotic appeal to morons" (Fig. 9.18). The sound of advertising, one journal contributor complained, was now that of clashing cymbals. Everyone was "yelling at the top of his voice" and "screaming . . . in guttural Gothic." Others complained of "faked-up photography," "high-pressure stunts," "chattering radio contests," and "deliberate falsehoods." The president of the American Association of Advertising Agencies warned that "a wave of ill-considered advertising" was bringing the country to "the verge of national nausea."[103]

Such aversions and forebodings did not disturb some copywriters. They had adapted their style to the desperately competitive atmosphere of the early depression and to the "spasms of worry" experienced by their clients. Accepting a narrow view of themselves as hardnosed peddlers of goods, they looked to each month's sales records for pride and justification. But many agency leaders, even during the depression, were unable to accept so limited a self-image. A vice-president in one leading agency confessed to a fellow executive that, while his first years with the agency had been "the most inspiring years of his business career," now "the glow of pride" in his work was gone. The reason, his colleague concluded, was that "gradually, insidiously, advertising has lost the element of serving the public." The *Printers' Ink* columnist "Groucho" grumbled that depression fears had transformed advertising leaders from "professionals who stimulated and improved public taste" into "scared-to-death panderers to a lower and lower kind of taste." A year later, he began reporting conversations with manufacturers who were "sick and tired of talking boob nonsense" and who were "getting hungry to get a little self-respect back when they read their own ads."[104]

Advertisers had been right, nearly everyone agreed, to respond to the depression by putting on the "overalls" of hard work. But in the hysteria of the times, some had distractedly pulled a clown suit or a "medicine man's garb" out of the wardrobe instead. "Monstrous headlines," "childish balloons," and unbelievable comic strips had turned advertising into a circus. In the "discouraging" years since 1929, Bruce Barton confessed in 1934, "you have seen silly advertisements, dishonest advertisements, disgusting advertisements." In late 1933, Raymond Levy, an agency vice-president, warned colleagues that the profession had "slipped backwards a decade" in only three years. His appeal to avoid national ridicule by halting the trend back toward the teachings of P. T. Barnum brought *Advertising Age* requests for nearly 5,000 reprints. One letter in *Advertising Age,* inspired by Levy's article "The Writing on the Wall," reminded advertising men how long they had struggled to "gain caste as a profession."[105]

It would be a mistake to characterize the advertising trade as split into two entirely separate camps, with the guardians of respectability uncompromisingly confronting the hardboiled "vulgarians" of the advertising-in-overalls school. Many who excoriated advertising for its mid-1930s abuses had also, on other occasions, praised the depression's "healthy" effect in bringing a new appreciation of the need for hard work, practicality, and down-to-earth selling. No efforts to regain self-esteem and an image of public service could ignore the need to wage a courageous, shirt-sleeved battle against the dangerous forces and attitudes unleashed by the depression.

Success, Advertising Men, and the Courage Quotient

In 1932 a writer in *Printers' Ink* made one more dramatic attempt to convince advertisers that they should defend their business futures by investing more money in the weaponry of advertising. After familiarizing readers with the "battleground upon which the sales struggle of these times must be waged," he warned ominously: "The business graveyard is crowded with headstones bearing the epitaph, 'Too scared to fight.'"[106]

Encapsulated in these brief phrases lay all the elements of the advertising trade's reaffirmation of the success creed in the face of depression conditions. The graveyard metaphor suggested the ultimate stakes involved: present business competition was truly a life-or-death struggle. This "fight" could best be understood through military analogies to weapons and battlegrounds. And, as in every war, judgments about the behavior of groups and individuals were phrased in moral terms. Failure stemmed from cowardice—from the behavior of those who were "too scared." The key to success was courage.

The equation of success with courage dominated the verbal and visual imagery of the advertising trade press in the early 1930s and frequently spilled over into the tableaux of national advertising. Thus, the messages of guilt embodied in the parables of the Skinny Kid and the Unraised Hand and the invitations to satisfy one's ambitions through minor consumer satisfactions in parables of the Democracy of Goods were accompanied by other messages reaffirming the moral necessity of hard work and of courageous commitment to the quest for economic success whatever the odds. In all of these appeals, copywriters recognized the centrality of the success creed to the dilemmas of depression-era Americans. But advertisers made no effort to learn popular attitudes in order to mirror them. Rather, they invested themselves with a responsiblity for moral leadership. By implicitly defining all other responses to the depression as cowardly, they sought to give a recommitment to hard work the force of a moral imperative. The appeal to courage did not invite a close examination of circumstances; rather it short-circuited any depression-inspired questions about the functioning and credibility of the American dream.

As early as the fall of 1930, publishers and advertising agencies began to exhort manufacturers by equating advertising appropriations with courage. What was "on trial" during the depression, editorialized *Printers' Ink,* was not advertising, but "the courage and resourcefulness of its users." A contributor to the journal, while attacking the "weak-kneed" cutbacks of many advertisers, praised the "intestinal fortitude" of the cigarette companies for their large appropriations. Publishers calculatingly addressed their ads to "advertisers who have maintained their courage" and to "men who are *not* afraid of the Dark." By 1932 journal editors and advertising agencies were celebrating those who maintained large advertising appropriations as "Captains Courageous" and offering them "Medals for Bravery."[107]

If advertising agents and the trade press frequently took advertisers to task for a lack of courage, they did not spare themselves from criticism. In fact, some advertising leaders indulged in rhetorical orgies of self-flagellation. Advertising people had grown soft and slack from the ease of good times, they confessed. The depression had come as a well-deserved slap in the face. "We took an awful licking that was coming to us," admitted BBDO. In *Advertising and Selling* an advertising manager reflected: "The thing that appalls me is our lack of courage." Trade journals went out of their way to repeat characterizations of the trade as cowardly, weak-willed, anemic, and effeminate. "We are not men, but jellyfish," quoted *Tide* with seeming approval from an ad in a specialized business journal. Were advertisers going to allow themselves to gain a reputation as "quitters"?[108]

Very quickly the language of the journals took on the formulaic character of a halftime pep talk. Dozens of advertising men volunteered to play the role of coach, dutifully excoriating the team for its previous failures, threatening its members with the shame of being labelled "quitters," and then promising a comeback based on a show of manliness and courage. A number of these self-appointed "coaches" fondly recalled the hard times in the past which had honed their own competitive instincts and insured their subsequent success. Claude Hopkins, now in semiretirement from his celebrated copywriting career, recalled that his "greatest advances" had been made under "sink or swim" conditions. The depression was a good thing, he argued, in a "Thanks, I needed that!" interpretation.[109] The Blackman advertising agency confidently recommended its services to new clients on the basis of the lessons it had learned during the "dark days" of the panic of 1907 and the slump of 1921. It had been a distinct advantage, the agency implied, to have been born into the mettle-testing world of the 1907 panic. Again and again, editorials and articles in the trade press defined courage as the acceptance of harsh realities, the recapturing of the will to succeed, and the recognition that "there is no substitute for work."[110]

As the end of the 1931–1932 school year approached, copywriters for the Hamilton Watch Company urged parents to "be thankful they are graduating in a Tough Year!" The tableau recounted a story of a 1929 reunion of men who had graduated in the year of the 1907 panic. These men had confessed that they were "eternally thankful" for the experience of having graduated when "jobs were few and dollars were tight," Hamilton Watches noted reassuringly. "They pitied the fellows who had missed the moulding lessons of their early struggles by graduating into a too soft and ready world!" The depression would assure graduates of 1932 the greatest likelihood of success, the ad implied.[111] In ads for Plymouth cars, Walter P. Chrysler testified to just such a benefit from the current depression. "In prosperous times we never could have done it," he insisted. The depression had brought the "adverse conditions" that had prompted his company to discover that "necessity was the mother of *invention* and that the seemingly impossible *could be done.*" The story of the new Plymouth was "a story written in sweat," boasted Chrysler, "the sweat of hard work—and plenty of it."[112]

Thus, advertisers argued to themselves and to the public, the depression had actually improved the functioning of the success ethic. By enforcing a tough discipline it had shaped men's character. More significantly, the intensified competition of the depression had reestablished the highly selective, "quality-control" process of an unrelenting economic struggle for survival. As early as December 1929, *Printers' Ink* predicted a major role for advertising in the coming "test period" in "weeding out the unfit brands." A 1932 *Business Week* ad which predicted an impending business upturn still took delight in warning that recovery would continue to enforce the "stern principle of the survival of the fittest." "Every far-sighted business concern," the prediction concluded enthusiastically, would equip itself with "a sharper set of teeth for the bloody battle that is bound to be fought for a bite of the consumer's dollar."[113]

The prevalence of calls to battle in the trade press of the early 1930s—the repeated appeals for a show of courage, of fortitude, of "guts"—accurately reflected the siege mentality of advertising agents in this era. Few Americans faced such unrelenting pressure to maintain a posture of optimism while suffering drastic losses and public criticism. Even the leaders of the few agencies that did not suffer major losses of clients and appropriations still could not escape the realization that the entire profession had been thrown on the defensive. Pressured by a consumer movement and by legislative initiatives, ridiculed by popular parodies, attacked by colleagues for tastelessness and low ethics, and conscious of a mounting public skepticism, advertising men easily identified with heroic portrayals of men fighting with their backs to the wall, of men driven back upon their deepest inner resources. Those who continued to write copy and plan illustrations, moreover, were increasingly conscious of themselves as survivors of yearly decimations of their ranks. In their natural instinct to justify their survival as part of a selection of the "fittest," they hastened to clothe themselves in the moral raiment of courage and to make sure that perspiration from hard work glistened visibly on their brows. Pictorially, they fixed upon panoramas that expressed Nature's moral empathy for their anxieties and insecurities and upon characters whose body language spoke eloquently of their own anguished determination. These scenes and gestures, etched in lines of both hope and frustration, emerged as two of the most striking visual clichés of the depression era: "sunbeams that banish shadows" and "the clenched fist."

Economic Sunbeams: Reassurance and Inspiration

The struggle for business survival had suggested a need to get more fully in tune with the tastes of the people. But depression pressures had also intensified the preoccupation of advertising men with their own plight. Abuses within the advertising trade threatened to undermine their proper influence and to wound their professional vanity. Having put on their overalls and rolled up their sleeves, advertising leaders still felt the need to reaffirm their ideological premises and assert their beneficent social role. Some found catharsis in an outpouring of anxiously phrased, and often visually melodramatic, tableaux of self-reassurance and inspiration. Many of these appeared in the trade press. But the tensions and insecurities that lay behind them often surfaced in national consumer advertising as well. As inspirational messages, published for the ostensible purpose of lifting the profession and the public out of psychological and economic depression, these ads helped the trade cling to a fading image of broad social power and public service. Advertising men could pull on overalls and buckle to their task, these ads implied, without necessarily confining themselves to roles as carnival barkers or high-pressure salesmen.

The ads of reassurance and inspiration that appeared in the advertising trade press between 1930 and 1934 were as finely tuned to the yearnings and sensitivities of their audience as any batch of advertising copy. Agencies sought to gain repute and attract clients by striking a noble stance and contributing a "public service" at their own expense. They hoped to do so by saying first, or most strikingly and convincingly, what they believed that everybody would agree "needed to be said." Opportunely, they would perform this public service of expressing latent feelings simply by consulting their own hopes and anxieties and presenting them sincerely and creatively.

As the depression deepened, the inspirational voices of mutual reassurance began to soar above the clatter of the advertising press. "Bad Times Are Good Times to be Born in," *Business Week* reassured potential advertisers searching for causes for optimism. Business was "in great shape for a hard fight," reported BBDO confidently. During the forced "diet" of the depression, it had "taken off

9.19, 9.20. In two of the many versions of the shadows-to-sunbeams motif, advertising organizations visually introduced the gloom of depression only to promise a bright prosperity waiting to be found.

a lot of fat."[114] N. W. Ayer won the plaudits of publishers and other advertising agencies for its 1932 message to fellow businessmen entitled "People are still *People!*" Whether stocks and budgets rose or fell, Ayer observed comfortingly, fundamental human needs and desires continued unabated.[115]

Inspirational depression tableaux often adopted a visual "sunbeams that banish shadows" motif. In majestic natural panoramas, dominated by vast expanses of sky, heavy clouds cast deep shadows over the landscape. But radiant beams, just emerging from behind the clouds, flooded part of the terrain with light. Sometimes human figures, dwarfed by the natural setting, emerged from the "shadows" or gazed expectantly into the beams of light (Figs. 9.19, 9.20). To introduce the reader immediately to the metaphorical association of clouds and shadows with the depression, and light beams with returning prosperity, these tableaux carried such captions and headlines as "The Sun of Better Business begins to Shine!" and "When the sun shines again who'll be in the shade?"[116]

Some of the shadow and sunbeam motifs sought merely to dramatize the assertion that a particular publication or city had escaped the dark impact of the depression. "It is not raining everywhere," these ads insisted. Others offered the consolation of a "silver linings" message. The "stern necessity" of the depression

CLOUDS . . . THUNDER . . . RAIN

9.21. *Floods of letters from the business community praised the Geyer-Cornell agency for its series of philosophical ads of reassurance.*

Under the burning sun the earth shrivels and e
up, but after the storm it is renewed and fertile. Then e
man who breathes its fresh damp breath feels stirring in
the old, old urge to dig . . . The fields in which we wor
fertile, and there is the better knowledge of how to dig v

enabled those advertisers and journals with "real strength" to forge ahead, Fairchild Publications explained. In a series of stark, double-truck illustrations, the Geyer-Cornell agency drew upon images of clouds and shadows ("Out of the Shadow of Yesterday"; "Clouds . . . Thunder . . . Rain . . . and the Good Fresh Earth") to muse about eternal rejuvenation. An "understanding born in the shadow," Geyer-Cornell promised, would come in on the flood tide to bring a "new usefulness of man to man" (Fig. 9.21). *Advertising and Selling* reported that corporate advertising managers had filled the floors of its publishing office "ankle-deep with letters of praise for this inspirational copy."[117]

Meanwhile, the advertising tableaux of inspiration and boosterism spilled out of the trade press and into consumer magazines and newspapers. Corporate

leaders appreciated the circulation of inspiriting messages within narrow business circles; but they looked even more favorably upon those businesses, agencies, and publishers who bought advertising space to help restore optimism (and generous buying habits) to the public as well. If, as the advertising writer Kenneth Goode argued, "mismanaged morale" was the most significant cause of the depression, then advertising might reclaim its larger responsibilities and reassert its power by rousing the nation out of its psychological and economic slump. In ads headlined "Look Ahead" and "Get Readjusted," Metropolitan Life Insurance offered readers of newspapers and popular magazines "unselfish" messages of reassurance and advice. The Bank of America joined the cheerleaders for prosperity by depicting a man with a shovel confidently leading Uncle Sam "Back to the Good Times."

The New Haven Railroad called readers to "Climb Out of the Depression," and the Missouri Pacific headlined its ads "Prosperity Bound." The trade's appetite for messages of reassurance seemed insatiable. The advertising journals welcomed each new inspirational ad with pathetic gratitude. When the Packard Motor Company ran an anti-hoarding ad that proclaimed "To buy today is a patriotic duty," *Printers' Ink* offered the company effusive congratulations on its unselfishness.[118]

Was advertising mirroring the attitudes of the American people in such morale-boosting campaigns? Certainly people hoped that the depression would soon come to an end. But advertisers and other business spokesmen had confidently predicted the "turning of the corner" so many times by 1932 that messages of reassurance must have increasingly confronted a skeptical public.[119] The popular magazine *Ballyhoo* made uproarious fun of such ads as Missouri Pacific's "Prosperity Bound" and lampooned morale-boosting campaigns with such proposals as "Smile us into Prosperity . . . wear a *Smilette*" (a device proposed by *Ballyhoo* to pull up the corners of the wearer's mouth).[120] The plain fact was that whatever attitudes the public may have adopted, manufacturers and advertising leaders wanted to hear such messages of inspiration to bolster their own convictions. They did not seek feedback from the consumer audience because they were not interested in reflecting its views. They wanted to exercise moral leadership.

Was it paradoxical that advertisements of reassurance, often illustrated in a spacious, romantic mode that contrasted sharply with the tabloid formats, should have flourished during the hardboiled era of advertising-in-overalls? I think not. With many agencies turning out "vulgar" and "moronic" copy, the ads of reassurance afforded copywriters an outlet for expressions of their continuing aspiration to see themselves as agents of uplift and public service. Moreover, the inspirational ads themselves often exuded an aura of perspiring, conscientious zeal which actually reinforced the mystique of redemptive hard work that had so captivated the advertising trade during the depression.

Clenched Fists

Folklore and convention depict the typical American as naturally hard-working and courageous. But popular literature, from melodramas and movies to comic strips and posters, has required that these qualities be strikingly dramatized on occasions when good Americans are forced back on their inner resources by threats or obstacles. We all know the appropriate gestures for such occasions: the undaunted worker rolls up his sleeves; the unconquerable defender of the right doubles his fists. Uncle Sam, particularly during wartime, often does both. So did the surrogates of advertising men in advertising tableaux of the early 1930s.

But a slight nuance distinguished the depression gestures. The man seeking to fulfill the dream of success in depression advertising tableaux did not simply bare his arm and double his fist in proud confidence. Rather, he *clenched* his fist, squeezing the fingers and thumb together, almost in desperation. Sometimes his accompanying facial grimaces further revealed the mixed elements of anguish and determination in such gestures. Through the image of the clenched fist, increasingly visible first in the trade press and then in the general circulation magazines of the early 1930s, advertising men invited Americans to join them in a cathartic response to the depression's challenges to the American dream.

The power of this familiar and evocative gesture, as of the rhetorical appeals to courage that frequently accompanied it, lay in its capacity to reduce all choices to a narrow, morally charged pair of alternatives. The gesture posited a scenario with two choices: confronted with the discouraging obstacles of the depression, the American "Everyman" either courageously clenched his fists, rolled up his sleeves, and struggled determinedly onward, or he slunk away from the battlefield in cowardice, confessing himself to be a quitter who was "too scared to fight." Finding the appeal to courage and determination, as dramatized in the clenched fist, an effective rallying cry and an appealing self-image, advertisers paraded this imagery before the consuming public. They did so partly out of a compulsion toward self-expression and partly out of a hope of exercising their responsiblities for leadership. Despite all the talk about a skeptical and disillusioned public, advertisers assumed that readers would share their sentiments and appreciate their empathy.

The penchant of advertisers for the imagery of the clenched fist may also have stemmed almost unconsciously from their simultaneous efforts to pump up the morale of their sales forces. In corporate sales bulletins during the early 1930s sales managers and their executives intensified their "pep talks" to struggling salesmen and field representatives. These harangues fiercely reasserted the validity of the success creed. E. R. Squibb and Sons, seeking to rally its salesmen to the "intestinal stamina, hard work, long hours, mental and physical exhaustion" now necessary for success, confronted them with the clenched fist challenge: "Courage, Men! The day of the survival of the fittest is here, and I know you belong to that select group which can take it 'on the chin' and then win out in the final round." The Metropolitan Life Insurance Company bluntly told its agents that none of them had lost his job or suffered reduced earnings "for reasons not within his own control." In a pointed reaffirmation of the success creed, it admonished agents that "the year ahead can be as good a year as the individual agent wills it to be."[121] By 1933 Metropolitan Life was throwing out the "quitter" challenge to its field men: "You were expected to succeed; not to fail. Either you are going to measure up to this larger opportunity, or you are not. If you do not you will have to admit defeat. . . . Are you going to plow ahead, pay the price, and overcome all discouragements and rebuffs, or are you going to give up?"[122]

The commingled determination, self-pity, and frustration portrayed so poignantly in some of the tableaux of clenched fists was best expressed verbally in an editorial entitled "Doing the Job" in *Printers' Ink Monthly* in April 1933. Advertisers were not making much money nowadays, the editorial complained, but they could still obtain "a sort of fierce satisfaction" by "sailing right into a tough job, pushing right on through obstacles." Certainly it would be easier, the editor continued, "to acknowledge defeat" and "retire to some quiet spot." But the courageous ad man would accept "grief, fighting, and worry" in quest of "the almost holy satisfaction that comes from accomplishment." Predictably, the edi-

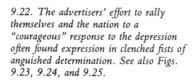

9.22. The advertisers' effort to rally themselves and the nation to a "courageous" response to the depression often found expression in clenched fists of anguished determination. See also Figs. 9.23, 9.24, and 9.25.

torial concluded by pledging ad men to continue the eternal struggle. "Advertisers in these United States are hardboiled fighters who get satisfactory rewards out of doing the job."[123]

This mood of besieged, teeth-gritting determination increasingly characterized the ads in the trade and business press in 1932 and 1933 (Fig. 9.22). Accepting the American Can Company's prediction of a coming era of "relentless competition, of savage battles for sales," one publication warned: "If you are going to keep your head above water this year, you must not only get your share of the business—*you must get more than your share.*" The Newell-Emmett advertising agency advised readers that "the *battle* for markets is just beginning." Powers Accounting Machines, in an ad captioned "Until you see the whites of their eyes," portrayed contemporary businessmen as analogues of the Bunker Hill "tradesmen and farmers . . . nerve-tensed . . . huddled behind inadequate straw and earth over a century ago." "We said it in 1920 and we repeat it in 1932," proclaimed the Henri, Hurst and McDonald agency; "it's the last drop of blood . . . the last ounce of power . . . the last 2 per cent that wins."[124]

Such appeals for a clenched-fist response were not limited to ads aimed at businessmen. The Young and Rubicam agency sought to elicit contributions for a committee to mobilize relief for the unemployed by displaying the man who deserved such relief with his sleeve rolled up and his fist clenched. "Of course, *We can do it!*" proclaimed the ad's headline. In an Ethyl Gasoline ad, an all-American boy clenched his fist in frustrated determination in a tableau that seemed vividly to connote the failed father syndrome of the depression. As other cars whizzed past father and son in their tired old car with listless gasoline, the son, with his fist clenched, reproached his father for his inadequacy: "Gee, Pop—They're All Passing You" (Fig. 9.23).[125] In "The Boy Deserves His Turn," the father in a Penn

9.23. Father, the consumer, is reproached by his son, whose clenched fist expresses his determination not to be "left behind" because of the depression's frustrating constraints.

THE BOY DESERVES HIS TURN

THE PENN MUTUAL LIFE INSURANCE COMPANY
WM. A. LAW, PRESIDENT • INDEPENDENCE SQUARE, PHILADELPHIA

9.24. This father, his ambitions displaced onto his son, conveys in a single gesture his determination that, even if competition has intensified, success can still be gained.

Mutual Life Insurance ad now expressed his hope of fulfillment through his son's success by adopting the cliché of the clenched fist. As his son in a football uniform knelt on the sidelines with his fist clenched, awaiting his chance to play, the father projected his own clenched fist over the boy's shoulder. "The competition of the present day can try men's souls," the text noted empathetically. "But sons will face competition, in all probability, even more rigorous." The father's clenched fist met the challenge by responding, figuratively: "This is the way that we must all face the challenges and frustrations of the depression" (Fig. 9.24).[126]

We should hardly find it surprising that the tableaux of the era did not include comparable examples of girls reproaching their fathers with clenched fists or of mothers with clenched fists anticipating tests of fortitude for their children. In conformance with the mystique of sweaty, hardboiled virility with which the advertising trade responded to the depression, the image of the clenched fist was a thoroughly masculine icon. It symbolized the ad men's self-conscious reaction against the "effeminacy" of the soft, overly pretty advertising they imputed to the late 1920s. Fists connoted rolled-up sleeves, brawny forearms, hard work, and the rest of the blue-collar imagery to which these white-collar manipulators of symbols seemed invariably to turn when they felt compelled to reassert a "masculine" commitment to the production ethic. The rhetoric of "hardtack copy" and the imagery of clenched fists suggested a revolt against the ignominy of pandering to the feminine qualities of their audience.

Still, a slight nuance of effeminacy did characterize many depression images of the clenched fist. These were clenched fists, not merely doubled fists. The intensity of closure, while not connoting hysteria as clenched hands might have

Watchman, what of the Night?

1700 B.C.

In the seven years of plenty man grew fat.

In the seven years of famine he grew lean.

As he starved, he beat his breast. He reproached his God.

But this brought him no escape from the economic trap. He starved, he died.

1932 A.D.

Economic situations, we have learned meanwhile, do not respond to emotional treatment.

Economically, this is a day of night.

Shall we huddle in frightened groups, with cries and lamentations?

Or shall we take our bearings by compass and march through darkness toward the dawn?

The Paul Cornell Company
Incorporated
Advertising and Marketing
580 Fifth Avenue, New York

9.25. Should these businessmen, besieged by economic darkness, be hopeful or fearful? With a clenched fist, the Cornell agency empathized with their anxiety and challenged them to march with courage "toward the dawn."

suggested in women, still betrayed a sense of anxiety, a feeling of being backed against the wall. So, too, did the "clenched faces" that often accompanied clenched fists or even substituted for them in the tableaux. They bespoke the anguish of working under intense pressures—both psychological and economic. Copywriters found one outlet for the expression of such anxieties in depression ads for the All-Year Club of Southern California. Promoting vacations as last-minute reprieves from nervous breakdowns, these tableaux throbbed with sincere empathy. "*Bake out* your troubles," suggested one. "Here's Something they *can't* take away from you," consoled another.[127] In 1932 an advertising executive alluded metaphorically to the "grimaces" of depression advertising, a phrase that can be applied more literally than he intended to the illustrations that emerged from the milieu he described: "Hard times have brought increased competition. The manufacturer has gotten nervous. He has put upon advertising a strain greater than it can bear. And his advertising, as a result, has assumed the grotesque attitudes and grimaces of a man tested beyond his strength."[128]

The clenched faces and clenched fists of advertising tableaux did not confess an unbearable strain, but they did suggest an almost desperate anxiety. In the Paul Cornell agency's "Watchman, what of the Night?" the clenched fist and clenched faces of the model businessmen seemed to express an ever-hopeful but obviously besieged fortitude. "Shall we huddle in frightened groups, with cries and lamentations?" read the text. "Or shall we take our bearings by compass and march through darkness towards the dawn?" (Fig. 9.25).[129] Disembodied fists strained with seeming desperation to crack tough nuts or squeeze the juice of "profit" out of a symbolic orange. Sometimes the face best expressed the clenched reaction to

TO FATHERS WHO WANT TO BE PROUD OF THEIR SONS

9.26. "Do all you can now to keep life from giving him an ugly break," Lionel urged this depression father. We don't see a father's clenched fist (as in Fig. 9.24), only the tense smile of a "clenched face."

intense pressure. Even attempted smiles on the part of proud but anxious fathers could be distorted almost into grimaces by clenched-fist determination. "Do you want your son to be keen-witted, quick-thinking, resourceful—or don't you care?" asked a Lionel Electric Train ad. The tone of voice was borrowed directly from the ad men's own "locker-room" harangues against "quitters." Obliquely alluding to depression circumstances, the Lionel ad reminded each father, "A lot depends on you. . . . Do all you can *now* to keep life from giving him an ugly break." The father depicted in the ad *did* care—so much so that his teeth clenched tightly behind his forced smile, as he resolved that this toy should prepare his son for the desperate fight for success that lay ahead (Fig. 9.26).[130]

No advertiser surpassed the Union Central Life Insurance Company in zealous expression of the clenched-fist response to the declining credibility of the success

A DAD FORGOT

that his boy stood only 1 chance in 43 . . .

PITIFULLY few boys get a really fair start in life these days. Figures prove it. The actual odds are 43 to 1 against a little fellow . . . *against his ever getting this fighting chance his Dad wants for him.*

Have you a small son? How old is he . . . 2, 3, perhaps 7 years? For his sake, look ahead now while there is still time to plan.

This you know with certainty: he'll face even stiffer competition than today's. For the worthwhile positions there will be college men. Ready, eager, they'll grasp the opportunities. And the going will be tough for the boy who has to go to work at high school age.

Will your lad be the one boy in forty-three to get a real chance in life? *He can be.*

You can *guarantee* today for your youngster a full college training. No matter what happens to you, however circumstances may

shift, you can be sure—*positive* that the needed money will be ready to see him through.

A plan developed by the old conservative Union Central Life Insurance Company removes every single doubt. You don't need wealth, or large salary or luck to follow this Union Central plan. Under it your investment is surprisingly small if you act now, while your boy is young.

As the first step, write for a booklet that tells all about this simple plan.

It tells you also what it costs to send a boy through any one of the country's 300 leading colleges. Figures on tuition, board and room, clothes, even incidentals, are given.

This manual, "A Place in the Sun," will be sent to you *free*, with no obligation. Simply send the coupon at the right direct to the home office. In justice to your boy, do this today.

$100,000 MORE LIFE INCOME AWAITS YOUR BOY IF HE GOES THROUGH COLLEGE

The Union Central Life Insurance Company
Dept. A-6   Cincinnati, Ohio

Please send me free the new manual for college costs, "A Place in the Sun"

Name

Address   City

County   State
Copr. 1933 by The Union Central Life Insurance Company

THE UNION CENTRAL LIFE INSURANCE COMPANY
ORGANIZED IN 1867 . . . MORE THAN $300,000,000 IN ASSETS

9.27. The depression had lengthened the odds against success, this bleak scene reminded fathers. They could rescue the American dream for their sons only by buying insurance.

creed. Union Central was not one of the giants in the insurance business; as an advertiser it had spent little more than $10,000 during its sixty-five year history. But in 1932, perhaps sensing the appeal of messages that encouraged middle-class fathers to project their thwarted ambitions onto their children, the company began advertising a savings plan to insure the college education of depression-reared sons. Copywriters for the J. Walter Thompson agency infused each Union Central ad with all the elements of the clenched-fist syndrome: the specter of intense competition; the challenge to "quitters"; the reaffirmation of the principle of the survival of the fittest; and the summons to courage and determination.[131]

With alarming headlines, Union Central sought to capture the mood of a besieged middle class. "A Dad Forgot . . . that his boy stood only 1 chance in 43," one ad warned (Fig. 9.27). "Against what odds will you ask your boy to fight?"

challenged another. In conversational, man-to-man tones, the ads reminded each father that his son would "face a fiercer, tougher fight than you or I ever did."[132] But while they acknowledged emphatically that "pitifully few boys get a really fair start in life these days," the Union Central ads refused to sanction resignation. The company offered a free pamphlet entitled "A Place in the Sun," which would explain how a college education could provide sons of the depression an "even break." Meanwhile, by buying life insurance, fathers could display a clenched-fist determination to give their sons "a running start in life." Agency copywriters beguiled fathers with pleasing but ensnaring affirmations, employing the ambiguous "you" to address each father individually. "Your boy will never quit. You know that. . . . He's not that kind."[133] Did a father, the ads insinuated, dare show less faith than his admiring and innocent son in the American promise of success? Surely this test demanded a moral response, a courageous, hard-fisted resolve.

In "The Lonely Uphill Struggle you would like to save your boy," Union Central adroitly added icon to rhetoric. It employed the visual imagery of the clenched fist to dramatize its reaffirmation of the success creed as an act of moral defiance of the depression. In the tableau, an unsuccessful young job seeker, collar turned up and eyes vacantly staring into space, turned wearily away from the employment agency. "You see so many of them," confided the text, "boys braving the handicap of lack of education . . . fighting their way uncertain, confused." But the young man, though temporarily thwarted, wore no expression of defeat. His clenched fist, in which he apparently grasped the want-ads, assured readers that, like all Americans, he was no quitter. He offered a clear reproach to any father who would deprive a courageous and determined son of an equal opportunity in the ongoing fight for success, who would leave him faced with "the lonely uphill struggle" (Fig. 9.28).[134]

Did the visual cliché of the clenched fist, and the many textual expressions of the same theme, mirror the attitudes of consumers or flatter them with a self-image to which they aspired? Carolyn Bird has suggested that an image of the slumped shoulders of "the retreating father" may characterize depression realities much more accurately than the clenched fist.[135] Even resigned or retreating fathers might wish to imagine themselves fighting courageously, against overwhelming odds, with fists and faces clenched in determination. But advertisers possessed no evidence that this was the case. They made no attempts to test whether the public wanted to identify with the spate of agonized grimaces and tension-filled fists. In fact, evidence from trade journals indicates that they *presumed* the public wished to see escapist scenes with joyful, chirping birds or grinning, carefree people.[136] The almost compulsive frequency with which advertisers turned away from what they presumed the public wanted, in order to confront themselves and their readers with clenched fists and faces, suggests that they felt more of an obligation to preach lessons of fortitude to the masses than to mirror their thoughts and desires. Their penchant for the verbal and visual imagery of the clenched fist may also indicate that these words and images, like the panoramas of clouds and sunbeams, played a therapeutic role in providing advertising writers with a mode of self-expression and an instrument of morale-boosting for themselves and the business leaders whom they served.

THE LONELY UPHILL STRUGGLE
you would like to save your boy

You see so many of them—boys braving the handicap of lack of education.... Fighting their way uncertain, confused. . . .

If you and I were starting out like these boys today, we'd realize how much tougher the going has become since our time. There's a college graduate for every opening now. Trained and ready—the kind of man every business and profession looks for!

It's men like these that *your* brave little boy will face, when he grows up. *College men!*

Will he meet them on even ground?

Or will he have to fight desperately hard, like the untrained boys we see around us, struggling uphill alone?

An old, conservative insurance company, The Union Central Life, has worked out a plan for your boy.

Is he two, seven, ten years old right now? Then—this plan *makes sure* he'll have the money to complete his education. However circumstances may change, whatever happens to you, it guarantees him funds to finish high school, to go on through college.

Today, when your boy is young, just a few dollars a month will let

you follow the plan. Your present life insurance can be the starting point. So keep this protection in force.

Then—learn what it will cost to send your boy to college. The Union Central Life has gathered cost figures on board and room, tuition, clothes, incidentals, at each of 300 colleges. They are printed in the booklet, "A Place in the Sun". It is yours—*free!*

Send for a copy. With it full facts about the Union Central Education Plan will reach you. In mailing the coupon you incur no obligation. For your boy's sake, send it in. Today!

14 COLLEGE MEN
WIN SUCCESS
FOR EVERY ONE
UNTRAINED MAN
WHO SUCCEEDS

The Union Central Life Insurance Company
Dept. S-7   Cincinnati, Ohio
*Please send me free the new manual on my
boy's future, "A Place in the Sun"*

Name

Address   City

County   State
Copr. 1932 by The Union Central Life Insurance Company

THE UNION CENTRAL LIFE INSURANCE COMPANY
ORGANIZED IN 1867 .... MORE THAN $300,000,000 IN ASSETS

9.28. Want ads in his clenched fist, this unemployed youth turned a re-proachful glance upon all fathers who might quit on their sons in the struggle to overcome the depression's odds.

Are they really <u>well</u>-known?

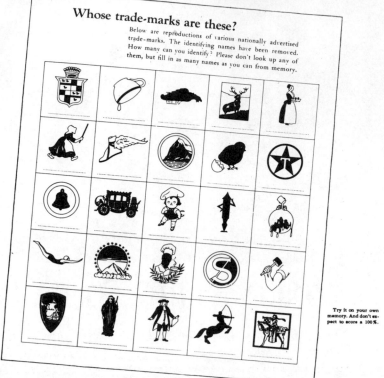

Whose trade-marks are these?

Below are reproductions of various nationally advertised trade-marks. The identifying names have been removed. How many can you identify? Please don't look up any of them, but fill in as many names as you can from memory.

Try it on your own memory. And don't expect to score a 100%.

This piece of paper FOUND OUT!

A manufacturer asked us, "How well-known do you suppose our trade-mark is?" We refused to "suppose." We found out. For this purpose Newell-Emmett invented this unusual type of questionnaire. It was so much like a game, people enjoyed filling it out. It was widely circulated under careful control. The results were exceptionally interesting. We found out the standing of each trade-mark and the relative standing of all twenty-five. We have recorded the results of this investigation in a brief which we will be very glad to send to anyone who requests it.

NEWELL-EMMETT CO., 40 E. 34th St., New York

Please send the results of your recent trade-mark investigation to:

NEWELL-EMMETT COMPANY ∕ ∕ ∕ ∕ ADVERTISING
"NOT HOW MUCH, BUT HOW WELL"

10.1. Literacy in trademarks was only the most visible aspect of a rising public familiarity with advertising motifs and parables. Nostalgic readers will find the answers in note 1, page 413.

THE THERAPEUTICS OF ADVERTISING

By the end of the 1920s, the identification of advertising slogans had become *Americans were assimilated into a new culture* a popular parlor game in some circles of American society. Agency studies indicated that a majority of Americans were literate in the ideogrammatic language of advertising trademarks (Fig. 10.1).[1] But the new advertising of the 1920s and 1930s taught more than a mere literacy in slogans and trademarks, it also familiarized people with an entire "vocabulary" of repeated visual motifs and social parables. Through advertising, Americans increasingly schooled themselves in a new "language"—a language that promised to assimilate them into a culture of high technology, complex economic and social relationships, and urbane sophistication.

Cities were mushrooming in size, mass production spewed forth a new profusion of goods, and the depression revealed how disturbances in the complex network of social and economic relationships could reverberate in every corner of the society, calling traditional assumptions and values into question. During both prosperity and depression, a society of *more people* (now more densely clustered) and *more things* (now available in bewildering varieties) required participation in a new intricacy of economic transactions and social interactions. In short, people had to operate on a complex new scale. Advertising provided the idioms to explain and celebrate life on this new scale. It was the "slang" that Americans learned in order to stay "up-to-date."

Advertising spoke a language of urbanity. To learn it, just as to learn the language of another national culture, was to experience a transformation—to acquire new perspectives, accept new assumptions, and undergo an initiation into new modes of thinking. Although advertising, like cinema, may not qualify as a language in the sense of possessing discoverable rules of grammar and a consistent syntax—or of being reducible to such linguistic units as phonemes—still it established and disseminated a vocabulary of visual images and verbal patterns that acculturated people into life on a complex urban scale.[2]

The mode of acculturation to modern complexity was one of accommodation, not compulsion. The language of advertising as it pursued its mission of modernity was, if anything, eclectic. It was a "living language," one shaped as much by changing inflections and gestures as by a verbal and visual vocabulary. Far from anticipating the abstract functionality of a computer language—seemingly appropriate for nationalizing a complex system of mass distribution—advertisers blended an imagery of modernity with the gestures and intonations of a person-to-person, conversational tone of voice that belied the very nature of mass communications. The world of radio and popular music had a word for this fusion of apparent intimacy with mass appeal; it was called "crooning."[3]

If we separate crooning as a mode of address from its usual association with the love song, we may find it provocative to view advertisers not only as "apostles of modernity" and "mediators of modernity" but also as "crooners" of modern refrains. Advertising writers did not share the relative insulation from direct public response enjoyed by such other apostles of modernity as engineers, scientists, or even architects. Advertisers could not insist on a spare, efficient, streamlined mode of discourse. The trials of the depression had reminded them again of the pangs and discontents that accompanied the "progress" of the modern economy; radio increasingly brought forth new evidence of a public hunger for personalized relationships with the wider world. Less sanguine than they had once been about cultural uplift of the consumer masses, advertising leaders accommodated themselves to a role which had been gradually acquiring clarity with the emergence of modern advertising—that of mediator and adviser. In the service of modernity, they would console, befriend, and reassure the public as well as stimulate and guide it. For an audience both enamored of modernity and discomfited by its complexity and impersonality, "crooning" seemed an appropriate way to express the new language of modern advertising.

Urbanity and Complexity: The Problem of Scale

The great parables and recurrent visual clichés of the ads of the 1920s and 1930s exemplify advertising's role as a language of urban complexity. The parable of the First Impression presupposed the anonymity and ambiguities of urban society. Significant other people in a person's life, the parable assumed, would not be part of a known, ongoing community. Acculturation to such a society often involved an "emotionally painful" transition. "For most people, in most places, through major portions of time," sociologist Lyn Lofland reminds us, "dealing with other human beings has meant dealing with personally known others." The parable of the First Impression sought to acculturate the audience to a new life on vastly expanded scale.[4] Now that people frequently confronted each other as urban strangers, they could expect their fates to be determined by fleeting judgments based on first impressions. The parable ushered the reader into the modern consciousness required in a world in which "the individual not only plans what he will do but also plans who he will be."[5] Phrases such as "Your Future is your own making" and *"Your Masterpiece—Yourself"* and persistent images of mirrors and judgmental eyes embodied this modern consciousness in the language of advertising.[6]

The parable of the Democracy of Goods, including its dramatic depression versions, promised compensations for the lack of self-sufficiency and personal control inherent in the scale of a life lived among the multitudes. This parable offered consumers a sense of significant participation in the society, on an equality with the most privileged citizens, through specific and often trivial acts of consumption. In so doing, it brushed aside the question of whether average citizens could hope to retain the qualities of political participation and economic self-determination that they might have enjoyed in a society of smaller scale. Images of the self-sufficient frontiersman and the democratic New England town meeting had always embodied as much myth as historical substance. But the parable of the Democracy of Goods helped screen out the realization that, even as ideals, these images had been made anachronistic simply by the scale of urban society. The parable encouraged readers to assume that they could finesse the new complexities of scale by seeking the satisfactions of "democratic" participation through consumption alone.

Other visual clichés and social parables offered similar lessons in adaptation to urban complexity. Visual motifs of office windows, family circles, futuristic cities, and eternal villages reinforced long-standing formulas for emotional adaptation to urban life. They implicitly proposed a bifurcation of lives and environs in which havens of security, intimacy, and simple pleasures would compensate for, and make tolerable, the anonymity and competitive insecurities of urban complexity. Numinous evocations of precious moments and tender sentiments offered similar psychic compensations to ease adaptation to new complexities of life on a larger scale. Even the parable of Civilization Redeemed never sought to discourage acculturation to the most hectic rhythms of urban life. On the contrary, it offered reassurance that the costs of moving away from Nature to the tensions and temptations of modern life could be entirely avoided through use of the proper product.

The parable of the Captivated Child, along with its elaborations in the parables of the Unraised Hand and the Skinny Kid, also educated parents in urbane sophistication. These parables taught the language and techniques of control through manipulation, a style of nurture appropriate to a more complex, interdependent society. In order for masses of people to live in close proximity without authoritarian rule, it was necessary for people to learn to control others and to be controlled through the "captivating" rewards of consumer products and pleasures. The parable of the Captivated Child appropriately condemned disruptive forms of behavior such as cranky fussing by the child and ill-tempered "forcing" by the parent. Both clashed with the urbane model of other-directed, adaptive social relationships needed for the smooth functioning of a complex society.

In less didactic ways than in the social parables, advertising spoke the language of urbanity through biases of content and style. The advertisers' propensity for the depiction of social elites reinforced a tendency to favor scenes of urban occupations, pastimes, and pleasures. Even those couples that readers glimpsed

10.2. Advertising's "language of urbanity" spoke in the accents of a fashionable elite. Auto showrooms provided luxurious settings for radiant beams.

The New Marmon 78 ($1895) and the New Marmon 68 ($1395) are on view at all of the leading automobile shows

motoring past eternal villages in the countryside and the businessmen who sought respite from the depression in Southern California vacations and scenes of nature's eternal rejuvenation, were refreshing themselves for a return to the hectic pace of urban business and society. Advertising's model American commuted to a downtown office. His favorite sport was golf, played in a pastoral setting that offered the compensatory satisfactions characteristic of successful adaptation to a life of urban tensions.[7] His wife adopted the latest cosmopolitan fashions and reveled in the variety of goods and activities offered by a complex urban environment. When not enfolded in the family circle, advertising's typical couple found their pleasures amid such habitual urban haunts as the hotel, the nightclub, and the palatial consumer showroom (Figs. 10.2, 10.3).[8]

Only with Rollins Hosiery . . . .

can you enjoy this perfect assurance of style and wearing quality . . . . . .

Walk when you will—dance til you're ready to drop—enjoy perfect confidence every moment you are wearing Rollins Runstop Hosiery; confidence born of flashing beauty, correct colors, flattering grace. But, more important still is the confidence instilled by this stocking's flawless appearance, free of embarrassing garter runs.

There is more than style and beauty in the fine silk of Rollins Runstop Hosiery. There is practical economy also—extra long life added to the joy of luxury. An exclusive Runstop feature makes Rollins unparalleled in security and durability.

Now you can indulge your fancy in the many colors Fashion favors. Longer wear prevents the need for quick replacement.

The dependability of Rollins enables you to establish a definite hosiery budget beyond which you need not go.

No runs caused by garter pull can pass below the dainty red dotted line of the Runstop at the hem. Look for this delicate, yet important, Runstop. It identifies Rollins and cannot be seen, even with the shortest skirt. The Runstop also affords protection to those wearing round garters—it stops all runs caused by pulling at the tops with sharp finger nails.

Rollins is sold only by reliable merchants—never by house-to-house canvassers. Sheerest chiffon or the rich-looking heavier weights may be had in new gleaming colors. Ask for Rollins at the store that serves you.

A leader in the Rollins line for men is the fine silk sock known as Rollins "400" with TRI-PLI toe and heel, reinforced to give unequalled wearing satisfaction. Our complete line of children's hosiery is remarkable for good looks and durability.

ROLLINS HOSIERY MILLS, Des Moines, Iowa

Eastern: Des Moines and Boone, Ia.
Cable Address: Rollins Des Moines
Southwestern Division: 575½ Lawrence St., San Francisco: 167 Mission St.

The distinctive Rollins Runstop at the hem (always a dainty red dotted line) positively identifies Rollins Runstop Hosiery—stops all garter runs and is out of sight even when worn with the shortest skirt.

Fill out the coupon and we will gladly forward to you, free, one cake of Rollins Silk Hosiery Soap. Also we'll send you the name of the merchant nearest featuring Rollins.

Mail this today

ROLLINS HOSIERY MILLS, Des Moines, Iowa, Dept. J4.

Kindly send me, free of charge, one cake of Rollins Silk Hosiery Soap, and name of nearest dealer featuring Rollins Hosiery.

Your Dealer's Name...........(Must be given)
Name...........(Must be given)
Address...........
City...........Store...........

Rollins Answers the Gift Question

ROLLINS RUNSTOP

Miles of wear in every pair

© R. H. M. 1927

10.3. Consumer surrogates joined the fashionable urban elite in luxurious hotels. Note the familiar contrast of the female knee bend and male solidity.

In style, even more than in content, advertising tableaux of the 1920s and 1930s often spoke to readers in a language of urbanity. Appropriating many of the motifs of modern art, advertising illustrations frequently adopted a tense, motion-charged urban vernacular. Their eye-catching, sometimes surrealistic juxtapositions of objects introduced readers into the visual language of the city with its contrasts and discontinuities. Such images conveyed the excitement of a complex environment and suggested the power of sophisticated denizens of such surroundings to remove image fragments from their original contexts and reorder them into new configurations and new meanings—a truly urban perception of the possibilities of imposing order in the midst of seemingly chaotic complexity. Even the tendency of advertisements to deny the actual processes of production—

10.4. *Against the back-drop of radiating beams and nostalgic country scenes, Campbell's offered urban readers an image of miraculous transformation rather than an education in actual production processes.*

to illustrate the soup can emerging directly and miraculously from the ripe tomato of the fields—may be seen as a replication of urban modes of thought (Fig. 10.4). Urbanites had quickly and contentedly shed knowledge of the production processes behind a variety of commodities such as food, cloth, and energy.[9]

The consoling, reassuring inflections of advertising's language of modernity became evident in its diagnosis of, and prescriptions for, "nerves." As we have seen, advertisers of the 1920s had pioneered the discovery of new social and physical afflictions. The intense competition of the early 1930s had inspired a fresh inventiveness in such research.[10] Still, most of these infirmities had captured the concern of only a single advertiser. The problems of nerves, by contrast, commanded the attention of a large variety of advertisers who proposed antidotes ranging from specific brands of coffee and breakfast cereal to radios and linoleum floors.[11] Advertisements obviously identified "jangled nerves" as a core problem of the culture.

"Nerves" was an urban disease, a by-product of modernity. Since the nineteenth century, American critics had identified the rise of a "collective nervous crisis" with the tempo and complex scale of urban life. Neurasthenia had been characterized as a predominantly "metropolitan" disease.[12] Advertising men did not discover this malady anew in the 1920s and 1930s, but their sensitivity to this "problem" and their prescriptions for relief confirmed their commitment to an urban frame of mind. Far from suggesting that people seek to avoid the modern pressures and urban milieus that fostered "jangled nerves," advertisements brought news of products that would keep nerves "focused," "healthy," and under control to cope with such conditions. The model which they proposed to the public was not the rural fugitive from urban tensions, nor even the exemplar of calm detachment, but the individual who was up on his toes, with nerves stimulated but under control. For instance, the depression image of the clenched fist honored the man who had chosen not to seek respite but to focus his nervous tension in preparation for economic battle.

pushing modern life at the reader

Advertising men thus stepped forward as advisers in adaptation to a metropolitan way of life. The pressures and tempo of modern life constantly increased, they reminded readers. Life was now being lived "to a pattern" everywhere. The new pattern was urban—and it was inevitable. Acceptance of the advertiser's advice would lead to "healthy nerves" and thus to the capacity to live the fuller life of the metropolitan elites.[13]

The Camel cigarettes campaign of the mid-1930s crowned this wellspring of advice and reassurance with a promise to cure an urban ill with a product symptomatic of the urban tempo itself. Cigarettes, Michael Schudson reminds us, were the "fast-food" of the tobacco industry, adapted, as pipes and plug tobacco were not, to a quick, urban life. Yet Camels, against backdrops of crowded sidewalks, warned of the impact of "high-speed modern living" with its "rush and tension" on the nerves and digestive system. Characterizing cigarettes as cure rather than symptom, Camels promised to soothe nerves and have the "pleasant effect" of "promoting digestion."[14] In this and similar campaigns, advertisers recognized "nerves" as a symptom of people's difficulties in adapting to the complicated interactions of modernity. As one of the "helping professions" they offered therapeutic advice: the product would enable consumers to adjust easily and happily to the intensities of a new, complex scale of life.

Proliferating Choices
and the Vacuum of Advice

Urban tempos and complexities were not the only features of modernity that could prove disconcerting as well as exciting. During the 1920s and 1930s a proliferation in products, brands, and styles of goods presented consumers with a multiplicity of choices. Everything from hosiery and fingernail polish to radios and cameras now came in a profusion of shapes, sizes, models, and colors. Even within the conservative confines of British merchandising, one writer has noted, a single London department store in 1937 offered consumers a choice among 135 toothpastes and 10,763 kinds of stockings. Advertising prided itself on expanding the frontiers of human freedom by informing consumers of such new choices in products. More choices, moreover, created more leverage for advertising. The greater the variety of brands, Neil Harris suggests, the more consumers found their interest in "the object's symbolic properties" stimulated. Increased choices and heightened attention to symbolic properties brought consumers new burdens and anxieties of decision-making. Advertisers quickly embraced a broader advisory role in helping people cope with an enlarged freedom of choice.[15]

The advertising trade invariably interpreted the proliferation of consumer choices as evidence of the progress of freedom. *Advertising and Selling* suggested that the number of items of merchandise for sale provided an authoritative "index of a civilization." An agency director of research triumphantly announced that the American consumer had attained a "greater freedom of choice in satisfying his wants, and more power to exercise that freedom" than had existed in "any other society, past or present." Each choice represented an act of individualization, one advertising woman argued. She noted approvingly that people were beginning to choose even the wood and nails for their houses by trademark and added contentedly, "We are expressing our individuality in more details."[16]

Urbane advertising men and women thus greeted the complexities of expanding choices with sincere enthusiasm. They judged themselves supremely capable of making appropriate choices. Each new opportunity to do so brought greater freedom. But when they contemplated the capabilities of the average consumer, they quickly recognized the burdens they must shoulder as a "helping profession." The typical consumer lacked their sophistication, suffered from daily anxieties about a number of minor product choices, and—most deplorable of all—was likely to be a woman. "Alone . . . she faces this problem," commiserated the A&P grocery chain, as it compared the businessman's wealth of expert advisers in decision-making with the lonely ineptitude of his wife as she faced the task of selecting food. (See Fig. 8.18). A consumer, one agency man noted, now had to choose among a greater variety of goods than many a factory purchasing agent of only a few years before.[17] The problem was compounded, one agency man observed, by the "more or less chaotic condition of mind" of women caught in a confusion of goods and values. Periodicals like *American Home* regularly stepped forward to offer advice to women "bewildered before the task of sifting and choosing just those things they really want, just those things in harmony with each other."[18] The proliferation of choices had created a vacuum of advice.

Broad social and demographic changes intensified the impact of this deficiency of advice. Mobility, generational discontinuities, more complex forms of social interaction, and the separation of city dwellers from the shared knowledge of small communities had disrupted informal, intrafamily, and intracommunity channels of advice. The "acids of modernity," as Walter Lippmann characterized the undermining of traditional truths and authoritative standards, had devalued elements of handed-down social wisdom.[19] Advertising itself had contributed eagerly to the diffusion of those "acids," and it made no apology. People needed the kind of advice that would acculturate them to modernity. Advertisers welcomed the inexperienced and insecure mother—isolated from, or properly distrustful of, out-of-date family and community advice—who yearned for authoritative information about proper child care.[20] And although they often deplored the fickleness and conformity of women who did not know what they wanted and "cheerfully abandoned all power of individual judgment," still they recognized that consumers might well fail to realize the benefits of technological and stylistic advances until advertising actively advised them. The woman with a broom certainly felt a "vague unspoken desire" for relief from drudgery. But she could not have imagined a vacuum cleaner, much less demanded one, without the advice of advertising.[21]

Society needed more advice, advertisers often observed, simply because the complexity of consumer choices had revealed new dimensions of public incompetence. "Most people are bewildered and uncertain at the drug counter," noted the Norwich Pharmacal Company. "There are so many brands. So many grades."[22] Parke, Davis and Co., a manufacturer of pharmaceutical products, described the plight of a mother of three who had found herself "half distracted, just making decisions." Confident that readers would identify with this woman's bewilderment, Parke, Davis and Co. had her confess her dilemma: "You see, I used to be all confused. I would go into the drug store and see rows and rows of products, all different. I suppose most of them were good—but how could I *know?* . . . I almost wore my mind out trying to decide."[23] This harried mother's mind had "smoothed right out," however, the company assured readers, when she had "decided once and for all" not to attempt such confusing decisions herself but to "let the Parke-Davis label decide *for* her."[24]

The proliferation of choices in color and style particularly exposed the growing incompetence of consumers. People liked the range of colors available in clothing, towels, and kitchen appliances, but they lacked the ability to select harmonious color ensembles. The Armstrong Cork Company reported floods of requests for decorating counsel. Holeproof Hosiery lamented that a majority of men lacked color consciousness. Martex, a manufacturer of towels, worried that many women would choose towels that would bring color disharmony to their bathrooms. When they later learned that their choices were incorrect and in poor taste, they might turn against the whole idea of towels as a "style item" and go back to treating them as a mundane convenience product.[25]

In response to the confusions and incompetencies revealed by the new complexity of goods, advertisers offered new forms of expert advice. Holeproof Hosiery and the House of Kuppenheimer devised point-of-sale advertisements in the form of color wheels and charts that would provide the consumer with "authentic style advice." Martex towels created a Martex Towel Color Guide to ease the consumer's problem of selection and eliminate "any possibility of color disharmony."[26] One paint manufacturer publicized an aid to "amateurs" in the form of a "revolving dial with slots" that would display correct five-color combinations. With this "sure-fire method" women could not err in choosing color schemes and would thus take on painting projects more confidently. Women made more errors in choosing hosiery colors than in any other accessory, Holeproof Hosiery explained. The company's Color Assistance chart, it assured sales clerks, "invariably brings back a woman a second and third time for more advice."[27]

Advertisers also discovered a vacuum of advice in areas in which the delicacy of the topic inhibited person-to-person conversation about offensive personal characteristics or new products for feminine hygiene. Recognizing the implications of the slogan "Even your best friend won't tell you," advertisers of soaps, deodorants, pimple preparations, and mouthwashes rushed to offer mass advice in the form of warnings of personal offenses of which the consumer might be unaware. Such "impolite copy" was not resented by consumers, a George Batten agency executive asserted. People would resent being told about such failings by someone they knew personally. But they gladly tolerated "intimate little scoldings" from advertisers. The very anonymity of advertisements made them perfect vehicles for such necessary, but hard to come by, advice.[28]

The advantages of anonymous advice had proved a particular boon in the realm of feminine hygiene, advertisers concluded. Ads by Zonite Products, manufacturer of an antiseptic douche, reminded readers of the desperate dearth of advice. "Isn't it less embarrassing for young married women to find out for themselves about Feminine Hygiene?" asked Zonite. "It's not because her friends *won't* tell . . . perhaps they are not sure themselves about Feminine Hygiene," suggested another Zonite headline.[29] The company's ads sympathized with the plight of the troubled, even frightened, "young wife without a confidante." Even in the most well-meaning families, Zonite observed, the informal network of advice often broke down: "Mother and daughter. It is one of nature's closest kinships, yet how often is there a gulf between! The responsibility is chiefly that of the older woman. When apart from her daughter, she is full of good resolutions, planning to speak frankly. But when they are together she finds it increasingly difficult to approach delicate subjects, made still more delicate by the old-fashioned custom of avoidance."[30] And if advice about birth control often fell short of women's needs, so too, according to Kotex, did advice about menstruation. Young girls between ten and fourteen desperately needed information and advice, but "thousands of mothers—courageous—intimate—in all things but this" would prove "too timid to meet this problem."[31]

Such deficiencies of advice gave advertisers the opportunity to dispense the needed counsel in conjunction with their product. Kotex offered to come to the rescue of reticent mothers and "free this task of enlightenment from the slightest embarrassment" with booklets entitled *Preparing for Womanhood* and *Marjorie May's Twelfth Birthday*. Concluding that its scientific aura was sufficiently established, Kotex dismissed the formidable "Ellen J. Buckland, Registered Nurse" and engaged the friendlier, chattier, "Mary Pauline Callender" to sign its advertising copy. As both authoritative adviser and personal confidante, Mary Pauline promised that her booklets would provide the kind of "intimate little chat between mother and daughter" that embarrassment and intergenerational distance had inhibited. The mother in a Lysol ad also confessed the superior competence of the expert commercial adviser: "Read this little book *carefully,* dear," she told her daughter. "It explains things so much better than I can" (Fig. 10.5).[32] The "disinfectant" douches, such as Zonite and Lysol, had to offer their mass advice very carefully in order not to violate the law or offend good taste. Not daring to use the phrase "birth control," they employed circumlocutions. Their ads promoted booklets which, while touting the product, promised "scientific" advice on

"Read this little book *carefully*, dear. . . . It explains things so much better than I can"

THERE IS much misinformation about feminine hygiene—a subject so vital to health and happiness that it behooves every woman to beware of unprofessional advice and to learn the *facts*.

As a contribution to the proper understanding and practice of scientific bodily care, the makers of "Lysol" Disinfectant offer a booklet which gives the facts—frankly, explicitly and reliably. Its name is "*The Scientific Side of Health and Youth*" and its author is a woman physician who

has combined sympathetic appreciation of woman's intimate problems with professional knowledge and experience.

The position of "Lysol" Disinfectant is self in the field of feminine hygiene is indicative of the trustworthy nature of this booklet. For 30 years "Lysol" Disinfectant has been the standard personal antiseptic in doctors' offices, hospitals and homes. Its quality never varies. Every drop is potent. And today it has no substitute where complete disinfection is imperative.

Send for the booklet today. It is free. It will reach you in a plain envelope. It will contribute to your peace of mind. Use the coupon below.

In the meantime, play safe in any immediate use of an antiseptic for personal cleansing and protection. Insist on "Lysol" Disinfectant—and "Lysol" Disinfectant alone. It is safe. It is *sure*. And it *cleanses* as it *kills germs*. Buy a bottle today.

Made by Lysol, Incorporated, *a division of* Lehn & Fink Products Company. *Sole distributors*, Lehn & Fink, Inc., Bloomfield, N. J.

Clip the coupon now before you forget.

LEHN & FINK, Inc., *Sole distributors*.
Department 28   Bloomfield, New Jersey.
Please send me, free, your booklet,
"The Scientific Side of Health and Youth."

Name ....

Street ....

City .... State ....

Woman's Home Companion February 1927

10.5. Advertisers quickly filled any vacuums of advice. Lysol invited mothers to confess their incompetence and turn to the authority of the company's "sympathetic" expert on "intimate problems."

how a woman could avoid "premature old age and a needlessly unhappy marriage."[33]

Lehn and Fink, having previously advertised Lysol primarily as a household disinfectant, decided in the mid-1920s to openly recognize that most women actually purchased it for use in birth control. The company converted its advertising to subtle advice on the importance of maintaining health, beauty, and "sane living habits" by avoiding "mistakes." Offers of a booklet on feminine hygiene increased coupon returns from the ads by 159 percent in one year. The booklet promised to tell "What feminine hygiene really is"—this for the sake of those who were not astute enough to realize that the repeated promises of Lysol's capacity to "*kill germs*" were meant to be read as "kill sperm."[34] A new germicidal douche introduced by Lehn and Fink in 1931 promoted its booklet with a promise of insider advice. In the role of confidante, Lehn and Fink asked insinuatingly, "Does the disinfectant you now use do what you think it does?" And Lysol made its promise of advice more specific than ever in 1932 when it publicized a new infirmity called "calendar fear"—the fear "brought on by some slight, easily avoided feminine irregularity. . . . *Fear* that feeds on itself until the minor indisposition looms as a major crisis."[35]

Their ingenuity in offering much-sought-after advice in areas surrounded by taboos, and their contributions to uplift in the promotion of cleanliness, toothbrushing, and technological victories over drudgery, easily convinced most advertising writers of the beneficence—even the indispensability—of their role as advisers. Since the public sometimes remained inert and unenlightened, the need for advice and uplift seemed to justify whatever small deceptions and manipulations might be necessary to awaken people to their own best interests. If what women wanted in choosing color ensembles was "authority"—the confidence that "they're *right*"—then advertisements should not hesitate to dictate correctness. If the public wanted its advice in the form of intimate conversations and romantic daydreams rather than factual data, advertisers should not hesitate to coat their advice with sentiment in order to help the consumer make necessary choices.[36]

The saga of No. 7 Duco car polish demonstrated the advantages of not being too inflexible to provide one kind of advertising "advice" demanded by the public. The Dupont company had first advised consumers about the new Duco paint for automobiles in 1924. At that time, its ads had stressed that soil and grease could easily be wiped off the durable Duco finish with plain soap and water. "Duco is waterproof, weatherproof, and sunproof," the ads proclaimed. "Mud, grease, and oil can be wiped away without a stain." According to Dupont, however, car owners refused to take advantage of the paint's new qualities. They liked to "polish" their cars for special occasions, or perhaps merely to experience a feeling of participation in the "production" and repeated re-creation of this prized possession—to help make it "theirs." In any event, Dupont reported with apparent dismay, people "had become accustomed to putting something out of a bottle on a rag and refused to be satisfied with other methods." In short, the public demanded a special "polish," despite the adequacy of soap and water alone.[37]

In response, Dupont produced No. 7 Duco Polish. At the same time, it quietly forgot about Duco's easy-cleaning finish. In fact, it discovered a hitherto unrecognized threat to Duco car finish in the form of "traffic film"—an "accumulation of oily, sticky particles of dirt." Under headlines warning that "It takes more than soap and water to remove *traffic film,*" the company depicted automobile owners happily anointing their cars with No. 7 Duco Polish. Dupont had produced the polish that people wanted and, through its advertising, had also provided them with a new, manifest justification for the rubbing and buffing they enjoyed—the blight of soap-and-water–resistant "traffic film."[38]

Other advertisers concluded that they could serve the public's need for advice less by intimate confidences or scientific revelations than by the imposition of arbitrary authority. Such "advice" was particularly helpful in contending with complex choices. One copywriter advocated the "snob appeal" because of its power to relieve middle-class women of unwanted conflicts of decision-making. It could satisfy the craving for a "guarantee of quality" by the woman "vacillating helplessly between this brand and that—uncomfortably aware of the fact that she has no reliable standards by which to judge for herself."[39] The ads paraded a legion of "experts" and "specialists" before the housewife to meet her (presumably) desperate need for "authentic" and "authoritative" advice. The National Electric Light Association decided she needed an authoritative plan for her entire house, endorsed by Thomas Edison. Jean Carroll empathetically expressed the consumer's plea for authority by entitling her advice column for Packer's Tar Soap, "*Please* tell me. . . ." Other advertisers similarly concluded that the consumer, faced with a choice among eight shades of nail polish or twenty variations of "nude" in hosiery, would appreciate advice that told her that "one alone is right."[40]

Advertising Advice and Added Values

By the 1920s advertisers had come to recognize a public demand for broad guidance—not just about product attributes, but about taste, social correctness, and psychological satisfactions. Young mothers did not know how to manage a house or raise their children. Advertising was "sweet music" to their ears. Women constantly revealed that "they really don't know very much about, or are uncertain about" their relations with suitors and husbands. They welcomed guidance on how to carry on a courtship or reawaken a husband's interest as well as advice about the specific qualities of a soap or lotion. Above all, people simply lacked reliable advice on how to live life at its best. Advertisers invited them to try out various techniques vicariously as they watched their surrogates in the advertising tableaux use the product.[41] When advertisers blended sentiment into soap advertising, they helped people achieve enhanced enjoyment by giving "color and perfume" to a mundane thing. In giving products subjective as well as utilitarian values, *Printers' Ink* proclaimed, advertising helped people "to enjoy life." One major agency defined the role of advertising even more sweepingly: "We are going to make living worth while."[42]

When we listen to the advertising leaders of the 1920s and 1930s discuss their role as public advisers, and particularly when we eavesdrop on their "backstage" gossip about the public's benighted need for guidance, we are likely to dismiss their claims to an important advising function as pretentious, manipulative, and even fraudulent. But however we judge the quality of their counsel, we can hardly disregard the existence of the "vacuum of advice" they rushed to fill. A complexity of choices did bring new burdens of decision-making in this wider exercise of freedom. In 1933 Robert Lynd, the sociologist and reformer, painted a picture of the growing dilemma of consumers that differed little from descriptions in the advertising journals: "A sharp increment both in the volume and variety of consumers' goods available, necessitates choices among more kinds of ways of carrying on familiar processes than any previous generation has faced."[43]

Lynd proposed government grading of a variety of products to make choices simpler and more rational. But most advertising leaders recognized a threat in such bureaucratic and scientific aids to decision-making. Consumers, they argued, did not want their choices of goods reduced to tedious exercises in cold calculation. They *did* want advice, but they didn't want all the romance taken out of life. Advertisements, full of glamor and emotion, could provide such helpful "advice" by inducing consumers to arrive at what ad executive Leo Burnett later characterized as "premade decisions." Unlike Lynd's dreary government grades, the ads offered authoritative advice without neglecting the broader, more "romantic" counsel about family relationships, personal behavior, and social expectations that the public also seemed to crave.[44]

The efficacy of the "premade decision" was particularly important in the case of what theorists now classify as "experience goods"—products whose qualities and consequences can be determined only by use, not by examination prior to purchase.[45] In fact, the very "utility" of some of these products is likely to be influenced by the persuasiveness of advertising, both before and after purchase. A significant part of the consumer's satisfaction in using goods ranging from automobiles to cold cream stems from such subjective experiences as feelings of sexual attractiveness, enhanced manliness, or social belonging. Martin Mayer labels these "added values"—qualities added to the products by the advertising itself.[46] The implicit promises of the ads induce consumers to experience satisfactions they would not have obtained otherwise. By creating a strong expectation of certain subjective satisfactions from a particular brand, and thus inducing a trusting premade decision, the advertisement enhances the value of the product to the consumer. It also helps banish indecision in realms of purchasing activity in which products are so similar or mundane that agonized decision-making would be unproductive. Some people want more choices in brands; but others find the increasing variety a troublesome barrier to quick decisions. Ads that offer the latter a premade decision help them deal with unwanted complexities.

Did advertisers, then, provide consumers with truly needed advice in the form of premade decisions? Did advertisements, by instilling a brand preference—through whatever emotional, irrational, or "seductive" tactics—relieve consumers of a host of trivial decisions? There are serious objections to the theory that they did. It would be more persuasive if advertisements only touted a single brand among the many choices. What about the consumer confusion induced by torrents of ads for rival brands? We do not know whether people effectively employed advertising advice during this era to help them reduce complexity through premade decisions or whether they reacted to rival appeals with bewilderment.

But we do know, from more recent studies, that people often use advertising as a mode of reassurance to reduce anxiety. Leon Festinger reports that people pay more attention to ads for a given brand *after* purchasing that brand than they do before. Raymond Bauer and Stephen Greyser, on the basis of a massive attitude survey, report that consumers rate ads more favorably when they advertise brands that the consumer already uses or prefers. Respondents noted that certain ads reminded them "of the pleasures of using the product." Bauer and Greyser conclude that for certain people ads provide reassurance of the correctness of their original buying decision. John Treasure goes on to argue that the central task of advertising is often the "reinforcement of the buying habit" for a brand through reassurance, and Paul Carpenter, in *The New Languages,* suggests that the "main effect" of advertisements is "to increase pleasure in the consumption of the product."[47]

Advertising advice also provided another functional service, despite the self-interested bias of specific ads. As retail selling gradually took on mass proportions—with larger stores, huge inventories of a wide variety of brands, and fewer clerks per customer—customers found point-of-sale advice less available. Customers who had previously relied on the recommendations of the corner grocer and the local druggist were thrown back on their own resources. With profits in large retail stores dependent on rapid turnover, clerks needed to make sales quickly and could spare less time to help shoppers with buying decisions. From the managerial viewpoint, the resulting increase in consumer incompetence and indecision was intolerable. For mass distribution to be cost-efficient, one agency president concluded, "the customer must know in advance *what* he needs and must *ask for it.*"[48] The cost of distribution could only be reduced, the president of the American Association of Advertising Agencies argued, "by shifting some of the selling effort into buying initiative."[49] By persuasively advising consumers, advertising sought to simplify the retail selling problem and keep the new freedom of choice from degenerating into a chaos of bewilderment.

Toward a New Incompetence

If advertising streamlined mass selling and relieved consumers of the anxieties of numerous trivial decisions, did it simultaneously, as its spokesmen claimed, help people surmount the new complexities of life? Did its "advice" enhance the competence of the average consumer? Advertisers liked to describe their function as one of education. Advertisements not only improved tastes; they made the consumer "a more competent buyer." Ads spoke of the modern woman buyer as "Armed with new Knowledge—sure of her new skill."[50] But, of what did the consumer's new skills consist? Were the shortcuts to decision-making offered by advertising advice a clear gain in competence in the face of complexity? Or did consumers merely increase their dependence on services and technological amenities they did not really comprehend?

The Lord and Thomas agency set forth an intriguing analysis of these issues in a 1936 ad in *Fortune.* Entitled "It's all Greek to Me," the ad warned advertisers,

"You can't 'get technical' with the average man on the street." Members of the average family had "a deep *admiration* for machinery," the agency continued, but they were bored and overwhelmed by efforts to explain it. Already, many families depended on a variety of devices—"radios, automobiles, heating systems, washers"—which they could operate by turning the right switches but which they did not really understand.[51] What "advice" should the advertiser supply consumers about such products?

Give them "a *dramatic clue* to the essential nature of the mechanism," counseled Lord and Thomas. Fire their imaginations. Reject explanations of the technical "profundities" of radio in favor of evocative phrases like Magic Brain. This would enable them to perceive the new RCA Victor radio as "a miraculous instrument." Dramatize the qualities of General Motors' car engines by proclaiming their Knee-Action—even if this phrase was useless as a literal description or explanation. Provide them with all they needed or wanted to know about the "cold-making mechanism" of the new Frigidaire by labeling it a Meter-Miser.[52] In short, give consumers such competence as they seemed to want and to be capable of acquiring—the competence to speak of the results of technology by reciting the proper slogans. Door-to-door canvassers for the Daniel Starch Advertising Service noted how often housewives spoke of certain brands in the exact phrases used in the advertisements. The Starch Service assumed that the most successful campaigns were those that educated consumers by inducing them to adopt the advertiser's formula for talking and thinking about the product.[53]

In the wake of Charles Lindbergh's solo transatlantic flight in 1927, writers in the advertising trade journals explored the issue of advertising advice and public competence in the context of a slightly tangential issue. A Western Union promotional campaign had encouraged proud Americans to send Lindbergh a congratulatory telegram. It invited them, if they wished, to choose from a variety of "canned" messages prepared for their convenience. Amos Bradbury, who frequently wrote humorous commentaries for *Printers' Ink,* greeted the Western Union campaign with mock gratitude: "to think that a great corporation, almost miraculously reading my thoughts, should have . . . (left) nothing for me to do but check a number and sign my name." But, reflecting on the specialization of the new age, Bradbury concluded derisively that it was only appropriate that "a giant public utility . . . had designated a man to tell me just what I wanted to say at the proudest moment of my life."[54]

A Western Union executive quickly turned the tables on Bradbury. Adopting the familiar arguments of many advertising writers, he explained that Western Union would have done the public a disservice by adopting Bradbury's "haughty and superior scorn." The demand for the canned telegram came from consumers, he contended. After company clerks had noticed the incompetence and embarrassment of the average citizen, Western Union had finally taken pity on the "honest folk to whom the task of writing even the simplest message is as terrifying as the facing of machine-gun fire." Public gratitude for such advice was confirmed when "something like seven out of ten of them promptly adopted one of the suggestions." Western Union, he concluded triumphantly, "could scarcely maintain its service or the integrity of its dividend record if it confined its employment to the nimble-witted minority . . . instead of extending patient helping hands to the inarticulate and ungrammatical majority."[55] There the argument rested—with the verdict clearly in favor of Western Union. Advice in the form of canned messages had momentarily made the public competent to congratulate Lindbergh—eloquently and grammatically. The question of whether the beneficiaries of such "advice" had gained a more permanent competence was never asked. Nor was the question of whether some Western Union customers, presented with a shortcut in the form of a choice of various "correct" messages, were not thereby dissuaded from composing their own telegrams.

Advice in the form of premade telegrams, of course, was not exactly the same as advertising advice that offered customers "dramatic clues" and "premade decisions." But the issue of the relation of advice to competence was the same. Advertisements often advised the consumer by asserting that a particular brand was "correct." Such advice might reduce the bother in making a trivial decision. But the consumer's acceptance of the notion that there was one correct make of silverware, or style of hosiery, or brand of motor oil, also reinforced the idea that there were correct and incorrect choices in other products. Such advice fostered a need for more and more advice about correctness. Advertising "educated" the consumer to accept certain premade decisions—not to practice making decisions. Reliance on such "authoritative" advice simply created a continuing dependence.

Of course, advertising hardly bore major responsibility for the increase of public incompetence in the face of technological sophistication. Undoubtedly, the agencies were right in arguing that most people wanted dramatic, easy-to-grasp clues about what the product would do for them and did not want explanations of how it worked. Nevertheless, advertisers did contribute to a growth of consumer incompetence by perceiving a growing "inferiority complex"—the sense of a declining ability to judge in the face of technological specialization. Exploiting this discovery, advertising encouraged public incompetence most clearly by glorifying the role of the expert in areas that were *not* technological. In activities extending from the choice of hosiery colors to the proper upbringing of children, copywriters exalted the authority of the specialist. "Does Mother *really* know best?" asked the pharmaceutical firm of Parke, Davis and Company. "Do love and instinct really equip us to cope with the complex problems of mental and physical readjustment?"[56] Thousands of other ads exalted experts and repeated the refrain. People needed expert advice on how to set a table or properly entertain guests. They should consult experts on how to avoid color disharmonies, how to create a proper impression in business contacts, and how to avoid marital frictions and disillusionment. Incessant warnings of the social necessity to be "correct" reminded consumers how prone they were to error. And a "single fault," as Gloria Vanderbilt testified in a Holeproof Hosiery ad, might "outweigh a thousand perfections." Advice from an expert represented the only secure defense against social disapproval.[57]

Kathryn Weibel observes that ads implied that women needed professional experts and authority figures to give them directions "in the most mundane aspects of buying and life." But the inadequacy ascribed to women was only one salient example of the wider public incompetence that advertisers assumed, and sought to reinforce, by their constant celebration of experts. Counseling in interpersonal relations by scientific experts had become "a characteristic part of the

American Way" by the 1930s, Warren Susman observes. The new advertising of the 1920s and 1930s made a significant contribution to that development.[58]

Advertising did not singlehandedly manufacture a public demand for mass advice on the management of interpersonal relations. The popularity of media "sob sisters" and "advice to the lovelorn" columns since early in the century testified to an authentic popular need. Alert advertising writers merely recognized the insatiability of this need and attempted to fill the vacuum of advice by proposing specific products as panaceas. The cumulative impact of their ads, however, did more than passively reflect popular yearnings. Through constant reminders, their ads reinforced readers' suspicions of their own inadequacies and intensified their need to depend on expert advice. Like restless fingers picking away at a scab, the ads repeatedly reopened the reader's psychological wounds.

Such advertising advice aimed at the same effect that Jeffrey Meikle has ascribed to the streamlined designs in vogue in the 1930s. By enclosing the product's mechanisms within the simple, smooth lines of a streamlined casing, Meikle explains, the industrial designer provided the user with "a feeling of confidence in the face of complexity."[59] Ads often aimed at the same temporary effect by offering assurances of "correctness" in style or "dramatic clues" to the essence of the product. Advertising experts frequently reminded copywriters of the importance of leaving the consumer "with the feeling that he has done his own thinking, made up his own mind." A woman liked to believe that she was "exercising her own independent judgment." She might even be persuaded that she was achieving a greater "knack in cooking" by using food out of cans.[60] Advertising advice offered consumers an increasingly desired *feeling* of competence. But the means by which that feeling was attained—the reliance on expert authority, the adoption of ready-made short cuts to avoid the drudgery of thought and activity, and the understanding of products through "dramatic clues"—were likely also to entail increased dependence. Advice itself could promote incompetence.

The "Re-personalization"
of American Life

In the January 1930 issue of *Better Homes and Gardens* the buoyant, chatty narrator of a Procter and Gamble advertisement related a heartwarming story. As a result of ads that had publicized her previous nineteen "actual visits to P and G homes," she was no longer a stranger to the average housewife. On her most recent visit to a randomly selected consumer, she had no sooner introduced herself than "Bobby's Mother" had "opened the door wide." "'Come in,' she invited smilingly, 'I've read every single P and G Naphtha story. And I've often wished on your trips that you would find me.'" (For an earlier ad in the same series, see Fig. 1.2.)[61]

We may be tempted to dismiss this delightful modern fairytale—in which the consumer plays Cinderella to the advertiser's Prince—as an archetypal copywriter's fantasy. But, if we ignore for a moment the copywriter's blissful vision of an audience of compulsive and credulous ad readers, we may count this tableau as one of many signs that the new advertising had recognized another vacuum it might fill. People seemed to suffer from an insufficient sense of "the personal" in modern life. They hungered to be addressed as individuals, in personal tones. They craved a sense of personal contact with persons outside of their sphere of acquaintance whose actions might affect them or whose activities they might enjoy vicariously. They even liked to "personalize" the products they used and to obtain advertising advice about those products from persons they felt they "knew."

In a certain sense, American advertising had incorporated a "personalized" approach long before the 1920s. Trade characters such as "Sunny Jim" and "Phoebe Snow" had represented Force Cereal and the Lackawanna Railroad in the early twentieth century; ads for manufactured products had featured a distinguished portrait of the founder of the firm. But the trade characters had been highly stylized caricatures of the model consumer, and the cameos of bewhiskered manufacturers sought simply to associate the product with the founder's personal integrity. No one was likely to mistake these stereotyped characters or dignified gentlemen for confidantes and personal advisers. By the 1920s, modern advertising had begun to respond to the public thirst for personalized mass communication in more subtle ways.

From a variety of sources, advertising leaders perceived a limitless public demand to be addressed personally, to obtain intimate confidences and advice. Responses to the movies had impressed everyone with the public hunger for "mass gossip," and especially for those personal details that could give one a sense of "knowing" celebrities intimately and participating vicariously in their lives. The meteoric rise of *True Story* and the tabloids jolted advertisers into realizing that newspaper advice-to-the-lovelorn columnists, extending back to the turn-of-the-century innovations of Pulitzer and Hearst, offered lessons for effective advertising. From Beatrice Fairfax to Dorothy Dix, these ladies (some of whom were pseudonyms for a series of writers) had attracted tons of mail from eager correspondents. *True Story* and the tabloids were now demonstrating the popularity of "first person" stories with which people could identify even more readily.[62]

Of all the media, however, it was radio that impressed advertisers most forcefully with the public craving for personal relationships through the media. Advertisers learned early that listeners formed personal attachments to radio personalities who were "guests" in their homes. Those who offered information and personal advice were bombarded with intimate letters. "Betty Crocker" had been invented in 1921 to sign company letters to housewives who responded to a contest with "questions that in more neighborly communities had been asked over the back fence." But it was radio that made Betty Crocker come alive. As regional cooking schools gave way to radio talks in 1924 and 1925, Blanche Ingersoll became Betty Crocker's radio voice and then indoctrinated other regional Betty Crockers in the proper tone for the "friendly visit" on radio. An experiment with the "chatty" style on the "Betty Crocker School of the Air" in Buffalo, according to General Mills' historian James Gray, attracted "letters by the

10.6, 10.7. Personal advisers gave advertising an opportunity to use conversational copy, establish a personal "face," and dispense sympathetic advice. Such confidantes as Dorothy Dix for Lux soap and Mary Dale Anthony for S.O.S. scouring pads stimulated floods of intimate letters from readers.

tens of thousands." Within a year, thirteen Betty Crockers were speaking over regional radio networks, offering friendly advice and reassurance. Eventually, Betty was signing replies to over 4,000 letters a day.[63]

Advertising leaders were impressed and a bit astonished by the number and intimacy of the letters that poured in whenever a media personality like Betty Crocker, real or invented, invited personal communications. When Postum introduced the friendly advisor "Carrie Blanchard" in search of a "personal note," it soon reported that this fictitious public confidante was receiving "more letters than a movie star."[64] *True Story* found its readers eager to submit intimate first-person stories of their "real life experience." Personalized cooking correspondents, like "Mary Hale Martin" for Libby Products, found that nearly half of the flood of incoming letters required personal replies. The General Electric Company, in evaluating its entrance into radio, noted that many of the 136,000 letters that greeted its first series of broadcasts "were of so confidential a character—so intimate revelations of personal trials and aspirations—as to testify to the widening acceptance of 'G-E' as in truth 'The Initials of a Friend.'"[65]

"You think Im a flapper but I *can* keep house"

"If we get married, I'll keep my house better than mother does hers. But I'm not going to turn into a slave. You *men!* You think drudgery is a sign of good housekeeping."

By MARY DALE ANTHONY

Leave it to the modern girl to speak her mind. She's painfully frank, sometimes, but I've found that she's usually mighty capable, too .... alert and eager to learn .... looking for new time-savers. Girls today want more leisure, and they get it by using short cuts.

Mary Dale Anthony
Adviser on kitchen and household clean-ing problems to thou-sands of women.

By the end of the 1920s, advertising agencies were routinely creating fictitious personal advisers and sponsoring helpful, personalized experts for their clients (Figs. 10.6, 10.7). Having rediscovered the appeal of the confidential adviser that had worked so effectively in the heyday of Lydia Pinkham's Vegetable Com-pound, advertisers employed "Ruth Miller" for Odo-ro-no, "Nurse Ellen J. Buckland" and "Mary Pauline Callender" for Kotex, "Marjorie Mills" for Lux, "Mary Dale Anthony" for S.O.S., "Janet Gray" for Lewis and Conger, "Mary Hale Martin" for Libby's, "Aunt Ellen" for Griswold Cast Iron Cooking Uten-sils, "Helen Chase" for Camay, and more than a dozen others. Even the U.S. Bureau of Home Economics had its "Aunt Sammy" on radio. The J. Walter Thompson agency described Mary Hale Martin's chatty "write me" column in the Libby ads as "brimful of real 'heart interest.'" After inventing Janet Gray, the author of first-person advice from an up-to-date housekeeper, the Batten agency discovered that she had spurred such interest that it had become advisable to take legal steps to protect the use of her name.[66] The "intimate, personal tone" of Ruth Miller's chats with consumers "induced thousands and thousands of women to write her letters of the most confidential sort." The authors of these intimate, advice-seeking letters received "personally signed" replies from the hand of a Mary Hale Martin, an Aunt Ellen, or a Helen Chase.[67]

Advertisers often described the outpouring of confidential correspondence from consumers with bemused contempt. They were amazed at the credulity of people and their eagerness to discuss their personal lives and daily problems with invented commercial characters. Some correspondents, they observed, insisted on perceiving even the most obviously fictional trade characters as real human beings. Ad writers continually marveled over the provinciality and self-abasement revealed in the pathetic appeals for personal recognition and trivial forms of advice.[68] But they realized that personalized copy might overcome the ineffectiveness of advertisements that seemed to be talking to a crowd.

Copy experts steadily urged their colleagues to visualize the audience as "*one person at a time*" and to talk to each reader "just as you would if you were seated before a cheery log fire or chatting over tea cups."[69] Conversational copy, in the mouth of a chatty commercial persona, did just that. Scarcely anyone, either in the advertising trade or outside, objected to the illusion of human intimacy, the "atmosphere of pseudo-gemeinschaft" that such ads often succeeded in creating. Edward Bok, the crusading editor of the early twentieth-century *Ladies' Home Journal*, had once campaigned zealously against the Lydia Pinkham ads for the fraud of soliciting personal letters to Mrs. Pinkham long after the company's founder had died. But no muckraker of the 1920s sought to expose the "bored young men struggling for the feminine touch" who often wrote the copy for the fictitious public confidantes of the new advertising.[70]

Quite the contrary. The simulation of one-to-one personal conversation between personalized emissaries of the corporations and individual consumers steadily gained favor among advertisers. By the early 1930s the "dulcet, friendly voices" of commercial personalities were saturating the airwaves. Among the first to become celebrated radio confidantes were Don McNeill (of the Breakfast Club) and Mary Margaret McBride. Advertisers eagerly recruited such personalities and observed attentively the tons of unsolicited personal mail that poured in to characters on the new radio soap operas. In 1933, the "Voice of Experience," a radio adviser on intimate problems, broke a record by eliciting more than 6,500 letters on a single day.[71] Another program entitled "Your Lover" featured a male voice against the background of muted organ music in a virtual parody of the "one person at a time" approach: "Hello, young lady. Yes, I mean you. . . . It's grand to be with you. And it's sweet of you to let me have the thrill of talking to you. . . . Come over here near me—won't you. . . . Just for a minute let's forget everyone else in the world."[72]

"Your Lover" also delivered the commercial message in the same intimate style. Such programs carried to an extreme the illusion of direct personal contact which the medium of radio created so vividly. Trade journals like *Tide* might deplore the mawkish excesses of "Your Lover" and its willingness to play on the "sick daydreams of . . . maladjusted women," but they also reported the "heavy mail" this program had inspired and rarely failed to take notice of new personalized approaches that attracted masses of listeners.[73]

Advertising leaders also intently observed the growth of that aspect of the consumption ethic which Reuel Denney has characterized as "the consumption of other people's personalities."[74] Long before scholars confirmed their perceptions, they recognized a public fascination with the intimate details of the private lives of the heroes of biographical sketches. Leo Lowenthal was to conclude in 1941 that the heroes of magazine biographies over the previous two decades had evolved from educational models to pseudo-individualized acquaintances of the reader whose private lives and consumption habits helped sustain "a dream world of the masses." Advertising writers had not required a systematic content analysis to reach this conclusion. The testimonial had risen to new popularity, noted a *Printers' Ink* contributor in 1926, because the public had acquired an insatiable appetite for idols and "cannot see enough of them."[75]

President Stanley Resor of the J. Walter Thompson agency placed "personality advertising" in a larger historical context. Like the tabloids and confession magazines, he suggested, "personality advertising" was meeting a powerful human need which had neither atrophied nor found fulfillment in modern life. People, Resor asserted, were "eternally searching for authority." Democracy was new; it failed to satisfy the masses' desire to express "instinctive veneration for 'their betters.'"[76] Advertising, by offering personalities for consumption, helped people cope with a modern, bureaucratized life in which authority and vivid personal relationships had become attenuated.

By the early 1930s advertisers had thoroughly accepted the idea of a public hunger for personalized communications, and new experiments in the "personal touch" steadily proliferated. Advertising agencies convinced several company presidents to shed their dignity and become familiar friends to the public through "personalized . . . racy, man-to-man talks."[77] After the bellhop, Johnny, created a sensation with his "Call-l-l . . . for-r-r Philip Mah-ra-hiss!" paging calls on radio commercials, Philip Morris had to recruit and train "a whole corps of midget 'Johnnies' to meet the demand for 'personal appearances.'" Wrigley's Gum began running ads in the personals column of the classified ads: "*Ella*—Notice how strong Edgar's teeth are getting? We've been giving him Wrigley's gum after every meal. Why don't you try it with Jim? *Lucille.*" In mock outrage at such tactics, *Advertising Age* complained, "Every time we rush eagerly through too much agate type in the hope of busting in on someone's private heartache, we come out with nothing better than a command to . . . bathe with another kind of soap."[78] Sears, Roebuck and Co. asked farmers for a chance "to pull up a chair and talk things over with you folks." "The main idea," it told its rural radio audience, "is just to . . . *visit*. Are you going to be home?"[79]

The Schenley Whiskey Company perfected the folksy mode of personalized advertising messages in the mid-1930s. Ads for its Wilken Family Blended Whiskey combined candid photographs with colloquial commentary. After rambling on about Granny's sugar cookies and Ma's "juicy hot mince pie," Pa Wilken (the name was taken from a Schenley ad agency employee) explained to each "neighbor" in the reading audience how the personable Wilken folks loaded their boat with family whiskey on the way to the consumer: "This photo shows you the Wilken Family giving a hand loading her up. It's me checking the number of cases with the captain, and my brother William wheeling a load up the gangplank. My brother-in-law Tom don't show up so good but you can make out the back part of him inside the barge bending over like."[80] Other Wilken tableaux introduced the reader to sons Harry, Jr., and William and to the family dog, Jessie. When a single Schenley newspaper ad in 1937 gossiped about Jessie's quintuplet puppies, 45,000 people wrote to request a photograph.[81]

Given the rage for the personal touch, it was perhaps inevitable that advertising writers would eventually seek to "personalize" the product itself. "When all else fails I'm your best Friend," promised the protagonist of a Lucky Strike Cigarette ad—the product itself. A Lucky was a "better friend than others," it promised the reader, because "in personal tragedies, minor or major, a Lucky stands you in good stead."[82] *Printers' Ink* praised new techniques of bringing the ingredients of products to life by depicting them as "little characters with names," and noted that people liked to identify trains by nicknames rather than numbers. Trade journal writers, marveling over "the almost human personality" that photographs had bestowed on some products, called on copywriters to find the "face" that lay embedded in every product. The task of advertising, one critic reminded his colleagues, was "to lift things out of the commonplace." The copywriter and artist could do this by giving the product personality and "radiance." People were not much interested in things as things. They took pleasure in seeing inanimate things come alive.[83]

At one extreme, therefore, the "re-personalization" of life through advertising involved a tacit recognition of an unvanquished public propensity for animism— the belief that all objects are alive. People wished to see their car as a tiger, or as a family pet, or as a "care-free vagabond." Perhaps that would help bring things back to a comprehensible scale. An individual "personality" might emancipate the product from its association with a complex and obscure process of mass production and imbue it with "human meaning" once again. At least they might draw greater comfort from products whose "friendliness and intimacy" were suggested by such descriptions as "sudsy," "crunchy-crisp," and "tangy."[84]

Most experiments in personalizing products brought a favorable public response, no matter how transparent the pretense of intimacy. Even disenchantment with the false pretenses of "pseudo-gemeinschaft" and the "feigning of personal concern" in the mass media seemed only to stimulate a greater hunger for personal connection, a "craving for reassurance." Robert Merton notes that the striking success of the Kate Smith war bond marathons on radio during World War II stemmed largely from the fact that listeners, despite their distrust of the "commercial duplicity" of other media "friends," really believed that Kate (who frequently delivered commercials herself) was talking to them personally and that she would probably answer the phone herself when they called in their bond pledge. "I feel I know Kate," one typical listener responded in Merton's survey. "She was speaking straight to me," confirmed another. Direct mail advertisers, who kept the most precise records of consumer responses, gave "tremendous emphasis" to a variety of ingenious devices for creating "the impression of a personal message."[85] Americans of the 1920s and 1930s may have seen themselves, as John Burnham has suggested, as living in an Age of Crowds. They may also have glorified the mounting complexities of technology and social interaction that characterized the age. Perhaps for those very reasons, as Burnham notes, they also displayed an intense interest in "personal, introspective accounts of private experiences."[86]

Perhaps more than any other institution, American advertising adapted itself to the possibilities for exercising both a dynamic and a stabilizing influence during such an age. Advertising served preeminently as the spokesman for modernism. It exalted technological advances and disseminated the good news of progress to the millions. It promoted urban lifestyles and sought to educate consumers to master the new complexities of social interaction. But the very social and technological changes which advertising glorified also placed a burden of proof on those who wished to reassure an anxious public that society still operated on a comprehensible human scale—a scale within which people could expect their individual needs to be recognized and catered to.

Finessing the Complexities of Scale

Advertising accepted the challenge presented by a new, "dehumanizing" scale of life. If people wanted to enjoy the benefits of modern technology without relinquishing any of the emotional satisfactions of a simpler life, advertising would attempt to give them what they wanted. As acutely as any other institution, advertising recognized people's psychological discomforts with the increasing complexity and impersonality of much of modern life. Advertising not only propagandized for modern, urban civilization; it also offered compensation for its discontents. Adopting a therapeutic mission, advertising provided comforting reassurances to those who anxiously watched the institutions of their society assume a larger, more complex, and more impersonal scale.

The new efficiencies of scale need bring no deficiencies of personal satisfaction, advertising promised. Americans could enjoy the urban tempo without paying the cost of frayed nerves. They could exercise an expanded freedom of choice in products and still feel "correct," reassured by simplified and dramatized forms of advice. If people experienced depersonalization in some aspects of their lives, advertising and the commercial media offered many compensatory varieties of "personal contact." If they feared a loss of individualism, the ads proclaimed that a correct choice of mass-merchandised products would provide exclusivity and the expression of "individual taste."

One mode of response by Americans to the modernization of their society in the nineteenth and early twentieth centuries had been to split life into two distinct spheres: the hard, rational, competitive, and impersonal realm of work and economic transactions; and the soft, sentimental, intimate world of home, family, and warm personal friendships. Presumably, such a bifurcation met people's psychological needs by preserving havens of intimate social relationships in the midst of growing complexity and bureaucratization. But people did not prove amenable to so rigid a compartmentalization of their lives. Their desires for psychological gratification and personal interaction spilled messily over from the world of private intimacy into the public realm of economic transactions.

Although sometimes dismayed by the irrationalities that this human predilection introduced into the business of selling goods, advertising leaders gradually abandoned any reservations about fusing advertising with entertainment. If the average person demanded psychic satisfactions and reassurance along with modern goods, and wanted to "be amused rather than instructed," then crooning undoubtedly represented the proper, therapeutic tone of voice. As Ernest Dichter reported from a survey in the early 1940s, people wanted more commercials delivered as "Bing Crosby does it."[87] Advertising leaders wished to retain a professional, rational, and business-like demeanor in carrying out their own "productive" function. But they adopted a bemused, canny tolerance toward a public that was unwilling or unable to confine its passion for personalized interaction to the narrow sphere of home and close acquaintanceship. Advertisers were the first experts of the advancing mass society to recognize the depth of public discomfort with rigid compartmentalization—the desire of people to integrate their lives by understanding and experiencing their entire social environment within a personal, comprehensible scale.

In response, advertising adopted a therapeutic role. It assured readers that all the apparent psychological costs of scale could be finessed. Individual Americans never need feel themselves diminished or alienated, whatever the scale of life. They could enjoy every modern artifact and style without losing the reassuring emotional bonds of the village community. Individual advertisers and agencies did not set themselves this broad therapeutic task. Rather, it emerged as the cumulative by-product of individual merchandising strategies that proved successful in selling products. No longer patent medicine "hawkers," advertising men had now become broader social therapists who offered, within the advertising tableaux themselves, balms for the discontents of modernity.

Does this mean that advertising, as society's "Mirror, mirror on the wall," provided benign, therapeutic deceptions rather than reflections of social reality? If we focus on the cast of characters in the tableaux—the French maids and the office-window imperialists—we will certainly be impressed primarily by the ads' distortions of social circumstances. If we focus on their specific prescriptions and advice—their promises of equality and autonomy through acts of consumption—we will be most impressed by their manipulative evasions, their efforts to finesse the problems of modernity. But if we focus on the perceptions of social and cultural dilemmas revealed in the tableaux, we will discover accurate, expressive images of underlying "realities" of American society in the 1920s and 1930s reflected in advertising's elusive mirror.

A single tableau will serve to recapitulate the reassuring, therapeutic resolutions that advertising offered for such core dilemmas of the society as the challenges of complexity to a sense of personal competence and control, of massive institutions to a sense of human scale, of mass merchandising to individual identity, of economic change to the success creed, of "overcivilization" to the simple virtues of nature, and of the engulfing crowd to individual freedom and autonomy.

In 1928 the Reo Motor Car Company invited readers vicariously to sit behind the wheel of the new Reo Flying Cloud and gaze expectantly out over the open road and rolling green hills of the tableau (Fig. 10.8). Observing that with modern advances, "twenty million automobiles crowd the once open roads . . . it's hard

—and the Roads That Once Were Open
Will be Open Once Again

Twenty million automobiles crowd the once open roads.

A hundred million people seeking freedom from the drabness of daily life ride up and down the modern version of the trails of pioneers.

Yet still there throbs in every vein, the old American call to romance and adventure, still the lure of going somewhere to meet the thrill of the unexpected.

But it's hard to get beyond the multitude in ordinary cars. There are so many of them. They fill so much of highways that were lonely yesterday.

There is a way to leave the crowds behind. There is a car so swift, so comfortable, so dependable, that you can reach and cross the farthest horizon with ease.

It is the Reo Flying Cloud of 1929.

Roads that once were open are open roads again when you drive this pleasure car.

For the Reo Flying Cloud laughs at sluggish traffic as it alertly beats the rest to every opening.

Hour after hour, it will hit a higher average speed to take you farther than the average car can cruise.

Gayly it takes the roughest roads, the steepest climbs, the widest plains.

With a zest that's all its own, it sails you out to the roads that are still open, while making the roads that once were open seem uncrowded because it does so many things better.

There's a new Reo Flying Cloud of 1929 ready for you to test. Try it out in every way you wish. Let it tell its story to you in its own sweet-running way. It will show you how the roads that once were open will be open once again.

1929 REO FLYING CLOUDS
REO MOTOR CAR COMPANY · Lansing, Michigan

10.8. Reo vicariously recaptured for readers that thrill of freedom and mastery evoked by the "open road." As the answer to roads clogged by "twenty million automobiles," Reo would "leave the crowds behind."

to get beyond the multitudes," Reo assured readers that modern technology would overcome the apparent barriers to individual freedom and fulfillment. "There is a way to leave the crowds behind," proclaimed Reo in defiance of the new scale and congestion of modern life. "There is a car so swift, so comfortable, so dependable, that you can reach and cross the farthest horizon with ease." Since

MAN ALIVE! . . . Have you forgotten the *fun* of driving?

Away ahead of the crowd. Where the breeze is clear and cool. Where the only sound is the purr of your motor and the excited little laugh of her beside you. You squeeze your foot to the floorboards and leap clear of the coming hill. Then glide down the path of your headlights with the whistle of wind in your ears.

Have you forgotten? Ethyl hasn't!

Drive to the nearest Ethyl pump and tell them to "fill 'er up." The night is young—and your car will be, as soon as it gets the feel of Ethyl's life-restoring power. Park your hats at home and let's go places!

* * *

P. S. May we add that people who use Ethyl regularly through the year find that *it also saves them money in lessened repair bills.* Ethyl Gasoline Corporation, New York City.

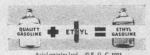

Ethyl contains lead. © E. G. C. 1933

DOUBLY TESTED

This emblem on a pump (or its globe) is the mark of the world's highest quality motor fuel. Ethyl Gasoline is tested at the time of its mixing, and again through samples taken from pumps, to maintain its high standards of anti-knock, volatility, and freedom from harmful gum and sulphur. Look for the Ethyl emblem. If the emblem is not there, it is not Ethyl Gasoline.

NEXT TIME STOP AT THE ETHYL PUMP

10.9. *Advertising's ultimate parable finessed problems apparently created by the scale of crowded, modern society and its threats to individualism and personal mastery. The product promised each reader a place "out front."*

"the Reo Flying Cloud laughs at sluggish traffic as it alertly beats the rest to every opening," all potential consumers could rest assured that for them, "Roads that Once Were Open Will Be Open Once Again."[88]

Was Reo's promise an evasion? An illusion? Certainly, by focusing on the individual rather than the collective effects of consumer purchases, it slyly finessed the problem of scale and the realities of mass society—just as had the *Ladies' Home Journal* ad which assured every reader that "Elizabeth Arden is personally interested in you."[89] But Reo may have "mirrored" the predominant American response to the technological promises and psychological discomforts of modernity nonetheless. F. Scott Fitzgerald, a favorite novelist of the era and of contemporary advertising writers, made a similar assessment of American aspirations toward an "open road." Generalizing from his protagonist, Jay Gatsby, to the wider society, Fitzgerald contemplated Gatsby's tragic belief "in the green light, the orgiastic future that year by year recedes before us." "It eluded us then," Fitzgerald's narrator mused philosophically, "but that's no matter—tomorrow we will run faster, stretch out our arms farther. . . . And one fine morning— . . . . So we beat on, boats against the current, borne back ceaselessly into the past."[90]

In scores of parables and visual clichés, advertising had served as the society's "green light," beckoning consumers to join in a cost-free progress toward modernity (Fig. 10.9). Advertising's "green light" was less ineffable than Fitzgerald's, its vision less commensurate to a "capacity for wonder."[91] But it expressed in more material, technological terms the promise of an open road accessible to consumers who would run faster, stretch out their arms farther. Far from being "borne back ceaselessly into the past," consumers would retain every amenity of the smaller, more personal scale of life in the past as they accelerated forward into modernity. The cumulative, crowning parable of advertising amplified the American dream by proclaiming, "You can have it all." In the truth of that proposition, most Americans devoutly wished to believe.

NOTES

Introduction

1. N. W. Ayer and Son, *The American Scene: An Exhibition of Art in Advertising* [pamphlet, Philadelphia, 1926], in N. W. Ayer and Son Archives, New York City. For similar prophecies, see *Printers' Ink,* June 23, 1927, p. 41; *Advertising Age,* June 7, 1937, p. 8.

2. Robert S. Lynd and Helen Merrell Lynd, *Middletown in Transition* (New York, 1937), pp. 489–94.

3. *Advertising and Selling,* Sept. 8, 1926, p. 27; Jan. 25, 1928, p. 26. The contemporary futurist, Jib Fowles, has concluded that advertising so inherently portrays people's unfulfilled needs and aspirations rather than their present circumstances that he relies entirely on advertisements to define the prospective social agenda of any given era. (Jib Fowles, *Mass Advertising as Social Forecast: A Method for Futures Research* [Westport, Conn., 1976], pp. 55, 63–80).

4. Jacques Ellul, *Propaganda,* trans. Konrad Kellen and Jean Lerner (New York, 1965), pp. 74–76.

5. Michael Schudson, *Advertising, the Uneasy Persuasion: Its Dubious Impact on American Society* (New York, 1984), pp. 214–18.

6. Bruce Kuklick, "Myth and Symbol in American Studies," *American Quarterly* 24 (Oct. 1972): 444; Jay Mechling, "Advice to Historians on Advice to Mothers," *Journal of Social History* 9 (Fall 1975): 44–63; Herbert J. Gans, *Popular Culture and High Culture* (New York, 1974), pp. 32, 35.

7. I have borrowed the term *reality check* from Frank W. Fox, "Advertising and the Second World War" (Ph.D. diss., Stanford Univ., 1973), p. 30. Fox's first chapter provides an excellent summary and analysis of the problems and possibilities of interpreting advertising as a social mirror. Another perceptive assessment of the relation of advertising to social reality is Schudson, *Advertising, the Uneasy Persuasion.*

8. *Printers' Ink,* June 30, 1927, p. 54; Frank W. Fox, "Advertisements as Documents in Social and Cultural History" (M.A. thesis, Univ. of Utah, 1969), p. vi.

9. "Corning Glass Ware" (Advertising 215), p. 11, Harvard Business School Case Studies, reel 11, HBS Archives.

10. *Harvard Awards, 1929* (New York, 1930), p. 30, Harvard Awards Archives, Baker Library, Harvard School of Business.

11. *Saturday Evening Post,* May 7, 1930, p. 122; Oct. 4, 1930, p. 160; Mar. 7, 1931, p. 44; *Tide,* Feb. 1934, p. 62.

12. Walter Benjamin, "The Work of Art in the Age of Mechanical Reproduction," in Benjamin, *Illuminations,* trans. Harry Zohn (New York, 1968), pp. 239–43.

13. George Lakoff and Mark Johnson, *Metaphors We Live By* (Chicago, 1980), pp. 5–6; Edmund Carpenter, "Our New Languages: The Mass Media," in *Languages of the Mass Media,* ed. Irving and Harriet A. Deer (Boston, 1965), pp. 1–13. See also Jerome L. Singer, *Daydreaming and Fantasy* (London, 1976), p. 172; and Schudson, *Advertising, the Uneasy Persuasion.*

14. I rely here on the counsel of Peter Burke in *Popular Culture in Early Modern Europe* (London, 1978), pp. 77–78, who observes that "historians can never trust their documents completely. . . . The point about the different classes of documents . . . is not that they are worthless, but that they are distorted and distortion can to some degree be allowed for—indeed, it is the historian's traditional business to do so."

One   Apostles of Modernity

1. In describing the superficially self-evident role of advertising as the logical extension of the process of modernization, I have drawn my definition of modernization from the following sources: Richard D. Brown, *Modernization: The Transformation of American Life, 1600–1865* (New York, 1976); Alex Inkeles and David H. Smith, *Becoming Modern: Individual Change in Six Developing Countries* (Cambridge, Mass., 1974); Daniel Lerner, *The Passing of Traditional Society* (Glencoe, Ill., 1958); and Thomas L. Haskell, *The Emergence of Professional Social Science: The American Social Science Association and the Nineteenth Century Crisis of Authority* (Urbana, Ill., 1977). I explore the complicated relationship between modernization and modern advertising further in Chapter 10.

2. In *The Visible Hand: The Managerial Revolution in American Business* (Cambridge, Mass., 1977), pp. 235–36, 266, 281–83, Alfred D. Chandler, Jr., employs the terms "velocity of flow" and "velocity of throughput" to describe how administrative coordination and integration in large businesses created gains of productivity and decreases in unit costs by ensuring a steady and rapid flow of materials through the industrial plant to the ultimate consumer. Velocity of flow was more important than economies of scale, he argues, in rationalizing the entire mass production–mass distribution system and ensuring higher productivity.

3. George E. Mowry, *The Urban Nation, 1920–1960* (New York, 1965), pp. 3, 11.

4. Earnest Elmo Calkins, "Business Has Wings," *Atlantic Monthly,* Mar. 1927, p. 313; Printers' Ink, *Fifty Years, 1888–1938* (New York, 1938), p. 325.

5. *Advertising and Selling,* Sept. 19, 1928, p. 28.

6. *Advertising and Selling,* June 29, 1927, p. 14; July 27, 1927, p. 13; and June 13, 1928, p. 23; *Printers' Ink Monthly,* Apr. 1926, p. 23.

7. *Advertising and Selling,* Apr. 20, 1927, pp. 20, 44, 52; May 5, 1926, p. 19; Oct. 29, 1930, p. 80; July 27, 1927, p. 13.

8. Robert S. Lynd and Helen Merrell Lynd, *Middletown: A Study in American Culture* (New York, 1929), pp. 40–41, 45–46, 57–58, 70–71.

9. For the best survey of the rise of national advertising to its modern institutional shape between the 1880s and 1920, see Daniel Pope, *The Making of Modern Advertising* (New York, 1983), pp. 4–8 and passim.

10. Noel L. Griese, "AT&T: Origins of the Nation's Oldest Continuous Institutional Advertising Campaign," *Journal of Advertising* 6 (1977): 18–22; J. D. Ellsworth, "The Start of General Magazine Advertising," typed ms., Jan. 1931, Box 1066, AT&T Archives, New York City; Roland Marchand, "Creating the Corporate Soul," convention paper, Organization of American Historians, Apr. 1980.

11. Printers' Ink, *Fifty Years,* pp. 205, 241–42, 244; *Advertising and Selling,* Sept. 8, 1926,

p. 29; July 13, 1927, p. 27. The branding of coal was ingeniously pioneered by a dealer who printed his name on thousands of orange cardboard disks which he scattered amidst the coal so that a householder would be reminded of the brand with nearly every shovelful.

12. Printers' Ink, *Fifty Years*, p. 249; *Saturday Evening Post*, Sept. 1, 1923, pp. 140, 143; Sept. 8, 1923, pp. 57, 135–36; Sept. 15, 1923, pp. 47, 124; Sept. 22, 1923, p. 45; Aug. 22, 1925, p. 131.

13. *Printers' Ink*, Dec. 13, 1917, p. 148; Printers' Ink, *Fifty Years*, pp. 288–90, 294; Theodore MacManus, *The Sword Arm of Business* (New York, 1927), p. xv; Otis A. Pease, *The Responsibilities of American Advertising* (New Haven, Conn., 1958), p. 17; Stephen Vaughn, *Holding Fast the Inner Lines: Democracy, Nationalism, and the Committee on Public Information* (Chapel Hill, N.C., 1980), pp. 141–43, 147, 190–92; J. Walter Thompson Co., *News Bulletin*, Aug. 5, 1918, p. 2, JWT Archives, New York City. This *News Bulletin* or *News Letter* was published under different titles between 1916 and 1929 for distribution within the agency. It will be cited subsequently as *JWT News Bulletin* or *JWT News Letter* to distinguish it from the externally distributed *J. Walter Thompson News Bulletin*.

14. Pease, *Responsibilities*, pp. 11–13; Frank Presbrey, *The History and Development of Advertising* (Garden City, N.Y., 1929), p. 567; Printers' Ink, *Fifty Years*, pp. 308–309, 320, 340.

15. Pope, *Modern Advertising*, pp. 22–29; *Printers' Ink*, Jan. 20, 1927, p. 165; Aug. 22, 1928, p. 29; and Oct. 11, 1928, p. 131; James Rorty, "'Art' and the Ad Man," *The Nation*, Jan. 23, 1934, p. 93.

16. *JWT News Bulletin*, Mar. 15, 1921, p. 1; Ed Roberts, "BBDO Short History," n.p., typescript, Batten, Barton, Durstine and Osborn (BBDO) Archives, New York City; Quentin James Schultze, "Advertising, Science, and Professionalism, 1885–1917" (Ph.D. diss., Univ. of Illinois, Urbana-Champaign, 1978), pp. 2–3, 21.

17. Sidney Hyman, *The Lives of William Benton* (Chicago, 1969), p. 86; *Advertising and Selling*, June 2, 1926, p. 29.

18. George Batten Company, *News Letter*, Oct. 6, 1925, p. 5, BBDO Archives; *Saturday Evening Post*, Oct. 31, 1931, p. 44; John Tebbel, *George Horace Lorimer and the Saturday Evening Post* (Garden City, N.Y., 1948), p. 117; Earnest Elmo Calkins, *Business the Civilizer* (Boston, 1928), pp. 230–31, p. 192. The Index of Advertisers first appeared in the *Post* issue of Mar. 20, 1926.

19. *JWT News Letter*, Apr. 15, 1926, p. 94; *Advertising and Selling*, Nov. 17, 1926, p. 73; *Printers' Ink*, Apr. 7, 1927, p. 123; Presbrey, *Development of Advertising*, p. 604.

20. *Judicious Advertising*, Apr. 1925, p. 50; *Printers' Ink*, June 17, 1926, p. 17; Nov. 18, 1926, pp. 223–24; Dec. 9, 1926, pp. 189–90; June 2, 1927, p. 33; and Dec. 15, 1927, pp. 203–204; *Advertising and Selling*, June 1, 1927, p. 28; GWC to L. B. Slocum, Sept. 28, 1933, Ford File, N. W. Ayer and Son Archives, New York City.

21. *Printers' Ink*, Feb. 10, 1927, p. 44; Sept. 13, 1928, p. 28; *Advertising and Selling*, June 30, 1926, p. 21.

22. Schultze, "Advertising, Science, and Professionalism," pp. 92–93, 98–99, 119, 169, 174–84.

23. George R. Creel, *How We Advertised America* (New York, 1920), pp. 157, 165; Pease, *Responsibilities*, p. 17; T. R. Nevett, *Advertising in Britain: A History* (London, 1982), pp. 143–44; George Batten Company, *News Letter*, Nov. 28, 1927, p. 8; Daniel Pope, "The Advertising Industry and World War I," *The Public Historian* 2 (1980): 5, 15–17, 19–21.

24. Leo Burnett, *Communications of an Advertising Man* (Chicago, 1961), pp. 272–73; The Blackman Company, "Art with an Advertising Accent," *Harvard Awards*, 5 vols., vol. 4, pt. 2, p. 3 ms. division, Baker Library, Harvard Business School.

25. Bruce Barton, *The Man Nobody Knows* (Indianapolis, 1925); Alice Payne Hackett and James Henry Burke, *80 Years of Best Sellers* (New York, 1977), p. 101; *Printers' Ink,* Feb. 25, 1926, p. 41, and Mar. 11, 1926, p. 33; *Judicious Advertising,* Apr. 1925, p. 50; *Advertising and Selling,* Dec. 14, 1927, p. 56.

26. Presbrey, *Development of Advertising,* pp. 610–11, 616–17.

27. *Printers' Ink,* Nov. 4, 1926, pp. 3–6, 198–200; *Advertising and Selling,* Nov. 3, 1926, pp. 21, 56.

28. J. H. Plumb, "The Acceptance of Modernity," in Neil McKendrick, John Brewer, and J. H. Plumb, *The Birth of a Consumer Society: The Commercialization of Eighteenth-Century England* (London, 1982), p. 316.

29. *Webster's New International Dictionary of the English Language,* 2nd ed. (Springfield, Mass., 1934), p. 1577.

30. Printers' Ink, *Fifty Years,* pp. 174–75, 182, 236; Pease, *Responsibilities,* pp. 34–35; Pope, *Modern Advertising,* pp. 236–41; T. J. Jackson Lears, "From Salvation to Self-Realization," in Richard Wightman Fox and T. J. Jackson Lears, eds., *The Culture of Consumption* (New York, 1983), p. 18.

31. Printers' Ink, *Fifty Years,* p. 205; *Advertising Age,* Nov. 22, 1937, p. 41.

32. Printers' Ink, *Fifty Years,* p. 362; *Printers' Ink Monthly,* June 1936, p. 45; Richard W. Pollay, "The Subsidizing Sizzle: A History of Print Advertising, 1900–1980," *Journal of Marketing* 49 (1985). Pollay raises a provocative question when he reports that his content analysis survey indicates that the marketing orientation (which has characterized modern advertising) began to fade again after the 1950s. It may be, however, that advertisers merely became more sophisticated in their techniques for pursuing that orientation.

33. *Ladies' Home Journal,* Apr. 1926, p. 164; Oct. 1926, p. 219; July 1928, p. 66; *Saturday Evening Post,* June 30, 1928, p. 51; *Good Housekeeping,* Jan. 1927, p. 152; *Printers' Ink,* Nov. 15, 1928, p. 193.

34. *Printers' Ink,* Apr. 28, 1932, p. 6.

35. Robert Wiebe, *The Search for Order, 1877–1920* (New York, 1967), pp. 52, 55, 111; Daniel Bell, *The Cultural Contradictions of Capitalism* (New York, 1976), p. 147; T. J. Jackson Lears, *No Place of Grace: Antimodernism and the Transformation of American Culture, 1880–1920* (New York, 1981), pp. 7, 13, 17, 79; Richard Hofstadter, *The Age of Reform* (New York, 1955), pp. 35–37, 216–17, 223–25.

36. Wiebe, *Search for Order,* p. 42; Lears, "From Salvation to Self-Realization," p. 4.

37. "Minutes of Monday Evening Meeting," May 17, 1930, p. 3, and Sept. 30, 1930, p. 11, J. Walter Thompson Company (JWT) Archives, New York City.

38. *Printers' Ink,* Feb. 4, 1926, p. 37; "Minutes of Representatives Meeting," Nov. 15, 1927, p. 1, JWT Archives; *American Weekly,* Feb. 27, 1927, p. 21; *Saturday Evening Post,* Apr. 10, 1926, pp. 104–105; *Chicago Tribune,* Nov. 19, 1926, p. 38. On the prevalence of accusing judgments and "harsh social scrutiny," see also Stuart Ewen, *Captains of Consciousness: Advertising and the Social Roots of the Consumer Culture* (New York, 1976), pp. 34, 36, 38.

39. Frank Luther Mott, *American Journalism, a History: 1607–1960,* 3rd ed. (New York, 1962), p. 599; Julian Lewis Watkins, *The 100 Greatest Advertisements,* 2nd ed., rev. (New York, 1959), p. 205; Richard Weiner, *Syndicated Columnists,* 3rd ed. (New York, 1979), p. 78; "Minutes of Representatives Meeting," Aug. 30, 1927, p. 5, JWT Archives; *Saturday Evening Post,* Apr. 24, 1926, p. 94, and Oct. 9, 1926, p. 133. On the "evolution of Aunt Ellen" for Griswold Mfg. Co., see *Printers' Ink,* Feb. 11, 1926, p. 1. On the origins of the "Ruth Miller personality" for Odo-ro-no, see Case History Files, JWT Archives. Barton, Durstine and Osborn invented "Janet Gray" for Lewis and Conger household furnishings in 1927, and J. Walter Thompson created the persona of "Mary Hale Martin, Cooking Correspondent" for Libby products in 1923. "Helen Chase" appeared in Procter and Gamble ads for Camay Soap in the late 1920s.

See BBDO, "Status Binder, 1928," BBDO Archives; *JWT News Letter,* Jan. 31, 1924, p. 6; *Saturday Evening Post,* June 15, 1929, fourth cover.

40. *Printers' Ink,* Mar. 11, 1926, p. 97, and Dec. 10, 1931, p. 88; "Minutes of Representatives Meeting," Oct. 2, 1929, p. 7, JWT Archives; *Printers' Ink Monthly,* Mar. 1926, p. 42.

41. *Saturday Evening Post,* Apr. 10, 1926, p. 2; "Minutes of Representatives Meeting," Dec. 3, 1929, pp. 5, 8, JWT Archives.

42. "Minutes of Creative Staff Meeting," June 28, 1932, pp. 3–4, JWT Archives; *Printers' Ink,* Apr. 21, 1927, pp. 74–75; James F. Newcomb and Co., Inc., *Direct Reflections* (New York, 1929), p. 27; *Advertising and Selling,* Sept. 27, 1934, p. 24.

43. *JWT News Letter,* Apr. 10, 1924, p. 1; "Minutes of Creative Staff Meeting," June 28, 1932, pp. 4–5, JWT Archives.

44. *JWT News Letter,* Apr. 10, 1924, p. 1, Apr. 1, 1926, pp. 86–87; "Minutes of Representatives Meeting," Feb. 7, 1928, p. 2; Feb. 28, 1928, p. 4; June 28, 1932, pp. 5–6, JWT Archives; *Tide,* June 1928, p. 4; *Printers' Ink,* Dec. 13, 1928, p. 149.

45. "Minutes of Representatives Meeting," May 24, 1927, p. 2, JWT Archives; *Saturday Evening Post,* Jan. 18, 1930, p. 45.

46. *Ladies' Home Journal,* Oct. 1928, p. 117; "Minutes of Representatives Meeting," July 18, 1928, pp. 2–4, and June 28, 1932, p. 7, JWT Archives; *Tide,* Oct. 1928, pp. 4–5; *American Magazine,* Nov. 1928, p. 91.

47. *Delineator,* Nov. 1928, p. 37; *American Magazine,* Oct. 1928, p. 91.

48. "Minutes of Representatives Meeting," June 28, 1932, pp. 1–2, 7, and Feb. 13, 1930, p. 7, JWT Archives.

49. *Printers' Ink,* Nov. 10, 1927, p. 3.

50. Ibid., p. 4; *Literary Digest,* Nov. 19, 1921, p. 45; *Good Housekeeping,* Jan. 1923, p. 144.

51. Gerard B. Lambert, "How I Sold Listerine," *Fortune,* Sept. 1956, p. 111; *Printers' Ink,* Oct. 14, 1926, p. 28. For examples of the mature Listerine advertising formula, see *Better Homes and Gardens,* July 1929, p. 33, and *Saturday Evening Post,* June 29, 1929, p. 83, and Aug. 24, 1929, p. 74. The term *sociodrama* is taken from Hugh Dalziel Duncan, *Symbols in Society* (New York, 1968), pp. 33–34.

52. *Printers' Ink,* Oct. 4, 1926, p. 25.

53. Gerard B. Lambert, *All Out of Step* (Garden City, N.Y., 1956), p. 115; *Chicago Tribune,* Feb. 10, 1926, p. 31, and Feb. 24, 1926, p. 12; *Los Angeles Times,* Oct. 5, 1927, p. 10; *Tide,* Sept. 15, 1927, p. 7, and Mar. 15, 1928, p. 4; *Good Housekeeping,* Oct. 1928, p. 118; *Saturday Evening Post,* Oct. 19, 1929, p. 115; Lambert, "How I Sold Listerine," pp. 166, 168, 170.

54. Lambert, *All Out of Step,* p. 58; *Advertising and Selling,* Sept. 19, 1928, p. 92; *Saturday Evening Post,* May 16, 1925, p. 121; Advertising Case Study 289 (National Shoe Retailers' Association), p. 12, reel 11, Harvard Business School Archives; *Tide,* Apr. 1928, p. 5, and Apr. 1936, p. 74; *Printers' Ink,* Feb. 4, 1926, p. 27, and June 22, 1933, p. 40. By the early 1930s the "halitosis style" had become so ingrained in popular lore that several advertisers concluded that they could effectively use tongue-in-cheek parodies to give a humorous lift to their copy. The Wayne Oil Burner Corporation announced the invention of a new disease, "coalitosis," a malady bred by rival fuels. Life Savers, Inc., parodied Listerine with "mocking . . . but still serious" copy on eligible bachelors and lovely spinsters under such headlines as "At last! . . . The long silent best friend *speaks out!*" (*Tide,* Mar. 1932, p. 18, and Sept. 1932, p. 12). Advertising appears to have discovered "smog" in 1934, not as a term for air pollution but as a disease of women's skin, a "blistering, darkening, aging, and tarnishing" affliction engendered by "smoke, soot, gases, and grime" (*Tide,* Apr. 1934, p. 5).

55. *Printers' Ink,* Nov. 19, 1931, p. 104; James Webb Young, *Full Corn in the Ear* (Coava, New Mexico, 1959), n.p.

56. *JWT News Letter,* Nov. 11, 1926, p. 261.

57. *Advertising Age,* June 30, 1934, p. 23.
58. *Good Housekeeping,* Jan. 1922, p. 123.
59. Scrapbook 195 (Kotex), Lord and Thomas Archives, housed at Foote, Cone and Belding Communications, Inc., Chicago; "Minutes of Representatives Meeting," May 21, 1930, p. 12, JWT Archives.
60. Scrapbooks 195 and 205 (Kotex), Lord and Thomas Archives; the emphasis on *hour* and *moments* is mine.
61. *Printers' Ink,* Apr. 21, 1927, pp. 74–75; John Gunther, *Taken at the Flood: The Story of Albert D. Lasker* (New York, 1960) pp. 153–54.
62. Printers' Ink, *Fifty Years,* p. 367.
63. Marketing Case Study 396 (Jordan Motor Car Company), pp. 454 and 458, reel 120, Harvard Business School Archives; *Saturday Evening Post,* Jan. 9, 1926, p. 79; Jan. 30, 1926, p. 35; Apr. 3, 1926, p. 106.
64. *J. Walter Thompson News Bulletin,* Aug. 1923, p. 6. This bulletin for external distribution is cited by its full title to distinguish it from the confidential, internally distributed *JWT News Bulletin* and *JWT News Letter.*
65. Ibid.; *Judicious Advertising,* Apr. 1925, p. 23; *Printers' Ink,* Jan. 1, 1925, p. 58; *Tide,* Sept. 1929, p. 7; *Chicago Tribune,* Dec. 18, 1927, mag. sec., p. 8; Kenneth M. Goode, *How to Turn People into Gold* (New York, 1929), p. 72; *Advertising Age,* Sept. 16, 1931, p. 24; *Advertising and Selling Fortnightly,* Mar. 24, 1926, p. 24; *Ladies' Home Journal,* Dec. 1926, p. 197.
66. *Printers' Ink Monthly,* Mar. 1926, p. 27; *Printers' Ink,* June 3, 1926, p. 3, and Nov. 14, 1929, p. 94; *Advertising and Selling,* Feb. 18, 1931, p. 17; *Saturday Evening Post,* Mar. 20, 1926, pp. 58–59; *Good Housekeeping,* Aug. 1925, p. 101.
67. Pease, *Responsibilities,* p. 43. See also Stuart Ewen and Elizabeth Ewen, *Channels of Desire: Mass Images and the Shaping of American Consciousness* (New York, 1982), pp. 37, 42.

Two   Men of the People: The New Professionals

1. *Advertising and Selling Fortnightly,* Nov. 18, 1925, p. 24; Dec. 2, 1925, p. 34; Apr. 7, 1926, p. 20; *Printers' Ink,* Mar. 26, 1931, p. 113; Oct. 2, 1930, p. 75; Oct. 16, 1930, p. 160; *Tide,* Oct. 1932, p. 34; *Saturday Evening Post,* May 3, 1924, p. 71.
2. *Advertising and Selling,* Dec. 25, 1929, p. 50; July 23, 1930, p. 64; *Advertising Age,* Oct. 15, 1932, p. 17; Oct. 22, 1932, p. 1; *Advertising and Selling Fortnightly,* Mar. 24, 1926, p. 25; *Printers' Ink,* Aug. 16, 1928, p. 41; May 22, 1930, pp. 49–50, 52; Apr. 30, 1931, p. 124; Oct. 27, 1932, p. 6; Aug. 18, 1932, p. 82; Jeffrey Meikle, *Twentieth Century Limited* (Austin, Tex., 1979), p. 70.
3. On this model of professionalism, see Margali Sarfatti Larson, *The Rise of Professionalism: A Sociological Analysis* (Berkeley, 1977), pp. 16, 38–39, 50–51, 58–59; John B. Cullen, *The Structure of Professionalism* (New York, 1978), pp. 56, 76; and Wilbert E. Moore, *The Professions: Roles and Rules* (New York, 1970), pp. 10–11.
4. *Advertising and Selling,* June 27, 1928, p. 22; *Printers' Ink,* June 2, 1927, pp. 125–28.
5. *Advertising and Selling Fortnightly,* Apr. 21, 1926, p. 20; *Advertising and Selling,* Dec. 10, 1930, p. 28; *Printers' Ink Monthly,* Aug. 1930, pp. 108–109.
6. *J. Walter Thompson News Bulletin,* Dec. 1924, p. 8; Dec. 1925, pp. 29–30; *JWT News Letter,* Apr. 1, 1928, p. 133, JWT Archives, New York City; Harvard University,

Graduate School of Business Administration, *Harvard Advertising Awards, 1924–1928* (New York, 1930–1931), p. 1; *Advertising and Selling*, May 28, 1930, p. 29; May 27, 1931, p. 31.

7. *Advertising and Selling*, Mar. 7, 1928, p. 49; June 24, 1931, p. 53.

8. *Printers' Ink*, Jan. 9, 1930, p. 161; *Saturday Evening Post*, Mar. 9, 1929, p. 79.

9. *Judicious Advertising*, Apr. 1925, p. 53; *Printers' Ink*, July 16, 1925, pp. 155–56; Sept. 25, 1930, p. 72; *Printers' Ink Monthly*, Dec. 1925, pp. 84, 87.

10. *Advertising and Selling Fortnightly*, Apr. 21, 1926, p. 52; *Printers' Ink Monthly*, Dec. 1925, p. 41.

11. *Printers' Ink*, June 30, 1927, pp. 123–24; Mar. 3, 1932, p. 26; Dec. 20, 1928, p. 98; May 16, 1929, p. 151; James R. Adams, *Sparks Off My Anvil* (New York, 1938), pp. 95–96; *Advertising and Selling*, Jan. 18, 1934, p. 30.

12. *Advertising and Selling*, Aug. 20, 1930, p. 54. Listerine manufacturer Gerard Lambert expressed a similar viewpoint: "I wonder if anyone connected with them (the Harvard Awards) ever thought of giving a prize to the advertisement that brought in the most profit to the man who paid for the advertisement" (*Printers' Ink*, Nov. 10, 1927, p. 3).

13. *Advertising and Selling*, Oct. 15, 1930, p. 28; *Printers' Ink Monthly*, June 1925, pp. 29–30.

14. *Printers' Ink*, Jan. 14, 1926, pp. 4, 203; Nov. 4, 1926, p. 6; Feb. 6, 1930, p. 28; Oct. 27, 1932, pp. 3–4, 6, 85–87; Feb. 23, 1933, p. 41; *Printers' Ink Monthly*, Sept. 1933, pp. 13–14; *Advertising and Selling*, May 18, 1927, p. 80.

15. *Advertising and Selling*, June 1, 1927, p. 15; Sept. 5, 1928, p. 52; Mar. 4, 1931, p. 42; Mar. 16, 1933, pp. 13–14; *Printers' Ink*, May 12, 1927, p. 65; Sept. 1, 1927, p. 176; Jan. 23, 1930, p. 175.

16. *Advertising and Selling*, Oct. 2, 1929, p. 72; Mar. 4, 1931, p. 42; *Printers' Ink*, Sept. 16, 1926, p. 69; Apr. 14, 1927, p. 81; Oct. 27, 1932, p. 6.

17. *Advertising and Selling*, Oct. 29, 1930, p. 20.

18. *Printers' Ink*, Sept. 16, 1926, pp. 70, 77; Aug. 26, 1926, p. 155; Batten, Barton, Durstine and Osborn, *The Wedge* 33, no. 10 (1932), n.p.

19. *Advertising and Selling*, May 18, 1927, p. 89; Mar. 16, 1933, p. 14; Albert Lasker, *The Lasker Story: As He Told It* (Chicago, 1963), pp. 108–109; *Printers' Ink*, Feb. 4, 1926, p. 200; Sept. 16, 1926, p. 79; Oct. 3, 1929, p. 6; Dec. 19, 1929, p. 28.

20. *Printers' Ink*, Nov. 4, 1926, p. 196.

21. "Here is the Lever, Archimedes," n.d., Box 144, Bruce Barton Papers, Wisconsin State Historical Society (WSHS).

22. Agency secrecy and the multitude of possible criteria for measuring agency "size" insure that such a list can only represent a rough estimate. I have relied most heavily on figures for the amount and cost of advertising space in 1927 as reported in the J. Walter Thompson *JWT News Letter*, June 1, 1928, p. 138. Another source of evidence is a memo from Roy Durstine to Bruce Barton, July 28, 1927, estimating the square feet per person in floor space of a number of New York City agencies (Barton Papers, Box 144, WSHS). The top three agencies are particularly difficult to rank, although J. Walter Thompson had the largest international operation by far and certainly commanded first place by the early 1930s.

23. John L. Rogers, ed., *Who's Who in Advertising, 1931* (New York, 1931), p. xiv. The value of this volume, the only nationwide compilation for the 1925–1935 era, for a collective demographic portrait of national advertising leaders is severely restricted by its failure to include scores of the most influential copywriters, art directors, and agency principals of the period. A 1931 survey that does not include Albert Lasker, Raymond Rubicam, William Esty, Mark O'Dea, Fairfax Cone, Sterling Getchell, H. A. Batten, Gordon Seagrove, Frank Fletcher, William Flannery, and Frank Hummert, to mention only a few of the missing, hardly provides an adequate sample of advertising's creative elite.

24. "B.D.O. Personnel by Classifications," typescript in merger transition folder, BBDO Archives, New York City. See also, *Advertising and Selling*, May 4, 1927, p. 31, and BBDO ads in *Printers' Ink Monthly* for 1929.

25. "Minutes of Representatives Meetings, 1928," and "J. Walter Thompson Organizational Chart," JWT Archives, New York City; Bureau of Business Research, University of Detroit, *182 Advertising Men: A Preliminary Analysis of Detroit Advertising Personnel* (Detroit, 1928), p. 2. See also Kenyon and Eckhardt, Inc., promotion brochure c. 1931, Kenyon and Eckhardt Archives, New York City.

26. *Printers' Ink Monthly*, Aug. 1926, p. 35. A 1925 Barton, Durstine and Osborn ad included the names of six women among fifty-six "account representatives and department heads" (*Advertising and Selling Fortnightly*, Dec. 2, 1925, p. 31).

27. *Printers' Ink Monthly*, Oct. 1930, p. 49; Nov. 1930, p. 49; "Memorandum Book, 1930," Box 2, Dorothy Dignam Papers, Arthur and Elizabeth Schlesinger Library, Radcliffe College; U.S. Department of Commerce, Bureau of the Census, *Historical Statistics of the United States* (Washington, D.C., 1975), Part I, p. 299.

28. *Printers' Ink*, June 19, 1930, pp. 168–69; Jan. 29, 1931, p. 133; June 4, 1931, pp. 124–25; June 2, 1932, p. 88; "Trends in Advertising," p. 6, Box 1, folder 9, and "Club Achievements," B-29, folder 1, Advertising Women of New York Papers, Schlesinger Library; "Relations with Men's Club," Box 3, folder 16, and "Consumer Work," p. 1, Box 3, folder 15, Dignam Papers, Schlesinger Library.

29. Sidney Hyman, *The Lives of William Benton* (Chicago, 1969), p. 103; Dignam biographical sketch, Dorothy Dignam Papers, Wisconsin State Historical Society; Memorandum Books, Box 2, Dignam Papers, Schlesinger Library; "Trends in Advertising," p. 8, Box 1, folder 9, Advertising Women of N.Y. Papers; Bureau of Business Research, *182 Advertising Men*, pp. 3–5; *Printers' Ink*, June 5, 1930, p. 96; Jim Ellis, *Billboards to Buicks: Advertising as I Lived It* (New York, 1968), pp. 42, 49, 55.

30. Bernice Fitzgibbon, *Macy's, Gimbels and Me* (New York, 1967), p. 17; The Blackman Company, "Art With an Advertising Accent," in "Exhibits presented for the Harvard Advertising Awards," vol. 4, pt. 2, pp. 13–14, Harvard Award Archives, Baker Library; *Printers' Ink*, Dec. 27, 1928, p. 89.

31. "Trends in Advertising," p. 8, Box 1, folder 9, Dignam Papers, Schlesinger Library; *Printers' Ink*, June 9, 1927, pp. 91–92.

32. *Printers' Ink Monthly*, Aug. 1926, pp. 82, 86; *Printers' Ink*, Oct. 7, 1926, p. 112.

33. *Printers' Ink*, Dec. 27, 1928, p. 89; *Printers' Ink Monthly*, Aug. 1926, p. 35.

34. Dorothy Dignam, "Up the Ladder We Must Go," speech typescript, 1933, pp. 6, 13, Box 3, folder 19, Dignam Papers, Schlesinger Library; Dorothy Dignam, "Advertising Careers for Women," radio typescript, c. 1934, Box 1, Dignam Papers, WSHS.

35. *Advertising and Selling*, July 5, 1934, pp. 18–19. See also *Printers' Ink Monthly*, Aug. 1926, p. 85; "Minutes of Representatives Meeting," Oct. 21, 1930, p. 5, JWT Archives; *Printers' Ink*, Nov. 21, 1935, p. 20.

36. *J. Walter Thompson News Bulletin*, May 1930; *Advertising and Selling*, June 7, 1934, pp. 26–27; "Record of Our Annual Dinners and Dinner Dances," B-29, folder 1, Advertising Women of N.Y. Papers; Dignam, "Up the Ladder We Must Go," pp. 7, 13.

37. Daniel Pope and William Toll, "We Tried Harder: Jews in American Advertising," *American Jewish History* 72 (1922): 30–36.

38. Rogers, ed., *Who's Who in Advertising, 1931*, p. xv and passim.

39. Pope and Toll, "We Tried Harder," p. 29.

40. H. A. Batten, "Notes on Chapters 12–19," enclosure to Alice Kimberline to Ralph M. Hower, May 1, 1939, Ralph M. Hower Papers, Harvard Business School Archives, Baker Library; "Jewish Brains" (advertisement), *Printers' Ink*, Apr. 11, 1929, p. 193.

As late as 1940, during a desperate effort to keep from losing part of the Ford account, an executive of the Ayer agency assured Harry Bennett of Ford that no Jews were employed by the agency (Memo on loss of Lincoln-Zephyr Account to Maxon, Sept. 13, 1940, Ford file, N. W. Ayer and Son Archives, New York City).

41. Association of National Advertisers, *Report of Proceedings, 1930*, p. 3; "Creative Staff Meeting Minutes," Apr. 26, 1933, p. 5, JWT Archives; *Advertising and Selling*, July 13, 1927, p. 25; Feb. 6, 1929, p. 25; *Printers' Ink Monthly*, July 1926, p. 40.

42. "Criticism of 'History of an Advertising Agency,'" pp. 43–44, folder C, Hower Papers; "Interviews with Senator William Benton for Oral History," pp. 24–25, Oral History Research Office, Columbia University, Copyright 1975 by the Trustees of Columbia University in the City of New York; BBDO, "Ciphers at the Right," *The Wedge* 31, no. 12 (1931), n.p.

43. George Batten Company, *News Letter*, Feb. 26, 1924, p. 1.

44. *JWT News Letter*, Sept. 15, 1927, p. 406; *Printers' Ink*, Jan. 26, 1928, p. 113; Mar. 29, 1928, p. 82; Nov. 28, 1935, p. 37; *Advertising and Selling*, July 25, 1928, p. 57; *Judicious Advertising*, Mar. 1925, p. 58.

45. *Advertising and Selling*, Jan. 22, 1930, p. 31; June 11, 1930, p. 28; *Printers' Ink*, Jan. 26, 1928, p. 162; Mar. 29, 1928, p. 82.

46. Bureau of Business Research, *182 Advertising Men*, pp. 3–5; *Historical Statistics of the United States*, part I, p. 301; Hyman, *Lives of William Benton*, pp. 88, 112; Fitzgibbon, *Macy's, Gimbels and Me*, p. 41; *Printers' Ink Monthly*, Dec. 1931, p. 26. A 1935 questionnaire revealed that during that depression year one agency employed a copy chief at $50,000, two key writers at $18,000, and several others at $15,000. Average copy salaries in agencies ranged all the way from $3,600 to $12,000 *(Printers' Ink*, Oct. 17, 1935, p. 10).

47. William G. Lownds, Edward D. Chenery, and George J. Wiltshire, comps., *Advertising and Selling Digest* (New York, 1926), pp. 12–13; Roy S. Durstine, *This Advertising Business* (New York, 1928), p. 27; Fairfax M. Cone, *With All Its Faults: A Candid Account of Forty Years in Advertising* (Boston, 1969), pp. 124–25; *Printers' Ink*, Jan. 6, 1927, p. 93; Mar. 1, 1934, p. 68; Claude C. Hopkins, *My Life in Advertising* (New York, 1927), pp. 173–74.

48. James Webb Young, *Full Corn in the Ear* (Coava, N.M., 1959), n.p.; *Advertising and Selling*, Dec. 21, 1933, p. 22; Bruce Barton to Joseph A. Grazier, Dec. 4, 1956, Box 75, Barton Papers.

49. Chester Bowles, "The Reminiscences of Chester Bowles," pp. 22, 38–39, Oral History Research Office, Columbia University, Copyright 1976 by the Trustees of Columbia University in the City of New York; Fitzgibbon, *Macy's, Gimbels and Me*, pp. 27–28, 233; Dorothy Dignam, "Diary," Box 2, Dignam Papers, Schlesinger Library; *Printers' Ink*, July 21, 1932, pp. 18–19; J. Walter Thompson Co., "Forum," Jan. 7, 1936, pp. 7–8, JWT Archives; *Advertising and Selling*, Feb. 23, 1927, p. 72; Margaret Hopkins Memo, Nov. 22, 1927, BBDO Archives.

50. *Printers' Ink*, Sept. 16, 1926, pp. 182–83; May 27, 1926, pp. 184–85; Oct. 13, 1927, pp. 240–41; July 26, 1928, pp. 172–73; Apr. 28, 1927, pp. 197, 200–201; J. M. Campbell to Ralph M. Hower, Jan. 4, 1940, Hower Papers; *Printers' Ink Monthly*, July 1925, p. 24; Sept. 1931, p. 98.

51. JWT "Forum," Jan. 7, 1936, pp. 5–6, JWT Archives.

52. *Printers' Ink*, July 5, 1929, p. 151; *Advertising and Selling*, Apr. 17, 1929, pp. 28, 74.

53. JWT "Forum," Jan. 7, 1936, p. 8, JWT Archives.

54. An excellent overview of this process appears in Daniel Pope, *The Making of Modern Advertising* (New York, 1983), Chapter 4. See also Ralph M. Hower, *The History of an Advertising Agency* (Cambridge, Mass., 1939), pp. 91–93, 254–57.

55. *Advertising and Selling,* Aug. 19, 1931, pp. 26–27.

56. BBDO, *News Letter,* June 5, 1936, p. 5.

57. Hower, *History of an Advertising Agency,* pp. 401, 401n; *Printers' Ink,* May 24, 1934, pp. 46–47.

58. *Printers' Ink,* July 2, 1931, p. 48; Howard Williams Dickinson, *Crying Our Wares* (New York, 1929), pp. 66–67; George Batten Company, *News Letter,* Nov. 28, 1927, p. 8.

59. *Printers' Ink Monthly,* Dec. 1925, p. 48; Roy S. Durstine, "We're On the Air," *Scribner's,* May 1928, pp. 627–28; BBDO, "Account Status Binder" (Atwater Kent, Art Metal Construction Co., and Ethyl accounts), Sept. 1928, BBDO Archives; "Minutes of Creative Staff Meeting," Dec. 14, 1932, p. 1, and "Minutes of Representatives Meeting," Dec. 29, 1927, p. 1, JWT Archives; Milton H. Biow, *Butting In: An Adman Speaks Out* (Garden City, N.Y., 1964), pp. 33, 185.

60. Joseph Bensman, *Dollars and Sense: Ideology, Ethics and the Meaning of Work in Profit and Non-profit Organizations* (New York, 1967), pp. 22, 36, 40, 207. "The agency man, if he has a sense of humor, must suppress it," wrote Howard Dickinson in his reminiscences of agency life, except, perhaps, "in chummy personal visits with kindred spirits of the art or copy departments," (Dickinson, *Crying Our Wares,* pp. 168–69).

61. Giancarlo Buzzi, *Advertising: Its Cultural and Political Effects,* trans. B. David Garmize (Minneapolis, 1968), pp. 131–32.

62. BBDO, "Account Status Binder," Sept. 1928, passim.

63. *Printers' Ink Monthly,* Dec. 1931, p. 26.

64. Fitzgibbon, *Macy's, Gimbels and Me,* pp. 169, 211, 251, 253; Dickinson, *Crying Our Wares,* pp. 73, 96, 100–101.

65. *Printers' Ink,* May 6, 1926, p. 164; Jan. 2, 1930, pp. 101–4; Jan. 23, 1930, pp. 61–62; Feb. 27, 1930, pp. 84–85; Jan. 1, 1931, pp. 90–92; "Minutes of Creative Organization Staff Meeting," Mar. 5, 1932, pp. 11–15, JWT Archives; *Advertising and Selling,* Sept. 12, 1935, p. 20; *Tide,* Apr. 1930, p. 1.

66. *Printers' Ink,* Jan. 7, 1926, p. 10; Mar. 3, 1927, pp. 79–80; Dec. 5, 1929, p. 33; Dec. 19, 1929, p. 117; Mar. 31, 1932, p. 50; *Advertising and Selling,* Jan. 9, 1929, p. 18.

67. James F. Newcomb and Co., Inc., *Direct Reflections,* Feb. 1929, p. 18; BBDO, *The Wedge* 30, no. 8 (1930), n.p.; *Advertising and Selling,* Feb. 22, 1928, p. 51.

68. *Tide,* Feb. 1930, p. 2; *Printers' Ink,* Feb. 13, 1930, pp. 121–24; Feb. 20, 1930, p. 44.

69. Frank Irving Fletcher, *Lucid Interval: Confessions of a Custodian of the Convictions of Others* (New York, 1938), pp. 58–59.

70. *Printers' Ink,* May 6, 1926, p. 117; *Advertising and Selling,* Jan. 17, 1935, p. 44; "Minutes of Creative Organization Staff Meeting," March 5, 1932, p. 16, JWT Archives; *JWT News Letter,* Feb. 1, 1928, p. 59.

71. BBDO, *The Wedge* 30, no. 8 (1930), n.p.; *Advertising and Selling,* Jan. 17, 1935, p. 44; Newcomb and Co., *Direct Reflections,* Feb. 1929, pp. 18, 23; Raymond Rubicam, "Finding Success in Copywriting," speech typescript, 1934, Young and Rubicam, Inc., Archives, New York City; *Printers' Ink,* Oct. 11, 1934, p. 76.

72. *Tide,* Aug. 1928, p. 10; *Printers' Ink Monthly,* Feb. 1932, p. 66; *Printers' Ink,* July 19, 1934, p. 81.

73. For a sense of the diverse personalities involved, see: Adams, *Sparks Off My Anvil,* p. 58; *Printers' Ink,* June 4, 1931, pp. 41–42, and Sept. 29, 1932, p. 76; Hopkins, *My Life in Advertising,* pp. 50, 90, 97; Dickinson, *Crying Our Wares,* pp. 98–99; John Gunther, *Taken at the Flood: The Story of Albert D. Lasker* (New York, 1960), pp. 9, 15, 63–65; J. M. Campbell to Ralph M. Hower, Jan. 4, 1940, Hower Papers; Bureau of Business Research, *182 Advertising Men,* pp. 10–11; *Advertising and Selling,* July 14, 1926, p. 70, and July 8, 1931, p. 28; BBDO, "A Promotion Plan for BBDO," p. 13, typescript, 1933, BBDO Archives.

74. Cone, *With All Its Faults,* pp. 187, 191; Durstine, *This Advertising Business,* p. 176;

Rosser Reeves, *Reality in Advertising* (New York, 1961), p. 136; *Printers' Ink*, May 12, 1927, p. 152; Adams, *Sparks Off My Anvil*, p. 124; "Minutes of Creative Staff Meeting," May 4, 1932, p. 12, JWT Archives.

75. *Printers' Ink*, Jan. 20, 1927, p. 108; *Advertising and Selling*, Aug. 6, 1930, p. 52; Bensman, *Dollars and Sense*, p. 47; Adams, *Sparks Off My Anvil*, p. 93.

76. Cone, *With All Its Faults*, p. 88; *Advertising and Selling*, Dec. 14, 1926, p. 27; July 27, 1927, p. 27; Adams, *Sparks Off My Anvil*, pp. 150, 152; *Printers' Ink*, Mar. 10, 1927, p. 17.

77. Benton, "Interviews," p. 82. See also George Batten Company, *News Letter*, Nov. 28, 1927, p. 8, and Ellis, *Billboards to Buicks*, pp. 55, 83.

78. *Advertising Age*, May 28, 1932, p. 11.

79. Bureau of Business Research, *182 Advertising Men*, p. 2; *Printers' Ink Monthly*, July 1930, p. 46; *Printers' Ink*, Mar. 26, 1931, p. 113; Frederic Wakeman, *The Hucksters* (New York, 1946), p. 129; *Advertising Age*, July 5, 1937, p. 201.

80. *Printers' Ink*, Mar. 15, 1928, pp. 86–87; Oct. 16, 1930, p. 54; Bureau of Business Research, *182 Advertising Men*, p. 2; *Advertising Age*, Aug. 22, 1938, p. 12.

81. Fred Manchee, *The Huckster's Revenge: The Truth About Life on Madison Avenue* (New York, 1959), p. 183; *Batten's Wedge* 21, no. 19 (1927), n.p.; *Advertising and Selling*, Oct. 19, 1927, p. 49; Dec. 14, 1927, p. 85; *Printers' Ink*, Oct. 27, 1927, pp. 114–15; Stanley Burnshaw, interview with author, Feb. 13, 1980; Adams, *Sparks Off My Anvil*, p. 152; *Advertising and Selling*, Aug. 6, 1930, p. 52. The copywriters' fixation on the idea of the young advertising man burned out early by pressure appears occasionally to have inspired copy themes. A 1927 Postum ad declared: "The average man in America starts on the downhill road at the age of 31" (*American Magazine*, Feb. 1927, p. 94).

82. Hopkins, *My Life in Advertising*, p. 97; Gunther, *Taken at the Flood*, p. 13; Cone, *With All its Faults*, pp. 66, 72–73; Leo B. Ributto, "Jesus Christ as Business Statesman: Bruce Barton and the Selling of Corporate Capitalism," *American Quarterly* 33 (1981): 223, 233.

83. Hyman, *The Lives of William Benton*, pp. 98, 134, 158; Bowles, "Reminiscences," p. 43; Theodore McManus, *The Sword Arm of Business* (New York, 1927), pp. 4–5; *Tide*, Apr. 1927, p. 1.

84. Hopkins, *My Life in Advertising*, pp. 50, 90. See also T. J. Jackson Lears' surmise that even Bruce Barton may have doubted "the worth of his own vocation," in "From Salvation to Self-Realization: Advertising and the Therapeutic Roots of the Consumer Culture, 1880–1930," in Richard Wightman Fox and T. J. Jackson Lears, eds., *The Culture of Consumption* (New York, 1983), pp. 35–36.

85. Hopkins, *My Life in Advertising*, p. 97; *Printers' Ink Monthly*, June 1928, p. 72; *Printers' Ink*, Apr. 14, 1927, p. 81; Nov. 3, 1927, pp. 3–4; Feb. 4, 1932, p. 92; *Harvard Advertising Awards, 1924–1928*, p. 1; Russell Lynes, *A Surfeit of Honey* (New York, 1957), p. 32; Richard Sennett, *The Hidden Injuries of Class* (New York, 1972), pp. 225–27; BBDO, *The Wedge* 30, no. 13 (1930) n.p.; *Tide*, Dec. 1932, p. 22. See also Irwin Ross's similar explanation of the satisfactions of the public relations man in *The Image Merchants* (Garden City, N.Y., 1959), p. 250.

86. *Printers' Ink*, Mar. 19, 1931, p. 122.

87. Richard Steven Tedlow, "Keeping the Corporate Image: Public Relations and Business, 1900–1950" (Ph.D. diss., Columbia Univ., 1976), p. 173; *Tide*, June 1934, p. 11.

88. Bensman, *Dollars and Sense*, pp. 54, 207.

89. Kenneth E. Boulding, *The Image* (Ann Arbor, Mich., 1956), pp. 140–41.

90. Erving Goffman, *The Presentation of Self in Everyday Life* (Garden City, N.Y., 1959), p. 112; Erving Goffman, *Frame Analysis: An Essay on the Organization of Experience* (Cambridge, Mass., 1974), pp. 83–84, 87, 131–32, 136.

91. James Webb Young, *The Diary of an Ad Man* (Chicago, 1944), p. 156; "Minutes of Staff Meeting," Feb. 2, 1932, pp. 5–6, JWT Archives. See also *JWT News Letter*, Feb. 15, 1928, p. 83.

92. Goffman, *The Presentation of Self*, pp. 48, 112.

93. Ibid., pp. 112, 121, 170–71.

94. "Minutes of Creative Staff Meeting," Dec. 21, 1932, p. 9, JWT Archives.

95. Robert Koretz, interview with author, Aug. 1, 1980. See also Biow, *Butting In*, pp. 33–34, 185, 235. Biow quotes Lasker as reflecting, when he divested himself of his agency: "All the while I have allowed the client to think that I was the pupil and he was the teacher. All along I knew that I was the teacher and he was the pupil—and I just got sick of it."

96. For such jokes, see *Printers' Ink*, Sept. 9, 1926, p. 186; "Minutes of Representatives Meeting," Jan. 9, 1929, pp. 2–4, and "Minutes of Creative Staff Meeting," June 22, 1932, p. 3, JWT Archives; *Printers' Ink*, Dec. 8, 1927, p. 197; *Printers' Ink Monthly*, May 1928, p. 158; *JWT News Letter*, Mar. 1, 1928, pp. 90, 95; *Tide*, Aug. 1928, pp. 5–6; Jan. 1931, p. 9; Feb. 1931, p. 11; and *JWT News Bulletin*, May 27, 1922, pp. 8, 10. The "oldest profession" quip is attributed to Jerry W. Allen, a peripatetic ad man for large retail stores (personal communication).

97. *Printers' Ink Monthly*, Apr. 1932, p. 80. See also "Minutes of Creative Staff Meeting," June 22, 1932, p. 3, JWT Archives.

98. *Advertising and Selling*, Aug. 22, 1928, p. 21; *Printers' Ink*, Apr. 26, 1934, pp. 97–98; June 14, 1934, p. 52.

Three   Keeping the Audience in Focus

1. *JWT News Letter*, Jan. 15, 1928, p. 40, J. Walter Thompson Company (JWT) Archives, New York City.

2. Ibid., pp. 40–41.

3. *Printers' Ink*, Aug. 5, 1926, pp. 74–75; Dec. 8, 1927, p. 41; John Chapman, *Tell It to Sweeney: The Informal History of the New York "Daily News"* (Garden City, N.Y., 1961), pp. 133, 141–42.

4. *Printers' Ink*, Nov. 4, 1926, pp. 38–39; Dec. 2, 1926, pp. 54–55; Feb. 17, 1927, p. 13.

5. Mary Macfadden and Emile Gauvreau, *Dumbbells and Carrot Strips* (New York, 1953), pp. 218–19; George Gerbner, "The Social Role of the Confession Magazine," *Social Problems* 6 (1958): 29.

6. Macfadden and Gauvreau, *Dumbbells*, p. 223; *Chicago Tribune*, June 11, 1929, p. 13.

7. Macfadden and Gauvreau, *Dumbbells*, p. 223.

8. Ibid., pp. 222, 231; N. W. Ayer and Son, *American Newspaper Annual and Directory*, 1924 and 1927; Theodore Barnard Peterson, *Magazines in the Twentieth Century*, 2nd ed. (Urbana, Ill., 1964), p. 294. Later in the 1920s, while the *Ladies' Home Journal* was lowering its newsstand price to 10 cents, *True Story* brazenly raised its price to 25 cents.

9. *True Story*, Jan. 1926, pp. 64ff; *Chicago Tribune*, Feb. 9, 1926, p. 17.

10. Gerbner, "Social Role of the Confession Magazine," pp. 34–35, 37; *Chicago Tribune*, Feb. 9, 1926, p. 17.

11. *Printers' Ink*, Jan. 14, 1926, pp. 37–40; May 20, 1926, p. 35; Dec. 2, 1926, p. 37; June 23, 1927, pp. 54–55; July 7, 1927, pp. 62–63; June 14, 1928, pp. 38–39; Nov. 22, 1928, p. 55; *Chicago Tribune*, June 11, 1929, p. 13.

12. See, for example, the advertising in *True Story* for the issues of November 1925 and January 1926.

13. *Printers' Ink*, June 9, 1927, pp. 46–47; June 14, 1928, p. 40; May 2, 1929, pp. 46–47; *True Story*, Mar. 1928, passim.

14. "Minutes of Representatives Meeting," Sept. 8, 1927, pp. 5–6; Feb. 28, 1928, p. 4, JWT Archives.

15. *True Story*, Apr. 1928, p. 125; Feb. 1929, p. 95; Jan. 1930, p. 141; May 1930, p. 71; Mar. 1929, p. 113; *Chicago Tribune*, Sept. 20, 1931, part VI, p. 2; *Ladies' Home Journal*, July 1931, p. 90; *Good Housekeeping*, Mar. 1928, pp. 119, 126; *Tide*, June 1928, p. 4; *Delineator*, Aug. 1928, p. 79.

16. Frank Luther Mott, *American Journalism: A History: 1607–1960*, 3rd ed. (New York, 1962), pp. 666–69, 672; Simon Michael Bessie, *Jazz Journalism: The Story of the Tabloid Newspaper* (New York, 1938), pp. 143.

17. Bessie, *Jazz Journalism*, pp. 87, 94.

18. Ibid., pp. 100, 103; Chapman, *Tell It to Sweeney*, pp. 71–72, 81.

19. Mott, *American Journalism*, pp. 670–71; Bessie, *Jazz Journalism*, pp. 196–98; 201–202.

20. Bessie, *Jazz Journalism*, pp. 20, 25, 220; *Advertising and Selling*, Nov. 3, 1926, p. 29.

21. Chapman, *Tell It to Sweeney*, pp. 134–35.

22. *Advertising and Selling Fortnightly*, Mar. 24, 1926, p. 56; William G. Lownds, Edward D. Chenery, and George J. Wiltshire, comps., *Advertising and Selling Digest* (New York, 1926), p. 37.

23. *Printers' Ink*, Feb. 18, 1926, pp. 94–95; Dec. 8, 1927, pp. 74–75; *Chicago Tribune*, June 4, 1929, p. 25; *Advertising and Selling Fortnightly*, Mar. 24, 1926, p. 56; Chapman, *Tell It to Sweeney*, pp. 133, 140–44; *Printers' Ink Monthly*, Jan. 1927, p. 155; Mar. 1927, p. 163; Oct. 1927, p. 97.

24. *The American Weekly*, Mar. 28, 1926, passim.

25. *Chicago Tribune*, Jan. 17, 1928, p. 26; *Printers' Ink*, Oct. 18, 1928, pp. 106–7; *The American Weekly*, July 9, 1933, p. 33; *Advertising and Selling*, Feb. 14, 1935, p. 15.

26. *Printers' Ink*, May 14, 1925, p. 106; June 7, 1928, p. 101; June 12, 1930, pp. 142–43; "Minutes of Creative Staff Meeting," Dec. 7, 1932, pp. 9, 15–16; "Minutes of Representatives Meeting," Sept. 30, 1930, pp. 11–12; June 16, 1931, p. 8, JWT Archives.

27. "Minutes of Creative Staff Meeting," Dec. 7, 1932, p. 14; "Minutes of Representatives Meeting," May 5, 1931, pp. 6–9, JWT Archives; *Advertising Age*, June 6, 1938, p. 18.

28. *Printers' Ink*, July 17, 1930, p. 43; *Judicious Advertising*, July 1923, pp. 14–16.

29. *Printers' Ink*, Oct. 22, 1914, p. 58; Sept. 27, 1928, p. 79; *Ladies' Home Journal*, Sept. 1926, p. 94; Neil Harris, "The Drama of Consumer Desire," in *Yankee Enterprise: The Rise of the American System of Manufactures*, ed. Otto Mayr and Robert C. Post (Washington, D.C., 1981), p. 201; *Saturday Evening Post*, Nov. 9, 1929, p. 75; *Chicago Tribune*, Oct. 12, 1930, p. 19; "Minutes of Representatives Meeting," May 5, 1931, p. 5, JWT Archives; Walter Benjamin, "The Work of Art in the Age of Mechanical Reproduction," in Benjamin, *Illuminations*, trans. Harry Zohn (New York, 1968), pp. 228, 240.

30. André Bazin, *What is Cinema?*, trans. Hugh Gray (Berkeley, Calif., 1967), p. 166; Stanley Cavell, *The World Viewed: Reflections on the Ontology of Film*, enlarged ed. (Cambridge, Mass., 1979), pp. 202–205.

31. *Printers' Ink*, Nov. 4, 1926, pp. 38–39; Jan. 27, 1927, p. 61; Feb. 17, 1927, p. 13; Nov. 17, 1927, pp. 113–14; Dec. 22, 1927, pp. 69–72; *Advertising and Selling Fortnightly*, Apr. 7, 1926, p. 45; *Advertising and Selling*, Aug. 24, 1927, p. 18.

32. *Printers' Ink*, Jan. 29, 1925, p. 43; June 3, 1926, pp. 86–87; Nov. 25, 1926, pp. 102–103; *Advertising and Selling*, Feb. 9, 1927, p. 18; *Chicago Tribune*, June 12, 1929, p. 34; *Saturday Evening Post*, Feb. 6, 1926, p. 63.

33. *Advertising and Selling Fortnightly*, Apr. 21, 1926, pp. 74–75.

34. *Printers' Ink*, Nov. 12, 1931, p. 127; *Advertising and Selling Fortnightly*, Jan. 13, 1926, p. 6; Mar. 24, 1926, p. 5; *Advertising and Selling*, Jan. 29, 1931, p. 16; Mar. 1, 1934, p. 27; *Advertising Age*, May 18, 1936, p. 5; Mar. 7, 1938, p. 9.

35. *Advertising and Selling Fortnightly*, Feb. 10, 1926, p. 22; Mar. 10, 1926, pp. 86–87; "General Platform on Johnson and Johnson Baby Powder," pp. 11, 13, Case History

File, JWT Archives. The observations about the *Chicago Defender* and the *Pittsburgh Courier* are based on a survey of the issues of 1926 and 1927. During 1926 fewer than a dozen national advertisers purchased *any* ads in the *Chicago Defender*. Most of those that did appear were very small. Only Colgate Dental Cream prepared special "race copy"; except for face powders and hair dressings, the ads usually portrayed whites.

36. *Tide,* Aug. 1931, p. 31.

37. *Printers' Ink,* Nov. 4, 1926, pp. 38–39; Feb. 17, 1927, p. 13; Jan. 7, 1932, pp. 70–71; *Advertising and Selling Fortnightly,* Apr. 7, 1926, p. 45; *Advertising and Selling,* Dec. 12, 1928, p. 121.

38. *Advertising and Selling,* Aug. 24, 1927, p. 18; *Printers' Ink,* Nov. 25, 1926, pp. 102–103; May 20, 1926, pp. 146–47; *J. Walter Thompson News Bulletin,* May 1930, pp. 12–23; Edison Lamp Works of General Electric Company, *The Edison Blue Book* (Harrison, N. J., 1924), pp. 9–10.

39. Robert S. Lynd, "The People as Consumers," *Recent Social Trends in the United States,* 2 vols. (New York, 1933), 2: 896.

40. *Printers' Ink Monthly,* May 1930, pp. 39–40; "You really should see my morning mail," and "I hurried home from a weekend party" (proofs with schedules), Procter and Gamble Archives, Cincinnati. On identical copy for a range of class and mass publications, see also Scrapbooks 167, 195, 198, Lord and Thomas Archives, housed at Foote, Cone and Belding Communications, Inc., Chicago.

41. For examples of the use of this figure of speech, see *Advertising and Selling Fortnightly,* Apr. 21, 1926, pp. 58–59; *Printers' Ink,* May 6, 1926 p. 82; July 15, 1926, p. 1; May 31, 1928, pp. 30–31; Apr. 10, 1930, p. 129; *Advertising and Selling,* Nov. 28, 1928, p. 44; June 22, 1933, p. 16; George Batten Co., *News Letter,* Feb. 26, 1924, p. 3, Batten, Barton, Durstine and Osborn Archives, New York City.

42. *Printers' Ink,* Nov. 7, 1929, p. 133.

43. Batten, Barton, Durstine and Osborn, Inc. (BBDO), *News Letter,* Mar. 14, 1936, p. 8, BBDO Archives; *Printers' Ink,* June 12, 1930, p. 57; *Advertising and Selling,* May 16, 1928, p. 32; *Tide,* July 1932, p. 25; Dec. 1932, p. 31; Mar. 1936, p. 41.

44. BBDO, *News Letter,* Mar. 14, 1936, p. 8; *J. Walter Thompson News Bulletin,* Dec. 1924, pp. 18–21; "Minutes of Representatives Meeting," June 16, 1931, p. 6, JWT Archives; *Printers' Ink Monthly,* June 1932, p. 26; Christine Frederick, *Selling Mrs. Consumer* (New York, 1929), pp. 43–44; *Advertising and Selling,* Mar. 14, 1935, p. 9. On the tradition of women as fickle and emotional consumer mobs, see Rosalind H. Williams, *Dream Worlds: Mass Consumption in Late Nineteenth-Century France* (Berkeley, Calif., 1982), pp. 2, 258, 307; Neil Harris, "The Drama of Consumer Desire," pp. 193–94; Michael Barry Miller, *The Bon Marché: Bourgeois Culture and the Department Store, 1869–1920* (Princeton, 1981), pp. 177–78, 191–93, 203–205; Neil McKendrick, John Brewer, and J. H. Plumb, *The Birth of a Consumer Society: The Commercialization of Eighteenth-Century England* (London, 1982), pp. 11, 60.

45. *Printers' Ink,* May 31, 1934, p. 84. See also *Printers' Ink,* Nov. 19, 1931, p. 28; "Minutes of Representatives Meeting," May 5, 1931, p. 5, JWT Archives.

46. *Printers' Ink,* Aug. 11, 1927, p. 41; Oct. 20, 1932, p. 57; *Advertising and Selling,* May 13, 1931, p. 24; Sept. 13, 1934, p. 20; Feb. 14, 1935, p. 26; Aug. 29, 1935, p. 56; Aug. 15, 1935, p. 34; Frank Irving Fletcher, *Lucid Interval: Confessions of a Custodian of the Convictions of Others* (New York, 1938), p. 162; "Roxy" Rothafel, "Monday Evening Talks," May 5, 1930, p. 7, JWT Archives; Albert T. Poffenberger, *Psychology in Advertising* (Chicago, 1925), pp. 321–23; *Tide,* Feb. 1934, p. 5.

47. *Printers' Ink Monthly,* Feb. 1932, pp. 22–23; "Minutes of Representatives Meeting," June 4, 1930, p. 16; "Minutes of Staff Meeting," Aug. 25, 1931, p. 7; "Minutes of Creative Staff Meeting," Apr. 23, 1932, pp. 7, 12; *J. Walter Thompson News Bulletin,* Nov. 1930, p. 5, JWT Archives; *Printers' Ink,* Feb. 8, 1934, p. 108. For *Time*'s disavowal of tabloid appeal, see *Printers' Ink,* Dec. 23, 1926, pp. 82–83. Perhaps the

most judicious argument for the necessity of tabloid copy aimed at the "child mind" came from John Caples of BBDO, who pointed out that while many readers were smarter than a thirteen-year-old, they did not usually give an advertising message their "full attention or intelligence." He warned copywriters: "Your advertisement gets only a fraction of their intelligence. *And that intelligence is equal to the intelligence of a child" (Printers' Ink Monthly,* Aug. 1931, pp. 48, 66).

48. "Minutes of Representatives Meeting," Sept. 30, 1930, p. 12, JWT Archives.

49. *Printers' Ink,* Feb. 19, 1931, p. 90; "Minutes of Representatives Meeting," June 16, 1931, p. 8, JWT Archives.

50. *Advertising and Selling,* Mar. 15, 1934, p. 21; *Advertising Age,* Mar. 22, 1937, p. 50; George Gallup, "Newspaper Memorandum," Feb. 26, 1936, p. 4, Raymond Rubicam Copy Research Data, Young and Rubicam Archives, New York City; Kenneth M. Goode, *How to Turn People into Gold* (New York, 1929), p. 63.

51. *Printers' Ink,* Nov. 1, 1928, pp. 46–47; *Judicious Advertising,* Feb. 1925, p. 36; Barton, Durstine and Osborn, "Report on Field Study for American Radiator Company," in "Exhibits presented for the Harvard Advertising Awards," vol. 2, pp. 61–62, Harvard Award Archives, Baker Library; N. W. Ayer and Son, *In Behalf of Advertising* (Philadelphia, 1929), p. 170; *Printers' Ink,* Nov. 4, 1926, p. 97; July 28, 1927, p. 137; Oct. 20, 1932, p. 57.

52. Batten, Barton, Durstine and Osborn, Inc., *The Wedge* 29 (1929), no. 6, n.p.; *Printers' Ink Monthly,* Apr. 1926, p. 24; May 1928, pp. 33, 82; "Minutes of Staff Meeting," Sept. 1, 1931, pp. 1–2, JWT Archives; *Printers' Ink,* Apr. 21, 1932, p. 72; July 20, 1933, p. 79; *Advertising and Selling,* Dec. 14, 1927, p. 40.

53. *Advertising and Selling,* May 23, 1935, p. 37.

54. Ibid.; "Minutes of Creative Organization Staff Meeting," Mar. 5, 1932, p. 9, JWT Archives; James F. Newcomb Co., Inc., *Direct Reflections,* Feb. 1929, p. 28.

55. Quentin James Schultze, "Advertising, Science, and Professionalism" (Ph.D. diss., Univ. of Illinois at Urbana-Champaign, 1978), pp. 93–101; A. Michal McMahon, "An American Courtship: Psychologists and Advertising Theory in the Progressive Era," *American Studies* 13 (1972): 10–13; *Printers' Ink,* Jan. 27, 1927, pp. 178–79; *J.Walter Thompson News Bulletin,* Nov. 1930, p. 5; "Minutes of Staff Meeting," Aug. 25, 1931, p. 7; "Minutes, Monday Evening Meeting," Apr. 28, 1930, p. 20, JWT Archives. On the broader trend toward an interpretation of the mass public as irrational and incompetent to understand modern complexities, and on the rise of the term "attitudes" to characterize public notions that were not lucid or rationally developed, see Edward A. Purcell, Jr., *The Crisis of Democratic Theory: Scientific Naturalism and the Problem of Value* (Lexington, Ky., 1973), pp. 99, 106; and Donald Fleming, "Attitude: The History of a Concept," *Perspectives in American History* 1 (1967): 358–59.

56. N. W. Ayer and Son, Inc., *In Behalf of Advertising,* p. 86; *Printers' Ink,* Dec. 16, 1926, pp. 90–91; May 19, 1927, pp. 46–47; Mar. 15, 1928, p. 151; Sept. 6, 1938, p. 61; Lownds et al., comps., *Advertising and Selling Digest,* p. 15; *Tide,* June 1928, p. 5.

57. Carroll Rheinstrom, *Psyching the Ads: The Case Book of Advertising* (New York, 1929), p. 10; *Printers' Ink,* Oct. 9, 1930, p. 35; Gallup, "Newspaper Memorandum," p. 1; *Advertising and Selling,* May 12, 1932, p. 21.

58. *Printers' Ink,* Oct. 13, 1932, p. 47; "Minutes of Representatives Meeting," Sept. 8, 1927, pp. 5–6, JWT Archives. See also *Advertising and Selling Fortnightly,* Jan. 13, 1926, p. 52; Mar. 24, 1926, p. 28; *Printers' Ink,* Feb. 24, 1927, p. 82; Apr. 14, 1932, p. 115.

59. *Printers' Ink,* Mar. 12, 1931, pp. 54–55. See also *Printers' Ink,* Dec. 26, 1929, p. 137; Feb. 9, 1933, pp. 8–9; *Advertising and Selling,* July 18, 1935, p. 65.

60. *Printers' Ink,* Jan. 14, 1932, p. 6.

61. *Printers' Ink,* Apr. 18, 1929, p. 55; BBDO, *News Letter,* Mar. 14, 1936, p. 8; *Advertising and Selling,* May 23, 1935, p. 37; *JWT News Letter,* July 1, 1928, p. 1; George Batten Company, *News Letter,* Apr. 22, 1924, p. 8.

62. *Printers' Ink,* Jan. 27, 1927, pp. 178–79; *Printers' Ink Monthly,* May 1928, p. 82.

63. *Printers' Ink,* Oct. 31, 1935, pp. 42–43.

64. Theodore MacManus, *The Sword Arm of Business* (New York, 1927), p. 6; Bruce Barton to "Miss Mac," Jan. 14, 1937, Box 5, Bruce Barton Papers, Wisconsin State Historical Society; W. A. Swanberg, *Luce and His Empire* (New York, 1972), p. 143.

65. *Printers' Ink,* June 23, 1927, p. 89; Feb. 2, 1928, p. 123; Apr. 12, 1928, p. 105.

66. *Printers' Ink,* Aug. 26, 1926, p. 89.

67. Goode, *How to Turn People into Gold,* p. 33; Neil H. Borden, *Problems in Advertising* (New York, 1932), pp. 549–50; *Printers' Ink Monthly,* Mar. 1931, pp. 100, 103.

68. "1935 Advertising Campaign, Lydia E. Pinkham Medicine Co.," vol. 331, Lydia Estes Pinkham Medicine Company Papers, Arthur and Elizabeth Schlesinger Library, Radcliffe College; *Printers' Ink,* Feb. 19, 1931, pp. 90–91.

69. *Printers' Ink,* Jan. 5, 1928, pp. 60, 64, 72; Mar. 22, 1928, p. 113; July 16, 1931, p. 34; *Printers' Ink Monthly,* Jan. 1929, pp. 56, 58; Mar. 1931, pp. 37–38; *Advertising and Selling,* Nov. 12, 1930, p. 30; *Advertising Age,* Sept. 7, 1936, p. 2.

70. *J. Walter Thompson News Bulletin,* Dec. 1925, pp. 29–30; *Advertising and Selling,* May 23, 1935, p. 35.

71. *Judicious Advertising,* Mar. 1925, p. 58; *Philadelphia Record,* July 22, 1934, clipping B-29, box 1, folder 3, Advertising Women of New York Papers, Schlesinger Library; *Printers' Ink,* Mar. 29, 1928, p. 82; June 14, 1928, pp. 94–95; George Batten Co., *News Letter,* Nov. 23, 1925, p. 3. See also *Printers' Ink,* May 1, 1930, pp. 54–55; *Advertising and Selling,* July 25, 1928, p. 57; Nov. 12, 1930, p. 31.

72. *Printers' Ink Monthly,* June 1930, p. 38; *Printers' Ink,* Oct. 2, 1930, p. 75; "Minutes of Creative Staff Meeting," Nov. 2, 1932, p. 10, JWT Archives.

73. "A Promotion Plan for BBDO," typescript, 1933, pp. 8–9, BBDO Archives; *Printers' Ink,* June 23, 1932, pp. 46–47; Mar. 29, 1928, p. 82; June 14, 1928, pp. 94–95. For what is possibly an even earlier account of the same Exide Battery saga, see George Batten Co., *News Letter,* Nov. 23, 1925, p. 3.

74. *Printers' Ink,* July 7, 1927, p. 12; Aug. 11, 1927, p. 42; Jan. 26, 1928, p. 116; May 21, 1931, p. 116; Aug. 20, 1931, p. 118; Nov. 26, 1931, p. 108; Feb. 4, 1932, p. 3; Apr. 26, 1934, pp. 60–61; *Advertising and Selling,* Aug. 7, 1929, p. 18; Jan. 22, 1930, p. 31; May 25, 1933, p. 33; Nov. 8, 1934, p. 64.

75. *Printers' Ink,* Oct. 1, 1931, p. 133; "JWT Forum," January 7, 1936, p. 5, JWT Archives. The Ruthrauff and Ryan agency devised an ingenious technique for vicarious mingling. In its reception room it mounted two "striking composite photographs" of crowds at sporting events. An agency copy man, observed *Advertising Age,* could study these pictures and ask himself, "What is the common denominator?" (*Advertising Age,* May 26, 1934, p. 27).

76. *Advertising and Selling,* May 23, 1935, p. 35; *Printers' Ink,* Oct. 1, 1931, p. 133; July 7, 1932, p. 19; "Minutes of Representatives Meeting," Sept. 30, 1930, p. 11, JWT Archives.

77. "Minutes of Creative Staff Meeting," Apr. 23, 1932, pp. 1–10; "Minutes of Representatives Meeting," Sept. 8, 1927, pp. 5–6, JWT Archives; *Advertising and Selling,* Feb. 6, 1929, pp. 26, 78; *Printers' Ink,* May 16, 1929, p. 173.

78. *Printers' Ink,* Feb. 25, 1926, p. 42; Feb. 17, 1927, p. 28; Aug. 4, 1927, p. 99; July 19, 1928, p. 81; June 11, 1931, pp. 8–9; Henry C. Link, *The New Psychology of Selling and Advertising* (New York, 1932), p. 18; John Gunther, *Taken at the Flood: The Story of Albert D. Lasker* (New York, 1960), p. 206; Thomas L. Greer to Professor James A. Field, Oct. 26, 1921, and Greer to Professor Gilbert H. Tapley, Nov. 1, 1921, Research Department Correspondence, 1921–1925, JWT Archives; "Rural and Small Town Investigation, Putnam County, 1923" and "Rural and Small Town Investigation, Randolph County, Indiana, 1924," JWT Archives; "1925 Market Trends

Involving Squibb Products," E. R. Squibb and Sons Archives, Princeton, New Jersey. See also the research studies in "Exhibits presented for the Harvard Advertising Awards, Harvard Award Archives."

79. *Printers' Ink*, June 15, 1933, p. 4; Rheinstrom, *Psyching the Ads;* Harold J. Rudolph, *Four Million Inquiries from Magazine Advertising* (New York, 1936), pp. v, vi, 15, 23, 61, 73.

80. *JWT News Bulletin*, June 10, 1922, p. 8; Borden, *Problems in Advertising*, pp. 559, 561.

81. *Printers' Ink Monthly*, Jan. 1934, p. 62.

82. H. K. McCann Company, *McCann Practice: Copy Testing* (New York, 1930), p. 13; *Printers' Ink*, Jan. 14, 1932, pp. 97–98; *Advertising and Selling*, Sept. 3, 1930, p. 13.

83. *Advertising and Selling Fortnightly*, Mar. 24, 1926, p. 45; Apr. 7, 1926, p. 45; *Printers' Ink*, May 6, 1926, pp. 66–67; June 17, 1926, pp. 74–75.

84. *Chicago Tribune*, Nov. 16, 1926, p. 19; *Printers' Ink*, July 7, 1927, pp. 126–27.

85. *Tide*, Feb. 1934, p. 77.

86. According to contemporary studies, the Browns' electric refrigerator would have placed them among the top 13 percent of all Pittsburgh families and the top 15.5 percent of families in Appleton, Wisconsin. *Tide*, June 1931, pp. 27–28; *Printers' Ink*, May 28, 1931, p. 21; *Historical Statistics of the United States*, I, 301; Jeffrey L. Meikle, *Twentieth Century Limited: Industrial Design in America, 1925–1939* (Philadelphia, 1979), p. 8; Jesse F. Steiner, "Research Memorandum on Recreation in the Depression," *Social Science Research Council Bulletin*, no. 32 (1937), p. 46; George Horace Gallup, *The Gallup Poll: Public Opinion, 1935–1971*, 3 vols. (New York, 1972); 2: 936.

87. *Advertising and Selling*, Jan. 21, 1931, p. 22; *Printers' Ink*, Oct. 6, 1927, pp. 54–55.

88. *Printers' Ink*, Jan. 5, 1928, p. 33; Jan. 14, 1926, p. 194; Feb. 19, 1931, pp. 8–9; *Saturday Evening Post*, Oct. 13, 1928, p. 83.

89. BBDO, *The Wedge* 31 (1931), no. 12, n.p.; 32 (1932), no. 8, n.p.

90. *Saturday Evening Post*, Aug. 17, 1935, p. 25.

91. *Printers' Ink*, May 15, 1930, p. 10.

92. Frederick, *Selling Mrs. Consumer*, pp. 19, 98, 202, 206, 252–53.

93. Raymond A. Bauer, "The Communicator and the Audience, in *People, Society and Mass Communications*, ed. Lewis Anthony Dexter and David Manning White (New York, 1964), pp. 136–38; Ithiel De Sola Pool and Irwin Shulman, "Newsmen's Fantasies, Audiences, and Newswriting," *Public Opinion Quarterly* 23 (1959): 145–46, 157.

94. "Mr. Armistead's Memo," typescript, n.d., pp. 36–37, Box 30–61, N. W. Ayer and Son Archives, New York City; "A Promotion Plan for BBDO," typescript (1933), p. 5, BBDO Archives.

95. For an example of confessions of inability to isolate the specific causes of success or failure, see "Minutes of Creative Staff Meeting," June 8, 1932, p. 8, JWT Archives.

96. *Printers' Ink Monthly*, Mar. 1931, p. 100; James Rorty, "'Art' and the Ad Man," *The Nation*, Jan. 23, 1934, pp. 92–93.

97. "Minutes of Representatives Meeting," Nov. 19, 1929, pp. 9, 12, JWT Archives; Fletcher, *Lucid Interval*, pp. 158–59.

98. A broader discussion of the problematic nature of ads as historical documents appears in the Introduction.

99. Hugh Dalziel Duncan, *Symbols in Society* (New York, 1968), p. 83.

100. Duncan, *Symbols in Society*, p. 172.

101. Frederick, *Selling Mrs. Consumer*, p. 264. On consumers as ad writers' "gods," see "JWT Forum," Jan. 7, 1936, p. 10, JWT Archives.

102. *Printers' Ink*, May 14, 1925, p. 193; Nov. 4, 1926, pp. 142–43; Feb. 9, 1933, p. 8; May 31, 1934, p. 33; Aug. 30, 1934, p. 49; Dec. 20, 1934, p. 30; *Advertising and Selling*, Feb. 6, 1929, p. 48; *Printers' Ink Monthly*, Feb. 1925, p. 53.

103. "Minutes of Representatives Meeting," Jan. 16, 1929, p. 5; Apr. 3, 1929, p. 5; Sept. 30, 1930, p. 15; "Minutes of Creative Organization Staff Meeting," Mar. 5. 1932, pp. 9–10, JWT Archives; "Memorandum for Mr. W. J. O'Connor," Nov. 7, 1930, Box 1, John M. Shaw Papers, Wisconsin State Historical Society; G. Lynn Sumner, "Is the Advertising Dollar Decreasing in Effectiveness?" Association of National Advertisers, ed., *Report of Proceedings, 1926*, p. 2.

104. "Minutes of Staff Meeting," Oct. 20, 1931, p. 2, JWT Archives; *Printers' Ink*, Feb. 24, 1927, p. 60.

105. Fletcher, *Lucid Interval*, p. 157. Reprinted by permission of Harper and Row, Publishers, Inc.

106. *Printers' Ink*, Jan. 22, 1931, p. 58; Nov. 14, 1935, p. 72; "Minutes of Staff Meeting," Aug. 25, 1931, p. 6, JWT Archives.

107. Fletcher, *Lucid Interval*, p. 159.

108. Erving Goffman, *The Presentation of Self in Everyday Life* (New York, 1959), pp. 170–71.

109. Ibid., p. 214.

110. *Printers' Ink Monthly*, Feb. 1933, p. 71.

111. *Tide*, Nov. 1931, p. 25.

112. *Printers' Ink*, July 6, 1933, p. 4; *Advertising and Selling*, May 28, 1930, p. 29; June 30, 1926, p. 21; July 24, 1929, p. 40; Mar. 23, 1927, p. 40; *Printers' Ink*, Sept. 25, 1930, p. 72.

Four   Abandoning the Great Genteel Hope:
From Sponsored Radio to the Funny Papers

1. The characterization of radio as inherently intrusive is drawn from Raymond A. Bauer and Stephen A. Greyser, *Advertising in America: The Consumer View* (Boston, 1968), p. 239.

2. Roy Durstine, "We're On the Air," *Scribner's*, May 1928, p. 625; Robert Sklar, *Movie-Made America: A Cultural History of American Movies* (New York, 1975), pp. 4, 14–18, 30, 32.

3. David Potter, "The Historical Perspective," in *The Meaning of Commercial Television*, ed. Stanley T. Donner (Austin, Tex., 1967), p. 58; Carl Dreher, "How the Wasteland Began: The Early Days of Radio," *The Atlantic*, Feb. 1966, p. 57; Erik Barnouw, *A History of Broadcasting in the United States*, 3 vols. (New York, 1966), 1: 78; Sydney W. Head, *Broadcasting in America* (Boston, 1972), pp. 150–51.

4. *Printers' Ink*, Apr. 27, 1922, p. 201; Feb. 8, 1923, pp. 175–76; Feb. 22, 1923, p. 157; Mar. 1, 1923, pp. 103–104; *Advertising and Selling*, July 1922, pp. 22–23.

5. Head, *Broadcasting in America*, pp. 146–47; John W. Spalding, "1928: Radio Becomes a Mass Medium," *Journal of Broadcasting* 8 (1963–64):40.

6. *Printers' Ink*, May 6, 1926, pp. 137, 144; Sept. 16, 1926, pp. 167–68.

7. *Printers' Ink*, Mar. 25, 1926, p. 152; Apr. 1, 1926, pp. 136–39; Apr. 15, 1926, p. 92; Oct. 6, 1927, p. 25; Bernard Lichtenberg, *Advertising Campaigns* (New York, 1926), p. 141; N. W. Ayer and Son, "What About Radio?" typescript of booklet [May, 1931], pp. 7, 44, Box 30–61, N. W. Ayer and Son Archives, New York City; *Advertising and Selling Digest* (New York, 1926), pp. 23, 25; *Advertising and Selling*, Dec. 15, 1926, p. 19; *JWT News Letter* Apr. 24, 1924, p. 3, J. Walter Thompson Company Archives, New York City.

8. Stuart D. Brandes, *American Welfare Capitalism, 1880–1940* (Chicago, 1976), pp. 8, 31, 93; David Brody, "The Rise and Decline of Welfare Capitalism," in *Change and*

Continuity in Twentieth Century America: The 1920s, ed. John Braeman, Robert H. Bremner, and David Brody (Columbus, Ohio, 1968), pp. 150–52; Morrell Heald, *The Social Responsibilities of Business: Company and Community, 1900–1960* (Cleveland, 1970), pp. 40, 46, 61; Kim McQuaid, "Corporate Liberalism in the American Business Community," *Business History Review* 52 (1978): 345–46; Dreher, "How the Wasteland Began," p. 57.

9. *Saturday Evening Post,* Jan. 26, 1924, p. 61. See also *Saturday Evening Post,* Sept. 8, 1923, p. 83. On the high expectations of Americans in the early 1920s for radio as an agent of education and cultural uplift, see Clayton R. Koppes, "The Social Destiny of the Radio: Hope and Disillusionment in the 1920s," *South Atlantic Quarterly* 68 (1969): 364–68.

10. *Advertising and Selling,* June 16, 1926, p. 29.

11. *Judicious Advertising,* Mar. 1925, p. 73. See also *Advertising and Selling,* Feb. 8, 1928, p. 59; Ed Roberts, "BBDO Short History," 1925 entry, typescript, Batten, Barton, Durstine and Osborn Archives, New York City; BBDO, *News Letter,* Oct. 9, 1931, p. 11; Ayer, "What About Radio?" p. 75; Frank Atkinson Arnold, "Reminiscences," p. 58, Oral History Research Office, Radio Unit, Columbia University.

12. George W. Batten Co., *News Letter,* Mar. 17, 1925, p. 3, BBDO Archives.

13. *American Magazine,* Nov. 1926, p. 107; Dec. 1926, p. 105; *Saturday Evening Post,* Nov. 13, 1926, pp. 160–61; Feb. 9, 1929, p. 80; July 26, 1930, p. 71; *San Francisco Examiner,* Nov. 6, 1929, p. 8. An advertising manager described how the proper facial expression for such a radio or phonograph ad might inadvertently be achieved. While waiting for a male model to assemble his evening clothes, he related, one young woman posing for the ad had fallen asleep. The resulting picture had been particularly effective, as the woman "certainly did appear to be enchanted by the music"(*Printers' Ink Monthly,* Feb. 1927, p. 89).

14. *Printers' Ink,* Mar. 12, 1925, p. 76; Mar. 25, 1926, p. 152; May 29, 1930, p. 66; Oct. 6, 1927, pp. 25 26; Herman S. Hettinger, *A Decade of Radio Advertising* (Chicago, 1933), p. 131; Association of National Advertisers, *Report of Proceedings, 1927,* p. 8.

15. *Printers' Ink,* Apr. 2, 1925, pp. 113–15, 120; Apr. 1, 1926, pp. 136–39; May 6, 1926, p. 137; Sept. 29, 1927, p. 20; Howard Williams Dickinson, *Crying Our Wares* (New York, 1929), pp. 229–30, 238–39.

16. On secondary audiences, see Chapter 3.

17. Hettinger, *A Decade of Radio Advertising,* p. 219, Spalding, "1928," pp. 36–37, 40; *Printers' Ink,* Apr. 1, 1926, pp. 133–36; May 6, 1926, pp. 137, 144; July 21, 1927, p. 42; Sept. 29, 1927, p. 20; *Printers' Ink Monthly,* Feb. 1931, p. 40.

18. *Printers' Ink,* Nov. 3, 1927, p. 165; *JWT News Letter,* May 15, 1928, p. 175; *Advertising and Selling,* Feb. 9, 1927, p. 72; Durstine, "We're on the Air," p. 631.

19. "Minutes of Staff Meeting," Feb. 2, 1932, pp. 2, 4, JWT Archives.

20. Arnold, "Reminiscences," pp. 8, 17, 66; Spalding, "1928," pp. 32–33; *JWT News Letter,* Feb. 15, 1928, p. 83; Frank Allen Burt, *American Advertising Agencies* (New York, 1940), p. 18; Dickinson, *Crying Our Wares,* pp. 215, 217–18, 227.

21. *Printers' Ink,* Feb. 5, 1925, pp. 151–52; June 24, 1926, p. 18; *Advertising and Selling,* Feb. 9, 1927, p. 23; Dickinson, *Crying Our Wares,* pp. 234–37. See also Hadley Cantril and Gordon W. Allport, *The Psychology of Radio* (New York, 1935), pp. 96, 260.

22. Daniel J. Czitrom, *Media and the American Mind: From Morse to McLuhan* (Chapel Hill, N.C., 1982), p. 77.

23. *JWT News Letter,* Apr. 24, 1924, p.3; *Printers' Ink,* Aug. 18, 1927, p. 28; June 6, 1929, p. 121.

24. *JWT News Letter,* Nov. 15, 1923, p. 10.

25. Spalding, "1928," pp. 38, 41; *Advertising and Selling,* July 29, 1929, p. 36; Hettinger, *A Decade of Radio Advertising,* pp. 262–63.

26. "The Technique of Commercial Announcements in Radio Commercials," Advertising Case Study 499, p. 2, reel 12, Harvard Business School (HBS) Archives.

27. James Gray, *Business Without Boundary: The Story of General Mills* (Minneapolis, 1954), p. 160; "The Technique of Commercial Announcements," p. 3.

28. *Printers' Ink,* Feb. 5, 1925, pp. 1, 163, 166–67; Apr. 2, 1925, pp. 113, 120; Aug. 6, 1925, pp. 125–26

29. *Advertising and Selling Fortnightly,* Jan. 13, 1926, p. 22; *Advertising and Selling,* July 14, 1926, p. 21; Nov. 3, 1926, p. 32; Nov. 17, 1926, p. 72; Apr. 6, 1927, p. 82; *Saturday Evening Post,* May 7, 1927, p. 177; Bernard Lichtenberg, *Advertising Campaigns* (New York, 1926), pp. 318–320.

30. Jeffrey L. Meikle, *Twentieth Century Limited: Industrial Design in America, 1925–1939* (Philadelphia, 1979), pp. 12–14.

31. Lichtenberg, *Advertising Campaigns,* p. 321; *Advertising and Selling Digest* (1926), p. 98; "New England Gas Association," Advertising Case Study 301, p. 9, reel 11, HBS Archives; Batten, Barton, Durstine and Osborn, Inc., *The Wedge* 29 (1929), no. 4, n.p.; *Printers' Ink,* Jan. 13, 1927, pp. 78–79.

32. *Advertising and Selling,* Nov. 3, 1926, p. 32; Nov. 17, 1926, p. 72; Apr. 6, 1927, p. 82; Sept. 19, 1928, p. 28; Lichtenberg, *Advertising Campaigns,* pp. 319–20; *Judicious Advertising,* Apr. 1925, p. 103.

33. *Printers' Ink,* Nov. 24, 1927, p. 65.

34. *Advertising and Selling Digest,* p. 99.

35. Albert Davis Lasker, "The Reminiscences of Albert Davis Lasker," pp. 100, 102, 107, Oral History Research Office, Columbia University; *Advertising Age,* Apr. 30, 1930, p. 144; *Los Angeles Times,* Oct. 17, 1927, p. 4; Oct. 25, 1927, p. 4.

36. *Advertising and Selling,* Apr. 17, 1929, p. 27.

37. Lasker, "Reminiscences," pp. 107–110; Scrapbooks 8 and 9 (American Tobacco Co.), Lord and Thomas Archives, housed at Foote, Cone and Belding Communications, Inc., Chicago; *Los Angeles Times,* Oct. 31, 1927, p. 4.

38. *Advertising and Selling,* Feb. 23, 1927, p. 29.

39. *Printers' Ink,* Aug. 26, 1926, p. 197; *Advertising and Selling,* Nov. 2, 1927, p. 66; "JWT Forum," Feb. 4, 1936, p. 6, JWT Archives; *Tide,* Nov.-Dec. 1927, p. 5.

40. *Tide,* Aug. 1932, p. 13. For P. T. Barnum's effective use of controversy as an advertising tool, see Neil Harris, *Humbug* (Boston, 1973), pp. 23–25, 65–67.

41. Scrapbook 8 (American Tobacco Co.), Lord and Thomas Archives; *Printers' Ink,* Aug. 23, 1938, pp. 62–63; Dec. 20, 1928, p. 36; Otis A. Pease, *The Responsibilities of American Advertising* (New Haven, Conn., 1958), p. 62.

42. James F. Newcomb and Co., Inc., *Direct Reflections,* Jan. 1929, p. 31; *Printers' Ink,* Nov. 25, 1928, pp. 10, 12; Susan Wagner, *Cigarette Country: Tobacco in American History and Politics* (New York, 1971), pp. 58–60; *Saturday Evening Post,* Jan. 19, 1929, p. 97; Feb. 16, 1929, p. 140; Oct. 27, 1928, p. 108.

43. *Tide,* Jan. 1929, pp. 1–2; Scrapbook 9 (American Tobacco Co.), Lord and Thomas Archives.

44. Scrapbook 9 (American Tobacco Co.), Lord and Thomas Archives. A footnote on the ad identified the "one of our men" as Boatswain's Mate Aloys A. Wilson.

45. Ibid.

46. *Advertising and Selling,* Feb. 20, 1929, p. 29; Mar. 6, 1929, pp. 29, 37; Apr. 17, 1929, p. 17; *Tide,* Mar. 1929, p. 1; Pease, *Responsibilities,* pp. 51–52. George Thornley to Ralph M. Hower, Jan. 18, 1937, case no. 2, Hower Papers, Baker Library, Harvard Business School.

47. *Advertising and Selling,* Feb. 19, 1930, pp. 23–24; Scrapbook 6 (American Tobacco Co.), Lord and Thomas Archives; *Los Angeles Times,* Aug. 6, 1930, part II, p. 10; *San Francisco Examiner,* Jan. 27, 1930, p. 14; Jan. 13, 1930, p. 16; Jan. 20, 1930, p. 20.

48. Scrapbooks 8 and 9 (American Tobacco Co.), Lord and Thomas Archives; *True Story,* Feb. 1930, fourth cover; *San Francisco Examiner,* Jan. 7, 1930, p. 12; Jan. 21, 1930, p. 14; *Printers' Ink,* Apr. 10, 1930, pp 94–95.

49. *Advertising and Selling,* Mar. 6, 1929, p. 24; Mar. 9, 1927, p. 24; *Printers' Ink,* Jan. 12, 1928, pp. 3–4, 182; *Advertising and Selling,* Mar. 6, 1929, p. 37; Dec. 25, 1929, p. 29; Feb. 5, 1930, p. 29.

50. *Tide,* July 1930, p. 4; *Printers' Ink,* Mar. 30, 1933, p. 51; Sept. 15, 1932, p. 82; June 5, 1930, p. 76; *Advertising and Selling,* Aug. 20, 1930, p. 54; Henry C. Link, *The New Psychology of Selling and Advertising* (New York, 1932), p. 23.

51. *Chicago Tribune,* Feb. 28, 1926, magazine section, p. 6; *True Story,* Apr. 1928, p. 77; *Colliers',* Apr. 21, 1928, p. 37; *Saturday Evening Post,* May 12, 1928, p. 148; Feb. 15, 1930, p. 124; Jan. 10, 1931, p. 111; Apr. 19, 1930, p. 180; Sept. 13, 1930, p. 167; "Minutes of Representatives Meeting," May 21, 1930, pp. 3, 8, JWT Archives; *Ladies' Home Journal,* May 1931, p. 88.

52. *Printers' Ink,* May 2, 1929, p. 46; *Printers' Ink Monthly,* Mar. 1926, pp. 28, 42; *Judicious Advertising,* Feb. 1925, p. 33; *Chicago Tribune,* Feb. 19, 1926, p. 23; *Saturday Evening Post,* Mar. 9, 1929, p. 123; Apr. 26, 1930, p. 144; Sept. 15, 1930, p. 66; July 21, 1928, p. 1; Oct. 4, 1930, p. 83; July 20, 1929, p. 34; July 27, 1929, first cover; June 7, 1930, first cover; *American Weekly,* Mar. 7, 1926, p. 16; *Chicago Tribune,* Nov. 14, 1926, pt. 1, p. 5, pt. 2, p. 7.

53. *JWT News Letter,* Apr. 1, 1926, pp. 86–87; *Judicious Advertising,* Apr. 1925, p. 108.

54. Bauer and Greyser, *Advertising in America,* p. 239.

55. Cantril and Allport, *The Psychology of Radio,* p. 247. For a review of various techniques of "interwoven" and "interspersed" commercials, see *Printers' Ink,* Apr. 24, 1930, pp. 65–73.

56. *Printers' Ink,* Apr. 24, 1930, p. 73; May 29, 1930, p. 73; "Minutes of Representatives Meeting," Apr. 3, 1929, p. 2, JWT Archives. See also *Advertising and Selling,* June 9, 1929, p. 26.

57. "Minutes of Representatives Meeting," Feb. 16, 1928, pp. 10–11, JWT Archives.

58. "Minutes of Creative Staff Meeting," June 22, 1932, pp. 8–10; "Minutes of Representatives Meeting," Apr. 3, 1929, p. 7, JWT Archives; *Tide,* May 1929, p. 3; *Printers' Ink,* Apr. 24, 1930, p. 76.

59. "Minutes of Representatives Meeting," Aug. 6, 1929, p. 12, JWT Archives.

60. *Printers' Ink,* June 6, 1929, p. 114; "Minutes of Representatives Meeting," July 11, 1928, p. 3, JWT Archives; Roberts, "BBDO Short History," n.p. (Radio 3–4). On specific agencies, see also *Printers' Ink,* May 3, 1928, pp. 38–39; Apr. 17, 1930, pp. 66–67; June 5, 1930, pp. 78–79; *Advertising and Selling,* Oct. 28, 1931, p. 48.

61. Spalding, "1928," p. 33; *Printers' Ink,* May 23, 1929, pp. 82–83.

62. Durstine, "We're On the Air," p. 627; *Printers' Ink,* June 6, 1929, p. 121.

63. *Advertising and Selling,* July 24, 1929, p. 36; Aug. 7, 1929, p. 3; Oct. 30, 1929, p. 29; *Printers' Ink,* May 23, 1929, p. 142; June 13, 1929, pp. 179–180; *Fortune,* Sept. 1932, p. 37.

64. *Advertising Age,* Apr. 30, 1930, p. 158; Frank N. Stanton, "Psychological Research in the Field of Radio Listening," in *American Broadcasting: A Source Book on the History of Radio and Television,* ed. Lawrence W. Lichty and Malachi C. Topping (New York, 1975), pp. 429–30, 488; *Tide,* July 1930, p. 4; "The Technique of Commercial Announcements," p. 11; Hettinger, *A Decade of Radio Advertising,* pp. 222, 226–27, 230; *Printers' Ink,* Feb. 12, 1931, p. 85; *Fortune,* Sept. 1932, pp. 37, 39, 40–41; Ayer, "What About Radio?" p. 67; Dreher, "How the Wasteland Began," p. 58.

65. *Printers' Ink,* May 14, 1931, p. 68; Hettinger, *A Decade of Radio Advertising,* pp. 52, 113; *Advertising Age,* Apr. 20, 1932, p. 10; "Minutes of Representatives Meeting," Sept. 30,

1930, p. 14; Apr. 3, 1929, p. 5; Jan. 31, 1931, p. 13, JWT Archives; *Advertising and Selling,* Nov. 26, 1930, pp. 17–18.

66. *Tide,* Dec. 1931, p. 6; *Printers' Ink,* Apr. 9, 1931, p. 90; *Advertising and Selling,* May 26, 1932, p. 48.

67. *Printers' Ink,* Nov. 19, 1931, p. 12; Leo Lowenthal, "Biographies in Popular Magazines," in *Radio Research, 1942–1943,* ed. Paul Lazarsfeld and Frank M. Stanton (New York, 1979 [c. 1944]), p. 544; Stanton, "Psychological Research," p. 488; Durstine, "We're On the Air," p. 631.

68. Hettinger, *A Decade of Radio Advertising,* pp. 36, 265, 268, 312; Arnold, "Reminiscences," pp. 38–39; "The Technique of Commerical Announcements," pp. 7–8; Cantril and Allport, *The Psychology of Radio,* pp. 97, 247, 259; Durstine, "We're On the Air," p. 631. See also BBDO, *News Letter,* Oct. 16, 1931, p. 4.

69. "The Technique of Commercial Announcements," p. 9. For an example of the culmination of the folksy approach and the interweaving of the commercial with the program, see Advertising Case Study 519 (Morro Tobacco Co.), pp. 11–13, reel 12, HBS Archives.

70. Hettinger, *A Decade of Radio Advertising,* pp. 221–22, 256.

71. "Minutes of Creative Staff Meeting," Dec. 21, 1932, p. 5, JWT Archives; BBDO, "A Promotion Plan for BBDO," p. 19, typescript, 1933, BBDO Archives; *Printers' Ink,* Nov. 10, 1932, p. 56; *Advertising Age,* June 7, 1937, p. 16.

72. *Tide,* Oct. 1931, p. 10; Nov. 1932, p. 16; Sydney Hyman, *The Lives of William Benton* (Chicago, 1969), p. 143; "The Technique of Commercial Announcements," pp. 10, 13–15, 17–18; *Advertising and Selling,* June 9, 1932, pp. 24, 26; *Printers' Ink,* June 30, 1932, p. 46. Young and Rubicam prided itself on producing "the first show on the air in which the commercials were so much a part of the program that they couldn't be removed and preserve continuity" ("Some Notes on Y and R," typescript, p. 26, Young and Rubicam Archives, New York City).

73. Young and Rubicam, Inc., "Standard Practice, 1936," bound typescript, p. 93, Young and Rubicam Archives; Ayer, "What About Radio?" pp. 32, 38; *Printers' Ink,* Feb. 12, 1931, p. 85.

74. Hettinger, *A Decade of Radio Advertising,* p. 5; *Printers' Ink,* Sept. 14, 1933, p. 53; "The Radio Honeymoon is Over," Scrapbook 382, Lord and Thomas Archives; *Printers' Ink Monthly,* Mar. 1934, p. 55.

75. "Minutes of Representatives Meeting," July 8, 1930, pp. 3–4; "Minutes of Creative Staff Meeting," Dec. 21, 1932, pp. 4–5, JWT Archives.

76. (Philip Morris and Co.) "Advertising Case Study 527", pp. 21–22, reel 12, HBS Archives; *Fortune,* Sept. 1932, p. 37; Milton H. Biow, *Butting In; An Adman Speaks Out* (Garden City, N.Y., 1964), pp. 148–50.

77. George Gallup, "The Reminiscences of George Gallup," p. 44, Oral History Research Office, Columbia University, copyright 1976 by the Trustees of Columbia University in the City of New York; "Minutes of Staff Meeting," June 16, 1931, pp. 4–6; "Minutes of Creative Organization Staff Meeting," Mar. 12, 1932, p. 1, JWT Archives; Pease, *The Responsibilities of American Advertising,* p. 195.

78. *Advertising and Selling,* Sept. 27, 1927, p. 57; July 9, 1930, p. 26; *Advertising Age,* July 8, 1933, p. 2; *Printers' Ink Monthly,* Apr. 1926, p. 23; *Tide,* July 1930, p. 3; *Chicago Tribune,* June 14, 1929, p. 40; June 18, 1929, p. 26; Oct. 19, 1930, part 6, p. 2; *American Weekly,* Jan. 10, 1930, p. 19.

79. "Minutes of Representatives Meeting," Mar. 3, 1931, pp. 7–8, JWT Archives; *Printers' Ink,* July 14, 1932, pp. 19, 21; July 27, 1933, pp. 52–53; *Advertising Age,* Sept. 30, 1933, p. 3.

80. *Printers' Ink,* July 19, 1934, p. 40; "Minutes of Creative Organization Staff Meeting," Mar. 12, 1932, pp. 2–3, JWT Archives; *Tide,* June 1932, p. 14.

81. *Printers' Ink,* Sept. 22, 1932, pp. 38–39; July 19, 1934, pp. 40–41; *Printers' Ink Monthly,* June 1932, p. 40; BBDO, *News Letter,* Dec. 24, 1931, p. 11; *Chicago Tribune,* Mar. 13, 1932, pt. 8, p. 2.

82. *Printers' Ink,* Apr. 28, 1932, p. 6; "Minutes of Creative Organization Staff Meeting," Mar. 12, 1932, p. 4, JWT Archives. See also Pease, *Responsibilities of American Advertising,* p. 186. For examples of increasing experiments in introducing eavesdropping into other print media, see *Saturday Evening Post,* Oct. 17, 1936, p. 45; Nov. 7, 1936, pp. 1, 64.

83. "Minutes of Creative Organization Staff Meeting," Mar. 12, 1932, p. 6, JWT Archives.

84. BBDO, *Newsletter,* May 22, 1931, n.p.; *Advertising and Selling,* Feb. 3, 1932, p. 23; "Minutes of Creative Organization Staff Meeting," Oct. 11, 1932, p. 23, JWT Archives; "The Funny Paper Advts," *Fortune,* Apr. 1933, p. 98.

85. *Advertising Age,* Sept. 17, 1932, p. 12; *Advertising and Selling,* May 12, 1932, p. 19.

86. *Printers' Ink,* Aug. 4, 1932, pp. 41–43; *Advertising Age,* Oct. 21, 1933, p. 30; "Minutes of Creative Organization Staff Meeting," Oct. 5, 1932, p. 4, JWT Archives. For an example of the prevalence of comic-strip, cartoon, and sequence ads in the mass-circulation magazines, see *Saturday Evening Post,* Feb. 9, 1935, pp. 33, 35, 36, 37, 39, 42, 45, 48, 64, 73, 74.

87. *Printers' Ink,* Aug. 4, 1932, pp. 42–43; *Advertising Age,* Dec. 20, 1933, p. 11; *Printers' Ink Monthly,* Nov. 1931, p. 40.

88. *Printers' Ink Monthly,* July 1933, p. 49.

89. *Printers' Ink,* Apr. 28, 1932, p. 6; July 14, 1932, pp. 17, 19.

90. Quoted in Potter, "The Historical Perspective," pp. 60–61.

91. *Advertising Age,* Jan. 25, 1937, p. 44; see also the issue of Oct. 19, 1936, p. 1.

92. The phrase *inferred intimacy* is used to refer to a similar quality of television in Kurt Lang and Gladys Engel Lang, *Politics and Television* (Chicago, 1968), p. 205.

Five   The Consumption Ethic: Strategies of Art and Style

1. Arthur W. Page, "Public Relations," AT&T General Operating Conference, May 1928, p. 3, vol. 5, Arthur Page Papers, Wisconsin State Historical Society (WSHS); Arthur W. Page, "Public Relations and Sales," AT&T General Commercial Conference, June 1928, p. 8, in A. W. Page, "Talks and Papers," Box 2034, American Telephone and Telegraph Company Archives, New York City.

2. "General Publicity Conference, 1928," pp. 96, 101–102, Box 1310, AT&T Archives; Arthur Page, "Coordination of Sales and Advertising Activities," AT&T General Sales Conference, Jan.-Feb. 1929, p. 5, vol. 5, Arthur Page Papers, WSHS.

3. Page, "Public Relations," p. 3.

4. Ibid.

5. Page, "Public Relations and Sales," p. 5.

6. Ibid.; Page, "Coordination of Sales and Advertising Activities," p. 5.

7. American Telephone and Telegraph Company, "Conference Notes and Prepared Papers," General Publicity Conference, 1929, pp. 39–41, Box 1310, AT & T Archives; T. T. Cook, "Advertising of the American Telephone and Telegraph Company," p. 60, General Publicity Conference, 1928, Box 1310, AT&T Archives.

8. John M. Shaw, "Memorandum for Mr. W. J. O'Connor," Nov. 7, 1930, Box 1, John M. Shaw Papers, WSHS; John Brooks, *Telephone: The First Hundred Years* (New York, 1975), p. 265.

9. Brooks, *Telephone,* p. 173; Page, "Coordination of Sales and Advertising Activities," p. 5; Cook, "Advertising," p. 60; *Better Homes and Gardens,* Aug. 1929, p. 9; Oct. 1929, p. 9; Apr. 1930, p. 9; Oct. 1930, p. 9; *Ladies' Home Journal,* Nov. 1928, p. 230.

10. Page, "Coordination of Sales and Advertising Activities," p. 5; AT&T, "Conference Notes and Prepared Papers," p. 41.

11. Anne Hollander, *Seeing Through Clothes* (New York, 1978), pp. 350, 355, 357, 450.

12. *Advertising and Selling*, Dec. 12, 1928, p. 29; *Printers' Ink*, May 31, 1928, p. 17; Dec. 31, 1931, p. 17. See also Christine Frederick, *Selling Mrs. Consumer* (New York, 1929), pp. 52, 358, and Robert Lynd, "The People as Consumers," in President's Research Committee on Social Trends, *Recent Social Trends in the United States*, 2 vols. (New York, 1933), 2: 878.

13. *Advertising and Selling*, Oct. 1, 1930, p. 30; Feb. 6, 1929, pp. 18, 52; *Printers' Ink*, Apr. 5, 1928, p. 6; *Saturday Evening Post*, Feb. 9, 1924, passim. Eventually advertising experts even convinced a few manufacturers to introduce color solely for the purpose of giving the advertising agency an element of "news" or product distinctiveness to depict. This was the case with Sunoco "blue" gasoline in 1928 and Gillette Blue Blades in the early 1930s *(Printers' Ink*, Apr. 19, 1928, p. 145; Russell B. Adams, Jr., *King C. Gillette* [Boston, 1978], p. 173).

14. *Printers' Ink*, Apr. 21, 1927, pp. 7, 202, 205–206; July 7, 1927, p. 87; Jeffrey L. Meikle, *Twentieth Century Limited: Industrial Design in America, 1925–1939* (Philadelphia, 1979), p. 12; *Good Housekeeping*, Feb. 1925, p. 48; Apr. 1925, p. 167; *JWT News Letter*, No. 34, July 3, 1924, p. 10, J. Walter Thompson Company (JWT) Archives, New York City; George Batten Company, *News Letter*, June 24, 1924, p. 2, Batten, Barton, Durstine and Osborn (BBDO) Archives, New York City; *Saturday Evening Post*, Jan. 13, 1923, p. 100.

15. Albert T. Poffenberger, *Psychology in Advertising* (Chicago, 1925), pp. 260–70, 428–43; *Printers' Ink*, Sept. 15, 1927, p. 150.

16. *Printers' Ink Monthly*, Aug. 1928, p. 29; *Printers' Ink*, Feb. 17, 1927, p. 196.

17. *Printers' Ink Monthly*, Aug. 1928, pp. 30, 86; Meikle, *Twentieth Century Limited*, p. 17; *Printers' Ink*, Feb. 17, 1927, p. 196; *Ladies' Home Journal*, Jan. 1928, p. 128; *Good Housekeeping*, Feb. 1927, p. 225.

18. *Printers' Ink Monthly*, Aug. 1928, p. 86.

19. Bernice Fitzgibbon, *Macy's, Gimbels and Me* (New York, 1967), p. 314.

20. *Printers' Ink*, June 17, 1926, p. 106; Apr. 21, 1927, p. 7; *Better Homes and Gardens*, Nov. 1929, p. 72; *Good Housekeeping*, Sept. 1927, p. 190; *Saturday Evening Post*, May 19, 1928, p. 162; Apr. 25, 1931, p. 146; *Ladies' Home Journal*, Apr. 1931, p. 142; Earnest Elmo Calkins, *Business the Civilizer* (Boston, 1928), p. 255.

21. *Printers' Ink*, Apr. 21, 1927, p. 206; *Saturday Evening Post*, Mar. 22, 1930, p. 135; *Good Housekeeping*, Apr. 1927, p. 117; Jan. 1929, p. 172; Apr. 1929, p. 228; *Ladies' Home Journal*, Sept. 1929, p. 197.

22. *Saturday Evening Post*, May 19, 1928, p. 162; Feb. 16, 1929, p. 152; Kenneth Macgowan, *Behind the Screen: The History and Techniques of the Motion Picture* (New York, 1965), pp. 261–62.

23. *Printers' Ink Monthly*, Aug. 1928, p. 86; *Printers' Ink*, Apr. 21, 1927, p. 7. The Henri, Hurst, and McDonald booklet is quoted in a *Delineator* advertisement in *Printers' Ink*, July 28, 1927, pp. 30–31.

24. *Advertising and Selling*, May 2, 1928, pp. 66–67; *JWT News Letter*, July 1, 1927, p. 316; *Saturday Evening Post*, Nov. 10, 1928, pp. 124–25.

25. *Printers' Ink*, Jan. 12, 1928, p. 10; *Saturday Evening Post*, May 19, 1928, pp. 126–27; Sept. 20, 1930, pp. 98–99; *San Francisco Examiner*, Nov. 7, 1929, p. 4; *Printers' Ink*, Aug. 2, 1928, p. 93; *Good Housekeeping*, Feb. 1928, p. 229; *Ladies' Home Journal*, Oct. 1929, pp. 248–49; *Better Homes and Gardens*, Mar. 1928, fourth cover.

26. "Pepperell Manufacturing Company," Advertising Case Study 239, reel 11, Harvard Business School (HBS) Archives; *Printers' Ink Monthly*, May 1929, p. 78. Pequot quickly advertised sheets in such colors as "peach" as essential for bedroom harmony

(*Ladies' Home Journal*, Nov. 1928, p. 204). For the appropriation of this idea a year later by the conservative mail-order house of Montgomery Ward and Co., see Scrapbook 232, Lord and Thomas Archives, at Foote, Cone and Belding Communications, Inc., Chicago.

27. *Printers' Ink*, Apr. 16, 1931, p. 155. See also *Ladies' Home Journal*, July 1929, p. 32.

28. Meikle, *Twentieth Century Limited*, pp. 43, 73; *Tide*, Feb. 1931, p. 24; Apr. 1931, p. 13.

29. *Printers' Ink*, Dec. 17, 1931, pp. 97–98; Feb. 10, 1927, p. 144.

30. Meikle, *Twentieth Century Limited*, p. 12; *Saturday Evening Post*, May 23, 1925, p. 88; Apr. 17, 1926, pp. 58–59; May 1, 1926, p. 64; *Printers' Ink Monthly*, Dec. 1929, p. 44.

31. *Saturday Evening Post*, Jan. 5, 1929, p. 55; Jan. 26, 1929, pp. 40–41; Mar. 23, 1929, p. 54; Sept. 20, 1930, p. 45.

32. *Saturday Evening Post*, Dec. 6, 1928, p. 118; July 21, 1928, p. 116; *Printers' Ink*, Dec. 6, 1928, p. 18.

33. "Minutes of Representatives Meeting," June 4, 1929, pp. 7–9, JWT Archives.

34. *Saturday Evening Post*, May 5, 1928, p. 136.

35. "Minutes of Representatives Meeting," June 4, 1929, pp. 7–9, JWT Archives; *Printers' Ink*, Feb. 10, 1927, p. 144; *Advertising and Selling*, May 16, 1928, p. 32; Calkins, *Business the Civilizer*, pp. 249, 251, 253. On the conception of advertising agents as representatives or "ambassadors" of a consumer constituency, see Chapter 2.

36. *Printers' Ink*, Sept. 25, 1930, pp. 72–73.

37. *Advertising and Selling*, Mar. 19, 1930, p. 69; July 24, 1929, p. 40; *Printers' Ink*, July 6, 1933, p. 4.

38. *Printers' Ink*, Apr. 8, 1926, p. 25.

39. *Printers' Ink Monthly*, Apr. 1928, pp. 128–29; *Printers' Ink*, Apr. 21, 1927, pp. 7, 202; Apr. 5, 1928, p. 6; Carroll Rheinstrom, *Psyching the Ads: The Case Book of Advertising* (New York, 1929), pp. 156, 180.

40. *Printers' Ink*, Oct. 7, 1926, p. 3; Nov. 15, 1928, p. 17.

41. *Printers' Ink*, Nov. 18, 1926, p. 98, *Advertising and Selling*, June 1, 1927, p. 16; Oct. 19, 1927, p. 59; Hollander, *Seeing Through Clothes*, pp. 359–61. For a fuller discussion of advertising men's views of their predominantly female audience, see Chapter 3.

42. Rheinstrom, *Psyching the Ads*, p. 272.

43. On the implications of the Colonel's Lady and Judy O'Grady figure of speech, see Chapter 3.

44. *Printers' Ink Monthly*, Mar. 1930, p. 95; Lynd, "The People as Consumers," pp. 898, 904. The *Buyer's Manual* is quoted in Lynd, p. 879.

45. Lynd, "The People as Consumers," p. 879; *Printers' Ink*, Nov. 15, 1928, pp. 17–18.

46. *Tide*, Dec. 1929, p. 2; *True Story*, May 1929, p. 74; June 1929, p. 181; *Saturday Evening Post*, June 23, 1928, p. 1; July 21, 1928, p. 116; Sept. 28, 1929, fourth cover.

47. *Printers' Ink*, Oct. 20, 1927, p. 69; *Saturday Evening Post*, Mar. 23, 1929, p. 157; Sept. 28, 1929, p. 36.

48. *Saturday Evening Post*, Oct. 12, 1929, p. 115. See also *Printers' Ink*, Apr. 16, 1931, p. 155.

49. *Saturday Evening Post*, June 15, 1929, p. 41; Theodore Menten, *Advertising Art in the Art Deco Style* (New York, 1975), pp. 28–32.

50. Calkins, *Business the Civilizer*, p. 255; *Los Angeles Times*, Aug. 17, 1930, preview section, p. 4; *Printers' Ink Monthly*, Mar. 1930, p. 96; Aug. 1931, p. 34; *American Weekly*, June 21, 1931, p. 8; *Ladies' Home Journal*, July 1931, p. 85; *Printers' Ink*, Sept. 15, 1927, p. 154; Jan. 12, 1928, p. 10; *Saturday Evening Post*, Mar. 22, 1930, p. 92.

51. *Saturday Evening Post*, May 19, 1928, fourth cover; Sept. 1, 1928, fourth cover.

52. *Saturday Evening Post*, Sept. 28, 1929, fourth cover; May 10, 1930, fourth cover.

53. *Printers' Ink Monthly*, Mar. 1926, pp. 29, 94–95; *Saturday Evening Post*, Oct. 6, 1928, p. 2.

54. *Chicago Tribune*, Nov. 1, 1926, p. 27; Nov. 10, 1926, p. 13; *Printers' Ink Monthly*, Mar. 1926, p. 95.

55. *Chicago Tribune*, Oct. 12, 1930, pt. 2, p. 2; *Ladies' Home Journal*, Sept. 1929, p. 138; *Saturday Evening Post*, Oct. 11, 1930, p. 132; *Printers' Ink*, Apr. 10, 1930, pp. 25–26; June 12, 1930, pp. 28–29, 33–34; May 21, 1931, p. 44; *Saturday Evening Post*, June 12, 1926, p. 100; *Chicago Tribune*, Oct. 12, 1930, pt. 2, p. 9; *Delineator*, Oct. 1928, p. 131; *Printers' Ink*, June 12, 1930, p. 57; May 29, 1930, p. 131; *Printers' Ink Monthly*, Mar. 1930, p. 34; *Tide*, Aug. 1932, p. 9; Oct. 1932, pp. 16–17; Mar. 1933, p. 39.

56. *Printers' Ink Monthly*, Oct. 1929, p. 41; *Advertising and Selling*, Nov. 14, 1928, p. 18.

57. *Printers' Ink Monthly*, Mar. 1930, p. 34; *Printers' Ink*, Dec. 2, 1926, p. 198; *Tide*, Aug. 1932, pp. 9–10.

58. On the early role of the department store as "a subtle adviser on personal taste, a joiner who fit individual temperament with proper merchandise," see Neil Harris, "The Drama of Consumer Desire," in *Yankee Enterprise: The Rise of the American System of Manufactures,* ed. Otto Mayr and Robert C. Post (Washington, D.C., 1981), pp. 199–200.

59. *Printers' Ink*, Nov. 15, 1928, pp. 18–19; Dec. 20, 1928, pp. 57–58, 60; June 12, 1930, pp. 29, 33–34, 36; June 14, 1934, p. 84; Lynd, "The People as Consumers," p. 878; *Printers' Ink Monthly*, May 1930, p. 56; Mar. 1931, p. 98; Meikle, *Twentieth Century Limited*, p. 17; *Saturday Evening Post*, June 12, 1926, p. 100.

60. *Printers' Ink Monthly*, June 1929, pp. 82, 85.

61. *Advertising and Selling*, Nov. 14, 1928, p. 18.

62. *Saturday Evening Post*, Mar. 22, 1930, p. 135; Sept. 1, 1928, fourth cover. See also *Los Angeles Times*, Aug. 27, 1930, p. 5.

63. *Printers' Ink Monthly*, May 1929, p. 78; *Saturday Evening Post*, May 25, 1929, p. 188; *Tide*, July 1929, p. 7; *Chicago Tribune*, Oct. 12, 1930, picture section, pt. 2, p. 9; *Printers' Ink*, May 29, 1930, p. 131; July 19, 1928, p. 3.

64. Frederick, *Selling Mrs. Consumer*, p. 38; *True Story*, June 1929, p. 181; *Printers' Ink*, Aug. 6, 1931, p. 80; *Advertising Age*, Mar. 16, 1936, p. 4; *Ladies' Home Journal*, May 1926, p. 117; Jan. 1927, p. 86; June 1927, p. 220; Aug. 1929, p. 116; *Photoplay Magazine*, Feb. 1929, p. 80.

65. Advertising agents particularly prided themselves on providing the public with cultural uplift and introducing a higher level of artistic sophistication. See *Advertising and Selling*, Dec. 1, 1926, p. 52; May 15, 1929, p. 35; *Printers' Ink*, Nov. 25, 1926, pp. 128–29; *Advertising Age*, June 4, 1932, p. 5; *Printers' Ink Monthly*, May 1925, p. 66.

66. *Tide*, Dec. 1928, p. 1; *Printers' Ink Monthly*, June 1928, p. 37.

67. *Tide*, Dec. 1928, p. 2; Poffenberger, *Psychology in Advertising*, pp. 428ff.; *Saturday Evening Post*, Jan. 14, 1928, p. 53; *Printers' Ink*, Sept. 2, 1926, p. 76. The psychologist Albert Poffenberger also exposed the class dimensions of "feeling-tone" in color: "the higher the social status, the higher is the standing of green and the lower is the standing of yellow" (Poffenberger, *Psychology in Advertising*, p. 441).

68. *Printers' Ink Monthly*, June 1926, p. 27; June 1928, p. 37; *Printers' Ink*, May 13, 1926, p. 44; Nov. 18, 1926, pp. 145–46, 150; June 13, 1929, pp. 129–30; *Advertising and Selling*, Dec. 1, 1926, p. 32.

69. *Advertising and Selling Fortnightly*, Mar. 24, 1926, p. 37.

70. David Gebhard, "The Moderne in the U.S., 1920–1941," *Architectural Association Quarterly* 2 (1970): 7; Meikle, *Twentieth Century Limited*, p. 154; *Advertising and Selling*, Apr. 4, 1928, p. 24.

71. *Printers' Ink*, July 26, 1929, p. 170.

72. *Printers' Ink*, Nov. 12, 1925, pp. 57–58; July 26, 1929, p. 170.

73. *Printers' Ink*, Mar. 18, 1926, p. 147; *Printers' Ink Monthly*, Feb. 1929, pp. 49, 128; Apr.

1930, p. 90; Ann Uhry Abrams, "From Simplicity to Sensation: Art in American Advertising," *Journal of Popular Culture* 10 (1976): 626.

74. *Printers' Ink Monthly*, Feb. 1928, p. 35; *Printers' Ink*, June 20, 1929, p. 19; Apr. 24, 1930, pp. 105–106; 108; Paul H. Nystrom, *Economics of Fashion* (New York, 1928), p. 119; Kathryn Weibel, *Mirror, Mirror: Images of Women Reflected in Popular Culture* (Garden City, N.Y., 1977), p. 204.

75. *Printers' Ink Monthly*, Aug. 1926, p. 24; Feb. 1930, pp. 40–41, 74; Jan. 1930, pp. 35, 78.

76. Nystrom, *Economics of Fashion*, p. 218; Elizabeth Kendall, *Where She Danced* (New York, 1979), pp. 208–209; Hollander, *Seeing Through Clothes*, pp. 153–55, 339–41.

77. Eugene Lunn, *Marxism and Modernism: An Historical Study of Lukács, Brecht, Benjamin, and Adorno* (Berkeley, Calif., 1982), pp. 16, 34–36, 60, 143, 262; Daniel Bell, *The Cultural Contradictions of Capitalism* (New York, 1976), pp. 46–49, 112, 118; *Advertising and Selling*, June 13, 1928, p. 46; *Printers' Ink Monthly*, June 1928, p. 37.

78. *Advertising and Selling*, June 13, 1928, p. 46.

79. *Printers' Ink Monthly*, Feb. 1929, p. 132; *Advertising and Selling*, June 13, 1928, pp. 46, 50; *Printers' Ink*, Feb. 26, 1931, pp. 25–26; Meyer Shapiro, "Style," in *Anthropology Today*, ed. A. L. Kroeber (Chicago, 1953), p. 287; T. J. Jackson Lears, "From Salvation to Self-Realization: Advertising and the Therapeutic Roots of the Consumer Culture, 1880–1930," in *The Culture of Consumption*, ed. Richard Wightman Fox and T. J. Jackson Lears (New York, 1983), p. 22; Earnest Elmo Calkins, *And Hearing Not* (New York, 1946), p. 239.

80. *Advertising and Selling Fortnightly*, Mar. 10, 1926, p. 27; *Printers' Ink Monthly*, Feb. 1929, pp. 131–32; *Advertising and Selling*, Oct. 30, 1929, p. 18; *Printers' Ink*, June 5, 1930, p. 89; Helen Woodward, *It's an Art* (New York, 1938), pp. 88–89.

81. *Advertising and Selling*, July 11, 1928, p. 66; *Printers' Ink*, Mar. 18, 1926, p. 146; *Printers' Ink Monthly*, Apr. 1928, p. 44; Dec. 1928, p. 35; Feb. 1930, pp. 40, 74; Apr. 1930, pp. 39–40.

82. *Advertising and Selling*, July 11, 1928, p. 66; *Printers' Ink Monthly*, Nov. 1929, p. 39.

83. *JWT News Letter*, Aug. 1, 1927, p. 34; *Advertising and Selling*, July 25, 1928, p. 54.

84. *Advertising and Selling*, Oct. 3, 1928, p. 27; July 10, 1929, p. 20; Dec. 1, 1926, p. 32; *Printers' Ink Monthly*, June 1925, p. 30.

85. *Advertising and Selling*, May 30, 1928, pp. 19–20, 68.

86. Ibid., pp. 19, 70.

87. *Advertising and Selling*, Dec. 12, 1928, p. 104; July 10, 1929, p. 20; Aug. 18, 1932, p. 21; Jan. 25, 1928, p. 26; *Printers' Ink*, Mar. 5, 1931, p. 122; *Printers' Ink Monthly*, Jan. 1932, pp. 21–22; June 1935, pp. 19, 61.

88. *Printers' Ink Monthly*, Dec. 1928, p. 35; *Advertising and Selling*, June 27, 1928, p. 58.

89. *Printers' Ink Monthly*, Apr. 1930, p. 34; *Advertising and Selling*, Aug. 30, 1934, p. 25.

90. *Printers' Ink*, June 21, 1928, p. 158; *Advertising and Selling*, Mar. 2, 1932, p. 22; May 26, 1932, p. 15; *Printers' Ink Monthly*, Apr. 1932, pp. 22–23; *Advertising Age*, Jan. 20, 1932, p. 5.

91. John Willett, *Art and Politics in the Weimar Period: The New Sobriety, 1917–1933* (New York, 1978), pp. 134, 137, 141; "Minutes of Creative Staff Meeting," Feb. 1, 1933, pp. 1–2, JWT Archives; *Printers' Ink Monthly*, June 1928, p. 37.

92. *Advertising and Selling*, May 14, 1930, p. 94; *Printers' Ink*, Apr. 8, 1926, p. 183; June 17, 1926, p. 88; Oct. 13, 1927, pp. 118–19; *Printers' Ink Monthly*, Apr. 1928, p. 151; Sept. 1930, p. 63; George Batten Company, *News Letter*, Jan. 13, 1925, pp. 4–6; Susan Sontag, *On Photography* (New York, 1977), p. 87. On the photograph's triumph over reality, see also Daniel Boorstin, *The Image, or What Happened to the American Dream* (New York, 1962), pp. 13–14, 170.

93. *Advertising and Selling*, Jan. 25, 1927, p. 42; Apr. 30, 1930, p. 67; *Printers' Ink*, Feb. 24, 1927, p. 130; Aug. 18, 1927, pp. 158, 162; May 16, 1929, pp. 89, 92; *Printers' Ink Monthly*, July 1928, p. 42.

94. *Printers' Ink Monthly*, Feb. 1928, p. 41; *JWT News Letter*, Apr. 23, 1926, p. 103; Mar. 1, 1928, pp. 103–104.

95. *The Hoover Newsy News*, Aug. 12, 1931, pp. 2–3, The Hoover Company Archives, North Canton, Ohio; *Saturday Evening Post*, Nov. 21, 1931, p. 82; *Printers' Ink Monthly*, Apr. 1930, pp. 41–42; *Printers' Ink*, Sept. 25, 1925, p. 74; May 16, 1929, p. 92; June 6, 1929, p. 140; Apr. 3, 1930, p. 118; Aug. 6, 1931, p. 56; *Tide*, Oct. 1931, p. 7; Albert Lasker, *The Lasker Story as He Told It* (Chicago, 1963), p. 23; *J. Walter Thompson News Bulletin*, Nov. 1930, p. 118.

96. *Printers' Ink*, Apr. 3, 1930, p. 118.

97. *Printers' Ink Monthly*, July 1933, p. 61; Sept. 1930, p. 63; Sontag, *On Photography*, pp. 3, 24, 52, 153, 169.

98. *Printers' Ink*, May 20, 1926, p. 127; *Advertising and Selling*, Nov. 17, 1926, pp. 32, 66; Theodore Barnard Peterson, *Magazines in the Twentieth Century*, 2nd ed. (Urbana, Ill., 1964), p. 351; *Judicious Advertising*, Apr. 1925, p. 103; "Minutes of Representatives Meeting," Dec. 23, 1930, p. 6, JWT Archives.

99. *Printers' Ink*, Apr. 3, 1930, pp. 84, 89; Aug. 7, 1930, pp. 10, 12; *Tide*, Dec. 1928, p. 8.

100. *Printers' Ink Monthly*, Apr. 1926, p. 23; *Printers' Ink*, May 19, 1927, p. 64; *Advertising and Selling*, Aug. 16, 1934, p. 31.

101. Stephen Baker, *Visual Persuasion: The Effect of Pictures on the Subconscious* (New York, 1961), n.p. (p. 4); Marshall McLuhan, *The Mechanical Bride: Folklore of Industrial Man* (New York, 1951), pp. v–vi, 75; James Monaco, *How to Read a Film: The Art, Technology, Language, History, and Theory of Film and Media* (New York, 1977), pp. 144–45; *Advertising and Selling*, Feb. 6, 1929, p. 38. See also Otis A. Pease, *The Responsibilities of American Advertising* (New Haven, Conn., 1958), pp. 132–33.

102. It has been the gradual maturation of this perception among advertisers that has led Judith Williamson to conclude that advertising is uncontrollable. Those who seek restrictions on the "verbal content or 'false claims' of ads," she notes, fail to recognize that "there is no way of getting at their use of images and symbols. And it is precisely these that do the work of the ad anyway" (Judith Williamson, *Decoding Advertisements: Ideology and Meaning in Advertising* [London, 1978], p. 175).

103. *Advertising and Selling*, Sept. 5, 1928, pp. 19–20; Frederick, *Selling Mrs. Consumer*, pp. 79–81, 246. See also *Advertising Age*, Jan. 13, 1934, p. 13.

104. Meikle, *Twentieth Century Limited*, pp. 12–13, 106; "Chevrolet Motors Co.," Advertising Case Study 526, reel 12, p. 48, HBS Archives; *Printers' Ink*, June 25, 1931, p. 92; May 3, 1928, p. 57.

105. Warren I. Susman, "'Personality' and the Making of Twentieth-Century Culture," in *New Directions in American Intellectual History*, ed. John Higham and Paul K. Conkin (Baltimore, 1979), p. 216; *Judicious Advertising*, Apr. 1925, p. 50; *Printers' Ink*, June 17, 1926, pp. 17–19; Nov. 18, 1926, pp. 223–24; Dec. 9, 1926, pp. 189–90; Dec. 15, 1927, pp. 203–204; *Advertising and Selling*, July 14, 1926, p. 10.

106. *Chicago Tribune*, Nov. 2, 1926, p. 19.

107. *Chicago Tribune*, Jan. 8, 1928, picture section, p. 2; *Advertising and Selling*, June 1, 1927, p. 28; Dorothy Dignam to Mr. Surrick, Feb. 2, 1927, Box 1, Dorothy Dignam Papers, Wisconsin State Historical Society (WSHS).

108. *Chicago Tribune*, Dec. 1, 1927, p. 9.

109. Frederick, *Selling Mrs. Consumer*, p. 6; Dorothy Dignam to Mr. Stinson, Nov. 11, 1936, and "Features of Interest to Women in the Ford V-8 for 1937" (typed sheet), Box 1, Dignam Papers, WSHS; *San Francisco Examiner*, Nov. 13, 1929, p. 11; July 9, 1933, p. 22; *Chicago Tribune*, Dec. 18, 1927, picture section, p. 7; Paul [illegible]

to Frank L. Scott, Jan. 9, 1940, Ford Folder, N. W. Ayer and Son Archives, New York City.

110. Albert L. Roe, "Bankers and Thrift in the Age of Affluence," *American Quarterly* 17 (1965): 620, 624–25, 630.

111. On this point, see also Stuart and Elizabeth Ewen, *Channels of Desire: Mass Images and the Shaping of American Consciousness* (New York, 1982), pp. 51, 148–49, 237.

112. George Batten Co., *News Letter,* June 23, 1925, p. 4; Aug. 25, 1925, p. 5; Fitzgibbon, *Macy's, Gimbels and Me,* p. 16.

113. Bruce Barton, *The Man Nobody Knows* (Indianapolis, Ind., 1925), p. 180; *Printers' Ink,* Dec. 19, 1935, p. 91; *Advertising and Selling,* Jan. 6, 1932, p. 3; Aug. 29, 1935, p. 36. For other insights into "advertisers' unease in a consumer culture," see Lears, "From Salvation to Self-Realization," p. 20.

114. *Advertising and Selling,* May 2, 1928, pp. 23, 66, 68.

115. Rosalind H. Williams, *Dream Worlds: Mass Consumption in Late Nineteenth-Century France* (Berkeley, Calif., 1982), p. 269.

116. *Printers' Ink Monthly,* May 1928, pp. 29–30, 91; *Advertising and Selling,* June 29, 1927, p. 21; July 27, 1927, p. 65; *Printers' Ink,* Sept. 30, 1926, pp. 133–34; *Advertising Age,* May 21, 1932, p. 11.

117. *Better Homes and Gardens,* Sept. 1930, p. 7; *Advertising and Selling,* June 2, 1926, p. 20.

118. On the idea of an "inherent contradiction" in the process of modernization, see Williams, *Dream Worlds,* p. 269, and Bell, *The Cultural Contradictions of Capitalism,* pp. xi–xiii, 11–13, 33, 37, 80–84.

119. *Printers' Ink,* Dec. 6, 1928, p. 19; *Saturday Evening Post,* May 21, 1927, p. 186; July 16, 1927, p. 138.

120. *Better Homes and Gardens,* Oct. 1929, p. 56; *San Francisco Examiner,* Jan. 26, 1930, p. 25; Frederick, *Selling Mrs. Consumer,* p. 252; Pease, *The Responsibilities of American Advertising,* pp. 41-42.

121. *Advertising and Selling,* Mar. 21, 1928, p. 29; *American Magazine,* Nov. 1929, p. 123; *Saturday Evening Post,* Apr. 9, 1927, pp. 88–89; May 14, 1927, pp. 124–25; *Printers' Ink,* Oct. 6, 1927, pp. 54–55; *Better Homes and Gardens,* Apr. 1930, pp. 9, 57; Aug. 1930, p. 9; *Ladies' Home Journal,* Oct. 1928, p. 84.

122. *Saturday Evening Post,* Aug. 16, 1924, pp. 62–63; Apr. 9, 1927, p. 116; *Tide,* Aug. 1929, p. 2; *Printers' Ink,* May 19, 1927, p. 144; June 23, 1927, pp. 62–63; *Better Homes and Gardens,* Aug. 1930, p. 57.

123. *Saturday Evening Post,* Oct. 6, 1928, p. 51.

124. *Printers' Ink,* June 17, 1926, p. 176; Dec. 5, 1929, p. 72; Howard Williams Dickinson, *Crying Our Wares* (New York, 1929), p. 102. See also Bruce Barton's elaboration of this philosophy in *Printers' Ink,* Oct. 3, 1929, pp. 3–4.

125. *Saturday Evening Post,* Feb. 21, 1931, pp. 60–61.

126. *Advertising Age,* July 12, 1937, pp. 14–15.

127. On the conception of women as driven by instincts toward "uncontrollable consumption" while men remained "uncorrupted," see Ewen and Ewen, *Channels of Desire,* pp. 149–50.

128. *Printers' Ink,* June 30, 1932, p. 86.

Six   Advertisements as Social Tableaux

1. *Chicago Tribune,* June 23, 1929, picture section, p. 4.

2. This approach parallels studies in the tradition of Leo Lowenthal's "Biographies in Popular Magazines," in *Radio Research, 1942–1943,* ed. Paul F. Lazarsfeld and Frank N. Stanton (New York, 1944), pp. 507–48.

3. Jack W. McCullough, "Edward Kilanyi and American Tableaux Vivants," *Theatre Survey* 16 (1975): 25–28.

4. Barbara Welter, "The Cult of True Womanhood," *American Quarterly* 18 (1966): 151–74; Kathryn Kish Sklar, *Catherine Beecher: A Study in American Domesticity* (New Haven, Conn., 1973), pp. 135–38, 152–54, 160–63; Christopher Lasch, *Haven in a Heartless World* (New York, 1977), pp. 5–6.

5. Christine Frederick, *Selling Mrs. Consumer* (New York, 1929), pp. 29–31, 53, 245–46; *Saturday Evening Post*, Mar. 8, 1930, p. 84; June 1, 1929, pp. 114–15; *American Magazine*, July 1927, p. 183; *Printers' Ink*, Nov. 27, 1930, pp. 98–99.

6. I have come across over 45 such designations in the trade press and in advertisements. Occasional additional variations included "general manager" and "first vice-president in charge of purchasing." For examples, see *Printers' Ink*, Apr. 8, 1926, p. 10; Jan. 12, 1928, pp. 94–95; *Advertising and Selling Fortnightly*, Mar. 24, 1926, p. 45; *Advertising and Selling*, June 2, 1926, p. 94; *Tide*, Dec. 1932, p. 40; *Saturday Evening Post*, Feb. 8, 1930, p. 88.

7. *Saturday Evening Post*, Mar. 24, 1928, p. 53.

8. *Saturday Evening Post*, Apr. 18, 1925, p. 184; Oct. 24, 1925, p. 211; Nov. 7, 1925, p. 97; *Advertising and Selling*, June 2, 1926, p. 94.

9. *Saturday Evening Post*, July 24, 1926, p. 37. See also *Saturday Evening Post*, May 4, 1929, p. 79.

10. *Saturday Evening Post*, Sept. 8, 1928, p. 93; May 5, 1928, p. 184; *Good Housekeeping*, Oct. 1927, p. 145.

11. *Saturday Evening Post*, July 18, 1931, p. 101; Oct. 10, 1931, p. 111; *Advertising Age*, July 23, 1932, p. 9; *Printers' Ink*, Oct. 13, 1932, p. 75.

12. Ruth Schwartz Cowan, "The Industrial Revolution in the Home: Household Technology and Social Change in the 20th Century," *Technology and Culture* 17 (1976): 23.

13. *Saturday Evening Post*, Apr. 8, 1933, p. 65.

14. *Ladies' Home Journal*, Mar. 1931, fourth cover.

15. Cowan, "The Industrial Revolution in the Home," p. 16.

16. *Chicago Tribune*, Nov. 16, 1926, p. 21.

17. *Saturday Evening Post*, Jan. 23, 1926, p. 102; Feb. 20, 1926, p. 74; Mar. 20, 1926, p. 145; Apr. 24, 1926, p. 94; May 22, 1926, p. 171; June 26, 1926, p. 124; July 24, 1926, p. 54; Oct. 9, 1926, p. 133.

18. For examples see *American Magazine*, Mar. 1926, p. 117; Apr. 1928, p. 121; *Saturday Evening Post*, July 21, 1928, p. 111; July 14, 1928, p. 143; Nov. 3, 1928, p. 38; *Tide*, Feb. 1935, p. 31.

19. Cowan, "The Industrial Revolution in the Home," p. 13; *Saturday Evening Post*, May 24, 1924, p. 107; Apr 25, 1925, p. 48; May 2, 1925, p. 42; Sept. 19, 1925, p. 171; Nov. 21, 1925, p. 106; July 10, 1926, pp. 50–51; June 18, 1927, p. 95; June 1, 1929, pp. 58–59; "Album 1918–1948," insertion for August 1925, and *The Ibaisaic*, July 28, 1927, p. 3, The Hoover Company Archives, North Canton, Ohio.

20. *Printers' Ink*, Jan. 20, 1927, p. 98; Apr. 26, 1928, p. 121; *Printers' Ink Monthly*, Apr. 1933, p. 47; *Advertising and Selling*, June 30, 1926, p. 47; Mar. 12, 1936, p. 2.

21. See, for example, *Saturday Evening Post*, Aug. 20, 1927, p. 95; Oct. 23, 1926, p. 59; Sept. 18, 1926, p. 83; *Advertising and Selling*, Dec. 25, 1929, pp. 62–63.

22. *Saturday Evening Post*, July 23, 1927, p. 98.

23. "Less Work for Mother and Better Food for All," Box 34–31, N. W. Ayer and Son, Inc., Archives, New York City; *Saturday Evening Post*, Aug. 23, 1924, p. 104; Jan. 3, 1925, pp. 76–77; June 5, 1926, pp. 142–43; Aug. 10, 1929, p. 144; *Better Homes and Gardens*, Oct. 1929, p. 111; Dec. 1929, p. 63; Mar. 1930, p. 97; *Woman's Home Companion*, July 1928, p. 103.

24. Roland Barthes, *Mythologies*, trans. Annette Lavers (London, 1972), p. 51; *Tide*,

Aug. 1935, p. 15; John Berger et al., *Ways of Seeing* (London, 1972), pp. 46–47; Frederick, *Selling Mrs. Consumer*, pp. 189–91; *Printers' Ink Monthly*, Aug. 1932, p. 29; *Redbook*, Sept. 1935, p. 73.

25. *Printers' Ink Monthly*, July 1932, p. 3; *Ladies' Home Journal*, Jan. 1931, p. 29. For examples of this "mirror image of woman," see *American Weekly*, July 8, 1928, p. 15; *Photoplay Magazine*, Dec. 1928, p. 93; *Saturday Evening Post*, Sept. 18, 1926, p. 57; *Delineator*, Jan. 1932, p. 63; Apr. 1932, p. 3; *Chicago Tribune*, Feb. 21, 1926, magazine section, p. 6; *Printers' Ink*, June 3, 1926, p. 2; *Printers' Ink Monthly*, July 1928, p. 7; Jan. 1933, p. 73. On the tradition of the mirror in art and its relation to women, see Anne Hollander, *Seeing Through Clothes* (New York, 1978), pp. 393–405. On women and mirrors in advertising, see Stuart Ewen, "Advertising as a Way of Life," *Liberation*, Jan. 1975, p. 31, and Stuart Ewen, *Captains of Consciousness: Advertising and the Social Roots of the Consumer Culture* (New York, 1976), pp. 177–80. Since beauty and health were so difficult to retain, a Kellogg's All-Bran ad commented, it was no wonder that women's mirrors so often revealed "the furtive glances of the afraid" (*Chicago Tribune*, Nov. 19, 1926, p. 38).

26. *Saturday Evening Post*, Dec. 3, 1927, p. 33; *American Magazine*, Sept. 1931, p. 14; *True Story*, Apr. 1933, p. 7; *Tide*, Oct. 1932, p. 46; *Ladies' Home Journal*, July 1931, p. 113; Apr. 1933, p. 37.

27. *American Magazine*, June 1926, p. 92; *Ladies' Home Journal*, Feb. 1931, p. 114; Apr. 1931, p. 97; May 1931, p. 148; July 1931, p. 113; *True Story*, June 1933, p. 18; *Better Homes and Gardens*, June 1930, p. 89. On the tradition of beauty as a woman's "duty" and as available to all, see Lois W. Banner, *American Beauty* (Chicago, 1983), pp. 9, 16, 205–208, 249, 264.

28. *Chicago Tribune*, Jan. 15, 1928, picture section, p. 6; *Saturday Evening Post*, Feb. 2, 1929, p. 30; Feb. 16, 1929, p. 32; Mar. 16, 1929, p. 34; May 25, 1929, p. 42; James R. Adams, *Sparks Off My Anvil* (New York, 1958), p. 97. The Fisher Body girl also appeared occasionally in ads for other products. See, for example, *Saturday Evening Post*, May 11, 1929, p. 70; Mar. 16, 1929, pp. 80–81; Mar. 23, 1929, p. 163.

29. *Saturday Evening Post*, June 19, 1926, p. 127; July 27, 1935, p. 25; *American Magazine*, Mar. 1926, p. 117; *McCall's*, July 1928, p. 44; *Ladies' Home Journal*, Sept. 1926, p. 166; Oct. 1926, p. 55.

30. *Printers' Ink Monthly*, Aug. 1926, p. 87; *Printers' Ink*, May 12, 1927, p. 88.

31. *Printers' Ink*, Aug. 25, 1927, p. 18; *Advertising and Selling Fortnightly*, Mar. p. 10, 1926, p. 27; *Printers' Ink Monthly*, Feb. 1929, p. 132. For salient examples of the woman as modern art object, see *American Weekly*, Feb. 20, 1927, p. 24; Apr. 17, 1927, p. 19; *Chicago Tribune*, Dec. 21, 1927, p. 24; Nov. 10, 1926, p. 8; June 28, 1929, p. 17; Oct. 3, 1930, p. 10; *Saturday Evening Post*, Feb. 18, 1928, p. 2; Jan. 5, 1929, pp. 72–73; Mar. 22, 1930, p. 137; *Los Angeles Times*, July 21, 1929, part III, p. 3; Aug. 10, 1930, part III, p. 5; Aug. 13, 1930, part II, p. 8; *True Story*, May 1930, p. 107.

32. For instance, compared with the women in the department store ad on page 24 of the *Chicago Tribune*, June 12, 1929, the woman photographed on the following page appeared to have no neck at all. See also *Saturday Evening Post*, Aug. 6, 1927, p. 142; Dec. 8, 1928, p. 139; Apr. 6, 1929, p. 48; May 4, 1929, p. 217; Sept. 14, 1929, p. 168. A contemporary advertising woman estimated that the camera could only distort a model to appear about one head higher than her real stature, whereas drawings regularly elongated her figure more strikingly (*Advertising and Selling*, Oct. 24, 1935, p. 30).

33. Paul H. Nystrom, *Economics of Fashion* (New York, 1928), p. 466.

34. Elizabeth Kendall, *Where She Danced* (New York, 1979), pp. 208–209; Hollander, *Seeing Through Clothes*, pp. 339–41.

35. Erving Goffman, *Gender Advertisements* (New York, 1979), pp. 45–47.

36. Ibid., p. 45. For examples of the two common types of gender-specific stances, see

Saturday Evening Post, Mar. 2, 1929, p. 92; June 22, 1929, pp. 124, 129; June 29, 1929, pp. 4, 36; Aug. 10, 1929, p. 63; Aug. 17, 1929, pp. 60, 176; Aug. 24, 1929, p. 40; *Collier's,* May 26, 1928, p. 49. Arthur William Brown, a prolific illustrator for *Saturday Evening Post* fiction and for advertisements, created a kind of visual formula out of such contrasts in stance. See *Saturday Evening Post,* June 15, 1929, pp. 6–7; Nov. 2, 1929, p. 154; Nov. 15, 1930, pp. 3, 5; Nov. 22, 1930, pp. 16–17, 20.

37. *Chicago Tribune,* Nov. 10, 1926, p. 8; *Saturday Evening Post,* Sept. 11, 1926, p. 186; Nov. 13, 1926, p. 139; July 2, 1927, p. 42; Aug. 13, 1927, p. 78; Feb. 19, 1927, p. 48; June 1, 1929, pp. 114–15.

38. *American Magazine,* Oct. 1932, p. 1. See also *Saturday Evening Post,* Jan. 21, 1933, p. 75. On the "appropriation" of feminist demands to promote consumerism, see also Ewen, *Captains of Consciousness,* pp. 160–61.

39. *Printers' Ink Monthly,* June 1935, p. 52.

40. Ibid., Mar. 1930, fourth cover.

41. *American Magazine,* July 1927, p. 183; Mar. 1935, p. 141; *Saturday Evening Post,* Jan. 5, 1929, p. 75; Nov. 9, 1929, p. 172; *Better Homes and Gardens,* Jan. 1930, p. 9.

42. *Saturday Evening Post,* Oct. 29, 1927, p. 60; Jan. 24, 1931, p. 72; *Ladies' Home Journal,* Apr. 1931, p. 97; *American Magazine,* Sept. 1929, p. 183.

43. *Saturday Evening Post,* Jan. 23, 1926, p. 102; Aug. 11, 1934, pp. 44–45.

44. *Printers' Ink,* Mar. 22, 1934, pp. 56–57.

45. *American Weekly,* Nov. 10, 1929, p. 28; *Saturday Evening Post,* Feb. 6, 1926, p. 153; July 3, 1926, p. 32; Apr. 14, 1928, p. 93; Dec. 7, 1929, p. 76; Mar. 9, 1935, p. 99; *American Magazine,* Mar. 1926, p. 94; Sept. 1930, second cover.

46. *Advertising and Selling,* May 11, 1933, p. 6.

47. *Saturday Evening Post,* Apr. 11, 1925, p. 164; Oct. 10, 1925, p. 87; Feb. 10, 1934, p. 91; Oct. 6, 1928, pp. 140–41; May 4, 1935, p. 1; Mar. 16, 1935, pp. 67, 97; *American Magazine,* Aug. 1929, p. 163; *Printers' Ink Monthly,* Oct. 1925, p. 41; June 1928, pp. 19ff; *Advertising and Selling,* Sept. 19, 1928, p. 28.

48. *Fortune,* June 1933, p. 9; *Saturday Evening Post,* Feb. 23, 1929, pp. 98–99.

49. *Printers' Ink,* May 19, 1927, p. 10.

50. Ibid.

51. *American Magazine,* June 1931, p. 110; Aug. 1931, p. 110.

52. Paula S. Fass, *The Damned and the Beautiful: American Youth in the 1920s* (New York, 1977), p. 20.

53. For examples of such scenes, see *Saturday Evening Post,* Feb. 9, 1928, p. 140; Sept. 15, 1928, p. 69; Jan. 12, 1929, p. 1; Feb. 23, 1929, p. 2; Dec. 27, 1930, p. 80; *American Magazine,* Apr. 1926, p. 229; Sept. 1928, p. 119; Sept. 1930, p. 128; Feb. 1933, p. 108; *Better Homes and Gardens,* May 1930, p. 114; Mar. 1933, p. 42. See also *Printers' Ink,* Nov. 25, 1926, pp. 98–99.

54. Martha Wolfenstein and Nathan Leites, *Movies: A Psychological Study* (Glencoe, Ill., 1950), p. 103.

55. Fass, *The Damned and the Beautiful,* pp. 59–60.

56. Ibid., pp. 55, 63, 102; Scrapbook 379 (Electric Refrigeration Bureau, NELA), Lord and Thomas Archives, housed at Foote, Cone and Belding Communications, Inc., Chicago; *Saturday Evening Post,* Jan 23, 1926, p. 135; Feb. 6, 1926, p. 156; July 27, 1935, p. 35; May 1, 1926, p. 176; *American Magazine,* July 1933, pp. 109, 119.

57. *Printers' Ink,* Nov. 19, 1931, p. 5; *Saturday Evening Post,* Mar. 2, 1935, p. 41; Dec. 19, 1936, p. 48.

58. *Better Homes and Gardens,* Sept. 1929, p. 12; *Ladies' Home Journal,* Apr. 1931, p. 2; *Printers' Ink,* May 20, 1926, p. 1; Mar. 4, 1926, p. 115.

59. *Saturday Evening Post,* July 2, 1927, p. 65; May 9, 1931, p. 126; Jan. 30, 1937, p. 93; *Better Homes and Gardens,* Sept. 1928, p. 119; *American Magazine,* Sept. 1933, p. 97;

May 1934, p. 119. Stanley Cavell, in *The World Viewed* (Cambridge, Mass., 1979), p. 35, notes a similar absence of blacks in films acting as consumers and "making an ordinary purchase."

60. David M. Potter, *People of Plenty* (Chicago, 1954), pp. 103–107, 167.

61. *American Magazine*, Dec. 1926, p. 6; *Saturday Evening Post*, Jan. 7, 1928, p. 129; Aug. 7, 1926, pp. 72–73; *Ladies' Home Journal*, Apr. 1931, p. 37; "Minutes of Creative Staff Meeting," Oct. 26, 1932, pp. 8–10, J. Walter Thompson Company (JWT) Archives, New York City.

62. *San Francisco Examiner*, Aug. 5, 1928, p. 9; *Saturday Evening Post*, June 25, 1927, p. 167; Jan. 7, 1928, pp. 128, 163; Sept. 4, 1926, p. 95; Aug. 21, 1925, pp. 68–69; *American Magazine*, July 1926, p. 145.

63. *Saturday Evening Post*, July 10, 1926, p. 37; Nov. 13, 1926, pp. 160–61; Aug. 7, 1926, pp. 72–73; *Printers' Ink*, Dec. 12, 1929, p. 200; *American Magazine*, Oct. 1929, p. 110.

64. *Saturday Evening Post*, Jan. 23, 1926, p. 2; *Chicago Tribune*, Nov. 7, 1926, magazine section, p. 12; Nov. 14, 1925, pt. 9, p. 2; *The Ibaisaic*, Mar. 3, 1927, p. 4, The Hoover Company Archives; *American Magazine*, May 1931, p. 99; *Saturday Evening Post*, July 20, 1929, p. 1; Nov. 22, 1930, p. 45; *Ladies' Home Journal*, Feb. 1931, pp. 84–85.

65. *Chicago Tribune*, Nov. 7, 1926, magazine section, p. 12; June 27, 1929, p. 4; *Saturday Evening Post*, Aug. 7, 1926, pp. 72–73; *Ladies' Home Journal*, Apr. 1931, p. 37; *JWT News Letter*, May 13, 1926, pp. 119–20, JWT Archives; Carroll Rheinstrom, *Psyching the Ads: The Case Book of Advertising* (New York, 1929), pp. 37–38.

66. *Ladies' Home Journal*, July 1931, p. 27. See also *Chicago Tribune*, Nov. 7, 1926, magazine section, p. 12; Oct. 5, 1930, picture section, pt. 2, p. 12; *American Magazine*, Nov. 1930, p. 122; *Saturday Evening Post*, Jan. 29, 1927, p. 152; Sept. 3, 1927, p. 59; *True Story*, Mar. 1928, p. 79; May 1930, p. 151; Rheinstrom, *Psyching the Ads*, p. 38; *San Francisco Examiner*, Aug. 5, 1928, p. 9; *Better Homes and Gardens*, Oct. 1928, p. 57.

67. Martha Wolfenstein, "The Emergence of Fun Morality," *Journal of Social Issues* 7 (1951): 22–24.

68. *Saturday Evening Post*, May 14, 1927, p. 180; Dec. 25, 1933, p. 37; Feb. 19, 1927, p. 119; Mar. 17, 1928, pp. 98–99; Sept. 3, 1927, pp. 82–83; *American Magazine*, Aug. 1933, p. 76; *San Francisco Examiner*, Nov. 3, 1929, section ★ [*sic*], p. 7; Scrapbook 198 (*True Story* copy, Cellucotton Products Co.), Lord and Thomas Archives.

69. *True Story*, Apr. 1929, p. 85; Jan. 1930, pp. 31, fourth cover; May 1930, p. 12; *Photoplay Magazine*, Mar. 1929, p. 69.

70. *Advertising Age*, June 6, 1938, p. 18; *True Story*, June 1933, p. 17; May 1933, p. 51; Mar. 1933, p. 109; Mar. 1938, p. 123; Nov. 1925, p. 81; "Minutes of Representatives Meeting," May 5, 1931, pp. 6–7, JWT Archives. See also *Photoplay Magazine*, Jan. 1930, p. 11; Mar. 1930, p. 82; May 1930, p. 9.

71. Frank Wayne Fox, "Advertisements as Documents in Social and Cultural History" (M.A. thesis, University of Utah, June 1929), p. 56.

72. Caroline Bird, *The Invisible Scar* (New York, 1966), pp. 2, 317.

73. On the tendency of those in the higher classes to make rather fine distinctions among those social groups nearest to them in status, and then to group all those considerably lower into only one or two very broad categories, see Allison Davis, Burleigh B. Gardner, and Mary R. Gardner, *Deep South: A Social-Anthropological Study of Caste and Class* (Chicago, 1941), p. 65.

74. *Saturday Evening Post*, Nov. 6, 1926, p. 104; Sept. 7, 1928, p. 170; *Printers' Ink*, Apr. 26, 1929, pp. 30–31; *Ladies' Home Journal*, Oct. 1931, p. 134; Feb. 1933, p. 57; Dec. 1933, p. 49; Jan. 1933, p. 21; *The Ibaisaic*, Sept. 29, 1932, p. 8; Oct. 13, 1932, p. 16, The Hoover Company Archives. An example of the refusal to contemplate living circumstances inferior to the comfortable, single-family bungalow occurs in a long series of Procter and Gamble ads between 1926 and 1931. These "slice-of-life" ads,

entitled "Actual Visits to P & G Homes" or "Actual Letters from P & G Homes," promoted a laundry soap, a mass-market product that would logically seek its constituency among those of nearly every level of society. Yet not one tableau of the 32 that I located revealed a home of less than middle-class status. Not one "P & G home" was an urban apartment, a rented home, or a multi-family structure.

75. *Saturday Evening Post,* Oct. 6, 1928, p. 169; May 31, 1930, p. 122; Mar. 7, 1931, pp. 44, 53; *Printers' Ink,* Apr. 24, 1930, p. 13.

76. Jib Fowles, *Mass Advertising as Social Forecast: A Method for Futures Research* (Westport, Conn., 1976).

77. Cyril E. Black, *The Dynamics of Modernization: A Study in Comparative History* (New York, 1966), pp. 21–23; Marion J. Levy, Jr., *Modernization and the Structure of Societies* (Princeton, N.J., 1966), pp. 273–76; Roland Marchand, "Visions of Classlessness; Quests for Dominion: American Popular Culture, 1945–1960," in *Reshaping America: Society and Institutions, 1945–1960,* ed. Robert H. Bremner and Gary W. Reichard (Columbus, Ohio, 1982), pp. 165–70; Daniel Sutherland, *Americans and Their Servants: Domestic Service in the United States from 1800 to 1920* (Baton Rouge, La., 1981), p. 183; David M. Katzman, *Seven Days a Week, Women and Domestic Service in Industrializing America* (New York, 1975), pp. 47, 49.

78. Frederick, *Selling Mrs. Consumer,* p. 169.

79. *Printers' Ink Monthly,* May 1928, p. 23. The distinctions involved in such categorizations as "similar" or "somewhat dissimilar" are necessarily subjective. If the maid is shown alone, with no "lady of the house" present, I have counted her as "similar" as long as she is slender, young, white, and has the standard, finely etched features. If the lady of the house is also present in the picture, I have counted the maid as similar even if her hair color and hairdo are different, as long as she is of the same build, posture, and facial features as her mistress and her mistress' friends and is as young or younger.

80. Department of Commerce, U.S. Bureau of the Census, *Fifteenth Census, 1930, Occupations,* p. 582; *Sixteenth Census, 1940, Occupations,* pp. 90, 199, 222.

81. Katzman, *Seven Days a Week,* pp. 47, 49, 66, 71–82, 228, 286; Department of Commerce, U.S. Bureau of the Census, *Comparative Occupation Statistics for the United States, 1870 to 1940,* comp. Alba M. Edwards (Washington, D.C., 1943), p. 129; *Sixteenth Census, 1940, Occupations,* p. 199; Department of Commerce, U.S. Bureau of the Census, *Historical Statistics of the United States,* 2 vols. (Washington, D.C., 1975), 1: 43; *Saturday Evening Post,* May 15, 1926, p. 177.

82. Cowan, "Industrial Revolution in the Home," pp. 9–10; *Advertising and Selling,* May 4, 1927, p. 20; Katzman, *Seven Days a Week,* pp. 131–32, 145, 228, 278.

83. "Minutes of Representatives Meeting," Dec. 3, 1929, p. 6, JWT Archives. See also *American Magazine,* Aug. 1931, p. 18, and *Ladies' Home Journal,* Oct. 1931, p. 134.

84. Katzman, *Seven Days a Week,* p. 146.

85. Ibid., pp. 146, 149, 237, 240. For examples of the image of solicitous personal attendance, see *Saturday Evening Post,* Oct. 8, 1928, p. 99; June 4, 1927, pp. 108–109; July 20, 1927, p. 115; Apr. 9, 1927, p. 57; Nov. 12, 1927, p. 1; Aug. 2, 1930, p. 2; *Printers' Ink Monthly,* May 1928, pp. 23, 132.

Seven   The Great Parables

1. Sallie McFague TeSelle, *Speaking in Parables: A Study in Metaphor and Theology* (Philadelphia, 1975), pp. 75, 78; Eta Linnemann, *Jesus of the Parables,* trans. John Sturdy from the third edition (New York, 1966), p. 19; A. T. Cadoux, *The Parables of Jesus: Their Art and Use* (London, [1930]), p. 45. In *The Man Nobody Knows* (Indianapolis, 1925), advertising executive Bruce Barton recommended Jesus's parables as models for advertising writers; see pp. 140–46.

2. TeSelle, *Speaking in Parables,* pp. 70, 72, 79.

3. For comparisons of melodrama and tragedy, see John Cawelti, *Adventure, Mystery, and Romance* (Chicago, 1976), pp. 26, 38, 46.

4. Thomas J. J. Altizer, *Total Presence: The Language of Jesus and the Language of Today* (New York, 1980), p. 3; TeSelle, *Speaking in Parables,* p. 78.

5. James M. Robinson, in *Seminar on Parable, Myth, and Language, College of Preachers, 1967* (Cambridge, Mass., [1967]), p. 49.

6. Joseph Ferguson McFadyen, *The Message of the Parables* (London, [1933]), p. 59; Leo Spitzer, *A Method of Interpreting Literature* (Northampton, Mass., 1949), pp. 117–21.

7. *Saturday Evening Post,* Apr. 4, 1931, pp. 118–19.

8. This "tragedy of manners" represents a conflation of the following ads: *Saturday Evening Post,* June 15, 1929, p. 148; Nov. 9, 1929, p. 169; *Better Homes and Gardens,* Oct. 1929, p. 99; Aug. 1930, p. 49.

9. Warren I. Susman, "'Personality' and the Making of Twentieth-Century Culture," in *New Directions in American Intellectual History,* ed. John Higham and Paul K. Conkin (Baltimore, 1979), pp. 214–16; Daniel Rodgers, *The Work Ethic in Industrial America, 1850–1920* (Chicago, 1978), p. 38.

10. Paula S. Fass, *The Damned and the Beautiful: American Youth in the 1920s* (New York, 1977), pp. 230, 243.

11. *Saturday Evening Post,* Apr. 28, 1932, p. 143; Aug. 27, 1932, p. 77; *American Magazine,* Feb. 1928, pp. 2, 5; Nov. 1929, p. 167; Mar. 1931, p. 127.

12. *American Magazine,* Apr. 1932, p. 97; *Ladies' Home Journal,* Mar. 1931, p. 102; *Saturday Evening Post,* Feb. 20, 1926, p. 115. See also *Saturday Evening Post,* Apr. 28, 1931, p. 143; Nov. 20, 1926, p. 162; *American Magazine,* Nov. 1929, p. 162.

13. *American Magazine,* Aug. 1928, p. 149.

14. *Tide,* Nov. 1933, p. 6; *American Magazine,* Feb. 1931, p. 112; *Ladies' Home Journal,* Feb. 1927, p. 126; Mar. 1927, p. 54.

15. *American Magazine,* Nov. 1931, p. 89; June 1929, p. 189; Dec. 1929, p. 183.

16. *Better Homes and Gardens,* Aug. 1928, p. 60; Apr. 1930, p. 124. See also *Saturday Evening Post,* Mar. 1, 1930, p. 145.

17. *Collier's,* Apr. 16, 1927, p. 44; *Saturday Evening Post,* Nov. 9, 1929, p. 169; *Chicago Tribune,* Feb. 15, 1926, p. 7; *Better Homes and Gardens,* Mar. 1929, p. 145.

18. *Ladies' Home Journal,* Oct. 1928, p. 259, *Saturday Evening Post,* Mar. 11, 1922, p. 111; *Better Homes and Gardens,* June 1931, p. 9.

19. *Better Homes and Gardens,* July 1930, p. 6; Sept. 1930, p. 2.

20. *Saturday Evening Post,* Feb. 16, 1929, p. 152; *Better Homes and Gardens,* Oct. 1929, p. 99. See also *Better Homes and Gardens,* Dec. 1929, p. 73; Jan. 1930, p. 48.

21. Paul H. Nystrom, *Economics of Fashion* (New York, 1928), p. 140.

22. *Saturday Evening Post,* Aug. 27, 1932, p. 77; *Tide,* Nov. 1933, p. 6; *Saturday Evening Post,* Feb. 21, 1931, p. 74; Jan. 3, 1931, p. 1; *Better Homes and Gardens,* Mar. 1929, p. 67; *American Magazine,* Sept. 1927, pp. 116–17.

23. *Better Homes and Gardens,* Sept. 1930, p. 2.

24. *Saturday Evening Post,* Mar. 1, 1930, p. 2. See also *Saturday Evening Post,* Mar. 28, 1936, p. 81; *Delineator,* Aug. 1928, p. 68.

25. Robert S. Lynd and Helen Merrell Lynd, *Middletown: A Study of American Culture* (New York, 1929), p. 81.

26. *Saturday Evening Post,* Apr. 15, 1933, p. 68; June 30, 1928, p. 51.

27. T. J. Jackson Lears, *No Place of Grace: Antimodernism and the Transformation of American Culture, 1880–1920* (New York, 1981), pp. 34–37; Peter Berger, Brigitte Berger, and Hansfried Kellner, *The Homeless Mind: Modernization and Consciousness* (New York, 1973), pp. 77–78; Richard M. Huber, *The American Idea of Success* (New York, 1971), pp. 226–29; Susman, "Personality," pp. 218, 220.

28. Dale Carnegie, *How to Win Friends and Influence People,* 22nd ed. (New York, 1937), pp. 83–145; Huber, *The American Idea of Success,* pp. 237–38; *Photoplay Magazine,* June 1930, pp. 22, 135.

29. Martha Wolfenstein and Nathan Leites, *Movies: A Psychological Study* (Glencoe, Ill., 1950), pp. 189–190, 301. Rudolf Arnheim also found the radio soap operas replete with victims of undeserved accusations. See Rudolf Arnheim, "The World of the Daytime Serial," in *Radio Research, 1942–1943,* ed. Paul F. Lazarsfeld and Frank Stanton (New York, 1944), p. 49.

30. *Ladies' Home Journal,* July 1926, p. 62; Oct. 1926, p. 188; *Delineator,* Apr. 1932, p. 35.

31. *Ladies' Home Journal,* Sept. 1929, second cover; *JWT News Letter,* Oct. 1, 1929, p. 1, J. Walter Thompson Company (JWT) Archives, New York City.

32. *Saturday Evening Post,* Apr. 3, 1926, pp. 182–83; Nov. 6, 1926, p. 104; Apr. 16, 1927, p. 199; Scrapbook 54 (Brunswick-Balke-Collender), Lord and Thomas Archives, at Foote, Cone and Belding Communications, Inc., Chicago.

33. *Chicago Tribune,* Nov. 21, 1926, picture section, p. 2.

34. *Los Angeles Times,* July 14, 1929, part VI, p. 3; *Tide,* July 1928, p. 10; *Photoplay Magazine,* Mar. 1930, p. 1.

35. *American Magazine,* Mar. 1926, p. 112.

36. *Printers' Ink,* Oct. 10, 1929, p. 138.

37. *Tide,* Sept. 15, 1927, p. 5; *American Magazine,* Aug. 1929, p. 93; *True Story,* June 1929, p. 133; *Chicago Tribune,* Jan. 11, 1928, p. 16; Jan. 18, 1928, p. 15; Jan. 28, 1928, p. 7; *Photoplay Magazine,* Feb. 1929, p. 111.

38. *True Story,* May 1928, p. 83; June 1929, p. 133; *American Magazine,* Feb. 1930, p. 110; *Saturday Evening Post,* Aug. 23, 1930, p. 124.

39. *Los Angeles Times,* July 6, 1929, p. 3.

40. *Saturday Evening Post,* May 8, 1926, p. 59; *American Magazine,* May 1932, pp. 76–77. See also *Saturday Evening Post,* July 18, 1931, pp. 36–37; Aug. 1, 1931, pp. 30–31; *Better Homes and Gardens,* Mar. 1930, p. 77.

41. *Saturday Evening Post,* Nov. 10, 1928, p. 90; *True Story,* Aug. 1934, p. 57. See also *Chicago Tribune,* Oct. 8, 1930, p. 17; *American Magazine,* Aug. 1930, p. 77; *Woman's Home Companion,* May 1927, p. 96.

42. *American Magazine,* Feb. 1927, p. 130.

43. Henry James, *Hawthorne,* rev. ed. (New York, 1967 [c. 1879]), p. 55.

44. *Printers' Ink,* Nov. 24, 1927, p. 52.

45. On the requirements for "consumer citizenship," see Chapter 3.

46. Francesco M. Nicosia and Robert N. Mayer, "Toward a Sociology of Consumption," *The Journal of Consumer Research* 3(1976): 73; Roland Marchand, "Visions of Class-lessness; Quests for Dominion: American Popular Culture, 1945–1960," in *Reshaping America: Society and Institutions, 1945–1960,* ed. Robert H. Bremner and Gary W. Reichard (Columbus, Ohio, 1982), pp. 165–70.

47. *Saturday Evening Post,* Nov. 15, 1930, p. 123.

48. Ibid.

49. Ibid.

50. *American Magazine,* Feb. 1928, p. 85; Apr. 1931, p. 144; May 1931, p. 181; Oct. 1931, p. 167; *Ladies' Home Journal,* Mar. 1931, p. 149.

51. *Saturday Evening Post,* Jan. 26, 1929, p. 127; *American Magazine,* Apr. 1926, p. 189; Nov. 1926, p. 211; Sept. 1928, p. 177.

52. *American Magazine,* July 1928, p. 110; *Saturday Evening Post,* Dec. 27, 1924, p. 57; May 12, 1928, p. 146; Jan. 26, 1933, pp. 48–49; Jan. 21, 1933, p. 47.

53. *Saturday Evening Post,* June 3, 1933, p. 60; Aug. 5, 1933, p. 67.

54. *Saturday Evening Post,* Jan. 26, 1933, pp. 48–49; *Better Homes and Gardens,* Aug. 1931, p. 38; *Good Housekeeping,* Apr. 1928, p. 7.

55. *American Magazine,* Nov. 1926, p. 211.

56. *American Magazine,* Mar. 1927, p. 100; *Saturday Evening Post,* Mar. 6, 1926, pp. 164–65.

57. *Saturday Evening Post,* Jan. 31, 1931, p. 107; Feb. 28, 1931, p. 39.

58. *Saturday Evening Post,* Sept. 15, 1928, p. 57; Oct. 26, 1929, p. 43; *American Magazine,* Mar. 1927, p. 100; *Advertising Age,* Nov. 11, 1933, p. 10; *Tide,* Dec. 1932, p. 10.

59. *American Magazine,* Mar. 1932, p. 143; *Saturday Evening Post,* Feb. 21, 1931, p. 44; *Los Angeles Times,* Jan. 11, 1929, part II, p. 5; *Tide,* Jan. 1929, p. 2; "Minutes of Representatives Meeting," Jan. 9, 1929, pp. 2–4, JWT Archives. Camels later joined the parade with a "jangled nerves" appeal (*Tide,* June 1934, p. 52).

60. *Saturday Evening Post,* Mar. 27, 1926, p. 45; June 8, 1929, p. 136.

61. *Saturday Evening Post,* Jan. 2, 1926, p. 32; *American Magazine,* Mar. 1927, p. 100; Sept. 1926, p. 114. See also *Saturday Evening Post,* Apr. 10, 1926, p. 99.

62. *Saturday Evening Post,* Dec. 4, 1926, p. 203.

63. For another example of the reaffirmation in this era of the compatibility of technological progress with retention of the best qualities of the past, see John W. Ward, "The Meaning of Lindbergh's Flight," *American Quarterly* 10 (1958): 3–16.

64. *Saturday Evening Post,* Sept. 15, 1928, p. 150; *Ladies' Home Journal,* Sept. 1929, pp. 86–87; Oct. 1929, pp. 89, 221. On the advertising of commodities "as means of circumventing the ills of industrial life," see also Stuart Ewen, *Captains of Consciousness: Advertising and the Social Roots of the Consumer Culture* (New York, 1976), pp. 44, 78.

65. *Saturday Evening Post,* Jan. 9, 1926, p. 231.

66. *San Francisco Examiner,* Jan. 8, 1930, p. 10; *Chicago Tribune,* Mar. 17, 1932, p. 8.

67. This scene is a composite drawn from the following advertisements for Campbell Soups: *American Magazine,* Feb. 1929, p. 63; *Ladies' Home Journal,* May 1931, p. 33; *Saturday Evening Post,* Feb. 14, 1931, p. 25; Nov. 5, 1932, p. 25.

68. *Ladies' Home Journal,* May 1931, p. 33; *American Magazine,* Mar. 1931, p. 79.

69. Ruth Schwartz Cowan, "The Industrial Revolution in the Home: Household Technology and Social Change in the 20th Century," *Technology and Culture* 17 (1976): 16, 21–23; Fass, *The Damned and the Beautiful,* pp. 54–55, 87–89, 100–102.

70. *American Magazine,* Feb. 1927, p. 111.

71. *Saturday Evening Post,* May 21, 1927, p. 123; *American Magazine,* Mar. 1926, p. 117.

72. For examples of parents joining or solicitously watching their children at play, see *Saturday Evening Post,* July 10, 1926, pp. 50–51; Dec. 3, 1927, p. 175; June 1, 1929, pp. 58–59; *Ladies' Home Journal,* Apr. 1926, p. 106. For examples of the suppliant posture, see *Saturday Evening Post,* Dec. 7, 1935, p. 25; Scrapbook 279 (Electric Refrigeration Bureau), Lord and Thomas Archives; *American Magazine,* Mar. 1926, p. 117.

73. *Saturday Evening Post,* July 7, 1928, p. 80; *American Magazine,* Oct. 1931, p. 102.

74. *American Magazine,* Dec. 1928, p. 86; Feb. 1929, p. 63; *Saturday Evening Post,* Nov. 5, 1932, p. 25.

75. *McCall's,* Nov. 1928, p. 88; *Better Homes and Gardens,* Sept. 1930, p. 11; *Ladies' Home Journal,* Mar. 1931, p. 68; Mar. 1933, p. 67; *American Magazine,* Aug. 1932, second cover; *Saturday Evening Post,* June 7, 1930, p. 151; Oct. 22, 1932, p. 71; Jan. 6, 1934, second cover.

76. *American Magazine,* March 1935, p. 98; *Ladies' Home Journal,* Apr. 1931, p. 63; Nov. 1931, p. 69; *American Magazine,* Feb. 1929, p. 76.

77. See, for instance, *Saturday Evening Post,* Mar. 7, 1931, p. 127; *American Magazine,* Nov. 1931, p. 133; June 1932, p. 115; *Ladies' Home Journal,* Mar. 1931, p. 68; *McCall's,* Nov. 1928, p. 88; *Redbook,* Dec. 1939, p. 103.

78. *Chicago Tribune,* Oct. 16, 1930, p. 30; *American Magazine,* Dec. 1928, p. 86; Aug. 1932, second cover; *Ladies' Home Journal,* Apr. 1931, p. 63.

79. *American Magazine,* Nov. 1928, p. 80; Mar. 1935, p. 98. See also *Chicago Tribune,* Sept. 6, 1931, picture section, p. 2.

80. *American Magazine,* Jan. 1929, p. 97; Feb. 1929, p. 76; Mar. 1929, p. 76; Sept. 1928, p. 94; Nov. 1928, p. 80.

81. *Advertising and Selling,* Dec. 15, 1926, p. 62.

82. Martha Wolfenstein, "Trends in Infant Care," *American Journal of Orthopsychiatry* 23 (1952): 122–23; Fass, *The Damned and the Beautiful,* pp. 100, 102; Martha Wolfenstein, "The Emergence of Fun Morality," *Journal of Social Issues* 7 (1951): 15–25. On the rise of applied psychology in the 1920s and 1930s and the personnel management movement, see Donald S. Napoli, *Architects of Adjustment: The History of the Psychological Profession in the United States* (Port Washington, N.Y., 1981), pp. 5, 32–36, 38–40; Gerald E. Kahler and Alton C. Johnson, *The Development of Personnel Administration, 1923–1945* (Madison, Wis., 1971), pp. 19–22; and Loren Baritz, *The Servants of Power: A History of the Use of Social Science in American Industry* (Middletown, Conn., 1960), pp. 5–6, 14–17, 104–106, 118–121. In 1938 an advertising trade journal commented favorably on a university class to train executives of the "cooperative variety" who would "be able to develop harmonious industrial relations" because they had been taught "to remake their personality to fit the requirements of a world which is growing much smaller and therefore more difficult to live in." The parable of the Captivated Child had anticipated the need for malleability that modern conditions now dictated for pursuit of the American dream (*Advertising Age,* Oct. 24, 1938, p. 19).

83. On the defective measures of audience feedback in this era, see Chapter 3.

84. On the argumentative or confrontational qualities of the biblical parables, see Cadoux, *The Parables of Jesus,* pp. 12–13. For a similar view of advertising as "therapeutic," see T. J. Jackson Lears, "From Salvation to Self-Realization: Advertising and the Therapeutic Roots of the Consumer Culture, 1880–1930" in *The Culture of Consumption,* ed. Richard Wightman Fox and T. J. Jackson Lears (New York, 1983), pp. 3–38.

Eight   Visual Clichés: Fantasies and Icons

1. John G. Cawelti, *Adventure, Mystery, and Romance* (Chicago, 1976), pp. 6–9, 20–21, 30, 297; Vladimir Propp, *The Morphology of the Folktale,* ed. Svalava-Jakobson, trans. Laurence Scott (Bloomington, Ind., 1958), pp. 18–23.

2. Jerome L. Singer, *Daydreaming and Fantasy* (London, 1976), pp. 3, 53–55, 118–19.

3. Albert T. Poffenberger, *Psychology in Advertising* (Chicago, 1925), pp. 36, 570. Poffenberger drew heavily on the earlier work of Harry A. Hollingsworth in *Advertising and Selling: Principles of Appeal and Response* (New York, 1913).

4. Poffenberger, *Psychology,* pp. 555, 563–64; Raymond Firth, *Symbols, Public and Private* (London, 1972), p. 105; Sol Worth, in *Studying Visual Communications,* ed. Larry Gross (Philadelphia, 1981), pp. 162, 179.

5. Earnest Elmo Calkins, *Business the Civilizer* (Boston, 1928), p. 141. See also E. H. Gombrich, "The Visual Image," *Scientific American,* Sept. 1972, p. 87.

6. *Printers' Ink,* Aug. 16, 1928, p. 69; *Saturday Evening Post,* June 7, 1930, pp. 76–77. See also *Saturday Evening Post,* May 10, 1930, p. 190.

7. Clifford Geertz, "Art as a Cultural System," *Modern Language Notes* 91 (1976): 1498–99. See also Gombrich, "The Visual Image," p. 87; *Advertising and Selling Fortnightly.* Dec. 2, 1925, p. 30.

8. *Institutional Advertisements,* vol. I, pp. 11, 13, 24, 50, 168, Box 1251, American Telephone and Telegraph Company (AT&T) Archives, New York City.

9. For examples of immense windows and individual panes, see *Saturday Evening Post,* Nov. 30, 1929, p. 78; Feb. 10, 1934, p. 39; May 18, 1935, p. 77; *Printers' Ink,* June 21,

1928, pp. 142–43; June 20, 1929, p. 11; Apr. 16, 1931, p. 30; *Printers' Ink Monthly*, Sept. 1930, pp. 17, 29; Mar. 1931, p. 10. For unobstructed views, see *Tide*, Jan. 1936, p. 71; *American Magazine*, Feb. 1927, p. 163; *Saturday Evening Post*, Mar. 14, 1925, pp. 130–31; Calkins, *Business the Civilizer*, p. 119.

10. Examples of the window-on-the-factory motif were common throughout the 1920s. Very few appeared after 1929.

11. For examples, see *Saturday Evening Post*, June 14, 1924, p. 70; Jan. 23, 1926, p. 1; June 4, 1927, p. 203; Sept. 8, 1928, p. 106; Aug. 24, 1929, p. 156; *True Story*, Jan. 1929, p. 131; *Printers' Ink Monthly*, Jan. 1928, p. 116; Apr. 1928, p. 129; June 1928, p. 133; *Advertising and Selling*, Feb. 9, 1927, p. 49; Apr. 17, 1929, p. 53; Nov. 27, 1929, p. 20.

12. *Saturday Evening Post*, Nov. 30, 1929, pp. 78–79; Batten, Barton, Durstine and Osborn, Inc., "Account Status Binder" (1928), BBDO Archives, New York City.

13. For examples of the view from the skyscraper office, see *Saturday Evening Post*, Jan. 9, 1926, p. 255; June 27, 1928, p. 85; Oct. 20, 1928, p. 180; Sept. 14, 1929, p. 247; Feb. 15, 1930, p. 134; July 11, 1931, pp. 58–59; *American Magazine*, Oct. 1930, p. 96; *Printers' Ink Monthly*, Dec. 1930, p. 13; Mar. 1931, p. 10; *Printers' Ink*, Apr. 16, 1931, p. 30.

14. *Saturday Evening Post*, Feb. 10, 1934, p. 39; *Printers' Ink Monthly*, Sept. 1930, p. 29; *Advertising and Selling*, July 28, 1926, pp. 54–55.

15. *Saturday Evening Post*, Oct. 27, 1928, p. 123; Apr. 23, 1927, p. 60; Sept. 22, 1928, p. 189; *Advertising and Selling Fortnightly*, Mar. 24, 1926, p. 26. See also *Collier's*, Oct. 13, 1928, p. 55; *Liberty*, Mar. 8, 1930, p. 29.

16. *Saturday Evening Post*, Feb. 8, 1930, p. 169; "A Message to Business Women" (1928), Pinkham Copy, vol. 369, Lydia Estes Pinkham Medicine Company Papers, Arthur and Elizabeth Schlesinger Library, Radcliffe College.

17. For examples, see *Saturday Evening Post*, Sept. 15, 1928, pp. 93, 194; Nov. 3, 1928, p. 160; Dec. 15, 1928, p. 161; *American Magazine*, Feb. 1928, p. 153; *Printers' Ink Monthly*, Mar. 1928, p. 135; *Printers' Ink*, May 17, 1934, pp. 42–43.

18. *Saturday Evening Post*, May 4, 1929, p. 95.

19. Anne Hollander, *Seeing Through Clothes* (New York, 1978), pp. 34–36; Herbert Collins, "The Sedentary Society," in *Mass Leisure*, ed. Eric Larrabee and Rolf Meyersohn (Glencoe, Ill., 1958), p. 20.

20. Barbara Welter, "The Cult of True Womanhood," *American Quarterly* 18 (1966): 171–74; Kathryn Kish Sklar, *Catherine Beecher: A Study in American Domesticity* (New Haven, Conn., 1973), pp. 135–38, 153–54; 160–63; Paula S. Fass, *The Damned and the Beautiful* (New York, 1977), pp. 116–17.

21. Fass, *The Damned and the Beautiful*, pp. 55, 63, 81, 89.

22. For examples of typical degrees of "soft focus," see *Saturday Evening Post*, June 19, 1926, p. 127; Sept. 29, 1928, pp. 96–97; Oct. 5, 1928, p. 92; Dec. 14, 1929, pp. 86–87; Mar. 8, 1930, p. 117; *Collier's*, Nov. 24, 1928, p. 35.

23. *Saturday Evening Post*, Mar. 31, 1928, p. 136; May 26, 1928, p. 134.

24. *Saturday Evening Post*, Sept. 29, 1928, p. 2; Dec. 15, 1928, p. 2; Dec. 8, 1928, p. 155; Scrapbook 379 (Arco–Petro Boilers), Lord and Thomas Archives,; at Foote, Cone and Belding Communications, Inc., Chicago.

25. For examples, see *Saturday Evening Post*, June 30, 1928, p. 140; Mar. 9, 1929, p. 1; Sept. 13, 1920, p. 153; Dec. 6, 1930, p. 36; Sept. 12, 1931, p. 43; *American Magazine*, Apr. 1931, p. 181; *Printers' Ink*, Feb. 25, 1931, p. 9; Oct. 1, 1931, pp. 14–15; Nov. 5, 1931, p. 15; Nov. 24, 1932, pp. 22–23; Feb. 8, 1934, p. 34; July 19, 1934, p. 37.

26. *Advertising and Selling*, Jan. 22, 1930, p. 47; May 25, 1933, p. 7; *Printers' Ink*, Nov. 20, 1930, pp. 14–15; Dec. 4, 1930, pp. 70–71.

27. For examples, see *Saturday Evening Post*, June 30, 1928, p. 140; Sept. 13, 1930, p. 153; *Chicago Tribune*, Sept. 21, 1931, p. 14; *Advertising and Selling*, May 13, 1931, p. 4.

28. For examples, see *Saturday Evening Post,* Oct. 6, 1928, p. 192; Dec. 6, 1930, p. 36; Nov. 2, 1935, p. 87; *Chicago Tribune,* Sept. 21, 1931, p. 14; *Printers' Ink,* Jan. 20, 1927, p. 24; Oct. 6, 1927, pp. 14–15; Feb. 25, 1931, p. 9.

29. *San Francisco Examiner,* Nov. 15, 1929, p. 11; *Saturday Evening Post,* Nov. 30, 1935, p. 87; Scrapbooks 55–56 (Brunswick-Balke-Collender) and Scrapbook 330 (RCA Victor), Lord and Thomas Archives.

30. George Lakoff and Mark Johnson, *Metaphors We Live By* (Chicago, 1980), pp. 14, 16, 42–43.

31. *San Francisco Examiner,* Nov. 5, 1929, p. 7; *Saturday Evening Post,* Jan. 9, 1932, p. 139; Dec. 8, 1934, p. 39; Dec. 28, 1935, p. 39; Sept. 18, 1937, p. 78; *Advertising and Selling,* Sept. 5, 1928, p. 32; *Fortune,* Jan. 1932, p. 92.

32. *Saturday Evening Post,* May 22, 1926, p. 42; Sept. 18, 1926, p. 66; Nov. 27, 1926, p. 96.

33. *Saturday Evening Post,* June 8, 1929, p. 155; *Los Angeles Times,* Aug. 25, 1930, p. 4; *Printers' Ink,* Sept. 17, 1931, pp. 58–59. See also *Tide,* Aug. 1932, p. 37; *Collier's,* Apr. 2, 1927, p. 42; May 12, 1928, p. 21.

34. *Saturday Evening Post,* Mar. 2, 1929, pp. 126–27; July 26, 1930, p. 131; Sept. 13, 1930, pp. 118–19; *Printers' Ink,* June 15, 1933, pp. 14–15; *Printers' Ink Monthly,* Aug. 1928, p. 38; *Tide,* Aug. 1932, p. 37.

35. *Saturday Evening Post,* Nov. 29, 1930, pp. 70–71. On the absence of human figures from interior photographs of the city, see William R. Taylor, "Psyching out the City," in *Uprooted Americans: Essays to Honor Oscar Handlin,* ed. Richard Bushman et al. (Boston, 1979), pp. 249, 257.

36. Hugh Ferriss, *The Metropolis of Tomorrow* (New York, 1929), p. 62. Despite this "warning," Ferriss's own romantic renderings of futuristic skyscraper cities contributed significantly to optimistic visions of human mastery in a complex but highly ordered urban life of the future. Advertising trade journals regularly employed Ferriss's renderings as illustrations.

37. Taylor, "Psyching out the City," pp. 248–49, 255, 280.

38. Lewis Atherton, *Main Street on the Middle Border* (Bloomington, Ind., 1954), pp. xv, 32, 336, 352–53. Atherton cites a 1930 survey of abandoned places which revealed that within the previous eighty-five years some 2,200 villages had vanished in the state of Iowa alone.

39. For examples, see *Saturday Evening Post,* Sept. 18, 1926, p. 93; Nov. 20, 1926, p. 203; Aug. 13, 1927, p. 136; May 18, 1929, p. 175; June 8, 1929, p. 69; June 22, 1929, p. 59; Apr. 12, 1930, p. 1; Oct. 18, 1930, p. 153.

40. *Saturday Evening Post,* May 31, 1930, p. 57; Sept. 6, 1930, p. 55.

41. *Squibb Sales Bulletin* 9 (1933): 369, E. R. Squibb and Company Archives, Princeton, N.J.

42. *Saturday Evening Post,* Sept. 22, 1928, p. 107.

43. *Tide,* May 1936, p. 70; *Advertising and Selling,* Feb. 27, 1936, p. 106; Apr. 23, 1936, p. 69; Jan. 30, 1936, p. 11.

44. *Printers' Ink,* Sept. 27, 1928, p. 92. For a rare example of the inclusion of specific New Testament imagery, see *Saturday Evening Post,* Dec. 7, 1929, p. 102.

45. Leo Spitzer, *A Method of Interpreting Literature* (Northampton, Mass., 1949), pp. 117–122.

46. Marghanita Laski, "Advertising—Sacred and Profane," *The Twentieth Century* 165 (1959): 119, 122; Rudolph Otto, *The Idea of the Holy,* trans. John W. Harvey (London, 1923), pp. 6–7, 20, 31.

47. Laski, "Advertising—Sacred and Profane," p. 125.

48. Ibid., p. 128; *Printers' Ink Monthly,* May 1926, p. 75.

49. *American Weekly,* July 23, 1933, p. 13; *Saturday Evening Post,* Mar. 6, 1926, pp. 112–13; Oct. 10, 1931, pp. 78–79; Sept. 28, 1929, pp. 88–89; Aug. 29, 1931, p. 75; *Advertising and Selling,* Jan. 23, 1929, p. 69; *Printers' Ink Monthly,* Dec. 1934, p. 37; Nov. 1932, p. 20.

50. *Tide,* Mar. 15, 1928, p. 10; *Saturday Evening Post,* May 12, 1928, pp. 100–101; Aug. 22, 1931, pp. 50–51; June 21, 1930, p. 61; Nov. 14, 1931, pp. 100–101; *Printers' Ink,* Apr. 12, 1928, pp. 89, 92.

51. *Printers' Ink,* Jan. 21, 1926, p. 142; Feb. 24, 1927, p. 130. Although exaggeration was often a "dangerous thing" in advertising because it undermined credibility, one trade journal writer observed, "when confined to the illustration" exaggeration visualized "something which no words, no matter how cunningly they are strung together, can adequately picture" (*Advertising and Selling Fortnightly,* Dec. 2, 1925, p. 30).

52. *Printers' Ink Monthly,* Mar. 1926, pp. 30–31; Rosalind H. Williams, *Dream Worlds: Mass Consumption in Late Nineteenth-Century France* (Berkeley, Calif., 1982), pp. 188, 191–93.

53. For examples, see *Saturday Evening Post,* Mar. 13, 1926, p. 188; June 14, 1930, p. 81; Scrapbook 330 (RCA Victor), Lord and Thomas Archives; *Printers' Ink Monthly,* May 1926, p. 138; Dec. 1934, p. 37; *Advertising and Selling,* Feb. 28, 1935, p. 4.

54. Bruce Barton to Louise MacLeod, Jan. 14, 1937, Box 5, Bruce Barton Papers, Wisconsin State Historical Society; *Printers' Ink,* Feb. 19, 1931, pp. 90–91; Apr. 21, 1932, p. 72; *Saturday Evening Post,* Dec. 30, 1933, p. 43. *J. Walter Thompson News Bulletin,* Nov. 1930, p. 5; "Minutes of Representatives Meeting," June 4, 1930, p. 16, JWT Archives, New York City; BBDO, *News Letter,* March 14, 1936, pp. 7–8, BBDO Archives, New York City. See also the discussion of advertisers' views of the consumer audience in Chapter 3.

55. Raymond Williams, *Culture and Society: 1780–1950* (New York, 1958), p. 319.

56. Vachel Lindsay, *The Art of the Motion Picture* (New York, 1915), pp. 2, 39, 41.

57. Jonathan Price, *The Best Thing on TV* (New York, 1978), p. 121.

58. For several classic "in its presence" refrigerator tableaux, see *Saturday Evening Post,* Nov. 13, 1926, p. 157; Sept. 24, 1927, p. 117; Oct. 22, 1927, p. 160; Oct. 27, 1928, p. 135; July 25, 1931, pp. 44–45; *Los Angeles Times,* Aug. 26, 1930, p. 9. Even in the company showroom, the opened refrigerator door might disclose a full supply of food. See *Ladies' Home Journal,* Mar. 1928, p. 92.

59. *American Magazine,* Oct. 1927, p. 107; *Los Angeles Times,* Jan. 10, 1929, p. 7; *Saturday Evening Post,* June 1, 1929, pp. 40–41; Sept. 24, 1927, p. 117; July 6, 1935; p. 39; Nov. 22, 1930, p. 37.

60. See, for example, *Good Housekeeping,* Oct. 1928, p. 115; *Saturday Evening Post,* June 5, 1926, p. 62; Oct. 22, 1927, p. 160; Oct. 27, 1928, p. 135; July 25, 1931, pp. 44–45; Mar. 23, 1935, p. 92; Mar. 9, 1929, p. 47; *American Magazine,* Nov. 1927, p. 109. In the last two advertisements cited, the wife combined the two variants by adopting the salesman's demonstration stance before her friends.

61. *American Magazine,* Apr. 1930, p. 97; *Saturday Evening Post,* Dec. 5, 1931, p. 65; Dec. 13, 1930, pp. 70–71; *San Francisco Examiner,* Nov. 1, 1929, p. 7. The company's house organ described one of these tableaux of rapt attention as "an illustration of sentiment exquisitely portrayed" (*The Ibaisaic,* Nov. 13, 1930, p. 8).

62. *American Magazine,* July 1926, p. 135.

63. *Tide,* May 1933, p. 12; *American Magazine,* Oct. 1927, p. 127.

64. For examples, see *San Francisco Examiner,* Nov. 26, 1929, p. 8; *Saturday Evening Post,* Dec. 12, 1925, p. 109; Dec. 4, 1926, p. 118; Nov. 5, 1927, p. 88; Dec. 20, 1930, p. 42; Nov. 28, 1931, pp. 42–43; *American Magazine,* Dec. 1926, p. 177.

65. *Printers' Ink,* Dec. 26, 1935, pp. 16–17. See also *Saturday Evening Post,* Dec. 19, 1925, p. 136; Dec. 12, 1925, p. 87; Nov. 23, 1929, p. 92.

66. *Better Homes and Gardens*, Mar. 1930, p. 53. For quite different kinds of poignant moments, see *Chicago Tribune*, Feb. 14, 1926, magazine section, pt. 2, pp. 2, 4; *Advertising and Selling*, Feb. 28, 1935, p. 21.

67. *American Weekly*, Mar. 14, 1926, p. 19; *True Story*, Mar. 1929, p. 73.

68. *Printers' Ink*, June 23, 1927, p. 154.

69. For examples of a variety of "radiant beams," see *Saturday Evening Post*, Oct. 27, 1928, pp. 70–71; Mar. 16, 1929, p. 155; June 22, 1929, p. 71; Aug. 24, 1929, p. 69; Sept. 28, 1929, p. 83; Dec. 21, 1929, p. 47; May 3, 1930, p. 61; *Printers' Ink*, Apr. 3, 1930, p. 163.

70. *Printers' Ink*, Jan. 28, 1926, pp. 99, 104; Feb. 24, 1927, pp. 126–127, 129.

71. *Advertising and Selling*, Oct. 10, 1935, p. 33; Dec. 12, 1928, p. 25; July 10, 1929, p. 85; *Saturday Evening Post*, Mar. 30, 1929, p. 97; *Printers' Ink*, Nov. 5, 1931, p. 2.

72. Hollander, *Seeing Through Clothes*, pp. 47–48.

73. Elizabeth Kendall, *Where She Danced* (New York, 1979), p. 173.

74. *Advertising and Selling*, May 18, 1927, p. 9; *Saturday Evening Post*, May 15, 1926, p. 175; Taylor, "Psyching out the City," pp. 247–48, 257, 285.

75. For examples of the city as castle, see *Saturday Evening Post*, Feb. 27, 1926, p. 70; Mar. 6, 1926, p. 97; June 19, 1926, p. 100; Feb. 27, 1930, p. 161; Sept. 27, 1930, p. 161; Nov. 22, 1930, p. 74; *Advertising and Selling*, Oct. 31, 1928, p. 35.

76. For examples, see *Saturday Evening Post*, May 26, 1928, pp. 122–23; Mar. 16, 1929, p. 74; June 8, 1929, p. 164; July 13, 1929, p. 83; Sept. 7, 1929, p. 172; Oct. 26, 1929, p. 94; *Printers' Ink*, Sept. 13, 1928, p. 69; Dec. 18, 1930, p. 5; *Printers' Ink Monthly*, Aug. 1930, pp. 113–14; *San Francisco Examiner*, July 7, 1933, p. 9.

77. *Chicago Tribune*, Nov. 30, 1926, p. 15; *Advertising and Selling*, Nov. 10, 1932, p. 12; *Saturday Evening Post*, Oct. 19, 1929, p. 147; May 4, 1929, p. 51.

78. *Saturday Evening Post*, Dec. 4, 1926, p. 189; Dec. 29, 1928, p. 87; May 18, 1929, p. 164; Nov. 30, 1929, p. 108; May 10, 1930, p. 51.

79. *Saturday Evening Post*, June 14, 1930, p. 119; May 27, 1933, fourth cover; *Printers' Ink Monthly*, July 1930, p. 72; *Delineator*, Jan. 1930, p. 69; *Good Housekeeping*, Mar. 1936, p. 208.

80. *Tide*, May 1928, p. 7; *San Francisco Examiner*, Mar. 11, 1926, p. 13.

81. *Saturday Evening Post*, Jan. 23, 1926, p. 127.

82. *Printers' Ink Monthly*, Mar. 1926, p. 30; *Advertising and Selling*, Dec. 12, 1928, p. 25; *Printers' Ink*, Apr. 14, 1927, pp. 18–19; Jan. 12, 1928, pp. 4, 179; Mar. 15, 1928, p. 81; Sept. 28, 1928, pp. 138–39; June 13, 1929, p. 178; *Advertising and Selling Fortnightly*, Dec. 2, 1925, p. 30; Apr. 21, 1926, p. 29.

83. Clifford Geertz, *The Interpretation of Cultures* (New York, 1973), p. 127; T. J. Jackson Lears, *No Place of Grace: Antimodernism and the Transformation of American Culture, 1880–1920* (New York, 1981), pp. 33, 208, 301.

Nine   Advertising in Overalls: Parables and Visual Clichés of the Depression

1. *Advertising and Selling Fortnightly*, Apr. 7, 1926, p. 9; *Printers' Ink*, Jan. 7, 1926, pp. 118–19.

2. *Advertising and Selling*, Nov. 27, 1929, p. 18.

3. Ibid., Nov. 13, 1929, p. 17; Nov. 27, 1929, pp. 17–19, 58.

4. *Tide*, Nov. 1929, p. 8; Dec. 1929, pp. 4–5; *San Francisco Examiner*, Nov. 7, 1929, p. 33. "Let's Go To Work" received a Harvard Award for 1929 as "a helpful message at a needed moment" which readers had admired for its "timeliness, common sense,

and good humor." The awards committee, however, cited no evidence for its generalizations about reader reaction. The award to Erwin, Wasey corroborated the argument by critics that the Harvard Awards remained oblivious to the question of whether a "good ad" had any practical effect (Harvard University, Graduate School of Business Administration, *Harvard Advertising Awards, 1929*, [New York, 1930], pp. 8–9).

5. *Printers' Ink,* Dec. 12, 1929, p. 58.

6. *Advertising and Selling,* Apr. 16, 1930, p. 40. For figures on the decline in advertising lineage, see *Printers' Ink,* Nov. 10, 1932, p. 111, and Frank Luther Mott, *American Journalism: A History, 1607–1960,* 3rd ed. (New York, 1962), p. 675.

7. *Advertising and Selling,* July 8, 1931, pp. 3, 67.

8. Ibid., June 24, 1931, p. 23; June 9, 1932, p. 32; Ralph M. Hower, *The History of an Advertising Agency* (Cambridge, Mass., 1939), p. 201; Fred Manchee, *The Huckster's Revenge* (New York, 1959), p. 173; Robert Koretz, untitled manuscript in Mr. Koretz's possession; John Gunther, *Taken at the Flood; The Story of Albert B. Lasker* (New York, 1960), p. 209; Jim Ellis, *Billboards to Buicks: Advertising—As I Lived It* (New York, 1968), p. 93.

9. *Printers; Ink,* July 3, 1930, pp. 69–71; Oct. 29, 1931, p. 70; Apr. 30, 1931, pp. 106–107; May 28, 1931, pp. 54–55; *Advertising and Selling,* Oct. 14, 1931, p. 48; Apr. 28, 1932, p. 17; July 7, 1932, p. 27.

10. *Printers' Ink,* June 11, 1931, pp. 3, 6, 121–22; Nov. 5, 1931, p. 112; Nov. 13, 1931, pp. 17–18; Oct. 31, 1935, p. 48.

11. Frank Allen Burt, *American Advertising Agencies* (New York, 1940), p. 1; *Printers' Ink,* Nov. 5, 1931, pp. 4, 112, 114; Nov. 12, 1931, p. 18; *Advertising and Selling,* May 25, 1933, p. 32; Apr. 12, 1934, pp. 19, 34, 36; *Advertising Age,* Aug. 12, 1933, p. 4.

12. *Better Homes and Gardens,* June 1931, p. 87; Mar. 1933, p. 8; Apr. 1933, fourth cover; *Saturday Evening Post,* July 4, 1931, p. 32; Feb. 11, 1933, p. 35; Feb. 25, 1933, p. 76; Aug. 24, 1935, p. 1; *Chicago Tribune,* Mar. 14, 1932, p. 7.

13. *Better Homes and Gardens,* Oct. 1931, pp. 5, 57; Feb. 1932, p. 65; *Saturday Evening Post,* May 17, 1930, p. 52; *American Magazine,* Feb. 1932, p. 142.

14. N. W. Ayer and Son, Inc., "What About Radio?" typescript of booklet [May 1931], Box 30–61, Ayer & Son Archives, New York City; "Minutes of Representatives Meeting," Apr. 14, 1931, p. 6, J. Walter Thompson Company (JWT) Archives, New York City; *Advertising Age,* Apr. 30, 1932, p. 10; *Advertising and Selling,* May 26, 1932, p. 48; Sept. 29, 1932, p. 44; Herman Hettinger, *A Decade of Radio Advertising* (Chicago, 1933), pp. 113, 272; *Saturday Evening Post,* Dec. 10, 1932, p. 51; *Printers' Ink,* Sept. 15, 1932, p. 33; *Fortune,* Sept. 1932, p. 37.

15. *Saturday Evening Post,* Nov. 19, 1927, p. 67; Jan. 14, 1928, p. 79; Dec. 1, 1928, p. 51; *American Magazine,* Nov. 1930, p. 8; *Saturday Evening Post,* Jan. 9, 1932, p. 85; June 25, 1932, p. 33; *Good Housekeeping,* Mar. 1933, p. 105.

16. *American Magazine,* Jan. 1932, p. 75; Aug. 1933, p. 1; *Saturday Evening Post,* June 25, 1932, p. 33; *Ladies' Home Journal,* Sept. 1933, p. 5.

17. *American Magazine,* Jan. 1933, p. 1. See also *Better Homes and Gardens,* Aug. 1933, p. 33; *Saturday Evening Post,* Feb. 6, 1932, p. 45; July 29, 1933, p. 1.

18. *Saturday Evening Post,* Nov. 15, 1930, p. 125; Nov. 22, 1930, p. 127; Dec. 6, 1930, p. 150; Oct. 10, 1931, p. 100; Oct. 24, 1931, p. 76; Nov. 7, 1931, p. 58; Nov. 21, 1931, p. 87; Oct. 8, 1932, p. 80; Oct. 22, 1932, p. 70; *American Magazine,* Jan. 1933, p. 117.

19. *Saturday Evening Post,* Jan. 16, 1932, p. 105; Mar. 5, 1932, p. 127; Apr. 2, 1932, p. 97; May 2, 1932, p. 100.

20. Ibid., Oct. 8, 1932, p. 38; Jan. 17, 1931, p. 30; June 3, 1933, p. 75; *American Magazine,* June 1931, p. 113. See also *American Magazine,* Feb. 1931, p. 131; *Liberty,* Mar. 26, 1932, p. 47; *Redbook,* May 1933, p. 95.

21. *Better Homes and Gardens,* June 1933, p. 33; *New Outlook,* Jan. 1933, p. 68; *Saturday Evening Post,* Apr. 9, 1932, p. 129; Aug. 27, 1932, p. 77; *American Magazine,* Oct. 1932, p. 68; Feb. 1933, p. 9. See also *Saturday Evening Post,* June 27, 1931, p. 141.

22. *Advertising Age,* May 14, 1932, p. 1.

23. *Saturday Evening Post,* Aug. 19, 1923, pp. 38–39; Oct. 14, 1933, p. 55; Mar. 28, 1931, p. 113; *Better Homes and Gardens,* Apr. 1933, p. 33.

24. *American Magazine,* June 1933, p. 87; *Literary Digest,* Apr. 15, 1933, p. 25.

25. *Saturday Evening Post,* Feb. 18, 1933, p. 75; Dec. 8, 1934, p. 3; *Good Housekeeping,* Apr. 1933, p. 1; *American Magazine,* Jan. 1935, p. 1. See also *American Magazine,* June 1935, p. 1.

26. *Tide,* Jan. 1936, p. 71; *Good Housekeeping,* Feb. 1933, p. 1; *Saturday Evening Post,* May 28, 1932, p. 45; *Ladies' Home Journal,* Apr. 1933, p. 1.

27. "Monday Evening Talk," Mar. 24, 1930, p. 7, JWT Archives; *The Ibaisaic,* Oct. 13, 1932, p. 16, The Hoover Company Archives, North Canton, Ohio.

28. *Ladies' Home Journal,* Apr. 1933, p. 1; *Saturday Evening Post,* Oct. 28, 1933, p. 85. See also *Ladies' Home Journal,* June 1933, p. 95.

29. *The Ibaisaic,* Sept. 1, 1932, pp. 6–7; Apr. 13, 1933, p. 11; *American Magazine,* Nov. 1932, p. 83; *Saturday Evening Post,* May 13, 1933, p. 71.

30. *The Ibaisaic,* Oct. 13, 1932, p. 16; Sept. 1, 1932, pp. 6–7; *Advertising and Selling,* Mar. 2, 1933, p. 21. At J. Walter Thompson, Aminta Casseres argued that consumers gained enjoyment from opportunities to glimpse the luxuries of the rich ("Minutes of Representatives Meeting," Oct. 21, 1930, pp. 3–4, JWT Archives).

31. *Printers' Ink,* Nov. 5, 1931, p. 1; *Tide,* Mar. 1935, p. 15; Sept. 1935, p. 15; *McCall's,* Oct. 1934, p. 75; Nov. 1934, p. 39; *Saturday Evening Post,* Aug. 19, 1933, pp. 38–39; *Ladies' Home Journal,* Mar. 1931, p. 93; May 1931, p. 71.

32. *Ladies' Home Journal,* Nov. 1933, p. 47; *Good Housekeeping,* Jan. 1933, p. 111; "Account History, Royal Baking Powder Company," Case History Files, JWT Archives; *Saturday Evening Post,* Dec. 2, 1933, p. 42; *Tide,* Jan. 1936, p. 71.

33. *The Ibaisaic,* Sept. 1, 1932, pp. 6–7.

34. *American Magazine,* Oct. 1933, p. 97; *Saturday Evening Post,* Feb. 18, 1933, p. 35.

35. *American Magazine,* Apr. 1929, p. 212; Nov. 1929, pp. 191, 198; Feb. 1930, p. 145; *Saturday Evening Post,* June 8, 1929, p. 57; Feb. 28, 1931, pp. 118–19; *Ladies' Home Journal,* Sept. 1933, p. 80; Dec. 1933, p. 53; Nov. 1933, p. 135; *Liberty,* Jan. 28, 1933, p. 31.

36. *Parents' Magazine,* Nov. 1931, p. 59; *Saturday Evening Post,* Feb. 28, 1931, pp. 118–19; Aug. 29, 1931, p. 87; *Ladies' Home Journal,* Nov. 1933, p. 135.

37. *Saturday Evening Post,* Sept. 3, 1932, p. 50.

38. Ibid., Jan. 30, 1932, p. 79; Nov. 11, 1933, p. 36. See also *Delineator,* Oct. 1932, p. 47; Nov. 1932, p. 45.

39. *Saturday Evening Post,* Sept. 3, 1932, p. 45.

40. Ibid.

41. *Ladies' Home Journal,* Sept. 1931, p. 81; *Saturday Evening Post,* Mar. 18, 1933, p. 90; *American Magazine,* Mar. 1935, p. 169; Nov. 1935, p. 131. See also *Saturday Evening Post,* Jan. 11, 1936, p. 29.

42. *McCall's,* September–November issues for 1928 through 1935. In 1931 an additional five advertisements employed the issue of underweight and refusal to eat as a secondary theme. This theme had appeared only once as a secondary theme in the September through November issues of 1928 and twice in the same period of 1929.

43. *Chicago Tribune,* Sept. 24, 1931, p. 16; Sept. 13, 1931, picture section, pt. 2, p. 4; *American Magazine,* Apr. 1935, p. 125; *San Francisco Examiner,* July 14, 1933, p. 11; *American Magazine,* Mar. 1932, p. 89; *Good Housekeeping,* Feb. 1932, p. 217; Feb. 1933, p. 127; Mar. 1934, p. 116; *Ladies' Home Journal,* Sept. 1933, p. 80.

44. *American Magazine,* July 1931, p. 116; May 1931, p. 134; *Saturday Evening Post,* Oct.

10, 1931, p. 94; May 21, 1932, p. 85; June 20, 1931, p. 125; July 23, 1932, p. 73.

45. *Saturday Evening Post,* May 21, 1932, p. 85. The results of a Gallup study and a coupon check suggested that the Cocomalt ads had attracted much higher than average reader interest (*Advertising Age,* May 14, 1932, p. 7).

46. *Printers' Ink,* Oct. 1, 1931, pp. 86–87; Aug. 18, 1932, pp. 22–23; Aug. 23, 1930, p. 90; Mar. 3, 1932, p. 26; *Printers' Ink Monthly,* Dec. 1931, p. 50; *Fortune,* Apr. 1933, p. 3; "Minutes of Creative Staff Meeting," Mar. 29, 1933, pp. 6–7, JWT Archives.

47. *Printers' Ink,* Feb. 5, 1931, pp. 77–78; Dec. 11, 1930, pp. 17–18, 87; Jan. 15, 1931, pp. 3, 133; Jan. 12, 1933, p. 25.

48. *Printers' Ink Monthly,* May 1932, p. 38; May 1933, pp. 28–29; July 1933, p. 28; *Printers' Ink,* Apr. 2, 1931, p. 149; Oct. 4, 1934, p. 34; *Advertising Age,* Nov. 4, 1933, p. 21; *Advertising and Selling,* June 22, 1933, p. 22.

49. *Printers' Ink Monthly,* June 1931, pp. 29–30; May 1933, p. 28; *Advertising and Selling,* Aug. 5, 1931, p. 23; *Printers' Ink,* Dec. 11, 1930, p. 18; Nov. 10, 1932, pp. 10, 12; Oct. 1, 1931, pp. 38–39; Dec. 17, 1931, p. 135; July 6, 1933, pp. 3–4; *Advertising and Selling,* Feb. 19, 1930, p. 26; July 5, 1934, p. 3; Jeffrey Meikle, *Twentieth Century Limited: Industrial Design in America, 1925–1939* (Philadelphia, 1979), p. 70.

50. *Tide,* Dec. 1933, p. 17; *Printers' Ink,* Apr. 12, 1934, p. 50.

51. *Printers' Ink Monthly,* June 1931, pp. 29–30; *Saturday Evening Post,* Nov. 7, 1931, p. 2; John M. Shaw, "What Are We Selling, Anyway?" typescript, Box 2, John M. Shaw Papers, Wisconsin State Historical Society.

52. *Advertising and Selling,* Dec. 9, 1931, p. 21; *Advertising Age,* Nov. 18, 1933, p. 24; *Tide,* Dec. 1933, p. 17.

53. *Printers' Ink,* Feb. 23, 1933, p. 3; *Advertising and Selling,* Nov. 24, 1932, p. 21; Aug. 30, 1934, p. 24; *Printers' Ink Monthly,* Sept. 1933, pp. 22–23; Frank Wayne Fox, "Advertisements as Documents in Social and Cultural History" (M.A. thesis, University of Utah, 1969), p. 156.

54. *Printers' Ink,* Dec. 11, 1930, pp. 18–19; *Printers' Ink Monthly,* Jan. 1933, p. 30; July 1932, p. 60.

55. *Printers' Ink Monthly,* Apr. 1934, p. 36; Helen Woodward, *It's An Art* (New York, 1938), p. 87.

56. *Advertising and Selling,* Aug. 30, 1934, p. 26; Oct. 10, 1935, p. 36; *Printers' Ink Monthly,* July 1932, p. 60.

57. Advertising and Selling, Aug. 30, 1934, p. 25; Nov. 24, 1932, p. 21; [H. A. Batten], "Criticism of *History of An Advertising Agency,*" p. 21, folder C, Ralph M. Hower Papers, Baker Library, Harvard Graduate School of Business.

58. Otis A. Pease, *The Responsibilities of American Advertising* (New Haven, Conn., 1958), pp. 60–66; *Chicago Tribune,* Mar. 31, 1932, p. 13; *Printers' Ink,* Mar. 12, 1931, pp. 130–31; Apr. 7, 1932, p. 8; Albert D. Lasker, "A Call for Dedication to Fundamentals in Advertising," typescript of address, June 10, 1935, p. 8, Foote, Cone and Belding Communications, Inc., Information Center, Chicago. For trade approval of another competitive campaign, see *Advertising Age,* Mar. 12, 1932, p. 4.

59. *Advertising and Selling,* Aug. 30, 1934, pp. 24–25; *Advertising Age,* Apr. 23, 1932, p. 12; Dec. 30, 1933, p. 10. For examples of the increasing proportion of "comic-strip" and continuity ads, see the issues of the *Saturday Evening Post* for Feb. 9, 1935, and Aug. 10, 1935.

60. *Printers' Ink,* Sept. 7, 1933, pp. 61–63; *True Story,* Aug. 1934, pp. 3, 5, 9; *Advertising and Selling,* Sept. 14, 1933, p. 16; *Tide,* Oct. 1932, p. 13.

61. *Printers' Ink Monthly,* May 1932, p. 33; *Advertising and Selling,* Aug. 1939, p. 20; *Printers' Ink,* Apr. 12, 1934, p. 73; *Advertising and Selling,* June 9, 1932, p. 15; Aug. 30, 1934, p. 26. For an example of the regular violation of the integrity of advertising illustrations, see *Saturday Evening Post,* Feb. 2, 1935, throughout.

62. *Advertising and Selling,* Dec. 7, 1933, p. 34. See also *Advertising Age,* Aug. 3, 1936, p. 26.

63. *Advertising and Selling*, July 6, 1933, p. 18; Dec. 7, 1933, p. 64; Dec. 21, 1933, p. 19; *Fortune*, Apr. 1935, p. 134; *McCall's*, Oct. 1932, p. 2; *Tide*, Sept. 1932, p. 19.

64. *Advertising and Selling*, Feb. 3, 1932, p. 26; Sept. 14, 1933, p. 16; *Printers' Ink Monthly*, Aug. 1934, pp. 16–18; *The Ibaisaic*, Mar. 24, 1934, pp. 16–17; *Judicious Advertising*, Feb. 1925, p. 18. For examples of the new technique, see *Saturday Evening Post*, Apr. 6, 1935, pp. 80–81, and May 4, 1935, pp. 72–73.

65. *Printers' Ink*, May 5, 1932, p. 96; *Advertising and Selling*, May 12, 1932, p. 22; June 22, 1933, p. 16; *Printers' Ink Monthly*, June 1935, p. 30; "Minutes of Creative Staff Meeting," Mar. 1, 1933, pp. 1–3, JWT Archives; *Advertising Age*, July 8, 1935, p. 24.

66. *Printers' Ink Monthly*, May 1933, throughout; Oct. 1933, pp. 66–67; Mar. 1935, p. 42; *Printers' Ink*, Sept. 15, 1932, p. 38; Sept. 22, 1932, p. 50; Oct. 20, 1932, p. 48; Nov. 24, 1932, p. 63; July 19, 1934, p. 17; *Advertising and Selling*, Apr. 11, 1935, p. 23.

67. *Advertising and Selling*, Feb. 17, 1932, p. 22; May 12, 1932, p. 54; *Printers' Ink*, Nov. 19, 1931, p. 125; Apr. 21, 1932, p. 44. See also *Printers' Ink*, Nov. 10, 1932, pp. 56–57.

68. *Printers' Ink*, Apr. 14, 1932, p. 115; "Minutes of Representatives Meeting," Apr. 3, 1929, p. 5; Jan. 13, 1931, p. 13; Oct. 6, 1931, pp. 9–10, JWT Archives.

69. *Printers' Ink*, Jan. 12, 1933, p. 25; Dec. 11, 1930, pp. 18–19.

70. *Saturday Evening Post*, May 5, 1934, p. 1; May 12, 1934, p. 53; Apr. 13, 1935, pp. 106–107; May 4, 1935, pp. 46–47; Aug. 17, 1935, pp. 36–37. See also *Saturday Evening Post*, July 21, 1934, p. 35; July 28, 1934, p. 66; Aug. 25, 1934, p. 4.

71. Sidney Hyman, *The Lives of William Benton* (Chicago, 1969), pp. 114–16; Fairfax M. Cone, *With All Its Faults* (Boston, 1969), p. 64.

72. William Benton, "Interview" (July 1968), pp. 93–94, Oral History Research Office, Columbia University, copyright 1975 by the Trustees of Columbia University in the City of New York; "Advertising, Volume I," p. 190, Vol. 328, Lydia Estes Pinkham Medicine Company Papers, Arthur and Elizabeth Schlesinger Library, Radcliffe College.

73. *Tide*, June 1936, p. 13; *Printers' Ink*, Sept. 15, 1932, p. 12; Cone, *For All Its Faults* p. 64; Lasker, "A Call for Dedication to Fundamentals in Advertising," p. 8; "Advertising, Volume I," p. 192, Vol. 328, Pinkham Papers.

74. *Saturday Evening Post*, Apr. 23, 1932, p. 119; May 7, 1932, p. 33; Jan. 13, 1934, pp. 84–85; *Printers' Ink*, Apr. 7, 1932, p. 8; *Advertising Age*, Dec. 3, 1932, p. 4; *Tide*, Jan. 1933, pp. 9–10.

75. *Advertising and Selling*, Aug. 16, 1934, p. 52; Woodward, *It's An Art*, p. 87.

76. *Advertising and Selling*, June 23, 1932, p. 26.

77. Maxwell Sackheim, *My First 65 Years in Advertising* (Blue Ridge Summit, Pa., 1975), pp. 62, 74–75; John Caples, interview with author, July 12, 1978; *Printers' Ink*, Aug. 25, 1927, p. 117; *Advertising and Selling*, July 20, 1933, p. 32. For a list of Ruthrauff and Ryan's mid-1920s accounts, which included a variety of correspondence schools, proprietary medicines, therapeutic and health devices, and publishers such as the Macfadden Publications, see the *Agency List of the Standard Advertising Register* (Skokie, Ill., 1925), pp. 366–67.

78. Caples, interview, July 12, 1978; *Tide*, May 1933, p. 17; *American Magazine*, Feb. 1931, p. 131; "Minutes of Representatives Meeting," June 21, 1927, p. 4; May 14, 1929, pp. 3–6; Dec. 3, 1929, p. 12, JWT Archives.

79. *Tide*, May 1933, p. 17; *Advertising and Selling*, May 11, 1933, p. 55.

80. *Printers' Ink*, Nov. 17, 1932, pp. 8–9; *Advertising Age*, Jan 9, 1932, p. 11; *Printers' Ink Monthly*, Jan. 1933, p. 30; *Advertising and Selling*, Jan. 4, 1934, p. 37.

81. *Advertising Age*, Jan. 9, 1932, p. 11; Dec. 30, 1933, p. 8; *Advertising and Selling*, Sept. 28, 1933, p. 27; Jan. 4, 1934, pp. 23, 37; *Printers' Ink*, Sept. 28, 1933, pp. 56–57; *Tide*, Jan. 1934, pp. 30, 32; *Printers' Ink Monthly*, Oct. 1933, p. 86. See also *Fortune*, Jan. 1934, p. 7.

82. *American Weekly,* Nov. 3, 1929, p. 18; *Saturday Evening Post,* Aug. 3, 1929, p. 107; Nov. 23, 1929, p. 151; *McCall's,* July 1930, p. 37; Sept. 1930, p. 70; *Good Housekeeping,* Jan. 1932, p. 153, *Ladies' Home Journal,* Apr. 1931, p. 99.

83. *Advertising and Selling,* Feb. 1, 1934, p. 37; *Printers' Ink,* May 12, 1932, pp. 46–47; *Printers' Ink Monthly,* Nov. 1931, p. 40.

84. *Printers' Ink,* Apr. 13, 1933, p. 12; *Advertising and Selling,* Oct. 14, 1931, pp. 20, 21; Russell B. Adams, Jr., *King C. Gillette* (Boston, 1978), p. 168.

85. *Advertising and Selling,* Oct. 14, 1931, p. 60; *Tide,* Jan. 1931, p. 22; Sept. 1931, pp. 27–28; Adams, *Gillette,* p. 169; *American Magazine,* Mar. 1932, p. 8; *Chicago Tribune,* Mar. 2, 1932, p. 19; *Saturday Evening Post,* Jan. 16, 1932, p. 12; Feb. 13, 1932, p. 37.

86. *True Story,* Aug. 1934, p. 1; Adams, *Gillette,* p. 177; *American Magazine,* June 1934, p. 11; July 1934, p. 9; Aug. 1934, p. 11; *Saturday Evening Post,* June 9, 1934, p. 91.

87. *Tide,* Aug. 1932, p. 30; Chester Bowles, "The Reminiscences of Chester Bowles" (1963), p. 34, Oral History Research Office, Columbia University, copyright 1976 by the Trustees of Columbia University in the City of New York; Hyman, *The Lives of William Benton,* pp. 130, 140–42, 150.

88. Young and Rubicam, Inc., *Young and Rubicam House Advertising, 1926–1934,* throughout; "Some Notes on Young and Rubicam, Inc., 1923–1948," typescript (1948), p. 5; "Notes on Young and Rubicam in 1934," typescript; "Brief History of Young and Rubicam, Inc.," typescript, pp. 6–10; Young and Rubicam, *Standard Practice* (1936), pp. 67, 69–70, 72; "Raymond Rubicam Copy Research Data," looseleaf binder (1935), Young and Rubicam Archives, New York City; George Horace Gallup, "The Reminiscences of George Gallup," pp. 58, 89, Oral History Research Office, Columbia University, copyright 1976 by the Trustees of Columbia University in the City of New York.

89. Ed Roberts, "BBDO Short History," typescript, p. 4; "BBDO History," typescript, Aug. 7, 1930, n.p., Batten, Barton, Durstine and Osborn (BBDO) Archives, New York City; *Advertising and Selling,* Feb. 17, 1932, p. 31; June 9, 1932, p. 25.

90. *Printers' Ink,* Oct. 27, 1927, pp. 115, 166–67; Robert Koretz, interview with author, Aug. 1, 1980; *Tide,* May 1929, pp. 7–8.

91. Mary Jane Higby, *Tune in Tomorrow* (New York, 1968), pp. 129–30, 139; Madeleine Edmondson and David Rounds, *From Mary Noble to Mary Hartman,* 2nd ed. (New York, 1976), pp. 43–46; *Tide,* Jan. 1935, p. 72; *Printers' Ink,* May 11, 1933, pp. 78–79; May 3, 1934, p. 74; *Fortune,* May 1934, p. 7.

92. *Tide,* Sept. 1933, pp. 12–13; Aug. 1935, p. 49; *Fortune,* Nov. 1947, p. 230; *Advertising Age,* Aug. 19, 1935, p. 1; Ellis, *Billboards to Buicks,* p. 93.

93. *Ballyhoo,* Aug. 1931, p. 29; Sept. 1931, p. 30; May 1932, p. 3.

94. *Tide,* Oct. 1931, p. 20; Feb. 1932, p. 19; *Printers' Ink,* Oct. 1, 1931, p. 101; Nov. 26, 1931, p. 96; Nov. 17, 1932, p. 4; *Fortune,* Jan. 1932, p. 109.

95. *Printers' Ink,* Apr. 28, 1932, p. 69; Aug. 4, 1932, p. 41; Nov. 17, 1932, p. 4; *Advertising and Selling,* Nov. 25, 1931, p. 17; Jan. 19, 1933, p. 21.

96. *Printers' Ink,* Aug. 11, 1927, pp. 57, 60; Sept. 29, 1927, pp. 187–88; Nov. 3, 1927, pp. 4, 6; Nov. 1, 1928, p. 187; *Advertising and Selling,* Apr. 6, 1927, p. 27; Aug. 24, 1927, p. 40; Sept. 7, 1927, p. 68; Sept. 21, 1927, p. 20; Oct. 5, 1927, p. 32; Nov. 2, 1927, p. 64; Jan. 11, 1928, p. 19; Mar. 28, 1928, second cover.

97. *Printers' Ink,* Oct. 4, 1928, pp. 34, 38; *Advertising and Selling,* Oct. 28, 1931, pp. 30, 38; Pease, *The Responsibilities of American Advertising,* p. 100.

98. *Advertising and Selling,* Dec. 21, 1933, p. 18; May 24, 1934, p. 72; June 7, 1934, p. 27; BBDO, *News Letter,* Mar. 30, 1935, p. 5; *Printers' Ink,* Aug. 2, 1934, p. 76; May 10, 1934, p. 90; *Advertising and Selling,* Nov. 25, 1931, p. 17; Mar. 2, 1932, pp. 26–27; *Printers' Ink Monthly,* Oct. 1934, p. 21; Aug. 1935, p. 13; *Printers' Ink,* Apr. 19, 1934, pp. 75–76; Apr. 19, 1934, p. 7; *Tide,* Mar. 1934, p. 5; *Advertising Age,* Mar. 23, 1935, p. 6.

99. *Printers' Ink Monthly,* Aug. 1935, p. 13; *Printers' Ink,* July 6, 1933, p. 89; Mar. 8, 1934, p. 3; Pease, *Responsibilities of American Advertising,* pp. 115–18; *Advertising Age,* July 15, 1933, p. 17.

100. *Advertising and Selling,* Sept. 1, 1932, p. 23; Aug. 16, 1934, p. 23; Pease, *The Responsiblities of American Advertising,* pp. 116–19.

101. *Printers' Ink,* Mar. 8, 1934, pp. 104–105.

102. Ibid., May 31, 1934, p. 32; Nov. 14, 1935, pp. 69, 71; *Advertising and Selling,* Feb. 17, 1932, p. 21; Sept. 13, 1934, p. 8; BBDO, *The Wedge,* vol. 31, no. 9 (1931), n.p.; *Advertising Age,* May 13, 1935, p. 6.

103. *Advertising and Selling,* June 24, 1931, p. 28; Apr. 14, 1932, p. 18; Aug. 30, 1934, p. 28; *Printers' Ink Monthly,* Aug. 1931, pp. 46, 72; *Printers' Ink,* May 7, 1931, pp. 57–58; Nov. 19, 1931, p. 124; Feb. 15, 1934, p. 7; May 31, 1934, p. 34.

104. "JWT Forum," Feb. 4, 1936, p. 1, JWT Archives; *Printers' Ink,* Sept. 8, 1932, p. 64; Mar. 8, 1934, p. 50; July 19, 1934, p. 58. See also *Printers' Ink Monthly,* Aug. 1932, p. 38; *Advertising Age,* May 4, 1936, p. 4.

105. *Advertising Age,* Dec. 2, 1933, p. 15; Dec. 16, 1933, p. 6; *Printers' Ink,* Nov. 14, 1935, p. 69.

106. *Printers' Ink,* Oct. 27, 1932, p. 73.

107. Ibid., Sept. 18, 1930, p. 150; Oct. 23, 1930, pp. 68, 72, 178–79; July 24, 1930, p. 10; July 10, 1930, p. 154; May 5, 1932, p. 94; *Advertising and Selling,* Nov. 26, 1930, p. 1; Mar. 18, 1931, p. 13; Jan. 20, 1932, p. 30; May 26, 1932, p. 29.

108. BBDO, *The Wedge,* vol. 30, no. 9 (1930), n.p.; vol. 31, no. 14 (1931), n.p.; *Advertising and Selling,* May 26, 1932, p. 22; Jan. 6, 1932, p. 31; Sept. 16, 1931, p.31; *Advertising Age,* Oct. 7, 1933, p. 3; *Tide,* July 1934, p. 6.

109. *Advertising and Selling,* May 12, 1932, p. 20.

110. Ibid., June 24, 1931, p. 59; July 8, 1931, pp. 15–16; *Printers' Ink,* Jan. 7, 1932, p. 114; *Advertising Age,* Oct. 7, 1933, p. 3.

111. *Saturday Evening Post,* May 21, 1932, p. 74.

112. Ibid., April 23, 1932, p. 119; May 7, 1932, p. 33; June 4, 1932, p. 31. See also Oct. 13, 1934, p. 91; Jan. 11, 1936, pp. 54–55.

113. *Printers' Ink,* Dec. 12, 1929, p. 211; *Advertising Age,* Oct. 8, 1932, p. 13. See also *Printers' Ink,* Apr. 3, 1930, p. 10; Sept. 11, 1930, p. 3; *Advertising and Selling,* May 12, 1932, p. 20; *American Magazine,* Apr. 1933, p. 128.

114. *Printers' Ink,* Dec. 18, 1930, p. 69; July 9, 1931, p. 113; Sept. 17, 1931, pp. 54–55.

115. Ibid., May 19, 1932, pp. 50–51. See also *Advertising and Selling,* Mar. 2, 1932, p. 2; May 26, 1932, p. 2; *Printers' Ink,* Oct. 27, 1932, p. 101; Sept. 28, 1933, p. 77; May 1, 1930, pp. 138–39; Feb. 16, 1933, pp. 46–47.

116. *Printers' Ink,* June 2, 1932, pp. 8–9; Oct. 20, 1932, pp. 8–9; Sept. 28, 1933, pp. 66–67; *Advertising and Selling,* Jan. 7, 1931, p. 4. See also *Advertising and Selling,* Nov. 26, 1930, p. 3; *Printers' Ink,* May 12, 1932, pp. 30–31; *American Magazine,* Apr. 1931, pp. 176–77.

117. *Fortune,* Nov. 1933, p. 133; Mar. 1934, p. 131; Apr. 1934, p. 169; *Printers' Ink Monthly,* Apr. 1935, pp. 58–59; *Advertising and Selling,* Oct. 12, 1933, pp. 8–9; Jan. 4, 1934, pp. 8–9; Oct. 26, 1933, p. 21; Jan. 18, 1934, p. 25.

118. *Advertising and Selling,* Mar. 2, 1932, p. 48; Feb. 2, 1933, p. 32; *American Magazine,* Jan. 1931, p. 77; *Saturday Evening Post,* Dec. 27, 1930, p. 52; Aug. 27, 1932, p. 73; *Printers' Ink,* Sept. 3, 1931, p. 122; May 5, 1932, p. 90; *Advertising Age,* Mar. 5, 1932, p. 10. See also *Chicago Tribune,* Oct. 14, 1930, p. 11.

119. For examples of attempts to mark an impending "turning of the corner," see *Printers' Ink,* Jan. 1, 1931, p. 3; Oct. 6, 1932, pp. 8–9; Oct. 20, 1932, p. 55; *Saturday Evening Post,* Nov. 5, 1932, p. 46; *Better Homes and Gardens,* July 1931, pp. 48–49; *Printers' Ink Monthly,* July 1933, p. 68.

120. *Ballyhoo*, Nov. 1931, p. 6; Dec. 1931, pp. 10–11; June 1932, p. 7. *Advertising and Selling* could hardly suppress a snicker upon learning that the American Society of Beauty Culturists had asserted that if women would only "paint their lips on with a slight upturn at each end (smile) the period of readjustment would soon be ended" (*Advertising and Selling*, Mar. 16, 1932, p. 27).

121. *Squibb Sales Bulletin*, June 18, 1932, p. 201; Oct. 24, 1931, n.p., E. R. Squibb and Sons Archives, Princeton, N.J.; *Metropolitan Underwriter*, Dec. 1931, p. 1, Metropolitan Life Insurance Company Archives, New York City.

122. *Metropolitan Underwriter*, Aug. 1933, p. 1.

123. *Printers' Ink Monthly*, Apr. 1933, p. 46.

124. *Business Week*, Apr. 12, 1933, p. 3; June 17, 1933, p. 2; *Advertising Age*, Jan. 9, 1932, p. 13; *Fortune*, Apr. 1932, p. 103; Jan. 1933, p. 85; Mar. 1933, p. 97; Apr. 1933, p. 3.

125. *Saturday Evening Post*, Nov. 21, 1931, p. 61; *Tide*, Nov. 1931, p. 11; *Fortune*, Feb. 1933, second cover.

126. *Saturday Evening Post*, Aug. 19, 1933, p. 75.

127. Ibid., Dec. 17, 1932, p. 59; Scrapbooks 1 and 61 (All-Year Club of Southern California), Lord and Thomas Archives, at Foote, Cone and Belding Communications, Inc., Chicago. All-Year Club ads had traditionally encouraged vacationers to look into business opportunities in California during their stay. Beginning in 1931 they carried the warning, "Come to Southern California for a glorious vacation. Do not come seeking employment lest you be disappointed."

128. *Advertising and Selling*, Nov. 24, 1932, p. 19. See also *Printers' Ink*, Mar. 22, 1934, p. 45.

129. *Fortune*, Sept. 1932, p. 92.

130. Ibid., Aug. 1932, p. 71; Feb. 1933, p. 24; *Saturday Evening Post*, Mar. 14, 1932, p. 169; Dec. 3, 1932, p. 75. By contrast, the Lionel Train ads of the previous Christmas season had not yet adopted any of the anxiety about the son's success that the tableaux of 1932 expressed both verbally and visually. A December 1931 Lionel ad spoke of the son's "wistful look" and his "thrill of expectancy." The ad concluded, "There's fun for him and fun for you in the ownership of a Lionel Electric Railroad" (*Saturday Evening Post*, Dec. 5, 1931, p. 135).

131. *Advertising Age*, Apr. 16, 1932, p. 5; *American Magazine*, June 1932, p. 3; Feb. 1933, p. 7; *Saturday Evening Post*, Oct. 8, 1932, p. 83; June 3, 1933, p. 43.

132. *American Magazine*, Apr. 1933, p. 99; June 1932, p. 3; *Saturday Evening Post*, July 9, 1932, p. 43.

133. *Saturday Evening Post*, June 4, 1932, p. 75; Feb. 4, 1933, p. 67; Mar. 4, 1933, p. 4; Apr. 1, 1933, p. 71.

134. Ibid., Nov. 5, 1932, p. 87.

135. Carolyn Bird, *The Invisible Scar* (New York, 1955), pp. 41–42, 49–50. See also Studs Terkel, *Hard Times* (New York, 1970), pp. 106–11, 119–21; Samuel H. Stouffer and Paul F. Lazarsfeld, *Research Memorandum on the Family in the Depression* (New York, 1971: reprint of 1937 edition), pp. 94–95, 113–14; Ruth Shonle Cavan and Katherine Howland Ranch, *The Family and the Depression* (Chicago, 1971: reprint of 1938 edition), pp. 61, 94, 111.

136. *Printers' Ink Monthly*, June 1933, p. 37; *Printers' Ink*, July 10, 1930, p. 105; Apr. 28, 1932, pp. 73–74; Oct. 13, 1932, p. 1; "Monday Evening Talk," Mar. 24, 1930, p. 11, JWT Archives.

Ten   The Therapeutics of Advertising

1. Christine Frederick, *Selling Mrs. Consumer* (New York, 1929), p. 336; *Fortune*, Apr. 1932, p. 21. The products and companies represented by the trademarks on the

Newell-Emmett quiz are as follows, reading left to right: *Top row:* Cadillac Motor Car Company; Maxwell House Coffee; Mobiloil "Gargoyle" Lubricating Oils (Vacuum Oil Company); Hartford Fire Insurance Company; Baker's Cocoa and Chocolate (Walter Baker Company). *Second row:* Old Dutch Cleanser (Cudahy Company); Goodyear Tire and Rubber Company; Prudential Life Insurance Company; The Bon Ami Company; Texaco Gasoline (The Texas Company). *Third row:* American Telephone and Telegraph Company; Fisher Body Corporation; Campbell Soup Company; Wrigley's Spearmint Gum; Sherwin-Williams Paint Company. *Fourth row:* The Jantzen Company (swimsuits); Paramount Pictures; Cream of Wheat Company; Swift and Company; Arm and Hammer Baking Soda (Church and Dwight Company). *Fifth row:* Plymouth Motor Cars (Chrysler Motors); Mazola (Corn Products Refining Company); Quaker Oats Company; Chase Brass and Copper Company; Hart, Schaffner and Marx.

2. Christian Metz, *Language and Cinema,* trans. Donna Jean Umiker-Sebeok (The Hague, 1974), pp. 27, 38; Peter Wollen, *Signs and Meaning in the Cinema,* 3rd ed. (Bloomington, Ind., 1972), p. 120; David Novitz, *Pictures and Their Use in Communication: A Philosophical Essay* (The Hague, 1977), pp. 86, 97, 106.

3. See Chapter 4, under "Crooners and Commercials."

4. Lyn Lofland, *A World of Strangers: Order and Action in Urban Public Space* (New York, 1973), pp. 4, 23, 178–79.

5. Peter L. Berger, Brigitte Berger, and Hansfried Kellner, *The Homeless Mind: Modernization and Consciousness* (New York, 1973), p. 74.

6. *Saturday Evening Post,* June 21, 1924, pp. 82–83; *Ladies' Home Journal,* Nov. 1928, p. 170.

7. A statistical survey of two issues per year of the *Saturday Evening Post* and two issues per year of *McCall's* from 1925 through 1935 revealed a clear bias toward urban settings for uses of leisure time, despite the frequent association of products with vacations. Golf outscored all other sports as a background setting for automobile ads. It ranked above tennis, fishing, polo, and even beach scenes among choices for the depiction of leisure in the ads.

8. *Saturday Evening Post,* July 25, 1931, pp. 44–45; Mar. 23, 1935, p. 92; Nov. 14, 1931, p. 140; Jan. 7, 1928, pp. 128, 163; Jan. 14, 1928, p. 58; *Ladies' Home Journal,* Dec. 1931, p. 38.

9. For an intriguing discussion of the surrealist nature of advertising, see Judith Williamson, *Decoding Advertisements: Ideology and Meaning in Advertising* (London, 1978), pp. 128–31, 134. Williamson also discusses perceptively the evasion of the processes of production as an element in the distortion of actual social and economic relationships. I would add that the desire not to be reminded of those processes reflected an urban as well as a class perspective. On the evasion or "mystification" of the processes of production, see also Stuart Ewen, *Captains of Consciousness: Advertising and the Social Roots of the Consumer Culture* (New York, 1976), pp. 105, 199.

10. *Saturday Evening Post,* Mar. 10, 1934, p. 72; *Advertising Age,* Nov. 18, 1933, p. 28.

11. *Saturday Evening Post,* Mar. 26, 1926, p. 45; Apr. 9, 1927, p. 116; Mar. 10, 1934, p. 47; June 9, 1934, pp. 70–71; *Liberty,* Oct. 11, 1930, p. 4; Harvard University, Graduate School of Business Administration, *The Harvard Advertising Awards, 1929,* (New York, 1930).

12. T. J. Jackson Lears, *No Place of Grace: Antimodernism and the Transformation of American Culture, 1880–1920* (New York, 1981), pp. 47–51.

13. *Saturday Evening Post,* Mar. 3, 1934, p. 28; Mar. 31, 1934, p. 39; *JWT News Letter,* July 1, 1926, pp. 1–2, J. Walter Thompson Company (JWT) Archives, New York City. In *The Harried Leisure Class* (New York, 1970), p. 25, Staffan Burenstam Linder notes that it is "hardly surprising" that a high consumption society with a shortage of time for consumption would come to "greatly admire those who are capable of maintaining a high tempo without breaking down."

14. Michael Schudson, *Advertising, the Uneasy Persuasion: Its Dubious Impact on American Society* (New York, 1984), pp. 198–99; *Saturday Evening Post,* Mar. 14, 1936, p. 36; Mar. 28, 1936, p. 34; Apr. 11, 1936, p. 63. See also *Saturday Evening Post* for May 12, 1934, p. 39; Mar. 7, 1935, pp. 72, 73; *Tide,* Mar. 1934, p. 18; May 1934, p. 6; June 1934, p. 52; *Advertising Age,* Apr. 6, 1936, p. 19.

15. Denys Thompson, *Voice of Civilization: An Enquiry into Advertising* (London, 1943), p. 167; Neil Harris, "The Drama of Consumer Desire," in *Yankee Enterprise,* ed. Otto Mayr and Robert C. Post (Washington, D.C., 1981), p. 204.

16. *Printers' Ink,* Feb. 19, 1931, p. 85; *Advertising and Selling,* July 25, 1928, p. 29; Frederick, *Selling Mrs. Consumer,* p. 339.

17. *Saturday Evening Post,* April 21, 1928, p. 174; *Judicious Advertising,* Apr. 1925, p. 77.

18. "Minutes of Representatives Meeting," Sept. 30, 1930, p. 7, JWT Archives; *Printers' Ink,* Sept. 13, 1928, pp. 150–51; Oct. 27, 1927, pp. 30–31; *Judicious Advertising,* Apr. 1925, p. 9.

19. Walter Lippmann, *A Preface to Morals* (New York, 1929), pp. 51–67.

20. *J. Walter Thompson Company News Bulletin,* Jan. 1925, p. 10; Case History Files, "Cream of Wheat," and "Johnson and Johnson," c. 1926, JWT Archives.

21. *Advertising and Selling,* Feb. 15, 1934, p. 24; BBDO, *The Wedge,* vol. 29, no. 4 (1929), n.p.; *Printers' Ink,* May 6, 1926, p. 158; Sept. 16, 1926, pp. 6, 8; Apr. 7, 1927, p. 77; Sept. 14, 1933, p. 94; Earnest Elmo Calkins, *Business the Civilizer* (Boston, 1928), pp. 14–15.

22. *Good Housekeeping,* Feb. 1933, p. 113.

23. *Saturday Evening Post,* Nov. 8, 1930, pp. 74–75.

24. Ibid.

25. *Printers' Ink Monthly,* Aug. 1930, pp. 32, 93; *Printers' Ink,* Sept. 10, 1931, p. 108.

26. *Printers' Ink Monthly,* Mar. 1929, p. 73; *Printers' Ink,* Dec. 20, 1928, pp. 170–71; Sept. 10, 1931, p. 108, June 14, 1934, p. 84.

27. *Printers' Ink Monthly,* July 1929, p. 54; Mar. 1929, p. 73. See also *Ladies' Home Journal,* May 1929, p. 214.

28. *Printers' Ink,* Apr. 28, 1927, p. 89. For an archetypal example of the application of the advantages of anonymous intimate advice, see *Chicago Tribune,* Sept. 17, 1931, p. 10.

29. *Better Homes and Gardens,* Feb. 1930, p. 119; Mar. 1930, p. 103.

30. *True Story,* Mar. 1928, p. 1; May 1928, p. 1; Jan. 1926, p. 73.

31. Scrapbooks 203 and 212 (Kotex), Lord and Thomas Archives, at Foote, Cone and Belding Communications, Inc., Chicago; *Good Housekeeping,* Mar. 1933, p. 157.

32. *Good Housekeeping,* Mar. 1933, p. 157; *Ladies' Home Journal,* Oct. 1927, p. 11; Feb. 1933, p. 108; Scrapbooks 203 and 205 (Kotex), Lord and Thomas Archives. See also *Parents' Magazine,* Aug. 1935, p. 49; Oct. 1935, p. 69.

33. *True Story,* Jan. 1928, p. 73; Batten, Barton, Durstine and Osborn, Inc., "Status Binder" (September 1928), n.p., BBDO Archives, New York City; *American Magazine,* Jan. 1927, p. 81; Oct. 1927, p. 161.

34. BBDO, "Status Binder," n.p.; *American Magazine,* Jan. 1927, p. 81.

35. *Advertising and Selling,* Sept. 16, 1931, p. 27; *American Weekly,* Oct. 16, 1932, p. 16.

36. *Printers' Ink,* June 10, 1926, p. 132; Aug. 6, 1931, pp. 18–20; Dec. 15, 1932, p. 27; Bernard Lichtenberg, *Advertising Campaigns* (New York, 1926), pp. 330, 335–38.

37. *Printers' Ink,* Feb. 18, 1926, pp. 177, 180.

38. Ibid.; *Saturday Evening Post,* July 14, 1928, p. 54; Sept. 8, 1928, p. 81.

39. *J. Walter Thompson News Bulletin,* Mar. 1923, pp. 11, 13; "Minutes of Staff Meeting," Sept. 1, 1931, pp. 8–9; "Minutes of Meeting in Lecture Hall," Jan. 3, 1934, p. 8, JWT Archives.

40. *Ladies' Home Journal,* Apr. 1929, p. 179; Aug. 1929, p. 74; *Good Housekeeping,* Sept. 1927, pp. 94, 239; Scrapbook 167 (Holeproof Hosiery), Lord and Thomas Archives; *Good Housekeeping,* June 1927, p. 252; *Saturday Evening Post,* May 26, 1928, p. 1; "Minutes of Representatives Meeting," Dec. 19, 1928, pp. 11–14, JWT Archives.

41. *Advertising Age,* Sept. 9, 1933, p. 11; "Minutes of Representatives Meeting," Sept. 30, 1930, p. 18, JWT Archives.

42. *Printers' Ink,* Nov. 1, 1928, p. 86; July 9, 1936, p. 44; Aug. 25, 1932, p. 44; *Advertising and Selling,* July 4, 1935, p. 36; BBDO, *The Wedge,* vol. 32, no. 4 (1932), n.p.

43. Robert Lynd, "The People as Consumers," in President's Research Committee on Social Trends, *Recent Social Trends in the United States* (New York, 1933), vol. 2, p. 910.

44. Leo Burnett, *Communications of an Advertising Man* (Chicago, 1961), p. 49; *Printers' Ink,* July 7, 1932, pp. 19–20; Aug. 25, 1932, p. 44; Nov. 1, 1928, pp. 85–86; "Minutes of Creative Staff Meeting," Nov. 2, 1932, pp. 1–2, JWT Archives.

45. Philip Nelson, "The Economic Value of Advertising," pp. 47, 51, and Yale Brozen, "Is Advertising a Barrier to Entry," p. 80, in *Advertising and Society,* ed. Yale Brozen (New York, 1974).

46. Ibid.; Martin Mayer, *Madison Avenue, U.S.A.* (New York, 1958), pp. 310–15. See also Richard W. Pollay, "The Identification and Distribution of Values Manifest in Print Advertising, 1900–1980," Working Paper No. 921 (1983), History of Advertising Archives Series, University of British Columbia.

47. Leon Festinger, *A Theory of Cognitive Dissonance* (Evanston, Ill., 1957), pp. 48–52; Raymond A. Bauer and Stephen A. Greyser, *Advertising in America* (Boston, 1968), pp. 288–90, 324, 339; John A. P. Treasure, "How Advertising Works," in Brozen, ed., *Advertising and Society,* p. 162; Edmund Carpenter, "The New Languages: Mass Media," in *Languages of the Mass Media,* ed. Irving and Harriet Deer (Boston, 1965), p. 4.

48. *J. Walter Thompson News Bulletin,* Dec. 1924, pp. 2–4.

49. John Benson, "Serving the Consumer in Advertising," p. 2 (address at Bok Dinner, Feb. 15, 1927), Harvard Award Archives.

50. *Tide,* July 1928, p. 12; *Printers' Ink,* June 10, 1926, p. 132; May 19, 1927, p. 153; *Judicious Advertising,* Jan. 1925, p. 59; *Better Homes and Gardens,* Jan. 1931, p. 9; *Saturday Evening Post,* Sept. 8, 1928, p. 93.

51. *Fortune,* Apr. 1936, p. 173. Not only had the complexities of new production processes overwhelmed the average consumer's "common sense craft judgment," observes William Leiss, but many commodities now consisted of so ambiguous a "collection of objective and imputed characteristics," and human needs had become so sophisticated and fragmented, that it was difficult to connect a specific product with a specific need. Advertisers rushed to offer seemingly authoritative advice about such connections. See Leiss, *The Limits to Satisfaction: An Essay on the Problems of Needs and Commodities* (Toronto, 1976), pp. 15, 79, 82, 89, 92.

52. *Fortune,* Apr. 1936, p. 173.

53. "Minutes of Meeting in Lecture Hall," Feb. 7, 1934, p. 5, JWT Archives.

54. *Printers' Ink,* June 16, 1927, pp. 69–70.

55. *Printers' Ink,* Dec. 8, 1927, pp. 49–50.

56. *Saturday Evening Post,* May 6, 1933, p. 91.

57. Scrapbook 167 (Holeproof Hosiery), Lord and Thomas Archives. For examples of the emphasis on the expert and the importance of being "correct," see *American Magazine,* Apr. 1926, p. 104; May 1929, p. 90; *Saturday Evening Post,* July 10, 1926, p. 90; Feb. 16, 1929, p. 2; Advertising Case 289 (National Shoe Retailers Assn.), reel 11, Harvard Business School Archives; *Printers' Ink,* Dec. 15, 1932, p. 27; "Minutes of Creative Organization Staff Meeting," Mar. 19, 1932, pp. 9–11, JWT Archives.

58. Kathryn Weibel, *Mirror, Mirror: Images of Women Reflected in Popular Culture* (Garden City, N.Y., 1977), p. 167; Warren I. Susman, ed., *Culture and Commitment, 1929–1945* (New York, 1973), pp. 16–17.

59. Jeffrey L. Meikle, *Twentieth Century Limited: Industrial Design in America, 1925–1939* (Philadelphia, 1979), p. 186.

60. *Tide,* Apr. 1927, p. 1; George Burton Hotchkiss, *Advertising Copy* (New York, 1924), p. 380; *Advertising Age,* Jan. 30, 1932, p. 10.

61. *Better Homes and Gardens,* Jan. 1930, p. 12. For a similar "experience" by "Helen Chase," see *Saturday Evening Post,* June 14, 1930, p. 2.

62. Lary May, *Screening Out the Past: The Birth of Mass Culture and the Motion Picture Industry* (New York, 1980), pp. 119, 154; Leo Lowenthal, "Biographies in Popular Magazines," in *Radio Research, 1942–1943,* ed. Paul Lazarsfeld and Frank N. Stanton (New York, 1944), p. 508; Simon Michael Bessie, *Jazz Journalism* (New York, 1938), pp. 48, 100–101; "Minutes of Creative Staff Meeting," Apr. 23, 1932, p. 7; "Minutes of Representatives Meeting," June 4, 1930, p. 8, JWT Archives; Frank Luther Mott, *American Journalism: A History, 1607–1960,* 3rd ed. (New York, 1962), p. 599. "Heart to Heart Talks" and "Side Talks with Girls" had also proved successful earlier in making the *Ladies' Home Journal* the "intimate friend" of readers. See John William Tebbel, *The Media in America* (New York, 1974), p. 338.

63. James Gray, *Business Without Boundary: The Story of General Mills* (Minneapolis, 1954), pp. 172–78, 182. On the "personalizing" qualities of radio, see Hadley Cantril and Gordon W. Allport, *The Psychology of Radio* (New York, 1935), pp. 72, 96.

64. Harvard University, Graduate School of Business Administration, *Harvard Advertising Awards, 1924–1928* (New York, 1930), p. 57.

65. *True Story,* Jan. 1926, p. 65; *JWT News Letter,* Feb. 21, 1924, pp. 5–6; Jan. 31, 1924, p. 6; General Electric Company, *General Electric Publicity, 1924* (Schenectady, N.Y., 1924), p. 80.

66. *JWT News Letter,* Jan. 31, 1924, p. 6; BBDO, "Status Binder," n.p.

67. "Odo-ro-no Account History," Case History Files, JWT Archives; *Printers' Ink,* Aug. 18, 1927, p. 18; *JWT News Letter,* Jan. 31, 1924, p. 6.

68. *Printers' Ink,* Jan. 21, 1926, p. 52; June 18, 1931, p. 134; *JWT News Letter,* Feb. 21, 1924, pp. 5–6; "Odo-ro-no Account History," Case History Files, JWT Archives.

69. *Printers' Ink Monthly,* Mar. 1926, p. 24; *Advertising and Selling,* Dec. 7, 1933, p. 42; *Printers' Ink,* Dec. 27, 1934, p. 34; Apr. 2, 1931, pp. 64–65; *Judicious Advertising,* Feb. 1925, p. 33.

70. On Bok's crusade against the posthumous personalization of Lydia Pinkham, see Helen Woodward, *The Lady Persuaders* (New York, 1960), p. 89; *Tide,* June 1929, p. 1; and Sarah Stage, *Female Complaints: Lydia Pinkham and the Business of Women's Medicine* (New York, 1979), pp. 163–64. For one of the very rare expressions of qualms about simulated friendship with the consumer, see *Printers' Ink,* Aug. 23, 1934, p. 80.

71. *Tide,* Feb. 1931, p. 8; Jan. 1933, p. 20; May 1933, p. 40; June 1933, p. 42; Nov. 1933, p. 15; Feb. 1934, p. 3; Alfred Lief, *It Floats: The Story of Procter and Gamble* (New York, 1958), pp. 172–73, 179; Kurt Lang and Gladys Engel Lang, *Politics and Television* (Chicago, 1968), p. 205; Morleen Betz Rouse, "Daytime Radio Programming for the Homemaker, 1926–1956," *Journal of Popular Culture* 12 (1979): 319.

72. *Tide,* June 1934, pp. 27–28.

73. Ibid.; *Tide,* Nov. 1933, p. 15; May 1934, p. 66; Feb. 1931, p. 8.

74. Reuel Denney, *The Astonished Muse* (Chicago, 1957), p. 249.

75. *Judicious Advertising,* Jan. 1925, p. 14; Leo Lowenthal, "The Triumph of Mass Idols," in Lowenthal, *Literature, Popular Culture and Society* (Englewood Cliffs, N.J., 1961), pp. 116, 133; *Printers' Ink,* Dec. 9, 1926, p. 6.

76. *Printers' Ink,* Dec. 13, 1928, pp. 150, 152; Apr. 11, 1929, pp. 145–48; James Webb Young, *The Diary of an Ad Man* (Chicago, 1944), p. 228.

77. *Tide,* Oct. 1932, pp. 15–16; *Saturday Evening Post,* Jan. 13, 1934, pp. 84–85; *Printers'*

Ink, Jan. 4, 1934, p. 74; "Minutes of Representatives Meeting," Aug. 30, 1927, p. 5, JWT Archives.

78. Milton H. Biow, *Butting In; An Adman Speaks Out* (Garden City, N.Y., 1964), p. 150; *Printers' Ink Monthly*, Feb. 1935, p. 42; *Advertising Age*, Oct. 18, 1937, p. 12.

79. *Printers' Ink*, Nov. 14, 1935, p. 68.

80. Scrapbook 342 (Schenley Whiskey), Lord and Thomas Archives.

81. *Advertising Age*, Oct. 4, 1937, p. 29. See also *Chicago Tribune*, Sept. 17, 1937, p. 15; Oct. 1, 1937, p. 32; Oct. 14, 1937. p. 35.

82. *Tide*, Mar. 1935, p. 64.

83. *Printers' Ink*, Nov. 17, 1927, pp. 41–42; May 22, 1930, p. 139; June 6, 1929, p. 163; *Judicious Advertising*, Mar. 1925, pp. 47–48; *Printers' Ink Monthly*, May 1928, pp. 37, 88; Aug. 1928, p. 50.

84. *Printers' Ink*, Sept. 15, 1921, p. 18; *Saturday Evening Post*, May 26, 1928, p. 70; May 21, 1932, p. 101; Thompson, *Voice of Civilisation*, p. 110.

85. Robert K. Merton, *Mass Persuasion: The Social Psychology of a Bond Drive* (Westport, Conn., 1971 [c. 1946]), pp. 40, 61, 63, 81–83, 120, 142–43; Henry C. Link, *The New Psychology of Selling and Advertising* (New York, 1932), p. 144. On the importance of names in ads, see "Minutes of Representatives Meeting," Dec. 3, 1929, JWT Archives.

86. John Chynoweth Burnham, "The New Psychology: From Narcissism to Social Control," in *Change and Continuity in Twentieth Century America: The 1920s*, ed. John Braeman, Robert H. Bremner, and David Brody (Columbus, Ohio, 1968), pp. 367–68. Advertising increasingly supplied "personal" accounts in scores of tableaux such as that entitled "Very, Very Intimate . . . and Heard at the Ritz" (*Photoplay Magazine*, Apr. 1930, p. 102). See also *Delineator*, Feb. 1930, p. 76; Apr. 1930, pp. 6–7.

87. *Advertising and Selling*, May 30, 1928, p. 25; Ernest Dichter, "On the Psychology of Radio Commercials," in *Radio Research, 1942–1943*, ed. Paul F. Lazarsfeld and Frank N. Stanton, p. 477.

88. *Saturday Evening Post*, June 9, 1928, p. 69.

89. *Ladies' Home Journal*, Nov. 1928, p. 170. See also *Redbook*, Feb. 1934, p. 71.

90. F. Scott Fitzgerald, *The Great Gatsby* (New York, 1925), p. 182.

91. Ibid.

BIBLIOGRAPHICAL ESSAY

This essay makes no attempt to encompass all of my sources, primary and secondary. For a guide to many of the specific collections, periodicals, articles, and books I have consulted, the reader must rely on the extensive Notes to the text chapters. Here I intend to review only sources that I found central to my understanding of the history and content of American advertising, and to point out sources that significantly broadened my background in the field or stimulated my conceptual approach.

The archival sources for the history of American advertising prior to World War II are as yet incompletely collected and identified. Only after much of my research was completed did I discover the existence of the verbatim minutes of staff meetings at the J. Walter Thompson agency in New York City and the vault of Lord and Thomas scrapbooks retained by Foote, Cone and Belding Communications, Inc., in Chicago. Undoubtedly many significant collections of materials remain in private hands, unknown to scholars; and some may still repose undetected in agency storerooms. Led by the J. Walter Thompson Company, the agencies are only now beginning to create formal historical archives. Whereas manufacturing corporations may find that an emphasis on their historical accomplishments is valuable in public relations and image-creation, most agencies sense that they can best appeal to prospective clients as future-minded organizations, riding the wave of change. A bias toward an ahistorical, or even antihistorical, outlook has been the result.

Within the agencies, aside from such rare treasures as occasional case files, status reports, and staff minutes, the most valuable materials are often the confidential or limited-distribution house organs. Written for a limited audience of insiders and with some of the naive frankness that characterized the advertising industry of that era, the house organs at J. Walter Thompson and Batten, Barton, Durstine and Osborn are often revealing. Reports of investigations and copies of speeches by agency leaders have also been occasionally retained. Some agencies, such as

N. W. Ayer and Son and Foote, Cone and Belding have retained extensive collections of their finished products (the Ayer advertisements have been donated to the Smithsonian); but these agencies have retained few materials that reveal the conscious strategies and creative processes that underlay these finished products.

The corporate advertisers themselves have often devoted more attention and resources to the preservation of their own histories. Yet many of their archives are startlingly deficient in materials that bear on the development of advertising and public relations strategies. I have found the fullest collections at the American Telephone and Telegraph Company, E. R. Squibb and Sons, General Electric, Metropolitan Life Insurance, and Hoover Worldwide Corporation. Several manufacturers of consumer goods have rejected my requests to inspect their historical records on the ground that nothing has been retained. Such denials of access may be understandable attempts to defend corporate privacy and avoid inconvenience, or they may originate with company officials who simply do not know the extent of their company's archives or do not appreciate the variety of materials that a perceptive scholar can profitably use. Students of the history of advertising will need to continue to press for access to such archives.

Scholars who hope to supplement the sparse archival sources on the pre–World War II history of American advertising with extensive materials from autobiographies, collected papers, and oral histories in established library collections will be largely disappointed. The Bruce Barton Papers at the Wisconsin State Historical Society are regretably thin in correspondence from the 1920s and 1930s. The Dorothy Dignam Papers at the Wisconsin State Historical Society and at the Arthur and Elizabeth Schlesinger Library provide interesting insights into the career of an exceptional woman copywriter, but they afford only occasional glimpses into the creative processes in the accounts on which she worked. The oral histories of William Benton, Chester Bowles, and George Gallup at the Oral History Research Office at Columbia University (OHRO) give only brief attention to their work in advertising agencies. "The Reminiscences of Albert Davis Lasker" at the OHRO gives little attention to advertising in the 1920s and 1930s. The Lydia Estes Pinkham Medicine Company Papers at the Schlesinger Library provide some basis for statistical analysis, as Richard Pollay has demonstrated in "Lydiametrics: Applications of Econometrics to the History of Advertising," *Journal of Advertising History*, no. 2 (1979), pp. 3–19. But only in a few instances do they afford insights into the development of advertising content by this atypical national advertiser.

Most of the autobiographies by agency leaders and copywriters of the era favor an anecdotal format. Historical scholars will find most of them infuriatingly vague in dates and chronology and almost invariably superficial in their tendency to move quickly from incident to incident, rarely exploring any campaign or issue in depth. Of those which give any significant attention to the 1920s or 1930s, Fairfax Cone's *With All Its Faults* (Boston, 1969) is the best. Others of value include James R. Adams, *Sparks Off My Anvil* (New York, 1958); Milton Biow, *Butting In: An Adman Speaks Out* (Garden City, N.Y., 1964); Leo Burnett, *Communications of an Advertising Man* (Chicago, 1961); Howard Williams Dickinson, *Crying Our Wares* (New York, 1929); Bernice Fitzgibbon, *Macy's, Gimbels and Me* (New York, 1967); Frank Irving Fletcher, *Lucid Interval: Confessions of a Custodian of the Convictions of Others* (New York, 1938); Claude C. Hopkins, *My Life in Advertising* (New York, 1927); Gerard B. Lambert, *All Out of Step* (Garden City, N.Y., 1956); Albert Lasker, *The Lasker Story: As He Told It* (Chicago, 1963); and James Webb Young, *Full Corn in the Ear* (Coava, New Mexico, 1959). Two biographies, John Gunther's *Taken at the Flood: The Story of Albert D. Lasker* (New York, 1960) and Sidney Hyman's *The Lives of William Benton* (Chicago, 1969), are more helpful. Although his analysis is drawn from observations in the post–World War II years, Joseph Bensman, a sociologist and former advertising executive, offers one of the most perceptive insights into the milieu of the advertising agency in *Dollars and Sense: Ideology, Ethics and the Meaning of Work in Profit and Non-profit Organizations* (New York, 1967).

Given the unevenness of archival sources and the scarcity of good memoirs, the fullest sources on the advertising profession and advertising strategies of the 1920s and 1930s remain the trade journals—especially *Advertising Age, Advertising and Selling, Judicious Advertising, Printers' Ink, Printers' Ink Monthly,* and *Tide.* Many of the trade journal articles were written by advertising managers and agency leaders and were often self-serving and uncritical. But because they were written for other professionals rather than the general public, they often expose with striking frankness the internal debates within the trade.

In the interpretation of American advertising from a historical perspective, the essential starting place is Otis A. Pease's *The Responsibilities of American Advertising* (New Haven, Conn. 1958), which impressively pioneered the broad study of the industry in its cultural and political contexts. Prior to that, Ralph M. Hower's exhaustive study of N. W. Ayer and Son, *The History of an Advertising Agency* (Cambridge, Mass., 1939), had stood as the only historical study based on extensive scholarly research. Hower's work is very valuable for its description of the structure and evolution of an agency in the late nineteenth and early twentieth century, but its analysis of the period after 1920 is weak because of a foreshortened historical perspective and the evident limitations of its status as a company-authorized history. Among the other early histories of American advertising, which are mainly descriptive, the best are James Playsted Wood, *The Story of Advertising* (New York, 1958); Frank Presbrey, *The History and Development of Advertising* (New York, 1929), by an agency president of the 1920s; and "Printers' Ink Fifty Years, 1888–1938," published by *Printers' Ink* magazine as its April 1938 issue.

The appearance of Pease's study in 1958 marked the first flowering of a new perception of the historical significance of advertising as a central institution in American culture, a perception that had emerged from David Potter's *People of Plenty* (Chicago, 1955). Although few historians expanded immediately upon the initial work of Potter and Pease, Daniel Boorstin issued another call to historians to attend to the neglected field of advertising in his Pulitzer Prize-winning *The Americans: The Democratic Experience* (New York, 1973). In his discussion of "consumption communities," Boorstin emphasized the role of advertising as "one of the most characteristic and most vigorous of American institutions." The challenges that Potter, Boorstin, and Pease issued to other historians began to find a widespread response only in the middle 1970s. In 1975, Frank W. Fox published his monograph, *Madison Avenue Goes to War: The Strange Military Career of Amer-*

ican Advertising (Provo, Utah, 1975), which demonstrated how a content analysis of advertising might be linked to an analysis of the professional, economic, and political agendas of the advertising industry and thus used to illuminate advertising's cultural and political role during World War II. Previously, Fox had more extensively set forth his analysis of the significance of advertisements as historical documents in his dissertation, "Advertising and the Second World War" (Stanford University, 1973), and his M.A. thesis, "Advertisements as Documents in Social and Cultural History" (University of Utah, 1969). In 1976, Stuart W. Ewen further explored the significance of advertising in *Captains of Consciousness: Advertising and the Social Roots of the Consumer Culture* (New York, 1976), in which he offered an interpretation of American advertising in the 1920s as a conspiracy by the corporate elite to "shape a culture" and impose its consciousness on the working class. Meanwhile, Professor Richard W. Pollay revived the call for scholarly attention to the history of advertising in "The Importance, and the Problems, of Writing the History of Advertising," *Journal of Advertising History* 1 (1977): 3–5, and in "Wanted: A History of Advertising," *Journal of Advertising Research* 18 (1978): 63–68.

A very recent surge of scholarly attention suggests that the historical role of advertising is finally attracting the attention of a wider group of perceptive scholars. Daniel Pope's *The Making of Modern Advertising* (New York, 1983), provides the first broadly interpretive account of the institutional development of American advertising between the 1880s and the 1920s. Quentin James Schultze, in "Advertising, Science, and Professionalism, 1885–1917" (his Ph.D. dissertation, University of Illinois, Urbana-Champaign, 1978), provides additional details on this period. Michael Schudson's *Advertising, the Uneasy Persuasion: Its Dubious Impact on American Society* (New York, 1984) perceptively traces the evolving functions of advertising in American culture from a sociologist's perspective. Neil Harris, in "The Drama of Consumer Desire," in *Yankee Enterprise: The Rise of the American System of Manufactures,* ed. Otto Mayr and Robert C. Post (Washington, D.C., 1981), pp. 189–216, describes the rise of "shopping rituals" and a "consumer sensibility" as he explores the emerging relationships between "objects of consumer desire and the creation of personality." And T. J. Jackson Lears' essay, "From Salvation to Self-Realization: Advertising and the Therapeutic Roots of the Consumer Culture, 1880–1930," in *The Culture of Consumption,* ed. Richard Wightman Fox and T. J. Jackson Lears (New York, 1983), pp. 3–38, brings a new sophistication to the historical interpretation of the role of advertising in the shaping of modern American culture. Stephen Fox, in *The Mirror Makers: A History of American Advertising and Its Creators* (New York, 1984), has updated the earlier work of Wood and Presbrey by providing a highly readable survey of the history of American advertising with an emphasis on leading personalities. Two provocative essays on the historical evolution of American consumer culture which appeared just as this book went to press are William R. Leach, "Transformations in a Culture of Consumption: Women and Department Stores, 1890–1925," *Journal of American History* 71 (1984): 317–42, and T. J. Jackson Lears, "Some Versions of Fantasy: Toward a Cultural History of American Advertising, 1880–1930," *Prospects* 9 (1984): 349–405. The findings of Richard Pollay's extensive longitudinal content analysis surveys, now beginning to appear articles as "The Subsiding Sizzle: A History of Print Advertising, 1900–1980," *Journal of Marketing* 49 (1985), promise to pose new challenges to interpreters of the historical role of advertising content.

In developing my own approach, I have drawn not only upon this bonanza of new interpretive work in the field of advertising but also upon several important older essays and upon stimulating work in adjacent or related fields. Among the most provocative of earlier essays on the interpretation of advertising are Marghanita Laski, "Advertising—Sacred and Profane," *The Twentieth Century* 165 (1959): 118–159; Leo Spitzer, "American Advertising Explained as Popular Art," in Spitzer, *A Method of Interpreting Literature* (Northampton, Mass., 1949), pp. 102–149; and Raymond Williams, "The Magic System," *New Left Review*, no. 4 (1960). pp. 27–32. I have benefitted greatly from the insights of those who have studied other emerging "professions" that closely paralleled the development of advertising during this period—especially Jeffrey L. Meikle's model study of industrial designers in *Twentieth Century Limited* (Philadelphia, 1979) and Richard S. Tedlow's perceptive monograph, *Keeping the Corporate Image: Public Relations and Business, 1900–1950* (Greenwich, Conn., 1979).

Common sense has persistently directed our attention to the seemingly obvious connection between advertising and the rise of a "consumption ethic." But recent studies from a variety of disciplinary perspectives invite a more sophisticated exploration of that historical relationship. Rosalind H. Williams' *Dream Worlds: Mass Consumption in Late Nineteenth-Century France* (Berkeley, Calif., 1982) offers a sage analysis of the emergence of mass consumption as a focus of intellectual debate. T. J. Jackson Lears reflects on this issue in *No Place of Grace: Antimodernism and the Transformation of American Culture* (New York, 1981), and Michael Schudson examines the functional role of advertising in American society in *Advertising, the Uneasy Persuasion* (New York, 1984). Michael Barry Miller provides a striking case study of the institutionalization of the new ethic in *The Bon Marché: Bourgeois Culture and the Department Store, 1869–1920* (Princeton, N.J., 1981). Stimulating economic, sociological, historical, and anthropological approaches to the nature of consumption appear in Mary Tew Douglas, *The World of Goods* (New York, 1983); William Leiss, *The Limits to Satisfaction: An Essay on the Problem of Needs and Commodities* (Toronto, 1976); Staffan Burenstam Linder, *The Harried Leisure Class* (New York, 1970); Francesco M. Nicosia and Robert N. Mayer, "Toward a Sociology of Consumption," *Journal of Consumer Research* 3 (1976): 65–75; and in the essays in Richard Wightman Fox and T. J. Jackson Lears, eds., *The Culture of Consumption* (New York, 1983). More extended historical perspectives appear in Neil McKendrick, John Brewer, and J. H. Plumb, *The Birth of a Consumer Society: The Commercialization of Eighteenth-Century England* (London, 1982), and in Stuart and Elizabeth Ewen, *Channels of Desire: Mass Images and the Shaping of American Consciousness* (New York, 1982). Robert S. Lynd's "The People as Consumers," in *Recent Social Trends in the United States,* vol. 2 (New York, 1933), pp. 857–911, continues to be of value.

Recent content analyses of advertisements have taken a wide variety of methodological and interpretive forms. These range from Judith Williamson's intensive application of structuralist and neo-Marxist theory in *Decoding Advertisements: Ideology and Meaning in Advertising* (London, 1978) and Varda Langholz

Leymore's structuralist analysis of binary elements in *Hidden Myth: Structure and Symbolism in Advertising* (London, 1975) to the emphasis on an analysis of rhetoric in Gunnar Andrén et al., *Rhetoric and Ideology in Advertising* (Stockholm, 1978) and to the statistical approaches of Trevor Millum's *Images of Women: Advertising in Women's Magazines* (London, 1975) and Richard Pollay's study of broad categories of strategy and appeal in his essay, "The Subsiding Sizzle: A History of Print Advertising, 1900–1980," *Journal of Marketing* 49(1985). All methods have their drawbacks: the more intensive and subjective approaches often read more into each ad than most observers will find plausible; the statistical approaches, by confining themselves to objective and numerable properties, face the problem of placing the countable elements of ads in categories that are not so general as to lead to vagueness or so narrow as to lead to precision at the expense of significance. In my own eclectic approach, I have drawn occasionally upon the methods developed in the works noted above. I have also made use of the insights developed by Erving Goffman in *Gender Advertisements* (New York, 1929), by Frank W. Fox in *Madison Avenue Goes to War* (Provo, Utah, 1975), and by Marshall McLuhan in *The Mechanical Bride: Folklore of Industrial Man* (New York, 1951). For all of its idiosyncrasies, *The Mechanical Bride,* which McLuhan wrote when he still considered the content of media significant, attains greater insights into advertising content than his later work.

In seeking to understand the visual messages of advertising, I have often turned for guidance to interpreters of other visual arts. Anne Hollander's *Seeing Through Clothes* (New York, 1978) offers particularly stimulating insights into the interpretation of high and popular art. The prolific works of the art historians Erwin Panofsky, Millard Meiss, Mario Praz, and Meyer Schapiro, although they interpret art works created for different purposes and often in the context of specific biblical or mythological texts, help train the eye to make a more probing observation of visual artifacts. I turned also to such guides to visual interpretation as Rudolf Arnheim, *Visual Thinking* (Berkeley, Calif., 1969); Stephen Baker, *Visual Persuasion: The Effect of Pictures on the Subconscious* (New York, 1961); John Berger et al., *Ways of Seeing* (London, 1972); Clifford Geertz, "Art as a Cultural System," *Modern Language Notes* 91 (1976): 1473–99; E. H. Gombrich, *Art and Illusion,* 3rd ed. (London, 1968); and E. H. Gombrich, "The Visual Image," *Scientific American,* Sept. 1972, pp. 82–96.

In interpreting advertising within the particular cultural context of the 1920s and 1930s, I turned not only to broad historical surveys and such notable contemporary analyses as Robert S. Lynd and Helen Merrell Lynd, *Middletown: A Study of American Culture* (New York, 1929) and *Middletown in Transition* (New York, 1937), but also to many narrowly focused, penetrating analyses of particular cultural phenomena and popular attitudes of the era. The most valuable among these were Ruth Schwartz Cowan, "The Industrial Revolution in the Home: Household Technology and Social Change in the 20th Century," *Technology and Culture* 17 (1976): 1–23; John Chynoweth Burnham, "The New Psychology: From Narcissism to Social Control," in *Change and Continuity in Twentieth-Century America: The 1920s,* ed. John Braeman, Robert H. Bremner, and David

Brody (Columbus, Ohio, 1968), pp. 351–98; Neil Harris, "Museums, Merchandising, and Popular Taste: The Struggle for Influence," in *Material Culture and the Study of American Life,* ed. Ian M. B. Quimby (New York, 1978), pp. 140–74; Clayton R. Koppes, "The Social Destiny of Radio: Hope and Disillusionment in the 1920s," *South Atlantic Quarterly* 68 (1969): 363–85; Mary P. Ryan, "The Projection of a New Womanhood: The Movie Moderns in the 1920s," in *Our American Sisters: Women in American Life and Thought,* ed. Jean E. Freeman and William G. Shade, 2nd ed. (Boston, 1976); John W. Spalding, "1928: Radio Becomes a Mass Advertising Medium," *Journal of Broadcasting* 8 (1963–64): 31–44; Bernard Sternsher, "Victims of the Great Depression: Self-Blame/Non-Self Blame, Radicalism and pre-1929 Experiences," *Social Science History* 1 (1977): 137–77; Warren I. Susman, "'Personality' and the Making of Twentieth-Century Culture," in *New Directions in American Intellectual History,* ed. John Higham and Paul K. Conkin (Baltimore, 1979), pp. 212–26; and William R. Taylor, "Psyching Out the City," in *Uprooted Americans: Essays to Honor Oscar Handlin,* ed. Richard Bushman et al. (Boston, 1979), pp. 245–78.

Somewhat broader in chronological dimension and topical scope, and crucial in setting the full historical context for analyzing advertising in the 1920s and 1930s, are Lois W. Banner, *American Beauty* (Chicago, 1983); Alfred D. Chandler, Jr., *The Visible Hand: The Managerial Revolution in American Business* (Cambridge, Mass., 1977); Paula A. Fass, *The Damned and the Beautiful: American Youth in the 1920s* (New York, 1977); Gunther Barth, *City People: The Rise of Modern City Culture in Nineteenth-Century America* (New York, 1980); Charles R. Hearn, *The American Dream and the Great Depression* (Westport, Conn., 1977); David M. Katzman, *Seven Days a Week: Women and Domestic Service in Industrializing America* (New York, 1978); Lary May, *Screening Out the Past: The Birth of Mass Culture and the Motion Picture Industry* (New York, 1980); George W. Mowry, *The Urban Nation, 1920–1940* (New York, 1965); Roderick Nash, *The Nervous Generation: American Thought, 1917-1930* (Chicago, 1969); Daniel T. Rodgers, *The Work Ethic in Industrial America, 1850–1920* (Chicago, 1978); Robert Sklar, *Movie-Made America: A Cultural History of American Movies* (New York, 1975); and Robert Wiebe, *The Search for Order, 1877–1920* (New York, 1967).

Analyses of the institutional structure and economic role of advertising are plentiful; many of these, however, do not contain an explicit historical dimension. Beyond the numerous contemporary analyses of the 1920s and 1930s, those appraisals of the functions of advertising that I have found most useful are Mark S. Albion and Paul W. Farris, *The Advertising Controversy: Evidence on the Economic Efforts of Advertising* (Boston, 1981); Neil Borden, *Problems in Advertising* (New York, 1932); Raymond A. Bauer and Stephen A. Greyser, *Advertising in America: The Consumer View* (Boston, 1968); Stephen A. Greyser and Raymond A. Bauer, "Americans and Advertising: Thirty Years of Public Opinion," *Public Opinion Quarterly* 30 (1968): 67–78; Larry Percy and Arch G. Woodside, eds., *Advertising and Consumer Psychology* (Lexington, Mass., 1983); Printers' Ink Publishing Co., ed., *Advertising: Today/Yesterday/Tomorrow* (New York, 1963); C. H. Sandage and Vernon Fryburger, eds., *The Role of Advertising* (Homewood, Ill., 1960); and

Julian L. Simon, *Issues in the Economics of Advertising* (Urbana, Ill., 1970). Philip Hanson's *Advertising and Socialism* (London, 1974) provides the basis for a useful comparative perspective.

It would be a wise author indeed who could pinpoint the sources of the underlying assumptions and broad theoretical frameworks that have influenced his interpretations. I have undoubtedly borrowed many ideas of which I am not consciously aware. I will simply confine myself to listing a few of those sources of conceptual ideas that I am conscious of having utilized. These include: Erving Goffman, *The Presentation of Self in Everyday Life* (Garden City, N.Y., 1959) and *Frame Analysis: An Essay on the Organization of Experience* (Cambridge, Mass., 1974); Clifford Geertz, *The Interpretation of Cultures* (New York, 1973); Daniel Bell, *The Cultural Contradictions of Capitalism* (New York, 1976); Peter L. Berger, Brigitte Berger, and Hansfried Kellner, *The Homeless Mind: Modernization and Consciousness* (New York, 1973); Susan Sontag, *On Photography* (New York, 1977); and Philip Rieff, *The Triumph of the Therapeutic: Uses of Faith After Freud* (New York, 1965). In arriving at various interpretive viewpoints, I also made use of Raymond A. Bauer, "The Obstinate Audience: The Influence Process from the Point of View of Social Communication," in *The Process and Effects of Mass Communication*, ed. Wilbur Schramm and Donald F. Roberts, revised ed. (Chicago, 1971), pp. 326–46; George Gerbner, "Communication and Social Environment," *Scientific American* 227 (1972): 153–60; George Gerbner, "The Social Role of the Confession Magazine," *Social Problems* 6 (1958): 29–40; Paul Hirsch, *The Structure of the Popular Music Industry* (Ann Arbor, Mich., 1968); Lyn Lofland, *A World of Strangers; Order and Action in Urban Public Space* (New York, 1973); Dean MacCannell, *The Tourist: A New Theory of the Leisure Class* (New York, 1976); Donald Fleming, "Attitude: The History of a Concept," *Perspectives in American History* 1 (1967): 287–375; and Meyer Schapiro, "Style," in *Anthropology Today*, ed. A. L. Kroeber (Chicago, 1953), pp. 287–312.

The best single bibliographical resource for the history of American advertising is Richard W. Pollay, *Information Sources in Advertising History* (Westport, Conn., 1979). Working papers with more recent bibliographies in selected fields are available from Professor Pollay at the History of Advertising Archives, University of British Columbia.

Sources for Illustrations

Endsheets

Top row, left to right

Diving Girl, registered trademark, owned by and used with permission of Jantzen, Inc.

Mayflower Ship on shield, registered trademark, of Plymouth Motor Cars, owned by and used with permission of the Chrysler Corporation.

Quaker Man, registered trademark, owned by and used with permission of the Quaker Oats Company.

Old Dutch Girl, registered trademark for Old Dutch Cleanser, owned by and used with permission of Purex Corporation.

Old Bell Symbol, registered trademark, owned by and used with permission of American Information Technologies Corporation, Bell Atlantic Corporation, Bell-South Corporation, Cincinnati Bell Inc., NYNEX Corporation, Pacific Telesis Group, Southern New England Telephone Company, Southwestern Bell Corporation and U S West, Inc.

Centaur, registered trademark of the Chase Brass and Copper Company, owned by and used with permission of the Standard Oil Company (SOHIO).

Second row, left to right

Carriage, registered trademark, owned by and used with permission of Fisher Body Corporation, Division of General Motors Corporation.

Rock Service Mark, registered trademark, owned by and used with permission of the Prudential Insurance Company of America.

Hartford Stag, registered trademark, owned by and used with permission of the Hartford Insurance Group.

Emblem with crown, registered trademark, owned by and used with permission of Cadillac Motor Car Division, General Motors Corporation.

Mountains, clouds and circle of stars, registered trademark, owned by and used with permission of Paramount Pictures Corporation.

Chef device, registered trademark for Cream of Wheat, owned by and used with permission of Nabisco, Inc.

Third row, left to right

Winged Foot, registered trademark, owned by and used with permission of Goodyear Rubber Company.

Cover the Earth, registered trademark, owned by and used with permission of the Sherwin-Williams Company.

Arm and Hammer, registered trademark, owned by and used with permission of Church and Dwight Co., Inc.

Spearman, registered trademark, owned by and used with permission of the Wm. Wrigley Jr. Company.

Gargoyle, registered trademark for Mobiloil Lubricating Oils, owned by and used with permission of Mobil Oil Corporation.

Cup and Drop device, registered trademark for Maxwell House Coffee, owned by and used with permission of General Foods Corporation.

Chapter 1

Fig. 1.1   *Good Housekeeping*, Oct. 1916, p. 11.

Fig. 1.2   *McCall's*, Aug. 1926, p. 4.

Fig. 1.3   *Ladies' Home Journal*, May 1919, p. 114.

Fig. 1.4   *Ladies' Home Journal*, Dec. 1923, p. 81.

Fig. 1.5   *Ladies' Home Journal*, May 1928, p. 77.

Fig. 1.6   *Ladies' Home Journal*, Nov. 1925, p. 91.

Fig. 1.7   *Ladies' Home Journal*, Oct. 1928, p. 117.

Fig. 1.8   *Good Housekeeping*, July 1923, p. 175.

Fig. 1.9   *Printers' Ink*, May 26, 1927, p. 170.

Fig. 1.10   *Saturday Evening Post*, July 18, 1925, p. 61.

Fig. 1.11   *Ladies' Home Journal*, Nov. 1927, p. 79.

Chapter 2

Fig. 2.1   *The Architectural Forum*, Oct. 1929, p. 461.

Fig. 2.2   *Advertising and Selling*, Nov. 10, 1932, p. 49.

Fig. 2.3   *Printers' Ink Monthly*, Aug. 1932, p. 35.

Fig. 2.4   *Printers' Ink Monthly*, Feb. 1936, p. 3.

Fig. 2.5   *Saturday Evening Post*, May 2, 1931, p. 71.

Fig. 2.6   *Printers' Ink Monthly*, Apr. 1928, pp. 67–69.

Chapter 3

Fig. 3.1   *True Story Magazine*, Apr. 1929, first cover. Reprinted with permission of *True Story Magazine*.

Fig. 3.2   *True Story Magazine*, Feb. 1929, p. 95.

Fig. 3.3   *True Story Magazine*, May 1930, p. 71.

Fig. 3.4   *The News* (New York), Mar. 1, 1920, p. 1, as reprinted in James Alvah Bessie, *Jazz Journalism* (New York, 1938), p. 86.

Fig. 3.5   *Fortune*, Feb. 1932, p. 111.

Fig. 3.6   *Printers' Ink*, July 7, 1927, p. 127.

Fig. 3.7   *Saturday Evening Post*, Oct. 13, 1928, p. 83.

Fig. 3.8   *Saturday Evening Post*, May 11, 1929, p. 149.

Fig. 3.9   *Saturday Evening Post*, Aug. 17, 1935, p. 25.

Chapter 4

Fig. 4.1   *Saturday Evening Post*, Sept. 18, 1926, p. 164.

Fig. 4.2   *American Magazine*, Feb. 1927, p. 119.

Fig. 4.3   *American Magazine*, May 1927, p. 161.

Fig. 4.4   From reproduction in *Fortune*, Nov. 1947, p. 115.

Fig. 4.5   *Saturday Evening Post*, Jan. 19, 1929, p. 97.

Fig. 4.6   *Life*, Mar. 15, 1929, pp. 30–31.

Fig. 4.7   *American Magazine*, Sept. 1930, p. 129.

Fig. 4.8   *Ladies' Home Journal*, Mar. 1931, p. 145.

Fig. 4.9   *Ladies' Home Journal*, Oct. 1928, pp. 44–45. Page 44, c. 1928, Family Media Inc., is reprinted with permission of *Ladies' Home Journal*.

Fig. 4.10   *Saturday Evening Post*, Feb. 2, 1929, p. 30.

Fig. 4.11   *Saturday Evening Post*, July 27, 1929, first cover. c. 1929, the Curtis Company. Reprinted by permission.

Fig. 4.12   *Printers' Ink*, Sept. 22, 1932, p. 100.

Fig. 4.13   *Advertising Age*, Oct. 29, 1932, p. 20.

Fig. 4.14   *Saturday Evening Post*, Mar. 14, 1936, p. 90.

Chapter 5

Fig. 5.1   *Better Homes and Gardens*, Oct. 1929, p. 9.

Fig. 5.2   *Saturday Evening Post*, Jan. 13, 1923, p. 100.

Fig. 5.3   *American Magazine*, Nov. 1928, p. 5.

Fig. 5.4   *Ladies' Home Journal*, Apr. 1927, p. 86.

Fig. 5.5   *Ladies' Home Journal*, Jan. 1927, p. 106.

Fig. 5.6   *House Beautiful*, Aug. 1928, p. 125.

Fig. 5.7   *Better Homes and Gardens*, July 1929, p. 79.

Fig. 5.8   *Saturday Evening Post*, June 6, 1931, p. 106.

Fig. 5.9   *Saturday Evening Post*, Mar. 22, 1930, p. 135.

Fig. 5.10   *House Beautiful*, Mar. 1928, p. 352.

Fig. 5.11   *Literary Digest*, Jan. 12, 1929, p. 35.

Fig. 5.12   *Saturday Evening Post*, Sept. 1, 1928, fourth cover.

Fig. 5.13   *Saturday Evening Post*, Oct. 6, 1928, p. 2.

Fig. 5.14   *American Magazine*, May 1930, p. 2.

Fig. 5.15   *Ladies' Home Journal*, Feb. 1929, p. 99.

Fig. 5.16   *Saturday Evening Post*, Nov. 19, 1927, p. 53.

Fig. 5.17   *Ladies' Home Journal*, May 1928, p. 98.

Fig. 5.18   *Good Housekeeping*, Dec. 1928, p. 255.

Fig. 5.19   *Saturday Evening Post*, Nov. 12, 1932, p. 62.

Fig. 5.20   *American Magazine*, Oct. 1927, p. 129.

Fig. 5.21   *Advertising and Selling Fortnightly*, Mar. 24, 1926, p. 37.

Fig. 5.22   *Woman's Home Companion*, May 1927, p. 104.

Fig. 5.23   *Advertising and Selling*, Apr. 18, 1929, p. 33.

Fig. 5.24   *Delineator*, Mar. 1932, p. 73.

Fig. 5.25   *Saturday Evening Post*, Nov. 21, 1931, p. 82.

Fig. 5.26   *Saturday Evening Post*, Mar. 8, 1930, p. 84.

Fig. 5.27   *Ladies' Home Journal*, Apr. 1927, p. 214.

Fig. 5.28   *Good Housekeeping*, Sept. 1928, p. 10.

Fig. 5.29   *American Magazine*, June 1929, p. 115.

Chapter 6

Fig. 6.1   *Saturday Evening Post*, Mar. 24, 1928, p. 53.

Fig. 6.2   *Ladies' Home Journal*, Mar. 1931, fourth cover.

Fig. 6.3   *Ladies' Home Journal*, Jan. 1926, p. 137.

Fig. 6.4   *Better Homes and Gardens*, Dec. 1929, p. 63.

Fig. 6.5   *Ladies' Home Journal*, Dec. 1926, p. 198.

Fig. 6.6   *Ladies' Home Journal*, Apr. 1927, p. 43.

Fig. 6.7   *Printers' Ink Monthly*, July 1932, p. 3.

Fig. 6.8   *Tide*, Feb. 1934, p. 75.

Fig. 6.9   *McCall's*, Mar. 1933, p. 111.

Fig. 6.10   *American Magazine*, May 1933, p. 10.

Fig. 6.11   *Saturday Evening Post*, Nov. 24, 1928, p. 34.

Fig. 6.12   *McCall's*, July 1928, p. 44.

Fig. 6.13   *Saturday Evening Post*, May 9, 1931, p. 2.

Fig. 6.14   *Saturday Evening Post*, Mar. 22, 1930, p. 137.

Fig. 6.15   *Saturday Evening Post*, May 4, 1929, p. 217.

Fig. 6.16   *Saturday Evening Post*, Dec. 8, 1928, p. 139.

Fig. 6.17   *Saturday Evening Post*, Mar. 2, 1929, p. 92.

Fig. 6.18   *Saturday Evening Post*, June 1, 1929, pp. 114–15.

Fig. 6.19   *American Magazine*, Oct. 1932, p. 1.

Fig. 6.20   *Saturday Evening Post*, Aug. 11, 1934, pp. 44–45.

Fig. 6.21   *Saturday Evening Post*, June 6, 1925, p. 149.

Fig. 6.22   *Saturday Evening Post*, Oct. 6, 1928, pp. 140–41.

Fig. 6.23   *American Magazine*, Jan. 1929, p. 2.

Fig. 6.24   *Saturday Evening Post*, May 9, 1931, p. 126.

Fig. 6.25   *Saturday Evening Post*, Nov. 13, 1926, pp. 160–61.

Fig. 6.26   *True Story Magazine*, May 1930, p. 12.

Fig. 6.27   *True Story Magazine*, Jan. 1930, fourth cover.

Fig. 6.28   *McCall's*, Aug. 1928, p. 73.

Fig. 6.29   *Saturday Evening Post*, May 31, 1930, p. 122.

Fig. 6.30   *Saturday Evening Post*, Nov. 14, 1931, p. 140.

Fig. 6.31   *Good Housekeeping*, Nov. 1929, p. 13.

Fig. 6.32   *Advertising and Selling*, May 18, 1927, p. 64.

Fig. 6.33   *Saturday Evening Post*, Apr. 9, 1927, p. 57.

Chapter 7

Fig. 7.1   *American Magazine*, Apr. 1928, p. 2.

Fig. 7.2   *American Magazine*, Aug. 1928, p. 149.

Fig. 7.3   *Saturday Evening Post*, Aug. 27, 1932, p. 77.

Fig. 7.4   *Saturday Evening Post*, June 30, 1928, p. 51.

Fig. 7.5   *Redbook*, June 1935, p. 86.

Fig. 7.6   *Saturday Evening Post*, Aug. 23, 1930, p. 124.

Fig. 7.7   *Saturday Evening Post*, May 8, 1926, p. 58.

Fig. 7.8   *Saturday Evening Post*, Aug. 5, 1933, p. 67.

Fig. 7.9   *Ladies' Home Journal*, Aug. 1931, p. 49.

Fig. 7.10   *Saturday Evening Post*, Sept. 15, 1928, p. 150.

Fig. 7.11   *American Magazine*, Feb. 1927, p. 1.

Fig. 7.12   *Ladies' Home Journal*, Apr. 1931, p. 99.

Chapter 8

Fig. 8.1   *Saturday Evening Post*, May 4, 1929, p. 51.

Fig. 8.2   *Saturday Evening Post*, June 7, 1930, pp. 76–77.

Fig. 8.3   *Saturday Evening Post*, Feb. 10, 1934, p. 39.

Fig. 8.4   *Saturday Evening Post*, June 14, 1924, p. 79.

Fig. 8.5   *Saturday Evening Post*, Nov. 30, 1929, p. 78.

Fig. 8.6   *Fortune*, Apr. 1934, p. 114.

Fig. 8.7   *Saturday Evening Post*, Sept. 22, 1928, p. 189.

Fig. 8.8   *Ladies' Home Journal*, Jan. 1928, p. 68.

Fig. 8.9   *Ladies' Home Journal*, Apr. 1931, p. 129.

Fig. 8.10   *Saturday Evening Post*, Sept. 15, 1934, p. 37.

Fig. 8.11   *Ladies' Home Journal*, Apr. 1928, p. 223.

Fig. 8.12   *Saturday Evening Post*, May 4, 1929, p. 95.

Fig. 8.13   *Printers' Ink Monthly*, Aug. 1930, p. 2.

Fig. 8.14   *Saturday Evening Post*, June 15, 1929, p. 134.

Fig. 8.15   *Ladies' Home Journal*, May 1928, p. 234.

Fig. 8.16   *Saturday Evening Post*, Jan. 10, 1925, pp. 82–83.

Fig. 8.17   *Saturday Evening Post*, Oct. 17, 1925, p. 150.

Fig. 8.18   *Saturday Evening Post*, Apr. 21, 1928, p. 174.

Fig. 8.19   *Saturday Evening Post*, Dec. 28, 1935, p. 39.

Fig. 8.20   *Fortune*, Jan. 1932, p. 92.

Fig. 8.21   *Saturday Evening Post*, Mar. 6, 1926, p. 97.

Fig. 8.22   *Saturday Evening Post*, Sept. 27, 1930, p. 161.

Fig. 8.23   *Saturday Evening Post*, Feb. 27, 1926, p. 70.

Fig. 8.24   *Saturday Evening Post*, Apr. 28, 1934, p. 58.

Fig. 8.25   *Saturday Evening Post*, Nov. 29, 1930, pp. 70–71.

Fig. 8.26   *Saturday Evening Post*, Jan. 12, 1935, p. 68.

Fig. 8.27   *Saturday Evening Post*, Aug. 29, 1925, p. 77.

Fig. 8.28   *Saturday Evening Post*, June 15, 1929, p. 73.

Fig. 8.29   *Saturday Evening Post*, Aug. 13, 1927, p. 136.

Fig. 8.30   *Advertising Age*, Feb. 17, 1936, p. 41.

Fig. 8.31   *Fortune*, Nov. 1931, p. 95.

Fig. 8.32   *Saturday Evening Post*, Oct. 19, 1929, p. 147.

Fig. 8.33   *Saturday Evening Post*, Mar. 14, 1936, p. 77.

Fig. 8.34   *Saturday Evening Post*, Dec. 30, 1933, p. 43.

Fig. 8.35   *Saturday Evening Post*, Sept. 24, 1927, p. 117.

Fig. 8.36   *Saturday Evening Post*, Nov. 22, 1930, p. 37.

Fig. 8.37   *Saturday Evening Post*, Mar. 23, 1935, p. 92.

Fig. 8.38   *Delineator*, Apr. 1930, p. 89.

Fig. 8.39   *Delineator*, Mar. 1930, p. 61.

Fig. 8.40   *Saturday Evening Post*, Feb. 2, 1929, p. 165.

Fig. 8.41   *Saturday Evening Post*, Mar. 1. 1924, p. 80.

Fig. 8.42   *Saturday Evening Post*, Sept. 8, 1928, p. 102.

Fig. 8.43   *Saturday Evening Post*, June 27, 1931, p. 70.

Fig. 8.44   *Saturday Evening Post*, Mar. 13, 1926, p. 143.

Fig. 8.45   *Good Housekeeping*, Aug. 1928, p. 137.

Fig. 9.20   *Advertising and Selling*, Feb. 3, 1932, p. 47.

Fig. 9.21   *Fortune*, Dec. 1933, pp. 110–11.

Fig. 9.22   *Fortune*, Feb. 1933, p. 24.

Fig. 9.23   *Fortune*, Feb. 1933, second cover.

Fig. 9.24   *Saturday Evening Post*, Aug. 19, 1933, p. 75.

Fig. 9.25   *Fortune*, Sept. 1932, p. 92.

Fig. 9.26   *Saturday Evening Post*, Dec. 3, 1932, p. 75.

Fig. 9.27   *American Magazine*, Apr. 1933, p. 99.

Fig. 9.28   *Saturday Evening Post*, Nov. 5, 1932, p. 87.

Chapter 10

Fig. 10.1   *Fortune*, Apr. 1932, p. 21.

Fig. 10.2   *Saturday Evening Post*, Jan. 14, 1929, p. 58.

Fig. 10.3   *Ladies' Home Journal*, June 1927, p. 206.

Fig. 10.4   *American Magazine*, Oct. 1929, p. 75.

Fig. 10.5   *Woman's Home Companion*, Feb. 1927, p. 53.

Fig. 10.6   *Ladies' Home Journal*, Mar. 1931, p. 102.

Fig. 10.7   *Ladies' Home Journal*, Mar. 1927, p. 182.

Fig. 10.8   *Saturday Evening Post*, June 9, 1928, p. 69.

Fig. 10.9   *Literary Digest*, Sept. 9, 1933, second cover.

Index

Page numbers in italics indicate illustrations

Designer: Steve Renick
Compositor: Interactive Composition
Text: 10/12 Bembo
Display: Optima
Printer: Hamilton Printing
Binder: Hamilton Printing